Programming in Ada
PLUS AN OVERVIEW OF ADA 9X
FOURTH EDITION

INTERNATIONAL COMPUTER SCIENCE SERIES

Consulting editor   **A D McGettrick**   University of Strathclyde

SELECTED TITLES IN THE SERIES

Programming in Ada
PLUS AN OVERVIEW OF ADA 9X
— FOURTH EDITION —

J.G.P. Barnes

ADDISON-WESLEY PUBLISHING COMPANY

WOKINGHAM, ENGLAND • READING, MASSACHUSETTS • MENLO PARK, CALIFORNIA • NEW YORK
DON MILLS, ONTARIO • AMSTERDAM • BONN • SYDNEY • SINGAPORE
TOKYO • MADRID • SAN JUAN • MILAN • PARIS • MEXICO CITY • SEOUL • TAIPEI

© 1994 Addison-Wesley Publishers Ltd.
© 1994 Addison-Wesley Publishing Company Inc.

The programs in this book have been included for their instructional value but are not guaranteed for any particular purpose. The publisher does not offer any warranties or representations, nor does it accept any liabilities with respect to the programs.

Many of the designations used by manufacturers and sellers to distinguish their products are claimed as trademarks. Addison-Wesley has made every attempt to supply trademark information about manufacturers and their products mentioned in this book.

Cover designed by Designers & Partners of Oxford
and printed by The Riverside Printing Co. (Reading) Ltd.
Typeset by Columns Design & Production Services Ltd, Reading.
Printed in the United States of America.

First edition published 1982. Reprinted 1982.
Second edition published 1984. Reprinted 1985 (twice), 1986 (twice), 1987 (twice) and 1988.
Third edition published 1989. Reprinted 1989, 1990 and 1991 (twice).
Combined edition (with LRM) published 1991. Reprinted 1992 and 1993 (twice).
Fourth edition printed 1993.

ISBN 0–201–62407–9

British Library Cataloguing in Publication Data
A catalogue record for this book is available from the British Library.

Library of Congress Cataloging in Publication Data applied for.

To Barbara

Foreword

The Ada language standard is now a decade old, and in the language world, such birthdays are generally celebrated by going through a revision process. The new version of the language is dubbed Ada 9X, reflecting the optimism that it will become a standard sometime in the 1990s. In fact, most handicappers are now betting that the X in Ada 9X will be 4.

The original Ada standard (Ada 83) has turned out to be a remarkably good language for the production of high-quality, highly reliable, industrial strength software. Inasmuch as every language seems to build up a surrounding culture, the Ada programming culture has developed as one that values highly readable programs where both the overall architecture of the system and the more detailed design, are captured explicitly in the structure, abstractions, and nomenclature of the source code. Subsystem interfaces, as embodied in package specifications, have become critical design elements in themselves, providing the stable framework around which the whole program is built.

But no technology stands still, and the 1980s have been a particularly active period of development in the areas of programming language technology and software development methodologies. Ada helped spearhead the development of object-oriented methodologies, fostered by its excellent support for data abstraction and program modularization, with information hiding and a strong separation of interface and implementation. Yet Ada 83 is fundamentally a static language; all data types and all subprogram bindings are fully determined prior to execution. Over the past decade, the software industry has moved toward a more dynamic model of program composition. The concepts of inheritance and polymorphism have emerged as mechanisms that can guarantee interface compatibility at compile time, while deferring the binding to particular data types or subprogram implementations to run time. This combination can preserve the reliability associated with compile time interface checking, while supporting more flexible composition and reuse of independently built subsystems.

Ada 9X builds on the excellent Ada 83 foundation of data abstraction and modularity, enhancing it to support type extension as part of inheritance, class-wide programming for polymorphism, and a hierarchical library unit name space. Together these enable a better representation within the language of the subsystem and abstraction hierarchies inherent in component-based, object-oriented programming. Accompanying these enhancements to the data abstraction and program structuring building blocks of the language, are enhancements to the concurrent programming facilities. Support has been added for efficient data-oriented synchronization, complementing the rendezvous-based synchronization model of Ada 83, and for asynchronous signaling, complementing the synchronous interaction model of Ada 83.

The publication of this new edition of John Barnes' classic text on Ada is an important milestone for the Ada 9X process. The 9X revision process actually began in 1988 with an initial call for user input on the goals for the revision, and the Ada 9X design team has been working full time since March of 1990 to meet those goals. John Barnes has been active in the process since the beginning, as an individual reviewer and sage, as head of the UK delegation to the ISO working group on Ada (WG9), where he made critical contributions toward building consensus for the object-oriented features of Ada 9X, and most recently as the author of the rationale that will accompany the proposed standard during balloting, a job that only someone with John's insight, perseverance, and indomitable good humour could pull off. With the publication of this book, John helps to celebrate the completion of the 9X design team's work of technically integrating the Ada 9X features into the language, while helping to start the essential process of integrating the Ada 9X features into the Ada culture.

The Ada 9X Reference Manual can tell a programmer what are the new features of Ada 9X. However, only an author with John's unique style can reveal not just what is new, but also why it is there and how it can be used as a broadened basis for the synthesis of highly reliable, and now more dynamic and extensible software systems.

S. Tucker Taft
August 1993

Preface

This book is about programming in Ada – both Ada 83, the original language and Ada 9X, the emerging new standard.

After a number of years of use, Ada is being revised in order to take account of feedback from existing users, the needs of new application areas and an increased understanding of the programming process. The revisions are quite extensive although strong upward compatibility has been achieved.

It thus seems appropriate for a new edition of this book that covers the new material in Ada 9X. It is clear, however, that Ada 83 will continue in use in its own right for many years. As a consequence the requirements of programmers will differ according to whether they are currently just concerned with Ada 83, in the process of considering how to prepare for the transition forward or indeed now starting to write in Ada 9X. This new edition aims to be helpful in all these situations.

Accordingly Chapters 2 to 16 concentrate on Ada 83 and are similar to those in earlier editions. But in anticipation of a transition to Ada 9X these chapters include details of where Ada 9X differs from Ada 83. These details are included as extra paragraphs and are marked in the margin by one, two or three icons according to their impact as follows.

An interesting remark, often the removal of some restriction or the addition of a related feature.

An incompatibility which might result in an existing Ada 83 program failing to compile in Ada 9X and thus needing to be changed.

An inconsistency which might result in an existing Ada 83 program continuing to compile and execute in Ada 9X but producing a different result. There are few of these but it is important that programmers are warned.

The entirely new Chapter 17 describes the main features of Ada 9X which are not encountered in the earlier chapters. These are principally the object oriented types, the hierarchical library and the protected type.

Thus the reader whose immediate need is to learn Ada 83 should read

Chapters 1 to 16 and ignore all marked paragraphs at least on a first reading. A programmer in the transition stage should take heed of the marked paragraphs especially if writing an Ada 83 program which is to be migrated to Ada 9X in due course. And finally, the eager reader wishing to know about Ada 9X will find the material in Chapter 17 of particular interest.

As I write, Ada 9X is still being given some final touches and it is possible that there might be small changes which impact on some aspects of the description in this book. However, I hope that such changes will be minor and restricted to fine detail such as the presentation of the syntax (included in Appendix 4) and terminology.

Note added during printing: One notable change to Ada 9X occurred just prior to its registration as an ISO Committee Draft. This concerns abstract types and subprograms (see Section 17.2.3). The word abstract is a sixth new reserved word. A tagged type is now explicitly indicated as abstract by the appearance of abstract following the is in its declaration. An abstract subprogram also uses abstract rather than <>. It is no longer required that at least one abstract subprogram be visible. A generic formal parameter can also be indicated as abstract with obvious matching rules.

Those who are familiar with earlier editions might care to note that the changes to Chapters 1 to 16 (other than the insertion of Ada 9X paragraphs) are broadly as follows

- Further Ada Issues arising since the third edition have been referenced and minor changes made to reflect such issues.

- A few additional exercises have been added mostly relating to interesting situations revealed by these further Ada Issues.

- The material on array aggregates has been rewritten once more (I really hate this topic) because the previously revised description was, frankly, incorrect. Third time lucky I hope.

- The section on the mathematical library has been updated to reflect the current Draft International Standard.

- An almost inevitable but small number of errors has been corrected. The most important was perhaps the misuse of the task type name Filter in the Sieve of Eratosthenes in Section 14.9 although this was corrected in reprintings of the third edition. The most curious was that the example of determining the storage size for an access collection in Section 15.4 used List instead of Link; this error had remained undetected since the first edition.

- The index has been expanded to give more information on the entries and a separate index has been added for the examples. The syntax index in Appendix 4 now also gives the entry for each use of each category.

- Finally, all program identifiers have been converted from all upper case into the more readable mixed form with only the first letter in upper case.

And now I must take this opportunity to thank all those who have helped with this exciting new edition. I am particularly grateful to all members of the Ada 9X Mapping team for many interesting discussions on detailed aspects of

Ada 9X. I must especially thank Tucker Taft, the leader of the Mapping team, and Bob Duff for their help in all areas by word of mouth, fax and electronic chat, and to Offer Pazzy for help in the fascinating area of protected types. I must also thank my colleagues on the Ada UK Ada 9X task group for their interaction and especially Bill Taylor and Brian Dobbing for many insightful remarks.

Big thanks are due to Bill Carlson of Intermetrics and to Christine Anderson of the US DoD for their continued encouragement and support and especially for enabling me to work with the Mapping team on writing material for the Ada 9X Rationale. I am particularly grateful for their permission to use some of that material as the foundation for parts of Chapter 17.

Finally, many thanks to my wife Barbara for putting up with me while I have been hiding away with my word processor and to friends at Addison-Wesley for spurring me on to make this text available as soon as possible.

J. G. P. Barnes
Reading
July 1993

Contents

Introduction

Ada is a high level programming language originally sponsored by the US Department of Defense for use in the so-called embedded system application area. (An embedded system is one in which the computer is an integral part of a larger system such as a chemical plant, missile or dishwasher.) In this introductory chapter we briefly trace the original development of Ada (and its successor Ada 9X), its place in the overall language scene and the general structure of the remainder of this book.

1.1 History

The story of Ada goes back to about 1974 when the United States Department of Defense realized that it was spending far too much on software. It carried out a detailed analysis of how its costs were distributed over the various application areas and discovered that over half of them were directly attributed to embedded systems.

Further analysis was directed towards the programming languages in use in the various areas. It was discovered that COBOL was the universal standard for data processing and FORTRAN was a similar standard for scientific and engineering computation. Although these languages were not modern, the fact that they were uniformly applied in their respective areas meant that unnecessary and expensive duplication was avoided.

The situation with regard to embedded systems was however quite different. The number of languages in use was enormous. Not only did each of the three Armed Services have their own favourite high level languages, but they also used many assembly languages as well. Moreover, the high level languages had spawned variants. It seemed that successive contracts had encouraged the development of special versions aimed at different applications. The net result was that a lot of money was being spent on an unnecessary number of compilers. There were also all the additional costs of training and maintenance associated with a lack of standardization.

It was therefore realized that standardization had to be established in the embedded system area if the costs were to be contained. The ultimate goal was, of course, a single language. In the short term a list of interim approved languages was introduced. This consisted of CMS-2Y, CMS-2M, SPL/1, TACPOL, JOVIAL J3, JOVIAL J73 and of course COBOL and FORTRAN for the other areas.

The first step in moving towards the development of a single standard was the writing of a document outlining the requirements. The first version was known as Strawman and was published in early 1975. After receiving comments from various sources it was refined and became Woodenman. A further iteration produced Tinman in June 1976. This was quite a specific document and identified the functionality required of the language.

At this stage many existing languages were evaluated against Tinman, partly to see whether one of them could be used as the ultimate standard, and partly to invoke detailed evaluation of the requirements themselves. As one might expect, none of the existing languages proved satisfactory; on the other hand the general impression was gained that a single language based on state-of-the-art concepts could be developed to meet the requirements.

The evaluation classified the existing languages into three categories which can be paraphrased as

'not appropriate' These languages were obsolete or addressed the wrong area and were not to be considered further. This category included FORTRAN and CORAL 66.

'not inappropriate' These languages were also unsatisfactory as they stood but had some interesting features which could be looked at for inspiration. This category included RTL/2 and LIS.

'recommended bases' These were the three languages Pascal, PL/I and Algol
68 and were seen as possible starting points for the
design of the final language.

At this point the requirements document was revised and reorganized to
give Ironman. Proposals were then invited from contractors to design a new
language starting from one of the recommended bases. Seventeen proposals
were received and four were chosen to go ahead in parallel and in competition.
The four contractors with their colour codings were CII Honeywell Bull
(Green), Intermetrics (Red), Softech (Blue) and SRI International (Yellow).
The colour codings were introduced so that the resulting initial designs could
be compared anonymously and hopefully therefore without bias.

The initial designs were delivered in early 1978 and many groups all over
the world considered their relative merit. The DoD judged that the Green and
Red designs showed more promise than Blue and Yellow and so the latter were
eliminated.

The development then entered its second phase and the two remaining
contractors were given a further year in which to refine their designs. The
requirements were also revised in the light of feedback from the initial designs
and became the final document Steelman[1].

The final choice of language was made on 2 May 1979 when the Green
language developed at CII Honeywell Bull by an international team led by Jean
Ichbiah was declared the winner.

The DoD then announced that the new language would be known as Ada in
honour of Augusta Ada Byron, Countess of Lovelace (1815–52). Ada, the
daughter of Lord Byron, was the assistant and patron of Charles Babbage and
worked on his mechanical analytical engine. In a very real sense she was
therefore the world's first programmer.

The development of Ada then entered a third phase. The purpose of this
was to expose the language to a significant cross section of eventual users in
order to allow them to comment on its suitability for their needs. Various
courses were given in the USA and Europe, and many teams then settled down
to carry out their evaluations. Some 80 general reports were written and
presented at a conference in Boston in October 1979. The general conclusion
was that Ada was good but a few areas needed further refinement. In addition,
nearly a thousand shorter technical language issue reports were received. After
all these reports had been considered the preliminary Ada design was revised
and this resulted in the publication in July 1980 of the first definitive version of
the language. It was then proposed to the American National Standards
Institute (ANSI) as a standard.

The ANSI standardization process occupied over two years and resulted in
a certain number of changes to Ada. Most of these were small but often of
subtle significance, especially for the compiler writer. The ANSI standard
Language Reference Manual (*LRM*) was finally published in January 1983 and
it is this edition which forms the main subject of this book[2].

ANSI then proposed to the International Standards Organization (ISO) that
Ada become an ISO standard. This resulted in the establishment of an ISO
working group which performed the required activities. Ada became ISO
standard 8652 in 1987. During this process (and since) a large number of

technical queries were and continue to be analysed by the so-called Ada Rapporteur Group (ARG) whose recommendations are passed for approval to both the ISO working group and the US DoD Ada Board, a federal advisory committee established to help the Ada Joint Program Office in its deliberations on how to reap the benefits of Ada. These recommendations are known as Ada Issues (AIs) and come in various categories.

The *LRM* is a complex document and it is not surprising that the ARG identified a number of gaps, ambiguities, inconsistencies, and the occasional plain error. Most of these are subtle and concern fine detail that will rarely impact on the average programmer. However, a few are of note, and they are referred to where appropriate as, for example, AI-6. These references have been inserted so that the reader will not be confused by apparent contradictions between the *LRM* and this book. The AIs are in the public domain, and are available through the various national standards bodies, ISO, the Ada Information Clearinghouse and other Ada related organizations.

The ISO working group has developed a number of secondary standards relating to Ada. An important one is that relating to mathematical functions, and the current Draft International Standard (DIS) is thus treated here very much as if it were part of the language standard.

1.2 Ada 9X

Time and technology do not stand still and accordingly, after several years use, it was decided that the Ada language standard should be revised in the light of experience and changing requirements. One major change was that Ada was now being used for many areas of application other than the embedded systems for which it was originally designed. Much had also been learnt about new programming paradigms such as Object Oriented Programming.

The DoD, as the agent of ANSI, the original proposers of the standard to ISO, established the Ada 9X project in 1988 under the management of Christine Anderson. The revision comprised a number of stages: the gathering of requests from the user community, the consolidation of these into a number of requirements, and then the mapping of these requirements into a revised language definition.

The requirements document was published in 1990[3]. It describes 41 specific Requirements plus 22 Study Topics which, as the name implies, cover areas that were not so well understood. The general goal of the revision was thus to satisfy all the Requirements and as many of the Study Topics as possible.

An interesting aspect of the requirements is that they cover a number of specialized application areas. It seemed likely that it would be too costly to implement a language meeting all these requirements in its entirety on every architecture. On the other hand, one of the strengths of Ada is its portability and the last thing wanted was the anarchy of uncontrolled subsets. As a consequence, Ada 9X comprises a Core language plus a small number of specialized Annexes. All compilers have to implement the core language and vendors can choose to implement zero, one or more annexes according to the needs of their markets.

Having established the requirements, the revised language design was contracted to Intermetrics under the technical leadership of Tucker Taft with continued strong interaction with the user community. (It is interesting to note that Intermetrics were the designers of the Red language in 1977.)

At the time of writing (mid 1993), the design of Ada 9X is essentially complete although the ISO standardization process will not finish until 1994/5. The first compilers will however be available in 1993 and it is thus now appropriate to consider the transition from the original language (which we refer to as Ada 83) to Ada 9X.

One important aspect of transition is compatibility; Ada 9X has been designed so that the great majority of Ada 83 programs will behave identically as Ada 9X programs. Indeed the theme of the whole 9X project was 'maximum positive impact' with 'minimum negative impact'. Nevertheless, no language revision has ever been totally upward compatible and indeed Ada 9X could not meet its requirements and be completely compatible. An important goal of this book is to indicate where the incompatibilities lie so that programmers are guided for the future.

1.3 Software engineering

It should not be thought that Ada is just another programming language. Ada is about Software Engineering, and by analogy with other branches of engineering it can be seen that there are two main problems with the development of software: the need to reuse software components as much as possible and the need to establish disciplined ways of working.

As a language, Ada (and especially Ada 9X) largely solves the problem of writing reusable software components (or at least through its excellent ability to prescribe interfaces, provides an enabling technology in which reusable software can be written).

Concerning the establishment of a disciplined way of working, it was realized twenty years ago that the language is just one component, although an important one, of the toolkit that every programmer (and his manager) should have available. It was therefore felt that additional benefit would be achieved if a uniform programming environment could also be established. And so, in parallel with the original language design, a series of requirements documents for an Ada Programming Support Environment (APSE) were developed. These were entitled Sandman, Pebbleman and finally Stoneman[4]. These documents are less detailed than the corresponding language documents because the state-of-the-art in this area was (and perhaps still is) in its infancy. A number of grandiose attempts to build an APSE were undertaken in the early 1980s. They failed for a number of reasons – the requirements were not well understood and moreover the hardware technology used for the larger projects, which would benefit most from an APSE, started to undergo a transformation from a central machine with dumb terminals to a distributed intelligent environment requiring a rather different approach.

The current situation (1993) is still somewhat confused. A number of excellent smaller environment systems have emerged with collections of so-called CASE (Computer Aided Software Engineering) tools. The successor to the original APSEs is PCTE+ (Portable Common Tools Environment); this focuses on the establishment of Public Tool Interfaces which are intended to allow tools to be moved between different environments. However, environments are really another story outside the scope of this book.

Returning to the consideration of Ada as a language, it is now clear after many years' use that Ada is living up to its promise of providing a language which can reduce the cost of both the initial development of software and its later maintenance. The main advantage of Ada is simply that it is reliable. The strong typing and related features ensure that programs contain few surprises; most errors are detected at compile time and of those that remain many are detected by run-time constraints. This aspect of Ada considerably reduces the costs and risks of program development compared for example with C and its derivatives such as C++. Even if Ada is seen as just another programming language, it reaches parts of the software development process that other languages do not reach.

The essence of Ada 9X, as we shall see, is that it adds extra flexibility to the inherent reliability of Ada 83, thereby producing an outstanding language suitable for the major development needs of applications that matter well into the next century.

1.4 Technical background

The evolution of programming languages has apparently occurred in a rather *ad hoc* fashion but with hindsight it is now possible to see a number of major advances. Each advance seems to be associated with the introduction of a level of abstraction which removes unnecessary and harmful detail from the program.

The first advance occurred in the early 1950s with high level languages such as Fortran and Autocode which introduced 'expression abstraction'. It thus became possible to write statements such as

```
X=A+B(I)
```

so that the use of the machine registers to evaluate the expression was completely hidden from the programmer. In these early languages the expression abstraction was not perfect since there were somewhat arbitrary constraints on the complexity of expressions; subscripts had to take a particularly simple form for instance. Later languages such as Algol 60 removed such constraints and completed the abstraction.

The second advance concerned 'control abstraction'. The prime example was Algol 60 which took a remarkable step forward; no language since then has made such an impact on later developments. The point about control abstraction is that the flow of control is structured and individual control points do not have to be named or numbered. Thus we write

    if X=Y **then** P:=Q **else** A:=B

and the compiler generates the gotos and labels which would have to be explicitly used in early versions of languages such as Fortran. The imperfection of early expression abstraction was repeated with control abstraction. In this case the obvious flaw was the horrid Algol 60 switch which has now been replaced by the case statement of languages such as Pascal. (The earlier case clause of Algol 68 had its own problems.)

The third advance was 'data abstraction'. This means separating the details of the representation of data from the abstract operations defined upon the data.

Older languages take a very simple view of data types. In all cases the data is directly described in numerical terms. Thus if the data to be manipulated is not really numerical (it could be traffic light colours) then some mapping of the abstract type must be made by the programmer into a numerical type (usually integer). This mapping is purely in the mind of the programmer and does not appear in the written program except perhaps as a comment. It is probably a consequence of this fact that software component libraries have not emerged except in numerical analysis. (Note that although much software is now sold it is at a different level and inevitably comprises whole programs and not components.) Numerical algorithms, such as those for finding eigenvalues of a matrix, are directly concerned with manipulating numbers and so these languages, whose data values are numbers, have proved appropriate. The point is that the languages provide the correct abstract values in this case only. In other cases, libraries are not successful because there is unlikely to be agreement on the required mappings. Indeed different situations may best be served by different mappings and these mappings pervade the whole program. A change in mapping usually requires a complete rewrite of the program.

Pascal introduced a certain amount of data abstraction as instanced by the enumeration type. Enumeration types allow us to talk about the traffic light colours in their own terms without our having to know how they are represented in the computer. Moreover, they prevent us from making an important class of programming errors – accidentally mixing traffic lights with other abstract types such as the names of fish. When all such types are described in the program as numerical types, such errors can occur.

Another form of data abstraction concerns visibility. It has long been recognized that the traditional block structure of Algol 60 is not adequate. For example, it is not possible in Algol 60 to write two procedures to operate on some common data and make the procedures accessible without also making the data directly accessible. Many languages have provided control of visibility through separate compilation; this technique is adequate for medium-sized systems, but since the separate compilation facility usually depends upon some external system, total control of visibility is not gained. The module of Modula is an example of an appropriate construction.

Ada was probably the first practical language to bring together these various forms of data abstraction.

Another language which made an important contribution to the development of data abstraction is Simula 67 with its concept of class. This leads us into the paradigm now known as Object Oriented Programming which is currently in vogue. There seems to be no precise definition of OOP, but its essence is a flexible form of data abstraction providing the ability to define new data abstractions in terms of old ones and allowing dynamic selection of types.

All types in Ada 83 are static and thus Ada 83 is not classed as a truly Object Oriented language but as an Object Based language. However, Ada 9X includes the essential functionality associated with OOP such as polymorphism and type extension.

We are, as ever, probably too close to the current scene to achieve a proper perspective. Data abstraction in Ada 83 seems to have been not quite perfect, just as Fortran expression abstraction and Algol 60 control abstraction were imperfect in their day. It remains to be seen just how well Ada 9X provides what we might call 'object abstraction'.

Ada is an important advance. Ada 83 has already shown the benefits of writing significant amounts of reusable software. The added flexibility of Ada 9X should provide additional opportunities and further encourage the development of a software components industry and the reuse of reliable software.

1.5 Structure and objectives of this book

Learning a programming language is a bit like learning to drive a car. Certain key things have to be learnt before any real progress is possible. Although we need not know how to use the windscreen washer, nevertheless we must at least be able to start the engine, engage gears, steer and brake. So it is with programming languages. We do not need to know all about Ada before we can write useful programs but quite a lot must be learnt. Moreover many virtues of Ada become apparent only when writing large programs just as many virtues of a Rolls-Royce are not apparent if we only use it to drive to the local shop.

This book is not an introduction to programming but an overall description of programming in Ada. It is assumed that the reader will have a significant knowledge of programming in some reasonable high level language. A knowledge of Pascal would be helpful but is certainly not necessary. A knowledge of C is probably better than nothing.

It should also be noted that this book strives to remain neutral regarding methods of program design and should therefore prove useful whatever techniques are used. However, certain features of Ada naturally align themselves with different design concepts such as Functional Decomposition (based on control flow) and Object Oriented Design (based on data abstraction) and will be mentioned as appropriate.

This book is primarily about programming in Ada 83, but in anticipation of a transition to Ada 9X it also includes details of where Ada 9X differs from Ada 83. These details are included as extra paragraphs and are marked in the margin as explained in the preface.

Chapter 2 gives a brief overview of some Ada concepts and is designed to give the reader a feel of the style and objectives of Ada. The rest of the book is in a tutorial style and introduces topics in a fairly straightforward sequence. By Chapter 7 we will have covered the traditional facilities of small languages such as Pascal. Chapters 8 to 16 cover modern and exciting material associated with data abstraction, programming in the large and parallel processing.

Finally, Chapter 17 describes the main features of Ada 9X which have not been encountered in the earlier chapters; naturally enough, these topics are largely the significant new additions rather than variations on existing themes.

Most sections contain exercises. It is important that the reader does most, if not all, of these since they are an integral part of the discussion and later sections often use the results of earlier exercises. Solutions to all the exercises will be found at the end of the book.

Most chapters conclude with a short checklist of key points to be remembered. Although incomplete, these checklists should help to consolidate understanding. Furthermore, the reader is encouraged to refer to the syntax in Appendix 4 which is organized to correspond to the order in which the topics are introduced.

This book covers all aspects of Ada 83 but does not explore every pathological situation. Its purpose is to teach the reader the effect of and intended use of the features of Ada. In two areas the discussion is incomplete; these are machine dependent programming and input–output. Machine dependent programming (as its name implies) is so dependent upon the particular implementation that only a brief overview seems appropriate. Input–output, although important, does not introduce new concepts but is rather a mass (mess?) of detail; again a simple overview is presented. Further details of these areas can be found in the *Language Reference Manual* (*LRM*) which is referred to from time to time.

Various appendices are provided in order to make this book reasonably self-contained; they are mostly based upon material drawn from the *Language Reference Manual*. Access to the *LRM*, which is the official definition of Ada, is recommended but should not be absolutely essential.

The discussion of Ada 9X, although by no means complete, covers the main features of the core language but not the specialized material in the annexes. Having become acquainted with Ada 83, this book should provide adequate information for a typical programmer wishing to exploit the main advantages of Ada 9X.

1.6 References

1 Defense Advanced Research Projects Agency (1978). *Department of Defense Requirements for High Order Computer Programming Languages – 'STEELMAN'* Arlington, Virginia.
2 United States Department of Defense (1983). *Reference Manual for the Ada Programming Language* (ANSI/MIL-STD-1815A). Washington DC.
3 Office of the Under Secretary of Defense for Acquisition (1990). *Ada 9X Requirements*. Washington DC.

4 Defense Advanced Research Projects Agency (1980). *Department of Defense Requirements for Ada Programming Support Environments – 'STONEMAN'.* Arlington, Virginia.

2 Ada Concepts

In this chapter we present a brief overview of some of the goals, concepts and features of Ada. Enough material is also given to enable the reader to create a framework in which the exercises and other fragments of program can be executed, if desired, before all the required topics (such as input–output) are discussed in depth.

2.1 Key goals

Ada is a large language since it addresses many important issues relevant to the programming of practical systems in the real world. It is, for instance, much larger than Pascal, which, unless extended in some way, is really only suitable for training purposes (for which it was designed) and for small personal programs. Some of the key issues in Ada are

- Readability – it is recognized that professional programs are read much more often than they are written. It is important therefore to avoid an over terse notation such as in APL which, although allowing a program to be written down quickly, makes it almost impossible to be read except perhaps by the original author soon after it was written.

- Strong typing – this ensures that each object has a clearly defined set of values and prevents confusion between logically distinct concepts. As a consequence many errors are detected by the compiler which in other languages (such as C) would have led to an executable but incorrect program.

- Programming in the large – mechanisms for encapsulation, separate compilation and library management are necessary for the writing of portable and maintainable programs of any size.

- Exception handling – it is a fact of life that programs of consequence are rarely perfect. It is necessary to provide a means whereby a program can be constructed in a layered and partitioned way so that the consequences of unanticipated events in one part can be contained.

- Data abstraction – as mentioned earlier, extra portability and maintainability can be obtained if the details of the representation of data can be kept separate from the specifications of the logical operations on the data.

- Tasking – for many applications it is important that the program be conceived as a series of parallel activities rather than just as a single sequence of actions. Building appropriate facilities into a language rather than adding them via calls to an operating system gives better portability and reliability.

- Generic units – in many cases the logic of part of a program is independent of the types of the values being manipulated. A mechanism is therefore necessary for the creation of related pieces of program from a single template. This is particularly useful for the creation of libraries.

2.2 Overall structure

One of the most important objectives of Software Engineering is to reuse existing pieces of program so that the effort of detailed new coding is kept to a minimum. The concept of a program library naturally emerges and an important aspect of a programming language is therefore its ability to express how to use the items in this library.

Ada recognizes this situation and introduces the concept of library units. A complete Ada program is conceived as a main program (itself a library unit) which calls upon the services of other library units. These library units can be thought of as forming the outermost lexical layer of the total program.

The main program takes the form of a procedure of an appropriate name. The service library units can be subprograms (procedures or functions) but they are more likely to be packages. A package is a group of related items such as subprograms but may be other entities as well.

Suppose we wish to write a program to print out the square root of some number such as 2.5. We can expect various library units to be available to provide us with a means of computing square roots and producing output. Our job is merely to write a main program to use these services as we wish.

For the sake of argument we will suppose that the square root can be obtained by calling a function in our library whose name is Sqrt. In addition we will suppose that our library includes a package called Simple_IO containing various simple input–output facilities. These facilities might include procedures for reading numbers, printing numbers, printing strings of characters and so on.

Our program might look like

```
with Sqrt, Simple_IO;
procedure Print_Root is
  use Simple_IO;
begin
  Put(Sqrt(2.5));
end Print_Root;
```

The program is written as a procedure called Print_Root preceded by a with clause giving the names of the library units which it wishes to use. The body of the procedure contains the single statement

```
Put(Sqrt(2.5));
```

which calls the procedure Put in the package Simple_IO with a parameter which in turn is the result of calling the function Sqrt with the parameter 2.5.

Writing

```
use Simple_IO;
```

gives us immediate access to the facilities in the package Simple_IO. If we had omitted this use clause we would have had to write

```
Simple_IO.Put(Sqrt(2.5));
```

in order to indicate where Put was to be found.

We can make our program more useful by making it read in the number whose square root we require. It might then become

```
with Sqrt, Simple_IO;
procedure Print_Root is
   use Simple_IO;
   X: Float;
begin
   Get(X);
   Put(Sqrt(X));
end Print_Root;
```

The overall structure of the procedure is now clearer. Between **is** and **begin** we can write declarations, and between **begin** and **end** we write statements. Broadly speaking, declarations introduce the entities we wish to manipulate and statements indicate the sequential actions to be performed.

We have now introduced a variable X of type Float which is a predefined language type. Values of this type are a set of certain floating point numbers, and the declaration of X indicates that X can have values only from this set. In our example a value is assigned to X by calling the procedure Get which is also in our package Simple_IO.

Some small scale details should be noted. The various statements and declarations all terminate with a semicolon; this is unlike some other languages such as Algol and Pascal where semicolons are separators rather than terminators. The program contains various identifiers such as **procedure**, Put and X. These fall into two categories. A few (63 in Ada 83 and 68 in Ada 9X) such as **procedure** and **is** are used to indicate the structure of the program; they are reserved and can be used for no other purpose. All others, such as Put and X, can be used for whatever purpose we desire. Some of these, notably Float in our example, have a predefined meaning but we can nevertheless reuse them if we so wish although it might be confusing to do so. For clarity in this book we write the reserved identifiers in lower case bold and capitalize the others. This is purely a notational convenience; the language rules do not distinguish the two cases except when we consider the manipulation of characters themselves. Note also how the underline character is used to break up long identifiers into meaningful parts.

Finally, observe that the name of the procedure, Print_Root, is repeated between the final **end** and the terminating semicolon. This is optional but is recommended so as to clarify the overall structure although this is obvious in a small example such as this.

Our program is still very simple; it might be more useful to enable it to cater for a whole series of numbers and print out each answer on a separate line. We could stop the program somewhat arbitrarily by giving it a value of zero.

```
with Sqrt, Simple_IO;
procedure Print_Roots is
   use Simple_IO;
   X: Float;
begin
   Put("Roots of various numbers");
   New_Line(2);
```

```
loop
   Get(X);
   exit when X = 0.0;
   Put(" Root of ");
   Put(X);
   Put(" is ");
   if X < 0.0 then
      Put("not calculable");
   else
      Put(Sqrt(X));
   end if;
   New_Line;
end loop;
New_Line;
Put("Program finished");
New_Line;
end Print_Roots;
```

The output has been enhanced by the calls of further procedures New_Line and Put in the package Simple_IO. A call of New_Line will output the number of new lines specified by the parameter (which is of the predefined type Integer); the procedure New_Line has been written in such a way that if no parameter is supplied then a default value of one is assumed. There are also calls of Put with a string as argument. This is in fact a different procedure from the one that prints the number X. The compiler knows which is which because of the different types of parameters. Having more than one procedure with the same name is known as overloading. Note also the form of the string; this is a situation where the case of the letters does matter.

Various new control structures are also introduced. The statements between **loop** and **end loop** are repeated until the condition X = 0.0 in the **exit** statement is found to be true; when this is so the loop is finished and we immediately carry on after **end loop**. We also check that X is not negative; if it is we output the message 'not calculable' rather than attempting to call Sqrt. This is done by the if statement; if the condition between **if** and **then** is true, then the statements between **then** and **else** are executed, otherwise those between **else** and **end if** are executed.

The general bracketing structure should be observed; **loop** is matched by **end loop** and **if** by **end if**. All the control structures of Ada have this closed form rather than the open form of Pascal which can lead to poorly structured and incorrect programs.

We will now consider in outline the possible general form of the function Sqrt and the package Simple_IO that we have been using.

The function Sqrt will have a structure similar to that of our main program; the major difference will be the existence of parameters.

```
function Sqrt(F: Float) return Float is
   R: Float;
begin
   -- compute value of Sqrt(F) in R
```

```
        return R;
    end Sqrt;
```

We see here the description of the formal parameters (in this case only one) and the type of the result. The details of the calculation are represented by the comment which starts with a double hyphen. The return statement is the means by which the result of the function is indicated. Note the distinction between a function which returns a result and is called as part of an expression, and a procedure which does not have a result and is called as a single statement.

The package Simple_IO will be in two parts: the specification which describes its interface to the outside world, and the body which contains the details of how it is implemented. If it just contained the procedures that we have used, its specification might be

```
package Simple_IO is
    procedure Get(F: out Float);
    procedure Put(F: in Float);
    procedure Put(S: in String);
    procedure New_Line(N: in Integer := 1);
end Simple_IO;
```

The parameter of Get is an **out** parameter because the effect of calling Get as in

```
Get(X);
```

is to transmit a value out from the procedure to the actual parameter X. The other parameters are all **in** parameters because the value goes in to the procedures.

Only a part of the procedures occurs in the package specification; this part is known as the procedure specification and just gives enough information to enable the procedures to be called.

We see also the two overloaded specifications of Put, one with a parameter of type Float and the other with a parameter of type String. Finally, note how the default value of 1 for the parameter of New_Line is indicated.

The package body for Simple_IO will contain the full procedure bodies plus any other supporting material needed for their implementation and which is naturally hidden from the outside user. In vague outline it might look like

```
with Text_IO;
package body Simple_IO is
    . . .
    procedure Get(F: out Float) is
        . . .
    begin
        . . .
    end Get;
    -- other procedures similarly
end Simple_IO;
```

The with clause shows that the implementation of the procedures in Simple_IO uses the more general package Text_IO. It should also be noticed how the full body of Get repeats the procedure specification which was given in the corresponding package specification. (The procedure specification is the bit up to but not including **is**.) Note that the package Text_IO really exists, whereas Simple_IO is a figment of our imagination made up for the purpose of our example. We will say more about Text_IO in Section 2.6.

The example in this section has briefly revealed some of the overall structure and control statements of Ada. One purpose of this section has been to stress that the idea of packages is one of the most important concepts in Ada. A program should be conceived as a number of components which provide services to and receive services from each other. In the next few chapters we will of necessity be dealing with the small scale features of Ada but in doing so we should not lose sight of the overall structure which we will return to in Chapter 8.

Perhaps this is an appropriate point to mention the special package Standard. This is a package which exists in every implementation and contains the declarations of all the predefined identifiers such as Float and Integer. We can assume access to Standard automatically and do not have to give its name in a with clause. It is discussed in detail in Appendix 2.

EXERCISE 2.2

1   In practice it is likely that the function Sqrt will not be in the library on its own but in a package along with other mathematical functions. Suppose this package has the identifier Simple_Maths and other functions are Log, Ln, Exp, Sin and Cos. By analogy with the specification of Simple_IO, write the specification of such a package. How would our program Print_Roots need to be changed?

2.3 Errors and exceptions

We introduce this topic by considering what would have happened in the example in the previous section if we had not tested for a negative value of X and consequently called Sqrt with a negative argument. Assuming that Sqrt has itself been written in an appropriate manner then it clearly cannot deliver a value to be used as the parameter of Put. Instead an exception will be raised. The raising of an exception indicates that something unusual has happened and the normal sequence of execution is broken. In our case the exception might be Constraint_Error which is a predefined exception declared in the package Standard. If we did nothing to cope with this possibility then our program would be terminated and no doubt the Ada Run Time System (that is the non-Ada magic that drives our program from the operating system) will give us a rude message saying that our program has failed and why. We can, however, look out for an exception and take remedial action if it occurs. In fact we could replace the conditional statement

```
        if X < 0.0 then
            Put("not calculable");
        else
            Put(Sqrt(X));
        end if;
```

by

```
        begin
            Put(Sqrt(X));
        exception
            when Constraint_Error =>
            Put("not calculable");
        end;
```

This fragment of program is an example of a block. If an exception is raised by the sequence of statements between **begin** and **exception**, then control immediately passes to the one or more statements following the handler for that exception and these are obeyed instead. If there were no handler for the exception (it might be another exception such as Storage_Error) then control passes up the flow hierarchy until we come to an appropriate handler or fall out of the main program, which then becomes terminated as we mentioned with a rude message from the Run Time System.

The above example is not a good illustration of the use of exceptions since the event we are guarding against can easily be tested for directly. Nevertheless it does show the general idea of how we can look out for unexpected events and leads us into a brief consideration of errors in general.

There are two underlying causes of errors in software as perceived externally: an incorrect software specification in which a possible sequence of external events has not been taken into consideration, and an incorrect implementation of the software specification itself. The first type of error can be allowed for to some extent by exception handlers. The second type leads to an incorrect Ada program.

From the linguistic viewpoint, an Ada program may be incorrect for various reasons. Four categories are recognized according to how they are detected.

- Some errors will be detected by the compiler – these will include simple punctuation mistakes such as leaving out a semicolon or attempting to violate the type rules such as mixing up colours and fish. In these cases the program will not be executed.

- Other errors are detected when the program is executed. An attempt to find the square root of a negative number or divide by zero are examples of such errors. In these cases an exception is raised as we have just seen and we have an opportunity to recover from the situation.

- There are also certain situations where the program breaks the language rules but there is no simple way in which this violation can be detected. For example a program should not use a variable before a value is assigned to it. If it does then the behaviour is quite unpredictable and the program is said to be erroneous.

- Finally there are situations where, for implementation reasons, the language does not prescribe the order in which things are to be done. For example the order in which the parameters of a procedure call are evaluated is not defined. If the behaviour of a program does depend on such an order then it is illegal and said to have an incorrect order dependency.

Care must be taken to avoid writing erroneous programs and those with incorrect order dependencies. In practice if we avoid clever tricks then all will usually be well.

We must mention at this point that Ada 9X uses a somewhat different classification for errors. It introduces the notion of a bounded error (the behaviour is not defined but there are bounds on the possibilities). A bounded error is thus not so bad as an erroneous execution. Many erroneous situations are classed as bounded errors in Ada 9X. Moreover, a program with an incorrect order dependency is simply considered to be not portable rather than illegal. Having said this we will ignore the subtlety of these changes throughout the rest of this book. Note that this is our first Ada 9X remark. It gets a single icon because it is of the category of interesting but it is not a compatibility hazard.

2.4 The type model

We have said that one of the key benefits of Ada is its strong typing. This is well illustrated by the enumeration type. Consider

```
declare
   type Colour is (Red, Amber, Green);
   type Fish is (Cod, Hake, Plaice);
   X, Y: Colour;
   A, B: Fish;
begin
   X := Red;      - - ok
   A := Hake;     - - ok
   B := X;        - - illegal
   . . .
end;
```

Here we have a block which declares two enumeration types Colour and Fish, and two variables of each type, and then performs various assignments. The declarations of the types gives the allowed values of the types. Thus the variable X can only take one of the three values Red, Amber or Green. The fundamental rule of strong typing is that we cannot assign a value of one type to a variable of a different type. So we cannot mix up colours and fish and thus our (presumably accidental) attempt to assign the value of X to B is illegal and will be detected during compilation.

There are two enumeration types predefined in the package Standard. One is

type Boolean **is** (False, True);

which plays a fundamental role in control flow. Thus the predefined relational operators such as < produce a result of this type and such a value follows **if** as we saw in the construction

if X < 0.0 **then**

in the example of Section 2.2. The other predefined enumeration type is Character whose values are the ASCII characters; this type naturally plays an important role in input–output. The literal values of this type include the printable characters and these are represented by placing them in single quotes thus 'X' or 'a' or indeed ''.

The other fundamental types are the numeric types. One way or another, all other data types are built out of enumeration types and numeric types. The two major classes of numeric types are the integer types and floating point types (there are also fixed point types which are rather obscure and deserve no further mention in this brief overview). All implementations will have the types Integer and Float used in Section 2.2. In addition, if the architecture is appropriate, an implementation may have other predefined numeric types, Long_Integer, Long_Float, Short_Float and so on.

One of the problems of numeric types is how to obtain both portability and efficiency in the face of variation in machine architecture. In order to explain how this is done in Ada we have to introduce the perhaps surprising concept of a derived type.

A derived type introduces a new type which is almost identical to an existing type except that it is logically distinct. If we write

type Light **is new** Colour;

then Light will, like Colour, be an enumeration type with literals Red, Amber and Green. However, values of the two types cannot be arbitrarily mixed since they are logically distinct. Nevertheless, in recognition of the close relationship, a value of one type can be converted to the other by explicitly using the destination type name. So we can write

```
declare
   type Light is new Colour;
   C: Colour;
   L: Light;
begin
   L := Amber;      – – the light amber, not the colour
   C := Colour(L);  – – explicit conversion
   . . .
end;
```

whereas a direct assignment

```
C := L;      – – illegal
```

would violate the strong typing rule and this violation would be detected during compilation.

Returning now to our numeric types, if we write

type Real **is new** Float;

then Real will have all the operations (+, – etc.) of Float and in general can be considered as equivalent. Now suppose we transfer our program to a different computer on which the predefined type Float is not so accurate and that Long_Float is necessary. Assuming that our program has been written using Real rather than Float then replacing our declaration of Real by

type Real **is new** Long_Float;

is the only change necessary. We can actually do better than this by directly stating the precision that we require, thus

type Real **is digits** 7;

will cause Real to be derived from the smallest predefined type with at least 7 decimal digits of accuracy.

The point of all this is that it is not good practice to use the type Float directly, and accordingly we will use our type Real in examples in future.

A similar approach is possible with integer types, but for a number of reasons the predefined type Integer has a fundamental place in the language and so we will continue to use it directly. We will say no more about numeric types for the moment except that all the expected operations apply to all integer and floating types.

Ada naturally enables the creation of composite array and record types and these are discussed in Chapters 6 and 11. There are also access types (the Ada name for pointer types) which allow list processing, and these are also discussed in Chapter 11. In conclusion we note that the type String which we encountered in Section 2.2, is in fact an array type whose components are of the enumeration type Character.

2.5 Generics

At the beginning of Section 2.2 we said that an important objective of Software Engineering is to reuse existing software components. However, the strong typing model of Ada rather gets in the way unless we have some method of writing software components which can be used for various different types. For example, the program to do a sort is largely independent of what it is sorting – all it needs is a rule for comparing the values. Record input–output is another example – the actions are quite independent of the contents of the records.

So we need a means of writing pieces of software which can be parameterized as required for different types. In Ada this is done by the generic mechanism. We can make a package or subprogram generic with respect to one or more parameters which can include types. Such a generic unit provides a template out of which we can create genuine packages and subprograms by so-called instantiation. The full details are quite extensive and will be dealt with in Chapter 13. However, we want to give the reader the immediate ability to do some input–output and the standard packages for this involve the generic mechanism.

The standard package for the input and output of floating point values in text form is generic with respect to the actual floating type. This is because we want a single package to cope with all the possible floating types such as the underlying machine types Float and Long_Float as well as our own portable type Real. Its specification is

```
generic
   type Num is digits <>;
package Float_IO is
   . . .
   procedure Get(Item: out Num; . . . );
   procedure Put(Item: in Num; . . . );
   . . .
end Float_IO;
```

where we have omitted various details relating to the format. The one generic parameter is Num and the notation **digits** <> indicates that it must be a floating point type and echoes the declaration of Real using **digits** 7 that we briefly mentioned in the last section.

In order to create an actual package to manipulate values of our type Real, we write

```
package Real_IO is new Float_IO(Real);
```

which creates a package with the name Real_IO where the formal type Num has been replaced throughout with our actual type Real. As a consequence, procedures Get and Put taking parameters of the type Real are created and we can then call these as required. But we are straying into the next section.

Another simple area where the Ada generic mechanism is used is for the mathematical library. This library, discussed in detail in Section 13.4, includes a generic package which contains among other things the various familiar elementary functions such as Sqrt. Its specification is

```
with Elementary_Functions_Exceptions;
generic
   type Float_Type is digits <>;
package Generic_Elementary_Functions is
```

```
function Sqrt(X: Float_Type) return Float_Type;
. . .  – – and so on
end;
```

Again there is a single generic parameter giving the floating type. In order to call the function Sqrt we must first instantiate the generic package much as we did for Float_IO, thus

```
package Real_Maths is
          new Generic_Elementary_Functions(Real);
use Real_Maths;
```

and we can then write a call of Sqrt directly. Note that the use clause for Real_Maths avoids us having to write Real_Maths.Sqrt everywhere.

The reader will have noticed that the generic package commences with a with clause for Elementary_Functions_Exceptions. This is another package which contains just the declaration of a single exception, Argument_Error, thus

```
package Elementary_Functions_Exceptions is
    Argument_Error: exception;
end Elementary_Functions_Exceptions;
```

This exception is raised if the parameter of a function such as Sqrt is unacceptable. This contrasts with our hypothetical function Sqrt introduced earlier which we assumed raised the predefined exception Constraint_Error when given a negative parameter. We will see later when we deal with exceptions in detail in Chapter 10 that it is generally better to declare and raise our own exceptions rather than use the predefined ones.

2.6 Input–output

The Ada language is defined in such a way that all input and output is performed in terms of other language features. There are no special intrinsic features just for input and output. In fact input–output is just a service required by a program and so is provided by one or more Ada packages. This approach runs the attendant risk that different implementations will provide different packages and program portability will be compromised. In order to avoid this, the *Language Reference Manual* describes certain standard packages that can be expected to be available. Other, more elaborate, packages may be appropriate to special circumstances and the language does not prevent this. Indeed very simple packages such as our purely illustrative Simple_IO may also be appropriate. Full consideration of input and output is deferred until Chapter 15 when we discuss interfaces between our program and the outside world in general. However, we will now briefly describe how to use some of the features so that the reader will be able to run some simple exercises. We will restrict ourselves to the input and output of simple text.

Text input–output is performed through the use of a standard package called Text_IO. Unless we specify otherwise, all communication will be through two standard files, one for input and one for output, and we will assume that (as is likely for most implementations) these are such that input is from the keyboard and output is to the screen. The full details of Text_IO cannot be described here but if we restrict ourselves to just a few useful facilities it looks a bit like

```
with IO_Exceptions;
package Text_IO is
    type Count is . . .  − − an integer type
    . . .
    procedure New_Line(Spacing: in Count := 1);
    procedure Set_Col(To: in Count);
    function Col return Count;

    . . .
    procedure Get(Item: out Character);
    procedure Put(Item: in Character);
    procedure Put(Item: in String);

    . . .
    − − the package Float_IO outlined in the previous section
    − − plus a similar package Integer_IO

    . . .
end Text_IO
```

Note first that this package commences with a with clause for IO_Exceptions. This is a further package which contains the declaration of a number of different exceptions relating to a variety of things which can go wrong with input–output. For toy programs the most likely to arise is probably Data_Error which would occur for example if we tried to read in a number from the keyboard but then accidentally typed in something which was not a number at all or was in the wrong format.

The next thing to note is the outline declaration of the type Count. This is an integer type having similar properties to the type Integer and almost inevitably derived from it (just as our type Real is likely to be derived from Float). The parameter of New_Line is of the type Count rather than plain Integer, although since the parameter will typically be a literal such as 2 (or be omitted so that the default of 1 applies) this will not be particularly evident.

The procedure Set_Col and function Col are useful for tabulation. The character positions along a line of output are numbered starting at 1. So if we write (and assuming use Text_IO;)

```
Set_Col(10);
```

then the next character output will go at position 10. A call of New_Line naturally sets the current position to 1 so that output commences at the beginning of the line. The function Col returns the current position and so

```
Set_Col(Col + 10);
```

will move the position on by 10 and thereby leave 10 spaces. Note that Col is an example of a function that has no parameters.

A single character can be output by for example

Put('A');

and a string of characters by

Put("This Is a string of characters");

A value of the type Real can be output in various formats. But first we have to instantiate the package Float_IO mentioned in the previous section and which is declared inside Text_IO. Having done that we can call Put with a single parameter, the value of type Real to be output, in which case a standard default format is used, or we can add further parameters controlling the format. This is best illustrated by a few examples, and we will suppose that our type Real was declared to have 7 decimal digits as in the example in Section 2.4.

If we do not supply any format parameters then an exponent notation is used with 7 significant digits, 1 before the point and 6 after (the 7 matches the precision given in the declaration of Real). There is also a leading space or minus sign. The exponent consists of the letter E followed by the exponent sign (+ or −) and then a two digit decimal exponent. The effect is shown by the following statements with the output given as a comment. For clarity the output is surrounded by quotes and s designates a space; in reality there are no quotes and spaces are spaces.

```
Put(12.34);      – – "s1.234000E+01"
Put(−987.65);    – – "−9.876500E+02"
Put(0.00289);    – – "s2.890000E−03"
```

We can override the default by providing three further parameters which give, respectively, the number of characters before the point, the number of characters after the point, and the number of characters after E. However, there is still always only one digit before the point. So

```
Put(12.34, 3, 4, 2);   – – "ss1.2340E+1"
```

If we do not want exponent notation then we simply specify the last parameter as zero and we then get normal decimal notation. So

```
Put(12.34, 3, 4, 0);   – – "s12.3400"
```

The output of values of type Integer follows a similar pattern. First we have to instantiate the generic package inside Text_IO which applies to all integer types with the particular type Integer thus

```
package Int_IO is new Integer_IO(Integer);
use Int_IO;
```

and (much as for the type Real), we can then call Put with a single parameter, the value of type Integer, in which case a standard default field is used, or we can add a further parameter specifying the field. The default field is the smallest that will accommodate all values of the type Integer allowing for a leading minus sign. Thus for a 16-bit implementation of Integer, the default field is 6. It should be noticed that if we specify a field which is too small then it is expanded as necessary. So

```
Put(123);       – – "sss123"
Put(–123);      – – "ss–123"
Put(123, 4);    – – "s123"
Put(123, 0);    – – "123"
```

That covers enough output for simple toy programs. The only input likely to be needed is of integer and real values and perhaps single characters. This is easily done by a call of Get with a parameter that must be a variable of the appropriate type, just as we wrote Get(X); in the simple program in Section 2.2.

A call of Get with a real or integer parameter will expect us to type in an appropriate number at the keyboard; this must have a decimal point if the parameter is real. It should also be noted that leading blanks (spaces) and newlines are skipped. A call of Get with a parameter of type Character will read the very next character, and this can be neatly used for controlling the flow of an interactive program, thus

```
C: Character;
. . .
Put("Do you want to stop? Answer Y if so. ");
Get(C);
if C = 'Y' then
. . .
```

That concludes our brief introduction to input–output which has inevitably been of a rather cookbook nature. Hopefully it has provided enough to enable the reader to drive such trial examples as desired as well as giving some further flavour to the nature of Ada.

EXERCISE 2.6

1 Which of the calls of Put discussed above would produce a different result with a 32-bit implementation of Integer?

2.7 Running a program

We are now in a position to put together a complete program using the proper input–output facilities and avoiding the non-portable type Float. As an

example we will rewrite the simple example of Section 2.2 and also use the
standard mathematical library. It becomes

```
with Text_IO, Generic_Elementary_Functions;
procedure Print_Roots is
   type Real is digits 7;
   X: Real;

   use Text_IO;
   package Real_IO is new Float_IO(Real);
   use Real_IO;

   package Real_Maths is new Generic_Elementary_Functions(Real);
   use Real_Maths;

begin
   Put("Roots of various numbers");
   . . .
   . . .       - - and so on as before
   . . .
end Print_Roots;
```

To have to write all that introductory stuff just to run a toy program each
time is rather a burden, so we will put it in a standard package of our own and
then compile it once so that it is permanently in our program library and can
then be accessed without more ado. We can write

```
with Text_IO, Generic_Elementary_Functions;
package Etc is
   type Real is digits 7;

   package Real_IO is new Text_IO.Float_IO(Real);
   package Int_IO is new Text_IO.Integer_IO(Integer);

   package Real_Maths is new Generic_Elementary_Functions(Real);
end Etc;
```

and having compiled Etc our typical program can look like

```
with Text_IO, Etc;
use Text_IO, Etc;
procedure Program is
   use Real_IO, Int_IO, Real_Maths;        - - as required
   . . .
   . . .
end Program;
```

Note that we can put the use clause for the packages mentioned in the with
clause immediately after the with clause. The reader will realize that the author

had great difficulty in identifying an appropriate and short name for our package Etc and hopes that he is forgiven for the pun on etcetera.

The reader should now be in a position to write complete simple programs. The exercises in this book have been written as fragments rather than complete programs for two reasons; one is that complete programs would take up a lot of space (and actually be rather repetitive) and the other is that Ada is really all about software components anyway.

Unfortunately it is not possible to explain how to call the Ada compiler and manipulate the program library because this depends upon the implementation and so we must leave the reader to find out how to do this last and vital step from the documentation for the implementation concerned.

EXERCISE 2.7

1   Write a program to output the ten times table. Make each column of the table 5 characters wide.

2   Write a program to output a table of square roots of numbers from 1 up to some limit specified by the user in response to a suitable question. Print the numbers as integers and the square roots to 5 decimal places in two columns. Use Set_Col to set the second column position so that the program can be easily modified. Note that a value N of type Integer can be converted to the corresponding Real value by writing Real(N).

2.8 Terminology

We conclude this introductory chapter with a few remarks on terminology. Every subject has its own terminology or jargon and Ada is no exception. (Indeed in Ada an exception is a kind of error, as we have seen!) A full glossary of terms will be found in Appendix 3.

Terminology will generally be introduced as required but before starting off with the detailed description of Ada it is convenient to mention a couple of concepts which will occur from time to time.

The term static refers to things that can be determined at compilation, whereas dynamic refers to things determined during execution. Thus a static expression is one whose value can be determined by the compiler such as

2 + 3

and a static array is one whose bounds are known at compilation time.

Sometimes it is necessary to make a parenthetic remark to the compiler where the remark is often not a part of the program as such but more a useful hint. This can be done by means of a construction known as a pragma. As an example we can indicate that we wish the compiler to optimize our program with emphasis on saving space by writing

> **pragma** Optimize(Space);

inside the region of program to which it is to apply. Alternatively we could write

> **pragma** Optimize(Time);

which indicates that speed of execution is the primary criterion.

Generally a pragma can appear anywhere that a declaration or statement can appear and in some other contexts also. Sometimes there may be special rules regarding the position of a particular pragma. For fuller details on pragmas see Appendix 1.

Ada 9X introduces slightly different terminology in order to increase clarity. We will use some of these terms in an informal way whenever it seems helpful. A good example is the idea of having different views of something such as occurs with renaming as will be described in Chapter 8.

Lexical Style

In the previous chapter, we introduced some concepts of Ada and illustrated the general appearance of Ada programs with some simple examples. However, we have so far only talked around the subject. In this chapter we get down to serious detail.

Regrettably it seems best to start with some rather unexciting but essential material – the detailed construction of things such as identifiers and numbers which make up the text of a program. However, it is no good learning a human language without getting the spelling sorted out. And as far as programming languages are concerned, compilers are usually very unforgiving regarding such corresponding and apparently trivial matters.

We also take the opportunity to introduce the notation used to describe the syntax of Ada language constructs. In general we will not use this syntax notation to introduce concepts but, in some cases, it is the easiest way to be precise. Moreover, if the reader wishes to consult the *LRM* then knowledge of the syntax notation is necessary. For completeness and easy reference the full syntax is given in Appendix 4.

3.1 Syntax notation

The syntax of Ada is described using a modified version of Backus–Naur Form
(BNF). In this, syntactic categories are represented by lower case names; some
of these contain embedded underlines to increase readability. A category is
defined in terms of other categories by a sort of equation known as a
production. Some categories are atomic and cannot be decomposed further –
these are known as terminal symbols. A production consists of the name being
defined followed by the special symbol ::= and its defining sequence.
  Other symbols used are

[ ]   square brackets enclose optional items,

{ }   braces enclose items which may be omitted, appear once or be
  repeated many times,

| a vertical bar separates alternatives.

In some cases the name of a category is prefixed by a word in italics. In such
cases the prefix is intended to convey some semantic information and can be
treated as a form of comment as far as the context free syntax is concerned.
Sometimes a production is presented in a form that shows the recommended layout.

3.2 Lexical elements

An Ada program is written as a sequence of lines of text containing the
following characters from the ISO 7-bit standard

• the alphabet A–Z

• the digits 0–9 various special characters " # & ' ( ) * + , – . / : ; < = > _ |

• the space character

The lower case alphabet may be used instead of or in addition to the upper
case alphabet, but the two are generally considered the same. (The only
exception is where the letters stand for themselves in character strings and
character literals.)
  Some other special characters such as ! may also be used in strings and
literals – these are in fact the remaining graphic characters of the ISO 7-bit
standard. Certain special characters may be used as alternatives to |, # and " if
these are not available. We will not bother with the alternatives and the extra
rules associated with them, but will stick to the normal characters in this book.
  Indeed these alternative characters are deprecated in Ada 9X and so there
is every reason to avoid them.
  We note incidentally that Ada 9X uses the larger ISO 8-bit character set
and so many more characters are allowed in strings and so on; but the general
program text rules are otherwise the same.

Moreover, AI–866 also allows an implementation of Ada 83 to use the ISO 8-bit Latin-1 standard and thereby extends AI-339 which only allowed such characters in comments. (This is our first example of an AI where the language is not quite as it seems from the *LRM*. See Section 1.1.)

The *LRM* does not prescribe how one proceeds from one line of text to the next. This need not concern us. We can just imagine that we type our Ada program as a series of lines using whatever mechanism the keyboard provides for starting a new line.

A line of Ada text can be thought of as a sequence of groups of characters known as lexical elements. We have already met several forms of lexical elements in Chapter 2. Consider for example

        Age := 43; – – John's age

This consists of five such elements

- the identifier **Age**
- the compound symbol :=
- the number **43**
- the single symbol ;
- the comment – – **John's age**

Other classes of lexical element are strings and character literals; they are dealt with in Chapter 6.

Individual lexical elements may not be split by spaces but otherwise spaces may be inserted freely in order to improve the appearance of the program. A most important example of this is the use of indentation to reveal the overall structure. Naturally enough a lexical element must fit on one line.

Particular care should be taken that the following compound delimiters do not contain spaces

        =>   used in aggregates, cases, etc.
        . .   for ranges
        **   exponentiation
        :=   assignment
        /=   not equals
        >=   greater than or equals
        <=   less than or equals
        <<   label bracket
        >>   the other label bracket
        <>   the 'box' for arrays and generics

However, spaces may occur in strings and character literals where they stand for themselves, and also in comments.

Note that adjacent identifiers and numbers must be separated from each other by spaces otherwise they would be confused. Thus we must write **end loop** rather than **endloop**.

3.3 Identifiers

We met identifiers in the simple examples in Chapter 2. As an example of the use of the syntax notation we now consider the following definition of an identifier

identifier ::= letter {[underline] letter_or_digit}

letter_or_digit ::= letter | digit

letter ::= upper_case_letter | lower_case_letter

This states that an identifier consists of a letter followed by zero, one or more instances of letter_or_digit optionally preceded by a single underline. A letter_or_digit is, as its name implies, either a letter or a digit. Finally a letter is either an upper_case_letter or a lower_case_letter. As far as this example is concerned the categories underline, digit, upper_case_letter and lower_case_letter are not decomposed further and so are considered to be terminal symbols.

In plain English this merely says that an identifier consists of a letter possibly followed by one or more letters or digits with embedded isolated underlines. Either case of letter can be used. What the syntax does not convey is that the meaning attributed to an identifier does not depend upon the case of the letters. In fact identifiers which differ only in the case of corresponding letters are considered to be the same. But, on the other hand, the underline characters are considered to be significant.

Ada 9X also allows a single trailing underline; partly for compatibility with non-Ada systems, and also to aid upgrade from Ada 83 to Ada 9X by providing new identifiers that could never have been used in Ada 83.

Ada does not impose any limit on the number of characters in an identifier. Moreover all are significant. There may however be a practical limit since an identifier must fit onto a single line and an implementation is likely to impose some maximum line length. Programmers are encouraged to use meaningful names such as Time_Of_Day rather than cryptic meaningless names such as T. Long names may seem tedious when first writing a program but in the course of its lifetime a program is read much more often than it is written and clarity aids subsequent understanding both by the original author and by others who may be called upon to maintain the program. Of course, in short mathematical or abstract subprograms, identifiers such as X and Y may be appropriate.

Identifiers are used to name all the various entities in a program. However, some identifiers are reserved for special syntactic significance and may not be reused. We encountered several of these in Chapter 2 such as **if**, **procedure** and **end**. There are 63 reserved words; they are listed in Appendix 1. For readability they are printed in boldface in this book, but that is not important. In program text they could, like all identifiers, be in either case or indeed in a mixture of cases – procedure, PROCEDURE and Procedure are all acceptable. Nevertheless, some discipline aids understanding, and a useful convention is to use lower case for the reserved words and leading upper case for all others. But this is a matter of taste.

There are minor exceptions regarding the reserved words **delta, digits** and **range**. As will be seen later, they are also used as attributes Delta, Digits and Range. However, when so used they are always preceded by a prime or single quote character and so there is no confusion.

There are five additional reserved words in Ada 9X namely **aliased, protected, requeue, tagged** and **until**. Clearly these are best avoided as identifiers in Ada 83 programs. Note also **access** and **Access** in Ada 9X.

Some identifiers such as Integer and True have a predefined meaning from the package Standard. These are not reserved and can be reused, although to do so is usually unwise since the program could become very confusing.

Note that Ada 9X introduces some new predefined identifiers in Standard such as Wide_Character and Wide_String. An existing Ada 83 program using such identifiers could be transformed to avoid a clash by systematically adding a trailing underline to the user's identifiers.

EXERCISE 3.3

1   Which of the following are not legal identifiers and why?

(a) Ada   (d) UMO164G   (g) X_
(b) fish&chips   (e) Time_ _Lag   (h) tax rate
(c) RATE-OF-FLOW   (f) 77E2   (i) goto

3.4 Numbers

Numbers (or numeric literals to use the proper jargon) take two forms according to whether they denote an integer (an exact whole number) or a real (an approximate and not usually whole number). The important distinguishing feature is that real literals always contain a decimal point whereas integer literals never do. Ada is strict on mixing up types. It is illegal to use an integer literal where the context demands a real literal and vice versa. Thus

Age: Integer := 43.0;

and

Weight: Real := 150;

are both illegal. (We are using a type Real rather than Float for reasons which were outlined in Section 2.4 and will be fully explained later.)

The simplest form of integer literal is simply a sequence of decimal digits. If the literal is very long it may be convenient to split it up into groups of digits by inserting isolated underlines thus

123_456_789

In contrast to identifiers such underlines are, of course, of no significance other than to make the literal easier to read.

The simplest form of real literal is a sequence of decimal digits containing a decimal point. Note that there must be at least one digit on either side of the decimal point. Again, isolated underlines may be inserted to improve legibility provided they are not adjacent to the decimal point; thus

```
3.14159_26536
```

Unlike most languages both integer and real literals can have an exponent. This takes the form of the letter E (either case) followed by a signed or unsigned decimal integer. This exponent indicates the power of ten by which the preceding simple literal is to be multiplied. The exponent cannot be negative in the case of an integer literal – otherwise it might not be a whole number. (As a trivial point an exponent of −0 is not allowed for an integer literal but it is for a real literal.)

Thus the real literal 98.4 could be written with an exponent in any of the following ways

```
9.84E1   98.4e0   984.0e−1   0.984E+2
```

Note that 984e−1 would not be allowed.

Similarly, the integer literal 1900 could also be written as

```
19E2   190e+1   1900E+0
```

but not as 19000e−1 nor as 1900E−0.

The exponent may itself contain underlines if it consists of two or more digits but it is unlikely that the exponent would be so large as to make this necessary. However, the exponent may not itself contain an exponent!

A final facility is the ability to express a literal in a base other than 10. This is done by enclosing the digits between # characters and preceding the result by the base. Thus

```
2#111#
```

is an integer literal of value $4 + 2 + 1 = 7$.

Any base from 2 to 16 inclusive can be used and, of course, base 10 can always be expressed explicitly. For bases above 10 the letters A to F are used to represent the superdigits 10 to 15. Thus

```
14#ABC#
```

equals $10 \times 14^2 + 11 \times 14 + 12 = 2126$.

A based literal can also have an exponent. But note carefully that the exponent gives the power of the base by which the simple literal is to be multiplied and not a power of ten – unless, of course, the base happens to be ten. The exponent itself, like the base, is always expressed in normal decimal notation. Thus

16#A#E2

equals $10 \times 16^2 = 2560$ and

2#11#E11

equals $3 \times 2 = 6144$.
 A based literal can be real. The distinguishing mark is again the point. (We can hardly say 'decimal point' if we are not using a decimal base! A better term is radix point.) So

2#101.11#

equals $4 + 1 + 1/2 + 1/4 = 5.75$ and

7#3.0#e−1

equals $3/7 = 0.\overset{\cdot}{4}2857\overset{\cdot}{1}$.
 The reader may have felt that the possible forms of based literal are unduly elaborate. This is not really so. Based literals are useful – especially for fixed point types since they enable the programmer to represent values in the form in which he or she thinks about them. Obviously bases 2, 8 and 16 will be the most useful. But the notation is applicable to any base and the compiler can compute to any base, so why not?
 Finally, note that a numeric literal cannot be negative. A form such as −3 consists of a literal preceded by the unary minus operator.

EXERCISE 3.4

1 Which of the following are not legal literals and why? For those that are legal, state whether they are integer or real literals.

(a) 38.6	(e) 2#1011	(i) 16#FfF#
(b) .5	(f) 2.71828_18285	(j) 1_0#1_0#E1_0
(c) 32e2	(g) 12#ABC#	(k) 27.4e_2
(d) 32e−2	(h) E+6	(l) 2#11#e−1

2 What is the value of the following?

(a) 16#E#E1	(c) 16#F.FF#E+2
(b) 2#11#E11	(d) 2#1.1111_1111_111#E11

3 How many different ways can you express the following as a numeric literal?

   (a) the integer 41   (b) the integer 150

   (Forget underlines, distinction between E and e, nonsignificant leading zeros and optional + in an exponent.)

3.5 Comments

It is important to add appropriate comments to a program to aid its understanding by someone else or yourself at a later date. We met some comments
in Chapter 2.

A comment in Ada is written as an arbitrary piece of text following two
hyphens (or minus signs – the same thing). Thus

```
– – this is a comment
```

The comment extends to the end of the line. There is no facility in Ada to
insert a comment into the middle of a line. Of course, the comment may be the
only thing on the line or it may follow some other Ada text. A long comment
needing several lines is merely written as successive comments.

```
– – this comment is spread
– – over
– – several
– – lines.
```

It is important that the leading hyphens are adjacent and are not separated by
spaces.

It should also be noted that AI-339 allows an implementation to permit a
comment to contain additional characters outside the ISO 7-bit standard.

EXERCISE 3.5

1 How many lexical elements are there in each of the following lines of text?

(a) X := X+2; – – add two to X
(b) – – that was a silly comment
(c) –
(d) – – – – – – – – – – – – –

2 Distinguish

(a) **delay** 2.0;
(b) **delay** 2.0;

CHECKLIST 3

The case of a letter is immaterial in all contexts except strings and
character literals.

Underlines are significant in identifiers but not in numeric literals.

Spaces are not allowed in lexical elements, except in strings, character literals and comments.

The presence or absence of a point distinguishes real and integer literals.

An integer may not have a negative exponent.

Numeric literals cannot be signed.

Scalar Types

This chapter lays the foundations for the small-scale aspects of Ada. We start by considering the declaration of objects, the assignment of values to them and the ideas of scope and visibility. We then introduce the important concepts of type, subtype and constraints. As examples of types, the remainder of the chapter discusses the numeric types 'Integer' and 'Real', enumeration types in general, the type 'Boolean' in particular, and the operations on them.

4.1 Object declarations and assignments

Values can be stored in objects which are declared to be of a specific type. Objects are either variables, in which case their value may change (or vary) as the program executes, or they may be constants, in which case they keep their same initial value throughout their life.

A variable is introduced into the program by a declaration which consists of the name (that is, the identifier) of the variable followed by a colon and then the name of the type. This can then optionally be followed by the := symbol and an initial value. The declaration terminates with a semicolon. Thus we might write

```
I: Integer;
P: Integer := 38;
```

This introduces the variable I of type Integer but gives it no particular initial value, and then the variable P and gives it the specific initial value of 38.

We can introduce several variables at the same time in one declaration by separating them by commas thus

```
I, J, K: Integer;
P, Q, R: Integer := 38;
```

In the second case all of P, Q and R are given the initial value of 38.

If a variable is declared and not given an initial value then great care must be taken not to use the undefined value of the variable until one has been properly given to it. If a program does use the undefined value in an uninitialized variable, its behaviour will be unpredictable; the program is said to be erroneous. As mentioned in Chapter 2, this means that the program is strictly illegal, but the compiler and run time system may not be able to tell us.

A common way to give a value to a variable is by using an assignment statement. In this, the identifier of the variable is followed by := and then some expression giving the new value. The statement terminates with a semicolon. Thus

```
I := 36;
```

and

```
P := Q+R;
```

are both valid assignment statements and place new values in I and P, thereby overwriting their previous values.

Note that := can be followed by any expression provided that it produces a value of the type of the variable being assigned to. We will discuss all the rules about expressions later, but it suffices to say at this point that they can consist of variables and constants with operations such as + and round brackets (parentheses) and so on just like an ordinary mathematical expression.

There is a lot of similarity between a declaration containing an initial value and an assignment statement. Both use := before the expression and the expression can be of arbitrary complexity.

An important difference, however, is that although several variables can be declared and given the same initial value together, it is not possible for an assignment statement to give the same value to several variables. This may seem odd but in practice the need to give the same value to several variables usually only arises with initial values anyway.

Perhaps we should remark at this stage that strictly speaking a multiple declaration such as

A, B: Integer := E;

is really a shorthand for

A: Integer := E;
B: Integer := E;

This means that in principle the expression E is evaluated for each variable. This is a subtle point and does not usually matter, but we will encounter some examples later where the effect is important.

A constant is declared in a similar way to a variable by inserting the reserved word **constant** after the colon. Of course, a constant must be initialized in its declaration otherwise it would be useless. Why? An example might be

Pi: **constant** Real := 3.14159_26536;

In the case of numeric types, and only numeric types, it is possible to omit the type from the declaration of a constant thus

Pi: **constant** := 3.14159_26536;

It is then technically known as a number declaration and merely provides a name for the number. The distinction between integer and real named numbers is made by the form of the initial value. In this case it is real because of the presence of the decimal point. It is usually good practice to omit the type when declaring numeric constants for reasons which will appear later. We will therefore do so in future examples. But note that the type cannot be omitted in numeric variable declarations even when an initial value is provided.

There is an important distinction between the allowed forms of initial values in constant declarations (with a type) and number declarations (without a type). In the former case the initial value may be any expression and is evaluated when the declaration is encountered at run time whereas in the latter case it must be a so-called universal expression which will almost inevitably be static and so evaluated at compilation time. Full details are deferred until Chapter 12.

EXERCISE 4.1

1 Write a declaration of a real variable R giving it an initial value of one.

2 Write appropriate declarations of real constants Zero and One.

3 What is wrong with the following declarations and statements?

    (a) **var** I: Integer;
    (b) G: **constant** := 981
    (c) P, Q: **constant** Integer;
    (d) P := Q := 7;
    (e) MN: **constant** Integer := M*N;
    (f) 2Pi: **constant**:= 2.0*Pi;

4.2 Blocks and scopes

Ada carefully distinguishes between declarations which introduce new identifiers and statements which do not. It is clearly only sensible that the declarations which introduce new identifiers should precede the statements which manipulate them. Accordingly, declarations and statements occur in separate places in the program text. The simplest fragment of text which includes declarations and statements is a block.

A block commences with the reserved word **declare**, some declarations, **begin**, some statements and concludes with the reserved word **end** and the terminating semicolon. A trivial example is

```
declare
    I: Integer := 0;    -- declarations here
begin
    I := I+1;           -- statements here
end;
```

A block is itself an example of a statement and so one of the statements in its body could be another block. This textual nesting of blocks can continue indefinitely.

Since a block is a statement it can be executed like any other statement. When this happens the declarations in its declarative part (the bit between **declare** and **begin**) are elaborated in order, and then the statements in the body (between **begin** and **end**) are executed in the usual way. Note the terminology: we elaborate declarations and execute statements. All that the elaboration of a declaration does is make the thing being declared come into existence and then evaluate and assign any initial value to it. When we come to the **end** of the block all the things which were declared in the block automatically cease to exist.

We can now see that the above simple example of a block is rather foolish; it introduces I, adds 1 to it but then loses it before use is made of the resulting value.

Another point to note is that the objects used in an initial value must, of course, exist. They could be declared in the same declarative part but the declarations must precede their use. For example

```
declare
   I: Integer := 0;
   K: Integer := I;
begin
```

is allowed, but

```
declare
   K: Integer := I;
   I: Integer := 0;
begin
```

is generally not. (We will see in a moment that this could have a valid but different meaning.)

This idea of elaborating declarations in order is important; the jargon is 'linear elaboration of declarations'.

Like other block structured languages, Ada also has the idea of hiding. Consider

```
declare
   I, J: Integer;
begin
   ...              – – here I is the outer one
   declare
      I: Integer;
   begin
      ...           – – here I is the inner one
   end;
   ...              – – here I is the outer one
end;
```

In this, a variable I is declared in an outer block and then redeclared in an inner block. This redeclaration does not cause the outer I to cease to exist but merely makes it temporarily invisible. In the inner block I refers to the new I, but as soon as we leave the inner block, this new I ceases to exist and the outer one again becomes visible.

We distinguish the terms 'scope' and 'visibility'. The scope is the region of text where the entity is potentially visible and it is visible at a given point if its identifier can be used to refer to it at that point. We will now illustrate these terms but a fuller discussion has to be left until Chapter 8.

In the case of a block the scope of a variable (or constant) extends from the start of its declaration until the end of the block. However, it is not visible in its own declaration nor in any inner block after the redeclaration of the same identifier. The regions of scope and visibility are illustrated by the following:

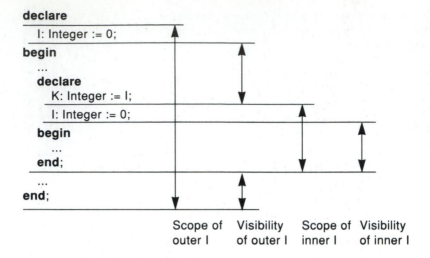

```
declare
    I: Integer := 0;
begin
    ...
    declare
        K: Integer := I;
        I: Integer := 0;
    begin
        ...
    end;
    ...
end;
```

Scope of outer I	Visibility of outer I	Scope of inner I	Visibility of inner I

The initial value of K refers to the outer I because it precedes the introduction of the inner I.

Thus

```
K: Integer := I;
I: Integer := 0;
```

may or may not be legal – it depends upon its environment.

EXERCISE 4.2

1   How many errors can you see in the following?

```
declare
    I: Integer := 7;
    J, K: Integer
begin
    J := I+K;
    declare
        P: Integer=I;
        I, J: Integer;
    begin
        I := P+Q;
        J := P–Q;
        K := I*J;
    end;
    Put(K);    – – output value of K
end;
```

4.3 Types

'A type is characterized by a set of values and a set of operations' (*LRM* 3.3).
In the case of the built-in type Integer, the set of values is represented by

   ..., −3, −2, −1, 0, 1, 2, 3, ...

and the operations include

   +, −, * and so on.

With two minor exceptions to be discussed later (arrays and tasks) every
type has a name which is introduced in a type declaration. (The built-in types
such as Integer are considered to be declared in the package Standard.)
Moreover, every type declaration introduces a new type quite distinct from any
other type.
   The set of values belonging to two distinct types are themselves quite
distinct, although in some cases the actual lexical form of the values may be
identical – which one is meant at any point is determined by the context. The
idea of one lexical form representing two or more different things is known as
overloading.
   Values of one type cannot be assigned to variables of another type. This is
the fundamental rule of strong typing. Strong typing, correctly used, is an
enormous aid to the rapid development of *correct* programs since it ensures
that many errors are detected at compilation time. (Overused, it can tie one in
knots; we will discuss this thought in Chapter 16.)
   A type declaration uses a somewhat different syntax to an object declaration
in order to emphasize the conceptual difference. It consists of the reserved word
type, the identifier to be associated with the type, the reserved word **is** and then
the definition of the type followed by the terminating semicolon. We can
imagine that the package Standard contains type declarations such as

   type Integer **is** ... ;

The type definition between **is** and ; gives in some way the set of values
belonging to the type. As a concrete example consider the following

   type Colour **is** (Red, Amber, Green);

(This is an example of an enumeration type and will be dealt with in more
detail in a later section in this chapter.)
   This introduces a new type called Colour. Moreover, it states that there are
only three values of this type and they are denoted by the identifiers Red,
Amber and Green.
   Objects of this type can then be declared in the usual way

   C: Colour;

An initial value can be supplied

```
C: Colour := Red;
```

or a constant can be declared

```
Default: constant Colour := Red;
```

We have stated that values of one type cannot be assigned to variables of another type. Therefore one cannot mix colours and integers and so

```
I: Integer;
C: Colour;
...
I := C;
```

is illegal. In older languages it is often necessary to implement concepts such as enumeration types by more primitive types such as integers and give values such as 0, 1 and 2 to variables named Red, Amber and Green. Thus in Algol 60 one could write

```
integer Red, Amber, Green;
Red := 0; Amber := 1; Green := 2;
```

and then use Red, Amber and Green as if they were literal values. Obviously the program would be easier to understand than if the code values 0, 1 and 2 had been used directly. But, on the other hand, the compiler could not detect the accidental assignment of a notional colour to a variable which was, in the mind of the programmer, just an ordinary integer. In Ada, as we have seen, this is detected during compilation thus making a potentially tricky error quite trivial to discover.

4.4 Subtypes

We now introduce subtypes and constraints. A subtype, as its name suggests, characterizes a set of values which is just a subset of the values of some other type known as the base type. The subset is defined by means of a constraint. Constraints take various forms according to the category of the base type. As is usual with subsets, the subset may be the complete set. There is, however, no way of restricting the set of operations of the base type. The subtype takes all the operations; subsetting applies only to the values.

As an example suppose we wish to manipulate dates; we know that the day of the month must lie in the range 1 .. 31 so we declare a subtype thus

```
subtype Day_Number is Integer range 1 .. 31;
```

We can then declare variables and constants using the subtype identifier in exactly the same way as a type identifier.

    D: Day_Number;

We are then assured that the variable D can take only integer values from 1 to 31 inclusive. The compiler will insert run-time checks if necessary to ensure that this is so; if a check fails then the Constraint_Error exception is raised.

It is important to realize that a subtype declaration does not introduce a new distinct type. An object such as D is of type Integer, and so the following is perfectly legal from the syntactic point of view.

    D: Day_Number;
    I: Integer;
    ...
    D := I;

Of course, on execution, the value of I may or may not lie in the range 1 .. 31. If it does, then all is well; if not then Constraint_Error will be raised. Assignment in the other direction

    I := D;

will, of course, always work.

It is not always necessary to introduce a subtype explicitly in order to impose a constraint. We could equally have written

    D: Integer **range** 1 .. 31;

Furthermore a subtype need not impose a constraint. It is perfectly legal to write

    subtype Day_Number **is** Integer;

although in this instance it is not of much value.

A subtype (explicit or not) may be defined in terms of a previous subtype

    subtype Feb_Day **is** Day_Number **range** 1 .. 29;

Any additional constraint must of course satisfy existing constraints

    Day_Number **range** 0 .. 10

would be incorrect and cause Constraint_Error to be raised.

The above examples have shown constraints with static bounds. This is not necessarily the case; in general the bounds can be given by arbitrary expressions and so the set of values of a subtype need not be static, that is known at compilation time. However, it is an important fact that a type is always static.

In conclusion then, a subtype does not introduce a new type but is merely a shorthand for an existing type with an optional constraint. However, in later chapters we will encounter several contexts in which an explicit constraint is not allowed; a subtype has to be introduced for these cases. We refer to a type or subtype name as a type mark and to the form consisting of a type mark followed by an optional constraint as a subtype indication as shown by the syntax

> type_mark ::= *type*_name | *subtype*_name
>
> subtype_indication ::= type_mark [constraint]

Thus we can restate the previous remark as saying that there are situations where a type mark has to be used whereas, as we have seen here, the more general subtype indication (which includes a type mark on its own) is allowed in object declarations.

The sensible use of subtypes has two advantages. It can ensure that programming errors are detected earlier by preventing variables from being assigned inappropriate values. It can also increase the execution efficiency of a program. This particularly applies to array subscripts as we shall see later.

We conclude this section by summarizing the assignment statement and the rules of strong typing. Assignment has the form

> Variable := expression;

and the two rules are

- both sides must have the same base type,
- the expression must satisfy any constraints on the variable; if it does not, the assignment does not take place, and Constraint_Error is raised instead.

Note carefully the general principle that type errors (violations of the first rule) are detected during compilation whereas subtype errors (violations of the second rule) are detected during execution by the raising of Constraint_Error. (A clever compiler might give a warning during compilation.)

We have now introduced the basic concepts of types and subtypes. The remaining sections of this chapter illustrate these concepts further by considering in more detail the properties of the simple types of Ada.

EXERCISE 4.4

1   Given the following declarations

I, J: Integer **range** 1 .. 10;

K : Integer **range** 1 .. 20;

which of the following assignment statements could raise Constraint_Error?

(a) I := J;
(b) K := J;
(c) J := K;

4.5 Simple numeric types

Perhaps surprisingly, a full description of the numeric types of Ada is deferred until much later in this book. The problems of numerical analysis (error estimates and so on) are complex and Ada is correspondingly complex in this area so that it can cope in a reasonably complete way with the needs of the numerical specialist. For our immediate purposes such complexity can be ignored. Accordingly, in this section, we merely consolidate a simple understanding of the two numeric types Integer and Real which we have been using as background for elementary examples. For the everyday programmer these two numeric types will probably suffice.

First a reminder. The type Integer is a genuine built-in Ada type. But as mentioned in Section 2.4, the type Real is not. It has to be declared somewhere in terms of one of the built-in floating point types. The reason for supposing that this has been done concerns portability and will be discussed when the truth about numeric types is revealed in more detail. For the moment, however, we will suppose that Real is the floating point type. (The author is not deceiving you but in fact encouraging good Ada programming practice.)

As we have seen, a constraint may be imposed on the type Integer by using the reserved word **range**. This is then followed by two expressions separated by two dots which, of course, must produce values of integer type. These expressions need not be literal constants. One could have

```
P: Integer range 1 .. I+J;
```

A range can be null as would happen in the above case if I+J turned out to be zero. Null ranges may seem pretty useless but they often automatically occur in limiting cases, and to exclude them would mean taking special action in such cases.

The minimum value of the type Integer is given by Integer'First and the maximum value by Integer'Last. These are our first examples of attributes. Ada contains various attributes denoted by a single quote followed by an identifier.

The value of Integer'First will depend on the implementation but will always be negative. On a two's complement machine it will be −Integer'Last−1 whereas on a one's complement machine it will be −Integer'Last. So on a typical 16-bit two's complement implementation we will have

```
Integer'First = −32768
Integer'Last = +32767
```

Of course, we should always write Integer'Last rather than +32767 if that is what we logically want. Otherwise program portability could suffer.

Two useful subtypes are

```
subtype Natural is Integer range 0 .. Integer'Last;
subtype Positive is Integer range 1 .. Integer'Last;
```

These are so useful that they are declared for us in the package Standard.

The attributes First and Last also apply to subtypes so

```
Positive'First = 1
Natural'Last = Integer'Last
```

We turn now to a brief consideration of the type Real. It is possible to apply constraints to the type Real to reduce the range and precision, but this takes us into the detail which has been deferred until later. There are also attributes Real'First and Real'Last. It is not really necessary to say any more at this point.

The other predefined operations that can be performed on the types Integer and Real are much as one would expect in a modern programming language. They are summarized below.

+, –   These are either unary operators (that is, taking a single operand) or binary operators taking two operands.

    In the case of a unary operator, the operand can be either integer or real; the result will be of the same type. Unary + effectively does nothing. Unary – changes the sign.

    In the case of a binary operator, both operands must be integer or both operands must be real; the result will be of the type of the operands. Normal addition or subtraction is performed.

*   Multiplication; both operands must be integer or both operands must be real; again the result is of the same type.

/   Division; both operands must be integer or both operands must be real; again the result is of the same type. Integer division truncates towards zero.

rem   Remainder; in this case both operands must be integer and the result is an integer. It is the remainder on division.

mod   Modulo; again both operands must be integer and the result is an integer. This is the mathematical modulo operation.

abs   Absolute value; this is a unary operator and the single operand may be integer or real. The result is again of the same type and is the absolute value. That is, if the operand is positive, the result is the same but if it is negative, the result is the corresponding positive value.

**   Exponentiation; this raises the first operand to the power of the second. If the first operand is of integer type, the second must be a positive integer or zero. If the first operand is of real type, the second can be any integer. The result is of the same type as the first operand.

In addition, we can perform the operations =, /=, <, <=, > and >= to return a Boolean result True or False. Again both operands must be of the same type. Note the form of the not equals operator /=.

Although the above operations are mostly straightforward a few points are worth noting.

It is a general rule that mixed mode arithmetic is not allowed. One cannot, for example, add an integer value to a real value; both must be of the same

type. A change of type from Integer to Real or vice versa can be done by using
the desired type name (or indeed subtype name) followed by the expression to
be converted in brackets.

So given

```
I: Integer := 3;
R: Real := 5.6;
```

we cannot write

```
I+R
```

but we must write

```
Real(I)+R
```

which uses real addition to give the real value 8.6, or

```
I+Integer(R)
```

which uses integer addition to give the integer value 9.

Conversion from real to integer always rounds rather than truncates, thus

```
1.4 becomes 1
1.6 becomes 2
```

but a value midway between two integers, such as 1.5, may be rounded up or
down according to the implementation.

This irritating lack of portability is cured in Ada 9X, which specifies that
rounding of such halves is always away from zero so that 1.5 always becomes
2 and −1.5 becomes −2.

There is a subtle distinction between **rem** and **mod**. The **rem** operation
produces the remainder corresponding to the integer division operation /.
Integer division truncates towards zero; this means that the absolute value of
the result is always the same as that obtained by dividing the absolute values
of the operands. So

```
  7 /  3  =  2
(−7)/  3  = − 2
  7 /(−3) = − 2
(−7)/(−3) =   2
```

and the corresponding remainders are

```
  7 rem  3  =  1
(−7) rem  3  = −1
  7 rem (−3) =  1
(−7) rem (−3) = −1
```

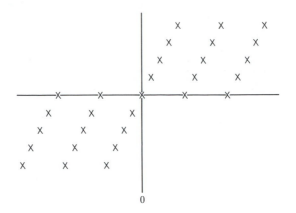

Figure 4.1 Behaviour of I **rem** 5 around zero.

The remainder and quotient are always related by

(I/J) * J + I **rem** J = I

and it will also be noted that the sign of the remainder is always equal to the sign of the first operand I (the dividend).

However, **rem** is not always satisfactory. If we plot the values of I **rem** J for a fixed value of J (say 5) for both positive and negative values of I we get the pattern shown in Figure 4.1.

As we can see, the pattern is symmetric about zero and consequently changes its incremental behaviour as we pass through zero.

The **mod** operation, on the other hand, does have uniform incremental behaviour as shown in Figure 4.2.

The **mod** operation enables us to do normal modulo arithmetic. For example

(A+B) **mod** n = (A **mod** n + B **mod** n) **mod** n

for all values of A and B both positive and negative. For positive n, A **mod** n is always in the range 0 .. n−1; for negative n, A **mod** n is always in the range n+1 .. 0. Of course, modulo arithmetic is only usually performed with a positive value for n. But the **mod** operator gives consistent and sensible behaviour for negative values of n also.

We can look upon **mod** as giving the remainder corresponding to division with truncation towards minus infinity. So

```
   7 mod   3  =  1
(−7) mod   3  =  2
   7 mod (−3) = −2
(−7) mod (−3) = −1
```

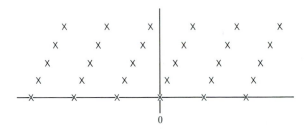

Figure 4.2   Behaviour of I **mod** 5 around zero.

In the case of **mod** the sign of the result is always equal to the sign of the second operand whereas with **rem** it is the sign of the first operand.

The reader may have felt that this discussion has been somewhat protracted. In summary, it is perhaps worth saying that integer division with negative operands is rare. The operators **rem** and **mod** only differ when just one operand is negative. It will be found that in such cases it is almost always **mod** that is wanted.

Finally some notes on the exponentiation operator ******. For a positive second operand, the operation corresponds to repeated multiplication. So

```
3**4 = 3*3*3*3 = 81
3.0**4 = 3.0*3.0*3.0*3.0 = 81.0
```

A very subtle point is that AI-868 (which contradicts AI-137) allows the repeated multiplications to be performed by appropriate squarings as an optimization although as we shall see when we come to Chapter 12 there can be slight differences in accuracy in the real case.

The second operand can be 0 and, of course, the result is then always the value one

```
3**0 = 1
3.0**0 = 1.0
0**0 = 1
0.0**0 = 1.0
```

The second operand cannot be negative if the first operand is an integer, as the result might not be a whole number. In fact, the exception Constraint_Error would be raised in such case. But it is allowed for a real first operand and produces the corresponding reciprocal

```
3.0**(−4) = 1.0/81.0 = 0.0123456780123...
```

We conclude this section with a brief discussion on combining operators in an expression. As is usual, the operators have different precedence levels and the natural precedence can be overruled by the use of brackets. Operators of the same precedence are applied in order from left to right. A subexpression in brackets obviously has to be evaluated before it can be used. But note that the order of evaluation of the two operands of a binary operator is not specified. The precedence levels of the operators we have met so far are shown below in increasing order of precedence

```
= /= < <= > >=
+ - (binary)
+ - (unary)
* / mod rem
** abs
```

Thus

```
A/B*C      means   (A/B)*C
A+B*C+D    means   A+(B*C)+D
A*B+C*D    means   (A*B)+(C*D)
A*B**C     means   A*(B*C)
```

In general, as stated above, several operations of the same precedence can be applied from left to right and brackets are not necessary. However, the syntax rules forbid multiple instances of the exponentiating operator without brackets. Thus we cannot write

```
A**B**C
```

but must explicitly write either

```
(A**B)**C   or   A**(B**C)
```

This restriction avoids the risk of accidentally writing the wrong thing. Note however that the well established forms

```
A-B-C   and   A/B/C
```

are allowed. The syntax rules similarly prevent the mixed use of **abs** and ** without brackets.

The precedence of unary minus needs care

```
-A**B   means   -(A**B)   rather than   (-A)**B
```

as in Algol 68. Also

```
A**-B   and   A*-B
```

are illegal. Brackets are necessary.

Note finally that the precedence of **abs** is, confusingly, not the same as that of unary minus. As a consequence we can write

```
- abs X   but not   abs - X
```

EXERCISE 4.5

1   Evaluate the expressions below given the following

I: Integer := 7;
J: Integer := –5;
K: Integer := 3;

(a) I*J*K   (e) J + 2 **rem** I
(b) I/J*K   (f) K**K**K
(c) I/J/K   (g) –J **mod** 3
(d) J + 2 **mod** I   (h) –J **rem** 3

2   Rewrite the following mathematical expressions in Ada. Use suitable identifiers of appropriate type.

(a) Mr^2 – moment of inertia of black hole
(b) b^2-4ac – discriminant of quadratic
(c) $^{4/3}\pi r^3$ – volume of sphere
(d) $p\pi a^4/8l\eta$ – viscous flowrate through tube

4.6 Enumeration types

Here are some examples of declarations of enumeration types starting with Colour which we introduced when discussing types in general

```
type Colour is (Red, Amber, Green);
type Day is (Mon, Tue, Wed, Thu, Fri, Sat, Sun);
type Stone is (Amber, Beryl, Quartz);
type Groom is (Tinker, Tailor, Soldier, Sailor,
                Rich_Man, Poor_Man, Beggar_Man, Thief);
type Solo is (Alone);
```

This introduces an example of overloading. The literal Amber can represent a Colour or a Stone. Both meanings of the same name are visible together and the second declaration does not hide the first whether they are declared in the same declarative part or one is in an inner declarative part. We can usually tell which is meant from the context, but in those odd cases when we cannot we can always qualify the literal by placing it in brackets and preceding it by an appropriate type mark (that is its type name or a relevant subtype name) and a single quote. Thus

```
Colour'(Amber)
Stone'(Amber)
```

Examples where this is necessary will occur later.

Although we can use Amber as an enumeration literal in two distinct enumeration types, we cannot use it as an enumeration literal and the identifier of a variable at the same time. The declaration of one would hide the other and they could not both be declared in the same declarative part. Later we will see that an enumeration literal can be overloaded with a subprogram.

There is no upper limit on the number of values in an enumeration type but there must be at least one. An empty enumeration type is not allowed.

Constraints on enumeration types and subtypes are much as for integers. The constraint has the form

range lower_bound_expression .. upper_bound_expression

and this indicates the set of values from the lower bound to the upper bound inclusive. So we can write

subtype Weekday **is** Day **range** Mon .. Fri;
D: Weekday;

or

D: Day **range** Mon .. Fri;

and then we know that D cannot be Sat or Sun.

If the lower bound is above the upper bound then we get a null range, thus

subtype Colourless **is** Colour **range** Amber .. Red;

Note the curious anomaly that we cannot have a null subtype of a type such as Solo (since it only has one value).

The attributes First and Last also apply to enumeration types and subtypes, so

Colour'First = Red
Weekday'Last = Fri

There are built-in functional attributes to give the successor or predecessor of an enumeration value. These consist of Succ or Pred following the type name and a single quote. Thus

Colour'Succ(Amber) = Green
Stone'Succ(Amber) = Beryl
Day'Pred(Fri) = Thu

Of course, the thing in brackets can be an arbitrary expression of the appropriate type. If we try to take the predecessor of the first value or the successor of the last then the exception Constraint_Error is raised. In the absence of this exception we have, for any type T and any value X,

$T'Succ(T'Pred(X)) = X$

and vice versa.

Another functional attribute is Pos. This gives the position number of the enumeration value, that is the position in the declaration with the first one having a position number of zero. So

    Colour'Pos(Red) = 0
    Colour'Pos(Amber) = 1
    Colour'Pos(Green) = 2

The opposite to Pos is Val. This takes the position number and returns the corresponding enumeration value. So

    Colour'Val(0) = Red
    Day'Val(6) = Sun

If we give a position value outside the range, as for example

    Solo'Val(1)

then Constraint_Error is raised.

Clearly we always have

    T'Val(T'Pos(X)) = X

and vice versa.

We also note that

    T'Succ(X) = T'Val(T'Pos(X) + 1)

they either both give the same value or both raise an exception.

It should be noted that these four attributes Succ, Pred, Pos and Val may also be applied to subtypes but are then identical to the same attributes of the corresponding base type.

It is probably rather bad practice to mess about with Pos and Val when it can be avoided. To do so encourages the programmer to think in terms of numbers rather than the enumeration values and hence destroys the abstraction.

Finally the operators =, /=, <, <=, > and >= also apply to enumeration types. The result is defined by the order of the values in the type declaration. So

    Red < Green is True
    Wed >= Thu   is False

The same result would be obtained by comparing the position values. So

    T'Pos(X) < T'Pos(Y)   and   X < Y

are always equivalent (except that X < Y might be ambiguous).

EXERCISE 4.6

1 Evaluate

   (a) Day'Succ(Weekday'Last)
   (b) Weekday'Succ(Weekday'Last)
   (c) Stone'Pos(Quartz)

2 Write suitable declarations of enumeration types for

   (a) the colours of the rainbow,
   (b) typical fruits.

3 Write an expression that delivers one's predicted bridegroom after eating a portion of pie containing N stones. Use the type Groom declared at the beginning of this section.

4 If the first of the month is in D where D is of type Day, then write an assignment replacing D by the day of the week of the Nth day of the month.

5 Why might X < Y be ambiguous?

4.7 The Boolean type

The Boolean type is a predefined enumeration type whose declaration can be considered to be

> **type** Boolean **is** (False, True);

Boolean values are used in constructions such as the if statement which we briefly met in Chapter 2. Boolean values are produced by the operators =, /=, <, <=, > and >= which have their expected meaning and apply to many types. So we can write constructions such as

> **if** Today = Sun **then**
>   Tomorrow := Mon;
> **else**
>   Tomorrow := Day'Succ(Today);
> **end if**;

The Boolean type (we capitalize the name in memory of the mathematician Boole) has all the normal properties of an enumeration type, so, for instance

> False < True = True !!
> Boolean'Pos(True) = 1

We could even write

and	F T		**or**	F T		**xor**	F T
F	F F		F	F T		F	F T
T	F T		T	T T		T	T F

Figure 4.3   Truth tables for **and**, **or** and **xor**.

   subtype Always **is** Boolean **range** True .. True;

although it would not seem very useful.
   The Boolean type also has other operators which are as follows

not   This is a unary operator and changes True to False and vice versa. It has the same precedence as **abs**.

and   This is a binary operator. The result is True if both operands are True, and False otherwise.

or   This is a binary operator. The result is True if one or other or both operands are True, and False only if they are both False.

xor   This is also a binary operator. The result is True if one or other operand but not both are True. (Hence the name – eXclusive OR.) Another way of looking at it is to note that the result is True if and only if the operands are different. (The operator is known as 'not equivalent' in some languages.)

   The effects of **and**, **or** and **xor** are summarized in the usual truth tables shown in Figure 4.3.
   The precedences of **and**, **or** and **xor** are equal to each other but lower than that of any other operator. In particular they are of lower precedence than the relational operators =, /=, <, <=, > and >=. This is unlike Pascal and as a consequence brackets are not needed in expressions such as

   P < Q **and** I = J

   However, although the precedences are equal, **and**, **or** and **xor** cannot be mixed up in an expression without using brackets (unlike + and – for instance). So

   B **and** C **or** D   is illegal

whereas

   I + J – K   is legal

We have to write

   B **and** (C **or** D)   or   (B **and** C) **or** D

in order to emphasize which meaning is required.

The reader familiar with other programming languages will remember that **and** and **or** usually have a different precedence. The problem with this is that the programmer often gets confused and writes the wrong thing. It is to prevent this that Ada makes them the same precedence and insists on brackets. Of course, successive applications of the same operator are permitted so

> B **and** C **and** D   is legal

and as usual evaluation goes from left to right although, of course, it does not matter in this case since the operator **and** is associative.

Take care with **not**. Its precedence is higher than **and**, **or** and **xor** as in other languages and so

> **not** A **or** B

means

> (**not** A) **or** B

rather than

> **not** (A **or** B)

which those familiar with logic will remember is the same as

> (**not** A) **and** (**not** B)

Boolean variables and constants can be declared and manipulated in the usual way.

> Danger: Boolean;
> Signal: Colour;
> ...
> Danger := Signal = Red;

The variable Danger is then True if the signal is Red. We can then write

> **if** Danger **then**
>   Stop_Train;
> **end if**;

Note that we do not have to write

> **if** Danger = True **then**

although this is perfectly acceptable; it just misses the point that Danger is already a Boolean and so can be used directly as the condition.

A worse sin is to write

```
if Signal = Red then
   Danger := True;
else
   Danger := False;
end if;
```

rather than

```
Danger := Signal = Red;
```

The literals True and False could be overloaded by declaring for example

type Answer **is** (False, Dont_Know, True);

but to do so might make the program rather confusing.

Finally, it should be noted that it is often clearer to introduce our own two-valued enumeration type rather than use the type Boolean. Thus instead of

Wheels_OK: Boolean;
...
if Wheels_OK **then**

it is much better (and safer!) to write

type Wheel_State is (Up, Down);
Wheel_Position: Wheel_State;
...
if Wheel_Position = Up **then**

since whether the wheels are OK or not depends upon the situation. OK for landing is different to being OK for cruising. The enumeration type removes any doubt as to which is meant.

EXERCISE 4.7

1   Write declarations of constants T and F having the values True and False.

2   Using T and F from the previous exercise, evaluate

(a) T **and** F **and** T   (d) (F = F) = (F = F)
(b) **not** T **or** T   (e) T < T < T < T
(c) F = F = F = F

3   Evaluate

(A /= B) = (A **xor** B)

for all combinations of values of Boolean variables A and B.

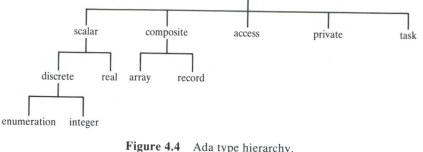

Figure 4.4   Ada type hierarchy.

4.8 Type classification

At this point we pause to consolidate the material presented in this chapter so far.

The types in Ada can be classified as shown in Figure 4.4. (Ada 9X uses a rather different classification but we will defer a comparison until Chapter 17 so as not to confuse the reader.)

This chapter has discussed scalar types. In Chapter 6 we will deal with the composite types but access, private and task types will be dealt with much later.

In Ada 9X there are also tagged types (for polymorphism and other Object Oriented goodies) and protected types (for passive task interaction); these are discussed in some detail in Chapter 17.

The scalar types themselves can be subdivided into real types and discrete types. Our sole example of a real type has been the type Real – the other real types are discussed in Chapter 12. The other types, Integer, Boolean and enumeration types in general are discrete types – the only other kinds of discrete types to be introduced are other integer types, again dealt with in Chapter 12, and character types which are in fact a form of enumeration type and are dealt with in Chapter 6.

The key abstract distinction between the discrete types and the real types is that the former have a clear-cut set of distinct separate (that is, discrete) values. The type Real, on the other hand, should be thought of as having a continuous set of values – we know in practice that a finite digital computer must implement a real type as actually a set of distinct values but this is an implementation detail, the abstract concept is of a continuous set of values.

The attributes Pos, Val, Succ and Pred apply to all discrete types (and subtypes) because the operations reflect the discrete nature of the values. We explained their meaning with enumeration types in Section 4.6. In the case of type Integer the position number is simply the number itself so

Integer'Pos(N) = N
Integer'Val(N) = N
Integer'Succ(N) = N+1
Integer'Pred(N) = N−1

The application of these attributes to integers does at first sight seem pretty futile, but when we come to the concept of generic units in Chapter 13 we will see that it is convenient to allow them to apply to all discrete types.

The attributes First and Last however apply to all scalar types and subtypes including real types.

Again we emphasize that Pos, Val, Succ and Pred for a subtype are identical to the corresponding operations on the base type, whereas in the case of First and Last this is not so.

Ada 9X introduces two new functional attributes for all scalar types and subtypes. These are Max and Min which take two parameters and return the maximum or minimum value respectively. Furthermore, despite our previous remarks about the continuous nature of real types, the attributes Pred and Succ also apply to all real types in Ada 9X. They return the adjacent implemented number.

Finally we note the difference between a type conversion and a type qualification.

Real(I)   − − conversion
Integer'(I)   − − qualification

In the case of a conversion we are changing the type, in the second, we are just stating it (usually to overcome an ambiguity). As a mnemonic aid *q*ualification uses a *q*uote.

In both cases we can use a subtype name and Constraint_Error could consequently arise. Thus

Positive(R)

would convert the value of the real variable R to integer and then check that it was positive, whereas

Positive'(I)

would just check that the value of I was positive. In both cases, of course, the result is the checked value and is then used in an overall expression; these checks cannot just stand alone.

4.9 Expression summary

All the operators introduced so far are shown in Table 4.1 grouped by precedence level.

Table 4.1   Scalar operators.

Operator	Operation	Operand(s)	Result
and	conjunction	Boolean	Boolean
or	inclusive or	Boolean	Boolean
xor	exclusive or	Boolean	Boolean
=	equality	any	Boolean
/=	inequality	any	Boolean
<	less than	scalar	Boolean
<=	less than or equals	scalar	Boolean
>	greater than	scalar	Boolean
>=	greater than or equals	scalar	Boolean
+	addition	numeric	same
−	subtraction	numeric	same
+	identity	numeric	same
−	negation	numeric	same
*	multiplication	Integer	Integer
		Real	Real
/	division	Integer	Integer
		Real	Real
mod	modulo	Integer	Integer
rem	remainder	Integer	Integer
**	exponentiation	Integer: Natural	Integer
		Real : Integer	Real
not	negation	Boolean	Boolean
abs	absolute value	numeric	same

In all the cases of binary operators except for **, the two operands must be of the same type.

We have actually now introduced all the operators of Ada except for one (&) although as we shall see in Chapter 6 there are further possible meanings to be added.

There are also two membership tests which apply to all scalar types (among others). These are **in** and **not in**. They are technically not operators although their precedence is the same as that of the relational operators =, /= and so on. They enable us to test whether a value lies within a specified range (including the end values) or satisfies a constraint implied by a subtype. The first operand is therefore a scalar expression, the second is a range or type mark and the result is, of course, of type Boolean. Examples are

```
I not in 1 .. 10
I in Positive
Today in Weekday
```

Note that this is one of the situations where we have to use a type mark rather than a subtype indication. We could not replace the last example by

> Today **in** Day **range** Mon .. Fri

although we could write

> Today **in** Mon .. Fri

Ada seems a bit curious here!

The test **not in** is equivalent to using **in** and then applying **not** to the result, but **not in** is usually more readable. So the first expression above could be written as

> **not** (I **in** 1 .. 10)

where the brackets are necessary.

The reason that **in** and **not in** are not technically operators is explained in Chapter 7 when we deal with subprograms.

There are also two short circuit control forms **and then** and **or else** which like **in** and **not in** are also not technically classed as operators.

The form **and then** is closely related to the operator **and**, whereas **or else** is closely related to the operator **or**. They may occur in expressions and have the same precedence as **and**, **or** and **xor**. The difference lies in the rules regarding the evaluation of their operands.

In the case of **and** and **or**, both operands are always evaluated but the order is not specified. In the case of **and then** and **or else** the left hand operand is always evaluated first and the right hand operand is only evaluated if it is necessary in order to determine the result.

So in

> X **and then** Y

X is evaluated first. If X is false, the answer is false whatever the value of Y so Y is not evaluated. If X is true, Y has to be evaluated and the value of Y is the answer.

Similarly in

> X **or else** Y

X is evaluated first. If X is true, the answer is true whatever the value of Y so Y is not evaluated. If X is false, Y has to be evaluated and the value of Y is the answer.

The forms **and then** and **or else** should be used in cases where the order of evaluation matters. A common circumstance is where the first condition protects against the evaluation of the second condition in circumstances that could raise an exception.

Suppose we need to test

I/J > K

and we wish to avoid the risk that J is zero. In such a case we could write

J /= 0 **and then** I/J > K

and we would then know that if J is zero there is no risk of an attempt to divide by zero. The observant reader will realize that this is not a very good example because one could usually write I>K*J (assuming J positive) – but even here we could get overflow. Better examples occur with arrays and access types and will be mentioned in due course.

Like **and** and **or**, the forms **and then** and **or else** cannot be mixed without using brackets.

We now summarize the primary components of an expression (that is the things upon which the operators operate) that we have met so far. They are

- identifiers   used for variables, constants, numbers and enumeration literals
- literals   such as 4.6, 2#101#
- type conversions   such as Integer(R)
- qualified expressions   such as Colour'(Amber)
- attributes   such as Integer'Last
- function calls   such as Day'Succ(Today)

A full consideration of functions and how they are declared and called has to be deferred until later. However, it is worth noting at this point that a function with one parameter is called by following its name by the parameter in brackets. The parameter can be any expression of the appropriate type and could include further function calls. We will assume for the moment that we have available a simple mathematical library containing familiar functions such as

```
Sqrt   square root
Log    logarithm to base 10
Ln     natural logarithm
Exp    exponential function
Sin    sine
Cos    cosine
```

In each case they take a Real argument and deliver a Real result.

We are now in a position to write statements such as

```
Root := (−B+Sqrt(B**2−4.0*A*C)) / (2.0*A);
Sin2x := 2.0*Sin(X)*Cos(X);
```

Finally a note on errors although this is not the place to deal with them in depth. The reader will have noticed that whenever anything could go wrong we have usually stated that the exception Constraint_Error will be raised. This is a general exception which applies to all sorts of violations of ranges. The only other exception which needs to be mentioned at this point is Numeric_Error. This will usually be raised if something goes wrong with the evaluation of an arithmetic expression itself before an attempt is made to store the result. An obvious example is an attempt to divide by zero. It might be thought that the distinction between these two exceptions was quite clear. However, consider on the one hand

    Integer'Succ(Integer'Last)

which might be expected to raise Constraint_Error, and on the other hand

    Integer'Last+1

which might be expected to raise Numeric_Error. In practice, the object code for these two expressions is likely to be the same. As a consequence, AI-387 concludes that Constraint_Error and Numeric_Error cannot be crisply distinguished and therefore must be considered to be the same exception; it recommends that implementations always raise Constraint_Error rather than Numeric_Error.

Ada 9X formalizes this position by declaring Numeric_Error as just a renaming of Constraint_Error.

As well as exceptions there are erroneous constructs and incorrect order dependencies as mentioned in Chapter 2. The use of a variable before a value has been assigned to it is an important example of an erroneous situation. Two cases which we have encountered so far where the order is not defined are

- The destination variable in an assignment statement may be evaluated before or after the expression to be assigned.
- The order of evaluation of the two operands of a binary operator is not defined.

(In the first case it should be realized that the destination variable could be an array component such as A(I+J) and so the expression I+J has to be evaluated as part of evaluating the destination variable; we will deal with arrays in Chapter 6.) Examples where these orders matter cannot be given until we deal with functions in Chapter 7.

EXERCISE 4.9

1   Rewrite the following mathematical expressions in Ada.

(a) $2\pi\sqrt{l/g}$ – period of a pendulum

(b) $\dfrac{m_{o}}{\sqrt{1-v^2/c^2}}$ – mass of relativistic particle

(c) $\sqrt{2\pi n}\, .n^n .e^{-n}$ – Stirling's approximation for $n!$ (integral n)

2   Rewrite **1** (c) replacing n by the real value x.

CHECKLIST 4

Declarations and statements are terminated by a semicolon.

Initialization, like assignment uses ':='.

Any initial value is evaluated for each object in a declaration.

Elaboration of declarations is linear.

An identifier may not be used in its own declaration.

Each type definition introduces a quite distinct type.

A subtype is not a new type but merely a shorthand for a type with a possible constraint.

A type is always static, a subtype need not be.

No mixed mode arithmetic.

Distinguish 'rem' and 'mod' for negative operands.

Exponentiation with a negative exponent only applies to real types.

Take care with the precedence of the unary operators.

A scalar type cannot be empty, a subtype can.

'Pos', 'Val', 'Succ' and 'Pred' on subtypes are the same as on the base type.

'First' and 'Last' are different for subtypes.

Qualification uses a quote.

Order of evaluation of binary operands is not defined.

Distinguish 'and', 'or' and 'and then', 'or else'.

5 Control Structures

This chapter describes the three bracketed sequential control structures of Ada. These are the if statement which we have briefly met before, the case statement and the loop statement. It is now recognized that these three control structures are not only necessary but also sufficient to be able to write programs with a clearly discernible flow of control without recourse to goto statements and labels. However, for pragmatic reasons, Ada does actually contain a goto statement and this is also described in this chapter.

The three control structures exhibit a similar bracketing style. There is an opening reserved word 'if', 'case' or 'loop' and this is matched at the end of the structure by the same reserved word preceded by 'end'. The whole is, as usual, terminated by a semicolon. So we have

if	**case**	**loop**
...	...	...
end if;	**end case;**	**end loop;**

In the case of the loop statement, the word 'loop' can be preceded by an iteration clause commencing with 'for' or 'while'.

5.1 If statements

The simplest form of if statement starts with the reserved word **if** followed by a Boolean expression and the reserved word **then**. This is then followed by a sequence of statements which will be executed if the Boolean expression turns out to be True. The end of the sequence is indicated by the closing **end if**. The Boolean expression can, of course, be of arbitrary complexity and the sequence of statements can be of arbitrary length.

A simple example is

```
if Hungry then
    Eat;
end if;
```

In this, Hungry is a Boolean variable and Eat is a subprogram describing the details of the eating activity. The statement Eat; merely calls the subprogram (subprograms are dealt with in detail in Chapter 7).

The effect of this if statement is that if variable Hungry is True then we call the subprogram Eat and otherwise we do nothing. In either case we then obey the statement following the if statement.

As we have said there could be a long sequence between **then** and **end if**. Thus we might break down the process into more detail

```
if Hungry then
    Cook;
    Eat;
    Wash_Up;
end if;
```

Note how we indent the statements to show the flow structure of the program. This is most important since it enables the program to be understood so much more easily. The **end if** should be underneath the corresponding **if** and **then** is best placed on the same line as the **if**.

Sometimes, if the whole statement is very short it can all go on one line

```
if X < 0.0 then X := −X; end if;
```

Note that **end if** will always be preceded by a semicolon. This is because the semicolons terminate statements rather than separate them as in Algol and Pascal. Readers familiar with those languages will probably feel initially that the Ada style is irksome. However, it is consistent and makes line by line program editing so much easier.

Often we will want to do alternative actions according to the value of the condition. In this case we add **else** followed by the alternative sequence to be obeyed if the condition is False. We saw an example of this in the last chapter

```
if Today = Sun then
   Tomorrow := Mon;
else
   Tomorrow := Day'Succ(Today);
end if;
```

Algol 60 and Algol 68 users should note that Ada is not an expression language and so conditional expressions are not allowed. We cannot write something like

```
Tomorrow :=
   if Today = Sun then Mon else Day'Succ(Today) end if;
```

The statements in the sequences after **then** and **else** can be quite arbitrary and so could be further nested if statements. Suppose we have to solve the quadratic equation

$$ax^2 + bx + c = 0$$

The first thing to check is a. If $a = 0$ then the equation degenerates into a linear equation with a single root $-c/b$. (Mathematicians will understand that the other root has slipped off to infinity.) If a is not zero then we test the discriminant $b^2 - 4ac$ to see whether the roots are real or complex. We could program this as

```
if A = 0.0 then
        -- linear case
else
   if B**2 - 4.0*A*C >= 0.0 then
        -- real roots
   else
        -- complex roots
   end if,
end if;
```

Observe the repetition of **end if**. This is rather ugly and occurs sufficiently frequently to justify an additional construction. This uses the reserved word **elsif** as follows

```
if A = 0.0 then
        -- linear case
elsif B**2 - 4.0*A*C >= 0.0 then
        -- real roots
else
        -- complex roots
end if;
```

This construction emphasizes the essentially equal status of the three cases and also the sequential nature of the tests.

The **elsif** part can be repeated an arbitrary number of times and the final

else part is optional. The behaviour is simply that each condition is evaluated in turn until one that is True is encountered; the corresponding sequence is then obeyed. If none of the conditions turns out to be True then the else part, if any, is taken; if there is no else part then none of the sequences is obeyed.

Note the spelling of **elsif**. It is the only reserved word of Ada that is not an English word (apart from operators such as **xor**). Note also the layout – we align **elsif** and **else** with the **if** and **end if** and all the sequences are indented equally.

As a further example, suppose we are drilling soldiers and they can obey four different orders described by

```
type Move is (Left, Right, Back, On);
```

and that their response to these orders is described by calling subprograms Turn_Left, Turn_Right and Turn_Back or by doing nothing at all respectively. Suppose that the variable Order of type Move contains the order to be obeyed. We could then write the following

```
if Order = Left then
   Turn_Left;
else
   if Order = Right then
      Turn_Right;
   else
      if Order = Back then
         Turn_Back;
      end if;
   end if;
end if;
```

But it is far clearer and neater to write

```
if Order = Left then
   Turn_Left;
elsif Order = Right then
   Turn_Right;
elsif Order = Back then
   Turn_Back;
end if;
```

This illustrates a situation where there is no **else** part. However, although better than using nested if statements, this is still a bad solution because it obscures the symmetry and mutual exclusion of the four cases ('mutual exclusion' means that by their very nature only one can apply). We have been forced to impose an ordering on the tests which is quite arbitrary and not the essence of the problem. The proper solution is to use the case statement as we shall see in the next section.

Contrast this with the quadratic equation. In that example, the cases were not mutually exclusive and the tests had to be performed in order. If we had tested $b^2 - 4ac$ first then we would have been forced to test a against zero in each alternative.

    There is no directly corresponding contraction for **then if** as in Algol 68. Instead the short circuit control form **and then** can often be used.

    So, rather than

```
if J > 0 then
   if I/J > K then
      Action;
   end if;
end if;
```

we can, as we have seen, write

```
if J > 0 and then I/J > K then
   Action;
end if;
```

EXERCISE 5.1

1   The variables Day, Month and Year contain today's date. They are declared as

```
Day: Integer range 1 .. 31;
Month: Month_Name;
Year: Integer range 1901 .. 2099;
```

    where

```
type Month_Name is (Jan, Feb, Mar, Apr, May, Jun, Jul, Aug, Sep, Oct, Nov, Dec);
```

    Write statements to update the variables to contain tomorrow's date. What happens if today is 31 Dec 2099?

2   X and Y are two real variables. Write statements to swap their values, if necessary, to ensure that the larger value is in X. Use a block to declare a temporary variable T.

5.2 Case statements

A case statement allows us to choose one of several sequences of statements according to the value of an expression. For instance, the example of the drilling soldiers should be written as

```
case Order is
   when Left => Turn_Left;
   when Right => Turn_Right;
   when Back => Turn_Back;
   when On => null;
end case;
```

All possible values of the expression must be provided for in order to guard against accidental omissions. If, as in this example, no action is required for one or more values then the null statement has to be used.

The null statement, written

null;

does absolutely nothing but its presence indicates that we truly want to do nothing. The sequence of statements here, as in the if statement, must contain at least one statement. (There is no empty statement as in Algol 60.)

It often happens that the same action is desired for several values of the expression. Consider the following

```
case Today is
   when Mon | Tues | Wed | Thu => Work;
   when Fri                     => Work; Party;
   when Sat | Sun               => null;
end case;
```

This expresses the idea that on Monday to Thursday we go to work. On Friday we also go to work and then go to a party. At the weekend we do nothing. The alternative values are separated by the vertical bar character. Note again the use of a null statement.

If several successive values have the same action then it is more convenient to use a range

```
when Mon .. Thu => Work;
```

Sometimes we wish to express the idea of a default action to be taken by all values not explicitly stated; this is provided for by the reserved word **others**. The above example could be rewritten

```
case Today is
   when Mon .. Thu  => Work;
   when Fri         => Work; Party;
   when others      => null;
end case;
```

It is possible to have ranges as alternatives. In fact this is probably a situation where the clearest explanation of what is allowed is given by the formal syntax[†].

```
case_statement ::=
   case expression is
      case_statement_alternative
      {case_statement_alternative}
   end case;
```

[†] In the production for case_statement_alternative, the vertical bar stands for itself and is not a metasymbol.

```
case_statement_alternative ::=
    when choice { | choice} => sequence_of_statements
choice ::= simple_expression | discrete_range | others |
    component_simple_name
discrete_range ::= discrete_subtype_indication | range
subtype_indication ::= type_mark [constraint]
type_mark ::= type_name | subtype_name
range ::= range_attribute | simple_expression .. simple_expression
```

We see that **when** is followed by one or more choices separated by vertical bars and that a choice may be a simple expression, a discrete range or **others**. (The syntax shows that a choice may be a component simple name; however this only applies to choices used in a different situation which we have not yet met and so can be ignored for the moment.) A simple expression, of course, just gives a single value – Fri being a trivial example. A discrete range offers several possibilities. It can be the syntactic form range which the syntax tells us can be two simple expressions separated by two dots – Mon .. Thu is a simple example; a range can also be given by a range attribute which we will meet in the next chapter. A discrete range can also be a subtype indication which as we know is a type mark (a type name or subtype name) followed optionally by an appropriate constraint. In this case the constraint has to be a range constraint which is merely the reserved word **range** followed by the syntactic form range. Examples of discrete ranges are

```
Mon .. Thu
Day range Mon .. Thu
Weekday
Weekday range Mon .. Thu
```

All these possibilities may seem unnecessary, but as we shall see later the form, discrete range, is used in other contexts as well as the case statement. In the case statement there is not usually much point in using the type name since this is known from the context anyway. Similarly there is not much point in using the subtype name followed by a constraint since the constraint alone will do. However, it might be useful to use a subtype name alone when that exactly corresponds to the range required. So we could rewrite the example as

```
case Today is
    when Weekday => Work;
                        if Today = Fri then
                            Party;
                        end if;
    when others => null;
end case;
```

although this solution feels untidy.

There are various other restrictions that the syntax does not tell us. One is that if we use **others** then it must appear alone and as the last alternative. As stated earlier it covers all values not explicitly covered by the previous alternatives (one is still allowed to write **others** even if there are no other cases to be considered!).

Another very important restriction is that all the choices must be static so that they can be evaluated at compilation time. Thus all expressions in choices must be static – in practice they will usually be literals as in our examples. Similarly, if a choice is simply a subtype such as Weekday then it too must be static.

Finally we return to the point made at the beginning of this section that all possible values of the expression after **case** must be provided for. This usually means all values of the type of the expression. This is certainly the case of a variable declared as of a type without any constraints (as in the case of Today). However, if the expression is of a simple form and belongs to a static subtype (that is one whose constraints are static expressions and so can be determined at compilation time) then only values of that subtype need be provided for. In other words, if the compiler can tell that only a subset of values is possible then only that subset need and must be covered. The simple forms allowed for the expression are the name of an object of the static subtype or a qualified or converted expression whose type mark is that of the static subtype.

In the case of our example, if Today had been of subtype Weekday then we would know that only the values Mon .. Fri are possible and so only these can and need be covered. Even if Today is not constrained we can still write our expression as a qualified expression Weekday'(Today) and then again only Mon .. Fri is possible. So we could write

```
case Weekday'(Today) is
    when Mon .. Thu  => Work;
    when Fri         => Work; Party;
end case;
```

but, of course, if Today happens to take a value not in the subtype Weekday (that is, Sat or Sun) then Constraint_Error will be raised. Mere qualification cannot prevent Today from being Sat or Sun. So this is not really a solution to our original problem.

As further examples, suppose we had variables

```
I: Integer range 1 .. 10;
J: Integer range 1 .. N;
```

where N is not static. Then we know that I belongs to a static subtype (albeit anonymous) whereas we cannot say the same about J. If I is used as an expression in a case statement then only the values 1 .. 10 have to be catered for, whereas if J is so used then the full range of values of type Integer (Integer'First .. Integer'Last) have to be catered for.

The above discussion on the case statement has no doubt given the reader the impression of considerable complexity. It therefore seems wise to summarize the key points which will in practice need to be remembered

- Every possible value of the expression after **case** must be covered once and once only.
- All values and ranges after **when** must be static.
- If **others** is used it must be last and on its own.

EXERCISE 5.2

1 Rewrite Exercise 5.1(**1**) to use a case statement to set the correct value in End_Of_Month.

2 A vegetable gardener digs in winter, sows seed in spring, tends the growing plants in summer and harvests the crop in the autumn or fall. Write a case statement to call the appropriate subprogram Dig, Sow, Tend or Harvest according to the month M. Declare appropriate subtypes if desired.

3 An improvident man is paid on the first of each month. For the first ten days he gorges himself, for the next ten he subsists and for the remainder he starves. Call subprograms Gorge, Subsist and Starve according to the day D. Assume End_Of_Month has been set and that D is declared as

    D: Integer **range** 1 .. End_Of_Month;

5.3 Loop statements

The simplest form of loop statement is

```
loop
    sequence_of_statements
end loop;
```

The statements of the sequence are then repeated indefinitely unless one of them terminates the loop by some means. So immortality could be represented by

```
loop
    Work;
    Eat;
    Sleep;
end loop;
```

As a more concrete example consider the problem of computing the base e of natural logarithms from the infinite series

$$e = 1 + 1/1! + 1/2! + 1/3! + 1/4! + \ldots$$

where

$$n! = n \times (n-1) \times (n-2) \ldots 3 \times 2 \times 1$$

A possible solution is

```
declare
    E: Real := 1.0;
    I: Integer := 0;
    Term: Real := 1.0;
begin
    loop
        I := I + 1;
        Term := Term / Real(I);
        E := E + Term;
    end loop;
    ...
```

Each time around the loop a new term is computed by dividing the previous term by I. The new term is then added to the sum so far which is accumulated in E. The term number I is an integer because it is logically a counter and so we have to write Real(I) as the divisor. The series is started by setting values in E, I and Term which correspond to the first term (that for which I = 0).

The computation then goes on for ever with E becoming a closer and closer approximation to *e*. In practice, because of the finite accuracy of the computer, Term will become zero and continued computation will be pointless. But in any event we presumably want to stop at some point so that we can do something with our computed result. We can do this with the statement

```
exit;
```

If this is obeyed inside a loop then the loop terminates at once and control passes to the point immediately after **end loop**.

Suppose we decide to stop after *N* terms of the series – that is when I = N. We can do this by writing the loop as

```
loop
    if I = N then exit; end if;
    I := I + 1;
    Term := Term / Real(I);
    E := E + Term;
end loop;
```

The construction

```
if condition then exit; end if;
```

is so common that a special shorthand is provided

    exit when condition;

So we now have

```
loop
   exit when I = N;
   I := I + 1;
   Term := Term / Real(I);
   E := E + Term;
end loop;
```

   Although an exit statement can appear anywhere inside a loop – it could be in the middle or near the end – a special form is provided for the frequent case where we want to test a condition at the start of each iteration. This uses the reserved word **while** and gives the condition for the loop to be continued. So we could write

```
while I /= N loop
   I := I + 1;
   Term := Term / Real(I);
   E := E + Term;
end loop;
```

The condition is naturally evaluated each time around the loop.

   The final form of loop allows for a specific number of iterations with a loop parameter taking in turn all the values of a discrete range. Our example could be recast as

```
for I in 1 .. N loop
   Term := Term / Real(I);
   E := E + Term;
end loop;
```

where I takes the values 1, 2, 3, ... N.

   The parameter I is implicitly declared by its appearance in the iteration scheme and does not have to be declared outside. It takes its type from the discrete range and within the loop behaves as a constant so that it cannot be changed except by the loop mechanism itself. When we leave the loop (by whatever means) I ceases to exist (because it was implicitly declared by the loop) and so we cannot read its final value from outside.

   We could leave the loop by an exit statement – if we wanted to know the final value we could copy the value of I into a variable declared outside the loop thus

```
if condition_to_exit then
   Last_I := I;
   exit;
end if;
```

The values of the discrete range are normally taken in ascending order. Descending order can be specified by writing

for I **in reverse** 1 .. N **loop**

but the range itself is always written in ascending order.

It is not possible to specify a numeric step size of other than 1. This should not be a problem since the vast majority of loops go up by steps of 1 and almost all the rest go down by steps of 1. The very few which do behave otherwise can be explicitly programmed using the while form of loop.

The range can be null (as for instance if N happened to be zero or negative in our example) in which case the sequence of statements will not be obeyed at all. Of course, the range itself is evaluated only once and cannot be changed inside the loop.

Thus

```
N := 4;
for I in 1 .. N loop
   ...
   N := 10;
end loop;
```

results in the loop being executed just four times despite the fact that N is changed to ten.

Our examples have all shown the lower bound of the range being 1. This, of course, need not be the case. Both bounds can be arbitrary dynamically evaluated expressions. Furthermore the loop parameter need not be of integer type. It can be of any discrete type, as determined by the discrete range.

We could, for instance, simulate a week's activity by

```
for Today in Mon .. Sun loop
   case Today is
      ...
   end case;
end loop;
```

This implicitly declares Today to be of type Day and obeys the loop with the values Mon, Tue, ... Sun in turn.

The other forms of discrete range (using a type or subtype name) are of advantage here. The essence of Mon .. Sun is that it embraces all the values of the type Day. It is therefore better to write the loop using a form of discrete range that conveys the idea of completeness

```
for Today in Day loop
   ...
end loop;
```

And again since we know that we do nothing at weekends anyway we could write

> **for** Today **in** Day **range** Mon .. Fri **loop**

or better

> **for** Today **in** Weekday **loop**

It is interesting to note a difference regarding the determination of types in the case statement and for statement. In the case statement, the type of a discrete range after **when** is determined from the type of the expression after **case**. In the for statement, the type of the loop parameter is determined from the type of the discrete range after **in**. The dependency is the other way round.

It is therefore necessary for the type of the discrete range to be unambiguous in the for statement. This is usually the case but if we had two enumeration types with two overloaded literals such as

> **type** Planet **is** (Mercury, Venus, Earth, Mars, Jupiter,
>   Saturn, Uranus, Neptune, Pluto);
> **type** Roman_God **is** (Janus, Mars, Jupiter, Juno, Vesta,
>   Vulcan, Saturn, Mercury, Minerva);

then

> **for** X **in** Mars .. Saturn **loop**

would be ambiguous and the compiler would not compile our program. We could resolve the problem by qualifying one of the expressions

> **for** X **in** Planet'(Mars) .. Saturn **loop**

or (probably better) by using a form of discrete range giving the type explicitly

> **for** X **in** Planet **range** Mars .. Saturn **loop**

When we have dealt with numerics in more detail we will realize that the range 1 .. 10 is not necessarily of type Integer. A general application of our rule that the type must not be ambiguous in a for statement would lead us to have to write

> **for** I **in** Integer **range** 1 .. 10 **loop**

However, this would be so tedious in such a common case that there is a special rule which applies to discrete ranges in for statements which says that if both bounds are integer literals then type Integer is implied. We can therefore conveniently write

> **for** I **in** 1 .. 10 **loop**

But note carefully that we cannot write

```
for I in –1 .. 10 loop
```

because –1 is not a literal as explained in Section 3.4. This perhaps surprising conclusion is confirmed by AI-148. We will return to this topic in Section 12.1.

In Ada 9X the special rule is slightly different so that a negated literal is allowed in this context without the explicit use of the type Integer.

Finally we reconsider the exit statement. The simple form encountered earlier always transfers control to immediately after the innermost embracing loop. But of course loops may be nested and sometimes we may wish to exit from a nested construction. As an example suppose we are searching in two dimensions

```
for I in 1 .. N loop
  for J in 1 .. M loop
    – – if values of I and J satisfy
    – – some condition then leave nested loop
  end loop;
end loop;
```

A simple exit statement in the inner loop would merely take us to the end of that loop and we would have to recheck the condition and exit again. This can be avoided by naming the outer loop and using the name in the exit statement thus

```
Search:
for I in 1 .. N loop
  for J in 1 .. M loop
    if condition_OK then
      I_Value := I;
      J_Value := J;
      exit Search;
    end if;
  end loop;
end loop Search;
– – control passes here
```

A loop is named by preceding it with an identifier and colon. (It looks remarkably like a label in other languages but it is not and cannot be 'gone to'.) The identifier must be repeated between the corresponding **end loop** and the semicolon.

The conditional form of exit can also refer to a loop by name

```
exit Search when condition;
```

EXERCISE 5.3

1 The statement Get(I); reads the next value from the input file into the integer variable I. Write statements to read and add together a series of numbers. The end of the series is indicated by a dummy negative value.

2 Write statements to determine the power of 2 in the factorization of N. Compute the result in Count but do not alter N.

3 Compute

$$g = \sum_{p=1}^{n} 1/p - \log n$$

(As $n \to \infty$, $g \to \gamma = 0.577215665...$)

5.4 Goto statements and labels

Many will be surprised that a modern programming language should contain a goto statement at all. It is now considered to be extremely bad practice to use goto statements because of the resulting difficulty in proving correctness of the program, maintenance and so on. And indeed Ada contains adequate control structures so that it should not normally be necessary to use a goto at all.

So why provide a goto statement? The main reason concerns automatically generated programs. If we try to transliterate (by hand or machine) a program from some other language into Ada then the goto will probably be useful. Another example might be where the program is generated automatically from some high-level specification. Finally there may be cases where the goto is the neatest way – perhaps as a way out of some deeply nested structure – but the alternative of raising an exception (see Chapter 10) could also be considered.

In order to put us off using gotos and labels (and perhaps so that our manager can spot them if we do) the notation for a label is unusual and stands out like a sore thumb. A label is an identifier enclosed in double angled brackets thus

```
<<The_Devil>>
```

and a goto statement takes the expected form of the reserved word **goto** followed by the label identifier and semicolon

```
goto The_Devil;
```

A goto statement cannot be used to transfer control into an if, case or loop statement nor between the arms of an if or case statement.

EXERCISE 5.4

1 Rewrite the nested loop of Section 5.3 using a label <<Search>> rather than naming the outer loop. Why is this not such a good solution?

5.5 Statement classification

The statements in Ada can be classified as shown in Figure 5.1.

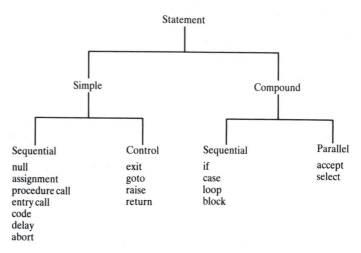

Figure 5.1 Classification of statements.

Further detail on the assignment statement is in the next chapter when we discuss composite types. Procedure calls and return statements are discussed in Chapter 7 and the raise statement which is concerned with exceptions is discussed in Chapter 10. The code statement is mentioned in Chapter 15. The remaining statements (entry call, delay, abort, accept and select) concern tasking and are dealt with in Chapter 14.

For completeness we note that there is an additional statement in Ada 9X, namely the requeue statement. This also concerns tasking and is dealt with in Chapter 17.

All statements can have one or more labels. The simple statements cannot be decomposed lexically into other statements whereas the compound statements can be so decomposed and can therefore be nested. Statements are obeyed sequentially unless one of them is a control statement (or an exception is implicitly raised).

CHECKLIST 5

Statement brackets must match correctly.

Use '**elsif**' where appropriate.

The choices in a case statement must be static.

All possibilities in a case statement must be catered for.

If '**others**' is used it must be last and on its own.

The expression after '**case**' can be qualified in order to reduce the alternatives.

A loop parameter behaves as a constant.

A named loop must have the name at both ends.

Avoid gotos.

Use the recommended layout.

Composite Types

In this chapter we describe the composite types which are arrays and records. We also complete our discussion of enumeration types by introducing characters and strings. At this stage we discuss arrays fairly completely but consider only simple forms of records. The more elaborate discriminated records which include variant records are deferred until Chapter 11.

6.1 Arrays

An array is a composite object consisting of a number of components all of the same type (strictly, subtype). An array can be of one, two or more dimensions. A typical array declaration might be

A: **array** (Integer **range** 1 .. 6) **of** Real;

This declares A to be a variable object which has six components, each of which is of type Real. The individual components are referred to by following the array name with an expression in brackets giving an integer value in the discrete range 1 .. 6. If this expression, known as the index value, has a value outside the range, then the exception Constraint_Error will be raised. We could set zero in each component of A by writing

for I **in** 1 .. 6 **loop**
    A(I) := 0.0;
end loop;

An array can be of several dimensions, in which case a separate range is given for each dimension. So

AA: **array** (Integer **range** 0 .. 2, Integer **range** 0 .. 3) **of** Real;

is an array of 12 components in total, each of which is referred to by two integer index values, the first in the range 0 .. 2 and the second in the range 0 .. 3. Each component of this two-dimensional array could be set to zero by a nested loop thus

for I **in** 0 .. 2 **loop**
    for J **in** 0 .. 3 **loop**
        AA(I, J) := 0.0;
    end loop;
end loop;

The discrete ranges do not have to be static: one could have

N: Integer := ... ;
B: **array** (Integer **range** 1 .. N) **of** Boolean;

and the value of N at the point when the declaration of B is elaborated would determine the number of components in B. Of course, the declaration of B might be elaborated many times during the course of a program – it might be inside a loop for example – and each elaboration will give rise to a new life of a new array and the value of N could be different each time. Like other declared objects, the array B ceases to exist once we pass the end of the block containing its declaration. Because of 'linear elaboration of declarations' both N and B could be declared in the same declarative part but the declaration of N would have to precede that of B.

The discrete range in an array index follows similar rules to that in a for statement. An important one is that a range such as 1 .. 6 implies type Integer so we could have written

   A: **array** (1 .. 6) **of** Real;

However, an array index could be of any discrete type. We could for example have

   Hours_Worked: **array** (Day) **of** Real;

This array has seven components denoted by Hours_Worked(Mon), ... Hours_Worked(Sun). We could set suitable values in these variables by

   for D **in** Weekday **loop**
      Hours_Worked(D) := 8.0;
   end loop;
   Hours_Worked(Sat) := 0.0;
   Hours_Worked(Sun) := 0.0;

If we only wanted to declare the array Hours_Worked to have components corresponding to Mon .. Fri then we could write

   Hours_Worked: **array** (Day **range** Mon .. Fri) **of** Real;

or (better)

   Hours_Worked: **array** (Weekday) **of** Real;

Arrays have various attributes relating to their indexes. A'First and A'Last give the lower and upper bound of the first (or only) index of A. So using our last declaration of Hours_Worked

   Hours_Worked'First = Mon
   Hours_Worked'Last = Fri

A'Length gives the number of values of the first (or only) index.

   Hours_Worked'Length = 5

A'Range is short for A'First .. A'Last. So

   Hours_Worked'Range is Mon .. Fri

The same attributes can be applied to the various dimensions of a multidimensional array by adding the dimension number in brackets. It has to be a static expression. So, in the case of our two-dimensional array AA we have

```
AA'First(1)   = 0
AA'First(2)   = 0
AA'Last(1)    = 2
AA'Last(2)    = 3
AA'Length(1) = 3
AA'Length(2) = 4
```

and

```
AA'Range(1)   is 0 .. 2
AA'Range(2)   is 0 .. 3
```

The first dimension is assumed if (1) is omitted. It is perhaps better practice to specifically state (1) for multidimensional arrays and omit it for one-dimensional arrays.

It is always best to use the attributes where possible in order to reflect relationships among entities in a program because it generally means that if the program is modified, the modifications are localized.

The Range attribute is particularly useful with loops. Our earlier examples are better written as

```
for I in A'Range loop
   A(I) := 0.0;
end loop;

for I in AA'Range(1) loop
   for J in AA'Range(2) loop
      AA(I, J) := 0.0;
   end loop;
end loop;
```

The Range attribute can also be used in a declaration. Thus

```
J: Integer range A'Range;
```

is equivalent to

```
J: Integer range 1 .. 6;
```

If a variable is to be used to index an array as in A(J) it is usually best if the variable has the same constraints as the discrete range in the array declaration. This will usually minimize the run-time checks necessary. It has been found that in such circumstances it is usually the case that the index variable J is assigned less frequently than the array component A(J) is accessed. We will return to this topic in Section 10.3.

The array components we have seen are just variables in the ordinary way. They can therefore be assigned to and used in expressions.

Like other variable objects, arrays can be given an initial value. This will often be denoted by an aggregate which is the literal form for an array value.

The simplest form of aggregate consists of a list of expressions giving the values of the components in order, separated by commas and enclosed in brackets. So we could initialize the array A by

A: **array** (1 .. 6) **of** Real := (0.0, 0.0, 0.0, 0.0, 0.0, 0.0);

In the case of a multidimensional array the aggregate is written in a nested form

AA: **array** (0 .. 2, 0 .. 3) **of** Real := ((0.0, 0.0, 0.0, 0.0),
                                                (0.0, 0.0, 0.0, 0.0),
                                                (0.0, 0.0, 0.0, 0.0));

and this illustrates that the first index is the 'outer' one. Or thinking in terms of rows and columns, the first index is the row number.

An aggregate must be complete. If we initialize any component of an array, we must initialize them all.

The initial values for the individual components need not be literals, they can be any expressions. These expressions are evaluated when the declaration is elaborated but the order of evaluation of the expressions in the aggregate is not specified.

An array can be declared as constant in which case an initial value is mandatory as explained in Section 4.1. Constant arrays are of frequent value as look-up tables. The following array can be used to determine whether a particular day is a working day or not

Work_Day: **constant array** (Day) **of** Boolean
          := (True, True, True, True, True, False, False);

An interesting example would be an array enabling tomorrow to be determined without worrying about the end of the week.

Tomorrow: **constant array** (Day) **of** Day
          := (Tue, Wed, Thu, Fri, Sat, Sun, Mon);

For any day D, Tomorrow (D) is the following day.

Finally, it should be noted that the array components can be of any type or subtype. Also the dimensions of a multidimensional array can be of different discrete types. An extreme example would be

Strange: **array** (Colour, 2 .. 7, Weekday **range** Tue .. Thu)
         of Planet **range** Mars .. Saturn;

EXERCISE 6.1

1 Declare an array F of integers with index running from 0 to N. Write statements to set the components of F equal to the Fibonacci numbers given by

$$F_0 = 0, \; F_1 = 1, \; F_i = F_{i-1} + F_{i-2} \qquad i > 1$$

2 Write statements to find the index values I, J of the maximum component of

     A: **array** (1 .. N, 1 .. M) **of** Real;

3 Declare an array Days_In_Month giving the number of days in each month. See Exercise 5.1(**1**). Use it to rewrite that example. See also Exercise 5.2(**1**).

4 Declare an array Yesterday analogous to the example Tomorrow above.

5 Declare a constant array Bor such that

     Bor(P, Q) = P **or** Q

6 Declare a constant unit matrix Unit of order 3. A unit matrix is one for which all components are zero except those whose indexes are equal which have value one.

6.2 Array types

The arrays we introduced in the last section did not have an explicit type name. They were in fact of anonymous type. This is one of the few cases in Ada where an object can be declared without naming the type – another case is with tasks.

Reconsidering the first example in the previous section, we could write

    type Vector_6 **is array** (1 .. 6) **of** Real;

and then declare A using the type name in the usual way

    A: Vector_6;

An advantage of using a type name is that it enables us to assign whole arrays that have been declared separately. If we also have

    B : Vector_6;

then we can write

    B := A;

which has the effect of

    B(1) := A(1); B(2) := A(2); ... B(6) := A(6);

although the order of assigning the components is not relevant.

On the other hand if we had written

    C: **array** (1 .. 6) **of** Real;
    D: **array** (1 .. 6) **of** Real;

then D := C; is illegal because C and D are not of the same type. They are of different types both of which are anonymous. The underlying rule is that every type definition introduces a new type and in this case the syntax tells us that an array type definition is the piece of text from **array** up to (but not including) the semicolon.

Moreover, even if we had written

C, D: **array** (1 .. 6) **of** Real;

then D := C; would still have been illegal. This is because of the rule mentioned in Section 4.1 that such a multiple declaration is only a shorthand for the two declarations above. There are therefore still two distinct type definitions even though they are not explicit.

Whether or not we introduce a type name for particular arrays depends very much on the abstract view of each situation. If we are thinking of the array as a complete object in its own right then we should use a type name. If, on the other hand, we are thinking of the array as merely an indexable conglomerate not related as a whole to other arrays then it should probably be of an anonymous type.

Arrays like Tomorrow and Work_Day of the last section are good examples of arrays which are of the anonymous category. To be forced to introduce a type name for such arrays would introduce unnecessary clutter and a possibly false sense of abstraction.

On the other hand, if we are manipulating lots of arrays of reals of length 6 then there is a common underlying abstract type and so it should be named.

The model for array types introduced so far is still not satisfactory. It does not allow us to represent an abstract view that embraces the commonality between arrays which have different bounds but are otherwise of the same type. In particular, it would not allow the writing of subprograms which could take an array of arbitrary bounds as an actual parameter. This is generally recognized as a major difficulty with the original design of Pascal. So the concept of an unconstrained array type is introduced in which the constraints for the indexes are not given. Consider

type Vector **is array** (Integer **range** <>) **of** Real;

(The compound symbol <> is read as 'box'.)

This says that Vector is the name of a type which is a one-dimensional array of Real components with an Integer index. But the lower and upper bounds are not given; **range** <> is meant to convey the notion of information to be added later.

When we declare objects of type Vector we must supply the bounds. We can do this in various ways. We can introduce an intermediate subtype and then declare the objects.

subtype Vector_5 **is** Vector(1 .. 5);
V: Vector_5;

Or we can declare the objects directly

```
V: Vector(1 .. 5);
```

In either case the bounds are given by an index constraint which takes the form of a discrete range in brackets. All the usual forms of discrete range can be used.

The index can also be given by a subtype name, thus

type P **is array** (Positive **range** <>) **of** Real;

in which case the actual bounds of any declared object must lie within the range implied by the index subtype Positive. Note that the index subtype must be given by a type mark and not by a subtype indication; this avoids the horrid double use of range which could otherwise occur as in

type Nasty **is array** (Integer **range** 1 .. 100 **range** <>) **of** ... ;

We can now see that when we wrote

type Vector_6 **is array** (1 .. 6) **of** Real;

this was really a shorthand for

subtype index **is** Integer **range** 1 .. 6;
type anon **is array** (index **range** <>) **of** Real;
subtype Vector_6 **is** anon(1 .. 6);

Another useful array type declaration is

type Matrix **is array** (Integer **range** <>, Integer **range** <>) **of** Real;

And again we could introduce subtypes thus

subtype Matrix_3 **is** Matrix(1 .. 3, 1 .. 3);
M: Matrix_3;

or the objects directly

M: Matrix(1 .. 3, 1 .. 3);

An important point to notice is that an array type or subtype must give all the bounds or none at all. It would be perfectly legal to introduce an alternative name for Matrix by

subtype Mat **is** Matrix;

in which no bounds are given, but we could not have a type or subtype that just gave the bounds for one dimension but not the other.

In all of the cases we have been discussing, the ranges need not have static bounds. The bounds could be any expressions and are evaluated when the index constraint is encountered. We could have

M: Matrix(1 .. N, 1 .. N);

and then the upper bounds of M would be the value of N when M is declared. A range could even be null as would happen in the above case if N turned out to be zero. In this case the matrix M would have no components at all.

There is a further way in which the bounds of an array can be supplied but this only applies to constant arrays which like other constants have to be given an initial value. The bounds can then be taken from the initial value if they are not supplied directly. The initial value can be any expression of the appropriate type but will often be an aggregate as shown in the previous section. The form of aggregate shown there consisted of a list of expressions in brackets. Such an aggregate is known as a positional aggregate since the values are given in position order. In the case of a positional aggregate used as an initial value and supplying the bounds, the lower bound is S'First where S is the subtype of the index. The upper bound is deduced from the number of components. (The bounds of positional aggregates in other contexts will be discussed in the next section.)

Suppose we had

type W **is array** (Weekday **range** <>) **of** Day;
Next_Work_Day: **constant** W := (Tue, Wed, Thu, Fri, Mon);

then the lower bound of the array is Weekday'First = Mon and the upper bound is Fri. It would not have mattered whether we had written Day or Weekday in the declaration of W because Day'First and Weekday'First are the same.

An important difference in Ada 9X is that the bounds of any array object, variable as well as constant, can be deduced from an initial value. Thus the restriction that it must be a constant array is lifted. Moreover, Ada 9X also allows the box notation with anonymous array types. So we can also write

Next_Work_Day: **array** (Weekday range <>) **of** Day :=
    (Tue, Wed, Thu, Fri, Mon);

and there is no need to declare the intermediate type W. Again the bounds are deduced from the aggregate and we have also chosen not to make the array a constant.

Using initial values to supply the bounds needs care. Consider

Unit_2: **constant** Matrix := ((1.0, 0.0), (0.0, 1.0));

intended to declare a 2 × 2 unit matrix with Unit_2(1, 1) = Unit_2(2, 2) = 1.0 and Unit_2(1, 2) = Unit_2(2, 1) = 0.0.

But disaster! We have actually declared an array whose lower bounds are Integer'First which is probably −32768 or some such number, but is certainly not 1.

If we declared the type Matrix as

type Matrix **is array** (Positive **range** <>, Positive **range** <>) **of** Real;

then all would have been well since Positive'First = 1.

So array bounds deduced from an initial value may lead to surprises.

We continue by returning to the topic of whole array assignment. In order to perform such assignment it is necessary that the array value and the array being assigned to have the same type and that the components can be matched. This does not mean that the bounds have to be equal, but merely that the number of components in corresponding dimensions is the same. In other words so that one array can be slid onto the other, giving rise to the term 'sliding semantics'. So we can write

```
V: Vector(1 .. 5);
W: Vector(0 .. 4);
...
V := W;
```

Both V and W are of type Vector and both have five components.

It is also valid to have

```
P: Matrix(0 .. 1, 0 .. 1);
Q: Matrix(6 .. 7, N .. N+1);
...
P := Q;
```

Equality and inequality of arrays follow similar sliding rules to assignment. Two arrays may only be compared if they are of the same type. They are equal if corresponding dimensions have the same number of components and the matching components are themselves equal. Note, however, that if the dimensions of the two arrays are not of the same length then equality will return False whereas an attempt to assign one array to the other will naturally cause Constraint_Error.

Although assignment and equality can only occur if the arrays are of the same type, nevertheless an array value of one type can be converted to another type if the component types and index types are the same. The usual notation for type conversion is used. So if we have

```
type Vector is array (Integer range <>) of Real;
type Row    is array (Integer range <>) of Real;

V: Vector(1 .. 5);
R: Row(0 .. 4);
```

then

```
R := Row(V);
```

is valid. In fact, since Row is an unconstrained type, the bounds of Row(V) are those of V. The normal assignment rules then apply. However, if the conversion uses a constrained type or subtype then the bounds are those of the type or subtype and the number of components in corresponding dimensions must be the same. Array type conversion is of particular value when subprograms from different libraries are used together as we shall see later.

There is a very subtle difference between Ada 83 and Ada 9X regarding when the check is made that the components of the array are of the same subtype in an array conversion. Remember that the component type could be constrained as in the array Strange at the end of the previous section. In Ada 83 the check that such constraints match is done at run time whereas in Ada 9X the check is at compile time. This means that some obscure Ada 83 programs will not compile in Ada 9X.

We conclude this section by observing that the attributes First, Last, Length and Range, as well as applying to array objects, may also be applied to array types and subtypes provided they are constrained (that is, have their bounds given). So

        Vector_6'Length = 6

but

        Vector'Length   is illegal

EXERCISE 6.2

1 Declare an array type Bbb corresponding to the array Bor of Exercise 6.1(**5**).

2 Declare a two-dimensional array type suitable for declaring operator tables on values of

        subtype Ring5 **is** Integer **range** 0 .. 4;

Then declare addition and multiplication tables for modulo 5 arithmetic. Use the tables to formulate the expression (A + B) * C using modulo 5 arithmetic and assign the result to D where A, B, C and D have been appropriately declared. See Section 4.5.

6.3 Array aggregates

In the previous sections we introduced the idea of a positional aggregate. There is another form of aggregate known as a named aggregate in which the component values are preceded by the corresponding index value and =>. (The symbol => is akin to the ☞ sign encountered in old railway timetables and used for indicating directions especially on the Paris Metro.) A simple example would be

        (1 => 0.0, 2 => 0.0, 3 => 0.0, 4 => 0.0, 5 => 0.0, 6 => 0.0)

with the expected extension to several dimensions. The bounds of such an aggregate are self-evident and so our problem with the unit 2 × 2 matrix of the previous section could be overcome by writing

```
Unit_2: constant Matrix :=(1 => (1 => 1.0, 2 => 0.0),
                           2 => (1 => 0.0, 2 => 1.0));
```

The rules for named aggregates are very similar to the rules for the alternatives in a case statement.

Each choice can be given as a series of alternatives each of which can be a single value or a discrete range. We could therefore rewrite some previous examples as follows

```
A: array (1 .. 6) of Real := (1 .. 6 => 0.0);
Work_Day: constant array (Day) of Boolean
          := (Mon .. Fri => True, Sat | Sun => False);
```

In contrast to a positional aggregate, the index values need not appear in order. We could equally have written

```
(Sat | Sun => False, Mon .. Fri => True)
```

We can also use **others** but then as for the case statement it must be last and on its own (and there do not have to be any more values). The use of **others** raises some problems since it must be clear what the totality of values is.

It should also be realized that although we have been showing aggregates as initial values, they can be used quite generally in any place where an expression of an array type is required. One way of supplying the context is by qualifying the aggregate as we did to distinguish between overloaded enumeration literals. In order to do this we must have an appropriate (constrained) type or subtype name. So we might introduce

```
type Schedule is array (Day) of Boolean;
```

and can then write an expression such as

```
Schedule'(Mon .. Fri => True, others => False)
```

which could be part of a larger expression or maybe an initial value as we shall see in a moment. (Note that when qualifying an aggregate we do not, as for an expression, need to put it in brackets because it already has brackets.)

Other contexts which supply the bounds will be met in due course when we discuss subprogram parameters and results in Chapter 7 and generic parameters in Chapter 13.

These same constrained contexts will also supply the bounds of a positional aggregate; like a named aggregate with **others**, the bounds of a positional aggregate are not self-evident although in this case the number of components is. The bounds of a positional aggregate are thus supplied by the context, or, if the context is unable to supply the bounds (as in the case of the initial value in the previous section) then the lower bound is by default taken to be S'First where S is the index subtype and the upper bound is then deduced from the number of components.

Array aggregates may not mix positional and named notation except that **others** may be used at the end of a positional aggregate. A positional aggregate with others follows the same general rules as for a named aggregate with **others**: it can only be used in a constrained context which provides the bounds.

The context of assignment (as well as a declaration with an initial value where the initial value is not being used to supply the bounds) needs special mention.

The destination object in such a context must be a constrained array (all array objects are constrained) and can therefore supply the bounds. A positional aggregate with or without **others** is thus allowed in such a context as expected. However, perhaps surprisingly, a named aggregate with **others** is not allowed in such a context at all (except in the trivial case when it just has **others** as the only choice).

So we cannot write

```
Work_Day: constant array (Day) of Boolean
            := (Mon .. Fri => True, others => False);  - - illegal
```

but we must instead write

```
Work_Day: constant array (Day) of Boolean
            := (True, True, True, True, True, others => False);
```

or change the context by using qualification and write

```
Work_Day: constant Schedule
            := Schedule'(Mon .. Fri => True, others => False);
```

The curious restriction regarding named aggregates with **others** after := does not apply in Ada 9X; so the first declaration is indeed allowed in Ada 9X.

Further insight might be obtained by another example. Consider

```
type Vector is array (Integer range < >) of Real;
V: Vector(1 .. 5) := (3 .. 5 => 1.0, 6 | 7 => 2.0);
```

which shows a named aggregate being assigned to V. The bounds of the named aggregate are self evident being 3 and 7 and the assignment causes the aggregate to slide as explained in the previous section so that the net result is that components V(1) .. V(3) have the value 1.0 and V(4) and V(5) have the value 2.0.

On the other hand, writing

```
V := (3 .. 5 => 1.0, others => 2.0);
```

has a rather different effect. It is not allowed in Ada 83 but in Ada 9X has the effect of setting V(3) .. V(5) to 1.0 and V(1) and V(2) to 2.0. The point is that the bounds of the aggregate are taken from the context and there is no sliding. Aggregates with **others** never slide.

Similarly, no sliding occurs in

V := (1.0, 1.0, 1.0, **others** => 2.0);

and this results in setting V(1) .. V(3) to 1.0 and V(4) and V(5) to 2.0. It is clear that care is necessary when using **others**.

The rules regarding the bounds of array aggregates seem very difficult and to be one of the most curious aspects of Ada. However, if you are very confused, do not be too worried at this point; we will return to this topic when we summarize a number of aspects of expressions in Section 16.1. Meanwhile, remember that an aggregate can always be qualified if in doubt.

Array aggregates really are rather complicated and we still have a few points to make. The first is that in a named aggregate all the ranges and values before => must be static (as in a case statement) except for one special situation. This is where there is only one alternative consisting of a single choice – it could then be a dynamic range or (unlikely) a single dynamic value. An example might be

A: **array** (1 .. N) **of** Integer := (1 .. N => 0);

This is valid even if N is zero (or negative) and then gives a null array and a null aggregate. The following example illustrates a general rule that the expression after => is evaluated once for each corresponding index value; of course it usually makes no difference but consider

A: **array** (1 .. N) **of** Integer := (1 .. N => 1/N);

If N is zero then there are no values and so 1/N is not evaluated and Numeric_Error (alias Constraint_Error) cannot occur. The reader will recall from Section 4.1 that a similar multiple evaluation also occurs when several objects are declared and initialized together.

In order to avoid awkward problems with null aggregates, a null choice is only allowed if it is the only choice. Foolish aggregates such as

(7 .. 6 | 1 .. 0 => 0)

are thus forbidden, and there is no question of the lower bound of such an aggregate.

Another point is that although we cannot mix named and positional notation within an aggregate, we can, however, use different forms for the different components and levels of a multidimensional aggregate. So the initial value of our matrix Unit_2 could also be written as

(1 => (1.0, 0.0),   or   ((1 => 1.0, 2 => 0.0),
  2 => (0.0, 1.0))   (1 => 0.0, 2 => 1.0))

or even as

```
   (1 => (1 => 1.0, 2 => 0.0),
    2 => (   0.0,      1.0))
```

and so on.

Note also that the Range attribute stands for a range and therefore can be used as one of the choices in a named aggregate. However, we cannot use the range attribute of an object in its own initial value. Thus

A: **array** (1 .. N) **of** Integer := (A'Range => 0); – – illegal

is not allowed. This is because an object is not visible until the end of its declaration. However, we could write

A: **array** (1 .. N) **of** Integer := (**others** => 0);

and this is probably better than repeating 1 .. N because it localizes the dependency on N.

A final point is that a positional aggregate cannot contain just one component because otherwise it would be ambiguous. We could not distinguish an aggregate of one component from a scalar value which happened to be in brackets. An aggregate of one component must therefore use the named notation. So instead of

A: **array** (1 .. 1) **of** Integer := (99); – – illegal

we must write

A: **array** (1 .. 1) **of** Integer := (1 => 99);

or even

A: **array** (N .. N) **of** Integer := (N => 99);

which illustrates the obscure case of an aggregate with a single choice and a single dynamic value being that choice.

The reader will by now have concluded that arrays in Ada are somewhat complicated. That is a fair judgement, but in practice there should be few difficulties. There is always the safeguard that if we do something wrong, the compiler will inevitably tell us. In cases of ambiguity, qualification solves the problems provided we have an appropriate type or subtype name to use. Much of the complexity with aggregates is similar to that in the case statement.

We conclude this section by pointing out that the named aggregate notation can greatly increase program legibility. It is especially valuable in initializing large constant arrays and guards against the accidental misplacement of individual values. Consider

```
   type Event is (Birth, Accession, Death);
   type Monarch is (William_I, William_II, Henry_I, ... ,
                    Victoria, Edward_VII, George_V, ... );
```

```
        ...
   Royal_Events: constant array (Monarch, Event) of Integer
     := ( William_I     => (1027, 1066, 1087),
          William_II    => (1056, 1087, 1100),
          Henry_I       => (1068, 1100, 1135),
          ...
          Victoria      => (1819, 1837, 1901),
          Edward_VII    => (1841, 1901, 1910),
          George_V      => (1865, 1910, 1936),
          ...                                    );
```

The accidental interchange of two lines of the aggregate causes no problems, whereas if we had just used the positional notation then an error would have been introduced and this might have been tricky to detect.

EXERCISE 6.3

1   Rewrite the declaration of the array Days_In_Month in Exercise 6.1(3) using a named aggregate for an initial value.

2   Declare a constant Matrix whose bounds are both 1 .. N where N is dynamic and whose components are all zero.

3   Declare a constant Matrix as in **2** but make it a unit matrix.

4   Declare a constant two-dimensional array which gives the numbers of each atom in a molecule of the various aliphatic alcohols. Declare appropriate enumeration types for both the atoms and the molecules. Consider methanol CH_3OH, ethanol C_2H_5OH, propanol C_3H_7OH and butanol C_4H_9OH.

6.4 Characters and strings

We now complete our discussion of enumeration types by introducing character types. In the enumeration types seen so far such as

type Colour **is** (Red, Amber, Green);

the values have been represented by identifiers. It is also possible to have an enumeration type in which some or all of the values are represented by character literals.

A character literal is a further form of lexical element. It consists of a single character within a pair of single quotes. The character must be one of the printable characters or it could be a single space. It must not be a control character such as horizontal tabulate or new line.

This is a situation where there is a distinction between upper and lower case letters. The character literals

'A', 'a'

are different.

So we could declare an enumeration type

type Roman_Digit **is** ('I', 'V', 'X', 'L', 'C', 'D', 'M');

and then

Dig: Roman_Digit := 'D';

All the usual properties of enumeration types apply.

Roman_Digit'First = 'I'
Roman_Digit'Succ('X') = 'L'
Roman_Digit'Pos'('M') = 6

Dig < 'L' = False

There is a predefined enumeration type Character which is (naturally) a character type. We can think of its declaration as being of the form

type Character **is** (*nul*, ... , '0', '1', '2', ... , 'A', 'B', 'C', ... , 'a', 'b', 'c', ... , *del*);

but for technical reasons which cannot be explained here the literals which are not actual character literals (such as *nul*) are not really identifiers either (which is why they are represented here in italics). It is, however, possible to refer to them as ASCII.Nul and so on (or under suitable circumstances to be discussed later as simply Nul). This predefined type Character represents the standard ASCII character set (the ISO 7-bit set) and describes the set of characters normally used for input and output; for its full declaration see Appendix 2. It is unfortunate that the type Character is hedged around with subtleties but in practice these do not matter. However, remember that AI-866 allows the type Character to represent the ISO 8-bit set commonly known as Latin-1.

An important difference in Ada 9X is that the type Character always represents the ISO 8-bit set (ISO 8859). Thus in Ada 83 Character'Pos(Character'Last) may be 127 whereas in Ada 9X it is always 255. This is one of the very few cases where Ada 9X is incompatible with Ada 83.

It should be noted that the introduction of both the type Roman_Digit and the predefined type Character results in overloading of some of the literals. An expression such as

'X' < 'L'

is ambiguous. We do not know whether we are comparing characters of the type Roman_Digit or Character. In order to resolve the ambiguity we must qualify one or both literals.

Character'('X') < 'L ' = False
Roman_Digit '('X ') < 'L' = True

As well as the predefined type Character there is also the predefined type String

type String **is array** (Positive **range** <>) **of** Character;

This is a perfectly normal array type and obeys all the rules of the previous section. So we can write

S: String (1 .. 7);

to declare an array of range 1 .. 7. In the case of a constant array the bounds can be deduced from the initial value thus

G: **constant** String := ('P ', 'I', 'G');

where the initial value takes the form of a normal positional aggregate. The lower bound of G (that is, G'First) is 1 since the index subtype of String is Positive and Positive 'First is 1.

An alternative notation is provided for a positional aggregate each of whose components is a character literal. This is the string. So we could more conveniently write

G: **constant** String := "PIG";

The string is the last lexical element to be introduced. It consists of a sequence of printable characters and spaces enclosed in double quotes. A double quote may be represented in a string by two double quotes so that"

('A', '"', 'B') = "A" "B"

The string may also have just one character or may be null. The equivalent aggregates using character literals have to be written in named notation.

(1 => 'A') = "A"
(1 .. 0 => 'A') = " "

Note how we have to introduce an arbitrary character in the null named form. Ada has some strange quirks!

Another rule about a lexical string is that it must fit onto a single line. Moreover it cannot contain control characters such as *soh*. And, of course, as with character literals, the two cases of alphabet are distinct in strings

"pig " /= "PIG"

In Section 6.6 we will see how to overcome the limitations that a string must fit onto a single line and yet cannot contain control characters.

A major use for strings is, of course, for creating text to be output. A simple sequence of characters can be output by a call of the (overloaded) subprogram Put. Thus

     Put ("The Countess of Lovelace");

will output the text

     The Countess of Lovelace

onto some appropriate file.

However, the lexical string is not reserved just for use with the built-in type String. It can be used to represent an array of any character type. We can write

     type Roman_Number **is array** (Positive **range** <>) **of** Roman_Digit;

and then

     Nineteen_Eighty_Four: **constant** Roman_Number := "MCMLXXXIV";

or indeed

     Four: **array** (1 .. 2) of Roman_Digit := "IV";

Ada 9X introduces extensions in this area. As well as the 8-bit type Character there is also the 16-bit type Wide_Character whose values are the codes of the ISO 10646 basic multilingual plane. This is of particular relevance for dealing with Eastern character sets. One consequence of the existence of Wide_Character is that an expression such as

     'X' < 'L'

is always ambiguous in Ada 9X since the literals are defined for both Character and Wide_Character. There is also an array type Wide_String defined as an array of the type Wide_Character.

EXERCISE 6.4

1   Declare a constant array Roman_To_Integer which can be used for table look-up to convert a Roman_Digit to its normal integer equivalent (e.g. converts 'C' to 100).

2   Given an object R of type Roman_Number write statements to compute the equivalent integer value V. It may be assumed that R obeys the normal rules of construction of Roman numbers.

6.5   Arrays of arrays and slices

The components of an array can be of any type (or subtype) for which we can declare objects. Thus we can declare arrays of any scalar type; we can also declare arrays of arrays. So we can have

> **type** Matrix_3_6 **is array** (1 .. 3) **of** Vector_6;

where, as in Section 6.2

> **type** Vector_6 **is array** (1 .. 6) **of** Real;

However, we cannot declare an array of unconstrained arrays (just as we cannot declare an object which is an unconstrained array). So we cannot write

> **type** Matrix_3_N **is array** (1 .. 3) **of** Vector; – – illegal

On the other hand, there is nothing to prevent us declaring an unconstrained array of constrained arrays thus

> **type** Matrix_N_6 **is array** (Integer **range** <>) **of** Vector_6;

It is instructive to compare the practical differences between declaring an array of arrays

> AOA: Matrix_3_6;   or   AOA: Matrix_N_6(1 .. 3);

and the similar multidimensional array

> MDA: Matrix(1 .. 3, 1 .. 6);

Aggregates for both are completely identical, for example

> ((1.0, 2.0, 3.0, 4.0, 5.0, 6.0),
> (4.0, 4.0, 4.0, 4.0, 4.0, 4.0),
> (6.0, 5.0, 4.0, 3.0, 2.0, 1.0))

but component access is quite different, thus

> AOA(I)(J)
> MDA(I, J)

where in the case of AOA the internal structure is naturally revealed. The individual rows of AOA can be manipulated as arrays in their own right, but the structure of MDA cannot be decomposed. So we could change the middle row of AOA to zero by

> AOA(2) := (1 .. 6 => 0.0);

but a similar technique cannot be applied to MDA.

Arrays of arrays are not restricted to one dimension, we can have a multidimensional array of arrays or an array of multidimensional arrays; the notation extends in an obvious way.

Arrays of strings are revealing. Consider

```
type String_Array is array (Positive range <>,
                            Positive range <>) of Character;
```

which is an unconstrained two-dimensional array type. We can then declare

```
Farmyard: constant String_Array := ("pig", "cat", "dog",
                                    "cow", "rat", "ass");
```

where the bounds are conveniently deduced from the aggregate. But note that we cannot have a ragged array where the individual strings are of different lengths such as

```
Zoo: constant String_Array := ("aardvark", "baboon",
          "camel", "dolphin", "elephant", ..., "zebra");  – – illegal
```

This is a real nuisance and means we have to pad the strings to be the same length

```
Zoo: constant String_Array := ("aardvark",
                               "baboon ",
                               "camel   ",
                               "dolphin ",
                               "elephant",
                               ...
                               "zebra   ");
```

The next problem is that we cannot select an individual one of the strings. We might want to output one and so attempt

```
Put(Farmyard(5));
```

hoping to print the text

```
rat
```

but this is not allowed since we can only select an individual component of an array which in this case is just one character.

An alternative approach is to use an array of arrays. A problem here is that the component in the array type declaration has to be constrained and so we have to decide on the length of our strings right from the beginning thus

```
type String_3_Array is array (Positive range <>) of String(1 .. 3);
```

and then

```
Farmyard: constant String_3_Array := ("pig", "cat", "dog",
                                       "cow", "rat", "ass");
```

With this formulation we can indeed select an individual string as a whole and so the statement Put(Farmyard(5)); now works. However, we still cannot declare our Zoo as a ragged array; we will return to this topic in Section 11.2 when another approach will be discussed.

We thus see that arrays of arrays and multidimensional arrays each have their own advantages and disadvantages. Neither is ideal; Ada arrays are rather restrictive and do not offer the flexibility of Algol 68.

A special feature of one-dimensional arrays is the ability to denote a slice of an array object. A slice is written as the name of the object (variable or constant) followed by a discrete range in brackets.

So given

```
S: String(1 .. 10);
```

then we can write S(3 .. 8) to denote the middle six characters of S. The bounds of the slice are the bounds of the range and not those of the index subtype. We could write

```
T: constant String := S(3 .. 8);
```

and then T'First = 3, T'Last = 8.

The bounds of the slice need not be static but can be any expressions. A slice would be null if the range turned out to be null.

The use of slices emphasizes the nature of array assignment. The value of the expression to be assigned is completely evaluated before any components are assigned. No problems arise with overlapping slices. So

```
S(1 .. 4) := "BARA";
S(4 .. 7) := S(1 .. 4);
```

results in S(1 .. 7) = "BARBARA". S(4) is only updated after the expression S(1 .. 4) is safely evaluated. There is no risk of setting S(4) to 'B' and then consequently making the expression "BARB" with the final result of

```
"BARBARB"
```

The ability to use slices is another consideration in deciding between arrays of arrays and multidimensional arrays. With our second Farmyard we can write

```
Pets: String_3_Array(1 .. 2) := Farmyard(2 .. 3);
```

which uses sliding assignment so that the two components of Pets are "cat" and "dog". Moreover, if we had declared the Farmyard as a variable rather than a constant then we could also write

Farmyard(1)(1 .. 2) := "ho";

which turns the "pig" into a "hog"! We can do none of these things with the old Farmyard.

EXERCISE 6.5

---

1   Write a single assignment statement to swap the first and second rows of AOA.

2   Declare the second Farmyard as a variable. Then change the cow into a sow.

3   Assume that R contains a Roman number. Write statements to see if the last digit of the corresponding decimal arabic value is a 4 and change it to a 6 if it is.

6.6   One-dimensional array operations

Many of the operators that we met in Chapter 4 may also be applied to one-dimensional arrays.

The Boolean operators **and, or, xor** and **not** may be applied to one-dimensional Boolean arrays. In the case of the binary operators, the two operands must have the same number of components and be of the same type. The underlying scalar operation is applied component by component and the resulting array is again of the same type. The lower bound of the result is equal to the lower bound of the left or only operand.

Consider

```
type Bit_Row is array (Positive range <>) of Boolean;
A, B: Bit_Row(1 .. 4);
C, D: array (1 .. 4) of Boolean;
T: constant Boolean := True;
F: constant Boolean := False;
```

then we can write

```
A := (T, T, F, F);
B := (T, F, T, F);

A := A and B;
B := not B;
```

and A now equals (T, F, F, F), and B equals (F, T, F, T). Similarly for **or** and **xor**. But note that C **and** D would not be allowed because they are of different (and anonymous) types because of the rule regarding multiple declarations (Section 4.1). This is clearly a case where it is appropriate to give a name to the array type because we are manipulating the arrays as complete objects.

Note that these operators also use sliding semantics, like assignment as explained in Section 6.2, and so only demand that the types and the number of components are the same. The bounds themselves do not have to be equal. However, if the number of components are not the same then, naturally, Constraint_Error will be raised.

Boolean arrays can be used to represent sets. Consider

```
type Primary is (R, Y, B);
type Colour is array (Primary) of Boolean;
C: Colour;
```

then there are $8 = 2 \times 2 \times 2$ values that C can take. C is, of course, an array with three components and each of these has value True or False; the three components are

C(R), C(Y)   and   C(B)

The 8 possible values of the type Colour can be represented by suitably named constants as follows

```
White    : constant Colour := (F, F, F);
Red      : constant Colour := (T, F, F);
Yellow   : constant Colour := (F, T, F);
Blue     : constant Colour := (F, F, T);
Green    : constant Colour := (F, T, T);
Purple   : constant Colour := (T, F, T);
Orange   : constant Colour := (T, T, F);
Black    : constant Colour := (T, T, T);
```

and then we can write expressions such as

Red **or** Yellow

which is equal to Orange and

not Black

which is White.

So the values of our type Colour are effectively the set of colours obtained by taking all combinations of the primary colours represented by R, Y, B. The empty set is the value of White and the full set is the value of Black. We are using the paint pot mixing colour model rather than light mixing. A value of True for a component means that the primary colour concerned is mixed in our pot. The murky mess we got at school from mixing too many colours together is our black!

The operations **or**, **and** and **xor** may be interpreted as set union, set intersection and symmetric difference. A test for set membership can be made by inspecting the value of the appropriate component of the set. Thus

C(R)

is True if R is in the set represented by C. We cannot use the predefined operation **in** for this. A literal value can be represented using the named aggregate notation, so

(R | Y => T, **others** => F)

has the same value as Orange. A more elegant way of doing this will appear in the next chapter.

We now consider the equality and relational operators. The operators = and /= apply to all types anyway and we gave the rules for arrays when we discussed assignment in Section 6.2.

The relational operators <, <=, > and >= may be applied to one-dimensional arrays of a discrete type. (Note discrete.) The result of the comparison is based upon the lexicographic (that is, dictionary) order using the defined order relation for the components. This is best illustrated with strings which we assume for the moment are unambiguously values of the type String. The following are all True

```
"CAT" < "DOG"
"CAT" < "CATERPILLAR"
"AZZ" < "B"
" "    < "A"
```

The strings are compared component by component until they differ in some position. The string with the lower component is then lower. If one string runs out of components as in CAT *versus* CATERPILLAR then the shorter one is lower. The null string is lowest of all.

If we assume that we have declared our type Roman_Number then

"CCL" < "CCXC"

is ambiguous since we do not know whether we are comparing type String or type Roman_Number. We must qualify one or both of the strings. This is done in the usual way but a string, unlike the bracketed form of aggregates, has to be placed in brackets otherwise we would get an ugly juxtaposition of a single and double quote. So

```
String'("CCL") < "CCXC"        is True
Roman_Number'("CCL") < "CCXC"  is False
```

Note that our compiler is too stupid to know about the interpretation of Roman numbers in our minds and has said that 250 < 290 is false. The only thing that matters is the order relation of the characters 'L' and 'X' in the type definition. In the next chapter we will show how we can redefine < so that it works 'properly ' for Roman numbers.

In the case of Ada 9X, the existence of Wide_String naturally means that "CCL" < "CCXC" is always ambiguous.

Of course, the relational operators also apply to general expressions and not just to literal strings

Nineteen_Eighty_Four < "MM"   is True

The relational operators can be applied to arrays of any discrete types. So

(1, 2, 3) < (2, 3)
(Jan, Jan) < (1 => Feb)

The predefined operators <=, > and >= are defined by analogy with <.

We finally introduce a new binary operator & which denotes catenation (or concatenation) of one-dimensional arrays. It has the same precedence as binary plus and minus. The two operands must be of the same type and the result is an array of the same type whose value is obtained by juxtaposing the two operands. The lower bound of the result is, as usual, the lower bound of the left operand. (If the left operand is null the result is simply the right operand.)

So

"CAT" & "ERPILLAR" = "CATERPILLAR"

String catenation can be used to construct a string which is too long to fit on one line

"This string goes" &
"on and on"

One or both operands of & can also be a single value of the component type. If the left operand is such a single value then the lower bound of the result is the lower bound of the subtype of the array index.

"CAT" & 'S' = "CATS"
'S' & "CAT" = "SCAT"
'S ' & 'S' = "SS"

This is useful for representing the control characters such as CR and LF in strings.

"First line" & ASCII.CR & ASCII.LF & "Next line"

Of course, it might be neater to declare

CRLF: **constant** String := (ASCII.CR, ASCII.LF);

and then write

"First line" & CRLF & "Next line"

The operation & can be applied to any one-dimensional array type and so we can apply it to our Roman numbers. Consider

```
R: Roman_Number(1 .. 5);
S: String(1 .. 5);

R := "CCL" & "IV";
S := "CCL" & "IV";
```

This is valid. The context tells us that in the first case we apply & to two Roman numbers whereas in the second we apply it to two values of type String. There is no ambiguity as in

```
B: Boolean := "CCL" < "IV";
```

EXERCISE 6.6

1　Write the eight possible constants White ... Black of the type Colour in ascending order as determined by the operator < applied to one-dimensional arrays.

2　Evaluate

    (a) Red **or** Green
    (b) Black **xor** Red
    (c) **not** Green

3　Show that **not** (Black **xor** C) = C is true for all values of C.

4　Why did we not write

    (Jan, Jan) < (Feb)

5　Put in ascending order the following values of type String: "ABC ", "123 ", "abc ", "Abc ", "abC ", "aBc ".

6　Given

```
C: Character;
S: String(5 .. 10);
```

What is the lower bound of

    (a) C & S
    (b) S & C
    (c) "" & S

7　Given

```
type T is array (1 .. 10) of Integer;
A: T;
```

What are the bounds of

(a) A(6 .. 10) & A(1 .. 5)
(b) A(6) & A(7 .. 10) & A(1 .. 5)

6.7 Records

As stated at the beginning of this chapter we are only going to consider the simplest form of record at this point. A fuller treatment covering variant records and so on is left until Chapter 11.

A record is a composite object consisting of named components which may be of different types. In contrast to arrays, we cannot have anonymous record types – they all have to be named. Consider

> **type** Month_Name **is** (Jan, Feb, Mar, Apr, May, Jun, Jul,
> Aug, Sep, Oct, Nov, Dec);

> **type** Date **is**
>   **record**
>   Day: Integer **range** 1 .. 31;
>   Month: Month_Name;
>   Year: Integer;
>   **end record**;

This declares the type Date to be a record containing three named components: Day, Month and Year.

We can declare variables and constants of record types in the usual way.

> D: Date;

declares an object D which is a date. The individual components of D can be denoted by following D with a dot and the component name. Thus we could write

> D.Day := 4;
> D.Month := Jul;
> D.Year := 1776;

in order to assign new values to the individual components.

Records can be manipulated as whole objects. Literal values can be written as aggregates much like arrays; both positional and named forms can be used. So we could write

> D: Date := (4, Jul, 1776);
> E: Date;

and then

> E := D;

or

E := (Month => Jul, Day => 4, Year => 1776);

The reader will be relieved to know that much of the complexity of array aggregates does not apply to records. This is because the number of components is always known.

In a positional aggregate the components come in order. In a named aggregate they may be in any order. In the particular example shown the use of a named aggregate avoids the necessity to know on which side of the Atlantic the record type was declared.

A named aggregate cannot use a range because the components are not ←
considered to be closely related and the vertical bar can only be used with components which have the same (base) type. The choice **others** can be used but again only when the remaining components are of the same type – and there must be some.

There is one extra possibility for records and that is that the positional and named notations can be mixed in one aggregate. But if this is done then the positional components must come first and in order (without holes) as usual. So in other words, we can change to the named notation at any point in the aggregate but must then stick to it. The above date could therefore also be expressed as

(4, Jul, Year => 1776)
(4, Year => 1776, Month => Jul)

and so on.

It is possible to give default expressions for some or all of the components in the type declaration. Thus

type Complex **is**
   rooord
      Rl: Real := 0.0;
      Im: Real := 0.0;
   end record;

or more succinctly

type Complex **is**
   record
      Rl, Im: Real := 0.0;
   end record;

declares a record type containing two components of type Real and gives a default expression of 0.0 for each. This record type represents a complex number $x + iy$ where Rl and Im are the values of x and y. The default value is thus (0, 0), the origin of the Argand plane. We can now declare

C1: Complex;
C2: Complex := (1.0, 0.0);

The object C1 will now have the values 0.0 for its components by default. In the case of C2 we have overridden the default values. Note that, irritatingly, even if there are default expressions, an aggregate must be complete even if it supplies the same values as the default expressions for some of the components.

In this case both components are the same type and so the following named forms are possible

```
(Rl | Im => 1.0)
(others => 1.0)
```

The only operations predefined on record types are = and /= as well as assignment of course. Other operations must be performed at the component level or be explicitly defined by a subprogram as we shall see in the next chapter.

A record type may have any number of components. It may pathologically have none in which case its declaration takes the form

```
type Hole is
   record
      null;
   end record;
```

The reserved word **null** confirms that we meant to declare a null record type. Null records have their uses but they will not be apparent yet.

Null records occur quite frequently in Ada 9X and so an abbreviated form is provided

```
type Hole is null record;
```

The components of a record type can be of any type; they can be other records or arrays. However, if a component is an array then it must be fully constrained (that is, its index must not contain <>) and it must be of a named type and not an anonymous type. And obviously a record cannot contain an instance of itself.

The components cannot be constants but the record as a whole can be. Thus

```
I: constant Complex := (0.0, 1.0);
```

is allowed and represents the square root of −1.

A more elaborate example of a record is

```
type Person is
   record
      Birth: Date;
      Name: String(1 .. 20) := (1 .. 20 => ' ');
   end record;
```

The record Person has two components, the first is another record, a Date, the second an array. The array which is a string of length 20 has a default value of all spaces.

We can now write

```
John: Person;
John.Birth := (19, Aug, 1937);
John.Name(1 .. 4) := "John";
```

and we would then have

```
John = ((19, Aug, 1937), "John            ")
```

The notation is as expected. The aggregates nest and for objects we proceed from left to right using the dot notation to select components of a record and indexes in brackets to select components of an array and ranges in brackets to slice arrays. There is no limit. We could have an array of persons

```
People: array (1 .. N) of Person;
```

and then have

```
People(6).Birth.Day := 19;
People(8).Name(3) := 'h';
```

and so on.

A final point concerns the evaluation of expressions in a record declaration. An expression in a constraint applied to a component is evaluated when the record type is elaborated. So our type Person could have

```
Name: String(1 .. N) := (others => ' ');
```

and the length of the component Name will be the value of N when the type Person is elaborated. Of course, N need not be static and so if the type declaration is in a loop, for example, then each execution of the loop might give rise to a type with a different size component. However, for each elaboration of the record type declaration all objects of the type will have the same component size.

On the other hand, a default expression in a record type is only evaluated when an object of the type is declared and only then if no explicit initial value is provided. Of course, in simple cases, like our type Complex, it makes no difference but it could bring surprises. For example suppose we write the component Name as

```
Name: String(1 .. N) := (1 .. N => ' ');
```

then the length of the component Name is the value of N when the record type is declared whereas when a Person is subsequently declared without an initial value, the aggregate will be evaluated using the value of N which then applies.

Of course, N may by then be different and so Constraint_Error will be raised. This is rather surprising; we do seem to have strayed into an odd backwater of Ada!

EXERCISE 6.7

1   Rewrite the solution to Exercise 6.1(**3**) using a variable D of type Date rather than three individual variables.

2   Declare three variables C1, C2 and C3 of type Complex. Write one or more statements to assign (a) the sum, (b) the product, of C1 and C2 to C3.

3   Write statements to find the index of the first person of the array People born on or after 1 January 1950.

CHECKLIST 6

Array types can be anonymous, but records cannot.

Aggregates must always be complete.

Distinguish constrained array types from unconstrained array types (those with '<>').

Named and positional notations cannot be mixed for array aggregates – they can for records.

An aggregate with '**others**' must have a context giving its bounds. It never slides.

A choice in an array aggregate can only be dynamic or null if it is the only choice.

The attributes 'First', 'Last', 'Length' and 'Range' apply to array objects and constrained array types and subtypes but not to unconstrained types and subtypes.

For array assignment to be valid, the number of components must be equal for each dimension – not the bounds.

The cases of alphabet are distinct in character literals and strings.

An aggregate with one component must use the named notation. This applies to records as well as to arrays.

A record component cannot be an anonymous array.

A default component expression is only evaluated when an uninitialized object is declared.

7 Subprograms

Subprograms are the conventional parameterized unit of programming. In Ada, subprograms fall into two categories: functions and procedures. Functions are called as components of expressions and return a value as part of the expression, whereas procedures are called as statements standing alone.

As we shall see, the actions to be performed when a subprogram is called are described by a subprogram body. Subprogram bodies are declared in the usual way in a declarative part which may for instance be in a block or indeed in another subprogram.

7.1 Functions

A function is a form of subprogram that can be called as part of an expression. In Chapter 4 we met examples of calls of functions such as Day'Succ, Sqrt and so on.

We now consider the form of a function body which describes the statements to be executed when the function is called. For example the body of the function Sqrt might have the form

```
function Sqrt(X: Real) return Real is
   R: Real;
begin
   - - compute value of Sqrt(X) in R
   return R;
end Sqrt;
```

All function bodies start with the reserved word **function** and the designator of the function being defined. If the function has parameters the designator is followed by a list of parameter specifications in brackets. If there are several specifications then they are separated by semicolons. Each specification gives the identifiers of one or more parameters followed by a colon and its type or subtype. The parameter list, if any, is then followed by the reserved word **return** and the type or subtype of the result of the function. In the case of both parameters and result the type or subtype must be given by a type mark and not by a subtype indication. This is an important example of a situation where an explicit constraint is not allowed; the reason will be mentioned later in this chapter.

The part of the body we have described so far is called the function specification. It specifies the function to the outside world in the sense of providing all the information needed to call the function.

After the specification comes **is** and then the body proper which is just like a block – it has a declarative part, **begin**, a sequence of statements, and then **end**. As for a block the declarative part can be empty, but there must be at least one statement in the sequence of statements. Between **end** and the terminating semicolon we may repeat the designator of the function. This is optional but, if present, must correctly match the designator after **function**.

It is often necessary or just convenient to give the specification on its own but without the rest of the body. In such a case it is immediately followed by a semicolon thus

```
function Sqrt(X: Real) return Real;
```

and is then correctly known as a function declaration – although often still carelessly referred to as a specification. The uses of such declarations will be discussed later.

The formal parameters of a function act as local constants whose values are provided by the corresponding actual parameters. When the function is called the declarative part is elaborated in the usual way and then the statements are executed. A return statement is used to indicate the value of the function call and to return control back to the calling expression.

Thus considering our example suppose we had

```
S := Sqrt(T + 0.5);
```

then first T + 0.5 is evaluated and then Sqrt is called. Within the body the parameter X behaves as a constant with the initial value given by T + 0.5. It is rather as if we had

```
X: constant Real := T + 0.5;
```

The declaration of R is then elaborated. We then obey the sequence of statements and assume they compute the square root of X and assign it to R. The last statement is **return** R; this passes control back to the calling expression with the result of the function being the value of R. This value is then assigned to S.

The expression in a return statement can be of arbitrary complexity and must be of the same type as and satisfy any constraints implied by the type mark given in the function specification. If the constraints are violated then, of course, the exception Constraint_Error is raised.

(Ada 9X is slightly more flexible in the case of a constrained array result type as explained at the end of this section.)

A function body may have several return statements. The execution of any of them will terminate the function. Thus the function Sign which takes an integer value and returns +1, 0 or −1 according to whether the parameter is positive, zero or negative could be written as

```
function Sign(X: Integer) return Integer is
begin
   if X > 0 then
      return +1;
   elsif X < 0 then
      return −1;
   else
      return 0;
   end if;
end Sign;
```

So we see that the last lexical statement of the body need not be a return statement since there is one in each branch of the statement. Any attempt to 'run' into the final end will raise the exception Program_Error. This is our first example of a situation giving rise to Program_Error; this exception is generally used for situations which would violate the run time control structure.

It should be noted that each call of a function produces a new instance of any objects declared within it (including parameters of course) and these disappear when we leave the function. It is therefore possible for a function to be called recursively without any problems. So the factorial function could be declared as

```
function Factorial(N: Positive) return Positive is
begin
   if N = 1 then
      return 1;
   else
      return N * Factorial(N−1);
   end if;
end Factorial;
```

If we write

```
F := Factorial(4);
```

then the function calls itself until, on the fourth call (with the other three calls all partly executed and waiting for the result of the call they did before doing the multiply) we find that N is 1 and the calls then all unwind and all the multiplications are performed.

Note that there is no need to check that the parameter N is positive since the parameter is of subtype Positive. So calling Factorial(−2) will result in Constraint_Error. Of course, Factorial(10_000) could result in the computer running out of space in which case Storage_Error would be raised. The more moderate call Factorial(20) would undoubtedly cause overflow and thus raise Numeric_Error (or the equivalent Constraint_Error − see Section 4.9).

A formal parameter may be of any type but the type must have a name. It cannot be an anonymous type such as

```
array (1 .. 6) of Real
```

In any event no actual parameter (other than an aggregate) could match such a formal parameter even if it were allowed since the actual and formal parameters must have the same type.

A formal parameter can, however, be an unconstrained array type such as

```
type Vector is array (Integer range <>) of Real;
```

In such a case the bounds of the formal parameter are taken from those of the actual parameter.

Consider

```
function Sum(A: Vector) return Real is
   Result: Real := 0.0;
begin
   for I in A'Range loop
      Result := Result + A(I);
   end loop;
   return Result;
end Sum;
```

then we can write

```
V: Vector(1 .. 4) := (1.0, 2.0, 3.0, 4.0);
S: Real;
...
S := Sum(V);
```

The formal parameter A then takes the bounds of the actual parameter V. So for this call we have

A'Range   is   1 .. 4

and the effect of the loop is to compute the sum of A(1), A(2), A(3) and A(4). The final value of Result which is returned and assigned to S is therefore 10.0.

The function Sum can be used to sum the components of a vector with any bounds. Ada thus overcomes one of the problems of original Pascal which insists that array parameters have static bounds. Of course, an Ada function could have a constrained array type as a formal parameter. However, remember that we cannot apply the constraint in the parameter list using a subtype indication as in

function Sum_6(A: Vector(1 .. 6)) **return** Real   – – illegal

but must use the name of a constrained array type such as

type Vector_6 **is array** (1 .. 6) **of** Real;

as a type mark as in

function Sum_6(A: Vector_6) **return** Real

An actual parameter corresponding to such a constrained formal array must have identical bounds; sliding is not allowed. This context is thus one of those like qualification which we recall from Section 6.3, will always supply the bounds of an aggregate. We could thus write

S := Sum_6((1.0, 2.0, 3.0, **others** => 0.0));

See the note at the end of this section regarding Ada 9X.

As another example consider

```
function Inner(A, B: Vector) return Real is
   Result : Real := 0.0;
begin
   for I in A'Range loop
      Result := Result + A(I)*B(I);
   end loop;
   return Result;
end Inner;
```

This computes the inner product of the two vectors A and B by adding together the sum of the products of corresponding components. This is our first example of a function with more than one parameter. Such a function is called by following the function name by a list of the expressions giving the values of the actual parameters separated by commas and in brackets. The order of evaluation of the actual parameters is not defined.

So

```
V: Vector(1 .. 3) := (1.0, 2.0, 3.0);
W: Vector(1 .. 3) := (2.0, 3.0, 4.0);
R: Real;
...
R := Inner(V, W);
```

results in R being assigned the value

$$1.0 * 2.0 + 2.0 * 3.0 + 3.0 * 4.0 = 20.0$$

Note that the function Inner is not written well since it does not check that the bounds of A and B are the same. It is not symmetric with respect to A and B since I takes (or tries to take) the values of the range A'Range irrespective of B'Range. So if the array W had bounds of 0 and 2, Constraint_Error would be raised on the third time round the loop. If the array W had bounds of 1 and 4 then no exception would be raised but the result might not be what we expected.

It would be nice to ensure the equality of the bounds by placing a constraint on B at the time of call but this cannot be done. The best we can do is simply check the bounds for equality inside the function body and perhaps explicitly raise Constraint_Error if they are not equal

```
if A'First /= B'First or A'Last /= B'Last then
    raise Constraint_Error;
end if;
```

(The use of the raise statement is described in detail in Chapter 10.)

We saw above that a formal parameter can be of an unconstrained array type. In a similar way the result of a function can be an array whose bounds are not known until the function is called. The result type can be an unconstrained array and the bounds are then obtained from the expression in the appropriate return statement.

As an example the following function returns a vector which has the same bounds as the parameter but whose component values are in the reverse order

```
function Rev(X: Vector) return Vector is
    R: Vector(X'Range);
begin
    for I in X'Range loop
        R(I) := X(X'First+X'Last–I);
    end loop;
    return R;
end Rev;
```

The variable R is declared to be of type Vector with the same bounds as X. Note how the loop reverses the value. The result takes the bounds of the expression R. Note that we have called the function Rev rather than Reverse; this is because **reverse** is a reserved word.

If a function returns a record or array value then a component can be immediately selected, indexed or sliced as appropriate without assigning the value to a variable. So we could write

Rev(Y)(I)

which denotes the component indexed by I of the array returned by the call of Rev.

It should be noted that a parameterless function call, like a parameterless procedure call, has no brackets. There is thus a possible ambiguity between calling a function with one parameter and indexing the result of a parameterless call; such an ambiguity could be resolved by, for example, renaming the functions as will be described in Chapter 8.

We conclude this section by mentioning a small difference between Ada 83 and Ada 9X in the case of parameters and results of a constrained array type such as Vector_6. In Ada 83, the bounds must match and sliding is not allowed. In Ada 9X, however, these cases are treated like assignment and so sliding is allowed. An array aggregate with **others** is still allowed in both contexts (and with the same meaning) although for different reasons. In Ada 83 it is allowed because the matching rules provide the bounds; in Ada 9X it is allowed because the assignment rules are themselves relaxed but on the other hand there is the overriding rule that aggregates with **others** never slide.

EXERCISE 7.1

1   Write a function Even which returns True or False according to whether its Integer parameter is even or odd.

2   Rewrite the factorial function so that the parameter may be positive or zero but not negative. Remember that the value of Factorial(0) is to be 1. Use the subtype Natural introduced in Section 4.5.

3   Write a function Outer that forms the outer product of two vectors. The outer product C of two vectors A and B is a matrix such that $C_{ij} = A_i.B_j$.

4   Write a function Make_Colour which takes an array of values of type Primary and returns the corresponding value of type Colour. See Section 6.6. Check that Make_Colour((R, Y)) = Orange.

5   Write a function Value which takes a parameter of type Roman_Number and returns the equivalent integer value. See Exercise 6.4(**2**).

6   Write a function Make_Unit that takes a single parameter N and returns a unit $N \times N$ real matrix. Use the function to declare a constant unit $N \times N$ matrix. See Exercise 6.3(**3**).

7 Write a function GCD to return the greatest common divisor of two nonnegative integers. Use Euclid's algorithm that

gcd $(x, y) =$ gcd $(y, x$ mod $y)$ y $\neq 0$
gcd $(x, 0) = x$

Write the function using recursion and then rewrite it using a loop statement.

8 Rewrite the function Inner to use sliding semantics so that it works providing the arrays have the same length. Raise Constraint_Error (as outlined above) if the arrays do not match.

7.2 Operators

In the last section we carefully stated that a function body commenced with the reserved word **function** followed by the designator of the function. In all the examples of the last section the designator was in fact an identifier. However, it can also be a character string provided that the string is one of the following language operators in double quotes.

and	**or**	**xor**		
=	**<**	**<=**	**>**	**>=**
+	**−**	**&**	**abs**	**not**
*	**/**	**mod**	**rem**	******

In such a case the function defines a new meaning of the operator concerned. As an example we can rewrite the function Inner of the last section as an operator.

```
function "*" (A, B: Vector) return Real is
   Result: Real := 0.0;
begin
   for I in A'Range loop
      Result := Result + A(I)*B(I);
   end loop;
   return Result;
end "*";
```

We call this new function by the normal syntax of uses of the operator "*". Thus instead of

```
R := Inner(V, W);
```

we now write

```
R := V*W;
```

This meaning of "*" is distinguished from the existing meanings of integer and real multiplication by the context provided by the types of the actual parameters V and W and the type required by R.

The giving of several meanings to an operator is another instance of overloading which we have already met with enumeration literals. The rules for the overloading of subprograms in general are discussed later in this chapter. It suffices to say at this point that any ambiguity can usually be resolved by qualification. Overloading of predefined operators is not new. It has existed in most programming languages for the past thirty years. What is new is the ability to define additional overloadings and indeed the use of the term 'overloading' is itself relatively new.

We can now see that the predefined meanings of all operators are as if there were a series of functions with declarations such as

> **function** "+" (Left, Right: Integer) **return** Integer;
> **function** "<" (Left, Right: Integer) **return** Boolean;
> **function** "<" (Left, Right: Boolean) **return** Boolean;

Moreover, every time we declare a new type, new overloadings of some operators such as "=" and "<" may be created.

Although we can add new meanings to operators we cannot change the ← syntax of the call. Thus the number of parameters of "*" must always be two and the precedence cannot be changed and so on. The operators "+" and "−" are unusual in that a new definition can have either one parameter or two parameters according to whether it is to be called as a unary or binary operator. Thus the function Sum could be rewritten as

```
function "+" (A: Vector) return Real is
   Result: Real := 0.0;
begin
   for I in A'Range loop
      Result := Result + A(I);
   end loop;
   return Result;
end "+";
```

and we would then write

> S := +V;

rather than

> S := Sum(V);

Function bodies whose designators are operators often contain interesting examples of uses of the operator being overloaded. Thus the body of "*" contains a use of "*" in A(I)*B(I). There is, of course, no ambiguity since the expressions A(I) and B(I) are of type Real whereas our new overloading is for type Vector. Sometimes there is the risk of accidental recursion. This particularly applies if we try to replace an existing meaning rather than add a new one.

Apart from the operator "=" there are no special rules regarding the types of the operands and results of new overloadings. Thus a new overloading of "<" need not return a Boolean result. On the other hand, the operator "=" can only be given new overloadings which return a value of type Boolean and then only under special circumstances which will be described in Chapter 9. Note that "/=" may never be explicitly redeclared – it always takes its meaning from "=".

The rules regarding "=" and "/=" are much more relaxed in Ada 9X. In fact there are no restrictions at all on new overloadings for "="; the result need not even be of type Boolean. However, if it is Boolean then a corresponding new overloading of "/=" is implicitly created. Moreover, new overloadings of "/=" are also allowed provided only that the result type is not Boolean.

The membership tests **in** and **not in** and the short circuit forms **and then** and **or else** cannot be given new meanings. That is why we said in Section 4.9 that they were not technically classed as operators.

Finally note that in the case of operators represented by reserved words, the characters in the string can be in either case. Thus a new overloading of **or** can be declared as "or" or "OR" or even "Or".

EXERCISE 7.2

1 Write a function "<" that operates on two Roman numbers and compares them according to their corresponding numeric values. That is, so that "CCL" < "CCXC". Use the function Value of Exercise 7.1(**5**).

2 Write functions "+" and "*" to add and multiply two values of type Complex. See Exercise 6.7(**2**).

3 Write a function "<" to test whether a value of type Primary is in a set represented by a value of type Colour. See Section 6.6.

4 Write a function "<=" to test whether one value of type Colour is a subset of another.

5 Write a function "<" to compare two values of the type Date of Section 6.7.

7.3 Procedures

The other form of subprogram is a procedure; a procedure is called as a statement. We have seen many examples of procedure calls where there are no parameters such as Work; Party; Action; and so on.

The body of a procedure is very similar to that of a function. The differences are

- a procedure starts with **procedure**,
- its name must be an identifier,
- it does not return a result,
- the parameters may be of three different modes **in**, **out** or **in out**.

The mode of a parameter is indicated by following the colon in the parameter specification by **in**, **out** or **in out**. If the mode is omitted then it is taken to be **in**. In the case of functions the only allowed mode is **in**; the examples earlier in this chapter omitted **in** but could have been written for instance, as

```
function Sqrt(X: in Real) return Real;
function "*" (A, B: in Vector) return Real;
```

The effect of the three modes is best summarized by quoting the *LRM* (Section 6.2).

in   The formal parameter is a constant and permits only reading of the value of the associated actual parameter.

in out   The formal parameter is a variable and permits both reading and updating of the value of the associated actual parameter.

out   The formal parameter is a variable and permits updating of the value of the associated actual parameter.

(The restriction that an **out** parameter cannot be read is relaxed in Ada 9X as explained at the end of this section.)
As a simple example of the modes **in** and **out** consider

```
procedure Add(A, B: in Integer; C: out Integer) is
begin
    C := A+B;
end Add;
```

with

```
P, Q: Integer;
...
Add(2+P, 37, Q);
```

On calling Add, the expressions 2+P and 37 are evaluated (in any order) and assigned to the formals A and B which behave as constants. The value of A+B is then assigned to the formal variable C. On return the value of C is assigned to the variable Q. Thus it is (more or less) as if we had written

```
declare
    A: constant Integer := 2+P;   – – in
    B: constant Integer := 37;    – – in
    C: Integer;                   – – out
```

```
        begin
          C:= A+B;                          – – body
          Q:= C;                            – – out
        end;
```

As an example of the mode **in out** consider

```
        procedure Increment(X: in out Integer) is
        begin
          X := X+1;
        end;
```

with

```
        I: Integer;
        ...
        Increment(I);
```

On calling Increment, the value of I is assigned to the formal variable X. The value of X is then incremented. On return, the final value of X is assigned to the actual parameter I. So it is rather as if we had written

```
        declare
          X: Integer := I;
        begin
          X := X+1;
          I := X;
        end;
```

For any scalar type (such as Integer) the modes correspond simply to copying the value **in** at the call or **out** upon return or both in the case of **in out**.

If the mode is **in** then the actual parameter may be any expression of the appropriate type or subtype. If the mode is **out** or **in out** then the actual parameter must be a variable. The identity of such a variable is determined when the procedure is called and cannot change during the call.

Suppose we had

```
        I: Integer;
        A: array (1 .. 10) of Integer;
        procedure Silly(X: in out Integer) is
        begin
          I := I+1;
          X:= X+1;
        end;
```

then the statements

```
        A(5) := 1;
        I := 5;
        Silly(A(I));
```

result in A(5) becoming 2, I becoming 6, but A(6) is not affected.

If a parameter is a composite type (such as an array or record) then the mechanism of copying, described above, may be used but alternatively an implementation may use a reference mechanism in which the formal parameter provides direct access to the actual parameter. A program which depends on the particular mechanism is erroneous. An example of such a program is given in the exercises at the end of this section. Note that because a formal array parameter takes its bounds from the actual parameter, the bounds are always copied in at the start even in the case of an **out** parameter. Of course, for simplicity, an implementation could always copy in the whole array anyway.

We now discuss the question of constraints on parameters.

In the case of scalar parameters the situation is as expected from the copying model. For an **in** or **in out** parameter any constraint on the formal must be satisfied by the actual at the beginning of the call. Conversely for an **in out** or **out** parameter any constraint on the variable which is the actual parameter must be satisfied by the value of the formal parameter upon return from the subprogram.

In the case of arrays the situation is somewhat different. If the formal parameter is a constrained array type, the bounds of the actual must be identical; it is not enough for the number of components in each dimension to be the same; the parameter mechanism is more rigorous than assignment. If, on the other hand, the formal parameter is an unconstrained array type, then, as we have seen, it takes its bounds from those of the actual. The foregoing applies irrespective of the mode of the array parameter. Similar rules apply to function results; if the result is a constrained array type then the expression in a return statement must have the same bounds. As an aside, one consequence of the parameter and result mechanism being more rigorous than assignment is that array aggregates with **others** are allowed as actual parameters and in return statements. On the other hand, as we saw in Section 6.3, they are not generally allowed in an assignment statement unless qualified.

Remember, however, that Ada 9X is slightly different. The parameter and result mechanism is like assignment but, on the other hand, the **others** rules for assignment are relaxed. The net effect is that an aggregate allowed as a parameter or in a return statement in Ada 83 is still allowed in Ada 9X.

In the case of the simple records we have discussed so far there are no constraints and so there is nothing to say. The parameter mechanism for other types will be discussed when they are introduced.

We stated above that an actual parameter corresponding to a formal **out** or **in out** parameter must be a variable. This includes the possibility of the actual parameter in turn being a formal parameter of some outer subprogram; but naturally an **out** parameter cannot be an actual parameter to a formal **in out** (or **in**) parameter because otherwise there might (will) be an attempt to read the **out** parameter.

(But these restrictions do not apply in Ada 9X because an **out** parameter can indeed be read in Ada 9X.)

A further possibility is that an actual parameter can also be a type conversion of a variable provided, of course, that the conversion is allowed. As an example, since conversion is allowed between any numeric types, we can write

```
R: Real;
...
Increment(Integer(R));
```

If R initially had the value 2.3, it would be converted to the integer value 2, incremented to give 3 and then on return converted back to 3.0 and assigned to R.

This conversion of **in out** or **out** parameters is particularly useful with arrays. Suppose we write a library of subprograms applying to our type Vector and then acquire from someone else some subprograms written to apply to the type Row of Section 6.2. The types Row and Vector are essentially the same; it just so happened that the authors used different names. Array type conversion allows us to use both sets of subprograms without having to change the type names systematically.

As a final example consider the following

```
procedure Quadratic(A, B, C: in Real; Root_1, Root_2:
                                       out Real; OK: out Boolean) is
    D: constant Real := B**2 – 4.0*A*C;
begin
    if D < 0.0 or A = 0.0 then
        OK := False;
        return;
    end if;
    Root_1 := (–B+Sqrt(D)) / (2.0*A);
    Root_2 := (–B–Sqrt(D)) / (2.0*A);
    OK := True;
end Quadratic;
```

The procedure Quadratic attempts to solve the equation

$$ax^2 + bx + c = 0$$

If the roots are real they are returned via the parameters Root_1 and Root_2 and OK is set to True. If the roots are complex (D < 0.0) or the equation degenerates (A = 0.0) then OK is set to False.

Note the use of the return statement. Since this is a procedure there is no result to be returned and so the word **return** is not followed by an expression. It just updates the **out** or **in out** parameters as necessary and returns control back to where the procedure was called. Note also that unlike a function we can 'run' into the **end**; this is equivalent to obeying **return**.

The reader will note that if OK is set to False then no value is assigned to the **out** parameters Root_1 and Root_2. The copy rule for scalars then implies that the corresponding actual parameters become undefined. In practice, junk values are presumably assigned to the actual parameters and this could possibly raise Constraint_Error if an actual parameter were constrained. This is probably bad practice and so it might be better to assign safe values such as 0.0 to the roots just in case. (In examples like this, the **out** mechanism does not seem so satisfactory as the simple reference mechanism of Algol 68 or Pascal.)

The procedure could be used in a sequence such as

```
declare
    L, M, N: Real;
    P, Q: Real;
    Status: Boolean;
begin
    – – sets values into L, M and N
    Quadratic(L, M, N, P, Q, Status);
    if Status then
        – – roots are in P and Q
    else
        – – fails
    end if;
end;
```

This is a good moment to emphasize the point made in Section 4.7 that it is often better to introduce our own two-valued enumeration type rather than use the predefined type Boolean. The above example would be clearer if we had declared

```
type Roots is (Real_Roots, Complex_Roots);
```

with other appropriate alterations.

We conclude this section by emphasizing that an **out** parameter cannot be treated as a proper variable since it cannot be read. Thus the statements of the above example could not be recast in the form

```
begin
    OK := D >= 0.0 and A /= 0.0;
    if not OK then
        return;
    end if;
    Root_1 := ... ;
    Root_2 := ... ;
end Quadratic;
```

because the Boolean expression **not** OK attempts to read the **out** parameter OK.

An exception to this rule is that the bounds of an **out** array can be read even though the components cannot. Remember that a formal array always takes its bounds from the actual array. A similar situation applies to discriminants of records which we will meet in Chapter 11.

The purely methodological restriction that an **out** parameter cannot be read proved somewhat irritating in Ada 83 and is thus relaxed in Ada 9X; an **out** parameter in Ada 9X is treated just like a variable without an initialization expression in its declaration. Thus the revised formulation of Quadratic just mentioned is indeed allowed in Ada 9X.

EXERCISE 7.3

1 Write a procedure Swap to interchange the values of the two real parameters.

2 Rewrite the function Rev of Section 7.1 as a procedure with a single parameter. Use it to reverse an array R of type Row.

3 Why is the following erroneous?

```
A: Vector(1 .. 1);

procedure P(V: Vector) is
begin
   A(1) := V(1)+V(1);
   A(1) := V(1)+V(1);
end;
...
A(1) := 1.0;
P(A);
```

4 Draw up a table showing what modes of formal parameter of an outer procedure are possible as actual parameters of various modes of a call of another procedure.

7.4 Named and default parameters

The forms of subprogram call we have been using so far have given the actual parameters in positional order. As with aggregates we can also use the named notation in which the formal parameter name is also supplied; the parameters do not then have to be in order.

So we could write

```
Quadratic(A => L, B => M, C => N, Root_1 => P, Root_2 => Q,
                                               OK => Status);
Increment(X => I);
Add(C => Q, A => 2+P, B => 37);
```

We could even write

```
Increment(X => X);
```

the scopes do not interfere.

This notation can also be used with functions

```
F := Factorial(N => 4);
S := Sqrt(X => T+0.5);
R := Inner(B => W, A => V);
```

The named notation cannot, however, be used with operators called with the usual infixed syntax (such as V*W) because there is clearly no convenient place to put the names of the formal parameters.

As with record aggregates, the named and positional notations can be mixed and any positional parameters must come first and in their correct order. However, unlike record aggregates, each parameter must be given individually and **others** may not be used. So we could write

Quadratic(L, M, N, Root_1 => P, Root_2 => Q, OK => Status);

The named notation leads into the topic of default parameters. It sometimes happens that one or more **in** parameters usually take the same value on each call; we can given a default expression in the subprogram specification and then omit it from the call.

Consider the problem of ordering a dry martini in the USA. One is faced with choices described by the following enumeration types

type Spirit **is** (Gin, Vodka);
type Style **is** (On_The_Rocks, Straight_Up);
type Trimming **is** (Olive, Twist);

The standard default expressions can then be given in a procedure specification thus

procedure Dry_Martini(Base: Spirit := Gin;
                          How: Style := On_The_Rocks;
                          Plus: Trimming := Olive);

Typical calls might be

Dry_Martini(How => Straight_Up);
Dry_Martini(Vodka, Plus => Twist);
Dry_Martini;
Dry_Martini(Gin, Straight_Up);

The first call uses the named notation; we get gin, straight up plus olive. The second call mixes the positional and named notations; as soon as a parameter is omitted the named notation must be used. The third call illustrates that all parameters can be omitted. The final call shows that a parameter can, of course, be supplied even if it happens to take the same value as the default expression; in this case it avoids using the named form for the second parameter.

Note that default expressions can only be given for **in** parameters. They cannot be given for operators but they can be given for functions designated by identifiers. Such a default expression (like a default expression for an initial value in a record type declaration) is only evaluated when required; that is, it is evaluated each time the subprogram is called and no corresponding actual parameter is supplied. Hence the default value need not be the same on each call although it usually will be. Default expressions are widely used in the standard input–output package to provide default formats.

Default expressions illustrate the subtle rule that a parameter specification of the form

P, Q: **in** Integer := E

is strictly equivalent to

P: in Integer := E;
Q: in Integer := E

(The reader will recall a similar rule for object declarations; it also applies to record components.) As a consequence, the default expression is evaluated for each omitted parameter in a call. This does not usually matter but would be significant if the expression E included a function call with side effects.

EXERCISE 7.4

1   Write a function Add which returns the sum of the two integer parameters and takes a default value of 1 for the second parameter. How many different ways can it be called to return N+1 where N is the first actual parameter?
2   Rewrite the specification of Dry_Martini to reflect that you prefer Vodka at weekends. Hint: declare a function to return your favourite spirit according to the global variable Today.

7.5 Overloading

We saw in Section 7.2 how new meanings could be given to existing language operators. This overloading applies to subprograms in general.

A subprogram will overload an existing meaning rather than hide it, provided that its specification is sufficiently different. Hiding will occur if the order and base types of the parameters and result (if any) are the same. A procedure cannot hide a function and vice versa. Note that the names of the parameters, their mode and the presence or absence of default expressions do not matter. Two or more overloaded subprograms may be declared in the same declarative part.

Subprograms and enumeration literals can overload each other. In fact an enumeration literal is formally thought of as a parameterless function with a result of the enumeration type. There are two classes of uses of identifiers – the overloadable ones and the non-overloadable ones. At any point an identifier either refers to a single entity of the non-overloadable class or to one or many of the overloadable class. A declaration of one class hides the other class and cannot occur in the same declaration list.

As we have seen, ambiguities arising from overloading can be resolved by qualification. This was necessary when the operator "<" was used with the strings in Section 6.4. As a further example consider the British Channel Islands; the larger three are Guernsey, Jersey and Alderney. There are woollen garments named after each island.

type Garment **is** (Guernsey, Jersey, Alderney);

and breeds of cattle named after two of them (the Alderney breed became extinct as a consequence of the Second World War).

type Cow **is** (Guernsey, Jersey);

and we can imagine (just) shops that sell both garments and cows according to

procedure Sell(G: Garment);
procedure Sell(C: Cow);

Although

Sell(Alderney);

is not ambiguous

Sell(Jersey);

is, since we cannot tell which subprogram is being called. We must write for example   ↗ *type name*

Sell(Cow'(Jersey));

We conclude by noting that ambiguities typically arise only when there are several overloadings. In the case here both Sell and Jersey are overloaded; in the example in Section 6.4 both the operator "<" and the literals 'X' and 'L' were overloaded.

EXERCISE 7.5

1   How else could Sell(Jersey); be made unambiguous?

7.6 **Declarations, scopes and visibility**

We said earlier that it is sometimes necessary or just convenient to give a subprogram specification on its own without the body. The specification is then followed by a semicolon and is known as a subprogram declaration. A complete subprogram, which always includes the full specification, is known as a subprogram body.

Subprogram declarations and bodies must, like other declarations, occur in a declarative part and a subprogram declaration must be followed by the corresponding body in the same declarative part.

An example of where it is necessary to use a subprogram declaration occurs with mutually recursive procedures. Suppose we wish to declare two procedures F and G which call each other. Because of the rule regarding linear elaboration of declarations we cannot write the call of F in the body of G until after F has been declared and vice versa. Clearly this is impossible if we just write the bodies because one must come second. However, we can write

```
procedure F( ... );      - - declaration of F

procedure G( ... ) is    - - body of G
begin
   F( ... );
end G;

procedure F( ... ) is    - - body of F repeats
begin                    - - its specification
   G( ... );
end F;
```

and then all is well.

If the specification is repeated then it must be given in full and the two must be the same. Technically we say that the two specifications must conform. Some slight variation is allowed. A numeric literal can be replaced by another numeric literal with the same value; an identifier can be replaced by a dotted name as described later in this section; the lexical spacing can be different. It is worth noting that the key reason for not allowing subtype indications in parameter specifications is to remove any problem regarding conformance since there is then no question of evaluating constraint expressions twice and possibly having different results because of side effects. No corresponding question arises with default expressions (which are of course written out twice) since they are only evaluated when the subprogram is called.

Another important case, where we have to write a subprogram declaration as well as a body, occurs in the next chapter when we discuss packages. Even if not always necessary, it is sometimes clearer to write subprogram declarations as well as bodies. An example might be in the case where many subprogram bodies occur together. The subprogram declarations could then be placed together at the head of the declarative part in order to act as a summary of the bodies to come.

Subprogram bodies and other declarations must not be mixed up in an arbitrary way. A body cannot, for example, be followed by object, type and number declarations. This ensures that small declarations are not 'lost' in between large bodies. The rules will be given in more detail when we discuss packages in the next chapter.

Note, however, that these methodological rules do not apply in Ada 9X.

Since subprograms occur in declarative parts and themselves contain declarative parts they may be textually nested without limit. The normal hiding rules applicable to blocks described in Section 4.2 also apply to declarations in subprograms. (The only complication concerns overloading as discussed in the previous section.) Consider

```
procedure P is
    I: Integer := 0;

  procedure Q is
      K: Integer := I;
      I: Integer;
      J: Integer;
  begin
      ...
  end Q;
    ...
end P;
```

Just as for the example in Section 4.2, the inner I hides the outer one and so the outer I is not visible inside the procedure Q after the declaration of the inner I.

However, we can always refer to the outer I by the so-called dotted notation, in which it is prefixed by the name of the unit immediately containing its declaration followed by a dot. So within Q we can refer to the outer I as P.I and so, for example, we could initialize J by writing

```
    J: Integer := P.I;
```

If the prefix is itself hidden then it can always be written the same way. Thus the inner I could be referred to as P.Q.I.

An object declared in a block cannot usually be referred to in this way since a block does not normally have a name. However, a block can be named in a similar way to a loop as shown in the following

```
Outer:
declare
    I: Integer := 0;
bogin
    ...
  declare
      K: Integer := I;
      I: Integer;
      J: Integer := Outer.I;
  begin
      ...
  end;
end Outer;
```

Here the outer block has the identifier Outer. Unlike subprograms, but like loops, the identifier has to be repeated after the matching **end**. Naming the block enables us to initialize the inner declaration of J with the value of the outer I.

Within a loop it is possible to refer to a hidden loop parameter in the same way. We could even rewrite the example in Section 6.1 of assigning zero to the elements of AA as

```
L:
for I in AA'Range(1) loop
   for I in AA'Range(2) loop
      AA(L.I, I) := 0.0;
   end loop;
end loop L;
```

although one would be a little crazy to do so!

It should be noted that the dotted form can always be used even if it is not necessary.

This notation can also be applied to operators and character literals. Thus the variable Result declared inside "*" can be referred to as "*".Result. And equally if "*" were declared inside a block B then it could be referred to as B. "*". If it is called with this form of name then the normal function call must be used

```
R := B. "*"(V, W);
```

Indeed, the functional form can always be used as in

```
R := "*"(V, W);
```

and we could then also use the named notation

```
R := "*"(A => V, B => W);
```

As we have seen, subprograms can alter global variables and therefore have side effects. (A side effect is one brought about other than via the parameter mechanism.) It is generally considered rather undesirable to write subprograms, especially functions, which have side effects. However, some side effects are beneficial. Any subprogram which performs input–output has a side effect on the file; a function delivering successive members of a sequence of random numbers only works because of its side effects; if we need to count how many times a function is called then we use a side effect; and so on. However, care must be taken when using functions with side effects that the program is correct since there are various circumstances in which the order of evaluation is not defined.

We conclude this section with a brief discussion of the hierarchy of **exit**, **return** and **goto** and the scopes of block and loop identifiers and labels.

A **return** statement terminates the execution of the immediately embracing subprogram. It can occur inside an inner block or inside a loop in the subprogram and therefore also terminate the loop. On the other hand an **exit** statement terminates the named or immediately embracing loop. It can also occur inside an inner block but cannot occur inside a subprogram declared in the loop and thereby also terminate the subprogram. A **goto** statement can transfer control out of a loop or block but not out of a subprogram.

As far as scope is concerned, identifiers of labels, blocks and loops behave as if they are declared at the end of the declarative part of the immediately embracing subprogram or block (or package or task body). Moreover distinct identifiers must be used for all blocks, loops and labels inside the same subprogram (or package or task body) even if some are in inner blocks. Thus two labels in the same subprogram cannot have the same identifier even if they are inside different inner blocks. This rule reduces the risk of goto statements going to the wrong label particularly when a program is amended.

CHECKLIST 7

Parameter and result subtypes must be given by a type mark and not a subtype indication.

A function must return a result and should not run into its final '**end**' although a procedure can.

The order of evaluation of parameters is not defined.

A default parameter expression is only evaluated when the subprogram is called and the corresponding parameter is omitted.

The actual and formal parameters of a constrained array type must have equal bounds.

Scalar parameters are copied. The mechanism for arrays and records is not defined.

Formal parameter specifications are separated by semicolons not commas.

---

8 Overall Structure

The previous chapters have described the small-scale features of Ada in considerable detail. The language presented so far corresponds to the areas addressed by languages of the 1960s and early 1970s, although Ada provides more functionality in those areas. However, we now come to the new areas which broadly speaking correspond to the concepts of data abstraction and programming in the large which were discussed in Chapter 1.

In this chapter we discuss packages (which is what Ada is all about) and the mechanisms for separate compilation. We also say a little more about scope and visibility.

8.1 Packages

One of the major problems with the traditional block structured languages, such as Algol and Pascal, is that they do not offer enough control of visibility. For example, suppose we have a stack represented by an array and a variable which indexes the current top element, a procedure Push to add an item and a function Pop to remove an item. We might write

```
Max: constant := 100;
S: array (1 .. Max) of Integer;
Top: Integer range 0 .. Max;
```

to represent the stack and then declare

```
procedure Push(X: Integer) is
begin
   Top := Top+1;
   S(Top) := X;
end Push;

function Pop return Integer is
begin
   Top := Top–1;
   return S(Top+1);
end Pop;
```

In a simple block structured language there is no way in which we can be given access to the subprograms Push and Pop without also being given direct access to the variables S and Top. As a consequence we cannot be forced to use the correct protocol and so be prevented from making use of knowledge of how the stack is implemented.

The Ada package overcomes this by allowing us to place a wall around a group of declarations and only permit access to those which we intend to be visible. A package actually comes in two parts: the specification which gives the interface to the outside world, and the body which gives the hidden details.

The above example should be written as

```
package Stack is                      – – specification
   procedure Push(X: Integer);
   function Pop return Integer;
end Stack;

package body Stack is                 – – body
   Max: constant := 100;
   S: array (1 .. Max) of Integer;
   Top: Integer range 0 .. Max;

   procedure Push(X: Integer) is
   begin
      Top := Top+1;
```

```
      S(Top) := X;
   end Push;

   function Pop return Integer is
   begin
      Top := Top-1;
      return S(Top+1);
   end Pop;

begin                                    – – initialization
   Top := 0;
end Stack;
```

The package specification (strictly declaration) starts with the reserved word **package**, the identifier of the package and **is**. This is then followed by declarations of the entities which are to be visible. It finishes with **end**, the identifier (optionally) and the terminating semicolon. In the example we just have the declarations of the two subprograms Push and Pop.

The package body also starts with **package** but this is then followed by **body**, the identifier and **is**. We then have a normal declarative part, **begin**, sequence of statements, **end**, optional identifier and terminating semicolon just as in a block or subprogram body.

In the example the declarative part contains the variables which represent the stack and the bodies of Push and Pop. The sequence of statements between **begin** and **end** is executed when the package is declared and can be used for initialization. If there is no need for an initialization sequence, the **begin** can be omitted. Indeed in this example we could equally and perhaps more naturally have performed the initialization by writing

```
   Top: Integer range 0 .. Max := 0;
```

Note that a package is itself declared and so is just one of the items in an outer declarative part (unless it is a library unit which is the outermost layer anyway).

The package illustrates another case where we need distinct subprogram declarations and bodies. Indeed we cannot put a body into a package specification. And moreover, if a package specification contains the specification of a subprogram, then the package body must contain the corresponding subprogram body. We can think of the package specification and body as being just one large declarative part with only some items visible. But, of course, a subprogram body can be declared in a package body without its specification having to be given in the package specification. Such a subprogram would be internal to the package and could only be called from within, either from other subprograms, some of which would presumably be visible, or perhaps from the initialization sequence.

The elaboration of a package body consists simply of the elaboration of the declarations inside it followed by the execution of the initialization sequence if there is one. The package continues to exist until the end of the scope in which it is declared. Entities declared inside the package have the same lifetime as the package itself. Thus the variables S and Top can be thought of as 'own' variables in the Algol 60 sense; their values are retained between successive calls of Push and Pop.

Packages may be declared in any declarative part such as that in a block, subprogram or indeed another package. If a package specification is declared inside another package specification then, as for subprograms, the body of one must be declared in the body of the other. But again both specification and body could be in a package body.

Apart from the rule that a package specification cannot contain bodies, it can contain any of the other kinds of declarations we have met.

Now to return to the use of our package. The package itself has a name and the entities in its visible part (the specification) can be thought of as components of the package in some sense. It is entirely natural therefore that, in order to call Push, we must also mention Stack. In fact the dotted notation is used. So we could write

```
declare
    package Stack is        – – specification
    ...                     – – and
    ...                     – – body
    end Stack;
begin
    ...
    Stack.Push(M);
    ...
    N := Stack.Pop;
    ...
end;
```

Inside the package we would call Push as just Push, but we could still write Stack.Push just as in the last chapter we saw how we could refer to a local variable X of procedure P as P.X. Inside the package we can refer to S or Stack.S, but outside the package Max, S and Top are not accessible in any way.

It would in general be painful always to have to write Stack.Push to call Push from outside. Instead we can write

```
use Stack;
```

as a sort of declaration and we may then refer to Push and Pop directly. The use clause could follow the declaration of the specification of Stack in the same declarative part or could be in another declarative part where the package is visible. So we could write

```
declare
    use Stack;
begin
    ...
    Push(M);
```

```
    ...
    N := Pop;
    ...
  end;
```

The use clause is like a declaration and similarly has a scope to the end of the block. Outside we would have to revert to the dotted notation. We could have an inner use clause referring to the same package – it would do no harm.

Two or more packages could be declared in the same declarative part. Generally, we could arrange all the specifications together and then all the bodies, or alternatively the corresponding specifications and bodies, could be together. Thus we could have spec A, spec B, body A, body B, or spec A, body A, spec B, body B.

The rules governing the order are simply

* linear elaboration of declarations,
* specification must precede body for same package (or subprogram),
* small items must generally precede big ones.

More precisely the last rule is that a body can only be followed by other bodies, subprogram and package (and task) specifications (strictly declarations) or indeed use clauses. The general intent of this rule is to prevent small items from being lost among big ones; the use clause is allowed as a 'big' item (as well as a small item) because it is very convenient to follow the declaration of a package by a corresponding use clause in the same declarative part.

The reader may recall that this last rule does not apply in Ada 9X.

Of course, the specification of a package may contain things other than subprograms. Indeed an important case is where it does not contain subprograms at all but merely a group of related variables, constants and types. In such a case the package needs no body. It does not provide any hiding properties but merely gives commonality of naming. (A body could be provided; its only purpose would be for initialization).

However, a package declared at the library level is only allowed to have a body in Ada 9X if it requires one for some reason such as providing the body for a subprogram declared in the specification. This avoids some awkward surprises which can occur as will be explained in Section 16.4.

As an example we could provide a package containing our type Day and some useful related constants.

```
package Diurnal is
  type Day is (Mon, Tue, Wed, Thu, Fri, Sat, Sun);
  subtype Weekday is Day range Mon .. Fri;
  Tomorrow: constant array (Day) of Day
                        := (Tue, Wed, Thu, Fri, Sat, Sun, Mon);
  Next_Work_Day: constant array (Weekday) of Weekday
                        := (Tue, Wed, Thu, Fri, Mon);
end Diurnal;
```

A final point. A subprogram cannot be called successfully during the elaboration of a declarative part if its body appears later. This did not prevent the mutual recursion of the procedures F and G in Section 7.6 because in that case the call of F actually only occurred when we executed the sequence of statements of the body of G. But it does prevent the use of a function in an initial value. So

```
function A return Integer;
I: Integer := A;
```

is illegal, and would result in Program_Error being raised.

A similar rule applies to subprograms in packages. If we call a subprogram from outside a package but before the package body has been elaborated, then Program_Error will be raised.

EXERCISE 8.1

1 The sequence defined by

$$X_{n+1} = X_n .5^5 \bmod 2^{13}$$

provides a crude source of pseudo random numbers. The initial value X_0 should be an odd integer in the range 0 to 2^{13}.
Write a package Random containing a procedure Init to initialize the sequence and a function Next to deliver the next value in the sequence.

2 Write a package Complex_Numbers which makes visible

• the type Complex,
• a constant $I = \sqrt{-1}$,
• functions +, −, *, / acting on values of type Complex.

See Exercise 7.2(**2**).

8.2 Library units

Many languages in the past have ignored the simple fact that programs are written in pieces, compiled separately and then joined together. Ada recognizes the need for separate compilation and provides two mechanisms – one top down and one bottom up.

The top down mechanism is appropriate for the development of a large coherent program which nevertheless, for various reasons, is broken down into subunits which can be compiled separately. The subunits are compiled after the unit from which they are taken. This mechanism is described in the next section.

The bottom up mechanism is appropriate for the creation of a program library where units are written for general use and consequently are written before the programs that use them. This mechanism will now be discussed in detail.

A library unit may be a subprogram specification or a package specification; the corresponding bodies are called secondary units. These units may be compiled individually or for convenience several could be submitted to the compiler together. Thus we could compile the specification and body of a package together but as we shall see it may be more convenient to compile them individually. As usual a subprogram body alone is sufficient to define the subprogram fully; it is then classed as a library unit rather than a secondary unit.

When a unit is compiled it goes into a program library. There will obviously be several such libraries according to user and project, etc. The creation and manipulation of libraries is outside the scope of this book. Once in the library, a unit can be used by any subsequently compiled unit but the using unit must indicate the dependency by a with clause.

As a simple example suppose we compile the package Stack. This package depends on no other unit and so it needs no with clause. We will compile both specification and body together so the text submitted will be

```
package Stack is
   ...
end Stack

package body Stack is
   ...
end Stack;
```

As well as producing the object code corresponding to the package, the compiler also places in the program library the information describing the interface that the package presents to the outside world; this is of course the information in the specification.

We now suppose that we write a procedure Main which will use the package Stack. Our procedure Main is going to be the main program in the usual sense. It will have no parameters and we can imagine that it is called by some magic outside the language itself. The Ada definition does not prescribe that the main program should have the identifier Main; it is merely a convention which we are adopting here because it has to be called something.

The text we submit to the compiler could be

```
with Stack;
procedure Main is
   use Stack;
   M, N: Integer;
begin
   ...
   Push(M);
   ...
   N := Pop;
   ...
end Main;
```

The with clause goes before the unit so that the dependency of the unit on other units is clear at a glance. A with clause may not be embedded in an inner scope.

On encountering a with clause the compiler retrieves from the program library the information describing the interface presented by the withed unit so that it can check that the unit being compiled uses the interface correctly. Thus if procedure Main tried to call Push with the wrong number or type of parameters then this will be detected during compilation. This thorough checking between separately compiled units is a major factor in the increased productivity obtained through using Ada.

If a unit is dependent on several other units then they can go in the one with clause, or it might be a convenience to use distinct with clauses. Thus we could write

> **with** Stack, Diurnal;
> **procedure** Main **is**
>
> ...

or equally

> **with** Stack;
> **with** Diurnal;
> **procedure** Main **is**
>
> ...

For convenience we can place a use clause after a with clause. Thus

> **with** Stack; **use** Stack;
> **procedure** Main **is**
>
> ...

and then Push and Pop are directly visible without more ado. A use clause in such a position can only refer to packages mentioned in the with clause.

Only direct dependencies need be given in a with clause. Thus if package P uses the facilities of package Q which in turn uses the facilities of package R, then, unless P also directly uses R, the with clause for P should mention only Q. The user of Q does not care about R and must not need to know since otherwise the hierarchy of development would be made more complicated.

Another point is that the with clause in front of a package or subprogram declaration will also apply to the body. It can but need not be repeated. Of course, the body may have additional dependencies which will need indicating with a with clause anyway. Dependencies which apply only to the body should not be given with the specification since otherwise the independence of the body and the specification would be reduced.

If a package specification and body are compiled separately then the body must be compiled after the specification. We say that the body is dependent on the specification. However, any unit using the package is dependent only on the specification and not the body. If the body is changed in a manner consistent with not changing the specification, any unit using the package will

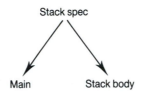

Figure 8.1   Dependencies between units.

not need recompiling. The ability to compile specification and body separately should simplify program maintenance.

The dependencies between the specification and body of the package **Stack** and the procedure **Main** are illustrated by the graph in Figure 8.1.

The general rule regarding the order of compilation is simply that a unit must be compiled after all units on which it depends. Consequently, if a unit is changed and recompiled then all dependent units must also be recompiled. Any order of compilation consistent with the dependency rule is acceptable.

There is one package that need not be mentioned in a with clause. This is the package **Standard** which effectively contains the declarations of all the predefined types such as **Integer** and **Boolean** and their predefined operations. It also contains an internal package **ASCII** containing constants defining the control characters such as **CR** and **LF**. We now see why the control characters were represented as **ASCII.CR** etc. in Chapter 6. By writing **use** **ASCII;** they can, of course, just be referred to as **CR**. The package **Standard** is described in more detail in Appendix 2.

Finally there are two important rules regarding library units. They must have distinct identifiers; they cannot be overloaded. Moreover they cannot be operators. These rules enable an Ada program library to be implemented quite easily on top of a basic filing system with simple identifiers.

The library mechanism in Ada 83 is flat; all library packages and subprograms are at the same level. In Ada 9X, however, a hierarchical structure with child units is introduced. This is described in detail in Chapter 17.

EXERCISE 8.2

1   The package D and subprograms P and Q and Main have correct with clauses as follows

specification of D	no with clause
body of D	**with** P, Q;
subprogram P	no with clause
subprogram Q	no with clause
subprogram Main	**with** D;

Draw a graph showing the dependencies between the units. How many different orders of compilation are possible?

8.3 Subunits

In this section we introduce a further form of secondary unit known as a subunit. The body of a package, subprogram (or task, see Chapter 14) can be 'taken out' of an immediately embracing library unit or secondary unit and itself compiled separately. The body in the embracing unit is then replaced by a body stub. As an example suppose we remove the bodies of the subprograms Push and Pop from the package Stack. The body of Stack would then become

```
package body Stack is
   Max: constant := 100;
   S: array (1 .. Max) of Integer;
   Top: Integer range 0 .. Max;
   procedure Push(X: Integer) is separate;    -- stub
   function Pop return Integer is separate;    -- stub
begin
   Top := 0;
end Stack;
```

The removed units are termed subunits; they may then be compiled separately. They have to be preceded by **separate** followed by the name of the parent unit in brackets. Thus the subunit Push becomes

```
separate (Stack)
procedure Push(X: Integer) is
begin
   Top := Top+1;
   S(Top) := X;
end Push;
```

and similarly for Pop.

In the above example the parent unit is (the body of) a library unit. The parent unit could itself be a subunit; in such a case its name must be given in full using the dotted notation starting with the ancestor library unit. Thus if R is a subunit of Q which is a subunit of P which is a library unit, then the text of R must start

```
separate (P.Q)
```

As with library units and for similar reasons, the subunits of a unit must have distinct identifiers. But, of course, this does not prevent subunits of different units having the same identifier. And again subunits cannot be operators.

A subunit is dependent on its parent (and any library units explicitly mentioned) and so must be compiled after them.

Visibility within a subunit is as at the corresponding body stub – it is exactly as if the subunit were plucked out with its environment intact (and indeed the compiler will store the relevant information on compiling the stub and retrieve it on compiling the subunit so that full type checking is maintained). As a consequence any with clause applying to the parent need not be repeated just because the subunit is compiled separately. However, it is possible to give the subunit access to additional library units by preceding it with its own with clauses (and possibly use clauses). Such clauses precede **separate**. So the text of R might commence

>**with** X; **use** X;
>**separate** (P.Q)
>...

A possible reason for doing this might be if we can then remove any reference to library unit X from the parent P.Q and so reduce the dependencies. This would give us greater freedom with the order of compilation; if X were recompiled for some reason then only R would need recompiling as a consequence and not also Q.

Note that a with clause only refers to library units and never to subunits. Finally observe that several subunits or a mixture of library units, library unit bodies and subunits can be compiled together.

EXERCISE 8.3

1   Suppose that the package Stack is written with separate subunits Push and Pop. Draw a graph showing the dependencies between the five units: procedure Main, procedure Push, function Pop, package specification Stack, package body Stack. How many different orders of compilation are possible?

8.4   Scope and visibility

We return once more to the topic of scope and visibility. In this section we summarize the major points which will be relevant to the everyday use of Ada. For some of the fine detail, the reader is referred to the *LRM*. It is perhaps worth mentioning that the *LRM* uses the term declarative region in order to explain the visibility and scope rules. Blocks and subprograms are examples of declarative regions and the scope rules associated with them were described in Sections 4.2 and 7.6. We now have to consider the effect of the introduction of packages.

A package specification and body together constitute a single declarative region. Thus if we declare a variable X in the specification then we cannot redeclare X in the body (except of course in an inner region such as a local subprogram).

In the case of a declaration in the visible part of a package, its scope extends from the declaration to the end of the scope of the package itself. Note that if the package is inside the visible part of another package then this means that, applying the rule again, the scope extends to the end of that of the outer package and so on.

In the case of a declaration in a package body (or in the private part of a package – to be described in the next chapter), its scope extends to the end of the package body.

In the case of the simple nesting of blocks and subprograms an entity is visible throughout its scope unless hidden by another declaration. We saw in Section 7.6 how even if it was hidden it could nevertheless in general be referred to by using the dotted notation where the prefixed name is that of the unit embracing the declaration. In essence, writing the name of the embracing unit makes the entity visible.

In the case of an entity declared in a package the same rules apply inside the package. But outside the package it is not visible unless we write the package name or alternatively write a use clause.

The identifiers visible at a given point are those visible before considering any use clauses plus those made visible by use clauses.

The basic rule is that an identifier in a package is made visible by a use clause provided the same identifier is not also in another package with a use clause and also provided that the identifier is not already visible anyway. If these conditions are not met then the identifier is not made visible and we have to continue to use the dotted notation.

A slightly different rule applies if all the identifiers are subprograms or enumeration literals. In this case they all overload each other unless of course their specifications clash (could hide each other) in which case they are not made visible. Thus an identifier made visible by a use clause can never hide another identifier although it may overload it.

The general purpose of these rules is to ensure that adding a use clause cannot invalidate an existing piece of text. We have only given a brief sketch here and the reader is probably confused. In practice there should be no problems since the Ada compiler will, we hope, indicate any ambiguities or other difficulties and things can always be put right by adding a qualifier or using a dotted name.

There are other rules regarding record component names, subprogram parameters and so on which are as expected. For example there is no conflict between an identifier of a record component and another use of the identifier outside the type definition itself. The reason is that although the scopes may overlap, the regions of visibility do not. Consider

```
declare
   type R is
      record
         I: Integer;
      end record;
   type S is
      record
         I: Integer;
      end record;
   AR: R;
   AS: S;
   I: Integer;
begin
```

```
        ...
    I := AR.I+AS.I;      – – legal
        ...
    end;
```

The scope of the I in the type R extends from the component declaration until the end of the block. However, its visibility is confined to within the declaration of R except that it is made visible by the use of AR in the selected component. Hence no conflict.

Similar considerations prevent conflict in named aggregates and in named parameters in subprogram calls.

Observe that a use clause can mention several packages and that it may be necessary for a package name to be given as a selected component itself. A use clause does not take effect until the semicolon. Suppose we have nested packages

```
    package P1 is
       package P2 is
          ...
       end P2;
       ...
    end P1;
```

then outside P1 we could write

```
    use P1; use P2;
```

or

```
    use P1, P1.P2;
```

but not

```
    use P1, P2;
```

We could even write **use** P1.P2; to gain visibility of the entities in P2 but not those in P1 – however, this seems an odd thing to do. Remember, moreover, that a use clause following a with clause can only refer to packages directly mentioned in the with clause.

In Ada 9X there is another form of use clause, the so-called use type clause. This allows us to make just the operators of a type visible. We will come back to this in a moment.

Earlier we mentioned the existence of the package Standard. This contains all the predefined entities but moreover every library unit should be thought of as being declared inside and at the end of Standard. This explains why an explicit use clause for Standard is not required. Another important consequence is that, provided we do not hide the name Standard by redefining it, a library unit P can always be referred to as Standard.P. Hence, in the absence of anonymous blocks, loops and overloading, every identifier in the program has a unique name commencing with Standard. Thus we could even pedantically refer to the predefined operators in this way

```
Four: Integer := Standard."+" (2, 2);
```

It is probably good advice not to redefine Standard!

8.5   Renaming

Certain entities can be renamed. As an example we can write

```
declare
    procedure S_Push(X: Integer) renames Stack.Push;
    function S_Pop return Integer renames Stack.Pop;
begin
    ...
    S_Push(M);
    ...
    N := S_Pop;
    ...
end;
```

A possible reason for doing this is to resolve ambiguities and yet avoid the use of the full dotted notation. Thus if we had two packages with a procedure Push (with an Integer parameter) then the use clause would be of no benefit since the full name would still be needed to resolve the ambiguity.

There is also a strong school of thought that use clauses are bad for you. Consider the case of a large program with many library units and suppose that the unit we are in has withed several packages. If we have use clauses for all these packages then it is not clear from which package an arbitrary identifier has been imported. In the absence of use clauses we have to use the full dotted notation and the origin of everything is then obvious. However, it is also commonly accepted that long meaningful identifiers should be generally used. A long meaningful package name followed by the long meaningful name of an entity in the package is often too much. However, we can introduce an abbreviation by renaming such as

```
V: Real renames Aeroplane_Data.Current_Velocity;
```

and then compactly use V in local computation and yet still have the full identification available in the text of the current unit.

As another example suppose we wish to use both the function Inner and the equivalent operator "*" of Chapter 7 without declaring two distinct subprograms. We can write

```
function "*" (X, Y: Vector) return Real renames Inner;
```

or

> **function** Inner(X, Y: Vector) **return** Real **renames** "*";

according to which we declare first.

Renaming of operators can also be used to avoid the use of prefixed notation in the absence of a use clause (which, as we mentioned, many consider to be evil). Thus suppose we are using the package Complex_Numbers of Exercise 8.1(**2**) but have not written a use clause. We would then have to write calls of "+" as for example

> C := Complex_Numbers."+"(A, B);

which is painful to say the least. We can avoid this by renaming

> **function** "+" (X, Y: Complex_Numbers.Complex)
>   **return** Complex_Numbers.Complex
>   **renames** Complex_Numbers."+";

and we can then simply write

> C := A + B;

This is still a bit of a nuisance and is made much easier in Ada 9X by the introduction of the use type clause which provides visibility of the operators of a type such as Complex but not other entities in the package. We can write

> **use type** Complex_Numbers.Complex;

and then we can use the operators in the normal infixed notation; the renaming is not necessary.

Renaming is also useful in the case of library units. Thus we might wish to have two or more overloaded subprograms and yet compile them separately. This cannot be done directly since library units must have distinct names. However, differently named library units could be renamed so that the user sees the required effect. The restriction that a library unit cannot be an operator can similarly be overcome. The same tricks can be done with subunits.

In Ada 83, a library unit can only be renamed as a local unit whereas in Ada 9X a library unit can also be renamed as another library unit.

If a subprogram is renamed, the number, base types and modes of the parameters (and result if a function) must be the same. This information can be used to resolve overloadings (as in the example of "*") and, of course, this matching occurs during compilation; we call this mode conformance. Rather strangely, any constraints on the parameters or result in the new subprogram are ignored; those on the original still apply.

On the other hand, the presence, absence or value of default parameters do not have to match. Renaming can be used to introduce, change or delete default expressions; the default parameters associated with the new name are those shown in the renaming declaration. Hence renaming cannot be used as a trick to give an operator default values. Similarly, parameter names do not have to match but naturally the new names must be used for named parameters of calls of the new subprogram.

An additional facility in Ada 9X is the ability to provide the body of a subprogram as simply a renaming of another subprogram. There is, however, an extra rule on the matching of parameters when renaming is used for this purpose. All constraints must statically match; this is called subtype conformance. The reason for requiring subtype conformance is so that a simple jump to the old subprogram can be compiled as the call to the new one.

The unification of subprograms and enumeration literals is further illustrated by the fact that an enumeration literal can be renamed as a parameterless function with the appropriate result. For example

```
function Ten return Roman_Digit renames 'X';
```

Renaming can also be used to partially evaluate the name of an object. Suppose we have an array of records such as the array People in Section 6.7 and that we wish to scan the array and print out the dates of birth in numerical form. We could write

```
for I in People'Range loop
    Put(People(I).Birth.Day); Put(":");
    Put(Month_Name'Pos(People(I).Birth.Month)+1);
    Put(":");
    Put(People(I).Birth.Year);
end loop;
```

It is clearly painful to repeat People(I).Birth each time. We could declare a variable D of type Date and copy People(I).Birth into it, but this would be very wasteful if the record were at all large. A better technique is to use renaming thus

```
for I in People'Range loop
    declare
        D: Date renames People(I).Birth;
    begin
        Put(D.Day); Put(":");
        Put(Month_Name'Pos(D.Month)+1);
        Put(":");
        Put(D.Year);
    end;
end loop;
```

Beware that renaming does not correspond to text substitution – the identity of the object is determined when the renaming occurs. If any variable in the name subsequently changes then the identity of the object does not change. Any constraints implied by the type mark in the renaming declaration are ignored; those of the original object still apply.

Renaming can be applied to objects (variables and constants), components of composite objects (including slices of arrays), exceptions (see Chapter 10), subprograms and packages. In the case of a package it takes the simple form

package P **renames** Stack;

Although renaming does not directly apply to types an almost identical effect can be achieved by the use of a subtype

subtype S **is** T;

or order to overcome a lack of standardization even

subtype Color **is** Colour;

Note also that renaming cannot be applied to a named number. This is partly because renaming requires a type name and named numbers do not have an explicit type name (we will see in Chapter 12 that they are of so-called universal types which cannot be explicitly named). Thus if we had a package Mathematical_Constants containing numbers such as Natural_E (the base of natural logarithms) then we would not be able to provide a local renaming for brevity. However, there is no need, we can just declare another named number

E: **constant** := Mathematical_Constants.Natural_E;

which is no disadvantage because the named numbers are not run-time objects anyway and so there is no duplication.

Finally note that renaming does not hide the old name nor does it ever introduce a new entity; it just provides another way of referring to an existing entity or, in other words, another view of it (that is why new constraints in a renaming declaration are ignored). Renaming can be very useful at times but the indiscriminate use of renaming should be avoided since the aliases introduced make program proving much more difficult.

EXERCISE 8.5

1   Declare a renaming of the literal Mon of type Day from the package Diurnal of Section 8.1.

2   Declare a renaming of Diurnal.Next_Work_Day.

3   Declare Pets as a renaming of the relevant part of the second Farmyard of Section 6.5.

CHECKLIST 8

Variables inside a package exist between calls of subprograms of the package.

A library unit must be compiled after other library units mentioned in its with clause.

A subunit must be compiled after its parent.

A body must be compiled after the corresponding specification.

A package specification and body form a single declarative region.

Do not redefine 'Standard'.

Renaming is not text substitution.

9 Private Types

We have seen how packages enable us to hide internal objects from the user of a package. Private types enable us to hide the details of the construction of a type from a user.

9.1 Normal private types

In Exercise 8.1(**2**) we wrote a package Complex_Numbers providing a type Complex, a constant I and some operations on the type. The specification of the package was

```
package Complex_Numbers is
    type Complex is
        record
            RI, Im: Real;
        end record;

    I: constant Complex:= (0.0, 1.0);

    function "+" (X: Complex) return Complex;   – – unary +
    function "–" (X: Complex) return Complex;   – – unary –

    function "+" (X, Y: Complex) return Complex;
    function "–" (X, Y: Complex) return Complex;
    function "*" (X, Y: Complex) return Complex;
    function "/" (X, Y: Complex) return Complex;
end;
```

The trouble with this formulation is that the user can make use of the fact that the complex numbers are held in cartesian representation. Rather than always using the complex operator "+", the user could also write things like

```
    C.Im := C.Im + 1.0;
```

rather than the more abstract

```
    C := C + I;
```

In fact, with the above package, the user has to make use of the representation in order to construct values of the type.

We might wish to prevent use of knowledge of the representation so that we could change the representation to perhaps polar form at a later date and know that the user's program would still be correct. We can do this with a private type. Consider

```
package Complex_Numbers is
    type Complex is private;
    I: constant Complex;
    function "+" (X: Complex) return Complex;
    function "–" (X: Complex) return Complex;
    function "+" (X, Y: Complex) return Complex;
    function "–" (X, Y: Complex) return Complex;
    function "*" (X, Y: Complex) return Complex;
    function "/" (X, Y: Complex) return Complex;
    function Cons(R, I: Real) return Complex;
```

```
function Rl_Part(X: Complex) return Real;
function Im_Part(X: Complex) return Real;

private
   type Complex is
      record
         Rl, Im: Real;
      end record;
   I: constant Complex := (0.0, 1.0);
end;
```

The part of the package specification before the reserved word **private** is the visible part and gives the information available externally to the package. The type Complex is declared to be private. This means that outside the package nothing is known of the details of the type. The only operations available are assignment, = and /= plus those added by the writer of the package as subprograms specified in the visible part.

We may also declare constants of a private type such as I in the visible part. The initial value cannot be given in the visible part because the details of the type are not yet known. Hence we just state that I is a constant; we call it a deferred constant.

After **private** we have to give the details of types declared as private and give the initial values of corresponding deferred constants.

A private type can be implemented in any way consistent with the operations visible to the user. It can be a record as we have shown; equally it could be an array, an enumeration type and so on; it could even be declared in terms of another private type. In our case it is fairly obvious that the type Complex is naturally implemented as a record; but we could equally have used an array of two components such as

```
type Complex is array (1 .. 2) of Real;
```

Having declared the details of the private type we can use them and so declare the constants properly and give their initial values.

It should be noted that as well as the functions +, −, * and / we have also provided Cons to create a complex number from its real and imaginary components and Rl_Part and Im_Part to return the components. Some such functions are necessary because the user no longer has direct access to the internal structure of the type. Of course, the fact that Cons, Rl_Part and Im_Part correspond to our thinking externally of the complex numbers in cartesian form does not prevent us from implementing them internally in some other form as we shall see in a moment.

The body of the package is as shown in the answer to Exercise 8.1(**2**) plus the additional functions which are trivial. It is therefore

```
package body Complex_Numbers is

   − − unary + −

   function "+" (X, Y: Complex) return Complex is
```

```
begin
   return (X.RI + Y.RI, X.Im + Y.Im);
end "+";
```

– – plus – * / similarly

```
function Cons(R, I: Real) return Complex is
begin
   return (R, I);
end Cons;

function RI_Part(X: Complex) return Real is
begin
   return X.RI;
end RI_Part;
```

– – Im_Part similarly

```
end Complex_Numbers;
```

The package Complex_Numbers could be used in a fragment such as

```
declare
   use Complex_Numbers;
   C, D: Complex;
   R, S: Real;
begin
   C := Cons(1.5, –6.0);
   D := C + I;                 – – Complex +
   R := RI_Part(D) + 6.0;   – – Real +
   ...
end;
```

Outside the package we can declare variables and constants of type Complex in the usual way. Note the use of Cons to create a complex literal. We cannot, of course, do mixed operations between our complex and real numbers. Thus we cannot write

```
C := 2.0 * C;
```

but instead must write

```
C := Cons(2.0, 0.0) * C;
```

If this is felt to be tedious we could add further overloadings of the operators to allow mixed operations.

Let us suppose that for some reason we now decide to represent the complex numbers in polar form. The visible part of the package will be unchanged but the private part could now become

```
private
   Pi: constant := 3.14159_26536;
   type Complex is
      record
         R: Real;
         Theta: Real range 0.0 .. 2.0*Pi;
      end record;
   I: constant Complex := (1.0, 0.5*Pi);
end;
```

Note how the constant Pi is for convenience declared in the private part; anything other than a body can be declared in a private part if it suits us – we are not restricted to just declaring the types and constants in full. Things declared in the private part are also available in the body.

The body of our package Complex_Numbers will now need completely rewriting. Some functions will become simpler and others will be more intricate. In particular it will be convenient to provide a function to normalize the angle θ so that it lies in the range 0 to 2π. The details are left for the reader.

However, since the visible part has not been changed the user's program will not need changing; we are assured of this since there is no way in which the user could have written anything depending on the details of the private type. Nevertheless, the user's program will need recompiling because of the general dependency rules explained in Section 8.2. This may seem slightly contradictory but remember that the compiler needs the information in the private part in order to be able to allocate storage for objects of the private type declared in the user's program. If we change the private part the size of the objects could change and then the object code of the user's program would change even though the source was the same.

An interesting point is that rather than declare a deferred constant we could provide a parameterless function

```
function I return Complex;
```

This has the slight advantage that we can change the value returned without changing the package specification and so having to recompile the user's program. Of course in the case of I we are unlikely to need to change the value anyway!

Finally note that between a private type declaration and the later full type declaration, the type is in a curiously half-defined state. Because of this there are severe restrictions on its use; it can only be used to declare deferred constants, other types and subtypes and subprogram specifications (also entries of tasks which we will meet in Chapter 14). It cannot be used to declare variables.

Thus we could write

```
type Complex_Array is array (Integer range <>) of Complex;
```

and then

   C: **constant** Complex_Array;

But until the full declaration is given we cannot declare variables of the type Complex or Complex_Array.

  However, we can declare the specifications of subprograms with parameters of the types Complex and Complex_Array and can even supply default expressions. Such default expressions can use deferred constants and functions; this is allowed because of course a default expression is only evaluated when a subprogram is called and this cannot occur until the body of the package has been declared and this is bound to be after the full type declaration.

  An interesting point with regard to deferred constants is that the syntax

   deferred_constant_declaration ::= identifier_list : **constant** type_mark;

shows that we cannot use an explicit constraint in their type declaration. This avoids the possibility of a constraint producing a different value when it is repeated in the subsequent full constant declaration. Thus the type marks have to conform just as in repeated subprogram specifications (see Section 7.6). In the case of the array C above the full declaration might be

   C: **constant** Complex_Array(1 .. 10) := ... ;

or even

   C: **constant** Complex_Array := ... ;

where in the latter case the bounds are taken from the initial value. If we wish to impose a constraint on the visible deferred constant declaration of C then we would have to introduce a subtype. Similar rules apply to discriminated records which we will discuss in Section 11.1.

  The rules in Ada 9X are more liberal. Any constant in a package specification can be deferred to the private part; it does not have to be of a private type. Moreover, a constraint is allowed in the deferred constant declaration; that in the full declaration must then, of course, match it statically.

  There are various other subtle points which need not concern the normal user but which are described in the *LRM*. However, the general rule is that you can only use what you know. Outside the package we know only that the type is private; inside the package and after the full type declaration we know all the properties implied by the declaration. Thus we see that we have two different views of the type according to where we are.

  As an example consider the type Complex_Array and the operator "<". (Remember that "<" only applies to arrays if the component type is discrete.) Outside the package we cannot use "<" since we do not know whether or not type Complex is discrete. Inside the package we find that it is not discrete and so still cannot use "<". If it had been discrete we could have used "<" after the full type declaration but of course we still could not use it outside. On the other hand slicing is applicable to all one-dimensional arrays and so can be used both inside and outside the package.

EXERCISE 9.1

1 Write additional functions "*" to enable mixed multiplication of real and complex numbers.

2 Rewrite the fragment of user program for complex numbers omitting the use clause.

3 Complete the package Rational_Numbers whose visible part is

```
package Rational_Numbers is

   type Rational is private;
   function "+" (X: Rational) return Rational;      -- unary +
   function "–" (X: Rational) return Rational;      -- unary –
   function "+" (X, Y: Rational) return Rational;
   function "–" (X, Y: Rational) return Rational;
   function "*" (X, Y: Rational) return Rational;
   function "/" (X, Y: Rational) return Rational;

   function "/" (X: Integer; Y: Positive) return Rational;
   function Numerator(R: Rational) return Integer;
   function Denominator(R: Rational) return Positive;

private
   ...
end;
```

A rational number is a number of the form N/D where N is an integer and D is a positive integer. For predefined equality to work it is essential that rational numbers are always reduced by cancelling out common factors. This may be done using the function GCD of Exercise 7.1(7). Ensure that an object of type Rational has an appropriate default value of zero.

4 Why does

```
function "/" (X: Integer; Y: Positive) return Rational;
```

not hide the predefined integer division?

9.2 Limited private types

The operations available on a private type can be completely restricted to those specified in the visible part of the package. This is done by declaring the type as limited as well as private thus

type T **is limited private**;

In such a case assignment and predefined = and /= are not available outside the package. However, the package may define a function "=" if the two parameters are of the same limited type; it must return a value of type Boolean. The operator /= always takes its meaning from = and so cannot be explicitly defined.

The reader will recall that the rules for = and /= are rather more liberal in Ada 9X. See Section 7.2.

An important consequence of the absence of assignment for limited types is that the declaration of an object cannot include an initial value; this in turn implies that a constant cannot be declared outside the defining package. Similarly a record component of a limited type cannot have a default initial expression. However, remember that the procedure parameter mechanism is not formally assignment and in fact we can declare our own subprograms with limited types as parameters of mode **in** or **in out** outside the defining package, and we can even supply default expressions for **in** parameters; parameters of mode **out** are however not allowed for a reason which will become apparent in the next section.

This last restriction does not apply in Ada 9X where we can write our own procedures with parameters of mode **out**.

The advantage of making a private type limited is that the package writer has complete control over the objects of the type – the copying of resources can be monitored and so on.

As a simple example consider the following

```
package Stacks is
   type Stack is limited private;
   procedure Push(S: in out Stack; X: in Integer);
   procedure Pop(S: in out Stack; X: out Integer);
   function "=" (S, T: Stack) return Boolean;
private
   Max: constant := 100;
   type Integer_Vector is array (Integer range <>) of Integer;
   type Stack is
      record
         S: Integer_Vector(1 .. Max);
         Top: Integer range 0 .. Max := 0;
      end record;
end;
```

Each object of type Stack is a record containing an array S and integer Top. Note that Top has a default initial value of zero. This ensures that when we declare a stack object, it is correctly initialized to be empty. Note also the introduction of the type Integer_Vector because a record component may not be an anonymous array.

The body of the package could be

```
package body Stacks is

   procedure Push(S: in out Stack; X: in Integer) is
   begin
      S.Top := S.Top+1;
      S.S(S.Top) := X;
   end Push;

   procedure Pop(S: in out Stack; X: out Integer) is
   begin
      X := S.S(S.Top);
      S.Top := S.Top-1;
   end Pop;

   function "=" (S, T: Stack) return Boolean is
   begin
      if S.Top /= T.Top then
         return False;
      end if;
      for I in 1 .. S.Top loop
         if S.S(I) /= T.S(I) then
         return False;
         end if;
      end loop;
      return True;
   end "=";

end Stacks;
```

This example illustrates many points. The parameter S of Push has mode **in out** because we need both to read from and to write to the stack. Further note that Pop cannot be a function since S has to be **in out** and functions can only have **in** parameters. However, "=" can be a function because we only need to read the values of the two stacks and not to update them.

The function "=" has the interpretation that two stacks are equal only if they have the same number of items and the corresponding items have the same value. It would obviously be quite wrong to compare the whole records because the unused components of the arrays would also be compared. It is because of this that the type Stack has been made limited private rather than just private. If it were just private then we could not redefine "=" to give the correct meaning.

But, of course, we can redefine "=" in Ada 9X under all circumstances and so we could have made it just private.

This is a typical example of a data structure where the value of the whole is more than just the sum of the parts; the interpretation of the array S depends on the value of Top. Cases where there is such a relationship usually need a limited private type.

A minor point is that we are using the identifier S in two ways: as the name of the formal parameter denoting the stack and as the array inside the record. There is no conflict because, although the scopes overlap, the regions of visibility do not as was explained in Section 8.4. Of course, it is rather confusing to the reader and not good practice but it illustrates the freedom of choice of record component names.

The package could be used in a fragment such as

```
declare
    use Stacks;
    St: Stack;
    Empty: Stack;
    ...
begin
    Push(St, N);
    ...
    Pop(St, M);
    ...
    if St = Empty then
    ...
    end if;
    ...
end;
```

Here we have declared two stacks St and Empty. Both are originally empty because their internal component Top has an initial value of zero. Assuming that we do not manipulate Empty then it can be used to see whether the stack St is empty or not by calling the function "=". This seems a rather dubious way of testing for an empty stack since there is no guarantee that Empty has not been manipulated. It would be better if Empty were a constant but as mentioned earlier we cannot declare a constant of a limited private type outside the package. We could however declare a constant Empty in the visible part of the package. A much better technique for testing the state of a stack would, of course, be to provide a function Empty and a corresponding function Full in the package.

We can write subprograms with limited private types as parameters outside the defining package despite the absence of assignment. As a simple example, the following procedure enables us to determine the top value on the stack without removing it.

```
procedure Top_Of(S: in out Stack; X: in out Integer) is
begin
    Pop(S, X);
    Push(S, X);
end;
```

The declaration of a function "=" does not have to be confined to the package containing the declaration of the limited type. The only point is that outside the package we cannot see the structure of the type. Furthermore, a composite type containing one or more components of a limited type is itself considered to be limited and so we could define "=" for such a type. Thus outside the package Stacks we could declare

    type Stack_Array **is array** (Integer **range** <>) **of** Stack;
    function "=" (A, B: Stack_Array) **return** Boolean;

where the definition of an appropriate body is left to the reader.

    Remember that within the private part (after the full type declaration) and within the body, any private type (limited or not) is treated in terms of how it is represented. Thus within the body of Stacks the type Stack is just a record type and so assignment and things consequential upon assignment (initialization and constants) are allowed. So we could declare a procedure Assign (intended to be used outside the package) as

    procedure Assign(S: **in** Stack; T: **out** Stack) **is**
    begin
       T := S;
    end;

    The parameter mechanism for a private type is simply that corresponding to how the type is represented. This applies both inside and outside the package. Of course, outside the package we know nothing of how the type is represented and therefore should make no assumption about the mechanism used.

    It is unfortunate that Ada does not separate the ability to permit assignment and redefinition of equality. For instance, it would be reasonable to allow assignment of stacks, but, of course, predefined equality is of no value. Equally in the case of a type such as Rational of Exercise 9.1(**2**), it would be quite reasonable to allow manipulation – including assignment – of values which were not reduced provided that equality was suitably redefined. We are therefore forced to use a procedural form such as Assign or reduce all values to a canonical form in which component by component equality is satisfactory. In the case of type Stack a suitable form would be one in which all unused elements of the stack had a standard dummy value such as zero.

    It is thus a great relief that we can redefine "=" in Ada 9X and are thus not forced to make a type limited when other considerations indicate that it should be just private. In fact Ada 9X separates the concepts of limited and private; they both relate to properties of views of the type. A limited type is one for which assignment is not predefined. A record type can be explicitly declared as limited by placing **limited** before **record** in its type declaration. Some types are inherently limited as we will see when we discuss task types in Section 14.6.

EXERCISE 9.2

1   Rewrite the specification of Stacks to include a constant Empty in the visible part.

2   Write functions Empty and Full for Stacks.

3   Rewrite the **function** "=" (S, T: Stack) using slices.

4 Write a suitable body for the function "=" applying to the type Stack_Array. Make it conform to the normal rules for array equality which we mentioned towards the end of Section 6.2.

5 Rewrite Assign for Stacks so that only the meaningful part of the record is copied.

6 Rewrite Stacks so that Stack is a normal private type. Ensure that predefined equality is satisfactory.

9.3 Resource management

An important example of the use of a limited private type is in providing controlled resource management. Consider the simple human model where each resource has a corresponding unique key. This key is then issued to the user when the resource is allocated and then has to be shown whenever the resource is accessed. So long as there is only one key and copying and stealing are prevented we know that the system is foolproof. A mechanism for handing in keys and reissuing them is usually necessary if resources are not to be permanently locked up. Typical human examples are the use of metal keys with safe deposit boxes, credit cards and so on.

Now consider the following

```
package Key_Manager is
   type Key is limited private;
   procedure Get_Key(K: in out Key);
   procedure Return_Key(K: in out Key);
   function Valid(K: Key) return Boolean;
   ...
   procedure Action(K: in Key; ... );
   ...
private
   Max: constant := 100;                          -- number of keys
   subtype Key_Code is Integer range 0 .. Max;
   type Key is
      record
         Code: Key_Code := 0;
      end record;
end;

package body Key_Manager is
   Free: array (Key_Code range 1 .. Key_Code'Last) of
                                    Boolean := (others => True);

   function Valid(K: Key) return Boolean is
   begin
      return K.Code /= 0;
   end Valid;
```

```
procedure Get_Key(K: in out Key) is
begin
  if K.Code = 0 then
    for I in Free'Range loop
      if Free(I) then
        Free(I) := False;
        K.Code := I;
        return;
      end if;
    end loop;
                                                    -- all keys in use

  end if;
end Get_Key;

procedure Return_Key(K: in out Key) is
begin
  if K.Code /= 0 then
    Free(K.Code) := True;
    K.Code := 0;
  end if;
end Return_Key;
...

procedure Action(K: in Key; ... ) is
begin
  if Valid(K) then
    ...
  end Action;

end Key_Manager;
```

The type Key is represented by a record with a single component Code. This has a default value of 0 which represents an unused key. Values from 1 .. Max represent the allocation of the corresponding resource. When we declare a variable of type Key it automatically takes an internal code value of zero. In order to use the key we must first call the procedure Get_Key; this allocates the first free key number to the variable. The key may then be used with various procedures such as Action which represents a typical request for some access to the resource guarded by the key.

Finally, the key may be relinquished by calling Return_Key. So a typical fragment of user program might be

```
declare
  use Key_Manager;
  My_Key: Key;
begin
  ...
  Get_Key(My_Key);
  ...
```

```
        Action(My_Key, ... );
        ...
        Return_Key(My_Key);
        ...
  end;
```

A variable of type Key can be thought of as a container for a key. When initially declared the default value can be thought of as representing that the container is empty; the type Key has to be a record because only record components can take default initial values. Note how the various possible misuses of keys are overcome.

- If we call Get_Key with a variable already containing a valid key then no new key is allocated. It is important not to overwrite an old valid key otherwise that key would be lost.

- A call of Return_Key resets the variable to the default state so that the variable cannot be used as a key until a new one is issued by a call of Get_Key. Note that the user is unable to retain a copy of the key because assignment is not valid since the type Key is limited.

The function Valid is provided so that the user can see whether a key variable contains the default value or an allocated value. It is obviously useful to call Valid after Get_Key to ensure that the key manager was able to provide a new key value; note that once all keys are issued, a call of Get_Key does nothing.

One apparent flaw is that there is no compulsion to call Return_Key before the scope containing the declaration of My_Key is left. The key would then be lost. This corresponds to the real life situation of losing a key (although in our model no one else can find it again – it is as if it were thrown into a black hole). To guard against this the key manager might assume (as in life) that a key not used for a certain period of time is no longer in use. Of course, the same key would not be reissued but the resource guarded might be considered reusable; this would involve keeping separate records of keys in use and resources in use and a cross-reference from keys to resources.

EXERCISE 9.3

1   Complete the package whose visible part is

```
package Bank is
    subtype Money is Natural;
    type Key is limited private;
    procedure Open_Account(K: in out Key; M: in Money);
        − − open account with initial deposit M
    procedure Close_Account(K: in out Key; M: out Money);
        − − close account and return balance
    procedure Deposit(K: in Key; M: in Money);
```

```
            - - deposit amount M
         procedure Withdraw(K: in out Key; M in out Money);
            - - withdraw amount M; if account does not contain M
            - - then return what is there and close account
         function Statement(K: Key) return Money;
            - - returns a statement of current balance
         function Valid(K: Key) return Boolean;
            - - checks the key is valid
      private
         ...
```

2 Assuming that your solution to the previous question allowed the bank the use of the deposited money, reformulate the private type to represent a home savings box or safe deposit box where the money is in a box kept by the user.

3 A thief writes the following

```
      declare
         use Key_Manager;
         My_Key: Key;
         procedure Cheat(Copy: in out Key) is
         begin
            Return_Key(My_Key);
            Action(Copy, ... );
               ...
         end;
      begin
         Get_Key(My_Key);
         Cheat(My_Key);
            ...
      end;
```

He attempts to return his key and then use the copy. Why is he thwarted?

4 A vandal writes the following

```
      declare
         use Key_Manager;
         My_Key: Key;
         procedure Destroy(K: out Key) is
         begin
            null;
         end;
      begin
         Get_Key(My_Key);
         Destroy(My_Key);
            ...
      end;
```

He attempts to destroy the value in his key by calling a procedure which does not update the **out** parameter; he anticipates that the copy back rule will result in a junk value being assigned to the key. Why is he thwarted?

CHECKLIST 9

For predefined equality to be sensible, the values should be in a canonical form.

An unlimited private type can be implemented in terms of another private type provided it is also unlimited.

A limited private type can be implemented in terms of any private type limited or not.

"/=" can never be defined – it always follows from "=". (It can sometimes be redefined in Ada 9X.)

"=" can be defined outside the package defining the limited private type concerned. (It can always be redefined in Ada 9X).

The rules apply transitively to composite types.

10 Exceptions

At various times in the preceding chapters we have said that if something goes wrong when the program is executed, then an exception, often 'Constraint_Error', will be raised. In this chapter we describe the exception mechanism and show how remedial action can be taken when an exception occurs. We also show how we may define and use our own exceptions. Exceptions concerned with interacting tasks are dealt with when we come to Chapter 14.

10.1 Handling exceptions

We have seen that if we break various language rules then an exception may be raised when we execute the program.

There are five predefined exceptions (declared in the package Standard) of which we have met four so far

Constraint_Error This generally corresponds to something going out of range.

Numeric_Error This can occur when something goes wrong with arithmetic such as an attempt to divide by zero. However, as explained in Section 4.9, AI-387 concludes that it is not always possible to distinguish this exception from Constraint_Error and recommends that Constraint_Error should always be raised in such circumstances.

Note further that Numeric_Error is just a renaming of Constraint_Error in Ada 9X.

Program_Error This will occur if we attempt to violate the control structure in some way such as running into the **end** of a function or calling a subprogram whose body has not yet been elaborated – see Sections 7.1 and 8.1.

Storage_Error This will occur if we run out of storage space as for example if we called our recursive function Factorial with a large parameter – see Section 7.1.

The other predefined exception is Tasking_Error. This is concerned with tasking and so is dealt with in Chapter 14.

If we anticipate that an exception may occur in a part of our program then we can write an exception handler to deal with it. For example, suppose we write

```
begin
   - - sequence of statements
exception
   when Constraint_Error =>
   - - do something
end;
```

If Constraint_Error is raised while we are executing the sequence of statements between **begin** and **exception** then the flow of control is interrupted and immediately transferred to the sequence of statements following the =>. The clause starting **when** is known as an exception handler.

As a trivial example we could compute Tomorrow from Today by writing

```
begin
   Tomorrow := Day'Succ(Today);
exception
```

```
  when Constraint_Error =>
     Tomorrow := Day'First;
end;
```

If Today is Day'Last (that is, Sun) then when we attempt to evaluate Day'Succ(Today), the exception Constraint_Error is raised. Control is then transferred to the handler for Constraint_Error and the statement Tomorrow := Day'First; is executed. Control then passes to the end of the block.

This is really a bad example. Exceptions should be used for rarely occurring cases or those which are inconvenient to test for at their point of occurrence. By no stretch of the imagination is Sunday a rare day. Over 14% of all days are Sundays. Nor is it difficult to test for the condition at the point of occurrence. So we should really have written

```
if Today = Day'Last then
   Tomorrow := Day'First;
else
   Tomorrow := Day'Succ(Today);
end if;
```

However, it is a simple example with which to illustrate the mechanism involved.

Several handlers can be written between **exception** and **end**. Consider

```
begin
   – – sequence of statements
exception
   when Numeric_Error | Constraint_Error =>
      Put("Numeric or Constraint Error occurred");
      ...
   when Storage_Error =>
      Put("Ran out of space");
      ...
   when others =>
      Put("Something else went wrong");
      ...
end;
```

In this example a message is output according to the exception. Note the similarity to the case statement. Each **when** is followed by one or more exception names separated by vertical bars. As usual we can write **others** but it must be last and on its own; it handles any exception not listed in the previous handlers. Note also that we have a common handler for Numeric_Error and Constraint_Error in accordance with AI-387.

But remember that Numeric_Error is just a renaming of Constraint_Error in Ada 9X and so the double handler is not necessary. However, the double handler is still allowed because Ada 9X permits an exception to be mentioned more than once in the same handler.

Exception handlers can appear at the end of a block, subprogram body, package body (or task body) and have access to all entities declared in the unit (called a frame in the *LRM* although we will continue to use the more informal term unit). The examples have shown a degenerate block in which there is no **declare** and declarative part; the block was introduced just for the purpose of providing somewhere to hang the handlers. We could rewrite our bad example to determine tomorrow as a function thus

```
function Tomorrow(Today: Day) return Day is
begin
   return Day'Succ(Today);
exception
   when Constraint_Error =>
      return Day'First;
end Tomorrow;
```

It is important to realize that control can never be returned directly to the unit where the exception was raised. The sequence of statements following => replaces the remainder of the unit containing the handler and thereby completes execution of the unit. Hence a handler for a function must generally contain a return statement in order to provide the 'emergency' result.

In particular, a goto statement cannot transfer control from a unit into one of its handlers or vice versa or from one handler to another. However, the statements of a handler can otherwise be of arbitrary complexity. They can include blocks, calls of subprograms and so on. A handler of a block could contain a goto statement which transferred control to a label outside the block and it could contain an exit statement if the block were inside a loop.

A handler at the end of a package body applies only to the initialization sequence of the package and not to subprograms in the package. Such subprograms must have individual handlers if they are to deal with exceptions.

We now consider the question of what happens if a unit does not provide a handler for a particular exception. The answer is that the exception is propagated dynamically. This simply means that the unit is terminated and the exception is raised at the point where the unit was invoked. In the case of a block we therefore look for a handler in the unit containing the block.

In the case of a subprogram, the call is terminated and we look for a handler in the unit which called the subprogram. This unwinding process is repeated until either we reach a unit containing a handler for the particular exception or come to the top level. If we find a unit containing a relevant handler then the exception is handled at that point. Alternatively we have reached the main program and have still found no handler – the main program is then abandoned and we can expect the run time environment to provide us with a suitable diagnostic message. (Unhandled exceptions in tasks are dealt with in Chapter 14.)

It is most important to understand that exceptions are propagated dynamically and not statically. That is, an exception not handled by a subprogram is propagated to the unit calling the subprogram and not to the unit containing the declaration of the subprogram – these may or may not be the same.

If the statements in a handler themselves raise an exception then the unit is terminated and the exception propagated to the calling unit; the handler does not loop.

EXERCISE 10.1

Note: these are exercises to check your understanding of exceptions. They do not necessarily reflect good Ada programming techniques.

1   Assuming that calling Sqrt with a negative parameter and attempting to divide by zero both raise Constraint_Error, rewrite the procedure Quadratic of Section 7.3 without explicitly testing D and A.

2   Rewrite the function Factorial of Section 7.1 so that if it is called with a negative parameter (which would normally raise Constraint_Error) or a large parameter (which would normally raise Storage_Error or Numeric_Error alias Constraint_Error) then a standard result of say −1 is returned. Hint: declare an inner function Slave which actually does the work.

10.2   Declaring and raising exceptions

Relying on the predefined exceptions to detect unusual but anticipated situations is usually bad practice because they do not provide a guarantee that the exception has in fact been raised because of the anticipated situation. Something else may have gone wrong instead.

As an illustration consider the package Stack of Section 8.1. If we call Push when the stack is full then the statement Top := Top+1; will raise Constraint_Error and similarly if we call Pop when the stack is empty then Top := Top−1; will also raise Constraint_Error. Since Push and Pop do not themselves have exception handlers, the exception will be propagated to the unit calling them. So we could write

```
declare
   use Stack;
begin
   ...
   Push(M);
   ...
   N := Pop;
   ...
exception
   when Constraint_Error =>
   − − stack manipulation incorrect?
end;
```

and misuse of the stack would then result in control being transferred to the handler for Constraint_Error. However, there would be no guarantee that the exception had arisen because of misuse of the stack; something else in the block could have gone wrong.

A better solution is to raise an exception specifically declared to indicate misuse of the stack. Thus the package could be rewritten

```
package Stack is
   Error: exception;
   procedure Push(X: Integer);
   function Pop return Integer;
end Stack;

package body Stack is
   Max: constant := 100;
   S: array (1 .. Max) of Integer;
   Top: Integer range 0 .. Max;

   procedure Push(X: Integer) is
   begin
      if Top = Max then
         raise Error;
      end if;
      Top := Top+1;
      S(Top) := X;
   end Push;

   function Pop return Integer is
   begin
      if Top = 0 then
         raise Error;
      end if;
      Top := Top-1;
      return S(Top+1);
   end Pop;

begin
   Top := 0;
end Stack;
```

An exception is declared in a similar way to a variable and is raised by an explicit raise statement naming the exception. The handling and propagation rules are just as for the predefined exceptions. We can now write

```
declare
   use Stack;
begin
   ...
   Push(M);
   ...
   N := Pop;
```

```
    ...
exception
   when Error =>
      - - stack manipulation incorrect
   when others =>
      - - something else went wrong
end;
```

We have now successfully separated the handler for misusing the stack from the handler for other exceptions.

Note that if we had not provided a use clause then we would have had to refer to the exception in the handler as Stack.Error; the usual dotted notation applies.

What could we expect to do in the handler in the above case? Apart from reporting that the stack manipulation has gone wrong, we might also expect to reset the stack to an acceptable state although we have not provided a convenient means of doing so. A procedure Reset in the package Stack would be useful. A further thing we might do is relinquish any resources that were acquired in the block and might otherwise be inadvertently retained. Suppose for instance that we had also been using the package Key_Manager of Section 9.3. We might then call Return_Key to ensure that a key declared and acquired in the block had been returned. Remember that Return_Key does no harm if called unnecessarily.

We would probably also want to reset the stack and return the key in the case of any other exception as well; so it would be as well to declare a procedure Clean_Up to do all the actions required. So our block might look like

```
declare
   use Stack, Key_Manager;
   My_Key: Key;

   procedure Clean_Up is
   begin
      Reset;
      Return_Key(My_Key);
   end;

begin
   Get_Key(My_Key);
   ...
   Push(M);
   ...
   Action(My_Key, ... );
   ...
   N := Pop;
   ...
   Return_Key(My_Key);
exception
   when Error =>
```

```
              Put("Stack used incorrectly");
              Clean_Up;
         when others =>
              Put("Something else went wrong");
              Clean_Up;
       end;
```

We have rather assumed that Reset is a further procedure declared in the package Stack but note that we could write our own procedure externally as follows:

```
    procedure Reset is
        Junk: Integer;
        use Stack;
    begin
        loop
            Junk := Pop;
        end loop;
    exception
        when Error =>
            null;
    end Reset;
```

This works by repeatedly calling Pop until Error is raised. We then know that the stack is empty. The handler needs to do nothing other than prevent the exception from being propagated; so we merely write **null**. This procedure seems a bit like trickery; it would be far better to have a reset procedure in the package.

Sometimes the actions that require to be taken as a consequence of an exception need to be performed on a layered basis. In the above example we returned the key and then reset the stack but it is probably the case that the block as a whole cannot be assumed to have done its job correctly. We can indicate this by raising an exception as the last action of the handler

```
    exception
        when Error =>
            Put("Stack used incorrectly");
            Clean_Up;
            raise Another_Error;
        when others =>
            ...
    end;
```

The exception Another_Error will then be propagated to the unit containing the block. We could put the statement

```
    raise Another_Error;
```

in the procedure Clean_Up.

Sometimes it is convenient to handle an exception and then propagate the same exception. This can be done by just writing

    raise;

This is particularly useful when we handle several exceptions with the one handler since there is no way in which we can explicitly name the exception which occurred.

So we might have

```
when others =>
    Put("Something else went wrong");
    Clean_Up;
    raise;
end;
```

The current exception will be remembered even if the action of the handler raises and handles its own exceptions such as occurred in our trick procedure Reset. However, note that there is a rule that we can only write **raise**; directly in a handler and not for instance in a procedure called by the handler such as Clean_Up.

Ada 9X provides additional facilities which enable a program to identify further information about the cause of an exception as will be explained in Chapter 17.

The stack example illustrates a legitimate use of exceptions. The exception Error should rarely, if ever, occur and it would also be inconvenient to test for the condition at each possible point of occurrence. To do that we would presumably have to provide an additional parameter to Push of type Boolean and mode **out** to indicate that all was not well, and then test it after each call. In the case of Pop we would also have to recast it as a procedure since a function cannot take a parameter of mode **out**.

The package specification would then become

```
package Stack is
    procedure Push(X: in Integer; B: out Boolean);
    procedure Pop(X: out Integer; B: out Boolean);
end;
```

and we would have to write

```
declare
    use Stack;
    OK: Boolean;
begin
    ...
    Push(M, OK);
    if not OK then ...        end if;
    ...
```

```
        Pop(N, OK);
        if not OK then ...        end if;
    end;
```

It is clear that the use of an exception provides a better structured program.

Note finally that nothing prevents us from explicitly raising one of the predefined exceptions. We recall that in Section 7.1 when discussing the function Inner we stated that probably the best way of coping with parameters whose bounds were unequal was to explicitly raise Constraint_Error.

EXERCISE 10.2

1 Rewrite the package Random of Exercise 8.1(**1**) so that it declares and raises an exception Bad if the initial value is not odd.
2 Rewrite your answer to Exercise 10.1(**2**) so that the function Factorial always raises Constraint_Error if the parameter is negative or too large.
3 Declare a function "+" which takes two parameters of type Vector and returns their sum using sliding semantics by analogy with the predefined one-dimensional array operations described in Section 6.6. Use type Vector from Section 6.2. Raise Constraint_Error if the arrays do not match.
4 Are we completely justified in asserting that Stack.Error could only be raised by the stack going wrong?

10.3 Checking and exceptions

In the previous section we came to the conclusion that it was logically better to check for the stack overflow condition ourselves rather than rely upon the built-in check associated with the violation of the subtype of Top. At first sight the reader may well feel that this would reduce the execution efficiency of the program. However this is not necessarily so, assuming a reasonably intelligent compiler, and this example can be used to illustrate the advantages of the use of appropriate subtypes.

We will concentrate on the procedure Push, similar arguments apply to the function Pop.

First consider the original package Stack of Section 8.1. In that we had

```
    ...
S: array (1 .. Max) of Integer;
Top: Integer range 0 .. Max;

procedure Push(X: Integer) is
begin
    Top := Top+1;
    S(Top) := X;
end Push;
```

If the stack is full (that is Top = Max) and we call Push then it is the assignment to Top that raises Constraint_Error. This is because Top has a range constraint. However, the only run-time check that needs to be compiled is that associated with checking the upper bound of Top. There is no need to check for violation of the lower bound since the expression Top+1 could not be less than 1 (assuming that the value in Top is always in range). Note moreover that no checks need be compiled with respect to the assignment to S(Top). This is because the value of Top at this stage must lie in the range 1 .. Max (which is the index range of S) – it cannot exceed Max because this has just been checked by the previous assignment and it cannot be less than 1 since 1 has just been added to its previous value which could not have been less than 0. So just one check needs to be compiled in the procedure Push.

On the other hand, if the variable Top had not been given a range constraint but just declared as

Top: Integer;

then although no checks would have been applied to the assignment to Top, nevertheless checks would have had to be compiled for the assignment to S(Top) instead in order to ensure that Top lay within the index range of S. Two checks would be necessary – one for each end of the index range.

So applying the range constraint to Top actually reduces the number of checks required. This is typical behaviour given a compiler with a moderate degree of flow analysis. The more you tell the compiler about the properties of the variables (and assuming the constraints on the variables match their usage), the better the object code.

Now consider what happens when we add our own test as in the previous section (and we assume that Top now has its range constraint)

```
procedure Push(X: Integer) is
begin
   If Top = Max then
      raise Error;
   end if;
   Top := Top+1;
   S(Top) := X;
end Push;
```

Clearly we have added a check of our own. However, there is now no need for the compiler to insert the check on the upper bound of Top in the assignment

Top := Top+1;

because our own check will have caused control to be transferred away via the raising of the Error exception for the one original value of Top that would have caused trouble. So the net effect of adding our own check is simply to replace a compiler check by our own; the object code is not less efficient.

There are two morals to this tale. The first is that we should tell the compiler the whole truth about our program; the more it knows about the properties of our variables, the more likely it is to be able to keep checks to the appropriate minimum. In fact this is just an extension of the advantage of strong typing discussed in Section 4.3 where we saw how arbitrary run-time errors can be replaced by easily understood compile-time errors.

The second moral is that introducing our own exceptions rather than relying upon the predefined ones need not reduce the efficiency of our program. In fact it is generally considered bad practice to rely upon the predefined exceptions for steering our program and especially bad to raise the predefined exceptions explicitly ourselves. It is all too easy to mask an unexpected genuine error that needs fixing.

It should also be noted that we can always ask the compiler to omit the run-time checks by using the pragma Suppress. This is described in Section 15.5.

Finally, an important warning. Our analysis of when checks can be omitted depends upon all variables satisfying their constraints at all times. Provided checks are not suppressed we can be reasonably assured of this apart from one nasty loophole. This is that we are not obliged to supply initial values in the declarations of variables in the first place. So they can start with a junk value which does not satisfy any constraints and may not even be a value of the base type. If such a variable is read before being updated then our program is erroneous and all our analysis is worthless. It is thus a good idea to initialize all variables unless it is perfectly obvious that updating will occur first.

EXERCISE 10.3

1   Consider the case of the procedure Push with explicit raising of Error but suppose that there is no range constraint on Top.

10.4 Scope of exceptions

To a large extent exceptions follow the same scope rules as other entities. An exception can hide and be hidden by another declaration; it can be made visible by the dotted notation and so on. An exception can be renamed

> Help: **exception renames** Bank.Alarm;

Exceptions are, however, different in many ways. We cannot declare arrays of exceptions, and they cannot be components of records, parameters of subprograms and so on. In short, exceptions are not objects and so cannot be manipulated. They are merely tags.

A very important characteristic of exceptions is that they are not created dynamically as a program executes but should be thought of as existing throughout the life of the program. This relates to the way in which exceptions are propagated dynamically up the chain of execution rather than statically up the chain of scope. An exception can be propagated outside its scope although of course it can then only be handled anonymously by **others**. This is illustrated by the following

```
declare
   procedure P is
      X: exception;
   begin
      raise X;
   end P;
begin
   P;
exception
   when others =>
            - - X handled here
end;
```

The procedure P declares and raises the exception X but does not handle it. When we call P, the exception X is propagated to the block calling P where it is handled anonymously.

It is even possible to propagate an exception out of its scope, where it becomes anonymous, and then back in again where it can once more be handled by its proper name. Consider (and this is really a crazy example)

```
declare
   package P is
      procedure F;
      procedure H;
   end P;

   procedure G is
   begin
      P.H;
   exception
      when others =>
         raise;
   end G;

   package body P is
      X: exception;

      procedure F is
      begin
         G;
      exception
         when X =>
            Put("Got it!");
      end F;
```

```
        procedure H is
        begin
           raise X;
        end H;

    end P;

begin
    P.F;
end;
```

The block declares a package P containing procedures F and H and also a procedure G. The block calls F in P which calls G outside P which in turn calls H back in P. The procedure H raises the exception X whose scope is the body of P. The procedure H does not handle X, so it is propagated to G which called H. The procedure G is outside the package P, so the exception X is now outside its scope; nevertheless G handles the exception anonymously and propagates it further by reraising it. G was called by F so X is now propagated back into the package and so can be handled by F by its proper name.

A further illustration of the nature of exceptions is afforded by a recursive procedure containing an exception declaration. Unlike variables declared in a procedure we do not get a new exception for each recursive call. Each recursive activation refers to the same exception. Consider the following artificial example

```
procedure F(N: Integer) is
   X: exception;
begin
  if N = 0 then
     raise X;
  else
     F(N–1);
  end if;
exception
  when X =>
     Put("Got it!");
     raise;
  when others =>
     null;
end F;
```

Suppose we execute F(4); we get recursive calls F(3), F(2), F(1) and finally F(0). When F is called with parameter zero, it raises the exception X, handles it, prints out a confirmatory message and then reraises it. The calling instance of F (which itself had N = 1) receives the exception and again handles it as X and so on. The message is therefore printed out five times in all and the exception is finally propagated anonymously. Observe that if each recursive activation had created a different exception then the message would only be printed out once.

In all the examples we have seen so far exceptions have been raised in statements. An exception can however also be raised in a declaration. Thus

```
N: Positive := 0;
```

would raise Constraint_Error because the initial value of N does not satisfy the range constraint 1 .. Integer'Last of the subtype Positive. An exception raised in a declaration is not handled by a handler (if any) of the unit containing the declaration but is immediately propagated up a level. This means that in any handler we are assured that all declarations of the unit were successfully elaborated and so there is no risk of referring to something that does not exist.

Finally, a warning regarding parameters of mode **out** or **in out**. If a subprogram is terminated by an exception then any actual parameter of a scalar type will not have been updated since such updating occurs on a normal return. For an array or record type the parameter mechanism is not so closely specified and the actual parameter may or may not have its original value. A program assuming a particular mechanism is of course erroneous. As an example consider the procedure Withdraw of the package Bank in Exercise 9.3(**1**). It would be incorrect to attempt to take the key away and raise an alarm as in

```
procedure Withdraw (K: in out Key; M: in out Money) is
begin
   if Valid (K) then
      if M > amount remaining then
         M := amount remaining;
         Free(K.Code) := True;
         K.Code := 0;
         raise Alarm;
      else
         ...
      end if;
   end if;
end Withdraw;
```

If the parameter mechanism were implemented by copy then the bank would think that the key were now free but would have left the greedy customer with a copy.

EXERCISE 10.4

1   Rewrite the package Bank of Exercise 9.3(**1**) to declare an exception Alarm and raise it when any illegal banking activity is attempted. Avoid problems with the parameters.

2   Consider the following pathological procedure

```
procedure P is
begin
   P;
exception
   when Storage_Error =>
      P;
end P;
```

What happens when P is called? To be explicit suppose that there is enough stack space for only N simultaneous recursive calls of P but that on the $N+1$th call the exception Storage_Error is raised. How many times will P be called in all and what eventually happens?

CHECKLIST 10

Do not use exceptions unnecessarily.

Use specific user declared exceptions rather than predefined exceptions where relevant.

Ensure that handlers return resources correctly.

Match the constraints on index variables to the arrays concerned.

Beware of uninitialized variables.

Out and in out parameters may not be updated correctly if a procedure is terminated by an exception.

'Numeric_Error' is obsolete.

11 Advanced Types

In this chapter we describe most of the remaining classes of types. These are discriminated record types, access types and derived types. Numeric types, which are explained in terms of derived types, are described in the next chapter and task types are described in Chapter 14.

11.1 Discriminated record types

In the record types we have seen so far there was no formal language dependency between the components. Any dependency was purely in the mind of the programmer as for example in the case of the limited private type Stack in Section 9.2 where the interpretation of the array S depended on the value of the integer Top.

In the case of a discriminated record type, some of the components are known as discriminants and the remaining components can depend upon these. The discriminants, which have to be of a discrete type, can be thought of as parameterizing the type and the syntax reveals this analogy.

As a simple example, suppose we wish to write a package providing various operations on square matrices and that in particular we wish to write a function Trace which sums the diagonal elements of a square matrix. We could contemplate using the type Matrix of Section 6.2.

```
type Matrix is array (Integer range < >, Integer range < >) of Real;
```

but our function would then have to check that the matrix passed as an actual parameter was indeed square. We would have to write something like

```
function Trace(M: Matrix) return Real is
   Sum: Real := 0.0;
begin
   if M'First(1) /= M'First(2) or M'Last(1) /= M'Last(2) then
      raise Non_Square;
   end if;
   for I in M'Range loop
      Sum := Sum + M(I, I);
   end loop;
   return Sum;
end Trace;
```

This is somewhat unsatisfactory; we would prefer to use a formulation which ensured that the matrix was always square and had a lower bound of 1. We can do this using a discriminated type. Consider.

```
type Square(Order: Positive) is
   record
      Mat: Matrix(1 .. Order, 1 .. Order);
   end record;
```

This is a record type having two components: the first, Order, is a discriminant of the discrete subtype Positive and the second, Mat, is an array whose bounds depend upon the value of Order.

Variables of type Square can be declared in the usual way but a value of the discriminant must be given as a constraint thus

```
M: Square(3);
```

The named form can also be used

```
M: Square(Order => 3);
```

The value provided as the constraint could be any dynamic expression but once the variable is declared its constraint cannot be changed. An initial value for M could be provided by an aggregate, but, perhaps surprisingly, this must be complete and repeat the constraint which must match, thus

```
M: Square(3) := (3, (1 .. 3 => (1 .. 3 => 0.0)));
```

However, we could not write

```
M: Square(N) := (M.Order, (M.Mat'Range(1) =>
                           (M.Mat'Range(2) => 0.0)));
```

in order to avoid repeating N because of the rule that we cannot refer to an object in its own declaration. However

```
declare
    M: Square(N);
begin
    M := (M.Order, (M.Mat'Range(1) =>
                    (M.Mat'Range(2) => 0.0)));
```

is perfectly valid. If we attempt to assign a value to M which does not have the correct discriminant value then Constraint_Error will be raised.

Constants can be declared as usual and, like array bounds, the discriminant constraint can be deduced from the initial value.

In Ada 9X, the discriminant of a variable as well as a constant can be deduced from an initial value. Thus array bounds and discriminants continue to follow the same rule in this respect.

We can, of course, introduce subtypes

```
subtype Square_3 is Square(3);
M: Square_3;
```

We can now rewrite our function Trace as follows

```
function Trace(M: Square) return Real is
    Sum: Real := 0.0;
begin
    for I in M.Mat'Range loop
        Sum := Sum + M.Mat(I, I);
    end loop;
    return Sum;
end Trace;
```

There is now no way in which a call of Trace can be supplied with a non-square matrix. Note that the discriminant of the formal parameter is taken from that of the actual parameter in a similar way to the bounds of an array. Discriminants of parameters have much in common with array bounds. For example a discriminant can be read even in the case of an **out** parameter. Again like arrays, the formal parameter could be constrained as in

> **function** Trace_3(M: Square_3) **return** Real;

but then the actual parameter would have to have a discriminant value of 3; otherwise Constraint_Error would be raised.

The result of a function could be of a discriminated type and, like arrays, the result could be a value whose discriminant is not known until the function is called. Thus we could write a function to return the transpose of a square matrix

```
function Transpose(M: Square) return Square is
   R: Square(M.Order);
begin
   for I in 1 .. M.Order loop
      for J in 1 .. M.Order loop
         R.Mat(I, J) := M.Mat(J, I);
      end loop;
   end loop;
   return R;
end Transpose;
```

A private type can also have discriminants and it must then be implemented in terms of a record type with corresponding discriminants. A good example is provided by considering the type Stack in Section 9.2. We can overcome the problem that all the stacks had the same maximum length of 100 by making Max a discriminant. Thus we can write

```
package Stacks is
   type Stack(Max: Natural) is limited private;
   procedure Push(S: in out Stack; X: in Integer);
   procedure Pop(S: in out Stack; X out Integer);
   function "=" (S, T: Stack) return Boolean;
private
   type Integer_Vector is array (Integer range < >) of Integer;
   type Stack(Max: Natural) is
      record
         S: Integer_Vector(1 .. Max);
         Top: Integer := 0;
      end record;
end;
```

Each variable of type Stack now includes a discriminant component giving the maximum stack size. When we declare a stack we must supply the value thus

> ST: Stack(100);

and as for the type Square the value of the discriminant cannot later be changed. Of course, the discriminant is visible and can be referred to as ST.Max although the remaining components are private.

The body of the package Stacks remains as before (see Section 9.2). Observe in particular that the function "=" can be used to compare stacks with different values of Max since it only compares those components of the internal array which are in use.

Although constants of the type Stack cannot be declared outside the defining package (because the type is limited private) we can declare a deferred constant in the visible part. Such a declaration need not supply a value for the discriminant since it will be given in the private part.

This is a good point to mention that discriminants bear a resemblance to subprogram parameters in several respects. The type or subtype of a discriminant must be given by a type mark and not by a subtype indication. This is so that the same simple conformance rules can be used when a discriminant specification has to be repeated in the case of a private type with discriminants, as illustrated by the type Stack above.

A conformance problem also arises in the case of deferred constants with discriminants which are analogous to the deferred array constants discussed in Section 9.1. Suppose we wish to declare a constant Stack with a discriminant of 3. We can omit the discriminant in the visible part and merely write

    C: **constant** Stack;

and then give the discriminant in the private part either as a constraint or through the mandatory initial value (or both)

    C: **constant** Stack(3) := (3, (1, 2, 3), 3);

However, if we wish to give the discriminant in the visible part then we must introduce a subtype to do so; we cannot use an explicit constraint in a subtype indication. Having introduced the subtype then the full constant declaration must also use it since the type marks must conform. Thus we can write

    subtype Stack_3 **is** Stack(3);
    C: **constant** Stack_3;

and then

    C: **constant** Stack_3 := (3, (1, 2, 3), 3);

in the private part.

As we mentioned in Section 9.1, Ada 9X is more liberal in this area. We can use an explicit constraint in both places but both occurrences must match statically.

It is possible to declare a type with several discriminants. We may for instance wish to manipulate matrices which although not constrained to be square nevertheless have both lower bounds of 1. This could be done by

```
type Rectangle(Rows, Columns: Positive) is
   record
      Mat: Matrix(1 .. Rows, 1 .. Columns);
   end record;
```

and we could then declare

```
R: Rectangle(2, 3);
```

or

```
R: Rectangle(Rows => 2, Columns => 3);
```

The usual rules apply: positional values must be given in order, named ones may be in any order, mixed notation can be used but the positional ones must come first.

Similarly to multidimensional arrays, a subtype must supply all the constraints or none at all. We could not declare

```
subtype Row_3 is Rectangle(Rows => 3);
```

in order to get the equivalent of

```
type Row_3(Columns: Positive) is
   record
      Mat: Matrix(1 .. 3, 1 .. Columns);
   end record;
```

In the examples we have shown, discriminants have been used in index constraints as the upper bounds of arrays; they can also be used as the lower bounds of arrays. In Section 11.3 we will describe how a discriminant can also be used to introduce a variant part. In these cases a discriminant must be used directly and not as part of a larger expression. So we could not declare

```
type Symmetric_Array(N: Positive) is
   record
      A: Vector(-N .. N);              - - illegal
   end record;
```

or

```
type Two_By_One(N: Positive) is
   record
      A: Matrix(1 .. N, 1 .. 2*N);     - - illegal
   end record;
```

EXERCISE 11.1

1   Suppose that M is an object of the type Matrix. Write a call of the function Trace whose parameter is an aggregate of type Square in order to determine the trace of M. What would happen if the two dimensions of M were not equal?

2   Rewrite the specification of Stacks to include a constant Empty in the visible part. See also Exercise 9.2(**1**).

3   Write a function Full for Stacks. See also Exercise 9.2(**2**).

4   Declare a constant Square of order N and initialize it to a unit matrix. Use the function Make_Unit of Exercise 7.1(**6**).

11.2   Default discriminants

The discriminant types we have encountered so far have been such that once a variable is declared, its discriminant cannot be changed. It is possible, however, to provide a default expression for a discriminant and the situation is then different. A variable can then be declared with or without a discriminant constraint. If one is supplied then that value overrides the default and as before the discriminant cannot be changed. If, on the other hand, a variable is declared without a value for the discriminant, then the value of the default expression is taken but it can then be changed by a complete record assignment.

Suppose we wish to manipulate polynomials of the form

$$P(x) = a_0 + a_1x + a_2x^2 + \dots a_nx^n$$

where $a_n \neq 0$ if $n \neq 0$.

Such a polynomial could be represented by

```
type Poly(N: Index) is
    record
        A: Integer_Vector(0 .. N);
    end record;
```

where

```
subtype Index is Integer range 0 .. Max;
```

but then a variable of type Poly would have to be declared with a constraint and would thereafter be a polynomial of that fixed size. This would be most inconvenient because the sizes of the polynomials may be determined as the consequences of elaborate calculations. For example, if we subtract two polynomials which have $n = 3$, then the result will only have $n = 3$ if the coefficients of x^3 are different.

However, if we declare

```
type Polynomial(N: Index := 0) is
   record
      A: Integer_Vector(0 .. N);
   end record;
```

then we can declare variables

```
P, Q: Polynomial;
```

which do not have constraints. The initial value of their discriminants would be zero because the default value of N is zero but the discriminants could later be changed by assignment. Note however that a discriminant can only be changed by a complete record assignment. So

```
P.N := 6;
```

would be illegal. This is quite natural since we cannot expect the array P.A to adjust its bounds by magic.

Variables of the type Polynomial could be declared with constraints

```
R: Polynomial(5);
```

but R would thereafter be constrained forever to be a polynomial with $n = 5$.

Initial values can be given in declarations in the usual way

```
P: Polynomial := (3, (5, 0, 4, 2));
```

which represents $5 + 4x^2 + 2x^3$. Note that despite the initial value, P is not constrained.

In practice we would make the type Polynomial a private type so that we could enforce the rule that $a_n \neq 0$. Observe that predefined equality is satisfactory and so we do not have to make it a limited private type. Both the private type declaration and the full type declaration must give the default expression for N.

Note once more the similarity to subprogram parameters; the default expression is only evaluated when required and so need not produce the same value each time. Moreover, the same conformance rules apply when it has to be written out again in the case of a private type.

If we declare functions such as

```
function "–" (P, Q: Polynomial) return Polynomial;
```

then it will be necessary to ensure that the result is normalized so that a_n is not zero. This could be done by the following function

```
function Normal(P: Polynomial) return Polynomial is
   Size: Integer := P.N;
```

```
   begin
      while Size > 0 and P.A(Size) = 0 loop
         Size := Size–1;
      end loop;
      return (Size, P.A(0 .. Size));
   end Normal;
```

This is a further illustration of a function returning a value whose discriminant is not known until it is called. Note the use of the array slice.

If default expressions are supplied then they must be supplied for all discriminants of the type. Moreover an object must be fully constrained or not at all; we cannot supply constraints for some discriminants and use the defaults for others.

The attribute Constrained can be applied to an object of a discriminated type and gives a Boolean value indicating whether the object is constrained or not. For any object of types such as Square and Stack which do not have default values for the discriminants this attribute will, of course, be True. But in the case of objects of a type such as Polynomial which does have a default value, the attribute may be True or False.

```
   P'Constrained = False
   R'Constrained = True
```

We mentioned above that an unconstrained formal parameter will take the value of the discriminant of the actual parameter. In the case of an **out** or **in out** parameter, the formal parameter will be constrained if the actual parameter is constrained (an **in** parameter is constant anyway). Suppose we declare a procedure to truncate a polynomial by removing its highest order term

```
   procedure Truncate (P: in out Polynomial) is
   begin
      P := (P.N–1, P.A(0 .. P.N–1));
   end;
```

Then given

```
   Q: Polynomial;
   R: Polynomial(5);
```

the statement

```
   Truncate(Q);
```

will be successful, but

```
   Truncate(R);
```

will result in Constraint_Error being raised.

We conclude this section by considering the problem of variable length strings. In Section 6.5 we noted, when declaring the Zoo, that the animals (or rather their names) all had to be the same length. The strong type model of Ada means that the type String does not have the flexibility found in cruder languages such as BASIC. However, with a bit of ingenuity, we can build our own flexibility by using discriminated records. There are a number of possibilities such as

```
subtype String_Size is Integer range 0 .. 80;

type V_String(N: String_Size := 0) is
  record
    S: String(1 .. N);
  end record;
```

The type V_String is very similar to the type Polynomial (the lower bound is different). We have chosen a maximum string size corresponding to a typical page width (or historic punched card).

We can now declare fixed or varying v-strings and make appropriate assignments

```
V: V_String := (5, "Hello");
```

We see that although we no longer have to pad the strings to a fixed length, we now have the burden of specifying the length explicitly. However, we can craftily write

```
function "+" (S: String) return V_String is
begin
  return (S'Length, S);
end "+";
```

and then

```
type V_String_Array is array (Positive range <>) of V_String;

Zoo: constant V_String_Array
       := (+"aardvark", +"baboon", +"camel", +"dolphin",
           +"elephant", ..., +"zebra");
```

Remember from Section 6.5 that we can declare an array of any type or subtype for which we can declare objects. Since v-strings have default discriminants we can declare unconstrained v-strings and hence arrays of them.

We thus see that we have more or less created a ragged array. However, there is a limit of 80 on our strings and, moreover, the storage space for the maximum size string is likely to be allocated irrespective of the actual string. We will return to the topic of ragged arrays when we discuss access types in Section 11.6.

EXERCISE 11.2

1 Declare a Polynomial representing zero (that is, $0x^0$).

2 Write a function "*" to multiply two polynomials.

3 Write a function "−" to subtract two polynomials. Use the function Normal.

4 Rewrite the procedure Truncate to raise Truncate_Error if we attempt to truncate a constrained polynomial.

5 What would be the effect of replacing the discriminant of the type Polynomial by (N: Integer := 0)?

6 Write a function "&" to concatenate two v-strings.

7 Write the converse unary function "+" which takes a V_String as parameter and returns the corresponding String. Use this function to output the camel.

11.3   Variant parts

It is sometimes convenient to have a record type in which part of the structure is fixed for all objects of the type but the remainder can take one of several different forms. This can be done using a variant part and the choice between the alternatives is governed by the value of a discriminant.

Consider the following

```
type Gender is (Male, Female);

type Person(Sex: Gender) is
    record
        Birth: Date;
        case Sex is
            when Male =>
                Bearded: Boolean;
            when Female =>
                Children: Integer;
        end case;
    end record;
```

This declares a record type Person with a discriminant Sex. The component Birth of type Date (see Section 6.7) is common to all objects of the type. However, the remaining components depend upon Sex and are declared as a variant part. If the value of Sex is Male then there is a further component Bearded whereas if Sex is Female then there is a component Children. Only men can have beards and only women (directly) have children.

Since no default expression is given for the discriminant all objects of the type must be constrained. We can therefore declare

John: Person(Male);
Barbara: Person(Female);

or we can introduce subtypes and so write

subtype Man **is** Person(Sex => Male);
subtype Woman **is** Person(Sex => Female);
John: Man;
Barbara: Woman;

Aggregates take the usual form but, of course, give only the components for the corresponding alternative in the variant. The value for a discriminant governing a variant must be static so that the compiler can check the consistency of the aggregate. We can therefore write

John := (Male, (19, Aug, 1937), False);
Barbara := (Female, (13, May, 1943), 2);

but not

S: Gender := Female;
...
Barbara := (S, (13, May, 1943), 2);

because S is not static but a variable.

The components of a variant can be accessed and changed in the usual way. We could write

John.Bearded := True;
Barbara.Children := Barbara.Children+1;

but an attempt to access a component of the wrong alternative such as John.Children would raise Constraint_Error.

Note that although the sex of objects of type Person cannot be changed, it need not be known at compilation time. We could have

S: Gender := ...
...
Chris: Person(S);

where the sex of Chris is not determined until he or she is declared. The rule that a discriminant must be static applies only to aggregates.

The variables of type Person are necessarily constrained because the type had no default expression for the discriminant. It is therefore not possible to assign a value which would change the sex; an attempt to do so would raise Constraint_Error. However, as with the type Polynomial, we could declare a default initial expression for the discriminant and consequently declare unconstrained variables. Such unconstrained variables could then be assigned values with different discriminants but only by a complete record assignment.

We could therefore have

```
type Gender is (Male, Female, Neuter);
```

```
type Mutant(Sex: Gender := Neuter) is
    record
        Birth: Date;
        case Sex is
            when Male =>
                Bearded: Boolean;
            when Female =>
                Children: Integer;
            when Neuter =>
                null;
        end case;
    end record;
```

Note that we have to write **null**; as the alternative in the case of Neuter where we did not want any components. In a similar way to the use of a null statement in a case statement this indicates that we really meant to have no components and did not omit them by accident.

We can now declare

```
M: Mutant;
```

The sex of this unconstrained mutant is neuter by default but can be changed by a whole record assignment.

Note the difference between

```
M: Mutant := (Neuter, (1, Jan, 1984));
```

and

```
N: Mutant(Neuter) := (Neuter, (1, Jan, 1984));
```

In the first case the mutant is not constrained but just happens to be initially neuter. In the second case the mutant is permanently neuter. This example also illustrates the form of the aggregate when there are no components in the alternative; there are none so we write none – we do not write **null**.

The rules regarding the alternatives closely follow those regarding the case statement described in Section 5.2. Each **when** is followed by one or more choices separated by vertical bars and each choice is either a simple expression or a discrete range. The choice **others** can also be used but must be last and on its own. All values and ranges must be static and all possible values of the discriminant must be covered once and once only. The possible values of the discriminant are those of its static subtype (if there is one) or type. Each alternative can contain several component declarations and as we have seen could also be null.

A record can only contain one variant part and it must follow other components. However, variants can be nested; the component lists in a variant part could themselves contain one variant part but again it must follow other components.

Also observe that it is unfortunately not possible to use the same identifier for components in different alternatives of a variant – all components of a record must have distinct identifiers.

It is perhaps worth emphasizing the rules regarding the changing of discriminants. If an object is declared with a discriminant constraint then it cannot be changed – after all it is a constraint just like a range constraint and so the discriminant must always satisfy the constraint. Because the constraint allows only a single value this naturally means that the discriminant can only take that single value and so cannot be changed.

The other basic consideration is that, for implementation reasons, all objects must have values for discriminant components. Hence if the type does not provide a default initial expression, the object declaration must and since it is expressed as a constraint the object is then consequently constrained.

There is a restriction on renaming components of a variable of a discriminated type. If the existence of the component depends upon the value of a discriminant then it cannot be renamed if the variable is unconstrained. (This only applies to variables and not to constants, see AI-738.) So we cannot write

```
C: Integer renames M.Children;
```

because there is no guarantee that the component M.Children of the mutant M will continue to exist after the renaming even if it does exist at the moment of renaming. However,

```
C: Integer renames Barbara.Children;
```

is valid because Barbara is a person and cannot change sex.

Note, amazingly, that we can write

```
Bobby: Man renames Barbara;
```

because the constraint in the renaming declaration is ignored (see Section 8.5). Barbara has not had a sex change – she is merely in disguise!

We have seen that a discriminant can be used as the bound of an array and also as the expression governing a variant. In a similar way it can also be used as the discriminant constraint of an inner component. We could declare a type representing rational polynomials (that is one polynomial divided by another) by

```
type Rational_Polynomial(N, D: Index := 0) is
   record
      Num: Polynomial(N);
      Den: Polynomial(D);
   end record;
```

The relationship between constraints on the rational polynomial as a whole and its component polynomials is interesting. If we declare

R: Rational_Polynomial(2, 3);

then R is constrained for ever and the components R.Num and R.Den are also permanently constrained with constraints 2 and 3 respectively. However

P: Rational_Polynomial := (2, 3, Num => (2, (−1, 0, 1)),
$\qquad\qquad\qquad\qquad\qquad$ Den => (3, (−1, 0, 0, 1)));

is not constrained. This means that we can assign complete new values to P with different values of N and D. The fact that the components Num and Den are declared as constrained does not mean that P.Num and P.Den must always have a fixed length but simply that for given N and D they are constrained to have the appropriate length. So we could not write

P.Num => (1, (1, 1));

because this would violate the constraint on P.Num. However, we can write

P := (1, 2, Num => (1, (1, 1)), Den => (2, (1, 1, 1)));

because this changes everything together. Of course we can always make a direct assignment to P.Num that does not change the current value of its own discriminant.

The original value of P represented $(x^2 − 1)/(x^3 − 1)$ and the final value represents $(x + 1)/(x^2 + x + 1)$ which is, in fact, the same with the common factor $(x − 1)$ cancelled. The reader will note the strong analogy between the type Rational_Polynomial and the type Rational of Exercise 9.1(**3**). We could write an equivalent function Normal to cancel common factors of our rational polynomials and the whole package of operations would then follow.

The remaining possible use of a discriminant is as part of the expression giving a default initial value for one of the other record components (but not another discriminant). Although the discriminant value may not be known until an object is declared, this is not a problem since the default initial expression is of course only evaluated when the object is declared and no other initial value is supplied.

However, we cannot use a discriminant for any other purpose. This unfortunately meant that when we declared the type Stack in the previous section we could not continue to apply the constraint to Top by writing

```
type Stack(Max: Natural) is
   record
      S: Integer_Vector(1 .. Max);
      Top: Integer range 0 .. Max := 0;      – – illegal
   end record;
```

since the use of Max in the range constraint is not allowed.

Finally, a discriminant need not be used at all. It could just be treated as one component of a record. This might be particularly relevant when we wish to have a type where some components are private and others are visible. As an interesting and extreme example we can reconsider the type Key of Section 9.3. We could change this to

> **type** Key(Code: Natural := 0) **is limited private**;

with

> **type** Key(Code: Natural := 0) **is**
>   **record**
>   **null**;
>   **end record**;

With this formulation the user can read the code number of his key, but cannot change it. There is, however, a small flaw whose detection and cure is left as an exercise. Note also that we have declared Code as subtype Natural rather than subtype Key_Code; this is because Key_Code is not visible to the user. Of course we could make Key_Code visible but this would make Max visible as well and we might not want the user to know how many keys there are.

    We conclude our discussion of discriminated records by recalling the rule in Section 6.5 that the components of an array can be of any type or subtype for which we can declare objects. So we can declare arrays of type Mutant and subtypes Man and Woman, but not of type Person.

EXERCISE 11.3

1   Write a procedure Shave which takes an object of type Person and removes any beard if the object is male and raises the exception Shaving_Error if the object is female.

2   Write a procedure Sterilize which takes an object of type Mutant and ensures that its sex is Neuter by changing it if necessary and possible and otherwise raises an appropriate exception.

3   Declare a type Object which describes geometrical objects which are either a circle, a square or a rectangle. A circle is characterized by its radius, a square by its side and a rectangle by its length and breadth.

4   Write a function Area which returns the area of an Object.

5   Rewrite the declaration of the type Polynomial of Section 11.2 so that the default initial value of a polynomial of degree n represents x^n. Hint: declare an auxiliary function returning an appropriate array value.

6   What is the flaw in the suggested new formulation for the type Key? Hint: remember that the user declares keys explicitly. Show how it can be overcome.

7   Write the specification of a package Rational_Polynomials. Make the type Rational_Polynomial private with visible discriminants. The functions should correspond to those of the package Rational_Numbers of Exercise 9.1(**3**).

11.4 Access types

In the case of the types we have met so far, the name of an object has been bound irretrievably to the object itself, and the lifetime of an object has been from its declaration until control leaves the unit containing the declaration. This is too restrictive for many applications where a more fluid control of the allocation of objects is desired. In Ada this can be done by access types. Objects of an access type, as the name implies, provide access to other objects and these other objects can be allocated in a manner independent of the block structure.

For those familiar with other languages, an access object can be thought of as a reference or pointer. The term reference has been brought into disrepute because of dangling references in Algol 68 and pointer has been brought into disrepute because of anonymous pointers in PL/I. Thus the new term access can be thought of as a polite term for reference or pointer. However, Ada access objects are strongly typed and, as we shall see, there are no dangling reference problems.

One of the simplest uses of an access type is for list processing. Consider

```
type Cell;
type Link is access Cell;

type Cell is
    record
        Value: Integer;
        Next: Link;
    end record;

L: Link;
```

These declarations introduce type Link which accesses Cell. The variable L can be thought of as a reference variable which can only point at objects of type Cell; these are records with two components, Value of type Integer and Next which is also a Link and can therefore access (point to or reference) other objects of type Cell. The records can therefore be formed into a linked list. Initially there are no record objects, only the single pointer L which by default takes the value **null** which points nowhere. We could have explicitly given L this default value thus

```
L: Link := null;
```

Note the circularity in the definitions of Link and Cell. Because of this circularity and the rule of linear elaboration it is necessary first to give an incomplete declaration of Cell. Having done this we can declare Link and then complete the declaration of Cell. Between the incomplete and complete declarations, the type name Cell can only be used in the definition of an access type. Moreover, the incomplete and complete declarations must be in the same list of declarations except for one case which we will mention in the next section.

Figure 11.1   An access object.

The accessed objects are created by the execution of an allocator which can (but need not) provide an initial value. An allocator consists of the reserved word **new** followed by either just the type of the new object or a qualified expression providing also the initial value of the object. The result of an allocator is an access value which can then be assigned to a variable of the access type.

So

    L := **new** Cell;

creates a record of type Cell and then assigns to L a designation of (reference to or pointer to) the object. We can picture the result as in Figure 11.1.

Note that the Next component of the record takes the default value **null** whereas the Value component is undefined.

The components of the object referred to by L can be accessed using the normal dotted notation. So we could assign 37 to the Value component by

    L.Value := 37;

Alternatively we could have provided an initial value with the allocator

    L := **new** Cell'(37, **null**);

The initial value here takes the form of a qualified aggregate, and as usual has to provide values for all the components irrespective of whether some have default initial expressions.

Of course, the allocator could have been used to initialize L when it was declared

    L: Link := **new** Cell'(37, **null**);

Distinguish carefully the types Link and Cell. L is of type Link which accesses Cell and it is the accessed type which follows **new**.

Suppose we now want to create a further record and link it to our existing record. We can do this by declaring a further variable

    N: Link;

and then executing

    N := **new** Cell'(10, L);
    L := N;

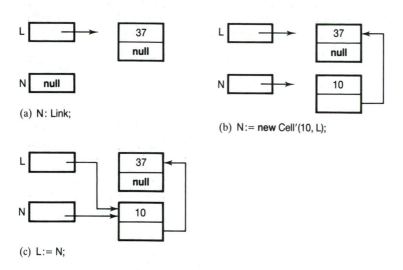

(a) N: Link;

(b) N:= **new** Cell'(10, L);

(c) L:= N;

Figure 11.2 Extending a list.

The effect of these three steps is illustrated in Figure 11.2.
Note how the assignment statement

    L := N;

copies the access values (that is, the pointers) and not the objects. If we
wanted to copy the objects we could do it component by component

    L.Value := N.Value;
    L.Next := N.Next;

or by using **all**

    L.**all** := N.**all**;

L.**all** refers to the whole object accessed by L. In fact we can think of L.Value
as short for L.**all**.Value. Unlike Pascal, dereferencing is automatic.
    Similarly

    L = N

will be true if L and N refer to the same object, whereas

    L.**all** = N.**all**

will be true if the objects referred to happen to have the same value.
    We could declare a constant of an access type but, of course, since it is a
constant we must supply an initial value

```
C: constant Link := new Cell'(0, null);
```

The fact that C is constant means that it must always refer to the same object. However, the value of the object could itself be changed. So

```
C.all := L.all;
```

is allowed but

```
C := L;
```

is not.

We did not really need the variable N in order to extend the list since we could simply have written

```
L := new Cell'(10, L);
```

This statement can be made into a general procedure for creating a new record and adding it to the beginning of a list

```
procedure Add_To_List(List: in out Link; V: in Integer) is
begin
    List := new Cell'(V, List);
end;
```

The new record containing the value 10 can now be added to the list accessed by L by

```
Add_To_List (L, 10);
```

The parameter passing mechanism for access types is defined to be by copy like that for scalar types. However, in order to prevent an access value from becoming undefined an **out** parameter is always copied in at the start. Remember also that an uninitialized access object takes the specific default value **null**. These two facts prevent undefined access values which could cause a program to go berserk.

The value **null** is useful for determining when a list is empty. The following function returns the sum of the Value components of the records in a list

```
function Sum(List: Link) return Integer is
    L: Link := List;
    S: Integer := 0;
begin
    while L /= null loop
        S := S+L.Value;
        L := L.Next;
    end loop;
    return S;
end Sum;
```

Observe that we have to make a copy of List because formal parameters of
mode **in** are constants. The variable L is then used to work down the list until
we reach the end. The function works even if the list is empty.

A more elaborate data structure is the binary tree. This consists of nodes
each of which has a value plus two subtrees one or both of which could be
null. Appropriate declarations are

```
type Node;
type Tree is access Node;

type Node is
   record
      Value: Real;
      Left, Right: Tree;
   end record;
```

As an interesting example of the use of trees consider the following
procedure Sort which sorts the values in an array into ascending order

```
procedure Sort(A: in out Vector) is
   I: Integer;
   Base: Tree := null;

   procedure Insert(T: in out Tree; V: Real) is
   begin
      if T = null then
         T := new Node'(V, null, null);
      else
         if V < T.Value then
            Insert(T.Left, V);
         else
            Insert(T.Right, V);
         end if;
      end if;
   end Insert;

   procedure Output(T: Tree) is
   begin
      if T /= null then
         Output(T.Left);
         A(I) := T.Value;
         I := I+1;
         Output(T.Right);
      end if;
   end Output;

begin                           -- body of Sort
   for J in A'Range loop
      Insert(Base, A(J));
   end loop;
   I := A'First;
   Output(Base);
end Sort;
```

The recursive procedure Insert adds a new node containing the value V to the tree T in such a way that the values in the left subtree of a node are always less than the value at the node and the values in the right subtree are always greater than (or equal to) the value at the node.

The recursive procedure Output copies the values at all the nodes of the tree into the array A by first outputting the left subtree (which has the smaller values) and then copying the value at the node and finally outputting the right subtree.

The procedure Sort simply builds up the tree by calling Insert with each of the components of the array in turn and then calls Output to copy the ordered values back into the array.

The access types we have met so far have referred to records. This will often be the case but an access type can refer to any type, even another access type. So we could have

```
type Ref_Int is access Integer;
R: Ref_Int := new Integer'(46);
```

Note that the value of the integer referred to by R is, perhaps inappropriately, denoted by R.**all**. So we can write

```
R.all := 13;
```

to change the value from 46 to 13.

It is most important to understand that all objects referred to by access types must be acquired through an allocator. We cannot write

```
C: Cell;
...
L: Link := C; - - illegal
```

This is to avoid the dangling reference problem of Algol 68 where it was possible to leave the scope of the referenced object while still within that of the referring object thus leaving the latter pointing nowhere.

This restriction does not apply in Ada 9X where it is possible for an access type to refer to a normal object. However, the rules in Ada 9X are such that dangling references still cannot occur. These and other forms of access types are discussed in more detail in Chapter 17.

In Ada, the accessed objects form a collection whose scope is that of the access type. The collection will cease to exist only when the scope is finally left but, of course, by then all the access variables will also have ceased to exist; so no dangling reference problems can arise.

If an object becomes inaccessible because no variables refer to it directly or indirectly then the storage it occupies may be reclaimed so that it can be reused by other objects. An implementation may (but need not) provide a garbage collector to do this.

Alternatively, there is a mechanism whereby a program can indicate that an object is no longer required; if, mistakenly, there are still references to such objects then the program is erroneous. For fuller details the reader is referred to Section 15.6. In this chapter we will assume that a garbage collector tidies up for us when necessary.

A few final points of detail. Allocators illustrate the importance of the rules regarding the number of times and when an expression is evaluated in certain contexts. For example, an expression in an aggregate is evaluated for each index value concerned and so

     A: **array** (1 .. 10) **of** Link := (1 .. 10 => **new** Cell);

creates an array of ten components and initializes each of them to access a different new cell. As a further example

     A, B: Link := **new** Cell;

creates two new cells (see Section 4.1), whereas

     A: Link := **new** Cell;
     B: Link := A;

naturally creates only one. Remember also that default expressions for record components, discriminants and subprogram parameters are re-evaluated each time they are required; if such an expression contains an allocator then a new object will be created each time.

If an allocator provides an initial value then this can take the form of any qualified expression. So we could have

     L: Link := **new** Cell'(N.**all**);

in which case the object is given the same value as the object referred to by N. We could have

     I: Integer := 46;
     R: Ref_Int := **new** Integer'(I);

in which case the new object takes the value of I; it does not matter that I is not an access object since only its value concerns us.

The type accessed could be constrained, so we could have

     type Ref_Pos **is access** Positive;

or equivalently

     type Ref_Pos **is access** Integer **range** 1 .. Integer'Last;

The values of the objects referred to are all constrained to be positive. We can write

     RP: Ref_Pos := **new** Positive'(10);

or even

> RP: Ref_Pos := **new** Integer'(10);

Note that if we wrote **new** Positive'(0) then Constraint_Error would be raised because 0 is not of subtype Positive. However, if we wrote **new** Integer'(0) then Constraint_Error is only raised because of the context of the allocator.

It is important to realize that each declaration of an access type introduces a new collection. Two collections can be of objects of the same type but the access objects must not refer to objects in the wrong collection. So we could have

> **type** Ref_Int_A **is access** Integer;
> **type** Ref_Int_B **is access** Integer;
> RA: Ref_Int_A := **new** Integer'(10);
> RB: Ref_Int_B := **new** Integer'(20);

The objects created by the two allocators are both of the same type but the access values are of different types determined by the context of the allocator and the objects are in different collections.

So, although we can write

> RA.**all** := RB.**all**;

we cannot write

> RA := RB;   – – illegal

EXERCISE 11.4

1 Write a

> **procedure** Append(First: **in out** Link; Second: **in** Link);

which appends the list Second (without copying) to the end of the list First. Take care of any special cases.

2 Write a function Size which returns the number of nodes in a tree.

3 Write a function Copy which makes a complete copy of a tree.

11.5   Access types and private types

A private type can be implemented as an access type. Consider once more the type Stack and suppose that we wish to impose no maximum stack size other than that imposed by the overall size of the computer. This can be done by representing the stack as a list

```
package Stacks is
  type Stack is limited private;
  procedure Push(S: in out Stack; X: in Integer);
  procedure Pop(S: in out Stack; X: out Integer);
private
  type Cell;
  type Stack is access Cell;
  type Cell is
    record
      Value: Integer;
      Next: Stack;
    end record;
end;

package body Stacks is

  procedure Push(S: in out Stack; X: in Integer) is
  begin
    S := new Cell'(X, S);
  end;

  procedure Pop(S: in out Stack; X: out Integer) is
  begin
    X := S.Value;
    S := S.Next;
  end;

end Stacks;
```

When the user declares a stack

```
S: Stack;
```

it automatically takes the default initial value **null** which denotes that the stack
is empty. If we call Pop when the stack is empty then this will result in
attempting to evaluate

```
null.Value
```

and this will raise Constraint_Error. The only way in which Push can fail is by
running out of storage; an attempt to evaluate

```
new Cell'(X, S)
```

could raise Storage_Error.

This formulation of stacks is one in which we have made the type limited
private. Predefined equality would merely have tested two stacks to see if they
were the same stack rather than if they had the same values, and assignment
would, of course, copy only the pointer to the stack rather than the stack itself.
The writing of an appropriate function "=" needs some care. We could attempt

```
function "=" (S, T: Stack) return Boolean is
   SS: Stack := S;
   TT: Stack := T;
begin
  while SS /= null and TT /= null loop
    SS := SS.Next;
    TT := TT.Next;
    if SS.Value /= TT.Value then
      return False;
    end if;
  end loop;
  return SS = TT;      - - True if both null
end;
```

but this does not work because we have hidden the predefined equality (and hence inequality) which we wish to use inside the body of "=" by the new definition itself. So this function will recurse indefinitely. The solution is to distinguish between the type Stack and its representation in some way. One possibility would be to make the type Stack a record of one component thus

```
type Cell;
type Link is access Cell;
type Cell is
   record
      Value: Integer;
      Next: Link;
   end record;
type Stack is
   record
      List: Link;
   end record;
```

so that we can distinguish between S, the Stack, and S.List, its internal representation.

In the previous section we stated that if we had to write an incomplete declaration first because of circularity (as in the type Cell) then there was an exception to the general rule that the complete declaration had to occur in the same list of declarations. The exception is that a private part and the corresponding package body are treated as a single list of declarations as far as this rule is concerned.

Thus, in either of the above formulations the complete declaration of the type Cell could be moved from the private part to the body of the package Stacks. This might be an advantage since it then follows from the dependency rules that a user program would not need recompiling just because the details of the type Cell are changed. In implementation terms it is possible to do this because it is assumed that values of all access types occupy the same space – typically a single word.

Finally, an access type could conversely refer to a private type. So we could have

```
type Ref_Stack is access Stack;
```

The only special point of interest is that if the accessed type is limited private
then an allocator cannot provide an initial value since this would be equivalent
to assignment and assignment is not allowed for limited types.

EXERCISE 11.5

1 Assuming that the exception Error is declared in the specification of Stacks, rewrite
   procedures Push and Pop so that they raise Error rather than Storage_Error and
   Constraint_Error.

2 Rewrite Push, Pop and "=" to use the formulation

   ```
   type Stack is
      record
         List: Link;
      end record;
   ```

   Ignore the possibility of exceptions.

3 Complete the package whose visible part is

   ```
   package Queues is
      Empty: exception;
      type Queue is limited private;
      procedure Join(Q: in out Queue; X: in Item);
      procedure Remove(Q: in out Queue; X: out Item);
      function Length(Q: Queue) return Integer;
   private
   ```

   Items join a queue at one end and are removed from the other so that a normal first-
   come-first-served protocol is enforced. An attempt to remove an item from an empty
   queue raises the exception Empty. Implement the queue as a singly linked list but
   maintain pointers to both ends of the list so that scanning of the list is avoided. The
   function Length returns the number of items in the queue; again, avoid scanning the
   list.

11.6   Access types and constraints

Access types can also refer to arrays and discriminated record types. In both
cases they can be constrained or not.
   Consider the problem of representing a family tree. We could declare

```
type Person;
type Person_Name is access Person;

type Person is
   record
```

```
        Sex: Gender;
        Birth: Date;
        Spouse: Person_Name;
        Father: Person_Name;
        First_Child: Person_Name;
        Next_Sibling: Person_Name;
    end record;
```

This model assumes a monogamous and legitimate system. The children are linked together through the component Next_Sibling and a person's mother is identified as the spouse of the father.

It might however be more useful to use a discriminated type for a person so that different components could exist for the different sexes and more particularly so that appropriate constraints could be applied. Consider

```
    type Person(Sex: Gender);
    type Person_Name is access Person;

    type Person(Sex: Gender) is
        record
            Birth: Date;
            Father: Person_Name(Male);
            Next_Sibling: Person_Name;
            case Sex is
                when Male =>
                    Wife: Person_Name(Female);
                when Female =>
                    Husband: Person_Name(Male);
                    First_Child: Person_Name;
            end case;
        end record;
```

The incomplete declaration of Person also gives the discriminants (and any default initial expressions); these must, of course, conform to those in the subsequent complete declaration. The component Father is now constrained always to access a person whose sex is male (or **null** of course). Similarly the components Wife and Husband are constrained; note that these had to have distinct identifiers and so could not both be Spouse. However, the components First_Child and Next_Sibling are not constrained and so could access a person of either sex. We have also taken the opportunity to save on storage by making the children belong to the mother only.

When the object of type Person is created by an allocator a value must be provided for the discriminant either through an explicit initial value as in

```
    Janet: Person_Name;
    ...
    Janet:= new Person'(Female, (22, Feb, 1967), John, others => null);
```

or by supplying a discriminant constraint thus

```
Janet := new Person(Female);
```

Note the subtle distinction whereby a quote is needed in the case of the full initial value but not when we just give the constraint. This is because the first takes the form of a qualified expression whereas the second is just a subtype indication. Note also the use of **others** in the aggregate; this is allowed because the last three components all have the same base type.

We could not write

```
Janet := new Person;
```

because the type Person does not have a default discriminant. However we could declare

```
subtype Woman is Person(Female);
```

and then

```
Janet := new Woman;
```

Such an object cannot later have its discriminant changed. This rule applies even if the discriminant has a default initial expression; objects created by an allocator are in this respect different to objects created by a normal declaration where, the reader will recall, a default initial expression allows unconstrained objects to be declared and later to have their discriminant changed.

On the other hand, we see that despite the absence of a default initial expression for the discriminant, we can nevertheless declare unconstrained objects of type Person_Name; such objects, of course, take the default initial value **null** and so no problem arises. Thus although an allocated object cannot have its discriminant changed, nevertheless an unconstrained access object could refer from time to time to objects with different discriminants.

The reason for not allowing an allocated object to have its discriminant changed is that it could be accessed from several constrained objects such as the components Father and it would be difficult to ensure that such constraints were not violated.

For convenience we can define subtypes

```
subtype Mans_Name is Person_Name(Male);
subtype Womans_Name is Person_Name(Female);
```

We can now write a procedure to marry two people.

```
procedure Marry(Bride: Womans_Name;
                Groom: Mans_Name) is
begin
   if Bride.Husband /= null or Groom.Wife /= null then
      raise Bigamy;
   end if;
```

```
      Bride.Husband := Groom;
      Groom.Wife := Bride;
   end Marry;
```

The constraints on the parameters are checked when the parameters are passed (remember that access parameters are always implemented by copy). An attempt to marry people of the wrong sex will raise Constraint_Error at the point of call. On the other hand an attempt to marry a nonexistent person will result in Constraint_Error being raised inside the body of the procedure. Remember that although **in** parameters are constants we can change the components of the accessed objects – we are not changing the values of Bride and Groom to access different objects.

A function could return an access value as for example

```
function Spouse(P: Person_Name) return Person_Name is
begin
   case P.Sex is
      when Male =>
         return P.Wife;
      when Female =>
         return P.Husband;
   end case;
end Spouse;
```

The result of such a function call can be directly used as part of a name so we can write

```
Spouse(P).Birth
```

to give the birthday of the spouse of P. (See the end of Section 7.1.) We could even write

```
Spouse(P).Birth := Newdate;
```

but this is only possible because the function delivers an access value. It could not be done if the function actually delivered a value of type Person rather than Person_Name. However, we cannot write

```
Spouse(P) := Q;
```

in an attempt to replace our spouse by someone else, whereas

```
Spouse(P).all := Q.all;
```

is valid and would change all the components of our spouse to be the same as those of Q.

The following function gives birth to a new child. We need the mother, the sex of the child and the date as parameters

```
function New_Child(Mother: Womans_Name;
                   Boy_Or_Girl:  Gender; Birthday: Date)
                                          return Person_Name is
   Child: Person_Name;
begin
   if Mother.Husband = null then
      raise Illegitimate;
   end if;
   Child := new Person(Boy_Or_Girl);
   Child.Birth := Birthday;
   Child.Father := Mother.Husband;
   declare
      Last: Person_Name := Mother.First_Child;
   begin
      if Last = null then
         Mother.First_Child := Child;
      else
         while Last.Next_Sibling /= null loop
            Last := Last.Next_Sibling;
         end loop;
         Last.Next_Sibling := Child;
      end if;
   end;
   return Child;
end New_Child;
```

Observe that a discriminant constraint need not be static – the value of Boy_Or_Girl is not known until the function is called. As a consequence we cannot give the complete initial value with the allocator because we do not know which components to provide. Hence we allocate the child with just the value of the discriminant and then separately assign the date of birth and the father. The remaining components take the default value null We can now write

```
Helen: Person_Name := New_Child(Barbara, Female, (28, Sep, 1969));
```

Access types can also refer to constrained and unconstrained arrays. We could have

```
type Ref_Matrix is access Matrix;
R: Ref_Matrix;
```

and then obtain new matrices with an allocator thus

```
R := new Matrix(1 .. 10, 1 .. 10);
```

Alternatively, the matrix could be initialized

```
R := new Matrix'(1 .. 10 => (1 .. 10 => 0.0));
```

but as for discriminated records we could not write just

    R := **new** Matrix;

because all array objects must have bounds. Moreover the bounds cannot be changed. However, R can refer to matrices of different bounds from time to time.

As expected we can create subtypes

    subtype Ref_Matrix_3 **is** Ref_Matrix(1 .. 3, 1 .. 3);
    R_3: Ref_Matrix_3;

and R_3 can then only reference matrices with corresponding bounds. Alternatively we could have written

    R_3: Ref_Matrix(1 .. 3, 1 .. 3);

Using

    subtype Matrix_3 **is** Matrix(1 .. 3, 1 .. 3);

we can then write

    R_3 := **new** Matrix_3;

This is allowed because the subtype supplies the array bounds just as we were allowed to write

    Janet := **new** Woman;

because the subtype Woman supplied the discriminant Sex.

This introduces another example of an array aggregate with **others**. Because the subtype Matrix_3 supplies the array bounds and qualifies the aggregate, we could initialize the new object as follows

    R_3 := **new** Matrix_3'(**others** => (**others** => 0.0));

The components of an accessed array can be referred to by the usual mechanism, so

    R(1, 1) := 0.0;

would set component (1, 1) of the matrix accessed by R to zero. The whole matrix can be referred to by **all**. So

    R_3.**all** := (1 .. 3 => (1 .. 3 => 0.0));

would set all the components of the matrix accessed by R_3 to zero. We can therefore think of R(1, 1) as an abbreviation for R.**all**(1, 1). As with records, dereferencing is automatic. We can also write attributes R'First(1) or alternatively R.**all**'First(1). In the case of a one-dimensional array slicing is also allowed.

We conclude this section by returning to the topic of ragged arrays. By analogy with the type V_String of Section 11.2, we can introduce a type A_String which uses an access type

> **type** A_String **is access** String;

and then

> **function** "+" (S: String) **return** A_String **is**
> **begin**
>   **return new** String'(S);
> **end** "+";

and

> type A_String_Array is array (Positive range <>) of A_String;
>
> Zoo: constant A_String_Array:=
>   (+"aardvark", +"baboon", ..., +"very long animal... ", ..., +"zebra");

With this formulation there is no limit on the length of the strings. But of course there is the overhead of the access value which is significant if the strings are short.

EXERCISE 11.6

1   Write a function to return a person's heir. Follow the normal rules of primogeniture – the heir is the eldest son if there is one and otherwise is the eldest daughter. Return **null** if there is no heir.

2   Write a procedure to divorce a woman. Divorce is only permitted if there are no children.

3   Modify the procedure Marry in order to prevent incest. A person may not marry their sibling, parent or child.

4   Write functions to return the number of children, the number of siblings, the number of grandchildren and the number of cousins of a person.

11.7 Derived types

It is perhaps worth mentioning right from the beginning that derived types are greatly extended in Ada 9X and form the foundation of the polymorphic type mechanism. Derived types in Ada 83 have a flavour of a concept not fully developed. As a consequence the discussion here, although correct as far as it goes for Ada 9X, provides a rather trivial view of the purpose of derived types.

Sometimes it is useful to introduce a new type which is similar in most respects to an existing type but which is nevertheless a distinct type. If T is a type we can write

type S **is new** T;

and then S is said to be a derived type and T is the parent type of S.

A derived type belongs to the same class of type as its parent. If T is a record type then S will be a record type and its components will have the same names and so on.

It will be remembered that the key things that distinguish a type are its set of values and its set of operations; we now consider these.

The set of values of a derived type is a copy of the set of values of the parent. An important instance of this is that if the parent type is an access type then the derived type is also an access type and they share the same collection. Note that we say that the set of values is a copy; this reflects that they are truly different types and values of one type cannot be assigned to objects of the other type; however, as we shall see in a moment, conversion between the two types is possible. The notation for literals and aggregates (if any) is the same and any default initial expressions for the type or its components are the same.

The operations applicable to a derived type are as follows. First, it has the same attributes as the parent. Second, unless the parent type, and consequently the derived type, are limited, assignment and predefined equality and inequality are also applicable. Third, a derived type will derive or inherit certain subprograms applicable to the parent type. (We say that a subprogram applies to a type if it has one or more parameters or a result of that type or one of its subtypes.) Such derived subprograms are implicitly declared at the place of the derived type definition but may be later redefined in the same declarative region.

If the parent type is a predefined type then the inherited subprograms are just the predefined subprograms. If the parent type is a user defined type then again there will be some predefined subprograms such as "<" and these will be inherited. If the parent type is itself a derived type then its inherited subprograms will be passed on again.

In addition, if the parent type is declared in the visible part of a package then any applicable subprograms declared in that visible part will also be inherited provided that the derived type is declared after the visible part. Thus the new subprograms only really 'belong' to the type in the sense that they can be inherited with it when we reach the end of the visible part.

Ada 9X is somewhat different; applicable subprograms in the private part are also inheritable. Moreover, subprograms become inheritable immediately after they are declared. This could lead to obscure inconsistencies.

We will now illustrate these rules with some examples. If we have

```
type Integer_A is new Integer;
```

then Integer_A will inherit all the predefined subprograms such as "+", "−" and "abs" as well as attributes such as First and Last.

If we derive a further type from Integer_A then these inherited subprograms are passed on again. However, suppose that Integer_A is declared in a package specification and that the specification includes further subprograms, thus

```
package P is
   type Integer_A is new Integer;
   procedure Increment(I: in out Integer_A);
   function "&" (I, J: Integer_A) return Integer_A;
end;
```

If we now have

```
type Integer_B is new Integer_A;
```

declared after the end of the specification (either outside the package or in its body) then Integer_B will inherit the new subprograms Increment and "&" as well as the predefined ones.

If we do not like one of the inherited subprograms then it can be redefined in the same declarative region. So we could write

```
package Q is
   type Integer_X is new Integer;
   function "abs" (X: Integer_X) return Integer_X;
end;
```

in which for some reason we have chosen to replace the predefined operator "abs" by a new version.

If we now write

```
type Integer_Y is new Integer_X;
```

after the end of the package specification, the new version of "abs" will be inherited rather than the original one.

There are a couple of other minor rules. We cannot derive from a private type until after its full type declaration. Also, if the parent type is itself a derived type declared in the visible part of a package (such as Integer_A) then a type derived from it (such as Integer_B) cannot be declared inside that visible part. This restriction does not apply if the parent type is not a derived type; but remember that a type so derived from such a parent will not inherit any new or replaced subprograms.

The second restriction does not apply in Ada 9X where, as we shall see, it is often convenient to declare a series of derived types in the same package.

Finally, it should be realized that the predefined types are not really a special case since they and the predefined subprograms are considered to be declared in the visible part of the package Standard.

Although derived types are distinct, the values can be converted from one to another using the same notation as was used for converting between numeric types. So given

```
type S is new T;
TX: T;
SX: S;
```

we can write

```
TX := T(SX);
```

or

```
SX := S(TX);
```

but not

```
TX := SX;      - - illegal
```

or

```
SX := TX;      - - illegal
```

If multiple derivations are involved then only the overall conversion is required; the individual steps need not be given. So if we have

```
type SS is new S;
type TT is new T;
SSX: SS;
TTX: TT;
```

then we can laboriously write

```
SSX := SS(S(TX));
```

and

```
TTX := TT(T(SX));
```

or merely

```
SSX := SS(TX);
```

and

```
TTX := TT(SX);
```

The introduction of derived types extends the possibility of conversion between array types discussed in Section 6.2. In fact a value of one array type can be converted to another array type if the component types are the same and the index types are the same or convertible to each other.

(The component types only have to statically match in Ada 9X.)

Having introduced conversion we can now describe the effective specification of a derived subprogram in more detail. It is obtained from that of the parent by simply replacing all instances of the parent base type in the original specification by the new derived type. Subtypes are replaced by equivalent subtypes with corresponding constraints and default initial expressions are converted by adding a type conversion. Any parameters or result of a different type are left unchanged. As an abstract example consider

```
type T is ... ;
subtype S is T range L .. R;

function F(X: T; Y: T := E; Z: Q) return S;
```

where E is an expression of type T and the type Q is quite unrelated. If we write

```
type TT is new T;
```

then it is as if we had also written

```
subtype SS is TT range TT(L) .. TT(R);
```

and the specification of the derived function F will then be

```
function F(X: TT; Y: TT := TT(E); Z: Q) return SS;
```

in which we have replaced T by TT, S by SS, added the conversion to the expression E but left the unrelated type Q unchanged. Note that the parameter names are naturally the same.

We can now rewrite the type Stack of Section 11.5 using a derived type as follows

```
type Cell;
type Link is access Cell;

type Cell is
  record
    Value: Integer;
```

```
      Next: Link;
   end record;

   type Stack is new Link;
```

It is now possible to write the function "=" thus

```
   function "=" (S, T: Stack) return Boolean is
      SL: Link := Link(S);
      TL: Link := Link(T);
   begin
      - - as the answer to Exercise 11.5(2)
   end "=";
```

An advantage of using a derived type rather than making the type Stack into a record of one component is that the procedures Push and Pop of Section 11.5 still work and do not have to be modified. This is because the type Stack is still an access type and shares its collection with the type Link.

Derived types are often used for private types and in fact we have to use a derived type if we want to express the private type as an existing type such as Integer.

Another use for derived types is when we want to use the operations of existing types, but wish to avoid the accidental mixing of objects of conceptually different types. Suppose we wish to count apples and oranges. Then we could declare

```
   type Apples is new Integer;
   type Oranges is new Integer;
   No_Of_Apples: Apples;
   No_Of_Oranges: Oranges;
```

Since Apples and Oranges are derived from the type Integer they both inherit "+". So we can write

```
   No_Of_Apples := No_Of_Apples+1;
```

and

```
   No_Of_Oranges := No_Of_Oranges+1;
```

but we cannot write

```
   No_Of_Apples := No_Of_Oranges;
```

If we did want to convert the oranges to apples we would have to write

```
   No_Of_Apples := Apples(No_Of_Oranges);
```

In the next chapter we will consider the numeric types in more detail but it is worth mentioning here that strictly speaking a type such as Integer has no literals. Literals such as 1 and integer named numbers are of a type known as universal integer and implicit conversion to any integer type occurs if the context so demands. Thus we can use 1 with Apples and Oranges because of this implicit conversion and not because the literal is inherited. Enumeration literals on the other hand do properly belong to their type and are inherited; in fact, as mentioned in Section 7.5, enumeration literals behave as parameterless functions and so can be considered to be inherited in the same way as any other applicable subprogram.

Returning to our apples and oranges suppose that we have overloaded procedures to sell them

```
procedure Sell(N: Apples);
procedure Sell(N: Oranges);
```

Then we can write

```
Sell(No_Of_Apples);
```

but

```
Sell(6);
```

is ambiguous because we do not know which fruit we are selling. We can resolve the ambiguity by qualification thus

```
Sell(Apples'(6));
```

When a subprogram is derived a new subprogram is not actually created. A call of the derived subprogram is really a call of the parent subprogram; **in** and **in out** parameters are implicitly converted just before the call; **in out** and **out** parameters or a function result are implicitly converted just after the call. So

```
My_Apples + Your_Apples
```

is effectively

```
Apples(Integer(My_Apples) + Integer(Your_Apples))
```

Derived types are in some ways an alternative to private types. Derived types have the advantage of inheriting literals but they often have the disadvantage of inheriting too much. For instance, we could derive types Length and Area from Real.

```
type Length is new Real;
type Area is new Real;
```

We would then be prevented from mixing lengths and areas but we would also have inherited the ability to multiply two lengths to give a length and to multiply two areas to give an area as well as hosts of irrelevant operations such as exponentiation. Of course, it is possible to redefine these operations to be useful or to raise exceptions but it is often simpler to use private types and just define the operations we need.

As a further example of the use of derived types, reconsider the package Bank of Exercise 9.3(**1**). In that package we declared

> **subtype** Money **is** Natural;

in order to introduce the meaningful identifier Money and also to ensure that monies were never negative. However, being only a subtype, we could still mix up monies and integers by mistake. It would be far better to write

> **type** Money **is new** Natural;

so that the proper distinction is made.

In the private part shown in the solution we should perhaps similarly have written

> **type** Key_Code **is new** Integer **range** 0 .. Max;

The above cases illustrate that we can derive from a subtype using either a type mark or the more general subtype indication. The derived type is then actually anonymous and is derived from the underlying base type. In the case of Key_Code it is as if we had written

> **type** anon **is new** Integer;
> **subtype** Key_Code **is** anon **range** 0 .. Max;

(where there was no need to write anon(0) .. anon(Max) because the literal 0 and the named number Max are of type universal integer and conversion is implicit). So Key_Code is not really a type at all but a subtype. The set of values of the new derived type is actually the full set of values of the type Integer. The derived operations "+", ">" and so on also work on the full set of values. So given

> K: Key_Code;

we can legally write

> K > −2

even though −2 could never be assigned to K. The Boolean expression is, of course, always true.

The reader may have felt that derived types are not very useful because in the examples we have seen there is usually an alternative mechanism open to us – usually involving record types or private types. However, one importance of derived types is that they are used to explain the mechanism for numeric types as we shall see in the next chapter. In truth, derived types are of fundamental importance to the capability to create types; this will become clearer as we proceed.

As we hinted at the beginning of this section, derived types play a very central role in Ada 9X as will be described in Chapter 17. On the other hand their importance with respect to the mechanism for numeric types is much less as we shall see in the next chapter.

We finish this chapter by mentioning a curious anomaly concerning the type Boolean which really does not matter so far as the normal user is concerned. If we derive a type from Boolean then the predefined relational operators =, < and so on continue to deliver a result of the predefined type Boolean whereas the logical operators **and**, **or**, **xor** and **not** are inherited normally and deliver a result of the derived type. We cannot go into the reason here other than to say that it is because of the fundamental nature of the type Boolean. However, it does mean that the theorem of Exercise 4.7(**3**) that **xor** and /= are equivalent only applies to the type Boolean and not to a type derived from it.

EXERCISE 11.7

1 Declare a package containing types Length and Area with appropriate redeclarations of the incorrect operations "*".

CHECKLIST 11

If a discriminant does not have a default expression then all objects must be constrained.

The discriminant of an unconstrained object can only be changed by a complete record assignment.

Discriminants can only be used as array bounds or to govern variants or as nested discriminants or in default initial expressions for components.

A discriminant in an aggregate and governing a variant must be static.

Any variant must appear last in a component list.

An incomplete declaration can only be used in an access type.

The scope of an accessed object is that of the access type.

If an accessed object has a discriminant then it is always constrained.

Functions returning access values can be used in names.

Access objects have a default initial value of 'null'.

An allocator in an aggregate is evaluated for each index value.

An allocator with a complete initial value uses a quote.

12 Numeric Types

We now come at last to a more detailed discussion of numeric types. There are two classes of numeric types in Ada: integer types and real types. The real types are further subdivided into floating point types and fixed point types.

There are two problems concerning the representation of numeric types in a computer. First, the range may be restricted and indeed many machines have hardware operations for various ranges so that we can chose our own compromise between range of values and space occupied by values. Second, it may not be possible to represent accurately all the possible values of a type. These difficulties cause problems with program portability because the constraints vary from machine to machine. Ada recognizes these difficulties and provides numeric types in such a way that a recognized minimum set of properties is provided; this enables the programmer to keep portability problems to a minimum.

We start by discussing integer types because these suffer only from range problems but not from accuracy problems.

For a number of reasons, Ada 9X takes a rather different approach in explaining numeric types although the effect from the normal user's point of view is much the same. The main difference is that the derived mechanism is not used as an underlying explanation (the model goes very slightly wrong at times). However, the main text of this book is about Ada 83 and so we have left the exposition in terms of the Ada 83 model and only mentioned situations where Ada 9X has a different effect that might impact on the normal user.

12.1 Integer types

All implementations of Ada have the predefined type Integer. In addition there may be other predefined types such as Long_Integer, Short_Integer and so on with a respectively longer or shorter range than Integer (could actually be the same as noted at the end of this section). The range of values of these predefined types will be symmetric about zero except for an extra negative value in two's complement machines (which now seem to dominate over one's complement machines). All predefined integer types have the same predefined operations that were described in Chapter 4 as applicable to the type Integer (except that the second operand of "**" is always just type Integer).

Thus we might find that on machine A we have types Integer and Long_Integer with

range of Integer:
    −32768 .. +32767   (i.e. 16 bits)

range of Long_Integer:
    −21474_83648 .. +21474_83647   (i.e. 32 bits)

whereas on machine B we might have types Short_Integer, Integer and Long_Integer with

range of Short_Integer:
    −2048 .. +2047   (i.e. 12 bits)

range of Integer:
    −83_88608 .. +83_88607   (i.e. 24 bits)

range of Long_Integer:
    −14073_74883_55328 .. +14073_74883_55327   (i.e. 48 bits)

For most purposes the type Integer will suffice on either machine and that is why we have simply used Integer in examples in this book so far. However, suppose we have an application where we need to manipulate signed values up to a million. The type Integer is inadequate on machine A and to use Long_Integer on machine B would be extravagant. We can overcome our problem by using derived types and writing (for machine A)

type My_Integer **is new** Long_Integer;

and then using My_Integer throughout the program. To move the program to machine B we just replace this one declaration by

type My_Integer **is new** Integer;

However, Ada enables this choice to be made automatically; if we write

> **type** My_Integer **is range** −1E6 .. 1E6;

then the implementation will implicitly choose the smallest appropriate type and it will be much as if we had written either

> **type** My_Integer **is new** Long_Integer **range** −1E6 .. 1E6;

or

> **type** My_Integer **is new** Integer **range** −1E6 .. 1E6;

So in effect My_Integer will be a subtype of an anonymous type derived from one of the predefined types and so objects of type My_Integer will be constrained to take only the values in the range −1E6 .. 1E6 and not the full range of the anonymous type. Note that the range must have static bounds since the choice of base type is made at compilation time.

If, out of curiosity, we wanted to know the full range we could use My_Integer'Base'First and My_Integer'Base'Last or, more neatly, My_Integer'Base'Range.

The attribute Base applies to any type or subtype and gives the corresponding base type. It can only be used to form other attributes as in this example. We could even go so far as to ensure that we could use the full range of the predefined type by writing

> **type** X **is range** −1E6 .. 1E6;
> **type** My_Integer **is range** X'Base'Range;

This would have the dubious merit of avoiding the constraint checks when values are assigned to objects of type My_Integer and would destroy the very portability we were seeking.

The attribute Base can indeed be used alone in Ada 9X and so we could write

> Var: X'Base;

This is of particular value in generic packages as is noted in Section 13.4. A rather minor additional point about Base is that it cannot be applied to composite types in Ada 9X. This is strictly an incompatibility although not significant.

We can convert between one integer type and another by using the normal notation for type conversion. Given

> **type** My_Integer **is range** −1E6 .. 1E6;
> **type** Index **is range** 0 .. 10000;
> M: My_Integer;
> I: Index;

then we can write

```
M := My_Integer(I);
I := Index(M);
```

On machine A a genuine hardware conversion is necessary but on machine B both types will be derived from Integer and the conversion will be null.

Note that, as mentioned in the last chapter, we can convert directly between related derived types and do not have to give each individual step. If this were not so we would have to write

```
M := My_Integer(Long_Integer(Integer(I)));
```

on machine A and

```
M := My_Integer(Integer(I));
```

on machine B and our portability would be lost.

The integer literals are considered to belong to a type known as universal integer. The range of this type is at least as large as any of the predefined integer types and it has all the usual operations of an integer type such as +, −, < and =. Integer numbers declared in a number declaration (see Section 4.1) such as

```
Ten: constant := 10;
```

are also of type universal integer. However, there are no universal integer variables and as a consequence most universal integer expressions are static. The initial value in a number declaration has to be a static universal expression. So

```
M: constant := 10;
MM: constant := M*M;
```

is allowed since M*M is a static universal expression. However,

```
N: constant Integer := 10;
NN: constant := N*N;
```

is not allowed since N*N is not a static expression of type universal integer but merely a static expression of type Integer.

Ada 9X is more liberal and allows the initial value to be any integer static expression so the second example is legal in Ada 9X.

It should be noted that certain attributes such as Pos in fact deliver a universal integer value and since Pos can take a dynamic argument it follows that certain universal integer expressions may actually be dynamic.

Conversion of integer literals, integer numbers and universal integer attributes to other integer types is automatic and does not require an explicit type conversion. Problems of ambiguity, however, demand that conversion of more general expressions has to be explicit.

The reader may recall that a range such as 1 .. 10 occurring in a for statement or in an array type definition is considered to be of type Integer. The full rule is in fact that the bounds must again be integer literals, integer numbers or universal integer attributes but not a more general expression. Note incidentally that specifying that the range is type Integer rather than any other integer type means that the predefined type Integer does have rather special properties.

We now see why we could not write

for I **in** –1 .. 10 **loop**

in Section 5.3. But we could introduce an integer number for –1 and then use that as the lower bound

Minus_One: **constant** := –1;
...
for I **in** Minus_One .. 10 **loop**

The rules in Ada 9X regarding conversions of universal integer expressions are slightly different and involve the introduction of a further fictitious type root integer which embraces all the predefined integer types. Conversion to this type root integer is preferred in the case of ambiguity. We will not bother with the details but one result is that we can write –1 in the above loop.

The use of integer type declarations which reflect the need of the program rather than the arbitrary use of Integer and Long_Integer is good practice because it not only encourages portability but also enables us to distinguish between different classes of objects as, for example, when we were counting apples and oranges in the last chapter.

Consideration of separation of classes is the key to deciding whether to use numeric constants (of a specific type) or named numbers (of type universal integer). If a literal value is a pure mathematical number then it should be declared as a named number. If, however, it is a value related naturally to just one of the program types then it should be declared as a constant of that type. Thus if we are counting oranges and are checking against a limit of 100 it is better to write

Max_Oranges: **constant** Oranges := 100;

rather than

Max_Oranges: **constant** := 100;

so that the accidental mixing of types as in

if No_Of_Apples = Max_Oranges **then**

will be detected by the compiler.

Returning to the question of portability it should be realized that complete portability is not easily obtained. For example, assume

```
type My_Integer is range -1E6 .. +1E6;
I, J: My_Integer;
```

and consider

```
I := 100000;
J := I*I;
```

In order to understand the behaviour it is most important to remember that My_Integer is really only a subtype of an anonymous type derived from Long_Integer on machine A or Integer on machine B. The derived operations +, −, *, / and so on have the anonymous type as operands and results and the subtype constraint is only relevant when we attempt to assign to J. So J := I*I; is effectively (on machine A)

```
J := anon(Long_Integer(I)*Long_Integer(I));
```

and the multiplication is performed with the operation of the type Long_Integer. The result is 1E10 and this is well within the range of Long_Integer. However, when we attempt to assign the result to J we get Constraint_Error.

On machine B on the other hand the type is derived from Integer and this time the result of the multiplication is outside the range of Integer. So Numeric_Error (Constraint_Error) is raised by the multiplication itself.

Thus, although the program fails in both cases the actual exception raised could be different. However, we recall from Section 11.1 that Numeric_Error and Constraint_Error should be treated as the same and so this example is somewhat irrelevant although it does illustrate another reason for not distinguishing the two exceptions.

A more interesting case is

```
I := 100000;
J := (I*I)/100000;
```

On machine A the intermediate product and final result are computed with no problem and moreover the final result lies within the range of J and so no exception is raised. But on machine B we again get Numeric_Error (alias Constraint_Error).

(The above analysis has ignored the possibility of optimization. The language allows the implementation to use a wider type in order to avoid Numeric_Error (Constraint_Error) provided that the correct result is obtained. However, the example is certainly valid if machine B did not have a type Long_Integer.)

It is also worth observing that AI-459 permits the limiting case where a type such as Long_Integer actually has the same range as Integer.

Finally, we note that the most negative and most positive values supported by the predefined integer types are given by System.Min_Int and System.Max_Int. These are, of course, implementation dependent and are numbers declared in the package System which is a predefined library package containing various such implementation dependent constants. Note carefully that these limits having nothing to do with the range of universal integer which is essentially infinite (AI-565); Min_Int and Max_Int concern the running program whereas universal integer is primarily a compilation issue.

EXERCISE 12.1

1   What types on machines A and B are used to represent

   type P **is range** 1 .. 1000;
   type Q **is range** 0 .. +32768;
   type R **is range** −1E14 .. +1E14;

2   Would it make any difference if A and B were one's complement machines with the same number of bits in the representations?

3   Given

   N: Integer := 6;
   P: **constant** := 3;
   R: My_Integer := 4;

   what is the type of

   (a) N+P   (d) N*N
   (b) N+R   (e) P*P
   (c) P+R   (f) R*R

4   Declare a type Longest_Integer which is the maximum supported by the implementation.

12.2 Real types

Integer types are exact types. Real types, however, are approximate and introduce problems of accuracy which have subtle effects. This book is not a specialized treatise on errors in numerical analysis and so we do not intend to give all the details of how the features of Ada can be used to minimize errors and maximize portability but will concentrate instead on outlining the basic principles.

Real types are subdivided into floating point types and fixed point types. Apart from the details of representation, the key abstract difference is that floating point values have a relative error whereas fixed point values have an absolute error. Concepts common to both floating and fixed point types are dealt with in this section and further details of the individual types are in subsequent sections.

There is a type universal real having similar properties to the type universal integer. Static operations on this type are notionally carried out with infinite accuracy during compilation. The real literals (see Section 3.4) are of type universal real. Real numbers declared in a number declaration such as

Pi: **constant** := 3.14159_26536;

are also of type universal real. (The reader will recall that the difference between an integer literal and a real literal is that a real literal always has a point in it.)

As well as the usual operations on a real type, some mixing of universal real and universal integer operands is also allowed. Specifically, a universal real can be multiplied by a universal integer and vice versa and division is allowed with the first operand being universal real and the second operand being universal integer; in all cases the result is universal real.

So we can write either

Two_Pi: **constant** := 2*Pi;

or

Two_Pi: **constant** := 2.0*Pi;

but not

Pi_Plus_Two: **constant** := Pi+2;

because mixed addition is not defined. Note that we cannot do an explicit type conversion between universal integer and universal real although we can always convert the former into the latter by multiplying by 1.0.

An important concept is the idea of a model number. When we declare a real type T we demand a certain accuracy. The implementation will, typically, use a greater accuracy just as an implementation of an integer type uses a base type which has a larger range than that requested. Corresponding to the accuracy requested will be a set of model numbers which are guaranteed to be exactly represented. Because the implemented accuracy will usually be higher, other values will also be represented. Associated with each value will be a model interval. If a value is a model number then the model interval is simply the model number. Otherwise the model interval is the interval consisting of the two model numbers surrounding the value. Special cases arise if a value is greater than the largest model number T'Large.

When an operation is performed the bounds of the result are given by the smallest model interval that can arise as a consequence of operating upon any values in the model intervals of the operands.

The relational operators =, > and so on are also defined in terms of model intervals. If the result is the same, whatever values are chosen in the intervals, then its value is clearly not in dispute. If, however, the result depends upon which values in the intervals are chosen then the result is undefined.

Some care is needed in the interpretation of these principles. A key point is that although we may not know where a value lies in a model interval, nevertheless it does have a specific value and should not be treated in a stochastic manner. There is perhaps some philosophical analogy here with Quantum Mechanics – the knowing of the specific value is the collapse of the wave packet! The behaviour of model numbers will be illustrated with examples in the next section and hopefully these remarks will then make more sense.

A very big difference in Ada 9X is that floating point model numbers are defined in terms of the implemented precision rather than the requested precision. Essentially, the model numbers in Ada 9X are what are called safe numbers in Ada 83 and the Ada 83 model numbers are abandoned. The main reason is to reflect the properties of the underlying hardware which is what is actually used to implement the types. Fixed point in Ada 9X is even more pragmatic and does not use the concept of model numbers at all.

EXERCISE 12.2

1   Given

> Two: Integer := 2;
> E: **constant** := 2.71828_18285;
> Max: **constant** := 100;

what is the type of

(a) Two*E   (d) Two*Two
(b) Two*Max   (e) E*E
(c) E*Max   (f) Max*Max

2   Given

> N: **constant** := 100;

declare a real number R having the same value as N.

12.3 Floating point types

Our discussion so far has been in terms of a type Real introduced in Section 2.4 This is not a predefined type but has been used to emphasize that the direct use of the predefined floating point types is not good practice.

In fact, in a similar way to integers, all implementations have a predefined type Float and may also have further predefined types Long_Float, Short_Float and so on with respectively more and less precision (could be the same, see

AI-459). These types all have the predefined operations that were described in Chapter 4 as applicable to the type Real.

So, as outlined earlier, we can derive our own type directly by

type Real **is new** Float;

or perhaps

type Real **is new** Long_Float;

according to the implemented precision but just as with the integer types it is better to state the precision required and allow the implementation to choose appropriately.

If we write

type Real **is digits** 7;

then we are asking the implementation to derive Real from a predefined type with at least 7 decimal digits of precision.

The precise behaviour is defined in terms of our model numbers. Suppose we consider the more general case.

type Real **is digits** D;

where D is a positive static integer expression. D is the number of decimal digits required and we first convert this to B, the corresponding number of binary digits giving at least the same relative precision. B has to be one more than the least integer greater than $D.\log_2 10$ or in other words

$$B{-}1 < 1 + (3.3219... \times D) < B$$

The binary precision B determines the model numbers; these are defined to be zero plus all numbers of the form

$$sign.mantissa.2^{exponent}$$

where

$sign$ is +1 or −1,
$\frac{1}{2} \le mantissa < 1$,
$-4B \le exponent \le +4B$

and the mantissa has exactly B digits after the binary point when expressed in base 2. The range of the exponent, which is an integer, has been chosen to be $\pm 4B$ somewhat arbitrarily after a survey of ranges provided by contemporary architectures.

When we say

type Real **is digits** 7;

we are guaranteed that the model numbers of the predefined floating point type chosen will include the model numbers for decimal precision 7.

As an extreme example suppose we consider

type Rough **is digits** 1;

Then D is 1 and so B is 5. The model numbers are values where the mantissa can be one of

$$^{16}/_{32}, {}^{17}/_{32}, ..., {}^{31}/_{32}$$

and the binary exponent lies in –20 .. 20.

The model numbers around one are

$$..., {}^{30}/_{32}, {}^{31}/_{32}, 1, 1{}^{1}/_{16}, 1{}^{2}/_{16}, 1{}^{3}/_{16}, ...$$

and the model numbers around zero are

$$..., -{}^{17}/_{32}.2^{-20}, -{}^{16}/_{32}.2^{-20}, 0, +{}^{16}/_{32}.2^{-20}, +{}^{17}/_{32}.2^{-20}, ...$$

Note the change of absolute accuracy at one and the hole around zero. By the latter we mean the gaps between zero and the smallest model numbers which in this case are 16 times the difference between them and the next model numbers. There is therefore a gross loss of accuracy at zero. These model numbers are illustrated in Figure 12.1.

The largest model numbers are

$$..., {}^{29}/_{32}.2^{20}, {}^{30}/_{32}.2^{20}, {}^{31}/_{32}.2^{20}$$

or

$$..., 950272, 983040, 1015808$$

Suppose we write

R: Rough := 1.05;

then without considering the actual predefined floating point type chosen for R the literal 1.05 will be converted to a number between 1 and $1{}^{1}/_{16}$ inclusive which are the model numbers surrounding 1.05 but we do not know which. So all we know is that the value of R lies in the model interval $[1, 1{}^{1}/_{16}]$.

If we compute

R := R*R;

then the computed mathematical result must lie between $1^2 = 1$ and $(1{}^{1}/_{16})^2 = {}^{289}/_{256} = 1{}^{33}/_{256}$. However, $1{}^{33}/_{256}$ is not a model number and so we take the next model number above as the upper bound of the result; this is $1{}^{3}/_{16}$. Hence all we can conclude is that R must now lie in the model interval $[1, 1{}^{3}/_{16}]$. And this is all we know! Type Rough indeed.

(a) around 1   ... × × × ×   ×   ×   × ...
                                      1

(b) around 0   ... × × × ×   ×   × × × × ...
                                      0

Figure 12.1 Model numbers of type Rough.

The result of

   R > 1.0

is not defined since 1>1 is false but $1^3/_{16} > 1$ is true.
   Similarly

   R = 1.0

is not defined since 1=1 is true but $1^3/_{16}=1$ is false.
   However

   R >= 1.0

is well defined and is true. So, perhaps surprisingly, the operations =, > and >= do not always have their expected relationship when applied to floating point types.

   The analysis we have just done should be understood to be in terms of predicting the values before executing the program. Of course, when the program actually runs, R has a genuine value and is not undefined in any way. Thus R > 1.0 will have the value true or the value false but will not be undefined; what is undefined is that we cannot beforehand, just given the pure Ada and without knowing any extraneous information about the implementation, predict which of true and false will be the value.

   In particular R = R is always true no matter what operations are performed. And similarly R − R is always zero. Hopefully the remark in the last section about Quantum Mechanics can now be appreciated. It is as if when we run the program we perform an observation on R and it then takes on an eigenvalue; but we cannot push the analogy too far.

   The crudity of the type Rough in the above example is extreme but illustrates the dangers of errors. The hole around zero is a particular danger − if a result falls in that hole then we say that underflow has occurred and all accuracy will be lost. Our value has gone down a black hole!

   In practice we will do rather better because the type Rough will undoubtedly be derived from a predefined type with more precision. Suppose that on a particular machine we just have a predefined type Float with D = 7. Then writing

   type Rough **is digits** 1;

is equivalent to

```
type anon is new Float;
subtype Rough is anon digits 1;
```

The type Rough is therefore really a subtype of the derived type anon and operations on values will be performed with the numbers of the type Float. In order to describe the mechanism more precisely we introduce the concept of safe numbers.

The safe numbers of a type are a superset of the model numbers and have similar computational properties. The safe numbers have the same number of digits B but the exponent range is $\pm E$ where E is at least equal to $4B$. Thus the safe numbers extend the reliable range and allow an implementation to take better advantage of the hardware. Another important difference between model numbers and safe numbers is that the safe numbers of a subtype are those of the base type whereas the model numbers of a subtype are those implied by the accuracy requested in its definition.

As an example, the safe numbers of the type Rough are the safe numbers of Float whereas the model numbers of Rough are those defined by $D = 1$. The operations apply to the safe numbers and it is these numbers that can be stored in objects of the type Rough.

The point of all this is that if we wish to write a portable program then we must stick to the properties of the model numbers, whereas if we wish to get the most out of an implementation then we can exploit the properties of the safe numbers. Note also that an implementation may provide additional numbers to the safe numbers; they cannot be relied upon in the sense that the language does not define their properties other than those implied by the model intervals or safe intervals.

As mentioned earlier, Ada 9X takes a rather different view. The model numbers are essentially what we have just described as safe numbers. The essence is to describe the behaviour in terms of the implemented hardware. Indeed the 9X model numbers are also defined in terms of the machine radix which might not be 2 (it is 16 on a hexadecimal machine).

As a minor point we could also impose a range constraint on a floating point subtype or object by for example

```
R: Rough range 0.0 .. 100.0;
```

or

```
subtype Positive_Real is Real range 0.0 .. Real'Last;
```

and so on. If a range is violated then Constraint_Error is raised.

As well as a type Real, we might declare a more accurate type Long_Real perhaps for the more sensitive parts of our calculation

```
type Long_Real is digits 12;
```

and then declare variables of the two types

```
R: Real;
LR: Long_Real;
```

as required. Conversion between these follows similar rules to integer types

```
R := Real(LR);
LR := Long_Real(R);
```

and we need not concern ourselves with whether Real and Long_Real are derived from the same or different predefined types.

Again in a similar manner to integer types, conversion of real literals, real numbers and universal real attributes to floating types is automatic but more general universal real expressions require explicit conversion.

More liberal rules apply in Ada 9X through the introduction of a type root real and conversion preference just as for integer types. As a consequence general universal real expressions can be implicitly converted.

Various attributes are available and can be used to help in writing more portable programs. For any type (or subtype) F (predefined or not) they are

F'Digits	the number of decimal digits, D,
F'Mantissa	the corresponding number of binary digits, B,
F'Emax	the maximum exponent, 4*F'Mantissa,
F'Small	the smallest possible model number, 2.0**(−F'Emax−1),
F'Large	the largest positive model number, 2.0**F'Emax*(1.0−2.0**(−F'Mantissa)),
F'Epsilon	the difference between 1.0 and the next model number above, 2.0**(1−F'Mantissa).

In addition there are attributes F'Safe_Emax, F'Safe_Small and F'Safe_Large which give the corresponding properties of the safe numbers of the type or subtype.

There are also the usual attributes F'First and F'Last which need not be model numbers or safe numbers but are the actual extreme implemented values of the type or subtype (AI-174).

Digits, Mantissa, Emax and Safe_Emax are of type universal integer; Small, Safe_Small, Large, Safe_Large and Epsilon are of type universal real; First and Last are of type F.

The attribute Base can again be used to enable us to find out about the implemented type. So Rough'Digits=1 and Rough'Base'Digits=7.

Of the above attributes, none apply in Ada 9X except for Digits. The reason is to avoid confusion with the change of interpretation. There are, however, similar attributes with identifiers such as Model_Mantissa, Model_Emax and so on which relate to the implemented properties.

We do not intend to say more about floating point but hope that the reader will have understood the principles involved. In general one can simply specify the precision required and all will work. But care is sometimes needed and the advice of a professional numerical analyst should be sought when in doubt. For further details the reader should consult the *LRM*.

EXERCISE 12.3

1   What is the value of Rough'Epsilon?

2   Compute the model interval in which the value of R must lie after

   type Real **is digits** 5;

   P: Real := 2.0;
   Q: Real := 3.0;
   R: Real := (P/Q)*Q;

3   What would be the effect of writing

   P: **constant** := 2.0;
   Q: **constant** := 3.0;
   R: Real := (P/Q)*Q;
   S: Real := Real((P/Q)*Q);

   Note that the answer is different in Ada 9X.

4   How many model numbers are there of type Rough?

5   The function

   function Hypotenuse(X, Y: Real) **return** Real **is**
   begin
      return Sqrt(X**2+Y**2);
   end;

   suffers from underflow if X and Y are small. Rewrite it to avoid this by testing X and Y against a suitable value and then rescaling if necessary.

6   Explain why B is not just the least integer greater than $D.\log_2 10$ but one more. Use the type Rough to illustrate your answer.

7   What is the ratio between the size of the hole around zero and the gap between the next model numbers for a general value of B?

8   Rewrite the function Inner of Section 7.1 using a local type Long_Real with 14 digits accuracy to perform the calculation in the loop.

9   Suppose that R of type Rough has the value $1\frac{1}{8}$. Compute the model interval of the results of R*R*R*R and (R*R)*(R*R). Comment on this with respect to the evaluation of R**4. See Section 4.5.

12.4 Fixed point types

Fixed point is normally used only in specialized applications or for doing approximate arithmetic on machines without floating point hardware.

The description of fixed point in Ada 9X is rather different although the effect from the point of view of the user is essentially identical except that the conversion rules are more liberal. In addition Ada 9X has special facilities for decimal types and these are dealt with in Chapter 17.

The general principle of derivation from predefined types applies also to fixed point. However, unlike the integer and floating point types, the predefined fixed point types are anonymous and so cannot be used directly but have to be used via a fixed point declaration. Such a declaration specifies an absolute error and also a mandatory range. It takes the form

type F **is delta** D **range** L .. R;

In effect this is asking for values in the range L to R with an accuracy of D which must be positive. D, L and R must be real and static. The above declaration is essentially equivalent to

type anon **is new** fixed;
subtype F **is** anon **range** anon(L) .. anon(R);

where fixed is an appropriate predefined and anonymous fixed point type.

A fixed point type (or subtype) is characterized by two attributes, a positive integer B and a positive real number *small*. B indicates the number of bits required for the number (apart from the sign) and *small* is the absolute precision. The model numbers are therefore zero plus all numbers of the form

sign.mantissa.small

where

sign is +1 or −1
$0 < mantissa < 2^B$

The definition

delta D **range** L .. R

implies a value of *small* which is the largest power of 2 less than or equal to D and a value of B which is the smallest integer such that L and R are no more than *small* from a model number.

As an example, if we have

type T **is delta** 0.1 **range** −1.0 .. +1.0;

then *small* will be $1/16$ and B will be 4. The model numbers of T are therefore

$$-{}^{15}/_{16}, -{}^{14}/_{16}, ..., -{}^1/_{16}, 0, +{}^1/_{16}, ..., +{}^{14}/_{16}, +{}^{15}/_{16}$$

Note carefully that L and R are actually outside the range of model numbers and are both exactly *small* from a model number; the definition just allows this.

If we have a typical 16-bit implementation then there will be a wide choice of predefined types from which T can be derived. The only requirement is that the model numbers of the predefined type include those of T. Assuming therefore that the predefined type will have $B = 15$, then at one extreme *small* could be 2^{-15} which would give us a much greater accuracy but the same range whereas at the other extreme *small* could be $1/16$ in which case we would have a much greater range but the same accuracy.

If we assume for the sake of argument that the implementation chooses the predefined type with the greatest accuracy then its model numbers will be

$$-(2^{15}-1)/2^{15}, \ ..., \ -1/2^{15}, \ 0, \ +1/2^{15}, \ ..., \ +(2^{15}-1)/2^{15}$$

The concept of safe numbers is also defined for fixed point types. The safe numbers of a type are the model numbers of its base type and the safe numbers of a predefined type are just its model numbers. So the safe numbers of T are the model numbers of the chosen predefined type. Similar remarks apply regarding portability as with floating point types. If we just assume the properties of the model numbers then portability is assured but we can also rely upon the safe numbers if we wish to get the best out of a particular implementation.

Returning to the type T, a different implementation might use just eight bits. Moreover using representation clauses (which will be discussed in more detail in Chapter 15) it is possible to give the compiler more precise instructions. We can say

    for T'Size **use** 5;

which will force the implementation to use the minimum five bits. Of course, it might be ridiculous for a particular architecture and in fact the compiler is allowed to refuse unreasonable representation clauses.

We can also override the rule that *small* is a power of 2 by using a representation clause. Writing

    for T'Size **use** 5;
    for T'Small **use** 0.1;

will result in the model numbers being

$$-1.5, \ -1.4, \ ..., \ -0.1, \ 0, \ +0.1, \ ..., \ +1.4, \ +1.5$$

In this case the predefined type has to have the same model numbers. This is because we have pinned down the possible implementation so tightly that there is only one *a priori* possible value for the predefined *small* anyway. However, and perhaps surprisingly, AI-341 states that specifying *small* via a representation clause always ensures that the selected predefined type will also have this value of *small*. In other words, any spare bits give extra range and not extra accuracy. This is yet another win for the accountants at the expense of the engineers!

The advantage of using the default standard whereby *small* is a power of 2 is that conversion between fixed point and other numeric types can be based on shifting. The use of other values of *small* will in general mean that conversion requires implicit multiplication and division.

It should be realized that the predefined fixed point types are somewhat ephemeral; they are not so much predefined as made up anonymously on the spot as required. However, an implementation is only formally required to have one anonymous predefined type. In such a case the *small* for the one type would inevitably be a power of 2 and so any attempt to specify a value of *small* which was not a multiple of this value would fail. Hence the sophisticated use of fixed point types is very dependent upon the implementation.

As we mentioned earlier, Ada 9X does not use the concepts of model and safe numbers in the description of fixed point. Nevertheless the value of *small* is defined in a very similar way and in essence is the *small* of the safe numbers. In other words the *small* in Ada 9X is simply *some* power of 2 not greater than the delta whereas in Ada 83 it is the largest power. But again the value of *small* can be explicitly given by a representation clause and need not be a power of 2.

A standard simple example is given by

```
Del: constant := 2.0**(–15);
type Frac is delta Del range –1.0 .. 1.0;
```

which will be represented as a pure fraction on a 16-bit two's complement machine. Note that it does not really matter whether the upper bound is written as 1.0 or 1.0–Del; the largest model number will be 1.0–Del in either case. Moreover, –1.0 is not a model number either; the model numbers are symmetric about zero (AI-147).

A good example of the use of a specified value for *small* is given by a type representing an angle and which uses the whole of a 16-bit word

```
type Angle is delta 0.1 range –Pi .. Pi;
for Angle'Small use Pi*2**(–15);
```

Note that the value given for the representation clause for Angle'Small must not exceed the value for delta which it overrides.

The arithmetic operations +, –, *, / and **abs** can be applied to fixed point values. Addition and subtraction can only be applied to values of the same type and, of course, return that type. Multiplication and division are allowed between different fixed types but always return values of an infinitely accurate type known as universal fixed. Such a value must be explicitly converted by a type conversion to a particular type before any further operation can be performed. Multiplication and division by type Integer are also allowed and these return a value of the fixed point type.

The behaviour of fixed point arithmetic is, like floating point arithmetic, defined in terms of the model numbers. Conversion of real literals and other universal real expressions to fixed point types follows similar rules to the floating types.

So given

    F, G: Frac;

we can write

    F := F+G;

but not

    F := F*G;   – – illegal in Ada 83

but must explicitly state

    F := Frac(F*G);

It should be noted that multiplication and division between a fixed point type and a universal real operand is not allowed. Moreover, because multiplication and division are defined between any pair of fixed point types it follows that automatic conversion of a simple universal real operand to match a fixed point operand is not possible because there is not a unique fixed point type to which it can be converted. The net result is that we cannot write

    F := Frac(0.5*F);   – – illegal in Ada 83

but must explicitly write

    F := Frac(Frac(0.5)*F);

On the other hand we can write

    F := F+0.5;

because addition is only allowed between the same fixed point types and so the universal real 0.5 is uniquely converted to type Frac. Note, moreover, that we can write

    F := 2*F;

because multiplication is defined between fixed point types and Integer (and not other integer types) and so the universal integer 2 is uniquely converted to type Integer.

Ada 9X is rather more liberal for two reasons. First, it does allow implicit conversion after multiplication and division provided the context determines a unique type. Secondly, the operands of multiplication and division are universal fixed. The effect is that the examples above marked as illegal in Ada 83 are indeed allowed in Ada 9X.

As a more detailed example we return to the package Complex_Numbers of Section 9.1 and consider how we might implement the package body using a polar representation. Any reader who gave thought to the problem will have realized that writing a function to normalize an angle expressed in radians to lie in the range 0 to 2π using floating point raises problems of accuracy since 2π is not a model number.

An alternative approach is to use a fixed point type. We can then arrange for π to be a model number. Another natural advantage is that fixed point types have uniform absolute error which matches the physical behaviour. The type Angle declared above is not quite appropriate because, as we shall see, it will be convenient to allow for angles of up to 2π.

The private part of the package could be

```
private
   Pi: constant := 3.14159_26536;
   type Angle is delta 0.1 range -4*Pi .. 4*Pi;
   for Angle'Small use Pi*2**(-13);
   type Complex is
      record
         R: Real;
         Theta: Angle range -Pi .. Pi;
      end record;
   I: constant Complex := (1.0, 0.5*Pi);
end;
```

The function for normalizing an angle to lie in the range of the component Theta (which is neater if symmetric about zero) could now be

```
function Normal(A: Angle) return Angle is
begin
   if A >= Pi then
      return A - Angle(2*Pi);
   elsif A < -Pi then
      return A + Angle(2*Pi);
   else
      return A;
   end if;
end Normal;
```

Note how we had to use the explicit type conversion in order to convert the universal real expression 2*Pi to type Angle; remember that automatic conversion of universal real values only applies to single items and not to general expressions. We could alternatively have written

```
   return A - Two_Pi;
```

where Two_Pi is a real number as declared in Section 12.2.

Another interesting point is that the values for Theta that we are using do not include the upper bound of the range +Pi; the function Normal converts this into the equivalent -Pi. Unfortunately we cannot express the idea of an open bound in Ada although it would be perfectly straightforward to implement the corresponding checks.

The range for the type Angle has been chosen so that it will accommodate the sum of any two values of Theta. This includes –2*Pi; however, making the lower bound of the range for Angle equal to –2*Pi is not adequate since there is no guarantee that the lower bound will be a model number – not even on a two's complement implementation. So to be on the safe side we squander a bit on doubling the range.

The various functions in the package body can now be written; we assume that we have access to appropriate trigonometric functions applying to the fixed point type Angle and returning results of type Real. So we might have

```
package body Complex_Numbers is
   function Normal ...   – – as above

   ...
   function "*" (X, Y: Complex) return Complex is
   begin
      return (X.R * Y.R, Normal(X.Theta + Y.Theta));
   end "*";

   ...
   function Rl_Part(X: Complex) return Real is
   begin
      return X.R * Cos(X.Theta);
   end Rl_Part;

   ...
end Complex_Numbers;
```

where we have left the more complicated functions for the enthusiastic reader.

We conclude by noting that the various attributes of a fixed point type or subtype F are as follows

F'Delta	the requested delta, D,
F'Mantissa	the number of bits, B,
F'Small	the smallest positive model number, *small*,
F'Large	the largest positive model number, $(2**F'Mantissa-1)*F'Small.$

In addition there are attributes F'Safe_Small and F'Safe_Large which give the corresponding properties of the safe numbers. Note that F'Safe_Small = F'Base'Small for fixed point types.

There are also the usual attributes F'First and F'Last which give the actual upper and lower bounds of the type or subtype and of course need not be model numbers.

Delta, Small, Safe_Small, Large and Safe_Large are of type universal real; Mantissa is of type universal integer; First and Last are of type F.

The attributes Mantissa, Large, Safe_Small and Safe_Large do not exist in Ada 9X because the description of fixed point is not based on model numbers at all.

EXERCISE 12.4

1   Given F of type Frac compute the model interval of F after

   F := 0.1;

2   Why could we not have written

   return A − 2.0*Pi;

   in the function Normal in order to avoid the explicit type conversion?

3   Write the following further function for the package Complex_Numbers implemented as in this section

   function "**" (X: Complex; N: Integer) **return** Complex;

   Remember that if a complex number z is represented in polar form (r, θ), then

   $$z^n \equiv (r, \theta)^n = (r^n, n\theta).$$

4   An alternative approach to the representation of angles in fixed point would be to hold the values in degrees. Rewrite the private part and the function Normal using a canonical range of 0.0 .. 360.0 for Theta. Make the most of a 16-bit word but use a power of 2 for *small*.

CHECKLIST 12

Use implicitly derived types for increased portability.

Beware of overflow in intermediate expressions.

Use named numbers or typed constants as appropriate.

Beware of underflow into the hole around floating point zero.

Beware of the relational operations with real types.

If in doubt consult a numerical analyst.

13 Generics

13.1 Declarations and instantiations 13.3 Subprogram parameters
13.2 Type parameters   13.4 The mathematical library

There are two major concepts in Ada which are static. These are types
and subprograms. By this statement we mean that all types and
subprograms are identified before program execution. The static nature
of these concepts increases the possibility of proving the correctness of
programs as well as simplifying implementation considerations. The idea
that types are static will be familiar from other languages. However,
many languages (such as Algol, Fortran and Pascal) have dynamic
procedures (at least as parameters to other procedures) and their absence
in Ada comes as a bit of a surprise.

In this chapter we describe the generic mechanism which allows us to
overcome the static nature of types and subprograms for many purposes
by a special form of parameterization which can be applied to
subprograms and packages. The generic parameters can be types and
subprograms as well as values and objects.

However, it should be noted that both subprograms and types can be
dynamically determined in Ada 9X. Experience showed that the static
nature of Ada 83 was too rigid for some applications. Nevertheless the
generic mechanism still has a very important role as a compile-time
mechanism of broad applicability as we shall see.

13.1 Declarations and instantiations

We often get the situation that the logic of a piece of program is independent of the types involved and it therefore seems unnecessary to repeat it for all the different types to which we might wish it to apply. A simple example is provided by the procedure Swap of Exercise 7.3(**1**)

```
procedure Swap(X, Y: in out Real) is
    T: Real;
begin
    T := X; X := Y; Y := T;
end;
```

It is clear that the logic is independent of the type of the values being swapped. If we also wanted to swap integers or Booleans we could of course write other procedures but this would be tedious. The generic mechanism allows us to overcome this. We can declare

```
generic
    type Item is private;
procedure Exchange(X, Y: in out Item);

procedure Exchange(X, Y: in out Item) is
    T: Item;
begin
    T := X; X := Y; Y := T;
end;
```

The subprogram Exchange is a generic subprogram and acts as a kind of template. The subprogram specification is preceded by the generic formal part consisting of the reserved word **generic** followed by a (possibly empty) list of generic formal parameters. The subprogram body is written exactly as normal but note that, in the case of a generic subprogram, we have to give both the body and the specification separately.

The generic procedure cannot be called directly but from it we can create an actual procedure by a mechanism known as generic instantiation. For example, we may write

```
procedure Swap is new Exchange(Real);
```

This is a declaration and states that Swap is to be obtained from the template described by Exchange. Actual generic parameters are provided in a parameter list in the usual way. The actual parameter in this case is the type Real which corresponds to the formal parameter Item. We could also use the named notation

```
procedure Swap is new Exchange(Item => Real);
```

So we have now created the procedure Swap acting on type Real and can henceforth call it in the usual way. We can make further instantiations

> **procedure** Swap **is new** Exchange(Integer);
> **procedure** Swap **is new** Exchange(Date);

and so on. We are here creating further overloadings of Swap which can be distinguished by their parameter types just as if we had laboriously written them out in detail.

Superficially, it may look as if the generic mechanism is merely one of text substitution and indeed in this simple case the behaviour would be the same. However, the important difference relates to the meaning of identifiers in the generic body but which are neither parameters nor local to the body. Such non-local identifiers have meanings appropriate to where the generic body is declared and not to where it is instantiated. If text substitution were used then non-local identifiers would of course take their meaning at the point of instantiation and this could give very surprising results.

As well as generic subprograms we may also have generic packages. A simple example is provided by the package Stack in Section 8.1. The trouble with that package is that it only works on type Integer although of course the same logic applies irrespective of the type of the values manipulated. We can also take the opportunity to make Max a parameter as well so that we are not tied to an arbitrary limit of 100. We write

```
generic
    Max: Positive;
    type Item is private;
package Stack is
    procedure Push(X: Item);
    function Pop return Item;
end Stack;

package body Stack is
    S: array (1 .. Max) of Item;
    Top: Integer range 0 .. Max;
    - - etc. as before but with Integer
    - - replaced by Item
end Stack;
```

We can now create and use a stack of a particular size and type by instantiating the generic package as in the following

```
declare
    package My_Stack is new Stack(100, Real);
    use My_Stack;
begin
    ...
    Push(X);
    ...
```

```
        Y := Pop;
        ...
    end;
```

The package My_Stack which results from the instantiation behaves just as a normal directly written out package. The use clause allows us to refer to Push and Pop directly. If we did a further instantiation

```
    package Another_Stack is new Stack(50, Integer);
    use Another_Stack;
```

then Push and Pop are further overloadings and can be distinguished by the type provided by the context. Of course, if Another_Stack was also declared with the actual generic parameter being Real, then we would have to use the dotted notation to distinguish the instances of Push and Pop despite the use clauses.

Both generic units and generic instantiations may be library units. Thus having put the generic package Stack in the program library an instantiation could itself be separately compiled just on its own thus

```
    with Stack;
    package Boolean_Stack is new Stack(200, Boolean);
```

If we added an exception Error to the package as in Section 10.2 so that the generic package declaration was

```
    generic
        Max: Positive;
        type Item is private;
    package Stack is
        Error: exception;
        procedure Push(X: Item);
        function Pop return Item;
    end Stack;
```

then each instantiation would give rise to a distinct exception and because exceptions cannot be overloaded we would naturally have to use the dotted notation to distinguish them.

We could, of course, make the exception Error common to all instantiations by making it global to the generic package. It and the generic package could perhaps be declared inside a further package

```
    package All_Stacks is
        Error: exception;
        generic
            Max: Positive;
            type Item is private;
        package Stack is
            procedure Push(X: Item);
```

```
      function Pop return Item;
   end Stack;
end All_Stacks;
```

package body All_Stacks **is**
   package body Stack **is**

     ...

   end Stack;
end All_Stacks;

This illustrates the binding of identifiers global to generic units. The meaning of Error is determined at the point of the generic declaration irrespective of the meaning at the point of instantiation.

The above examples have illustrated formal parameters which were types and also integers. In fact generic formal parameters can be values and objects much as the parameters applicable to subprograms; they can also be types and subprograms. As we shall see in the next sections, we can express the formal types and subprograms so that we can assume in the generic body that the actual parameters have the properties we require.

In the case of the familiar parameters which also apply to subprograms they can be of mode **in** or **in out** but not **out**. As with subprograms, **in** is taken by default as illustrated by Max in the example above.

An **in** generic parameter acts as a constant whose value is provided by the corresponding actual parameter. A default expression is allowed as in the case of parameters of subprograms; such a default expression is evaluated at instantiation if no actual parameter is supplied in the same way that a default expression for a subprogram parameter is evaluated when the subprogram is called if no actual parameter is supplied. Observe that an **in** generic parameter cannot be of a limited type; this is because assignment is not allowed for limited types and the mechanism of giving the value to the parameter is treated as assignment. Note that this is a different mechanism to that used for **in** subprogram parameters where limited types are allowed.

An **in out** parameter, however, acts as a variable renaming the corresponding actual parameter. The actual parameter must therefore be the name of a variable and its identification occurs at the point of instantiation using the same rules as for renaming described in Section 8.5. One such rule is that any constraints on the actual parameter apply to the formal parameter and any constraints implied by the formal type mark are, perhaps surprisingly, completely ignored. Another rule is that if any identifier in the name subsequently changes then the identity of the object referred to by the generic formal parameter does not change. Because of this there is a restriction that the actual parameter cannot be a component of an unconstrained discriminated record if the very existence of the component depends on the value of the discriminant. Thus if M is a Mutant as in Section 11.3, M.Children could not be an actual generic parameter because M could have its Sex changed. However, M.Birth would be valid. This restriction also applies to renaming itself.

It will now be realized that although the notation **in** and **in out** is identical to subprogram parameters the meaning is somewhat different. Thus there is no question of copying in and out and indeed no such thing as **out** parameters.

Inside the generic body, the formal generic parameters can be used quite freely except for one restriction. This arises because generic parameters (and their attributes) are not considered to be static. There are various places where an expression has to be static such as in the alternatives in a case statement or variant, and in the range in an integer type definition, or the number of digits in a floating point type definition and so on. In all these situations a generic formal parameter cannot be used because the expression would not then be static. A further consequence is that the type of the expression in a case statement and similarly the type of the discriminant in a variant may not be a generic formal type.

Some of these restrictions are relaxed in Ada 9X. Thus the type in a case statement or variant can be a generic formal provided there is an others clause – this ensures that all values are covered.

Our final example in this section illustrates the nesting of generics. The following generic procedure performs a cyclic interchange of three values and for amusement is written in terms of the generic procedure Exchange

```
generic
   type Thing is private;
procedure Cab(A, B, C: in out Thing);

procedure Cab(A, B, C: in out Thing) is
   procedure Swap is new Exchange(Item => Thing);
begin
   Swap(A, B);
   Swap(A, C);
end Cab;
```

Although nesting is allowed, it must not be recursive.

Finally, note that a generic unit may be renamed in Ada 9X although not in Ada 83. So we could write

```
generic procedure Taxi renames Cab;
```

although perhaps confusing for this example.

EXERCISE 13.1

1   Write a generic package declaration based on the package Stacks in Section 11.1 so that stacks of arbitrary type may be declared. Declare a stack S of length 30 and type Boolean. Use named notation.

2   Write a generic package containing both Swap and Cab.

13.2   Type parameters

In the previous section we introduced types as generic parameters. The examples showed the formal parameter taking the form

   type T **is private**;

In this case, inside the generic subprogram or package, we may assume that assignment and equality are defined for T. We can assume nothing else unless we specifically provide other parameters as we shall see in a moment. Hence T behaves in the generic unit much as a private type outside the package defining it; this analogy explains the notation for the formal parameter. The corresponding actual parameter must, of course, provide assignment and equality and so it can be any type except one that is limited.

A formal generic type parameter can take other forms. It can be

   type T **is limited private**;

and in this case assignment and equality are not available automatically. The corresponding actual parameter can be any type.

Either of the above forms could have discriminants

   type T(...) **is private**;

and the actual type must then have discriminants with the same types. The formal type must not have default expressions for the discriminants but the actual type can as we shall see later.

The formal parameter could also be one of

   type T **is** (<>);
   type T **is range** <>;
   type T **is digits** <>;
   type T **is delta** <>;

In the first case the actual parameter must be a discrete type – an enumeration type or integer type. In the other cases the actual parameter must be an integer type, floating point type or fixed point type respectively. Within the generic unit the appropriate predefined operations and attributes are available.

As a simple example consider

```
generic
   type T is (<>);
function Next(X: T) return T;

function Next(X: T) return T is
begin
   if X=T'Last then
      return T'First;
   else
      return T'Succ(X);
```

```
        end if;
    end Next;
```

The formal parameter T requires that the actual parameter must be a discrete type. Since all discrete types have attributes First, Last and Succ we can use these attributes in the body in the knowledge that the actual parameter will supply them.

We could now write

function Tomorrow **is new** Next(Day);

so that Tomorrow(Sun) = Mon.

An actual generic parameter can also be a subtype but an explicit constraint is not allowed; in other words the actual parameter must be just a type mark and not a subtype indication. The formal generic parameter then denotes the subtype. Thus we can have

function Next_Work_Day **is new** Next(Weekday);

so that Next_Work_Day(Fri) = Mon. Note how the behaviour depends on the fact that the Last attribute applies to the subtype and not to the base type so that Day'Last is Sun and Weekday'Last is Fri.

The actual parameter could also be an integer type so we could have

```
    subtype Digit is Integer range 0 .. 9;
    function Next_Digit is new Next(Digit);
```

and then Next_Digit(9) = 0.

Now consider the package Complex_Numbers of Section 9.1; this could be made generic so that the particular floating point type upon which the type Complex is based can be a parameter. It would then take the form

```
    generic
        type Real is digits <>;
    package Generic_Complex_Numbers is
        type Complex is private;
        -- as before
        I: constant Complex := (0.0, 1.0);
    end;
```

Note that we can use the literals 0.0 and 1.0 because they are of the universal real type which can be converted to whichever type is passed as actual parameter. The package could then be instantiated by for instance

```
    package My_Complex_Numbers is
                    new Generic_Complex_Numbers(My_Real);
```

A formal generic parameter can also be an array type. The actual parameter must then also be an array type with the same component type and constraints, if any, the same number of dimensions and the same index subtypes. Either both must be unconstrained arrays or both must be constrained arrays. If they are constrained then the index ranges must be the same for corresponding indexes.

It is possible for one generic formal parameter to depend upon a previous formal parameter which is a type. This will often be the case with arrays. As an example consider the simple function Sum in Section 7.1. This added together the elements of a real array with integer index. We can generalize this to add together the elements of any floating point array with any index type

```
generic
    type Index is (<>);
    type Floating is digits <>;
    type Vec is array (Index range <>) of Floating;
function Sum(A: Vec) return Floating;

function Sum(A: Vec) return Floating is
    Result: Floating := 0.0;
begin
    for I in A'Range loop
        Result := Result+A(I);
    end loop;
    return Result;
end Sum;
```

Note that although Index is a formal parameter it does not explicitly appear in the generic body; nevertheless it is implicitly used since the loop parameter I is of type Index.

We could instantiate this by

```
function Sum_Vector is new Sum(Integer, Real, Vector);
```

and this will give the function Sum of Section 7.1.

The matching of actual and formal arrays takes place after any formal types have been replaced in the formal array by the corresponding actual types. As an example of matching index subtypes note that if we had

```
type Vector is array (Positive range <>) of Real;
```

then we would have to use Positive (or an equivalent subtype) as the actual parameter for the Index.

The final possibility for formal type parameters is the case of an access type. The formal can be

```
type A is access T;
```

where T may but need not be a previous formal parameter. The actual parameter corresponding to A must then access T. Constraints on the accessed type must also be the same.

Observe that there is no concept of a formal record type. This is because the internal structure of records is somewhat arbitrary and the possibilities for matching would therefore be rare.

As a final example in this section we return to the question of sets. We saw in Section 6.6 how a Boolean array could be used to represent a set. Exercises 7.1(**4**), 7.2(**3**) and 7.2(**4**) also showed how we could write suitable functions to operate upon sets of the type Colour. The generic mechanism allows us to write a package to enable the manipulation of sets of an arbitrary type.

Consider

```
generic
    type Base is (<>);
package Set_Of is
    type Set is private;
    type List is array (Positive range <>) of Base;

    Empty, Full: constant Set;

    function Make_Set(X: List) return Set;
    function Make_Set(X: Base) return Set;
    function Decompose(X: Set) return List;

    function "+" (X, Y: Set) return Set;     - - union
    function "*" (X, Y: Set) return Set;     - - intersection
    function "-" (X, Y: Set) return Set;     - - symmetric difference
    function "<" (X: Base; Y: Set) return Boolean;  - - inclusion
    function "<=" (X, Y: Set) return Boolean;       - - contains
    function Size(X: Set) return Natural;           - - no of elements

private
    type Set is array (Base) of Boolean;

    Empty: constant Set := (Set'Range => False);
    Full: constant Set := (Set'Range => True);
end;
```

The single generic parameter is the base type which must be discrete. The type Set is made private so that the Boolean operations cannot be directly applied (inadvertently or malevolently). Aggregates of the type List are used to represent literal sets. The constants Empty and Full denote the empty and full set respectively. The functions Make_Set enable the creation of a set from a list of the base values or a single base value. Decompose turns a set back into a list.

The operators +, * and − represent union, intersection and symmetric difference; they are chosen as more natural than the underlying **or**, **and** and **xor**. The operator < tests to see whether a base value is in a set. The operator <= tests to see whether one set is a subset of another. Finally, the function Size returns the number of base values present in a particular set.

In the private part the type Set is declared as a Boolean array indexed by the base type (which is why the base type had to be discrete). The constants Empty and Full are declared as arrays whose elements are all False and all True respectively. The body of the package is left as an exercise.

Turning back to Section 6.6, we can instantiate the package to work on our type Primary by

```
package Primary_Sets is new Set_Of(Primary);
use Primary_Sets;
```

For comparison we could then write

```
subtype Colour is Set;
White: Colour renames Empty;
Black: Colour renames Full;
```

and so on.

We can use this example to explore the creation and composition of types. Our attempt to give the type Set the name Colour through a subtype is poor. We would really like to pass the name Colour in some way to the generic package as the type to be used. We cannot do this and retain the private nature of the type. But we can use the derived type mechanism to create a proper type Colour from the type Set

```
type Colour is new Set;
```

Recalling the rules for inheriting applicable subprograms from Section 11.7, we note that the new type Colour automatically inherits all the functions in the specification of Set_Of (strictly the instantiation Primary_Sets) because they all have the type Set as a parameter or result type.

However, this is a bit untidy; the constants Empty and Full will not have been inherited and the type List will still be as before.

One improvement therefore is to replace the constants Empty and Full by equivalent parameterless functions so that they will also be inherited. A better approach to the type List is to make it and its index type into further generic parameters. The visible part of the package will then just consist of the type Set and its applicable subprograms

```
generic
   type Base is (<>);
   type Index is (<>);
   type List is array (Index range <>) of Base;
package Nice_Set_Of is
   type Set is private;
   function Empty return Set;
   function Full return Set;
   ...
private
```

We can now write

```
type Primary_List is array (Positive range <>) of Primary;
```

```
package Primary_Sets is new Nice_Set_Of(Base => Primary,
                                         Index => Positive,
                                         List => Primary_List);
```

```
type Colour is new Primary_Sets.Set;
```

The type Colour now has all the functions we want and the array type has a name of our choosing. We might still want to rename Empty and Full thus

function White **return** Colour **renames** Empty;

or we can still declare White as a constant by

White: **constant** Colour := Empty;

As a general rule it is better to use derived types rather than subtypes because of the greater type checking provided during compilation; sometimes, however, derived types introduce a need for lots of explicit type conversions which clutter the program, in which case the formal distinction is probably a mistake and one might as well use subtypes.

We conclude by summarizing the general principle regarding the matching of actual to formal generic types which should now be clear. The formal type represents a class of types which have certain common properties and these properties can be assumed in the generic unit. The corresponding actual type must then supply these properties. The matching rules are designed so that this is assured by reference to the parameters only and without considering the details of the generic body. As a consequence the user of the generic unit need not see the body for debugging purposes. This notion of matching guaranteed by the parameters is termed the contract model.

Unfortunately there is an important violation of the contract model in the case of unconstrained types. If we have the basic formal type

type T **is private**;

then this can be matched by an unconstrained array type such as Vector provided that we do not use T in the generic unit in a way that would require the array to be constrained. The most obvious example is that we must not declare an object of type T. However, if we do make such a declaration then the error shows up in the body rather than in the instantiation which is against the principle of the contract model.

In a similar way the actual type could be an unconstrained discriminated type provided that T is not used in a way that would require constraints. Thus again we could not declare an unconstrained object of type T; but note that if the actual type has default discriminants then the defaults will be used in the generic body and then we will be able to declare an object. This interpretation is given in AI-37 and contrasts with the apparent statement in the *LRM*.

This violation of the contract model is cured in Ada 9X. The form

type T **is private**;

can only be matched by a type such as Integer, a constrained type such as Vector_6 or a record type with default discriminants. These types are collectively known as definite types as opposed to an indefinite type such as Vector. Moreover, Ada 9X introduces the new form

type T(<>) **is private**;

which can be matched by any type including an indefinite type, but then within the body such a formal type cannot be used to declare an (uninitialized), object. We will return to this topic in Chapter 17.

The attribute Constrained can be applied to the formal type T and gives a Boolean value indicating whether the actual type is a constrained type or not. Thus considering the types of Section 11.3, T'Constrained would be True if the actual parameter were Man but False if the actual parameter were Person or Mutant; in the last case the default constraint Neuter is irrelevant. Remember that the actual parameter must be a type mark and not a subtype indication.

Finally we recall that our use of generic formal parameters within the body is restricted by the rule that they are not static.

But as we mentioned in Section 13.1 there is some relaxation of this rule in Ada 9X.

EXERCISE 13.2

1   Instantiate Next to give a function behaving like **not**.

2   Rewrite the specification of the package Rational_Numbers so that it is a generic package taking the integer type as a parameter. See Exercise 9.1(**3**).

3   Rewrite the function Outer of Exercise 7.1(**3**) so that it is a generic function with appropriate parameters. Instantiate it to give the original function.

4   Write the body of the package Set_Of.

5   Rewrite the private part of Set_Of so that an object of the type Set is by default given the initial value Empty when declared.

13.3 Subprogram parameters

As mentioned earlier a generic parameter can also be a subprogram. There are a number of distinct characteristic applications of this facility and we introduce the topic by considering the classical problem of sorting.

Suppose we wish to sort an array into ascending order. There are a number of general algorithms that can be used but they do not depend on the type of the values being sorted. All we need is some comparison operation such as "<" which is defined for the type.

We might start by considering the specification

```
generic
    type Index is (<>);
    type Item is (<>);
    type Collection is array (Index range <>) of Item;
procedure Sort(C: in out Collection);
```

Although the body is largely irrelevant it might help to illustrate the problem to consider the following crude possibility

```
procedure Sort(C: in out Collection) is
   Min: Index;
   Temp: Item;
begin
   for I in C'First .. Index'Pred(C'Last) loop
      Min := I;
      for J in Index'Succ(I) .. C'Last loop
         if C(J) < C(Min) then Min := J; end if;      - - use of <
      end loop;
      Temp := C(I); C(I) := C(Min); C(Min) := Temp;
   end loop;
end Sort;
```

This trivial algorithm repeatedly scans the part of the array not sorted, finds the least component (which because of the previous scans will be not less than any component of the already sorted part) and then swaps it so that it is then the last element of the now sorted part. Note that because of the generality we have imposed upon ourselves, we cannot write

```
for I in C'First .. C'Last–1 loop
```

because we cannot rely upon the array index being an integer type. We only know that it is a discrete type and therefore have to use the attributes Index'Pred and Index'Succ which we know to be available since they are common to all discrete types.

However, the main point to note is the call of "<" in the body of Sort. This calls the predefined function corresponding to the type Item. We know that there is such a function because we have specified Item to be discrete and all discrete types have such a function. Unfortunately the net result is that our generic sort can only sort arrays of discrete types. It cannot sort arrays of floating types. Of course we could write a version for floating types by replacing the generic parameter for Item by

```
type Item is digits <>;
```

but then it would not work for discrete types. What we really need to do is specify the comparison function to be used in a general manner. We can do this by adding a fourth parameter which is a formal subprogram so that the specification becomes

```
generic
   type Index is (<>);
   type Item is private;
   type Collection is array (Index range <>) of Item;
   with function "<" (X, Y: Item) return Boolean;
procedure Sort(C: in out Collection);
```

The formal subprogram parameter is like a subprogram declaration preceded by **with**. (The leading **with** is necessary to avoid a syntactic ambiguity and has no other subtle purpose.)

We have also made the type Item private since the only common property now required (other than supplied through the parameters) is that the type Item can be assigned. The body remains as before.

We can now sort an array of any (unlimited) type provided that we have an appropriate comparison to supply as parameter. So in order to sort an array of our type Vector, we first instantiate thus

```
procedure Sort_Vector is
    new Sort(Integer, Real, Vector, "<");
```

and we can then apply the procedure to the array concerned

```
An_Array: Vector( ... );
...
Sort_Vector(An_Array);
```

Note carefully that our call of "<" inside Sort is actually a call of the function passed as actual parameter; in this case it is indeed the predefined function "<" anyway.

Passing the comparison rule gives our generic sort procedure amazing flexibility. We can, for example, sort in the reverse direction by

```
procedure Reverse_Sort_Vector is
    new Sort(Integer, Real, Vector, ">");
...
Reverse_Sort_Vector(An_Array);
```

This may come as a slight surprise but it is a natural consequence of the call of the formal "<" in

```
if C(J) < C(Min) then ...
```

being, after instantiation, a call of the actual ">". No confusion should arise because the internal call is hidden but the use of the named notation for instantiation would look curious

```
procedure Reverse_Sort_Vector is
                new Sort(Index    => Integer,
                         Item     => Real,
                     Collection   => Vector,
                         "<"      => ">");
```

We could also sort our second Farmyard of Section 6.5 assuming it to be a variable

```
subtype String_3 is String(1 .. 3);

procedure Sort_String_3_Array is
   new Sort(Positive, String_3, String_3_Array, "<");
...
Sort_String_3_Array(Farmyard);
```

The "<" operator passed as parameter is the predefined operation applicable to one-dimensional arrays described in Section 6.6.

The correspondence between formal and actual subprograms is such that the formal subprogram just renames the actual subprogram. Thus the matching rules regarding parameters, results and so on are as described in Section 8.5. In particular the constraints on the parameters are those of the actual subprogram and any implied by the formal subprogram are ignored. A parameterless formal function can also be matched by an enumeration literal of the result type just as for renaming.

Generic subprogram parameters (like generic object parameters) can have default values. These are given in the generic formal part and take two forms. In the above example we could write

with function "<" (X, Y: Item) **return** Boolean **is** <>;

This means that we can omit the corresponding actual parameter if there is visible at the point of *instantiation* a unique subprogram with the same designator and matching specification. With this alteration to Sort we could have omitted the last parameter in the instantiation giving Sort_Vector.

The other form of default value is where we give an explicit name for the default parameter. The usual rules for defaults apply; the default name is only evaluated if required by the instantiation but the binding of identifiers in the expression which is the name occurs at the point of *declaration* of the generic unit. In our example

with function "<" (X, Y: Item) **return** Boolean **is** Less_Than;

could never be valid because the specification of Less_Than must match that of "<" and yet the parameter Item is not known until instantiation. The only valid possibilities are where the formal subprogram has no parameters depending on formal types or the default subprogram is itself another formal parameter or an attribute. Thus we might have

with function Next(X: T) **return** T **is** T'Succ;

The same rules for mixing named and positional notation apply to generic instantiation as to subprogram calls. Hence if a parameter is omitted, subsequent parameters must be given using named notation. Of course, a generic unit need have no parameters in which case the instantiation takes the same form as for a subprogram call – the brackets are omitted.

As a final example of the use of our generic Sort (which we will assume now has a default parameter <> for "<"), we show how any type can be sorted provided we supply an appropriate rule.

Thus consider sorting an array of the type Date from Section 6.7. We write

type Date_Array **is array** (Positive **range** <>) **of** Date;

function "<" (X, Y: Date) **return** Boolean **is**
begin
  if X.Year /= Y.Year **then**
    return X.Year < Y.Year;
  elsif X.Month /= Y.Month **then**
    return X.Month < Y.Month;
  else
    return X.Day < Y.Day;
  end if;
end "<";

procedure Sort_Date_Array **is new** Sort(Positive, Date, Date_Array);

where the function "<" is passed through the default mechanism.

It might have been nicer to give our comparison rule a more appropriate name such as

function Earlier(X, Y: Date) **return** Boolean;

but we would then have to pass it as an explicit parameter; this might be considered better style anyway.

Formal subprograms can be used to supply further properties of type parameters in a quite general way. Consider the generic function Sum of the last section. We can generalize this even further by passing the adding operator itself as a generic parameter

generic
  type Index **is** (< >);
  type Item **is private**;
  type Vec **is array** (Index **range** <>) **of** Item;
  with function "+" (X, Y: Item) **return** Item;
function Apply(A: Vec) **return** Item;

function Apply(A: Vec) **return** Item **is**
  Result: Item := A(A'First);
begin
  for I **in** Index'Succ(A'First) .. A'Last **loop**
    Result := Result+A(I);
  end loop;
  return Result;
end Apply;

The operator "+" has been added as a parameter and Item is now just private and no longer floating. This means that we can apply the generic function to any binary operation on any type. However, we no longer have a zero value and so have to initialize Result with the first component of the array A and then iterate through the remainder. In doing this, remember that we cannot write

```
for I in A'First+1 .. A'Last loop
```

because the type Index may not be an integer type.

Our original function Sum of Section 7.1 is now given by

```
function Sum is new Apply(Integer, Real, Vector, "+");
```

We could equally have

```
function Prod is new Apply(Integer, Real, Vector, "*");
```

A very important use of formal subprograms is in mathematical applications such as integration. In traditional languages such as Algol and Pascal, this is done by passing subprograms as parameters to other subprograms. In Ada, subprograms can only be parameters of generic units and so we use the generic mechanism.

In Ada 9X, subprograms can indeed be parameters of other subprograms and so the traditional techniques can be used as shown in Chapter 17.

We could have a generic function

```
generic
   with function F(X: Real) return Real;
function Integrate(A, B: Real) return Real;
```

which evaluates

$$\int_a^b f(x)dx$$

In order to integrate a particular function we must instantiate Integrate with our function as actual generic parameter. Thus suppose we needed

$$\int_0^P e^t \sin t \; dt$$

We would write

```
function G(T: Real) return Real is
begin
   return Exp(T)*Sin(T);
end;

function Integrate_G is new Integrate(G);
```

and then our result is given by the expression

>   Integrate_G(0.0, P)

As we have seen the specification of the formal function could depend on preceding formal types. Thus we could extend our integration function to apply to any floating point type by writing

>   **generic**
>   **type** Floating **is digits** <>;
>   **with function** F(X: Floating) **return** Floating;
>   **function** Integrate(A, B: Floating) **return** Floating;

and then

>   **function** Integrate_G **is new** Integrate(Real, G);

In practice the function Integrate would have other parameters indicating the accuracy required and so on.

Examples such as this are often found confusing at first sight. The key point to remember is that there are two distinct levels of parameterization. First we fix the function to be integrated at instantiation and then we fix the bounds when we call the integration function thus declared. The sorting examples were similar; first we fixed the parameters defining the type of array to be sorted and the rule to be used at instantiation and then we fixed the actual array to be sorted when we called the procedure.

We conclude this section with an important philosophical remark. Generics provide an extremely powerful mechanism for parameterization. Moreover, this mechanism does not increase run-time costs because all type and subprogram identification is static. Thus Ada enables us to write reusable software of greater applicability without a penalty on run-time performance.

As we have already remarked, Ada 9X has additional dynamic capabilities whereby all type and subprogram matching is not static. This gives increased flexibility but at run-time cost. However, this cost is only incurred if the dynamic flexibility is used.

13.4   The mathematical library

EXERCISE 13.3

1   Instantiate Sort to apply to

>   **type** Poly_Array **is array** (Integer **range** < >) **of** Polynomial;

See Section 11.1. Define a sensible ordering for polynomials.

2 Instantiate Sort to apply to an array of the type Mutant of Section 11.3. Put neuter things first, then females, then males and within each class the younger first. Could we sort an array of the type Person from the same section?

3 Sort the array People of Section 6.7.

4 What happens if we attempt to sort an array of less than two components?

5 Describe how to make a generic sort procedure based on the procedure Sort of Section 11.4. It should have an identical specification to the procedure Sort of this section.

6 Instantiate Apply to give a function to "and" together all the components of a Boolean array.

7 Rewrite Apply so that a null array can be a parameter without raising an exception. Use this new version to redo the previous exercise.

8 Write a generic function Equals to define the equality of one-dimensional arrays of a limited private type. See Exercise 9.2(**4**). Instantiate it to give the function "=" applying to the type Stack_Array.

9 Given a function

> **generic**
>   **with function** F(X: Real) **return** Real;
>   **function** Solve **return** Real;

that finds a root of the equation $f(x) = 0$, show how you would find the root of

$$e^x + x = 7$$

The reader will be surprised to learn that the *LRM* says nothing about everyday mathematical functions such as Sqrt. This is in strong contrast to most languages such as Algol, Pascal and Fortran where the provision of standard mathematical functions is taken for granted.

However, the flexibility and generality of Ada is such that the specification of a suitable package is not immediately obvious. There are a number of conflicting requirements

- ease of casual use for simple calculations,
- ability to provide the ultimate in accuracy for serious numerical work,
- portability across different implementations.

Although numerical applications are in a minority, we will nevertheless consider the topic in some detail because it provides a good illustration of the use of generics and other key features of Ada.

The two packages to be described are the proposed ISO standard (DIS 11430). They were developed by the Ada-Europe and SIGAda working groups on Ada Numerics.

First there is an auxiliary package containing a single exception which is raised under appropriate circumstances. It has no body.

```
package Elementary_Functions_Exceptions is
   Argument_Error: exception;
end Elementary_Functions_Exceptions;
```

The main package is a generic package containing the mathematical functions themselves. Its specification is as follows

```
with Elementary_Functions_Exceptions;
generic
   type Float_Type is digits <>;
package Generic_Elementary_Functions is

   function Sqrt (X:            Float_Type) return Float_Type;
   function Log (X:             Float_Type) return Float_Type;
   function Log (X, Base:       Float_Type) return Float_Type;
   function Exp (X:             Float_Type) return Float_Type;
   function "**" (Left, Right:  Float_Type) return Float_Type;

   function Sin (X:             Float_Type) return Float_Type;
   function Sin (X, Cycle:      Float_Type) return Float_Type;
   function Cos (X:             Float_Type) return Float_Type;
   function Cos (X, Cycle:      Float_Type) return Float_Type;
   function Tan (X:             Float_Type) return Float_Type;
   function Tan (X, Cycle:      Float_Type) return Float_Type;
   function Cot (X:             Float_Type) return Float_Type;
   function Cot (X, Cycle:      Float_Type) return Float_Type;
   function Arcsin (X:          Float_Type) return Float_Type;
   function Arcsin (X, Cycle:   Float_Type) return Float_Type;
   function Arccos (X:          Float_Type) return Float_Type;
   function Arccos (X, Cycle:   Float_Type) return Float_Type;
   function Arctan (Y:          Float_Type; X: Float_Type := 1.0)
                                                     return Float_Type;
   function Arctan (Y: Float_Type; X: Float_Type := 1.0;
                             Cycle: Float_Type) return Float_Type;
   function Arccot (X: Float_Type; Y: Float_Type := 1.0)
                                                     return Float_Type;
   function Arccot (X: Float_Type; Y: Float_Type := 1.0;
                             Cycle: Float_Type) return Float_Type;

   function Sinh (X: Float_Type) return  Float_Type;
   function Cosh (X: Float_Type) return Float_Type;
   function Tanh (X: Float_Type) return Float_Type;
   function Coth (X: Float_Type) return  Float_Type;
   function Arcsinh (X: Float_Type) return   Float_Type;
   function Arccosh (X: Float_Type) return   Float_Type;
   function Arctanh (X: Float_Type) return   Float_Type;
   function Arccoth (X: Float_Type) return   Float_Type;

   Argument_Error: exception
      renames Elementary_Functions_Exceptions.Argument_Error;

end Generic_Elementary_Functions;
```

The single generic parameter is the floating type. The package might be instantiated with a predefined type such as Float or Long_Float but hopefully more likely with a user's own type such as Real

```
package Real_Elementary_Functions is
   new Generic_Elementary_Functions(Real);
```

The body could then choose an implementation appropriate to the accuracy of the user's type through the attribute Float_Type'Digits rather than necessarily using the accuracy of the predefined type from which the user's type has been derived. This could have significant timing advantages.

There is, however, a problem if the user has instantiated the package with a subtype such as

```
subtype Normal is Float range −1.0 .. +1.0;
```

which might occur if the user was dealing with data which was known to be in such a range. Now the body of the package will undoubtedly declare working variables for use in the algorithms and these will inevitably be declared simply as of the formal type Float_Type. Unfortunately these variables will have the constraints from the user's subtype and as a consequence even though the data and potential result of a function may be in range nevertheless some intermediate value might fall outside the range and cause Constraint_Error. It is therefore advisable not to instantiate the package with such a subtype and indeed some implementations may forbid this anyway.

The reader might wonder why the implementation could not declare a working type

```
type Local is digits Float_Type'Base'Digits;
```

in order to get back to the underlying type. Unfortunately this is not allowed because attributes of generic parameters are not static and the expression after **digits** must be static.

This difficulty is overcome in Ada 9X since we are allowed to use the attribute Base on its own as we mentioned in Section 12.1. We can therefore declare local variables of type Float_Type'Base. In fact in the Ada 9X version of this package all parameters and results are themselves of Float_Type'Base.

We continue by considering the individual functions in the package. The functions Sqrt and Exp need little comment except perhaps concerning exceptions. Calling Sqrt with a negative parameter will raise Argument_Error whereas calling Exp with a large parameter will raise Constraint_Error.

The general principle is that intrinsic mathematical restrictions raise Argument_Error whereas implementation range restrictions raise Constraint_Error.

Observe that the exception Argument_Error is declared in a separate non-generic package. This means that there is only one such exception which applies to all instantiations of the main package. The renaming declaration enables us to refer to the exception without reference to the package Elementary_Functions_Exceptions. We will meet this technique again when we discuss input–output in Chapter 15.

There are two overloadings of Log. That with a single parameter gives the natural logarithm to base *e*, whereas that with two parameters allows us to choose any base at all. Thus to find $\log_{10}2$, we write

    Log(2.0, 10.0)   – – 0.3010...

The reader may wonder why there is not just a single function with a default parameter thus

     function Log(X: Float_Type; Base: Float_Type :=
                       2.71828_18284_59045...) **return** Float_Type;

which would seem to give the desired result with less fuss. The reason concerns obtaining the ultimate in precision. Passing a default parameter means that the accuracy of the value of *e* used can only be that of the Float_Type. Using a separate function enables the function body to obtain the benefit of the full accuracy of a universal real named number (declared in the body of the package).

The restrictions on the parameters of Log are X > 0.0, Base > 0.0 and also Base /= 1.0. So Base could be 0.5 which is an amusing thought.

The function "**" effectively extends the predefined operator to allow non-integral exponents. Consequently the formal parameters are Left and Right to match (the other functions follow mathematical convention and use X and Y). The parameter Left must not be negative.

The trigonometric functions Sin, Cos, Tan and Cot also come in pairs like Log and for a similar reason. The single parameter versions assume the parameter is in radians whereas the second parameter allows the use of any unit by giving the number of units in a whole cycle. Thus to find the sine of 30 degrees, we write

    Sin(30.0, 360.0)   – – 0.5

because there are 360 degrees in a cycle.

In these functions the single parameter versions enable the highly accurate number Two_Pi to be used directly rather than being passed with less accuracy as a parameter.

Of the inverse functions, Arcsin and Arccos need no comment. However, Arctan has a default value of 1.0 for a second parameter (the Cycle then being third). This enables us to call Arctan with two parameters giving the classical *x*- and *y*-coordinates (thus fully identifying the quadrant). So

     Arctan(Y => –1.0, X => +1.0)   – – –Pi/4
     Arctan(Y => +1.0, X =>–1.0)   – – +3*Pi/4

Note carefully that the first parameter of Arctan is Y since it is the *x*-coordinate that is taken to be 1.0 by default. Arccot is very similar except that the parameters are naturally in the other order.

There are no obvious comments to make on the hyperbolic functions.

We now turn to an interesting illustration of the use of default subprogram parameters for conveniently passing properties of generic types. Although the example is of a rather mathematical nature it is hoped that the general principles will be appreciated. It follows on from the above elementary functions package and concerns the provision of similar functions but working on complex arguments. Suppose we want to provide the ability to compute Sqrt, Log, Exp, Sin and Cos with functions such as

```
function Sqrt(X: Complex_Type) return Complex_Type;
```

Many readers will have forgotten that this can be done or perhaps never knew. It is not necessary to dwell on the details of how such calculations are performed or their use; the main point is to concentrate on the principles involved. These computations use various operations on the real numbers out of which the complex numbers are formed. Our goal is to write a generic package which works however the complex numbers are implemented (cartesian or polar) and also allows any floating point type as the basis for the underlying real numbers.

Here are the formulae which we will need to compute.

Taking, $z \equiv x + iy \equiv r(\cos \theta + i \sin \theta)$, as the argument:

$$\text{sqrt } z = \sqrt{r} \,(\cos \theta/2 + i \sin \theta/2)$$
$$\log z = \log r + i \,\theta$$
$$\exp z = e^x(\cos y + i \sin y)$$
$$\sin z = \sin x \cosh y + i \cos x \sinh y$$
$$\cos z = \cos x \cosh y - i \sin x \sinh y$$

We thus see that we will need functions to decompose the complex number into both cartesian and polar forms plus Sqrt, Cos, Sin, Log, Exp, Cosh and Sinh applying to the underlying floating type. We also need to be able to put the result together from both cartesian and polar forms.

Our package Generic_Complex_Numbers (see Sections 9.1 and 13.2) is a good starting point. However, it only gives a cartesian view of a complex number and so needs augmenting with additional functions to provide a polar view. We will assume that this has been done and that the extra visible functions are

```
function Cons_Polar (R, Theta: Real) return Complex;
function "abs" (X: Complex) return Real;
function Arg (X: Complex) return Real;
```

The package Generic_Elementary_Functions described above provides all the operations we need on the underlying floating type. Now consider

```
generic
   type Real_Type is digits <>;
   type Complex_Type is private;
```

```
with function Cons(R, I: Real_Type) return Complex_Type is <>;
with function Cons_Polar(R, Theta: Real_Type) return
                                          Complex_Type is <>;
with function Rl_Part(X: Complex_Type) return Real_Type is <>;
with function Im_Part(X: Complex_Type) return Real_Type is <>;
with function "abs" (X: Complex_Type) return Real_Type is <>;
with function Arg (X: Complex_Type) return Real_Type is <>;

with function Sqrt (X: Real_Type) return Real_Type is <>;
with function Log (X: Real_Type) return Real_Type is <>;
with function Exp (X: Real_Type) return Real_Type is <>;
with function Sin (X: Real_Type) return Real_Type is <>;
with function Cos (X: Real_Type) return Real_Type is <>;
with function Sinh (X: Real_Type) return Real_Type is <>;
with function Cosh (X: Real_Type) return Real_Type is <>;

package Generic_Complex_Functions is

    function Sqrt(X: Complex_Type) return Complex_Type;
    function Log (X: Complex_Type) return Complex_Type;
    function Exp (X: Complex_Type) return Complex_Type;
    function Sin (X: Complex_Type) return Complex_Type;
    function Cos (X: Complex_Type) return Complex_Type;

end Generic_Complex_Functions;
```

This generic package looks extremely tedious to use. Apart from the obviously necessary parameters Real_Type and Complex_Type, it has 13 other functions as parameters. However, we note that they all have the default form <>. So, if at the point of instantiation, by good luck or careful planning, we happen to have all the functions visible with the correct names and matching types then we need not mention them in the instantiation. In other words we can pass all the properties of the types on the sly.

So we could write

```
type My_Real is digits 9;

package My_Elementary_Functions is
    new Generic_Elementary_Functions(Float_Type => My_Real);

package My_Complex_Numbers is
    new Generic_Complex_Numbers(Real => My_Real);

use My_Elementary_Functions, My_Complex_Numbers;

package My_Complex_Functions is
    new Generic_Complex_Functions(My_Real, Complex);

use My_Complex_Functions;
```

and *Hey presto!* it all works. Note that irritatingly the complex type is just Complex and not My_Complex. We could remedy this using a subtype or derived type as we did for the type Colour and the package Set_Of in Section

13.2. Another point to note is that we have to write the use clause for My_Elementary_Functions and My_Complex_Numbers before the instantiation of Generic_Complex_Functions otherwise the various exported functions would not be directly visible.

Of course it was not entirely an accident that the parameters matched. But if one of them had not then it could have been explicitly provided. For example the formal parameter for constructing a complex number from its cartesian form might have had the better name Cons_Cartesian rather than the rather abbreviated Cons. If that had been the case then the instantiation could be

```
package My_Complex_Functions is
  new Generic_Complex_Functions(My_Real, Complex, Cons_Cartesian
                                                      => Cons);
```

where we have used named notation for the extra parameter, although by coincidence it comes next anyway.

Another way to overcome the mismatch is to use renaming. This works because, as mentioned earlier, the matching of actual to formal generic subprogram parameters is defined in terms of renaming anyway. This is a bit tedious because the parameters and result type have to be written out in full and so we leave this as an exercise.

It should also be noted that matching would not have been possible at all if only a single (two parameter) function with default parameter had been provided for Log, Sin and so on in the package Generic_Elementary_Functions. Matching requires that the number of parameters be the same irrespective of any defaults.

As a final point, the astute reader may have realized that adding the polar functions to our package Generic_Complex_Numbers means that its body also needs access to some of the elementary functions applied to the underlying floating type. These can be provided via default parameters in a similar way.

A completely different approach to the whole exercise which applies to both Generic_Complex_Functions itself as well as to Generic_Complex_Numbers is to instantiate the elementary functions inside the bodies so that we do not have to pass the functions as parameters. This works but will result in wasteful and unnecessary multiple instantiations especially since we may well need them at the user level anyway. A possible advantage, however, is that there is then no risk that the wrong function is passed by default which would happen if the user were foolish enough to redeclare perhaps Log to have a completely different meaning (which might be something to do with logging a result). This would be both unfortunate and unlikely.

It is hoped that the general principles have been understood and that the mathematics has not clouded the issues. The principles are important but not easily illustrated with short examples. It should also be noted that although the package Generic_Elementary_Functions described above is exactly as the proposed standard, the complex number packages are just an illustration of how generics can be used.

Ada 9X has an additional mechanism whereby an instantiation of a generic package can be a parameter of a further generic package. This enables a

package such as Generic_Complex_Functions to be written in a much simpler
manner without the convoluted default parameters we have described. For
further details see Chapter 17.

Note also that Ada 9X does indeed define standard packages for complex
numbers and functions; they include rather more functions than we have
provided in our simple illustration.

EXERCISE 13.4

1   Write a body for the package Simple_Maths of Exercise 2.2(**1**) using an instantiation
    of Generic_Elementary_Functions. Raise Constraint_Error for all exceptional
    circumstances.

2   Write a body for the package Generic_Complex_Functions using the formulae defined
    above. Ignore exceptions.

3   Write the renaming of Cons required to overcome the parameter mismatch discussed
    above.

4   Rewrite the package Generic_Complex_Numbers adding the extra generic parameters
    to supply the required elementary functions. Implement the type Complex in cartesian
    form.

CHECKLIST 13

The generic mechanism is not text replacement; non-local name binding
would be different.

Object '**in out**' parameters are bound by renaming.

Object '**in**' parameters are always copied unlike parameters of
subprograms.

Subprogram generic parameters are bound by renaming.

Generic subprograms may not overload – only the instantiations can.

Generic subprograms always have a separate specification and body.

Formal parameters (and defaults) may depend upon preceding
parameters.

Generic formal parameters and their attributes are not static.

14 Tasking

The final major topic to be introduced is tasking. This has been left to the end, not because it is unimportant or particularly difficult, but because, apart from the interaction with exceptions, it is a fairly self contained part of the language.

14.1 Parallelism

So far we have only considered sequential programs in which statements are obeyed in order. In many applications it is convenient to write a program as several parallel activities which cooperate as necessary. This is particularly true of programs which interact in real time with physical processes in the real world, simulation programs (which mimic parallel activities in the real world), and programs which wish to exploit multiprocessor architectures directly.

In Ada, parallel activities are described by means of tasks. In simple cases a task is lexically described by a form very similar to a package. This consists of a specification describing the interface presented to other tasks and a body describing the dynamic behaviour of the task.

```
task T is        - - specification
   ...
end T;

task body T is   - - body
   ...
end T;
```

In some cases a task presents no interface to other tasks in which case the specification reduces to just

```
task T;
```

As a simple example of parallelism, consider a family going shopping to buy ingredients for a meal. Suppose they need meat, salad and wine and that the purchase of these items can be done by calling procedures Buy_Meat, Buy_Salad and Buy_Wine respectively. The whole expedition could be represented by

```
procedure Shopping is
begin
   Buy_Meat;
   Buy_Salad;
   Buy_Wine;
end;
```

However, this solution corresponds to the family buying each item in sequence. It would be far more efficient for them to split up so that, for example, mother buys the meat, the children buy the salad and father buys the wine. They agree to meet again perhaps in the car park. This parallel solution can be represented by

```
procedure Shopping is
   task Get_Salad;

   task body Get_Salad is
   begin
      Buy_Salad;
   end Get_Salad;
```

```
    task Get_Wine;

    task body Get_Wine is
    begin
        Buy_Wine;
    end Get_Wine;

begin
    Buy_Meat;
end Shopping;
```

In this formulation, mother is represented as the main processor and calls Buy_Meat directly from the procedure Shopping. The children and father are considered as subservient processors and perform the locally declared tasks Get_Salad and Get_Wine which respectively call the procedures Buy_Salad and Buy_Wine.

The example illustrates the declaration, activation and termination of tasks. A task is a program component like a package and is declared in a similar way inside a subprogram, block, package or indeed another task body. A task specification can also be declared in a package specification in which case the task body must be declared in the corresponding package body. However, a task specification cannot be declared in the specification of another task but only in the body.

The activation of a task is automatic. In the above example the local tasks become active when the parent unit reaches the **begin** following the task declaration.

Such a task will terminate when it reaches its final **end**. Thus the task Get_Salad calls the procedure Buy_Salad and then promptly terminates.

A task declared in the declarative part of a subprogram, block or task body is said to depend on that unit. It is an important rule that a unit cannot be left until all dependent tasks have terminated. This termination rule ensures that objects declared in the unit and therefore potentially visible to local tasks cannot disappear while there exists a task which could access them. (Note that a task cannot depend on a package – we will return to this later.)

It is important to realize that the main program is itself considered to be called by a hypothetical main task. We can now trace the sequence of actions when this main task calls the procedure Shopping. First the tasks Get_Salad and Get_Wine are declared and then when the main task reaches the **begin** these dependent tasks are set active in parallel with the main task. The dependent tasks call their respective procedures and terminate. Meanwhile the main task calls Buy_Meat and then reaches the **end** of Shopping. The main task then waits until the dependent tasks have terminated if they have not already done so. This corresponds to mother waiting for father and children to return with their purchases.

In the general case termination therefore occurs in two stages. We say that a unit is completed when it reaches its final **end**. It will subsequently become terminated only when all dependent tasks, if any, are also terminated. Of course, if a unit has no dependent tasks then it effectively becomes completed and terminated at the same time (but see Section 14.7).

EXERCISE 14.1

1   Rewrite procedure Shopping to contain three local tasks so that the symmetry of the situation is revealed.

14.2   The rendezvous

In the Shopping example the various tasks did not interact with each other once they had been set active except that their parent unit had to wait for them to terminate. Generally, however, tasks will interact with each other during their lifetime. In Ada this is done by a mechanism known as a rendezvous. This is similar to the human situation where two people meet, perform a transaction and then go on independently.

A rendezvous between two tasks occurs as a consequence of one task calling an entry declared in another. An entry is declared in a task specification in a similar way to a procedure in a package specification

```
task T is
    entry E( ... );
end;
```

An entry can have **in**, **out** and **in out** parameters in the same way as a procedure. It cannot however have a result like a function. An entry is called in a similar way to a procedure

```
T.E( ... );
```

A task name cannot appear in a use clause and so the dotted notation is necessary to call the entry from outside the task. Of course, a local task could call an entry of its parent directly – the usual scope and visibility rules apply.

The statements to be obeyed during a rendezvous are described by corresponding accept statements in the body of the task containing the declaration of the entry. An accept statement usually takes the form

```
accept E( ... ) do
    – – sequence of statements
end E;
```

The formal parameters of the entry E are repeated in the same way that a procedure body repeats the formal parameters of a corresponding procedure declaration. The **end** is optionally followed by the name of the entry. A

significant difference is that the body of the accept statement is just a sequence
of statements. Any local declarations or exception handlers must be provided
by writing a local block.

Note that the situation in Ada 9X is slightly different: exception handlers
are permitted as part of an accept statement but an inner block is still required
for declarations.

The most important difference between an entry call and a procedure call
is that in the case of a procedure, the task that calls the procedure also
immediately executes the procedure body whereas in the case of an entry, one
task calls the entry but the corresponding accept statement is executed by the
task owning the entry. Moreover, the accept statement cannot be executed
until a task calls the entry and the task owning the entry reaches the accept
statement. Naturally one of these will occur first and the task concerned will
then be suspended until the other reaches its corresponding statement. When
this occurs the sequence of statements of the accept statement is executed by
the called task while the calling task remains suspended. This interaction is
called a rendezvous. When the end of the accept statement is reached the
rendezvous is completed and both tasks then proceed independently. The
parameter mechanism is exactly as for a subprogram call; note that
expressions in the actual parameter list are evaluated before the call is issued.

We can elaborate our shopping example by giving the task Get_Salad two
entries, one for mother to hand the children the money for the salad and one to
collect the salad from them afterwards. We do the same for Get_Wine
(although perhaps father has his own funds in which case he might keep the
wine to himself anyway).

We can also replace the procedures Buy_Salad, Buy_Wine and Buy_Meat
by functions which take money as a parameter and return the appropriate
ingredient. Our shopping procedure might now become

```
procedure Shopping is
  task Get_Salad is
    entry Pay(M: in Money);
    entry Collect(S: out Salad);
  end Get_Salad;

  task body Get_Salad is
    Cash: Money;
    Food: Salad;
  begin
    accept Pay(M: in Money) do
      Cash := M;
    end Pay;

    Food := Buy_Salad(Cash);

    accept Collect(S: out Salad) do
      S := Food;
    end Collect;
  end Get_Salad;

  - - Get_Wine similarly
```

```
begin
   Get_Salad.Pay(50);
   Get_Wine.Pay(100);
   MM := Buy_Meat(200);
   Get_Salad.Collect(SS);
   Get_Wine.Collect(WW);
end Shopping;
```

The final outcome is that the various ingredients end up in the variables MM, SS and WW whose declarations are left to the imagination.

The logical behaviour should be noted. As soon as the tasks Get_Salad and Get_Wine become active they encounter accept statements and wait until the main task calls the entries Pay in each of them. After calling the function Buy_Meat, the main task calls the Collect entries. Curiously, mother is unable to collect the wine until after she has collected the salad from the children.

As a more abstract example consider the problem of providing a task to act as a single buffer between one or more tasks producing items and one or more tasks consuming them. Our intermediate task can hold just one item

```
task Buffering is
   entry Put(X: in Item);
   entry Get(X: out Item);
end;

task body Buffering is
   V: Item;
begin
   loop
      accept Put(X: in Item) do
         V := X;
      end Put;
      accept Get(X: out Item) do
         X := V;
      end Get;
   end loop;
end Buffering;
```

Other tasks may then dispose of or acquire items by calling

```
Buffering.Put( ... );
Buffering.Get( ... );
```

Intermediate storage for the item is the variable V. The body of the task is an endless loop which contains an accept statement for Put followed by one for Get. Thus the task alternately accepts calls of Put and Get which fill and empty the variable V.

Several different tasks may call Put and Get and consequently may have to be queued. Every entry has a queue of tasks waiting to call the entry – this queue is processed in a first-in–first-out manner and may, of course, be empty at a particular moment. The number of tasks on the queue of entry E is given by E'Count but this attribute may only be used inside the body of the task owning the entry.

An entry may have several corresponding accept statements (usually only one). Each execution of an accept statement removes one task from the queue.

Note the asymmetric naming in a rendezvous. The calling task must name the called task but not vice versa. Moreover, several tasks may call an entry and be queued but a task can only be on one queue at a time.

Entries may be overloaded both with each other and with subprograms and obey the same rules. An entry may be renamed as a procedure

    procedure Write(X: **in** Item) **renames** Buffering.Put;

This mechanism may be useful in avoiding excessive use of the dotted notation. An entry, renamed or not, may be an actual or default generic parameter corresponding to a formal subprogram.

An entry may have no parameters, such as

    entry Signal;

and it could then be called by

    T.Signal;

An accept statement need have no body as in

    accept Signal;

In such a case the purpose of the call is merely to effect a synchronization and not to pass information. However, an entry without parameters can have an accept statement with a body and vice versa. There is nothing to prevent us writing

    accept Signal **do**
      Fire;
    end;

in which case the task calling Signal is only allowed to continue after the call of Fire is completed. We could also have

    accept Put(X: Item);

although clearly the parameter value is not used.

There are few constraints on the statements in an accept statement. They may include entry calls, subprogram calls, blocks and further accept statements (but not for the same entry or one of the same family – see Section 14.8). On the other hand an accept statement may not appear in a subprogram body but must be in the sequence of statements of the task although it could be in a block or other accept statement. The execution of a **return** statement in an accept statement corresponds to reaching the final end and therefore terminates the rendezvous. Similarly to a subprogram body, a **goto** or **exit** statement cannot transfer control out of an accept statement.

A task may call one of its own entries but, of course, will promptly deadlock. This may seem foolish but programming languages allow lots of silly things such as endless loops and so on. We could expect a good compiler to warn us of obvious potential deadlocks.

This is a good moment to mention that, broadly speaking, there are two sorts of interaction problems in tasking. One is typified by the shopping example where the tasks need to communicate with each other by passing messages of some sort (the money and ingredients in that example). The other situation is typified by the buffering example where a shared resource (the variable V) is protected from arbitrary access by several tasks at a time by some protocol. Ada 83 uses the rendezvous to solve both classes of problem. However, it should be observed that Ada 9X introduces a completely new paradigm, the protected object, to solve shared resource problems. Protected objects avoid the need for additional slave tasks and have a number of other advantages which are discussed in Chapter 17.

EXERCISE 14.2

1 Write the body of a task whose specification is

```
task Build_Complex is
   entry Put_RI(X: in Real);
   entry Put_Im(X: in Real);
   entry Get_Comp(X: out Complex);
end;
```

and which alternately puts together a complex number from calls of Put_RI and Put_Im and then delivers the result on a call of Get_Comp.

2 Write the body of a task whose specification is

```
task Char_To_Line is
   entry Put(C: in Character);
   entry Get(L: out Line);
end;
```

where

```
type Line is array (1 .. 80) of Character;
```

The task acts as a buffer which alternately builds up a line by accepting successive calls of Put and then delivers a complete line on a call of Get.

14.3   Timing and scheduling

As we have seen, an Ada program may contain several tasks. Conceptually, it is best to think of these tasks as each having its own personal processor so that, provided a task is not waiting for something to happen, it will actually be executing.

In practice, of course, most implementations will not be able to allocate a unique processor to each task and indeed, in many cases, there will be only one physical processor. It will then be necessary to allocate the processor(s) to the tasks that are logically able to execute by some scheduling algorithm. This can be done in many ways.

One of the simplest mechanisms is to use time slicing. This means giving the processor to each task in turn for some fixed time interval such as 10 milliseconds. Of course, if a task cannot use its turn (perhaps because it is held up awaiting a partner in a rendezvous), then a sensible scheduler would allocate its turn to the next task. Similarly, if a task cannot use all of its turn then the remaining time could be allocated to another task.

Time slicing is somewhat rudimentary since it treats all tasks equally. It is often the case that some tasks are more urgent than others and in the face of a shortage of processing power this equality is a bit wasteful. The idea of a task having a priority is therefore introduced. A simple scheduling system would be one where each task had a distinct priority and the processor would then be given to the highest priority task which could actually run. Combinations of time slicing and priority scheduling are also possible. A system might permit several tasks to have the same priority and time slice between them.

Ada allows various scheduling strategies to be used. If an implementation has the concept of priority, then the priority of a task can be indicated by a pragma appearing somewhere in the task specification as for example

```
    task Buffering is
        pragma Priority(7);
        entry Put ...
        ...
    end;
```

In the case of the main program, which, as we have seen, is also considered to be a task, the pragma goes in its outermost declarative part.

The priority must be a static expression of the subtype Priority of the type Integer but the actual range of the subtype Priority depends upon the implementation. Note that the priority of a task is static and therefore cannot be changed in the course of execution of the program. A larger priority indicates a higher degree of urgency. Several tasks can have the same priority but on the other hand a task need not have an explicit priority at all.

The effect of priorities on the scheduling of Ada tasks is given by the following rule taken from the *LRM*.

'If two tasks with different priorities are both eligible for execution and could sensibly be executed using the same physical processors and the same other processing resources, then it cannot be the case that the task with the lower priority is executing while the task with the higher priority is not.'

Basically this says that scheduling must be preemptive – a higher priority task *always* preempts a lower priority task. This rule has been misinterpreted but AI-32 confirms that preemption is mandatory.

However, this rule says nothing about tasks whose priorities are not defined nor does it say anything about tasks with the same priority. The implementation is therefore free to do whatever seems appropriate in these cases. Moreover, nothing prevents an implementation from having Priority'First = Priority'Last in which case all tasks could be time sliced equally and the concept of priority disappears. The rule also contains the phrase 'could sensibly be executed using the same ... processing resources'; this is directed towards distributed systems where it may not be at all sensible for a processor in one part of the system to be used to execute a task in a different part of the system.

In the case of a rendezvous (and activation, to be discussed later), a complication arises because two tasks are involved. If both tasks have explicit priorities, the rendezvous is executed with the higher priority. If only one task has an explicit priority then the rendezvous is executed with at least that priority. If neither task has a defined priority then the priority of the rendezvous is not defined. Of course, if the accept statement contains a further entry call or accept statement then the rules are applied once more.

The rendezvous rules ensure that a high priority task is not held up just because it is engaged in a rendezvous with a low priority task. On the other hand, the order of accepting the tasks in an entry queue is always first-in-first-out and is not affected by priorities. If a high priority task wishes to guard against being held up because of lower priority tasks in the same entry queue, it can always use timed out or conditional calls as we shall see in the next section.

The use of priorities needs care. They are intended as a means of adjusting relative degrees of urgency and should not be used for synchronization. It should not be assumed that the execution of task A precludes the execution of task B just because task A has a higher priority than task B. There might be several processors or later program maintenance might result in a change of priorities because of different realtime requirements. Synchronization should be done with the rendezvous and priorities should be avoided except for fine tuning of responsiveness.

The priority rules of Ada 83 have been criticized for being too rigid and causing so-called priority inversion. However, Ada 9X allows greater flexibility and special regimes may be implemented.

A task may be held up for various reasons; it might be waiting for a partner in a rendezvous or for a dependent task to terminate. It can also be held up by executing a delay statement such as

delay 3.0;

This suspends the task (or main program) executing the statement for three seconds. The expression after the reserved word **delay** is of a predefined fixed point type Duration and gives the period in seconds. (The *LRM* says the task is suspended for 'at least' the duration specified. This is solely because, after the expiry of the interval, there might not be a processor immediately available to execute the task since in the meantime a higher priority task might have obtained control. It does not mean that the scheduler can leave the suspended task rotting indefinitely. If it has a higher priority than a task running when the interval expires then it will preempt.)

The type Duration is a fixed point type so that the addition of durations can be done without systematic loss of accuracy. If we add together two fixed point model numbers, we always get another model number; this does not apply to floating point. On the other hand, we need to express fractions of a second in a convenient way and so the use of a real type rather than an integer type is much more satisfactory.

Delays can be more easily expressed by using suitable constant declarations, thus

```
Seconds: constant Duration := 1.0;
Minutes: constant Duration := 60.0;
Hours: constant Duration := 3600.0;
```

We can then write for example

```
delay 2*Hours+40*Minutes;
```

in which the expression uses the rule that a fixed point value can be multiplied by an integer giving a result of the same fixed point type.

A delay statement with a zero or negative argument has no effect.

Although the type Duration is implementation defined we are guaranteed that it will allow durations (both positive and negative) of up to at least one day (86400 seconds). Delays of more than a day (which are unusual) would have to be programmed with a loop. At the other end of the scale, the smallest value of Duration, that is Duration'Small, is guaranteed to be not greater than 20 milliseconds. This should not be confused with System'Tick which gives the basic clock cycle and is, for example, and as confirmed by AI-201, the accuracy with which a delay statement must be executed (as opposed to being requested).

More sophisticated timing operations can be performed by using the predefined package Calendar whose specification is

```
package Calendar is

  type Time is private;

  subtype Year_Number is Integer range 1901 .. 2099;
  subtype Month_Number is Integer range 1 .. 12;
  subtype Day_Number is Integer range 1 .. 31;
  subtype Day_Duration is Duration range 0.0 .. 86_400.0;

  function Clock return Time;

  function Year(Date: Time) return Year_Number;
```

```
function Month(Date: Time) return Month_Number;
function Day(Date: Time) return Day_Number;
function Seconds(Date: Time) return Day_Duration;

procedure Split(Date: in Time;
                Year: out Year_Number;
                Month: out Month_Number;
                Day: out Day_Number;
                Seconds: out Day_Duration);

function Time_Of(Year: Year_Number;
                 Month: Month_Number;
                 Day: Day_Number;
                 Seconds: Day_Duration := 0.0) return Time;

function "+" (Left: Time; Right: Duration) return Time;
function "+" (Left: Duration; Right: Time) return Time;
function "−" (Left: Time; Right: Duration) return Time;
function "−" (Left: Time; Right: Time) return Duration;
function "<" (Left, Right: Time) return Boolean;
function "<=" (Left, Right: Time) return Boolean;
function ">" (Left, Right: Time) return Boolean;
function ">=" (Left, Right: Time) return Boolean;

Time_Error: exception;
            − − can be raised by Time_Of, +, and −

private
    − − implementation dependent
end Calendar;
```

A value of the private type Time is a combined time and date; it can be decomposed into the year, month, day and the duration since midnight of the day concerned by the procedure Split. Alternatively the functions Year, Month, Day and Seconds may be used to obtain the individual values. On the other hand, the function Time_Of can be used to build a value of Time from the four constituents; the seconds parameter has a default of zero. Note the subtypes Year_Number, Month_Number and Day_Number; the range of Year_Number is such that the leap year calculation is simplified. The exception Time_Error is raised if the parameters of Time_Of satisfy the constraints but nevertheless do not form a proper date. A careful distinction must be made between Time and Duration. Time is absolute but Duration is relative.

The current Time is returned by a call of the function Clock. The result is, of course, returned in an indivisible way and there is no risk of getting the time of day and the date inconsistent around midnight as there would be if there were separate functions delivering the individual components of the current time and date.

The various overloadings of "+", "−" and the relational operators allow us to add, subtract and compare times and durations as appropriate. Attempts to create a time outside the allowed range of years or to create a duration outside the implemented range will result in Time_Error being raised. Note the strange

formal parameter names Left and Right; these are the normal names for the
parameters of the predefined operators in the package Standard.

As an example of the use of the package Calendar suppose we wish a task
to call a procedure Action at regular intervals, every five minutes perhaps. Our
first attempt might be to write

```
loop
   delay 5*Minutes;
   Action;
end loop;
```

However, this is unsatisfactory for various reasons. First, we have not
taken account of the time of execution of the procedure Action and the
overhead of the loop itself, and secondly, we have seen that a delay statement
sets a minimum delay only (since a higher priority task may retain the
processor on the expiry of the delay). Furthermore, we might get preempted by
a higher priority task at any time anyway. So we will inevitably get a
cumulative timing drift. This can be overcome by writing for example

```
declare
   use Calendar;
   Interval: constant Duration := 5*Minutes;
   Next_Time: Time := First_Time;
begin
   loop
      delay Next_Time – Clock;
      Action;
      Next_Time := Next_Time + Interval;
   end loop;
end;
```

In this formulation Next_Time contains the time when Action is next to be
called; its initial value is in First_Time and it is updated exactly on each
iteration by adding Interval. The delay statement is then used to delay by the
difference between Next_Time and the current time obtained by calling Clock.
This solution will have no cumulative drift provided the mean duration of
Action plus the overheads of the loop and updating Next_Time and so on do
not exceed Interval. Of course, there may be a local drift if a particular call of
Action takes a long time or other tasks temporarily use the processors. Note
especially that an unbounded amount of local drift could occur if we were very
unlucky and the task was temporarily suspended between the call of Clock and
the actual issue of the delay statement; the delay would be incorrect by the
amount of time for which the task did not have a processor. In effect, we have
a race condition. Finally, there is one other condition that must be satisfied for
the required timing to be obtained: the interval has to be a safe number.

The nasty race condition can be avoided in Ada 9X by the use of a
variation of the delay statement. This takes the form

```
delay until Next_Time;
```

::: ::: where the expression after **delay until** is of the type Time. This works perfectly.
::: A very pedantic point is that the Ada 9X description of fixed point does
not use the concept of safe numbers. However, the message is the same, the
interval has to be exactly represented.

EXERCISE 14.3

1 Write a generic procedure to call a procedure regularly. The generic parameters
should be the procedure to be called, the time of the first call, the interval and the
number of calls. If the time of the first call passed as parameter is in the past use the
current time as the first time.

2 What is the least number of bits required to implement the type Duration?

14.4   Simple select statements

The select statement allows a task to select from one of several possible
rendezvous.
Consider the problem of protecting a variable V from uncontrolled access.
We might consider using a package and two procedures Read and Write

```
package Protected_Variable is
   procedure Read(X: out Item);
   procedure Write(X: in Item);
end;

package body Protected_Variable is
   V: Item;

   procedure Read(X: out Item) is
   begin
      X := V;
   end;

   procedure Write(X: in Item) is
   begin
      V := X;
   end;

begin
   V := initial value;
end Protected_Variable;
```

However this is generally unsatisfactory. For one thing, the initial value is
set in a rather arbitrary way. It would be better if somehow we could ensure
that a call of Write had to be done first. We could, of course, have an internal

state marker and raise an exception if Read is called first but this complicates
the interface. The major problem, however, is that nothing prevents different
tasks in our system from calling Read and Write simultaneously and thereby
causing interference. As a more specific example, suppose that the type Item is
a record giving the coordinates of an aircraft or ship

```
type Item is
   record
      X_Coord: Real;
      Y_Coord: Real;
   end record;
```

Suppose that a task A acquires pairs of values and uses a call of Write to store
them into V and that another task B calls Read whenever it needs the latest
position. Now assume that A is halfway through executing Write when it is
interrupted by task B which promptly calls Read. It is clear that B could get a
value consisting of the new x-coordinate and the old y-coordinate which would
no doubt represent a location where the vessel had never been. The use of such
inconsistent data for calculating the heading of the vessel from regularly read
pairs of readings would obviously lead to inaccuracies.

The reader may wonder how the task A could be interrupted by task B
anyway. In a single processor system with time slicing it may merely have
been that B's turn came at an unfortunate moment. Alternatively B might have
a higher priority than A; if B had been waiting for time to elapse before taking
the next reading by obeying a delay statement, then A might be allowed to
execute and B's delay might expire just at the wrong moment. In practical
realtime situations things are always happening at the wrong moment!

The proper solution is to use a task rather than a package, and entry calls
rather than procedure calls. Consider now

```
task Protected_Variable is
   entry Read(X: out Item),
   entry Write(X: in Item);
end;

task body Protected_Variable is
   V: Item;
begin
   accept Write(X: in Item) do
      V := X;
   end;
   loop
      select
         accept Read(X: out Item) do
            X := V;
         end;
      or
         accept Write(X: in Item) do
            V := X;
```

```
          end;
      end select;
    end loop;
  end Protected_Variable;
```

The body of the task starts with an accept statement for the entry Write; this ensures that the first call accepted is for Write so that there is no risk of the variable being read before it is assigned a value. Of course, a task could call Read before any task had called Write but the calls of Read will be queued until a call of Write has been accepted.

Having accepted a call of Write, the task enters an endless loop containing a single select statement. A select statement starts with the reserved word **select** and finishes with **end select**; it contains two or more alternatives separated by **or**. In this example each alternative consists of an accept statement – one for Read and one for Write.

When we encounter the select statement various possibilities have to be considered according to whether calls of Read or Write or both or neither have been made. We consider these in turn

- If neither Read nor Write has been called then the task is suspended until one or the other is called and then the corresponding accept statement is obeyed.

- If one or more calls of Read are queued but there are no queued calls of Write then the first call of Read is accepted and vice versa with the roles of Read and Write reversed.

- If calls of both Read and Write are queued then an arbitrary choice is made.

Thus each execution of the select statement results in one of its branches being obeyed and one call of Read or Write being dealt with. We can think of the task as corresponding to a person serving two queues of customers waiting for two different services. If only one queue has customers then the server deals with it; if there are no customers then the server waits for the first irrespective of the service required; if both queues exist, the server rather capriciously serves either and makes an arbitrary choice each time.

So each time round the loop the task Protected_Variable will accept a call of Read or Write according to the demands upon it. It thus prevents multiple access to the variable V since it can only deal with one call at a time but does not impose any order upon the calls. Compare this with the task Buffering in Section 14.2 where an order was imposed upon the calls of Put and Get.

Another point to notice is that this example illustrates a case where we have two accept statements for the same entry (Write). It so happens that the bodies are identical but they need not be.

The reader may wonder what the phrase 'arbitrary choice' means when deciding which alternative to choose. The intent is that there is no rule and the implementor is free to choose some efficient mechanism that nevertheless introduces an adequate degree of nondeterminism so that the various queues are treated fairly and none gets starved. A random choice with equal probability would be acceptable but hard to implement efficiently. The most important point is that a program must not rely on the selection algorithm used; if it does, it is erroneous.

A more complex form of select statement is illustrated by the classic problem of the bounded buffer. This is similar to the problem in Section 14.2 except that up to N items can be buffered. A solution is

```
task Buffering is
    entry Put(X: in Item);
    entry Get(X: out Item);
end;

task body Buffering is
    N: constant := 8;   – – for instance
    A: array (1 .. N) of Item;
    I, J: Integer range 1 .. N := 1;
    Count: Integer range 0 .. N := 0;
begin
    loop
        select
            when Count < N =>
            accept Put(X: in Item) do
                A(I) := X;
            end;
            I := I mod N+1; Count := Count+1;
        or
            when Count > 0 =>
            accept Get(X: out Item) do
                X := A(J);
            end;
            J := J mod N+1; Count := Count–1;
        end select;
    end loop;
end Buffering;
```

The buffer is the array A of length N which is a number set to 8 in this example. The variables I and J index the next free and last used locations of the buffer respectively and Count is the number of locations of the buffer which are full. Not only is it convenient to have Count, but it is also necessary in order to distinguish between a completely full and completely empty buffer which both have I = J. The buffer is used cyclically so I need not be greater than J. The situation in Figure 14.1 shows a partly filled buffer with Count = 5, I = 3 and J = 6. The portion of the buffer in use is shaded. The variables I and J are both initialized to 1 and Count is initialized to 0 so that the buffer is initially empty.

The objective of the task is to allow items to be added to and removed from the buffer in a first-in–first-out manner but to prevent the buffer from being overfilled or under-emptied. This is done with a more general form of select statement which includes the use of guarding conditions.

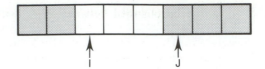

Figure 14.1 The bounded buffer.

Each branch of the select statement commences with

when condition =>

and is then followed by an accept statement and then some further statements. Each time the select statement is encountered all the guarding conditions are evaluated. The behaviour is then as for a select statement without guards but containing only those branches for which the conditions were true. So a branch will be taken and the corresponding rendezvous performed. After the accept statement a branch may contain further statements. These are executed by the server task as part of the select statement but outside the rendezvous.

So the guarding conditions are conditions which have to be true before a service can be offered. The accept statement represents the rendezvous with the customer and the giving of the service. The statements after the accept statement represent bookkeeping actions performed as a consequence of giving the service and which can be done after the customer has left but, of course, need to be done before the next customer is served.

In our example the condition for being able to accept a call of Put is simply that the buffer must not be full; this is the condition Count < N. Similarly we can accept a call of Get provided that the buffer is not empty; this is the condition Count > 0. The statements in the bodies of the accept statements copy the item to or from the buffer. After the rendezvous is completed, the index I or J as appropriate and Count are updated to reflect the change of state. Note the use of **mod** to update I and J in a cyclic manner.

Thus we see that the first time the select statement is executed, the condition Count < N is true but Count > 0 is false. Hence, only a call of Put can be accepted. This puts the first item in the buffer. The next time both conditions will be true so either Put or Get can be accepted, adding a further item or removing the one item. And so it goes on; allowing items to be added or removed with one of the guarding conditions becoming false in the extreme situations and thereby preventing overfilling or under-emptying.

A few points need emphasis. The guards are re-evaluated at the beginning of each execution of the select statement (but their order of evaluation is not defined). An absent guard is taken as true. If all guards turn out to be false then the exception Program_Error is raised. It should be realized that a guard need not still be true when the corresponding rendezvous is performed because it might use global variables and therefore be changed by another task. Later we will discuss an example where guards could change unexpectedly. In the example here, of course, nothing can go wrong. One guard is always true, so Program_Error can never be raised and they both only involve the local

variable Count and so cannot be changed between their evaluation and the
rendezvous.

For our next example consider again the task Protected_Variable. This
allowed either read or write access but only one at a time. This is somewhat
severe; the usual classical problem is to allow only one writer of course, but to
allow several readers together. A simple solution is shown below. It takes the
form of a package containing a local task

```
package Reader_Writer is
  procedure Read(X: out Item);
  procedure Write(X: in Item);
end;

package body Reader_Writer is
  V: Item;

  task Control is
    entry Start;
    entry Stop:
    entry Write(X: in Item);
  end;

  task body Control is
    Readers: Integer := 0;
  begin
    accept Write(X: in Item) do
      V := X;
    end;
    loop
      select
        accept Start;
        Readers := Readers+1;
      or
        accept Stop;
        Readers := Readers−1;
      or
        when Readers = 0 =>
        accept Write(X: in Item) do
          V := X;
        end;
      end select;
    end loop;
  end Control;

  procedure Read(X: out Item) is
  begin
    Control.Start;
    X := V;
    Control.Stop;
  end Read;
```

```
procedure Write(X: in Item) is
begin
   Control.Write(X);
end Write;

end Reader_Writer;
```

The task Control has three entries: Write to do the writing and Start and Stop associated with reading. A call of Start indicates a wish to start reading and a call of Stop indicates that reading has finished. The task is wrapped up in a package because we wish to provide multiple reading access. This can be done by providing a procedure Read which can then be called reentrantly; it also enforces the protocol of calling Start and then Stop.

So the whole thing is a package containing the variable V, the task Control and the access procedures Read and Write. As stated, Read enforces the desired calls of Start and Stop around the statement X := V; the procedure Write merely calls the entry Write.

The task Control declares a variable Readers which indicates how many readers are present. As before it begins with an accept statement for Write to ensure that the variable is initialized and then enters a loop containing a select statement. This has three branches, one for each entry. On a call of Start or Stop the count of number of readers is incremented or decremented. A call of Write can only be accepted if the condition Readers = 0 is true. Hence writing when readers are present is forbidden. Of course, since the task Control actually does the writing, multiple writing is prevented and, moreover, it cannot at the same time accept calls of Start and so reading is not possible when writing is in progress. However, multiple reading is allowed as we have seen.

Although the above solution does fulfil the general conditions it is not really satisfactory. A steady stream of readers will completely block out a writer. Since writing is probably rather important, this is not acceptable. An obvious improvement would be to disallow further reading if one or more writers are waiting. We can do this by using the attribute Write'Count in a guard so that the select statement now becomes

```
select
   when Write'Count = 0 =>
   accept Start;
   Readers := Readers+1;
or
   accept Stop;
   Readers := Readers-1;
or
   when Readers = 0 =>
   accept Write(X: in Item) do
      V := X;
   end;
end select;
```

The attribute Write'Count is the number of tasks currently on the queue for the entry Write. The use of the count attribute in guards needs care. It gives the value when the guard is evaluated and can well change before a rendezvous is accepted. It could increase because another task joins the queue – that would not matter in this example. But, as we shall see later, it could also decrease unexpectedly and this would indeed give problems. We will return to this example in a moment.

EXERCISE 14.4

1   Rewrite the body of the task Build_Complex of Exercise 14.2(**1**) so that the calls of Put_Rl and Put_Im are accepted in any order.

14.5   Timed and conditional rendezvous

There are also various other forms of select statement. It is possible for one or more of the branches to start with a delay statement rather than an accept statement. Consider

```
select
  accept Read( ... ) do
  ...
  end;
or
  accept Write( ... ) do
  ...
  end;
or
  delay 10*Minutes;
  - - time out statements
end select;
```

If neither a call of Read nor Write is received within ten minutes, then the third branch is taken and the statements following the delay are executed. The task might decide that since its services are no longer apparently required it can do something else or maybe it can be interpreted as an emergency. In a process control system we might be awaiting an acknowledgement from the operator that some action has been taken and after a suitable interval take our own emergency action

```
Operator.Call("Put out fire");

select
  accept Acknowledge;
```

```
or
    delay 1*Minutes;
    Fire_Brigade.Call;
end select;
```

A delay alternative can be guarded and indeed there could be several in a select statement although clearly only the shortest one with a true guard can be taken. It should be realized that if one of the accept statements is obeyed then any delay is cancelled – we can think of a delay alternative as waiting for a rendezvous with the clock. A delay is, of course, set from the start of the select statement and reset each time the select statement is encountered. Finally, note that it is the start of the rendezvous that matters rather than its completion as far as the time out is concerned.

Another form of select statement is one with an else part. Consider

```
select
    accept Read( ... ) do
    ...
    end;
or
    accept Write( ... ) do
    ...
    end;
else
    – – alternative statements
end select;
```

In this case the final branch is preceded by **else** rather than **or** and consists of just a sequence of statements. The else branch is taken at once if none of the other branches can be immediately accepted. A select statement with an else part is rather like one with a branch starting **delay** 0.0; it times out at once if there are no customers to be dealt with. A select statement cannot have both an else part and delay alternatives.

There is a subtle distinction between an accept statement starting a branch of a select and an accept statement anywhere else. In the first case the accept statement is bound up with the workings of the select statement and is to some extent conditional. In the second case, once encountered, it will be obeyed come what may. The same distinction applies to a delay statement starting a branch of a select statement and one elsewhere. Thus if we change the **or** to **else** in our emergency action to give

```
select
    accept Acknowledge;
else
    delay 1*Minutes;
    Fire_Brigade.Call;
end select;
```

then the status of the delay is quite different. It just happens to be one of a sequence of statements and will be obeyed in the usual way. So if we cannot accept a call of **Acknowledge** at once, we immediately take the else part. The fact that the first statement is a delay is fortuitous – we immediately delay for one minute and then call the fire brigade. There is no time out. We see therefore that the simple change from **or** to **else** causes a dramatic difference in meaning which may not be immediately obvious; so take care!

If a select statement has an else part then Program_Error can never be raised. The else part cannot be guarded and so will always be taken if all branches have guards and they all turn out to be false.

There are two other forms of select statement which are rather different; they concern a single entry call rather than one or more accept statements. The timed out entry call allows a sequence of statements to be taken as an alternative to an entry call if it is not accepted within the specified duration. Thus

```
select
   Operator.Call("Put out fire");
or
   delay 1*Minutes;
   Fire_Brigade.Call;
end select;
```

will call the fire brigade if the operator does not accept the call within one minute. Again, it is the start of the rendezvous that matters rather than its completion. Finally there is the conditional entry call. Thus

```
select
   Operator.Call("Put out fire");
else
   Fire_Brigade.Call;
end select;
```

will call the fire brigade if the operator cannot immediately accept the call.

The timed out and conditional entry calls are quite different to the general select statement. They concern only a single unguarded call and so these select statements always have exactly two branches – one with the entry call and the other with the alternative sequence of statements. Timed out and conditional calls apply only to entries. They do not apply to procedures or even to entries renamed as procedures.

Timed out and conditional calls are useful if a task does not want to be unduly delayed when a server task is busy. They correspond to a customer in a shop giving up and leaving the queue after waiting for a time or, in the conditional case, a highly impatient customer leaving at once if not immediately served.

Timed out calls, however, need some care particularly if the Count attribute is used. A decision based on the value of that attribute may be invalidated because of a timed out call unexpectedly removing a task from an entry queue. Consider for example the package Reader_Writer. As it stands the entry calls cannot be timed out because they are encapsulated in the procedures **Read** and **Write**. However, we might decide to provide further overloadings of these procedures in order to provide timed out facilities. We might add, for example

```
procedure Write(X: in Item; T: Duration; OK: out Boolean) is
begin
  select
    Control.Write(X);
    OK := True;
  or
    delay T;
    OK := False;
  end select;
end Write;
```

Unfortunately this is invalid. Suppose that one writer is waiting (so that Write'Count = 1) but the call is timed out between the evaluation of the guards and the execution of an accept statement. There are two cases to consider according to the value of Readers. If Readers = 0, then no task can call Stop since there are no current readers; a call of Start cannot be accepted because its guard was false and the expected call of Write will not occur because it has been timed out; the result is that all new readers will be unnecessarily blocked until a new writer arrives. On the other hand, if Readers > 0, then although further calls of Write correctly cannot be accepted, nevertheless further calls of Start are unnecessarily delayed until an existing reader calls Stop despite there being no waiting writers. We therefore seek an alternative solution.

The original reason for using Write'Count was to prevent readers from overtaking waiting writers. One possibility in cases of this sort is to make all the customers call a common entry to start with. This ensures that they are dealt with in order. This entry call can be parameterized to indicate the service required and the callers can then be placed on a secondary queue if necessary. This technique is illustrated by the solution which now follows. The package specification is as before

```
package body Reader_Writer is
  V: Item;
  type Service is (Read, Write);

  task Control is
    entry Start(S: Service);
    entry Stop_Read;
    entry Write;
    entry Stop_Write;
  end Control;

  task body Control is
    Readers: Integer := 0;
    Writers: Integer := 0;
  begin
    loop
      select
```

```
        when Writers = 0 =>
        accept Start(S: Service) do
          case S is
            when Read =>
              Readers := Readers+1;
            when Write =>
              Writers := 1;
          end case;
        end Start;
      or
        accept Stop_Read;
        Readers := Readers−1;
      or
        when Readers = 0 =>
        accept Write;
      or
        accept Stop_Write;
        Writers := 0;
      end select;
    end loop;
  end Control;

  procedure Read(X: out Item) is
  begin
    Control.Start(Read);
    X := V;
    Control.Stop_Read;
  end Read;

  procedure Write(X: in Item) is
  begin
    Control.Start(Write);
    Control.Writo;
    V := X;
    Control.Stop_Write;
  end Write;

end Reader_Writer;
```

We have introduced a variable Writers to indicate how many writers are in the system; it can only take values of 0 and 1. All requests initially call the common entry Start but have to wait until there are no writers. The count of readers or writers is then updated as appropriate. In the case of a reader it can then go ahead as before and finishes by calling Stop_Read. A writer, on the other hand, must wait until there are no readers; it does this by calling Write and then finally calls Stop_Write in order that the control task can set Writers back to zero. Separating Stop_Write from Write enables us to cope with time outs as we shall see; we also take the opportunity to place the actual writing statement in the procedure Write so that it is similar to the read case.

In this solution, the variable Writers performs the function of Write'Count in the previous but incorrect solution. By counting for ourselves we can keep the situation under control. The calls of Start and Write can now be timed out provided that we always call Stop_Read or Stop_Write once a call of Start has been accepted. The details of suitable overloadings of Read and Write to provide timed out calls are left as an exercise.

Note that the above solution has ignored the problem of ensuring that the first call is a write. This can be catered for in various ways, by using a special initial entry, for instance, or by placing the readers on a second auxiliary queue so that they are forced to wait for the first writer.

We finish this section by showing a rather slick alternative to the above

```
task Control is
   entry Start(S: Service);
   entry Stop;
end Control;

task body Control is
   Readers: Integer := 0;
begin
   loop
      select
         accept Start(S: Service) do
            case S is
               when Read =>
                  Readers := Readers+1;
               when Write =>
                  while Readers > 0 loop
                     accept Stop;            -- from readers
                     Readers := Readers-1
                  end loop;
            end case;
         end Start;

         if Readers = 0 then
            accept Stop;                      -- from the writer
         end if;
      or
         accept Stop;                         -- from a reader
         Readers:= Readers-1;
      end select;
   end loop;
end Control;

procedure Read(X: out Item) is
begin
   Control.Start(Read);
   X := V;
   Control.Stop;
end Read;

procedure Write(X: in Item) is
begin
```

```
      Control.Start(Write);
      V := X;
      Control.Stop;
   end Write;
```

The essence of this solution is that the writer waits in the rendezvous for any readers to finish and the whole of the writing process is dealt with in the one branch of the select statement. No guards are required at all and the control task only has two entries. A common Stop entry is possible because the structure is such that each accept statement deals with only one category of caller. A minor disadvantage of the solution is that less flexible timed calls are possible. Once the writer has been accepted by the call of Start, it is committed to wait for all the readers to finish.

As we mentioned earlier, the protected types of Ada 9X provide a better means of programming examples concerning protected access such as the package Reader_Writer. In particular, the problems with the Count attribute do not arise with protected objects as we shall see in Chapter 17.

EXERCISE 14.5

1   Write additional procedures Read and Write for the (penultimate) package
Reader_Writer in order to provide timed out calls. Take care with the procedure Write
so that the calls of the entries Start and Write are both timed out appropriately.

14.6   Task types and activation

It is sometimes useful to have several similar but distinct tasks. Moreover, it is often not possible to predict the number of such tasks required. For example, we might wish to create distinct tasks to follow each aircraft within the zone of control of an air traffic control system. Clearly, such tasks need to be created and disposed of in a dynamic way not related to the static structure of the program.

A template for similar tasks is provided by a task type declaration. This is identical to the simple task declarations we have seen so far except that the reserved word **type** follows **task** in the specification. Thus we may write

```
   task type T is
      entry E( ... );
   end T;

   task body T is
      ...
   end T;
```

The task body follows the same rules as before.

To create an actual task we use the normal form of object declaration. So we can write

    X: T;

and this declares a task X of type T. In fact the simple form of task declaration we have been using so far such as

    task Simple **is**
       ...
    end Simple;

is exactly equivalent to writing

    task type anon **is**
       ...
    end anon;

followed by

    Simple: anon;

Task objects can be used in structures in the usual way. Thus we can declare arrays of tasks

    AOT: **array** (1 .. 10) **of** T;

records containing tasks

    type Rec **is**
       record
          CT: T;
          ...
       end record;
    R: Rec;

and so on.

The entries of such tasks are called using the task object name; thus we write

    X.E(...);
    AOT(I).E(...);
    R.CT.E(...);

A most important consideration is that task objects are not variables but behave as constants. A task object declaration creates a task which is permanently bound to the object. Hence assignment is not allowed for task types and nor are the comparisons for equality and inequality. A task type is therefore another form of limited type (we call it inherently limited) and so could be used as the actual type corresponding to a formal generic parameter specified as limited private and as the actual type in a private part corresponding to a limited private type. Although task objects behave as constants, they cannot be declared as such since a constant declaration needs an explicit initial value. Subprogram parameters may be of task types; they are always passed by reference and so the formal and actual parameters always refer to the same task. As in the case of other limited types, outside their defining package, parameters of mode **out** are not allowed; of course there is no defining package in the case of task types anyway.

In Section 14.1 we briefly introduced the idea of dependency. Each task is dependent on some unit and there is a general rule that a unit cannot be left until all tasks dependent upon it have terminated.

A task declared as a task object (or using the abbreviated simple form) is dependent upon the enclosing block, subprogram or task body in which it is declared. Inner packages do not count in this rule – this is because a package is merely a passive scope wall and has no dynamic life. If a task is declared in a package (or nested packages) then the task is dependent upon the block, subprogram or task body in which the package or packages are themselves declared. For completeness, a task declared in a library package is said to depend on that package and we refer to it as a library task. After termination of the main program, the main environment task (which calls the main program) must wait for all library tasks to terminate. Only then does the program as a whole terminate (AI-222).

We saw earlier that a task becomes active only when the declaring unit reaches the **begin** following the declaration. The execution of a task can be thought of as a two-stage process. The first stage, known as activation, consists of the elaboration of the declarations of the task body whereas the second stage consists, of course, of the execution of its statements. During the activation stage the parent unit is not allowed to proceed. If several tasks are declared in a unit then their activations and the subsequent execution of their statements occur independently and in parallel. But it is only when the activation of all the tasks is complete that the parent unit can continue with the execution of the statements following the **begin** in parallel with the new tasks.

Note that the activation of a task (like the rendezvous) involves two tasks: the parent and itself. Similar priority rules apply as for the rendezvous so that the activation occurs at the higher of the priority of the task and that of its parent (if defined) and so on (AI-288).

The activation process is depicted in Figure 14.2 which illustrates the behaviour of a block containing the declarations of two tasks A and B

```
declare
   ...
   A: T;
   B: T;
   ...
begin
   ...
end;
```

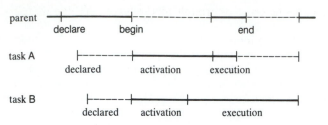

Figure 14.2 Task activation.

Time flows from left to right and a solid line indicates that a unit is actively doing something whereas a dashed line indicates that it exists but is suspended.

For the sake of illustration, we show task A finishing its activation after task B so that the parent resumes execution when task A enters its execution stage. We also show task A finishing its execution and therefore becoming completed and terminated before task B. The parent is shown reaching its **end** and therefore completing execution of the block after task A has terminated but before task B has terminated. The parent is therefore suspended until task B is terminated when it can then resume execution with the statements following the block.

The reason for treating task activation in this way concerns exceptions. The reader may recall that an exception raised during the elaboration of declarations is not handled at that level but immediately propagated. So an exception raised in the declarations in a new task could not be handled by that task at all. However, since it is clearly desirable that some means be provided for detecting such an exception, it is obvious that an exception has to be raised in the parent unit. In fact the predefined exception Tasking_Error is raised irrespective of the original exception. It would clearly make life rather difficult if this exception were raised in the parent unit after it had moved on in parallel and so it is held up until all the new tasks have been activated. The exception Tasking_Error is then raised in the parent unit as soon as it attempts to move on from the **begin**. Note that if several of the new tasks raise exceptions during activation then Tasking_Error is only raised once. Such tasks become completed (not terminated) and do not affect sibling tasks being simultaneously activated.

The other thing that can go wrong is that an exception can occur in the declarations of the parent unit itself. In this case any new tasks which have been declared (but of course will not have been activated because the parent unit has not yet reached its **begin**) will automatically become terminated and are never activated at all.

Task objects can be declared in a package and although not dependent upon the package are nevertheless set active at the **begin** of the package body. If the package body has no initialization statements and therefore no **begin**, then a null initialization statement is assumed. Worse, if a package has no body, then a body with just a null initialization statement is assumed. So the task Control in the package Reader_Writer of the previous section is set active at the end of the declaration of the package body.

Tasks can also be created through access types. We can write

   type Ref_T **is access** T;

and then we can create a task using an allocator in the usual way

   RX: Ref_T := **new** T;

The type Ref_T is a normal access type and so assignment and equality comparisons of objects of the type are allowed. The entry E of the task accessed by RX can be called as expected by

   RX.E(...);

Tasks created through access types obey slightly different rules for activation and dependency. They commence activation immediately upon evaluation of the allocator whether it occurs in a sequence of statements or in an initial value – we do not wait until the ensuing **begin**. Furthermore, such tasks are not dependent upon the unit where they are created but are dependent upon the block, subprogram body or task body containing the declaration of the access type itself. The strong analogies between tasks declared as objects and those created through an allocator are revealed when we consider tasks which are components of a composite object.

Suppose we have the following somewhat artificial type

   type R **is**
      record
         A: T;
         I: Integer := E;
         B: T;
      end record;

where A and B are components of some task type T and E is the default initial expression for the component I.

If we declare an object X of type R thus

   declare
      X: R;
   begin

then it is much as if we declared the individual objects

   declare
      XA: T;
      XI: Integer := E;
      XB: T;
   begin

using the rules explained above.

Now suppose we have an access type

type Ref_R **is access** R;

and create an object using an allocator

RR: Ref_R := **new** R;

The first thing that happens is that the various components are declared and the initial expression is evaluated and assigned to RR.I. It is only when this has been done that activation of the tasks RR.A and RR.B can commence; in a sense we wait until reaching **end record** by analogy with waiting until we reach **begin** in the case of directly declared objects. The component tasks are then activated in parallel but the parent unit is suspended and the access value is not returned until all the activations are complete just as we could not move past the **begin**. Similarly, if an exception is raised by the activation of one or both component tasks, then, on return from the allocator, Tasking_Error is raised just once in the parent unit. Such rogue tasks will then become completed but will not interfere with any other sibling component tasks. Finally, if the evaluation of E raises an exception in the parent unit then the component tasks will automatically become terminated without even being activated.

The reader will probably feel that the activation mechanism is somewhat elaborate. However, in practice, the details will rarely need to be considered. They are mentioned in order to show that the mechanism is well defined rather than because of their everyday importance.

Note that entries in a task can be called as soon as it is declared and even before activation commences – the call will just be queued. However, situations in which this is sensibly possible are rare.

An interesting use of task types is for the creation of agents. An agent is a task that does something on behalf of another task. As an example suppose a task Server provides some service that is asked for by calling an entry Request. Suppose also that it may take Server some time to provide the service so that it is reasonable for the calling task User to go away and do something else while waiting for the answer to be prepared. There are various ways in which the User could expect to collect his answer. He could call another entry Enquire; the Server task would need some means of recognizing the caller – he could do this by issuing a key on the call of Request and insisting that it be presented again when calling Enquire. This corresponds to taking something to be repaired, being given a ticket and then having to exchange it when the repaired item is collected later. An alternative approach which avoids the issue of keys, is to create an agent. This corresponds to leaving your address and having the repaired item mailed back to you. We will now illustrate this approach.

First of all we declare a task type as follows

```
task type Mailbox is
   entry Deposit(X: in Item);
   entry Collect(X: out Item);
end;
```

```
task body Mailbox is
   Local: Item;
begin
   accept Deposit(X: in Item) do
      Local := X;
   end;
   accept Collect(X: out Item) do
      X := Local;
   end;
end Mailbox;
```

A task of this type acts as a simple mailbox. An item can be deposited and collected later. What we are going to do is to give the identity of the mailbox to the server so that the server can deposit the item in the mailbox from which the user can collect it later. We need an access type

```
type Address is access Mailbox;
```

The tasks Server and User now take the following form

```
task Server is
   entry Request(A: Address; X: Item);
end;

task body Server is
   Reply: Address;
   Job: Item;
begin
   loop
      accept Request(A: Address; X: Item) do
         Reply := A;
         Job := X,
      end;

      - - work on job

      Reply.Deposit(Job);
   end loop;
end Server;

task User;

task body User is
   My_Box: Address := new Mailbox;
   My_Item: Item;
begin
   Server.Request(My_Box, My_Item);

   - - do something while waiting

   My_Box.Collect(My_Item);
end User;
```

In practice the user might poll the mailbox from time to time to see if the item is ready. This is easily done using a conditional entry call.

```
select
    My_Box.Collect(My_Item);
    – – item collected successfully
else
    – – not ready yet
end select;
```

It is important to realize that the agent serves several purposes. It enables the deposit and collect to be decoupled so that the server can get on with the next job. Moreover, and perhaps of more importance, it means that the server need know nothing about the user; to call the user directly would mean that the user would have to be of a particular task type and this would be most unreasonable. The agent enables us to factor off the only property required of the user, namely the existence of the entry Deposit.

If the decoupling property were not required then the body of the agent could be written as

```
task body Mailbox is
begin
    accept Deposit(X: in Item) do
        accept Collect(X: out Item) do
            Collect.X := Deposit.X;
        end;
    end;
end Mailbox;
```

The agent does not need a local variable in this case since the agent now only exists in order to aid closely coupled communication. Note also the use of the dotted notation in the nested accept statements in order to distinguish the two uses of X; we could equally have written X := Deposit.X; but the use of Collect is more symmetric.

14.7   Termination and exceptions

A task can become completed and then terminate in various ways as well as running into its final end. It will have been noticed that in many of our earlier examples, the body of a task was an endless loop and clearly never terminated. This means that it would never be possible to leave the unit on which the task was dependent. Suppose, for example, that we needed to have several protected variables in our program. We could declare a task type

```
task type Protected_Variable is
    entry Read(X: out Item);
```

```
      entry Write(X: in Item);
   end;
```

so that we can just declare variables such as

```
   PV: Protected_Variable;
```

and then access them by

```
   PV.Read( ... );
   PV.Write( ... );
```

However, we could not leave the unit on which PV depends without terminating the task in some way. We could, of course, add a special entry Stop and call it just before leaving the unit, but this would be inconvenient. Instead it is possible to make a task automatically terminate itself when it is of no further use by a special form of select alternative.

The body of the task can be written as

```
   task body Protected_Variable is
      V: Item;
   begin
      accept Write(X: in Item) do
         V := X;
      end;
      loop
        select
           accept Read(X: out Item) do
             X := V;
           end;
        or
           accept Write(X: in Item) do
             V := X;
           end;
        or
           terminate;
        end select;
      end loop;
   end Protected_Variable;
```

The terminate alternative is taken if the unit on which the task depends has reached its end and so is completed and all sibling tasks and dependent tasks are terminated or are similarly able to select a terminate alternative. In such circumstances all the tasks are of no use since they are the only tasks that could call their entries and they are all dormant. Thus the whole set automatically terminates.

In practice, this merely means that all service tasks should have a terminate alternative and will then quietly terminate themselves without more ado.

Strictly speaking, the initial Write should also be in a select statement with a terminate alternative otherwise we are still stuck if the task is never called at all.

A terminate alternative may be guarded. However, it cannot appear in a select statement with a delay alternative or an else part.

Selection of a terminate alternative is classified as normal termination – the task is under control of the situation and terminates voluntarily.

At the other extreme the abort statement unconditionally terminates one or more tasks. It consists of the reserved word **abort** followed by a list of task names as for example

    abort X, AOT(3), RX.**all**;

If a task is aborted then all tasks dependent upon it or a subprogram or block currently called by it are also aborted. If the task is suspended for some reason, then it immediately becomes completed; any delay is cancelled; if the task is on an entry queue, it is removed; other possibilities are that it has not yet even commenced activation or it is at an accept or select statement awaiting a partner. If the task is not suspended, then completion will occur as soon as convenient and certainly no new communication with the task will be possible. The reason for this somewhat vague statement concerns the rendezvous. If the task is engaged in a rendezvous when it is aborted, then we also have to consider the effect on the partner. This depends on the situation. If the called task is aborted, then the calling task receives the exception Tasking_Error. On the other hand, if the calling task is aborted, then the called task is not affected; the rendezvous carries on to completion with the caller in a somewhat abnormal state and it is only when the rendezvous is complete that the caller becomes properly completed. The rationale is simple; if a task asks for a service and the server dies so that it cannot be provided then the customer should be told. On the other hand, if the customer dies, too bad – but we must avoid upsetting the server who might have the database in a critical state.

Note that the above rules are formulated in terms of completing the tasks rather than terminating them. This is because a parent task cannot be terminated until its dependent tasks are terminated and if one of those is the caller in a rendezvous with a third party then its termination will be delayed. Thus completion of the tasks is the best that can be individually enforced and their termination will then automatically occur in the usual way.

The abort statement is very disruptive and should only be used in extreme situations. It might be appropriate for a command task to abort a complete subsystem in response to an operator command.

Another possible use for the abort statement might be in an exception handler. Remember that we cannot leave a unit until all dependent tasks are terminated. Hence, if an exception is raised in a unit, then we cannot tidy up that unit and propagate the exception on a layered basis while dependent tasks are still alive and so one of the actions of tidying up might be to abort all dependent tasks. Thus the procedure Clean_Up of Section 10.2 might do just this.

However, it is probably always best to attempt a controlled shutdown and only resort to the abort statement as a desperate measure. Statements in the command task might be as follows

```
select
    T.Closedown;
or
    delay 60*Seconds;
    abort T;
end select;
```

If the slave task does not accept the Closedown call within a minute, then it is ruthlessly aborted. We are assuming, of course, that the slave task polls the Closedown entry at least every minute using a conditional accept statement such as

```
select
    accept Closedown;
    – – tidy up and die
else
    – – carry on normally
end select;
```

If we cannot trust the slave to close down properly even after accepting the entry call, then the command task can always issue an abort after a due interval just in case. Aborting a task which has already terminated has no effect. So the command task might read

```
select
    T.Closedown;
    delay 10*Seconds;
or
    delay 60*Seconds;
end select;
abort T;
```

Of course, even this is not foolproof since the malevolent slave might continue for ever in the rendezvous itself

```
accept Closedown do
    loop
        Put("Can't catch me");
    end loop;
end;
```

Some minimal degree of cooperation is obviously needed!

The status of task T can be ascertained by the use of two attributes. Thus T'Terminated is true if a task is terminated. The other attribute, T'Callable, is true unless the task is completed or terminated or in the abnormal state pending final abortion. The use of these attributes needs care. For example, between discovering that a task has not terminated and taking some action based on that information, the task could become terminated. However, the reverse is not possible since a task cannot be restarted and so it is quite safe to take an action based on the information that a task has terminated.

In Section 14.1 we mentioned that if a task has no dependents then completion and termination effectively occur together. However, AI-441 notes that completion and termination might not be exactly simultaneous and so it is possible for both T'Terminated and T'Callable to be false even though T has no dependents.

As an illustration of the impact of abnormal termination and how it can be coped with, we will reconsider the task Control in the package Reader_Writer in Section 14.5 in its final form

```
task body Control is
   Readers: Integer := 0;
begin
   loop
      select
         accept Start(S: Service) do
            case S is
               when Read =>
                  Readers := Readers+1;
               when Write =>
                  while Readers > 0 loop
                     accept Stop;                -- from readers
                     Readers := Readers-1;
                  end loop;
            end case;
         end Start;
         if Readers = 0 then
            accept Stop;                         -- from the writer
         end if;
      or
         accept Stop;                            -- from a reader
         Readers := Readers-1;
      end select;
   end loop;
end Control;
```

Suppose that a reading task has called Start and is then aborted before it can call Stop. The variable Readers will then be inconsistent and can never be zero again. The next writer will then be locked out for ever. Similarly, if a writing task has called Start and is then aborted before it can call Stop, then all other users will be locked out for ever.

The difficulty we have run into is that our task Control assumes certain behaviour on the part of the calling tasks and this behaviour is not guaranteed. (We had a similar difficulty with our elementary solution to this example in Section 14.5 regarding the Count attribute and timed out entry calls.) We can overcome our new difficulty by the use of intermediate agent tasks which we can guarantee cannot be aborted.

The following shows the use of agents for the readers; a similar technique can be applied to the writers. The package body now becomes

```
package body Reader_Writer is
   V: Item;
   type Service is (Read, Write);

   task type Read_Agent is
      entry Read(X: out Item);
   end;

   type RRA is access Read_Agent;

   task Control is
      entry Start(S: Service);
      entry Stop;
   end;

   task body Control is
      – –as before
   end Control;

   task body Read_Agent is
   begin
      select
         accept Read(X: out Item) do
            Control.Start(Read);
            X := V;
            Control.Stop;
         end;
      or
         terminate;
      end select;
   end Read_Agent;

   procedure Read(X: out Item) is
      Task_007: RRA := new Read_Agent;
   begin
      Task_007.Read(X);
   end Read;

   procedure Write(X: in Item) is
   begin
      ...
   end Write;

end Reader_Writer;
```

If we now abort the task calling the procedure Read, then either the rendezvous with its agent (Task_007) will be in progress, in which case it will be completed, or the rendezvous will not be in progress, in which case there will be no interference. The agent therefore either does its job completely or not at all. Note that if we made the agent a direct task object (rather than an access to a task object), then aborting the task calling the procedure Read would also immediately abort the agent because it would be a dependent task. Using an access type makes the agent dependent on the unit in which the Reader_Writer is declared and so it can live on.

The agent task body contains a select statement with a terminate alternative. This ensures that if the user task is aborted between creating the agent and calling the agent then nevertheless the agent can quietly die when the unit on which it depends is left.

It is worth summarizing why the above solution works

- the agent is invisible and so cannot be aborted;
- if the calling task in a rendezvous is abnormally terminated, the called task (the agent) is not affected;
- the agent is an access task and is not dependent on the caller.

The moral is not to use abort without due care; or, as in life, if you cannot trust the calling tasks, use indestructible secret agents.

We finish this section by discussing a few remaining points on exceptions. The exception Tasking_Error is concerned with general communication failure. As we have seen, it is raised if a failure occurs during task activation and it is also raised in the caller of a rendezvous if the server is aborted. In addition, no matter how a task is completed, all tasks still queued on its entries receive Tasking_Error. Similarly calling an entry of a task that is already completed also raises Tasking_Error in the caller.

If an exception is raised during a rendezvous (that is as a consequence of an action by the called task) and is not handled by the accept statement, then it is propagated into both tasks as the same exception on the grounds that both need to know. Of course, if the accept statement handles the exception internally, then that is the end of the matter anyway.

It might be convenient for the called task, the server, to inform the calling task, the user, of some event by the explicit raising of an exception. In such a case it is likely that the server task will not wish to take any action and so a null handler will be required. So in outline we might write

```
begin
  select
    accept E( ... ) do
      ...
      raise Error;          -- tell user
      ...
    end E;
  or
    ...
  end select;
exception
  when Error =>
    null;                   -- server forgets
end;
```

Finally, if an exception is not handled by a task at all, then, like the main program, the task is abandoned and the exception is lost; it is not propagated to the parent unit because it would be too disruptive to do so. However, we might expect the run time environment to provide a diagnostic message. If it does not, it might be good practice for all significant tasks to have a general handler at the outermost level in order to guard against the loss of exceptions and consequential silent death of the task.

EXERCISE 14.7

1 Rewrite the task Buffering of Section 14.4 so that it has the following specification

```
task Buffering is
   entry Put(X: in Item);
   entry Finish;
   entry Get(X: out Item);
end;
```

The writing task calls Put as before and finally calls Finish. The reading task calls Get as before; a call of Get when there are no further items raises the global exception Done.

2 What happens in the following bizarre situation

```
task body Server is
begin
   accept E do
      abort Caller;
      raise Havoc;
   end E;
end Server;

task body Caller is
begin
   Server.E;
exception
   when Havoc =>
      Put("What a mess");
end Caller;
```

14.8   Resource scheduling

When designing tasks in Ada it is important to remember that the only queues over which we have any control are entry queues and that such queues are handled on a strictly first-in–first-out basis. This might be thought to be a problem in situations where requests are of different priorities or where later requests can be serviced even though earlier ones have to wait. (Note that in this section we will assume that calling tasks are not aborted.)

Requests with priorities can be handled by a family of entries. A family is rather like a one-dimensional array. Suppose we have three levels of priority given by

```
type Priority is (Urgent, Normal, Low);
```

and that we have a task Controller providing access to some action on a type Data but with requests for the action on three queues according to their priority. We could do this with three distinct entries but it is neater to use a family of entries. Consider

```
task Controller is
   entry Request(Priority) (D: Data);
end;

task body Controller is
begin
   loop
      select
         accept Request(Urgent) (D: Data) do
            Action(D);
         end;
      or
         when Request(Urgent)'Count = 0 =>
         accept Request(Normal) (D: Data) do
            Action(D);
         end;
      or
         when Request(Urgent)'Count = 0 and
               Request(Normal)'Count = 0 =>
         accept Request(Low) (D: Data) do
            Action(D);
         end;
      end select;
   end loop;
end Controller;
```

Request is a family of entries, indexed by a discrete range which in this case is the type Priority. Clearly this approach is only feasible if the number of priority values is small. If it is large, a more sophisticated technique is necessary. We could try checking each queue in turn thus

```
task body Controller is
begin
   loop
      for P in Priority loop
         select
            accept Request(P) (D: Data) do
               Action(D);
            end;
```

```
            exit;
         else
            null;
         end select;
      end loop;
   end loop;
end Controller;
```

Unfortunately this is not satisfactory since it results in the task Controller continuously polling when all the queues are empty. We need a mechanism whereby the task can wait for the first of any request. This can be done by a two-stage process; the calling task must first sign in by calling a common entry and then call the appropriate entry of the family. The details are left as an exercise for the reader.

We now illustrate a quite general technique which effectively allows the requests in a single entry queue to be handled in an arbitrary order. Consider the problem of allocating a group of resources from a set. We do not wish to hold up a later request that can be satisfied just because an earlier request must wait for the release of some of the resources it wants. We suppose that the resources are represented by a discrete type Resource. We can conveniently use the generic package Set_Of from Section 13.2

```
package Resource_Sets is new Set_Of(Resource);
use Resource_Sets;
```

and then

```
package Resource_Allocator is
   procedure Request(S: Set);
   procedure Release(S: Set);
end;

package body Resource_Allocator is
   task Control is
      entry First(S: Set; OK: out Boolean);
      entry Again(S: Set; OK: out Boolean);
      entry Release(S: Set);
   end;

   task body Control is
      Free: Set := Full;
      Waiters: Integer := 0;
      procedure Try(S: Set; OK: out Boolean) is
      begin
         if S <= Free then
            Free := Free–S;
            OK := True;       – – allocation successful
         else
            OK := False;      – – no good, try later
         end if;
      end Try;
```

```
            begin
              loop
                select
                  accept First(S: Set; OK: out Boolean) do
                    Try(S, OK);
                    if not OK then
                      Waiters := Waiters+1;
                    end if;
                  end;
                or
                  accept Release(S: Set) do
                    Free := Free+S;
                  end;
                  for I in 1 .. Waiters loop
                    accept Again(S: Set; OK: out Boolean) do
                      Try(S, OK);
                      if OK then
                        Waiters := Waiters−1;
                      end if;
                    end;
                  end loop;
                end select;
              end loop;
            end Control;

            procedure Request(S: Set) is
              Allocated: Boolean;
            begin
              Control.First(S, Allocated);
              while not Allocated loop
                Control.Again(S, Allocated);
              end loop;
            end Request;

            procedure Release(S: Set) is
            begin
              Control.Release(S);
            end Release;

        end Resource_Allocator;
```

This is another example of a package containing a control task; the overall structure is similar to that of the package Reader_Writer introduced in Section 14.4. The package Resource_Allocator contains two procedures Request and Release which have as parameters the set S of resources to be acquired or returned; the type Set is from the instantiation of Set_Of. These procedures call the entries of the task Control as appropriate.

The task Control has three entries: First, Again and Release. The entries First and Again are similar; as well as the parameter S giving the set of resources required, they also have an out parameter OK which indicates whether the attempt to acquire the resources was successful or not. The accept statements for First and Again are identical and call a common procedure Try.

This checks the set S against the set Free of available resources using the inclusion operator "<=" from (the instantiation of) Set_Of. If all the resources are available, Free is altered correspondingly using the symmetric difference operator "−" from Set_Of and OK is set True; if they are not all available, OK is set False. The entry Release returns the resources passed as the parameter S by updating Free using the union operator "+" from Set_Of. Note that the declaration of Free gives it the initial value Full which is also from Set_Of.

The entries First and Again are called by the procedure Request. It makes an immediate attempt to acquire the resources by a call of First; if they are not all available, the Boolean Allocated is set False and the request is queued by calling Again. This call is then repeated until successful. The entry Release is merely called by the procedure Release.

The body of Control is the inevitable select statement in a loop. It has two branches, one for First and one for Release. Thus a call of Release is always acceptable and a call of First is also accepted promptly except when the task is dealing with the consequences of Release. After a call of Release, the requests which could not be satisfied on their call of First and were consequently placed on the Again queue are reconsidered since the resources made available by the call of Release may be able to satisfy one or more requests at arbitrary points in the queue. The queue is scanned by doing a rendezvous with each call; a user which cannot be satisfied places itself back on the queue by a further call of Again in the procedure Request. In order that each user should have only one retry the scan is done by a loop controlled by the variable Waiters. This indicates how many callers have called First unsuccessfully and so are waiting in the system; it is initially zero and is incremented on an unsuccessful call of First and decremented on a successful call of Again. Note that we cannot use Again'Count; deadlock might arise if all the resources were released between a task unsuccessfully calling First and actually calling Again. The moral of the readers and writers example is thus echoed; avoid the Count attribute − we must count for ourselves.

The above solution is reasonably satisfactory although there is a risk of unfairness. Tasks could overtake each other in the race from the front of the queue to the back; a newcomer could also miss a turn.

Problems of such race conditions can be overcome in Ada 9X by the use of the requeue statement; this allows a task to end a rendezvous by making a further entry call (possibly for the same entry).

It is interesting to modify the above solution so that the requests are always satisfied in order. That is, a later request is always held up for an earlier one even if the resources they require are quite different. The essence of the solution is to allow only one waiting task in the system at a time. The modification is left as an exercise for the reader.

For this modified problem the following alternative solution is perhaps better. It has the merit of avoiding the task scheduling associated with the waiting task repeatedly calling Again. We show just the task Control and the procedure Request

```
task Control is
   entry Sign_In(S: Set);
   entry Request;
```

```
            entry Release(S: Set);
         end;

         task body Control is
            Free: Set := Full;
            Waiters: Integer range 0 .. 1 := 0;
            Wanted: Set;
         begin
            loop
               select
                  when Waiters = 0 =>
                  accept Sign_In(S: Set) do
                     Wanted := S;
                  end;
                  Waiters := Waiters+1;
               or
                  when Waiters > 0 and then Wanted <= Free =>
                  accept Request do
                     Free := Free–Wanted;
                  end;
                  Waiters := Waiters–1;
               or
                  accept Release(S: Set) do
                     Free := Free+S;
                  end;
               end select;
            end loop;
         end Control;

         procedure Request(S: Set) is
         begin
            Control.Sign_In(S);
            Control.Request;
         end Request;
```

In this solution we use a guarding condition which is true when the request can be honoured. A sign in call is required in order to hand over the parameter first because of course a guarding condition cannot depend upon the parameters of the actual entry call it is guarding. Note the short circuit condition which prevents the evaluation of Wanted when there is no waiting task. The variable Waiters should perhaps be a Boolean; it can only be zero or one.

EXERCISE 14.8

1 Modify the first form of the package Resource_Allocator so that requests are dealt with strictly in order.

2 Rewrite the task Controller as a package containing a task in a way which avoids continuous polling. The package specification should be

```
package Controller is
   procedure Request(P: Priority; D: Data);
end;
```

14.9   Examples of task types

In this final section on tasking we briefly summarize the main differences between packages and tasks and then give a number of examples which illustrate various ways in which task types can be used.

Tasks and packages have a superficial lexical similarity – they both have specifications and bodies. However, there are many differences

- A task is an active construction whereas a package is passive.
- A task can only have entries in its specification. A package can have anything except entries. A task cannot have a private part.
- A package can be generic but a task cannot. The general effect of a parameterless generic task can be obtained by a task type. Alternatively the task can be encapsulated by a generic package.
- A package can appear in a use clause but a task cannot.
- A package can be a library unit but a task cannot. However, a task body can be a subunit.

The overall distinction is that the package should be considered to be the main tool for structuring purposes whereas the task is intended for synchronization. Thus typical subsystems will consist of a (possibly generic) package containing one or more tasks. This general structure has as we have seen the merit of giving complete control over the facilities provided; internal tasks cannot be unwillingly aborted and entry calls cannot be unwillingly timed out if they are not visible.

The above broad differences between tasks and packages remain in Ada 9X. The only notable variation is that a task may have a private part in Ada 9X; such a private part may only contain entries and these entries are then local to the task and not visible outside.

Our first example illustrates the use of task types as private types by the following generic package which provides a general type Buffer

```
generic
   N: Positive;
   type Item is private;
package Buffers is
   type Buffer is limited private;
   procedure Put(B: in out Buffer; X: in Item);
```

```
        procedure Get(B: in out Buffer; X: out Item);
private
  task type Control is
    entry Put(X: in Item);
    entry Get(X: out Item);
  end;
  type Buffer is new Control;
end;

package body Buffers is

  task body Control is
    A: array (1 .. N) of Item;
    I, J: Integer range 1 .. N := 1;
    Count: Integer range 0 .. N := 0;
  begin
    loop
      select
        when Count < N =>
        accept Put(X: in Item) do
          A(I) := X;
        end;
        I := I mod N+1; Count := Count+1;
      or
        when Count > 0 =>
        accept Get(X: out Item) do
          X := A(J);
        end;
        J := J mod N+1; Count := Count-1;
      or
        terminate;
      end select;
    end loop;
  end Control;

  procedure Put(B: in out Buffer; X: in Item) is
  begin
    B.Put(X);
  end Put;

  procedure Get(B: in out Buffer; X: out Item) is
  begin
    B.Get(X);
  end Get;

end Buffers;
```

The buffer is implemented as a task object of a task type derived from Control so that when we declare an object of the type Buffer a new task is created which in turn declares the storage for the actual buffer. Calls of the procedures Put and Get access the buffer by calling the corresponding entries of the appropriate task. Note that the select statement contains a terminate alternative so that the task object automatically disappears when we leave the scope of its declaration. Moreover, the system is robust even if the calling task is aborted.

We could have dispensed with the derived type and have written directly

```
task type Buffer is
    entry Put(X: in Item);
    entry Get(X: out Item);
end;
```

thus illustrating that a task type declaration can give the full type corresponding to a limited private type – remember that a task type is limited. However, the derived type enables us to use two different names according to whether we are thinking about the buffer or the control aspects of the one concept.

We now come to an interesting demonstration example which illustrates the dynamic creation of task objects. The objective is to find and display the first few prime numbers using the Sieve of Eratosthenes.

This ancient algorithm works using the observation that if we have a list of all the primes below N so far, then N is also prime if none of these divide exactly into it. So we try the existing primes in turn and as soon as one divides N we discard N and try again with N set to $N+1$. On the other hand, if we get to the end of our list of primes without dividing N, then N must be prime, so we add it to our list and also start again with $N+1$.

Our implementation (reproduced by permission of Alsys) uses a separate task for each prime P which is linked (via an access value) to the previous prime task and next prime task as shown in Figure 14.3. Its duty is to take a trial number N from the previous task and to check whether it is divisible by its prime P. If it is, the number is discarded; if it is not, the number is passed to the next prime task. If there is no next prime task then P was the largest prime so far and N is a newly found prime; the P task then creates a new task whose duty is to check for divisibility by N and links itself to it. Each task thus acts as a filter removing multiples of its own prime value.

On the screen each task displays a frame containing its own prime and an inner box which displays the trial value currently being tested, if any. Figure 14.3 shows the situation when the primes 2, 3 and 5 have been found. The 5 task is testing 7 (which will prove to be a new prime), the 3 task is resting and waiting to receive another number from the 2 task, the 2 task (having just discarded 8) is testing 9 (which it will pass to the 3 task in a moment).

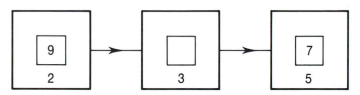

Figure 14.3   The Sieve of Eratosthenes.

The program comprises a package Frame containing subprograms which manipulate the display (the body of this package is not shown), a task type Filter which describes the activities of the prime tasks and a main program Sieve.

```
package Frame is
   type Position is private;
   function Make_Frame(Divisor: Integer) return Position;
   procedure Write_To_Frame(Value: Integer; Where: Position);
   procedure Clear_Frame(Where: Position);
private
   ...
end Frame;

use Frame;

task type Filter is
   entry Input(Number: Integer);
end Filter;

type A_Filter is access Filter;

function Make_Filter return A_Filter is
begin
   return new Filter;
end Make_Filter;

task body Filter is
   P: Integer;        – – prime divisor
   N: Integer;        – – trial number
   Here: Position;
   Next: A_Filter;
begin
   accept Input(Number: Integer) do
      P := Number;
   end;
   Here := Make_Frame(P);
   loop
      accept Input(Number: Integer) do
         N := Number;
      end;
      Write_To_Frame(N, Here);
      if N mod P /= 0 then
         if Next = null then
            Next := Make_Filter;
         end if;
         Next.Input(N);
      end if;
      Clear_Frame(Here);
   end loop;
end Filter;
```

```
procedure Sieve is
   First: A_Filter := new Filter;
   N: Integer := 2;
begin
   loop
      First.Input(N);
      N := N+1;
   end loop;
end Sieve;
```

The subprograms in the package Frame behave as follows. The function Make_Frame draws a new frame on the screen and permanently writes the divisor number (that is P for the task calling it) into the frame; the inner box is left empty. The function returns a value of the private type Position which identifies the position of the frame; this value is later passed as a parameter to the two other procedures which manipulate the inner box in order to identify the frame concerned. The procedure Write_To_Frame has a further parameter giving the value to be written in the inner box; the procedure Clear_Frame wipes the inner box clean.

The task type Filter is fairly straightforward. It has a single entry Input which is called by the preceding task to give it the next trial divisor except that the first call passes the value of P which identifies the task. Hence Filter has two accept statements, the first collects the value of P and the other is within the main loop. After collecting P it creates its frame (noting the position in Here) and then enters the loop and awaits a number N to test. Having collected N it displays it in the inner box and then tests for divisibility by P. If it is divisible, it clears the inner box and goes to the beginning of the loop for a new value of N. If N is not divisible by P, it makes a successor task if necessary and in any event passes the value of N to it by calling its entry Input. Only after the successor task has taken the value does it clear the inner box and go back to the beginning.

Note that the task Filter automatically creates its own storage when it is activated (just as the task Control in the previous example). It should also be noticed that the task does not know who it is until told; this is a characteristic of Ada task types since there is no way of parameterizing them.

The driving procedure Sieve makes the first task, sets N to 2 and then enters an endless loop giving the task successive integer values until the end of time (or some other limitation is reached).

The reader may wonder why we declared the function Make_Filter rather than simply writing

```
Next := new Filter;
```

within the body of the task Filter. The reason is that within a task body the name of the task refers to the current execution of the task and cannot be used as a type mark. Thus we could abort the current task or pass it as a parameter to a procedure by using the name Filter and this would refer to the task object currently executing the body.

In Ada 9X a task can be parameterized by discriminants and this example could then be rewritten so that each new task is declared with its divisor as a discriminant. This is left as an exercise for Chapter 17.

Our final example illustrates in outline a typical application using several processors. In recent years the cost of processors has fallen dramatically and for many applications it is now more sensible to use several individual processors rather than one very high performance processor. Indeed the finite value of the velocity of light coupled with the nonzero value of Planck's constant places physical limits to the performance that one can get from a single processor. We are then faced with the software organizational problem of how to use several processors effectively. For many applications this is hard, but for those where there is a replication of some sort it is often feasible. The processing of algorithms on arrays in graphics, signal processing and so on are good examples.

In Ada the task type gives us a natural means of describing a process which can be run in parallel on several processors simultaneously. For the moment we will suppose that we have a computer comprising several processors with a common address space. Thus when several tasks are active they really will be active and we assume that there are enough processors for all the tasks in the program to truly run in parallel.

Suppose we wish to solve the differential equation

$$\frac{\partial^2 P}{\partial x^2} + \frac{\partial^2 P}{\partial y^2} = F(x, y)$$

over a square region. The value of P is given on the boundary and the value of F is given throughout. The problem is to find the value of P at internal points of the region. This equation arises in many physical situations. One example might concern the flow of heat in a thin sheet of material; $P(x, y)$ would be the temperature of point (x, y) in the sheet and $F(x, y)$ would be the external heat flux applied at that point. However, the physics doesn't really matter.

The standard approach is to consider the region as a grid and to replace the differential equation by a corresponding set of difference equations. For simplicity we consider a square region of side N with unit grid. We end up with something like having to solve

$$4P(i, j) = P(i-1, j) + P(i+1, j) + P(i, j-1) + P(i, j + 1) - F(i, j) \qquad 0 < i, j < N$$

This equation gives a value for each point in terms of its four neighbours. Remember that the values on the boundary are known and fixed. We use an iterative approach (Gauss–Seidel) and allocate a task to each point (i, j). The tasks then repeatedly compute the value of their point from the neighbouring points until the values cease to change. The function F could be of arbitrary complexity. A possible program is as follows

```
procedure Gauss_Seidel is
   N: constant := 5;
   subtype Full_Grid is Integer range 0 .. N;
   subtype Grid is Full_Grid range 1 .. N–1;
```

```
type Real is digits 7;
type Matrix is (Integer range <>, Integer range <>) of Real;
P: Matrix(Full_Grid, Full_Grid);
Delta_P: Matrix(Grid, Grid);
Tolerance: constant Real := 0.0001;
Error_Limit: constant Real := Tolerance * (N–1)**2;
Converged: Boolean := False;
Error_Sum: Real;
pragma Shared(Converged);

function F(I, J: Grid) return Real is separate;

task type Iterator is
   entry Start(I, J: in Grid);
end;

Process: array (Grid, Grid) of Iterator;

task body Iterator is
   I, J: Grid;
   New_P: Real;
begin

   accept Start(I, J: in Grid) do
      Iterator.I := Start.I;
      Iterator.J := Start.J;
   end Start;

   loop
      New_P := 0.25 * (P(I–1, J) + P(I+1, J) + P(I, J–1) + P(I, J+1)
                                                       –F(I, J));

      Delta_P(I, J) := New_P – P(I, J);
      P(I, J) := New_P;
      exit when Converged;
   end loop;

end Iterator;

begin     – – of main program; the Iterator tasks are now active

   ...       – – initialize P and Delta_P

   for I in Grid loop
      for J in Grid loop
         Process(I, J).Start(I, J);      – – tell them who they are
      end loop;
   end loop;

   loop
      Error_Sum := 0.0;
      for I in Grid loop
         for J in Grid loop
            Error_Sum := Error_Sum + Delta_P(I, J)**2;
         end loop;
      end loop;
```

```
            Converged := Error_Sum < Error_Limit;
            exit when Converged;
         end loop;

         ...  − − output results

      end Gauss_Seidel;
```

The main task starts by telling the Iterator tasks who they are through the call of the entry Start. Thereafter the individual tasks execute independently and communicate through shared variables. The Iterator tasks continue until the Boolean Converged is set by the main task; they then exit their loop and terminate. The main task repeatedly computes the sum of squares of the errors from Delta_P (set by the Iterator tasks) and sets Converged accordingly. When stability is reached the main task outputs the results.

The normal way in which tasks communicate is through the rendezvous but there are occasions as here when this might prove too slow. In this example there are three shared objects; the Boolean Converged and the two arrays P and Delta_P. Ada discourages the use of shared variables on the grounds that optimization through holding values in registers is impeded. The rules in the *LRM* (to which the reader is referred) guarantee that sharing works only under certain circumstances. One such circumstance is that the pragma Shared is specified for the variables concerned. We have done this for Converged but the *LRM* appears to forbid this for composite objects. So our program is strictly erroneous but we will assume that our implementation keeps the arrays P and Delta_P in such a way that sharing works.

Ada 9X has somewhat more helpful pragmas for sharing arrays and records. We can write

```
      pragma Atomic_Components(Matrix);
```

and this ensures that all arrays of the type Matrix are such that reads and writes of individual components are indivisible.

The program as shown (with $N = 5$) requires 17 tasks and thus 17 processors. This is not unreasonable and of course the program is based on the assumption of one asynchronous processor per task. Nevertheless, the reader will observe a number of flaws. The convergence criterion is a bit suspect. It might be possible for waves of divergence to slurp around the grid in a manner which escapes the attention of the asynchronous main task − but this is unlikely. Another point is that the Iterator tasks might still be computing one last iteration while the main task is printing the results. It would be better to add a Stop entry so that the main task can wait until the Iterator tasks have finished their loops. Alternatively the array of tasks could be declared in an inner block and the main task could do the printing outside that block where it would know that the other tasks must have terminated. Thus

```
      begin     − − main program

         ...       − − initialize arrays
         declare
            Process: array (Grid, Grid) of Iterator;
```

begin   – – Iterator tasks active

...

...

end;   – – wait for Iterator tasks to terminate

...   – – output results

end Gauss_Seidel;

Many multiprocessor systems will not have a shared memory in which case a different approach is necessary. A naive first attempt might be to give each Iterator an entry which when called delivers the current value of the corresponding point of the grid. Direct *ad hoc* calls from one task to another in a casual design will quickly lead to deadlock. A better approach is to have two tasks per point; one to do the computation and one to provide controlled access to the point (much like the task type Protected_Variable of Section 14.4). We might use one physical processor for each pair of tasks.

It is hoped that our simple example has given the reader some glimpse of how tasking may be distributed over a multiprocessor system. It is a complex subject which is only now being addressed seriously. Of course our example had a ludicrously trivial computation in each task and the system (especially without shared memory) will spend much of its time on communication rather than computation. Nevertheless the principles should be clear. Note that we have not discussed how the different tasks become associated with the different processors; this lies outside the domain of the language itself.

We conclude by mentioning that Ada 9X introduces new concepts which relate to distributed systems; the details are outside the scope of this book.

EXERCISE 14.9

1   A boot repair shop has one man taking orders and three others actually repairing the boots. The shop has storage for 100 boots awaiting repair. The person taking the orders notes the address of the owner and this is attached to the boots; he then puts the boots in the store. Each repairman takes boots from the store when he is free, repairs them and then mails them.

Write a package Cobblers whose specification is

package Cobblers **is**
   procedure Mend(A: Address; B: Boots);
end;

The package body should contain four tasks representing the various men. Use an instantiation of the package Buffers to provide a store for the boots and agent tasks as mailboxes to deliver them.

2   Sketch a solution of the differential equations using two tasks for each point and no shared variables. Assume one physical processor per point and set the priorities so that the data manager task is of a higher priority than the iterator task. Evaluate and store Delta_P in the data task. The main program should use the same convergence rule as before. You will not need arrays (other than for the tasks) since the data will be distributed in the data manager tasks.

CHECKLIST 14

A task is active whereas a package is passive.

A task specification can contain only entries.

A task cannot be generic.

A task name cannot appear in a use clause.

Entries may be overloaded and renamed as procedures.

The 'Count' attribute can only be used inside the task owning the entry.

An accept statement must not appear in a subprogram.

Do not attempt to use priorities for synchronization.

Scheduling is preemptive.

The order of evaluation of guards is not defined.

A select statement can have just one of an else part, a single terminate alternative, one or more delay alternatives.

A terminate or delay alternative can be guarded.

Several alternatives can refer to the same entry.

Beware of the 'Count' attribute in guards.

Task types are limited.

A task declared as an object is dependent on a block, subprogram or task body but not an inner package.

A task created by an allocator is dependent on the block, subprogram or task body containing the access type definition.

A task declared as an object is made active at the following (possibly notional) '**begin**'.

A task created by an allocator is made active at once.

Do not use '**abort**' without good reason.

15 External Interfaces

In this chapter we consider various aspects of how an Ada program interfaces to the outside world. This includes obvious areas such as input–output, interrupt handling and so on, but we will also consider the mapping of our abstract Ada program onto an implementation. However, the discussion in this chapter cannot be exhaustive because many details of this area will depend upon the implementation. The intent, therefore, is to give the reader a general overview of the facilities available.

15.1 Input and output

Unlike many other languages, Ada does not have any intrinsic features for input–output. Instead existing general features such as subprogram overloading and generic instantiation are used. This has the merit of enabling different input–output packages to be developed for different application areas without affecting the language itself. On the other hand this approach can lead to a consequential risk of anarchy in this area; the reader may recall that this was one of the reasons for the downfall of Algol 60. In order to prevent such anarchy the *LRM* defines standard packages for input–output. We discuss the general principles of these packages in this and the next section. For further fine detail the reader should consult the *LRM*.

Two categories of input–output are recognized and we can refer to these as binary and text respectively. As an example consider

        I: Integer := 75;

We can output the binary image of I onto file F by

        Write(F, I);

and the pattern transmitted might be (on a 16-bit machine)

        0000 0000 0100 1011

In fact the file can be thought of as essentially an array of the type Integer. On the other hand we can output the text form of I by

        Put(F, I);

and the pattern transmitted might then be

        0011 0111 0011 0101

which is the representation of the characters '7' and '5' without parity bits. In this case the file can be thought of as an array of the type Character.

Input–output of the binary category is in turn subdivided into sequential and direct access and is provided by distinct generic packages with identifiers Sequential_IO and Direct_IO respectively. Text input–output (which is always sequential) is provided by the special non-generic package Text_IO. There is also a package IO_Exceptions which contains the declarations of the exceptions used by the three other packages. We will deal here first with Sequential_IO and then with Direct_IO and consider Text_IO in the next section.

The specification of the package Sequential_IO is as follows

```
        with IO_Exceptions;
        generic
           type Element_Type is private;
```

```
package Sequential_IO is
  type File_Type is limited private;
  type File_Mode is (In_File, Out_File);

  - - File management

  procedure Create(File: in out File_Type;
                   Mode: in File_Mode := Out_File;
                   Name: in String := "";
                   Form: in String := "");
  procedure Open(File: in out File_Type;
                 Mode: in File_Mode;
                 Name: in String;
                 Form: in String := "");
  procedure Close(File: in out File_Type);
  procedure Delete(File: in out File_Type);
  procedure Reset(File: in out File_Type;
                  Mode: in File_Mode);
  procedure Reset(File: in out File_Type);
  function Mode(File: in File_Type) return File_Mode;
  function Name(File: in File_Type) return String;
  function Form(File: in File_Type) return String;
  function Is_Open(File: in File_Type) return Boolean;

  - - Input and output operations

  procedure Read(File: in File_Type; Item: out Element_Type);
  procedure Write(File: in File_Type; Item: in Element_Type);
  function End_Of_File(File: in File_Type) return Boolean;

  - - Exceptions

  Status_Error: exception renames IO_Exceptions.Status_Error;
  Mode_Error: exception renames IO_Exceptions.Mode_Error;
  Name_Error: exception renames IO_Exceptions.Name_Error;
  Use_Error: exception renames IO_Exceptions.Use_Error;
  Device_Error: exception renames IO_Exceptions.Device_Error;
  End_Error: exception renames IO_Exceptions.End_Error;
  Data_Error: exception renames IO_Exceptions.Data_Error;

private
  - - implementation dependent
end Sequential_IO;
```

The package has a single generic parameter giving the type of element to be manipulated. Note that limited types (and that, thankfully, includes task types) cannot be handled since the generic formal parameter is private rather than limited private.

Externally a file has a name which is a string but internally we refer to a file by using objects of type File_Type. An open file also has an associated value of the enumeration type File_Mode; there are two possible values, In_File or Out_File according to whether read-only or write-only access is required. Read-write access is not allowed for sequential files. The mode of a file is originally set when the file is opened or created but can be changed later by a call of the procedure Reset. Manipulation of sequential files is done using various subprograms whose behaviour is generally as expected.

::: ::: ::: The enumeration type File_Mode has a third literal in Ada 9X, namely Append_File. This mode indicates that the file should be opened for writing like Out_File but positioned so that writing commences at the end of the file rather than the beginning.

As an example, suppose we have a file containing measurements of various populations and that we wish to compute the sum of these measurements. The populations are recorded as values of type Integer and the name of the file is "Census 47". (The actual conventions for the external file name are dependent upon the implementation.) The computed sum is to be written onto a new file to be called "Total 47". This could be done by the following program

```
with Sequential_IO;
procedure Compute_Total_Population is
   package Integer_IO is new Sequential_IO(Integer);
   use Integer_IO;

   Data_File: File_Type;
   Result_File: File_Type;
   Value: Integer;
   Total: Integer := 0;
begin
   Open(Data_File, In_File, "Census 47");

   while not End_Of_File(Data_File) loop
      Read(Data_File, Value);
      Total := Total+Value;
   end loop;
   Close(Data_File);

   - -now write the result

   Create(Result_File, Name => "Total 47");
   Write(Result_File, Total);
   Close(Result_File);
end Compute_Total_Population;
```

We start by instantiating the generic package Sequential_IO with the actual parameter Integer. The use clause enables us to refer to the entities in the created package directly.

The file with the data to be read is referred to via the object Data_File and the output file is referred to via the object Result_File of the type File_Type. Note that this type is limited private; this enables the implementation to use techniques similar to those described in Section 9.3 where we discussed the example of the key manager.

The call of Open establishes the object Data_File as referring to the external file "Census 47" and sets its mode as read-only. The external file is then opened for reading and positioned at the beginning.

We then obey the loop statement until the function End_Of_File indicates that the end of the file has been reached. On each iteration the call of Read copies the item into Value and positions the file at the next item. Total is then updated. When all the values on the file have been read, it is closed by a call of Close.

The call of Create creates a new external file named "Total 47" and establishes Result_File as referring to it and sets its mode by default to write-only. We then write our total onto the file and close it.

The procedures Create and Open have a further parameter Form; this is provided so that auxiliary implementation dependent information can be specified; the default value is a null string so its use is not mandatory. Note that the Name parameter of Create also has a default null value; such a value corresponds to a temporary file. The procedures Close and Delete both close the file and thereby sever the connection between the file variable and the external file. The variable can then be reused for another file. Delete also destroys the external file if the implementation so allows.

The overloaded procedures Reset cause a file to be repositioned at the beginning as for Open. Reset can also change the access mode so that, for example, having written a file, we can now read it.

The functions Mode, Name and Form return the corresponding properties of the file. The function Is_Open indicates whether the file is open; that is indicates whether the file variable is associated with an external file or not.

The procedures Read and Write automatically reposition the file ready for a subsequent call so that the file is processed sequentially. The function End_Of_File only applies to an input file and returns true if there are no more elements to be read.

If we do something wrong then one of the exceptions in the package IO_Exceptions will be raised. This package is as follows

```
package IO_Exceptions is
    Status_Error:    exception;
    Mode_Error:      exception;
    Name_Error:      exception;
    Use_Error:       exception;
    Device_Error:    exception;
    End_Error:       exception;
    Data_Error:      exception;
    Layout_Error:    exception;
end IO_Exceptions;
```

This is an example of a package that does not need a body. The various exceptions are declared in this package rather than in Sequential_IO so that the same exceptions apply to all instantiations of Sequential_IO. If they were inside Sequential_IO then each instantiation would create different exceptions and this would be rather more inconvenient in the case of a program manipulating files of various types since general purpose exception handlers would need to refer to all the instances. The renaming declarations on the other hand enable the exceptions to be referred to without use of the name IO_Exceptions. (A similar technique was used with the mathematical library in Section 13.4.)

The following brief summary gives the general flavour of the circumstances giving rise to each exception

Status_Error   File is open when expected to be closed or vice versa.

Mode_Error   File of wrong mode, for example, In_File when should be Out_File.

Name_Error   Something wrong with Name parameter of Create or Open.

Use_Error   Various such as unacceptable Form parameter or trying to print on card reader.

Device_Error   Physical device broken or not switched on.

End_Error   Malicious attempt to read beyond end of file.

Data_Error   Read or Get (see next section) cannot interpret data as value of desired type.

Layout_Error   Something wrong with layout in Text_IO (see next section) or Put overfills string parameter.

For fuller details of which exception is actually raised in various circumstances the reader is referred to the *LRM* and to the documentation for the implementation concerned.

We continue by considering the package Direct_IO which is very similar to Sequential_IO but gives us more flexibility by enabling us to manipulate the file position directly.

As mentioned earlier a file can be considered as a one-dimensional array. The elements in the file are ordered and each has an associated positive index. This ranges from 1 to an upper value which can change since elements can be added to the end of the file. Not all elements necessarily have a defined value in the case of a direct file as we shall see.

Associated with a direct file is a current index which indicates the position of the next element to be transferred. When a file is opened or created this index is set to 1 so that the program is ready to read or write the first element. The main difference between sequential and direct input–output is that in the sequential case this index is implicit and can only be altered by calls of Read, Write and Reset whereas in the direct case, the index is explicit and can be directly manipulated.

The extra facilities of Direct_IO are as follows. The enumeration type File_Mode has a third value Inout_File so that read-write access is possible; this is also the default mode when a new file is created (thus the Mode parameter of Create has a different default for direct and sequential files). The type and subtype

```
type Count is range 0 .. implementation_defined;
subtype Positive_Count is Count range 1 .. Count'Last;
```

are introduced so that the current index can be referred to and finally there are various extra subprograms whose specifications are as follows

```
procedure Read(File: in File_Type; Item: out Element_Type;
               From: Positive_Count);
procedure Write(File: in File_Type; Item: in Element_Type;
                To: Positive_Count);
procedure Set_Index(File: in File_Type;
                    To: in Positive_Count);
function Index(File: in File_Type) return Positive_Count;
function Size(File: in File_Type) return Count;
```

The extra overloadings of Read and Write first position the current index to the value given by the third parameter and then behave as before. A call of Index returns the current index value; Set_Index sets the current index to the given value and a call of Size returns the number of elements in the file. Note that a file cannot have holes in it; all elements from 1 to Size exist although some may not have defined values.

As an illustration of the manipulation of these positions we can alter our example to use Direct_IO and we can then write the total population onto the end of an existing file called "Totals". The last few statements then become

```
    – – now write the result

    Open(Result_File, Out_File, "Totals");
    Set_Index(Result_File, Size(Result_File)+1);
    Write(Result_File, Total);
    Close(Result_File);
end Compute_Total_Population;
```

Note that if we set the current index well beyond the end of the file and then write to it, the result will be to add several undefined elements to the file and then finally the newly written element.

Note also that the language does not define whether it is possible to write a file with Sequential_IO and then read it with Direct_IO or vice versa. This depends upon the implementation.

We conclude this section by noting that in Ada 9X the formal generic parameter of Sequential_IO takes the indefinite form mentioned in Section 13.2, thus

```
generic
    type Element_Type (<>) is private;
    package Sequential_IO is ...
```

whereas Direct_IO continues to take the definite form. As a consequence Sequential_IO can be instantiated with an unconstrained type such as String in Ada 9X whereas Direct_IO cannot. In principle both can be instantiated with String in Ada 83 although many implementations impose restrictions.

We should also mention that Ada 9X also has additional packages providing support for heterogenous stream input–output.

EXERCISE 15.1

1 Write a generic library procedure to copy a file onto another file but with the elements in reverse order. Pass the external names as parameters.

15.2 Text input–output

Text input–output, which we first met in Chapter 2, is the more familiar form and provides two overloaded procedures Put and Get to transmit values as streams of characters as well as various other subprograms such as New_Line for layout control. In addition the concept of current default files is introduced so that every call of the various subprograms need not tiresomely repeat the file name. Thus if F is the current default output file, we can write

```
Put("Message");
```

rather than

```
Put(F, "Message");
```

There are two current default files, one of mode Out_File for output, and one of mode In_File for input. There is no mode Inout_File in the package Text_IO.

When we enter our program these two files are set to standard default files which are automatically open; we can assume that these are attached to convenient external files such as an interactive terminal or (in olden days) a card reader and line printer. If we wish to use other files and want to avoid repeating the file names in the calls of Put and Get then we can change the default files to refer to our other files. We can also set them back to their original values. This is done with subprograms

```
function Standard_Output return File_Type;
function Current_Output return File_Type;
procedure Set_Output(File: File_Type);
```

with similar subprograms for input. The function Standard_Output returns the initial default output file, Current_Output returns the current default output file and the procedure Set_Output enables us to change the current default output file to the file passed as parameter.

Thus we could bracket a fragment of program with

```
F: File_Type;
...
Open(F, ... );
Set_Output(F);
```

```
    – – use Put
    Set_Output(Standard_Output);
```

so that having used the file F, we can reset the default file to its standard value.

The more general case is where we wish to reset the default file to its previous value which may, of course, not be the standard value. The reader may recall that the type File_Type is limited private and therefore values cannot be assigned; at first sight, therefore, it might not seem possible to make a copy of the original current value. However, with suitable contortion it can be done by using the parameter mechanism. We could write

```
    procedure Job(Old_File, New_File: File_Type) is
    begin
        Set_Output(New_File);
        Action;
        Set_Output(Old_File);
    end;
```

and then

```
    Job(Current_Output, F);
```

When we call Job, the present current value is preserved in the parameter Old_File from whence it can be retrieved for the restoring call of Set_Output. However, although this works, it does feel a bit like standing on one's head!

As an aside, Ada 9X treats the result of a function call as an object and so it can be renamed and it then behaves rather like an in parameter. So we can write

```
    Old_File: File_Type renames Currrent_Output;

    ...
    Set_Output(Old_File),
```

and there is no need to introduce an unnecessary subprogram.

The full specification of Text_IO is rather long and so only the general form is reproduced here

```
    with IO_Exceptions;
    package Text_IO is
        type File_Type is limited private;
        type File_Mode is (In_File, Out_File);

        type Count is range 0 .. implementation_defined;
        subtype Positive_Count is Count range 1 .. Count'Last;
        Unbounded: constant Count := 0;   – – line and page length

        subtype Field is Integer range 0 .. implementation_defined;
        subtype Number_Base is Integer range 2 .. 16;
        type Type_Set is (Lower_Case, Upper_Case);
```

– – File management

– – Create, Open, Close, Delete, Reset, Mode, Name,
– – Form and Is_Open as for Sequential_IO

– – Control of default input and output files

procedure Set_Output(File: **in** File_Type);
function Standard_Output **return** File_Type;
function Current_Output **return** File_Type;

– – Similarly for input

– – Specification of line and page lengths

procedure Set_Line_Length(To: **in** Count);
procedure Set_Page_Length(To: **in** Count);
function Line_Length **return** Count;
function Page_Length **return** Count;

– – also with File parameter

– – Column, line and page control

procedure New_Line(Spacing: **in** Positive_Count := 1);
procedure Skip_Line(Spacing: **in** Positive_Count := 1);
function End_Of_Line **return** Boolean:
procedure New_Page;
procedure Skip_Page;
function End_Of_Page **return** Boolean;
function End_Of_File **return** Boolean;
procedure Set_Col(To: **in** Positive_Count);
procedure Set_Line(To: **in** Positive_Count);
function Col **return** Positive_Count;
function Line **return** Positive_Count;
function Page **return** Positive_Count;

– – also with File parameter

– – Character input–output

procedure Get(File: **in** File_Type; Item: **out** Character);
procedure Get(Item: **out** Character);
procedure Put(File: **in** File_Type; Item: **in** Character);
procedure Put(Item: **in** Character);

– – String input-output

procedure Get(Item: **out** String);
procedure Put(Item: **in** String);
procedure Get_Line(Item: **out** String; Last: **out** Natural);
procedure Put_Line(Item: **in** String);

– – Generic package for input–output of integer types

generic
  type Num **is range** <>;

```
package Integer_IO is
   Default_Width: Field := Num'Width;
   Default_Base: Number_Base := 10;

   procedure Get(Item: out Num; Width: in Field := 0);
   procedure Put(Item: in Num;
                    Width: in Field := Default_Width;
                    Base: in Number_Base := Default_Base);
   procedure Get(From: in String; Item: out Num;
                    Last: out Positive);
   procedure Put(To: out String;
                    Item: in Num;
                    Base: in Number_Base := Default_Base);
end Integer_IO;

– – Generic packages for input–output of real types

generic
   type Num is digits <>;
package Float_IO is
   Default_Fore: Field := 2;
   Default_Aft: Field := Num'Digits-1;
   Default_Exp: Field := 3;

   procedure Get(Item: out Num; Width: in Field := 0);
   procedure Put(Item: in Num;
                    Fore: in Field := Default_Fore;
                    Aft: in Field := Default_Aft;
                    Exp: in Field := Default_Exp);
   procedure Get(From: in String;
                    Item: out Num;
                    Last: out Positive);
   procedure Put(To: out String;
                    Item: in Num;
                    Aft: in Field := Default_Aft;
                    Exp: in Field := Default_Exp);
end Float_IO;

generic
 type Num is delta <>;
package Fixed_IO is
   Default_Fore: Field := Num'Fore;
   Default_Aft: Field := Num'Aft;
   Default_Exp: Field := 0;
   – – then as for Float_IO
end Fixed_IO;

– – Generic package for input–output of enumeration types

generic
   type Enum is (<>);
package Enumeration_IO is
```

```
Default_Width: Field := 0;
Default_Setting: Type_Set := Upper Case;

procedure Get(Item: out Enum);
procedure Put(Item: in Enum;
                   Width: in Field := Default_Width;
                   Set: in Type_Set := Default_Setting);
procedure Get(From: in String;
                   Item: out Enum;
                   Last: out Positive);
procedure Put(To: out String;
                   Item: out Enum;
                   Set: in Type_Set := Default_Setting);
end Enumeration_IO;

-- Exceptions

Status_Error: exception renames IO_Exceptions.Status_Error;
...
Layout_Error: exception renames IO_Exceptions.Layout_Error;

private

-- implementation dependent

end Text_IO;
```

The types File_Type and File_Mode and the various file management procedures are similar to those for Sequential_IO since text files are of course sequential in nature.

Naturally enough, the additional mode Append_File also applies to text files in Ada 9X.

Procedures Put and Get occur in two forms for characters and strings, one with the file and one without; both are shown only for type Character.

In the case of type Character, a call of Put just outputs that character; for type String a call of Put outputs the characters of the string.

A problem arises in the case of numeric and enumeration types since there is not a fixed number of such types. This is overcome by the use of internal generic packages for each category. Thus for integer input–output we instantiate the package Integer_IO with the appropriate type thus

```
type My_Integer is range −1E6 .. +1E6;
...
package My_Integer_IO is new Integer_IO(My_Integer);
use My_Integer_IO;
```

For integer output, Put occurs in three forms, one with the file, one without and one with a string as the destination; only the last two are shown.

In the case of Put to a file, there are two format parameters Width and Base which have default values provided by the variables Default_Width and Default_Base. The default width is initially Num'Width which gives the smallest field which is adequate for all values of the type expressed with base

10 (including a leading space or minus). Base 10 also happens to be the initial default base. These default values can be changed by the user by directly assigning new values to the variables Default_Width and Default_Base (they are directly visible); remember that a default parameter is re-evaluated on each call requiring it and so the default obtained is always the current value of these variables. The integer is output as an integer literal without underlines and leading zeros but with a preceding minus sign if negative. It is padded with leading spaces to fill the field width specified; if the field width is too small, it is expanded as necessary. Thus a default width of 0 results in the field being the minimum to contain the literal. If base 10 is specified explicitly or by default, the value is output using the syntax of decimal literal; if the base is not 10, the syntax of based literal is used.

The attribute 'Width deserves attention. It is a property of the subtype of the actual generic type parameter and not that of the base type. Thus the default format is appropriate to the type as the user sees it and not to the predefined type from which it is derived. This is important for portability. So in the case of My_Integer, the attribute has the value 8 (7 digits for one million plus the space or sign).

The general effect is shown by the following sequence of statements where the output is shown in a comment. The quotes delimit the output and s designates a space. We start with the initial default values for the format parameters.

```
X: My_Integer := 1234;

...
Put(X);               – – "ssss1234"
Put(X, 5);            – – "s1234"
Put(X, 0);            – – "1234"
Put(X, Base => 8);   – – "s8#2322#"
Put(X, 11, 8);       – – "ssss8#2322#"
Default_Base := 8;
Put(X);              – – "s8#2322#"
```

In the case of Put to a string, the field width is taken as the length of the string. If this is too small, then Layout_Error is raised. Put to strings is useful for building up strings containing various bits and pieces and perhaps editing them before actually sending them to a file. It will be found that slices are useful for this sort of manipulation.

Similar techniques are used for real types. A value is output as a decimal literal without underlines and leading zeros but with a preceding minus sign if negative. If Exp is zero, then there is no exponent and the format consists of Fore characters before the decimal point and Aft after the decimal point. If Exp is nonzero, then a signed exponent in a field of Exp characters is output after a letter E with leading zeros if necessary; the exponent value is such that only one significant digit occurs before the decimal point. If the Fore or Exp parts of the field are inadequate, then they are expanded as necessary. Base 10 is always used and the value is rounded to the size of Aft specified.

The initial default format parameters for floating point types are 2, Num'Digits–1 and 3; this gives an exponent form with a space or minus sign plus single digit before the decimal point, Num'Digits−1 digits after the decimal point and a two-digit exponent. The corresponding parameters for fixed point types are Num'Fore, Num'Aft and 0; this gives a form without an exponent and the attributes give the smallest field such that all values of the type can be expressed with appropriate precision.

Enumeration types use a similar technique. A default field of zero is used. If the field has to be padded then the extra spaces go after the value and not before as with the numeric types. Upper case is normally used, but lower case may be specified. A value of a character type which is a character literal is output in single quotes.

Note the subtle distinction between Put defined directly for the type Character and for enumeration values

```
Text_IO.Put('X');
```

outputs the single character X, whereas

```
package Char_IO is new Text_IO.Enumeration_IO(Character);
...
Char_IO.Put('X');
```

outputs the character X between single quotes.

Input using Get works in an analogous way; a call of Get always skips line and page terminators. In the case of the type Character the next character is read. In the case of the type String, the procedure Get reads the exact number of characters as determined by the actual parameter. In the case of enumeration types, leading blanks (spaces or horizontal tabs) are also skipped; input is terminated by a character which is not part of the value or by a line terminator. Numeric types normally have the same behaviour but they also have an additional and optional Width parameter and if this has a value other than zero, then reading stops after this number of characters including skipped blanks. In the case of Get where the source is a string rather than a file, the value of Last indexes the last character read; the end of the string behaves as the end of a file.

The allowed form of data for reading an enumeration value is an identifier (case of letters being ignored), or a character literal in single quotes. The allowed form for an integer value is first and optionally a plus or minus sign and then according to the syntax of an integer literal which may be a based literal and possibly have an exponent (see Section 3.4). The allowed form for a real value is similarly an optional sign followed by a real literal (one with a radix point in it). If the data item is not of the correct form or not a value of the subtype Num then Data_Error is raised. The collector of Ada curiosities will note that Put cannot output integer based forms where the base is 10 such as

```
10#41#
```

although Get can read them. Similarly Put cannot output real based forms at all although Get can read them. On the other hand Get can read whatever Put can write.

A text file is considered as a sequence of lines. The characters in a line have a column position starting at 1. The line length on output can be fixed or variable. A fixed line length is appropriate for the output of tables, a variable line length for dialogue. The line length can be changed within a single file. It is initially not fixed. The lines are similarly grouped into pages starting at page 1.

On output a call of Put will result in all the characters going on the current line starting at the current position in the line. If, however, the line length is fixed and the characters cannot fit in the remainder of the line, a new line is started and all the characters are placed on that line starting at the beginning. If they still will not fit, Layout_Error is raised. If the length is not fixed, the characters always go on the end of the current line.

The layout may be controlled by various subprograms. In some cases they apply to both input and output files; in these cases if the file is omitted then it is taken to apply to the output case and the default output file is assumed. In most cases, a subprogram only applies to one direction and then omitting the file naturally gives the default in that direction.

The function Col returns the current position in the line and the procedure Set_Col sets the position to the given value. A call of Set_Col never goes backwards. On output extra spaces are produced and on input characters are skipped. If the parameter of Set_Col equals the current value of Col then there is no effect; if it is less then a call of New_Line or Skip_Line is implied.

The procedure New_Line (output only) outputs the given number of newlines (default 1) and resets the current column to 1. Spare positions at the end of a line are filled with spaces. The procedure Skip_Line (input only) similarly moves on the given number of lines (default 1) and resets the current column. The function End_Of_Line (input only) returns True if we have reached the end of a line.

The function Line_Length (output only) returns the current line length if it is fixed and zero if it is not. The procedure Set_Line_Length (output only) sets the line length fixed to the given value; a value of zero indicates that it is not to be fixed.

There are also similar subprograms for the control of lines within pages. These are Line, Set_Line, New_Page, Skip_Page, End_Of_Page, Page_Length and Set_Page_Length. Finally the function Page returns the current page number from the start of the file. There is no Set_Page.

The procedures Put_Line and Get_Line are particularly appropriate for manipulating whole lines. A call of Put_Line outputs the string and then moves to the next line (by calling New_Line). A call of Get_Line reads successive characters into the string until the end of the string or the end of the line is encountered; in the latter case it then moves to the next line (by calling Skip_Line); Last indexes the last character moved into the string. Successive calls of Put_Line and Get_Line therefore manipulate whole lines. However, AI-50 places a curious interpretation on Get_Line when the string is exactly the right length to accommodate the remaining characters on the line – it doesn't move to the next line! So, given a series of lines of length 80, successive calls of Get_Line with a string of length 80 (bounds 1 .. 80) return alternately lines of 80 characters and null strings (or in other words the value of Last is alternately 80 and 0). This unhelpful behaviour can be overcome by using a string of length 81 or calling Skip_Line ourselves after each call of Get_Line.

It will be found helpful to use slices with Get_Line and Put_Line; thus to copy a text file (with lines of less than 100 characters) and adding the string "– –" to each line we could write

```
S: String(1 .. 100);
N: Natural;
...
while not End_Of_File loop
  Get_Line(S, N);
  Put_Line("– –" & S(1 .. N));
end loop;
```

where we have assumed default files throughout.

The package Text_IO may seem somewhat elaborate but for simple output all we need is Put and New_Line and these are quite straightforward as we have seen.

EXERCISE 15.2

1   What do the following calls output? Assume the initial values for the default parameters.

(a) Put("Fred");
(b) Put(120);
(c) Put(120, 8);
(d) Put(120, 0);
(e) Put(–120, 0);

(f) Put(120, 8, 8);
(g) Put(–38.0);
(h) Put(0.07, 6, 2, 2);
(i) Put(3.14159, 1, 4);
(j) Put(9_999_999_999.9, 1, 1, 1);

Assume that the real values are of a type with **digits** = 6 and the integer values are of a type with 16 bits.

2   Write a body for the package Simple_IO of Section 2.2. Ignore exceptions.

15.3   Interrupts

An interrupt is another form of input. In Ada this can be achieved through the rendezvous mechanism. From within the program, an interrupt appears as an entry call performed by an external task whose priority is higher than that of any task in the program. The interrupt handler is then naturally represented in the program by a task with accept statements for the corresponding entry. The entry is identified as an interrupt by what is known as a representation clause giving the relevant hardware address.

As an example suppose a program wishes to act upon an interrupt arising from the closing of an electrical contact and the interrupt is associated with the address 8#72#. We could write

```
task Contact_Handler is
    entry Contact;
    for Contact use at 8#72#;
end;

task body Contact_Handler is
begin
    loop
        accept Contact do
            ...
        end;
    end loop;
end Contact_Handler;
```

The body of the accept statement corresponds to the direct response to the interrupt. The rule that the external mythical task has a priority higher than that of any software task ensures that the response takes precedence over ordinary tasks.

An interrupt entry will usually have no parameters but it can have **in** parameters through which control information is passed. An accept statement for an interrupt entry can also occur in a select statement.

The detailed behaviour of interrupt entry calls is somewhat dependent upon the implementation. They could for example appear as conditional entry calls and therefore be lost if the response task is not ready to execute the corresponding accept statement. The exact interpretation of the address in the representation clause is also dependent on the implementation.

Ada 9X provides an intrinsically more efficient method of handling interrupts based on protected objects. The technique we have just been describing can be considered obsolete and may well be removed from some future version of the language.

15.4   Representation clauses

In the last section we introduced the representation clause as a means of informing the compiler of additional information about the interrupt entry. Representation clauses take various forms and apply to various entities. Their general purpose is to provide the compiler with directions regarding how the entity is to be implemented. A representation clause must occur in the same declaration list as the declaration of the entity it refers to.

An address clause is of the form used for the entry. It can be used to assign an explicit address to an object, to indicate the start address of the code body of a subprogram, package or task, or as we have seen, to specify an interrupt to which an entry is to be linked.

A length clause allows us to specify the amount of storage to be allocated for objects of a type, for the collection of an access type and for the working storage of a task type. This is done by indicating the value of certain attributes. Thus

> **type** Byte **is range** 0 .. 255;
> **for** Byte'Size **use** 8;

ensures that objects of the type Byte occupy only 8 bits.

The space for access collections and tasks is indicated using the attribute Storage_Size. In these cases the unit is not bits but storage units. The number of bits in a storage unit is implementation dependent and is given by the constant Storage_Unit in the package System. Thus if we wanted to ensure that the access collection for

> **type** Link **is access** Cell;

will accommodate 500 cells then we write

> **for** Link'Storage_Size **use**
>   500 * (Cell'Size / System.Storage_Unit);

which assumes that Cell'Size is an exact multiple of Storage_Unit.

Similarly the data space for each task of a task type can be indicated by

> **for** Mailbox'Storage_Size **use** 128;

The value of *small* for a fixed point type can also be indicated by a length clause as was discussed in Section 12.4.

An enumeration representation clause can be used to specify, as an aggregate, the internal integer codes for the literals of an enumeration type. We might have a status value transmitted into our program as single bit settings, thus

> **type** Status **is** (Off, Ready, On);
> **for** Status **use** (Off => 1, Ready => 2, On => 4);

There is a constraint that the ordering of the values must be the same as the logical ordering of the literals. However, despite the holes, the functions Succ, Pred, Pos and Val always work in logical terms.

If these single bit values were autonomously loaded into our machine at location octal 100 then we could conveniently access them in our program by declaring a variable of type Status and placing it at that location using an address clause

> S: Status;
> **for** S **use at** 8#100#;

However, if by some hardware mishap a value which is not 1, 2 or 4 turns up then the program will be erroneous and its behaviour quite unpredictable. We will see how to overcome this difficulty in Section 15.6.

The final form of representation clause is used to indicate the layout of a record type. Thus if we have

```
type Register is range 0 .. 15;
type Opcode is ( ... );

type RR is
    record
        Code: Opcode;
        R1: Register;
        R2: Register;
    end record;
```

which represents a machine instruction of the RR format in the IBM System 370, then we can specify the exact mapping by

```
for RR use
    record at mod 2;
        Code at 0 range 0 .. 7;
        R1   at 1 range 0 .. 3;
        R2   at 1 range 4 .. 7;
    end record;
```

The optional alignment clause

```
    at mod 2;
```

indicates that the record is to be aligned on a double byte boundary; the alignment is given in terms of the number of storage units and in the case of the 370 a storage unit would naturally be one 8-bit byte.

The position and size of the individual components are given relative to the start of the record. The value after **at** gives a storage unit and the range is in terms of bits. The bit number can extend outside the storage unit; we could equally have written

```
    R1 at 0 range 8 .. 11;
```

If we do not specify the location of every component, the compiler is free to juggle the rest as best it can. However, we must allow enough space for those we do specify and they must not overlap unless they are in different alternatives of a variant. There may also be hidden components (array dope information for example) and this may interfere with our freedom.

We conclude this section by noting an important rule that only one representation clause is allowed for (a particular aspect of) any type. Moreover, any type derived from a type after the declaration of a representation clause will inherit that representation. Nevertheless we can have two types one derived from the other with different representations by placing the representation clauses after the derivation. So, in essence, derived types allow us to have different representations for essentially the same type and conveniently force us

::: to use explicit type conversions to transfer from one representation to another.
Ada 9X uniformly allows the attribute notation for setting all representation forms. Thus we can alternatively write

:::   **for** S'Address **use** 8#100#;

::: in order to set the address of the variable S of type Status and

:::   **for** RR'Alignment **use** 2;

::: to set the alignment of the record type RR. The forms using **at** are considered deprecated. The order of numbering of bits in a record type can be specified. Thus

:::   **for** RR'Bit_Order **use** Low _Order_First.

indicates little endian numbering as opposed to big endian using the Gulliverian vernacular.

15.5   Implementation considerations

It is hard to be specific in this area since so much depends upon the implementation. However, there is a package System which includes the values of various machine constants. Its specification is as follows

```
package System is
  type Address is implementation_defined;
  type Name    is implementation_defined_enumeration_type;

  System_Name  : constant Name := implementation_defined;

  Storage_Unit : constant := implementation_defined;
  Memory_Size  : constant := implementation_defined;

  -- system-dependent named numbers

  Min_Int      : constant := implementation_defined;
  Max_Int      : constant := implementation_defined;
  Max_Digits   : constant := implementation_defined;
  Max_Mantissa : constant := implementation_defined;
  Fine_Delta   : constant := implementation_defined;
  Tick         : constant := implementation_defined;

  -- other system-dependent declarations

  subtype Priority is Integer range implementation_defined;

  ...
end System;
```

The type Address is that used in an address clause and given by the corresponding attribute; it might be an integer type or possibly a record type.

The numbers Storage_Unit and Memory_Size give the size of a storage unit in bits and the memory size in storage units; both are of type universal integer. Min_Int and Max_Int give the most negative and most positive values of an integer type, Max_Digits is the largest number of decimal digits of a floating type and Max_Mantissa is the largest number of binary digits of a fixed type; they are all of type universal integer. Fine_Delta is a bit redundant since it always has the value 2.0**(–Max_Mantissa) and Tick is the clock period in seconds; they are both of type universal real.

The package System in Ada 9X is somewhat more extensive and in particular includes additional facilities for manipulating addresses and offsets.

Various pragmas enable us to set certain parameters of the implementation, and attributes enable us to read the value of certain parameters. The predefined pragmas and attributes are listed in Appendix 1 although an implementation is free to add others.

Note that the pragmas System_Name, Storage_Unit and Memory_Size are deleted in Ada 9X because experience showed them to be unnecessary.

Some pragmas enable us to guide the compiler regarding the balance of the implementation between integrity and efficiency and also between space and time.

The pragma Suppress can be used to indicate that the run-time checks associated with detecting conditions which could give rise to exceptions can be omitted if to do so would lead to a more efficient program. However, it should be remembered that a pragma is merely a recommendation and so there is no guarantee that the exception will not be raised. Indeed it could be propagated from another unit compiled with checks.

The checks corresponding to the exception Constraint_Error are Access_Check (checking that an access value is not null when attempting to access a component), Discriminant_Check (checking that a discriminant value is consistent with the component being accessed or a constraint), Index_Check (checking that an index is in range), Length_Check (checking that the number of components of an array match) and Range_Check (checking that various constraints are satisfied).

The checks corresponding to Numeric_Error are Division_Check (checking the second operand of /, **rem** and **mod**) and Overflow_Check (checking for numeric overflow).

Remember that Numeric_Error is simply a renaming of Constraint_Error in Ada 9X.

The check corresponding to Storage_Error is Storage_Check (checking that space for an access collection or task has not been exceeded).

The check corresponding to Program_Error is Elaboration_Check (checking that the body of a unit has been elaborated).

The pragma takes the form

    pragma Suppress(Range_Check);

in which case it applies to all operations in the unit concerned or it can list the types and objects to which it is to be applied. Thus

    pragma Suppress(Access_Check, Link);

indicates that no checks are to be applied when accessing objects of the access type Link.

The other pragmas in this category apply to the balance between speed and time. They are Controlled, Inline, Optimize and Pack; they are described in Appendix 1.

Finally, there are various machine dependent attributes defined for real types. For example there is the attribute Machine_Rounds which indicates whether rounding is performed for the type concerned. Another is the attribute Machine_Overflows which indicates whether Numeric_Error (Constraint_Error) is raised for computations which exceed the range of the type. If a program uses these attributes then care is required if portability is to be ensured.

15.6 Unchecked programming

Sometimes the strict integrity of a fully typed language is a nuisance. This particularly applies to system programs where, in different parts of a program, an object is thought of in different terms. This difficulty can be overcome by the use of a generic function called Unchecked_Conversion. Its specification is

```
generic
    type Source is limited private;
    type Target is limited private;
function Unchecked_Conversion(S: Source) return Target;
```

As an example, we can overcome our problem with possible erroneous values of the type Status of Section 15.4. We can receive the values into our program as values of type Byte, check their validity in numeric terms and then convert the values to type Status for the remainder of the program. In order to perform the conversion we first instantiate the generic function thus

```
function Byte_To_Status is
    new Unchecked_Conversion(Byte, Status);
```

and we can then write

```
B: Byte;
for B use at 8#100#;
S: Status;
...
case B is
    when 1 | 2 | 4 =>
        null;
    when others =>
        raise Bad_Data;
end case;

S := Byte_To_Status(B);
```

The effect of the unchecked conversion is nothing; the bit pattern of the source type is merely passed on unchanged and reinterpreted as the bit pattern of the target type. Clearly, certain conditions must be satisfied for this to be possible; an obvious one which may be imposed by the implementation is that the number of bits in the representations of the two types must be the same. We cannot get a quart into a pint pot.

A minor point is that the generic formal parameters of Unchecked_ Conversion in Ada 9X take the indefinite form with (<>) in a similar manner to Sequential_IO. Also the checking of status can be conveniently done using the Valid attribute after the conversion.

Another area where the programmer can be given extra freedom is in the deallocation of access types. As mentioned in Section 11.4 there may or may not be a garbage collector. In any event we may prefer to do our own garbage collection perhaps on the grounds that this gives us better timing control in a realtime program. We can do this with a generic procedure called Unchecked_Deallocation. Its specification is

```
generic
    type Object is limited private;
    type Name is access Object;
procedure Unchecked_Deallocation(X: in out Name);
```

If we take our old friend

```
type Link is access Cell;
```

then we can write

```
procedure Free is
    new Unchecked_Deallocation(Cell, Link);
```

and then

```
L: Link;
...
Free(L);
```

After calling Free, the value of L will be **null** and the cell will have been returned to free storage. Of course, if we mistakenly still had another variable referring to the cell then we would be in a mess; the program would be erroneous. If we use unchecked deallocation then the onus is on us to get it right. We should also insert

```
pragma Controlled(Link);
```

to tell the compiler that we are looking after ourselves and that any garbage collector should not be used for this access type.

In Ada 9X the formal generic parameter Object takes the indefinite form as expected.

The use of both these forms of unchecked programming needs care and it would be sensible to restrict the use of these generic subprograms to privileged parts of the program. Note that since both generic functions are library functions then any compilation unit using them must refer to them in a with clause. This makes it fairly straightforward for a tool to check for their use. And also for our manager to peer over our shoulders to see whether we are writing naughty programs!

15.7   Other languages

Another possible form of communication between an Ada program and the outside world is via other languages. These could be machine languages or other high level languages such as Fortran. The *LRM* prescribes general methods but the actual details will obviously depend so much upon the implementation that an outline description seems pointless and the reader is therefore referred to specific documentation for the implementation concerned.

16 Concluding Ada 83

This chapter covers various overall aspects of Ada. The first four sections consider in more detail and consolidate some important topics which have of necessity been introduced in stages throughout the book. There is then a section on the important issue of portability. Finally, we discuss the general topic of program design as it relates to Ada.

16.1   Names and expressions

The idea of a name should be carefully distinguished from that of an identifier. An identifier is a syntactic form such as Fred which is used for various purposes including introducing entities when they are declared. A name, on the other hand, may be more complex and is the form used to denote entities in general. In the *LRM* and in particular in the syntax rules, the term simple name is used to refer to an identifier other than when it is first introduced; we have not used this term since it seems unnecessarily pedantic.

Syntactically, a name starts with an identifier such as Fred or an operator symbol such as "+" and can then be followed by one or more of the following in an arbitrary order

* one or more index expressions in brackets; this denotes a component of an array,
* a discrete range in brackets; this denotes a slice of an array,
* a dot followed by an identifier, operator or **all**; this denotes a record component, an access value or an entity in a package, task, subprogram, block or loop,
* a prime and then an identifier, possibly indexed; this denotes an attribute,
* an actual parameter list in brackets; this denotes a function call.

A function call in a name must deliver an array, record or access value and must be followed by indexing, slicing, attribution or component selection. This is not to say that a function call must always be followed by one of these things; it could deliver a value as part of an expression, but as part of a name it must be so followed. This point is clarified by considering the assignment statement. The left hand side must be a name whereas the right hand side is an expression. Hence, as we saw in Section 11.6, we can write

        Spouse(P).Birth := Newdate;

but not

        Spouse(P) := Q;

although

        Q := Spouse(P);

is of course perfectly legal. (Ada is somewhat less consistent than Algol 68 in this respect.)

Names are just one of the primary components of an expression. The others are literals (numeric literals, enumeration literals, strings and **null**), aggregates, allocators, function calls (not considered as names), type conversions and qualified expressions as well as expressions in brackets. Expressions involving scalar operators were summarized in Section 4.9.

For convenience, all the operators and their predefined uses are shown in Table 16.1. They are grouped according to precedence level. We have also included the short circuit forms **and then** and **or else** and the membership tests **in** and **not in** although these are not technically classed as operators (they cannot be overloaded).

Note the careful distinction between Boolean which means the predefined type and 'Boolean' which means Boolean or any type derived from it. Similarly Integer means the predefined type and 'integer' means any integer type (including universal integer). Also 'floating' means any floating type plus universal real.

We recall from Chapter 12 that more liberal rules apply for fixed point multiplication and division in Ada 9X; the operands can be universal fixed.

Observe that the membership tests apply to any type and not just scalar types which were discussed in Section 4.9. Thus we can check whether an array or record has a particular subtype by using a membership test rather than testing the bounds or discriminant. So we can write

```
V in Vector_5      – – true, see Section 6.2
John in Woman      – – false, see Section 11.3
```

rather than

```
V'First = 1 and V'Last = 5
John.Sex = Female
```

which are equivalent.

Finally, remember that & can take either an array or a component for both operands so four cases arise.

The observant reader will notice that the syntax in Appendix 4 uses the syntactic form 'simple_expression' in some cases where 'expression' might have been expected. One reason for this is to avoid a potential ambiguity regarding the use of **in** as a membership test with ranges.

From time to time we have referred to the need for certain scalar expressions to be static. As explained in Chapter 2 this means that they can be evaluated at compilation time. An expression is static if all its constituents are one of the following

- a numeric or enumeration literal,
- a named number,
- a constant initialized by a static expression,
- a predefined operator,
- a static attribute or a functional attribute with static parameters,
- a qualified static expression provided that any constraint involved is static.

Note that renaming preserves staticness so a renaming of one of the above (for which renaming is allowed) is also an allowed constituent of a static expression (AI-1 and AI-438). However, membership tests and short circuit

Table 16.1 Predefined operators.

Operator	Operand(s)		Result
and or xor	Boolean		same
	one-dim Boolean array		same
and then or else	Boolean		same
= /=	any, not limited		Boolean
< <= > >=	scalar		Boolean
	one-dim discrete array		Boolean
in not in	scalar	range	Boolean
	any	type mark	Boolean
+ − (binary)	numeric		same
&	one-dim array ǀ component		same array
+ − (unary)	numeric		same
*	integer	integer	same
	fixed	Integer	same fixed
	Integer	fixed	same fixed
	fixed	fixed	univ fixed
	floating	floating	same
	univ real	univ integer	univ real
	univ integer	univ real	univ real
/	integer	integer	same
	fixed	Integer	same fixed
	fixed	fixed	univ fixed
	floating	floating	same
	univ real	univ integer	univ real
mod rem	integer	integer	same
**	integer	Natural	same integer
	floating	Integer	same floating
not	Boolean		same
	one-dim Boolean array		same
abs	numeric		same

forms are not allowed (AI-128). Observe that staticness only applies to scalar expressions and that all intermediate subexpressions must also be scalar (AI-219). This excludes bizarre examples such as 'a'&'b'='c'&'d' where the intermediate expressions are arrays although the result is scalar.

The rules are somewhat more liberal in Ada 9X and additional constituents are allowed in a static expression. Membership tests and short circuit control forms are static if their constituents are static; the bounds, length and range of static arrays are static and a type conversion is static provided that any constraint involved is static. Moreover generic formal types are treated more favourably with regard to case statements and variants as mentioned in Section 13.1.

The final point we wish to make about expressions concerns array bounds. If an expression delivers an array value then it will have bounds for each dimension. Such an expression can be used in various contexts which can be divided into categories according to the rules regarding the matching of the bounds.

The first category (sliding semantics) includes assignment and initialization in an object declaration. In these cases the bounds of the expression do not have to match the bounds of the object; all that matters is that the number of components in each dimension is the same. Thus as we saw in Section 6.2 we can write

```
V: Vector(1 .. 5);
W: Vector(0 .. 4);
...
V := W;
```

The same sliding rules apply in the case of the predefined equality and relational operators.

Array type conversion described in Section 6.2 also has sliding semantics if the destination type is constrained. However, if the type is unconstrained then the 'result' naturally takes the bounds of the operand.

The second category (matching semantics) includes using an array as an actual parameter, as a function result, as an initial value in an allocator or in a qualified expression. Again, the destination type may or may not be constrained. If it is constrained, then the bounds must exactly match; if it is not constrained, then the result takes the bounds of the expression. Thus if we had a function

```
function F return Vector_5 is
  V: Vector(1 .. 5);
  W: Vector(0 .. 4);
begin
  ...
```

then we could write **return** V but not **return** W. If, however, the specification had been

```
function F return Vector
```

then we could write either **return** V or **return** W.

⁞⁞⁞ Ada 9X is much more liberal and allows sliding for parameter passing, in allocators and for function results and indeed treats these situations just like type conversions. In particular therefore we can indeed write **return** W in the first example above. In fact the only situation in Ada 9X where matching is still required is type qualification; this is quite natural since qualification is, in essence, an assertion and it would be very wrong to change the value in any way.

There are complications with array aggregates. In the case of a named aggregate without **others** the bounds are evident; such an aggregate can be used in any of the above contexts. In the case of a positional aggregate without **others** the bounds are not evident although the number of components is; such an aggregate can also be used in any of the above contexts—in all the cases of the first category (sliding) and those of the second category (matching) with a constrained type the bounds are taken to be those required by the constraint—in cases of the second category with an unconstrained type the lower bound is given by S'First where S is the index subtype. If an aggregate (positional or named) contains **others**, then neither the bounds nor the number of components is evident. Such an aggregate can be used in a situation of the second category with a constrained type. Finally, a positional aggregate with **others** (or just **others** on its own) is also allowed in a situation of the first category; but remember that it takes its bounds from the destination and never actually slides.

⁞⁞⁞ Ada 9X also allows named aggregates with **others** in the last case as was explained in Section 6.3.

Finally, note that similar rules apply to nested aggregates; the context of the whole aggregate is applied transitively to its components.

EXERCISE 16.1

1 Given

```
L: Integer := 6;
M: constant Integer := 7;
N: constant := 8;
```

then classify the following as static or dynamic expressions and give their type.

(a) L+1
(b) M+1
(c) N+1

16.2 Type equivalence

It is perhaps worth emphasizing the rules for type equivalence. The basic rule is that every type definition introduces a new type. Remember the difference between a type definition and a type declaration. A type definition introduces a type whereas a type declaration also introduces an identifier referring to it. Thus

    type T **is** (A, B, C);

is a type declaration whereas

    (A, B, C)

is a type definition.

Most types have names but in a few cases a type may be anonymous. The obvious cases occur with the declarations of arrays and tasks. Thus

    A: **array** (I **range** L .. R) **of** C;

is short for

    type anon **is array** (I **range** <>) **of** C;
    A: anon(L .. R);

and

    task T **is** ...

is short for

    task type anon **is** ...
    T: anon;

More subtle cases occur where an apparent type declaration is actually only a subtype declaration. This occurs with array types, derived types and numeric types and so

    type T **is array** (I **range** L .. R) **of** C;

is short for

    subtype index **is** I **range** L .. R;
    type anon **is array** (index **range** <>) **of** C;
    subtype T **is** anon(L .. R);

and

    type S **is new** T constraint;

is short for

    type anon **is new** T;
    subtype S **is** anon Constraint;

and

        type T **is range** L .. R;

is short for

        type anon **is new** integer_type;
        subtype T **is** anon **range** L .. R;

where integer_type is one of the predefined integer types. Similar expansions apply to floating and fixed types.

When interpreting the rule that each type definition introduces a new type, remember that generic instantiation is equivalent to text substitution in this respect. Thus each instantiation of a package with a type definition in its specification introduces a distinct type. It will be remembered that a similar rule applies to the identification of different exceptions. Each textually distinct exception declaration introduces a new exception; an exception in a recursive procedure is the same for each incarnation but generic instantiation introduces different exceptions.

Remember also that multiple declarations are equivalent to several single declarations written out explicitly. Thus if we have

        A, B: **array** (I **range** L .. R) **of** C;

then A and B are of different anonymous types.

In summary then, Ada has named equivalence rather than the weaker structural equivalence of some languages such as Algol 68. As a consequence Ada gives greater security in the sense that more errors can be found during compilation. However, the Ada type model requires more care in program design. Overzealous use of lots of different types can lead to trouble and there are stories of programs that could never be got to compile.

An obvious area of caution is with numeric types (a novice programmer often uses lots of numeric types with great glee). Attempts to use different numeric types to separate different units of measurement (for example the lengths and areas of Exercise 11.7(**1**)) can lead to messy situations where either lots of overloadings of operators have to be introduced or so many type conversions are required that the clarity sought is lost by the extra clutter. Another problem is that each different numeric type will require a separate instantiation of the relevant package in Text_IO if input–output is required. An example of possible overuse of numeric types is in Text_IO itself where the distinct integer type Count (used for counting characters, lines and pages) is a frequent irritant.

So too many types can be unwise. However, the use of appropriate constraints (as explicit subtypes or directly) always seems to be a good idea. Remember that subtypes are merely shorthands for a base type plus constraint and as a consequence have structural equivalence. Thus, recalling an example in Section 4.4, we can declare

```
subtype Day_Number is Integer range 1 .. 31;
subtype Feb_Day is Day_Number range 1 .. 29;
D1: Integer range 1 .. 29;
D2: Day_Number range 1 .. 29;
D3: Feb_Day;
```

and then D1, D2 and D3 all have exactly the same subtype.

When to use a subtype and when to use a new type is a matter of careful judgement. The guidelines must be the amount of separation between the abstract concepts. If the abstractions are quite distinct then separate types are justified but if there is much overlap and thus much conversion then subtypes are probably appropriate. Thus we could make a case for Day_Number being a distinct derived type

```
type Day_Number is range 1 .. 31;
```

but we would find it hard to justify making Feb_Day not simply a subtype of Day_Number.

Another important distinction between types and subtypes is in their representation. The basic rule is that a subtype has the same representation as the base type whereas a derived type can have a different representation. Of course, the compiler can still optimize, but that is another matter.

It should also be remembered that checking subtype properties is generally a run-time matter. Thus

```
S: String(1 .. 4) := "ABC";
```

raises Constraint_Error although we can expect that any reasonable compiler would pick this up during compilation.

However, although checking that a value lies within a subtype remains a run-time matter in Ada 9X, static matching is generally required between subtypes. Examples are matching the component subtypes in array conversions (Section 6.2), the subtype conformance rules for renaming subprogram bodies (Section 8.5) and matching in deferred constants (Section 9.1).

16.3   Structure summary and the main program

Ada has four structural units in which declarations can occur; these are blocks, subprograms, packages and tasks. They can be classified in various ways. First of all packages and tasks have separate specifications and bodies; for subprograms this separation is optional; for blocks it is not possible or relevant since a block has no specification. We can also consider separate compilation: packages, tasks and subprogram bodies can all be subunits but only packages and subprograms can be library units. Note also that only packages and subprograms can be generic. Finally, tasks, subprograms and

Table 16.2 Properties of units.

Property	Blocks	Subprograms	Packages	Tasks
Separation	no	optional	yes	yes
Subunits	no	yes	yes	yes
Library units	no	yes	yes	no
Generic units	no	yes	yes	no
Dependent tasks	yes	yes	no	yes

blocks can have dependent tasks but packages cannot since they are only passive scope control units. These various properties of units are summarized in Table 16.2.

We can also consider the scope and nesting of these four structural units. (Note that a block is a statement whereas the others are declarations.) Each unit can appear inside any of the other units and this lexical nesting can in principle go on indefinitely, although in practical programs a depth of three will not often be exceeded. The only restrictions to this nesting are that a block, being a statement, cannot appear in a package specification but only in its body (and directly only in the initialization sequence) and of course none of these units can appear in a task specification but again only in its body. In practice, however, some of the combinations will arise rarely. Blocks will usually occur inside subprograms and task bodies and occasionally inside other blocks. Subprograms will occur as library units and inside packages and less frequently inside tasks and other subprograms. Packages will usually be library units or inside other packages. Tasks will probably nearly always be inside packages and occasionally inside other tasks or subprograms.

The *Language Reference Manual* is a little vague about the concept of an Ada program. This is perhaps to be expected since Ada is about software components, and undue concern regarding what constitutes a complete program is probably out of place particularly bearing in mind the growing concern with distributed and parallel systems. However, for simple systems we can regard a program as composed out of the library units in a particular program library. The *LRM* does not prescribe how the program is to be started but as discussed in Sections 2.2 and 8.2 we can imagine that one of the library units which is a subprogram (or an instance of a generic subprogram (AI-513)) is called by some magic outside the language itself. Moreover, we must imagine that this originating flow of control is associated with an anonymous task. The priority of this task can be set by the pragma Priority in the outermost declarative part of this main subprogram.

The main program will almost inevitably use dependent library units such as Text_IO. These have to be elaborated before the main program is entered and again we can imagine that this is done by our anonymous task. The order of these elaborations is not precisely specified but it must be consistent with the dependencies between the units. In addition, the pragma Elaborate can be used to ensure that a body is elaborated before a unit that calls it; this may be necessary to prevent Program_Error. Consider the situation mentioned at the end of Section 8.1 thus

```
package P is
   function A return Integer;
end P;

package body P is
   function A return Integer is
   begin
      return 0;
   end A;
end P;

with P;
package Q is
   I: Integer := P.A;
end Q;
```

The three units can be compiled separately and the requirements are that the body of P and the specification of Q must both be compiled after the specification of P. But there is no need for the body of P to be compiled before the specification of Q. However, when we come to elaborate the three units it is important that the body of P be elaborated before the specification of Q otherwise Program_Error will be raised. The dependency rules are not enough to ensure this and so we have to use the pragma Elaborate and write

```
with P;
pragma Elaborate(P);
package Q is
   I: Integer := P.A;
end Q;
```

The pragma immediately follows the context clause and can refer to one or more of the library units mentioned in the context clause.

If the dependencies and any pragmas Elaborate are such that no consistent order of elaboration exists then the program is illegal; if there are several possible orders and the behaviour of the program depends on the particular order then it is also illegal (since it then has an incorrect order dependency).

There are also pragmas Elaborate_All and Elaborate_Body in Ada 9X. The pragma Elaborate remains but is essentially replaced by Elaborate_All which is transitive; Elaborate_Body applied to a specification ensures that the body is immediately elaborated after the specification.

A further point is that whether a main program can have parameters or not or whether there are restrictions on their types and modes or indeed whether the main program can be a function is dependent on the implementation. Again this is in line with the view that Ada is about the open world of components rather than the closed world of complete programs. It may indeed be very convenient for a main program to have parameters, and for the calling and parameter passing to be performed by the magic associated with the interpretation of a statement in some non-Ada command language.

The above general description is confirmed by AI-222 which also summarizes a number of issues that have been clarified and then illustrates the effect of various rules by the following model

```
task body ... is
begin
  begin
    declare
      package Standard is    – – This is Appendix 2
        ...
      end;

      package body Standard is
        – – Library units and secondary units needed by
        – –    the main program and the main program
        – –    (procedure or function), in an order
        – –    consistent with the with clauses and any
        – –    pragmas Elaborate.
      begin
        – – Get parameters required by the main program,
        – –    if any.
        – – Call the main program.
      exception
        – – Handle any exceptions associated with main
        – –    program execution.
      end Standard;
    begin
      null;
    end;  – – Wait for library tasks to terminate.
  exception
    – – Handle any exceptions associated with library unit
    – –    elaboration.
  end;
  – – Close external files (optional).
  – – Communicate main program function result, if any.
end;
```

This model captures the following

- The environment task is expressed as an anonymous task.
- Library units and the main program are contained in the package Standard.
- Library units needed by the main program, corresponding library unit bodies and the main program are elaborated in an implementation defined order consistent with the with clauses and any Elaborate pragmas. These elaborations occur before the main program is called.
- Delay statements executed by the environment task during the elaboration of a library package delay the environment task.

- Tasks that depend on a library unit (and that are not designated by an access value) are started at the end of the declarative part of Standard and before the main program is called.

- After normal termination of the main program the environment task must wait for all library tasks to terminate. If all library tasks terminate, then the program as a whole terminates.

- If the main program terminates abnormally by the propagation of an exception then the exception is handled by the environment task. The environment task then waits for any library tasks to terminate. The effect of the environment task's exception handler on unterminated tasks is not defined. In particular, unterminated tasks can be aborted.

- If any external files are used by statements executed in library package bodies, then such operations are performed before execution of the main program begins. If external files are used by library tasks, then these files are processed in accordance with normal Ada semantics, whether or not execution of the main program has begun or has finished. After the main program and all library tasks have terminated (or if execution of the main program is abandoned because of an unhandled exception), any further effects on the external files are not defined; in particular, any files that have been left open may (but need not) be closed.

The reader is warned not to read more into the model than the points listed (it does not cover every subtlety). Nevertheless the model does help to dispel a certain mystery about the nature of the main program and its environment.

The main changes in Ada 9X in this area are as follows. There is a fifth structural unit, the protected object; there are additional and different pragmas for elaboration control; and a superstructure of partitions is added – a program in Ada 83 is a single partition in Ada 9X.

16.4 Visibility and program composition

The visibility and scope rules have been introduced by stages. The basic rules applicable to the simple block structure were introduced in Section 4.2 and further discussed in Section 7.6 when we considered the use of the dotted notation to provide visibility of an outer identifier which had been hidden by an inner redeclaration. The overloading rules were discussed in Section 7.2 and we recall that the use of identifiers fell into two categories: overloadable (subprograms) and not overloadable (the rest). We then considered the impact of packages in Section 8.4 and the rules regarding the use clause. We also noted in Section 10.3 that exceptions had some special characteristics. We do not intend to repeat all these rules here but rather to illustrate some of their effects particularly with regard to building programs from components.

We begin by recalling from Section 7.5 that enumeration literals behave much like parameterless functions. We could not therefore declare both an enumeration type and a parameterless function returning that type and with the same identifier as one of the literals in the same declarative region thus

```
type Colour is (Red, Amber, Green);
function Red return Colour;          – – illegal
```

although we could of course declare the function Red in an inner scope where
it would hide the literal Red (AI-330). A more subtle illustration is given by

```
package P is
    type Light is new Colour;
    function Red return Light;
end;
```

where (assuming Colour as above) the function Red replaces the literal Red of
the derived type Light. So if we then declared

```
type More_Light is new Light;
```

after the package specification then More_Light would inherit the function Red
rather than the literal Red (AI-2).

We will now discuss the visibility rules and similar properties of generic
packages in more detail. Reconsider the package Set_Of from Section 13.2

```
generic
    type Base is (<>);
package Set_Of is
    type Set is private;
    type List is array (Positive range <>) of Base;
    ...
end;
```

It is very important to grasp the difference between the rules for the
template (the generic text as written) and an instance (the effective text after
instantiation).

The first point is that the generic package is not a genuine package and in
particular does not export anything. So no meaning can be attached to
Set_Of.List outside the generic package and nor can Set_Of appear in a use
clause. Of course, inside the generic package we can indeed write Set_Of.List
if we wished to be pedantic or had hidden List by an inner redeclaration.

If we now instantiate the generic package thus

```
package Character_Set is new Set_Of(Character);
```

then Character_Set is a genuine package and so we can refer to
Character_Set.List outside the package and Character_Set can appear in a use
clause. In this case there is no question of writing Character_Set.List *inside*
the package because the inside text is quite ephemeral.

Another very important point concerns the properties of an identifier such
as List. Inside the generic template we can only use the properties common to
all possible actual parameters as expressed by the formal parameter notation.
Outside we can additionally use the properties of the particular instantiation.
So, inside we cannot write

```
S: List(1 .. 6) := "String";
```

because we do not know that the actual type is going to be a character type – it
could be an integer type. However, outside we can indeed write

```
S: Character_Set.List(1 .. 6) := "String";
```

because we know full well that the actual type is, in this instance, a character
type (AI-398 and AI-409).

Constructing a total program requires putting together various components
whose interfaces match much as we can put together hardware components by
the use of various plugs and sockets. In order for an entity from one
component to be used by another, its name must be exported from the
component declaring it and then imported into the component using it. Our
normal component is naturally a library package which will often be generic.
We will now summarize the various tools at our disposal.

Entities are exported by being in the visible part of a package.

Entities are imported by being generic parameters and also through with
clauses. Direct visibility is given by use clauses.

We have also seen that generic actual parameters can be imported into a
package and then used to create entities that are exported (the example List
above); we also noted that specific properties of the actual parameters were
reexported but not visible internally (the fact that the actual type was a
character type).

The Ada export and import rules work on groups of entities rather than
individual entities as in some languages. The Ada technique avoids clutter and
is very appropriate when the entities are highly cohesive (that is are strongly
related). However, if they are not cohesive then the coarse grouping is a
nuisance; there are various (not altogether satisfactory) techniques that can be
used to give finer control.

An obvious technique for giving finer control of entities exported from the
visible part of a package is simply to declare a hierarchical set of nested
packages

```
package Outer is
    package Inner1 is
    ...
    end;

    package Inner2 is
    ...
    end;
end;
```

We could then write

```
with Outer;
package User is
    use Outer.Inner1;
```

and then Inner2 and its internal entities will not be directly visible. Note that we cannot put the use clause immediately after the with clause because a use clause in such a position can only refer to the packages mentioned in the with clause itself.

There is no directly corresponding technique for grouping imported generic parameters. Sometimes we would like to only partially instantiate a generic package. Consider the more general function Integrate of Section 13.3

```
generic
    type Floating is digits <>;
    with function F(X: Floating) return Floating;
function Integrate(A, B: Floating) return Floating;
```

If we want to do lots of different integrations but all with the same floating type then it would be rather nice to fix the type parameter once and then only have to bother with the function parameter thereafter. This could be done if our generic function were rewritten as a nested generic thus

```
generic
    type Floating is digits <>;
package Generic_Integrate is
    generic
        with function F(X: Floating) return Floating;
    function Integrate(A, B: Floating) return Floating;
end Generic_Integrate;
```

We can then write

```
package Real_Integrate is new Generic_Integrate(Real);
use Real_Integrate;
```

and now we can instantiate the inner generic with our actual function G as in Section 13.3. This technique obviously works but we do have to impose a predetermined order on our partial parameterization.

Renaming is a useful (although somewhat heavy) tool for filtering visibility. We can import some entities into a package and then just rename those that we wish to reexport. As an example consider again the package Set_Of. Suppose we wish to instantiate this for type Character but only want the user to have access to Make_Set on single values, "+", "−" and Size on the grounds that the other operations are superfluous. (This is only an example!) We write and compile

```
with Set_Of;
package XYZ is new Set_Of(Character);
```

and then

```
with XYZ;
package Character_Set is
```

```
   subtype Set is XYZ.Set;
   function Make_Set(X: Character) return Set renames
                                          XYZ.Make_Set;
   function "+" (X, Y: Set) return Set renames XYZ."+";
   function "–" (X, Y: Set) return Set renames XYZ."–";
   function Size(X: Set) return Natural renames XYZ.Size;
end Character_Set;
```

The user can now access the reexported facilities from the package Character_Set without having visibility of the facilities of XYZ. Of course the user could still write **with** XYZ; and this would defeat the object of the exercise. However, it might be that our program library has additional tools which can hide library units without deleting them. Thus we see that the flat library structure of Ada without additional tools is not entirely adequate.

Note also that we had to use a subtype because we cannot rename a type. The subtype declaration also makes available the intrinsic ability to declare objects and perform assignment. However, if we wish to do equality comparisons then we must explicitly rename "=" as well thus

```
   function "=" (Left, Right: Set) return Boolean renames XYZ."=";
```

This also makes "/=" available as one would expect. The general rule therefore is that predefined operators can be imported by renaming but intrinsic properties which cannot be dealt with that way are available automatically. In order to properly comprehend the mechanism it must be realized that predefined operators such as "=" are implicitly declared immediately after the declaration of the type to which they refer.

Another example is provided by enumeration types; if we want to have visibility of the literals then they have to be renamed. So writing

```
   package C is
      type Colour is (Red, Amber, Green);
      – – predefined operators such as = and < applying to the
      – – type Colour are implicitly declared here
   end;

   with C;
   package P is
      subtype Light is C.Colour;
      function Red return Light renames C.Red;
      function Amber return Light renames C.Amber;
      function "<" (Left, Right: Light) return Boolean renames C."<";
   end;
```

will provide visibility (from P) of the literals Red and Amber but not Green and also of "<" but none of the other relational operators. Further details can be found in the *LRM*.

Rather simpler examples of the renaming technique for controlling visibility are given by the renaming of the exceptions declared in IO_Exceptions at the end of the three input–output packages.

Table 16.3 Compilation units.

Unit	Category	Depends on
package spec	library	
package body	secondary	[generic] package spec
subprogram spec	library	
subprogram body	library	
	secondary	[generic] subprogram spec
gen package spec	library	
gen subprogram spec	library	
subunit	secondary	package body I subprogram body I subunit
gen package instance	library	
gen subprogram instance	library	

We conclude this section be reconsidering the rules for order of compilation and recompilation of the units in a program library. The various different units are categorized as library units or secondary units as summarized in Table 16.3 which also shows their basic interrelationships.

The reader will recall from Chapter 8 that the compilation order is determined by the dependency relationships. A unit cannot be compiled unless all the units on which it depends have already been compiled. And contrariwise, if a unit is recompiled then all units depending upon it also have to be recompiled. The basic rules for dependency are

- A body is dependent on its specification.
- A subunit is dependent on its parent.
- A unit is also dependent on the specifications of units mentioned in its with clauses.

In addition, for implementation reasons, there are also the following auxiliary rules

- If a subprogram call is inlined using the pragma Inline (see Appendix 1) then the calling unit will be dependent upon the called subprogram body (as well as the specification).
- If several units are compiled together then the compiler may carry out fancy optimizations not otherwise possible and this may result in dependencies between the units.
- An implementation is also allowed to create other dependencies concerning generics; a unit containing an instantiation may be dependent on the generic body (as well as the specification) and on any subunits of that body (AI-408 and AI-506). An implementation may also require that a generic specification and body be compiled together and that a generic body and its stubs be compiled together.

The last rule says in effect that an implementation may require that the whole of a generic unit be compiled before any instantiation.

Ada 9X does not allow an implementation to impose these restrictions on generics. The philosophy of separation of specification and body (and subunits) was found difficult to implement in early compilers and so a permissive approach was taken in Ada 83. With experience it is now felt that Ada 9X should take a firmer attitude.

The basic rules for recompilation are as follows. A newly compiled library unit will replace an existing library unit (of any sort) with the same name. A secondary unit will be rejected unless there already exists a matching unit on which it can depend – a body is rejected unless its specification exists and a subunit is rejected unless its parent body or subunit exists. A successfully compiled secondary unit naturally replaces an existing one. If a unit is replaced then all units dependent on it are also deleted.

These fairly straightforward rules are complicated by the fact that a subprogram need not have a distinct specification and a package may not need a body.

If we start with an empty library and compile a procedure body P, then it will be accepted as a library unit (and not needing a distinct specification). If we subsequently compile a new version of the body then it will replace the previous library unit. If, however, we subsequently compile just the specification of P, then it will make the old body obsolete and we must then compile a new body which will now be classed as a secondary unit. In other words we cannot add the specification as an afterthought and then provide a new body perhaps in the expectation that units dependent just on the specification could avoid recompilation. Moreover, once we have a distinct specification and body we cannot join them up again – if we provide a new body which matches the existing distinct specification then it will replace the old body, if it does not match the specification then it will be rejected.

The situation is somewhat reversed in the case of a package. We remember that some packages do not need a body but that a body might be useful for initialization. There is a certain risk here since we will not get an error if we mistakenly forget to compile the missing but apparently not necessary body (a good implementation will give a warning). Note that once we have provided such a body, we can only get rid of it by providing a new specification and that will mean that all dependent units have to be recompiled. Of course, we can always provide an explicit null body.

The risk is removed in Ada 9X because a library package is only allowed to have a body if it requires one in order to satisfy language rules. One way of forcing a body to be required is to use the pragma Elaborate_Body.

Generics also have to be considered and we need to take care to distinguish between generic units and their instantiations. A generic subprogram always has a distinct specification but a generic package may not need a body. Note carefully that the body of a generic package or subprogram looks just like the body of a plain package or subprogram. It will be classed as one or the other according to the category of the existing specification (a body is rejected if there is no existing specification except in the case of a subprogram which we discussed above (AI-225)). An instantiation however is all in one lump, it is classed as a library unit in its own right and the

separation of specification and body does not occur. The notional body of a
generic instance cannot be replaced by a newly compiled plain body. For
example, suppose we first compile

```
generic
procedure GP;

procedure GP is
begin ... end GP;
```

and then separately compile

```
with GP;
procedure P is new GP;
```

and then submit

```
procedure P is
begin ... end P;
```

The result is that the new unit P will be accepted. However, it will be classed as a
library unit and completely replace the existing instantiation. It cannot be taken
as a new secondary unit since the instantiation is treated as one lump (AI-199).

We conclude by observing that we have been discussing the Ada language
rules regarding the behaviour of the program library. We can expect an
implementation to provide utility programs which manipulate the library in
additional ways. Any such facilities are outside the scope of this book and we must
hence refer the reader to the documentation for the implementation concerned.

A big change in Ada 9X is the introduction of a hierarchical library as
described in Chapter 17.

EXERCISE 16.4

1   Draw a dependency graph for the program Print_Roots modified to use the package
Simple_Maths as well as Simple_IO as described in Exercise 2.2(**1**). Assume that the
bodies of Simple_Maths and Simple_IO are as in the answers to Exercises 13.4(**1**) and
15.2(**2**). Assume also that our implementation requires generic units to be compiled as
a whole.

16.5   Portability

An Ada program may or may not be portable. In many cases a program will be
intimately concerned with the particular hardware on which it is running; this
is particularly true of embedded applications. Such a program cannot be

transferred to another machine without significant alteration. On the other hand it is highly desirable to write portable program libraries so that they can be reused in different applications. In some cases a library component will be totally portable; more often it will make certain demands on the implementation or be parameterized so that it can be tailored to its environment in a straightforward manner. This section contains general guidelines on the writing of portable Ada programs.

One thing to avoid is erroneous programs and those with incorrect order dependencies. They can be insidious. A program may work quite satisfactorily on one implementation and may seem superficially to be portable. However, if it happens to depend upon some undefined feature then its behaviour on another implementation cannot be guaranteed. A common example in most programming languages occurs with variables which accidentally are not initialized. It is often the case that the intended value is zero and furthermore many operating systems clear the program area before loading the program. Under such circumstances the program will behave correctly but may give surprising results when transferred to a different implementation. So the concept of erroneous programs is not confined to Ada. In the previous chapters we have mentioned various causes of such illegal programs. For convenience we summarize them here.

An important group of situations concerns the order of evaluation of expressions. Since an expression can include a function call and a function call can have side effects, it follows that different orders of evaluation can sometimes produce different results. The order of evaluation of the following is not defined

- the operands of a binary operator,
- the destination and value in an assignment,
- the components in an aggregate,
- the parameters in a subprogram or entry call,
- the index expressions in a multidimensional name,
- the expressions in a range,
- the guards in a select statement.

There is an important situation where a junk value can arise

- reading an uninitialized variable before assigning to it.

There are two situations where the language mechanism is not defined

- the passing of array, record and private parameters,
- the algorithm for choosing a branch of a select statement.

There are also situations where the programmer is given extra freedom to overcome the stringency of the type model; abuse of this freedom can lead to erroneous programs. Examples are

- suppressing exceptions,
- unchecked deallocation,
- unchecked conversion.

Finally, we recall from Section 16.3 that the order of elaboration of library units is not defined.

Numeric types are another important source of portability problems. The reason is, of course, the compromise necessary between achieving absolutely uniform behaviour on all machines and maximizing efficiency. Ada uses the concept of model numbers as the formalization of this compromise. In principle, if we rely only on the properties of the model numbers then our programs will be portable. In practice this is not easy to do; the reader will recall the problems of overflow in intermediate expressions discussed in Section 12.1.

There are various attributes which, if used correctly, can make our programs more portable. Thus we can use Base to find out what is really going on and Machine_Overflows to see whether Numeric_Error (Constraint_Error) will occur or not. But the misuse of these attributes can lead to very non-portable programs.

There is, however, one simple rule that can be followed. We should always declare our own real types and not directly use the predefined types such as Float. Ideally, a similar approach should be taken with integer types, but the language does encourage us to assume that the predefined type Integer has a sensible range.

Another area to consider is tasking. Any program that uses tasking is likely to suffer from portability problems because instruction execution times vary from machine to machine. This will affect the relative execution times of tasks as well as their individual execution times. In some cases a program may not be capable of running at all on a particular machine because it does not have adequate processing power. Hard guidelines are almost impossible to give but the following points should be kept in mind.

Take care that the type Duration is accurate enough for the application. Remember that regular loops cannot easily be achieved if the interval required is not a safe number.

Avoid the unsynchronized use of shared variables as far as possible. Sometimes, timing considerations demand quick and dirty techniques; consult your friendly realtime specialist if tempted. In simple cases the pragma Shared may be able to prevent interference between tasks.

The use of the abort statement will also give portability problems because of its asynchronous nature.

Avoid also the overuse of priorities. If you need to use priorities to obtain adequate responsiveness then the program is probably stretching the resources of the machine.

The finite speed of the machine leads to our final topic in this section – the finite space available. It is clear that different machines have different sizes and so a program that runs satisfactorily on one machine might raise Storage_Error on another. Moreover, different implementations may use different storage allocation strategies for access types and task data. We have seen how representation clauses can be used to give control of storage allocation and thereby reduce portability problems. However, the unconsidered use of recursion and access types is best avoided.

Programs in Ada 9X are rather more portable than in Ada 83. For example, as mentioned in Section 4.5, Ada 9X specifies that rounding of halves on conversion to an integer type is always away from zero whereas Ada 83 leaves this to the implementation. We must beware, however, that a program in Ada 83 may behave differently in Ada 9X because we were erroneously (and presumably unknowingly) relying on some undefined behaviour which happened to correspond to the behaviour of the implementation we were using. Thus we might have been relying on rounding of halves being towards zero and then in Ada 9X our program will go wrong. Of course, it was wrong anyway. The reader is therefore urged to take heed of such possibilities. Generally we might expect a well written program to move to Ada 9X with more ease than between different implementations of Ada 83; this will especially apply if the various notes in the previous chapters have been observed.

One key reason why Ada 9X is more portable is that many packages are defined in a standard library rather than being left up to the implementation as in Ada 83. For details the reader is referred to the Ada 9X Reference Manual.

EXERCISE 16.5

1   The global variable I is of type Integer and the function F is

```
function F return Integer is
begin
    I := I+1;
    return I;
end F;
```

Explain why the following fragments of program are unwise. Assume in each case that I is reset to 1.

(a) I := I+F;
(b) A(I) := F;
(c) AA(I, F) := 0;

16.6   Program design

This final section considers the question of designing Ada programs. As stated in Section 1.5, this book does not claim to be a treatise on program design. Indeed, program design is still largely an art and the value of different methods of design is often a matter of opinion rather than a matter of fact. We have therefore tried to stick to the facts of Ada and to remain neutral regarding design. Nevertheless much has been learnt about design methods over the last decade and many millions of lines of Ada programs have been designed and written. In particular, Object Oriented Design, which matches Ada well, has gained popularity. So although the general guidelines in this section must be treated with some caution there seems little reason to doubt their general validity. Note also that we are only addressing the question of design issues as they relate to Ada.

There are various low level and stylistic issues which are perhaps obvious. Identifiers should be meaningful. The program should be laid out neatly – the style used in this book is based on that recommended from the syntax in the *LRM*. Useful comments should be added. The block structure should be used to localize declarations to their use. Whenever possible a piece of information should only be written once; thus number and constant declarations should be used rather than explicit literals. And so on.

Programming is really all about abstraction and the mapping of the problem onto constructions in the programming language. We recall from Section 1.4 that the development of programming languages has been concerned with the introduction of various levels of abstraction and that Ada in particular introduces a degree of data abstraction not present in other practically used languages.

An important concept in design and the use of abstractions is information hiding. Information should only be accessible to those parts of a program that need to know. The use of packages and private data types to hide unnecessary detail is the cornerstone of good Ada programming. Indeed as we have stated before Ada is a language which aims to encourage the development of reusable software components; the package is the key component.

Designing an Ada program is therefore largely concerned with designing a group of packages and the interfaces between them. Often we will hope to use one or more existing packages. For this to be possible it is clear that they must have been designed with consistent, clean and sufficiently general interfaces. The difficulties are perhaps in deciding what items are sufficiently related or fundamental to belong together in a package and also how general to make the package. If a package is too general it might be clumsy and inefficient; if not general enough it will not be as useful as it might.

The interface to a package is provided by its specification; at least that provides the syntax of how to use the interface, the semantics must also be defined and that can only be provided by a natural language commentary. Thus consider the package Stack of Section 8.1; its specification (in the Ada sense) guarantees that it will provide subprograms Push and Pop with certain parameter and result types. However, the specification does not, of itself, guarantee that a call of Pop will in fact remove and deliver the top item from the stack. From the point of view of the language it would be quite acceptable for the package body to be

```
package body Stack is
   procedure Push(X: Integer) is
   begin
      null;
   end;
```

```
function Pop return Integer is
begin
   return 0;
end;
end Stack;
```

However, in our imagined future world of the software components industry, anyone selling such package bodies would soon go out of business.

We will now discuss some categories of related items that might make up useful packages.

A very simple form of package is one which merely consists of a group of related types and constants and has no body. The packages System and Ascii are in this category. A further example in Section 8.1 is the package Diurnal; this does not seem a good example – if it has an array Tomorrow then surely it should also have Yesterday. Better examples might be packages of related mathematical constants, conversion constants (metric to imperial say), tables of physical and chemical constants and so on. The last could be

```
package Elements is
   type Element is (H, He, Li, ... );
      – – beware of Indium – In is reserved!
   Atomic_Weight: array (Element) of Real
            := (1.008, 4.003, 6.940, ... );

   ...
end Elements;
```

Another case is where the package contains functions related by application area. An obvious example is the mathematical library discussed in Section 13.4. The individual functions in such a case are really independent although for efficiency Sin and Cos for example are likely to share a common procedure. The package body enables us to hide such a procedure from the user because its existence is merely an implementation detail.

Sometimes a package is needed in order to hide a benevolent side effect – an obvious example is the package Random in Exercise 8.1(**1**).

Packages such as Sequential_IO encapsulate a great deal of hidden information and provide a number of related services. A problem here is deciding whether to provide additional subprograms for convenience or to stick to only those absolutely necessary. The package Text_IO contains many convenience subprograms.

Many packages can be classified as a means of providing controlled access to some form of database. The database may consist of just one item as in the package Random or it could be the symbol tables of a compiler or a grand commercial style database and so on. The package Bank in Section 9.3 is another example.

An important use of packages is to provide new data types and associated operations. Obvious examples are the packages Complex_Numbers (Section 9.1), Rational_Numbers (Exercise 9.1(**3**)) and Queues (Exercise 11.5(**3**)). In such cases the use of private types enables us to separate the representation of the type from the operations upon it. In a way the new types can be seen as natural extensions to the language.

Packages of this sort raise the question of whether we should use operators rather than functions. Ada is not so flexible as some other languages; new operator forms cannot be introduced and the precedence levels are fixed. This ensures that over-enthusiastic use of operators cannot lead to programs that do not even look like Ada programs as can happen with languages such as POP-2. Even so Ada provides opportunities for surprises. We could write

```
function "−" (X, Y: Integer) return Integer is
begin
   return Standard."+" (X, Y);
end "−";
```

but it would obviously be very foolish to do so. Hence a good general guideline is to minimize surprises.

Operators should be considered for functions with a natural mathematical flavour. As a general rule the normal algebraic properties of the operators should be preserved if this is possible. Thus "+" and "*" should be commutative. Mixed type arithmetic is best avoided but there are situations where it is necessary.

The definitions of the operators in the package Complex_Numbers have the expected properties and do not allow mixed working. It would be nice if type conversion could be done by overloading the type name so that we could write Complex(2.0) rather than Cons(2.0, 0.0). However, Ada does not allow this. Type conversion of this form is restricted to the predefined and derived numeric types.

On the other hand, consider the operators in the predefined package Calendar in Section 14.3. Here the very essence of the problem requires mixed type addition but commutivity is preserved by providing two overloadings of "+".

When introducing mathematical types such as Complex and Rational it is always best to use private types. We will then need to provide constructor and selector functions as well as the natural operations themselves. It will usually be the case that construction and selection are best done with functional notation whereas the natural operations can be done with the operators. However, in the case of rational numbers the division operator "/" provides a natural notation for construction.

There is a general and difficult question of how much to provide in a package for a mathematical type. The bare minimum may be rather spartan and incur all users in unnecessary creation of additional subprograms. To be generous might make the package too cumbersome. For instance should we provide a relational operator and if so should we provide all four? Should input–output be included? Such questions are left for the reader to answer from his or her own experience according to the needs of the application.

Another important issue is storage allocation. This is well illustrated by a type such as Polynomial introduced in Section 11.1. If this is implemented using a discriminated record thus

```
type Polynomial(N: Index := 0) is
   record
      A: Integer_Vector(0 .. N);
   end record;
```

then in the case of unconstrained polynomials the compiler will (unless very clever) allocate the maximum space that could be required. Hence it is important that the range of the discriminant has a sensible upper bound. If we had written

      type Polynomial(N: Integer := 0) **is** ...

then each unconstrained polynomial would have had the space for an array of length Integer'Last and we would presumably soon run out of storage.

    If all the polynomials are to be fairly small, then using a discriminated record is probably satisfactory. On the other hand, if they are likely to be of greatly varying size then it is probably better to use access types. Indeed a mixed strategy could be used – a fixed array for the first few terms and then the use of an access type for the remainder. In order that such alternative implementation strategies can be properly organized and hidden from the user it is clear that the polynomial should be a private type. The design of a suitable package is left as an informal exercise for the reader.

    In designing packages there is the question of what to do when something goes wrong. This brings us to exceptions. Although not new to programming languages they are nevertheless not widely used except in PL/I and the experience with PL/I has not been satisfactory. However, exceptions in Ada are different to those in PL/I in one most important aspect. In Ada one cannot go back to the point where the exception was raised but is forced to consider a proper alternative to the part of the program that went wrong.

    Having said that, exceptions nevertheless need care. In Chapter 10 we warned against the unnecessary use of exceptions and in particular the casual raising of the predefined exceptions since we have no guarantee, when handling such an exception, that it was raised for the reason we had in mind.

    The first goal should always be to have clean and complete interfaces. As an example consider again the factorial function and the action to be taken when the parameter is illegal. We could consider

- printing a message,
- returning a default value,
- returning a status via a Boolean parameter,
- calling an error procedure,
- raising an exception.

Printing a message is highly unsatisfactory because it raises a host of detailed problems such as the identity of the file, the format of the message and so on. Moreover, it gives the calling program no control over the action it would like to take and some file is cluttered with messages. Furthermore, there is still the question of what to do after having printed the message.

    Another possibility is to return a default value such as −1 as in Exercise 10.1(**2**). This is not satisfactory since there is no guarantee that the user will check for this default value upon return. If we could rely upon the user doing so then we could equally rely upon the user checking the parameter of the function before calling it in the first place.

If we wish to return an auxiliary status value via another parameter then, as we saw when discussing Push and Pop in Section 10.2, we can no longer use a function anyway and would have to use a procedure instead. We also have to rely upon the caller again as in the case of the default value.

We could call a global procedure to be supplied by the user. This means agreeing on a standard name which is unsatisfactory. We cannot pass the error procedure as a parameter and to resort to the generic mechanism really is using a steam hammer to crack a nut. In any case we still have the problem, as with printing a message, of what to do afterwards and how to return finally from the function. It is highly naive to suppose that the program can just stop. The manager of the steelworks would not wish the control part of the program to stop just because of a minor error in some other part; there must be a way of carrying on.

There are only two ways out of a subprogram in Ada; back to the point of call or by a propagated exception (the global goto and label parameters of other languages are effectively replaced by the exception). We seem to have eliminated the possibility of returning to the point of call as not reliable and so have to come to the conclusion that the raising of an exception is the appropriate solution.

Another criterion we should consider when deciding whether to use exceptions is whether we expect the condition to arise in the normal course of events or not. If we do then an exception is probably wrong. As an example the end of file condition in the package Sequential_IO is tested for by a Boolean function and not an exception. We naturally expect to come to the end of the file and so must test for it – see the answer to Exercise 15.1(**1**).

On the other hand, if we are using the package Stack in say an interpreter for mathematical expressions, then, provided that the interpreter is written correctly, we know that the stack cannot underflow. An exception for this unexpected condition is acceptable. Note also that when using Sequential_IO, if we accidentally attempt to read after the end of the file then an exception (End_Error) is raised.

The raising of exceptions is, however, not a panacea. We cannot sweep the problem under the carpet in this way. The exception must be handled somewhere otherwise the program will terminate. In fact this is one of their advantages – if the user does nothing then the program will terminate safely, whereas if we return status values and the user does nothing then the program will probably ramble on in a fruitless way.

The indiscriminate use of **others** in an exception handler should be avoided. If we write **others** we are really admitting that anything could have gone wrong and we should take appropriate action; we should not use **others** as shorthand for the exceptions we anticipate.

Another major design area concerns the use of tasks. It is usually fairly clear that a problem needs a solution involving tasks but it is not always clear how the various activities should be allocated to individual tasks.

There are perhaps two major problems to be solved regarding the interactions between tasks. One concerns the transmission of messages between tasks, the other the controlling of access to common data by several tasks.

The rendezvous provides a natural mechanism for the closely coupled transmission of a message; examples are provided by the interaction between mother and the other members of her family in the procedure Shopping in Section 14.2 and by the interaction between the server and the customer in the package Cobblers of Exercise 14.9(**1**). If the transmission needs to be decoupled so that the sender can carry on before the message is received then some intermediary task is required. Examples are the task Buffering in Section 14.4 and the task type Mailbox in Section 14.6.

Controlled access to common data is, in Ada, also done by an intermediary task whereas in other languages it may use passive constructions such as monitors or low level primitives such as semaphores. The Ada approach usually provides a clearer and safer solution to the problem. An example is the task Protected_Variable in Section 14.4. Quite often the task is encapsulated in a package in order to enforce the required protocol; examples are the package Reader_Writer of Section 14.4 and the package Resource_Allocator of Section 14.8.

Ada 9X of course has protected objects for controlling access to common data. Protected objects, being passive, will have a better performance than tasks and are also easier to understand than monitors.

Sometimes the distinction between message passing and controlling data access is blurred; the task Buffering at the macro level is passing messages whereas at the micro level it is controlling access to the buffer.

Another categorization of tasks is between users and servers. A pure server task is one with entries but which calls no other tasks whereas a pure user has no entries but calls other tasks. The distinction is emphasized by the asymmetry of the naming in the rendezvous. The server does not know the names of user tasks whereas the user tasks must know the names of the server tasks in order to call their entries. Sometimes a task is part server and part user; an example is the task type Read_Agent in Section 14.7.

One problem when designing a set of interacting tasks is deciding which way round the entries are to go. Our intuitive model of servers and users should help. The entries belong in the servers. Another criterion is provided by the consideration of alternatives; if a task is to have a choice of rendezvous via a select statement then it must own the entries and therefore be a server. A select statement can be used to accept one of several entry calls but cannot be used to call one of several entries.

It cannot be emphasized too much that aborting tasks must not be done casually. The abort statement is for extreme situations only. One possible use is in a supervisory task where it may be desirable to close down a complete subsystem in response to a command from a human operator.

The reason for wishing to avoid abort is that it makes it very difficult to provide reliable services as we saw with the package Reader_Writer in Section 14.7. If we know that the users cannot be abnormally terminated then the fancy use of secret agents is not necessary; indeed that example should be considered as illustrating what can be done rather than what should be done.

A multitasking Ada program will often be seen as a set of cooperating tasks designed together. In such circumstances we can rely on the calling tasks to obey the necessary protocols and the design of the servers is then simplified.

The use of timed out entry calls also needs some care but is a very natural and common requirement in realtime systems. Services should where possible be able to cope with timed out calls.

Finally, there are generics and the whole question of parameterization. Should we write specific packages or very general ones? This is a familiar problem with subprograms and generics merely add a new dimension. Indeed, in the imagined future market for software components it is likely that packages of all sorts of generalities and performance will be available. We conclude by imagining a future conversation in our local software shop.

Customer: Could I have a look at the reader–writer package you have in the window?

Server: Certainly. Would you be interested in this robust version – proof against abort? Or we have this slick version for trusty callers. Just arrived this week.

Customer: Well – it's for a cooperating system so the new one sounds good. How much is it?

Server: It's 250 Eurodollars but as it's new there is a special offer with it – a free copy of this random number generator and 10% off your next certification.

Customer: Great. Is it validated?

Server: All our products conform to the highest standards. The parameter mechanism conforms to ES98263 and it has the usual international multitasking certificate.

Customer: OK, I'll take it.

Server: Will you take it as it is or shall I instantiate it for you?

Customer: As it is please. I prefer to do my own instantiation.

...

On this fantasy note we come to the end of this discussion of Ada 83. It is hoped that the reader will have gained some general understanding of the principles of Ada as well as a lot of the detail. Further understanding will come with use and the author hopes that he has in some small way prepared the reader for the successful use of a very good programming language.

In the next chapter we take another step forward and introduce the main new capabilities of Ada 9X.

17 Ada 9X

The main body of this book has been about Ada 83. However, we have mentioned some of the changes found in Ada 9X when discussing existing features largely in order to indicate where incompatibilities might lie in moving Ada 83 programs to Ada 9X. We also took the opportunity to introduce a few other improvements where they seemed to fit naturally with the topic in hand such as the use type clause in Section 8.5 and the delay until statement in Section 14.3.

In this chapter we discuss the main additional features introduced into Ada 9X. But first a few words on the strengths and weaknesses of Ada 83 which became apparent after some years of use.

17.1   Background

As we said in Chapter 1, one of the great strengths of Ada 83 is its reliability. The strong typing and related features ensure that programs contain few surprises; most errors are detected at compile time and many of those remaining are detected by constraint checks at run time. Moreover, the compile-time checking extends across compilation unit boundaries. This reliability aspect of Ada considerably reduces the costs and risks of program development (especially for large programs) compared with C or its derivatives such as C++.

However, after a number of years experience it became clear that some improvements were necessary in order to completely satisfy the present and the future needs of users from a whole variety of application areas. Four main areas were perceived as needing attention.

- Object oriented programming. Recent experience with other languages has shown the benefits of the object oriented paradigm. This gives rather more flexibility and, in particular, it enables a program to be extended without recompiling existing and tested parts of it.

- Program libraries. The library mechanism is one of Ada's great strengths. Nevertheless its flat structure is a hindrance to fine visibility control and to program extension without recompilation.

- Interfacing. Although Ada 83 does have facilities to enable it to interface to external systems written in other languages, these have not proved as flexible as they might. For example, it has proved particularly awkward to program call-back mechanisms which are very useful especially when using Graphical User Interfaces.

- Tasking. The Ada rendezvous model provides an advanced description of many paradigms. However, it has not proved entirely appropriate for shared data problems where a static monitor like approach brings performance benefits. Furthermore, Ada 83 has a rather rigid approach to priorities and it is not easy to take advantage of recent deeper understanding of scheduling theory which has emerged since Ada was first designed.

The first three topics are really all about flexibility and so a prime goal of the design of Ada 9X has been to give the language a more open and extensible feel without losing the inherent integrity and efficiency of Ada 83. That is to keep the Software Engineering but allow more flexibility.

As we shall see, the additions to Ada 9X which contribute to this more flexible feel are the extended or tagged types, the hierarchical library and the greater ability to manipulate pointers or references. The tagged types and hierarchical library together provide very powerful tools for programming by extension.

As a consequence, Ada 9X incorporates the benefits of object oriented languages without incurring the pervasive overheads of languages such as SmallTalk or the insecurity brought by the weak C foundation in the case of

C++. Ada 9X remains a very strongly typed language but provides the prime benefits of all key aspects of the object oriented paradigm.

In the case of the tasking model, the introduction of protected types allows a more efficient implementation of standard paradigms of shared data access. This brings the benefits of speed provided by low level primitives such as semaphores without the risks incurred by the use of such unstructured primitives. Moreover, the clearly data-oriented view brought by the protected types fits in naturally with the general spirit of the object oriented paradigm. Other improvements to the tasking model allow a more flexible response to interrupts and other changes of state.

Another area which sees considerable change is that of generics. These are largely consequential on changes to the type model but nevertheless deserve special mention because generics are one of the key facilities of Ada 83 which promote reuse.

Ada 9X also incorporates numerous other minor improvements reflecting feedback from the use of existing features and these have been addressed in earlier chapters of this book. Finally there are a number of specific new features addressing the needs of specialized applications and communities.

17.2   Object oriented programming

Object oriented programming is not easy to define. It stems from the general idea of programming around the concept of objects which are defined by a type and the operations upon the type (often called methods in some languages). This concept clearly already exists in the Ada 83 package and private type.

However, another vital aspect of object oriented programming that has attracted much attention is the extra flexibility obtained by a more dynamic attitude regarding types than that provided by the static view taken by Ada 83. There are a number of points.

- The ability to extend a type with new components and operations. This is known as type extension.

- The ability to identify a type at run time and to manipulate values of several specific types. This is called polymorphism (from the Greek *poly*, many, and *morphe*, form).

- The ability to choose an operation at run time. This is often called late binding because the choice of operation is made late in the compile-link-run process.

As we shall see, type extension in Ada 9X is provided through tagged types and also through child library units. Polymorphism is provided by class wide types. Late binding is provided by dispatching where the choice of subprogram to call is made at run time depending on the type of the parameters or possibly the type of the result of the subprogram call; late binding also occurs through a new form of access type which can reference subprograms.

17.2.1 Programming by extension

The key idea of programming by extension is the ability to declare a new type that refines an existing parent type by inheriting, modifying or adding to both the existing components and the operations of the parent type. A major goal is the reuse of existing reliable software without the need for recompilation and retesting.

Type extension in Ada 9X builds upon the existing Ada 83 concept of a derived type. In Ada 83, a derived type inherits the operations of its parent and can add new operations; however, it is not possible to add new components to the type. The whole mechanism is thus somewhat static. By contrast, in Ada 9X a derived type can also be extended to add new components. As we shall see, the mechanism is much more dynamic and allows greater flexibility through late binding and polymorphism.

The extra flexibility does, however, incur some run-time costs (although small) and moreover it is desirable to preserve the static functionality of existing programs using the existing form of derived types.

Accordingly in Ada 9X we allow record types to be extended on derivation provided they are marked as tagged. Private types implemented as records can also be tagged. As its name implies a tagged type has an associated tag. The word tag will be familiar to Pascal programmers where it denotes what we term a discriminant; as we shall see later the Ada 9X tag is effectively a hidden discriminant identifying the type and so the term is very appropriate.

As a very simple example we will reconsider the description of geometrical objects briefly considered in Exercise 11.3(**3**). All objects will have a position given by their x- and y-coordinates. So we declare

```
type Object is tagged
  record
      X_Coord: Real;
      Y_Coord: Real;
  end record;
```

and then we can declare

```
type Circle is new Object with
  record
      Radius: Real;
  end record;
```

and the type Circle then has the three components X_Coord, Y_Coord and Radius.

A private type can also be marked as tagged

```
type Shape is tagged private;
```

and the full type declaration must then (ultimately) be a tagged record

```
type Shape is tagged
  record ...
```

or derived from a tagged record such as Object. On the other hand we might wish to make visible the fact that the type Shape is derived from Object and yet keep the additional components hidden. In this case the visible declaration might be

    type Shape **is new** Object **with private**;

and the full declaration could be

    type Shape **is new** Object **with**
      record
          – – the private components
      end record;

In this last case it is not necessary for the full declaration of Shape to be derived directly from the type Object. There might be a chain of intermediate derived types; all that matters is that Shape is ultimately derived from Object.

Sometimes it is convenient to derive a new type without adding any further components. For example

    type Point **is new** Object **with null record**;

In this last case we have derived Point from Object but naturally not added any new components. However, since we are dealing with tagged types we have to explicitly add **with null record**; to indicate that we did not want any new components. This has the advantage that it is always clear from a declaration whether a type is tagged or not.

Just as in Ada 83, derived types inherit the operations which 'belong' to the parent type – these are called primitive operations in Ada 9X. User-written subprograms are classed as primitive operations if they are declared in the same package specification as the type and have the type as parameter or result (or have an access parameter referring to the type as will be explained later in Section 17.3.3). Note that, unlike Ada 83, subprograms in the private part are also inherited. This will be found helpful when we consider child packages.

Thus we might have declared a function giving the distance from the origin

```
function Distance(O: in Object) return Real is
begin
   return Sqrt(O.X_Coord**2 + O.Y_Coord**2);
end Distance;
```

The type Circle would then sensibly inherit this function. If however, we were concerned with the area of an object then we might start with

```
function Area(O: in Object) return Real is
begin
   return 0.0;
end Area;
```

which returns zero since a raw object has no area. This would also be inherited by the type Circle but would be inappropriate; it would be more sensible to explicitly declare

```
function Area(C: in Circle) return Real is
begin
   return Pi*C.Radius**2;
end Area;
```

which will override the inherited operation.

It is possible to convert a value from the type Circle to Object and vice versa. From circle to object is easy, we simply write

```
O: Object := (1.0, 0.5);
C: Circle := (0.0, 0.0, 34.7);
...
O := Object(C);
```

which effectively ignores the third component. However, conversion in the other direction requires the provision of a value for the extra component and this is done by an extension aggregate thus

```
C := (O with 41.2);
```

where the expression O is extended after **with** by the values of the extra components written just as in a normal aggregate. In this case we only had to give a value for the radius. We could have used named notation

```
C := (O with Radius => 41.2);
```

We now consider a more extensive example which illustrates the use of tagged types to build a system as a hierarchy of types and packages. We will see how this allows the system to be extended without recompilation of its central part.

Our system concerns the processing of reservation requests for Ada Airlines. We can imagine that there are a number of aspects to this; the creation of a reservation request by interaction with an operator; the processing of the request by some central system; and then reporting back to the operator indicating success or failure. There are three categories of travel, Basic, Nice and Posh. The better categories have options which can be requested when making the reservation. Nice passengers are given a choice of seat (Aisle or Window) and a choice of meal which can be Green (vegetarian), White (fish or fowl) or Red (for the carnivores). Posh passengers are also given onward personal ground transport (or Personal Onward Surface Help).

We concentrate on the part of the system that processes the requests and first consider how this might be done in Ada 83 using variant records.

```
package Ada_83_Reservations is

   type Category is (Basic, Nice, Posh);
```

```
type Position is (Aisle, Window);
type Meal_Type is (Green, White, Red);

type Reservation(C: Category) is
  record
    Flight_Number: Integer;
    Date_Of_Travel: Date;
    Seat_Number: String(1 .. 4) := "    ";
    case C is
      when Basic => null;
      when Nice | Posh =>
        Seat_Sort: Position;
        Food: Meal_Type;
        case C is
          when Basic | Nice => null;
          when Posh =>
            Destination: Address;
        end case;
    end case;
  end record;

procedure Make(R: in out Reservation);
procedure Select_Seat(R: in out Reservation);
procedure Order_Meal(R: in Reservation);
procedure Arrange_Limo(R: in Reservation);

end Ada_83_Reservations;
```

Each reservation request is represented as a discriminated record with the category of travel as the discriminant. Perhaps surprisingly, the structure and processing depend on this discriminant in a quite complex manner. One immediate difficulty is that we are more or less obliged to use nested variants because of the rule that all the components of a record have to have different identifiers. The body of the procedure Make might be

```
procedure Make(R: in out Reservation) is
begin
  Select_Seat(R);
  case R.C is
    when Basic => null;  -- no frills
    when Nice | Posh =>
      Order_Meal(R);
      case R.C is
        when Basic | Nice => null;
        when Posh =>
          Arrange_Limo(R);
      end case;
  end case;
end Make;
```

Observe that the parameters of Make and Select_Seat have mode **in out**. This is because Select_Seat updates the component Seat_Number with a string representing the chosen seat (or perhaps "full" if there are none available).

A problem with this approach is that the code is curiously complex due to the nested structure and consequently hard to maintain and error-prone. If we try to avoid the nested case statements then we have to repeat some of the code.

However, a more serious problem is that if, for example, we need to add a further seat category, perhaps Supersonic (which would mean adding another value to the type Category), then the whole system will have to be modified and recompiled. Existing reliable code will then be disturbed with the risk of subsequent errors.

In Ada 9X we can use a series of extended tagged types with a distinct procedure Make for each one. This completely eliminates the need for case statements and variants and indeed the type Category itself is no longer required because it is now inherent in the types themselves (it is implicit in the tag). The package specification now becomes

```
package New_Reservation_System is

    type Position is (Aisle, Window);
    type Meal_Type is (Green, White, Red);

    type Reservation is tagged
      record
          Flight_Number: Integer;
          Date_Of_Travel: Date;
          Seat_Number: String(1 .. 4) := "    ";
      end record;

    procedure Make(R: in out Reservation);
    procedure Select_Seat(R: in out Reservation);

    type Basic_Reservation is new Reservation with null record;

    type Nice_Reservation is new Reservation with
      record
          Seat_Sort: Position;
          Food: Meal_Type;
      end record;

    procedure Order_Meal(NR: in Nice_Reservation);

    -- now override inherited operation
    procedure Make(NR: in out Nice_Reservation);

    type Posh_Reservation is new Nice_Reservation with
      record
          Destination: Address;
      end record;

    procedure Arrange_Limo(PR: in Posh_Reservation);
```

```
        procedure Make(PR: in out Posh_Reservation);

   end New_Reservation_System;
```

In this formulation the variant record is replaced with the tagged type Reservation and three types derived from it. Note that Ada 9X allows a type to be derived in the same package specification as the parent and to inherit all the primitive operations but we cannot add any new primitive operations to the parent after a type has been derived from it. This is different to Ada 83 where the operations were not derivable until after the end of the package specification. This change allows the related types to be conveniently encapsulated all in the same package.

The type Basic_Reservation is simply a copy of Reservation (note **with null record**;) and could be dispensed with although it maintains equivalence with the Ada 83 version; Basic_Reservation inherits the procedure Make from Reservation. The type Nice_Reservation extends Reservation and provides its own procedure Make thus overriding the inherited version. The type Posh_Reservation further extends Nice_Reservation and similarly provides its own procedure Make. Thus instead of a single procedure Make containing complex case statements the Ada 9X solution distributes the logic for handling reservations to each specific reservation type without any repetition of code.

The package body is as follows

```
   package body New_Reservation_System is

      procedure Make(R: in out Reservation) is
      begin
         Select_Seat(R);
      end Make;

      procedure Make(NR: in out Nice_Reservation) is
      begin
         Make(Reservation(NR));    - - make as plain reservation
         Order_Meal(NR);
      end Make;

      procedure Make(PR: in out Posh_Reservation) is
      begin
         Make(Nice_Reservation(PR));   - - conversion
         Arrange_Limo(PR);
      end Make;

      procedure Select_Seat(R: in out Reservation) is separate;

      procedure Order_Meal(NR: in Nice_Reservation) is separate;

      procedure Arrange_Limo(PR: in Posh_Reservation) is separate;

   end New_Reservation_System;
```

Each distinct body for Make contains just the code relevant to the type and delegates additional processing back to its ancestor using an explicit type conversion. Note carefully that all type checking is static and so no run-time penalties are incurred with this structure (the variant checks have been avoided).

In the Ada 9X model a new reservation category such as Supersonic_Reservation can now be added without recompiling (and perhaps more importantly, without retesting) the existing code.

```
with New_Reservation_System;
package Supersonic_Reservation_System is

    type Supersonic_Reservation is
        new New_Reservation_System.Reservation with private;

    procedure Make(SR: in out Supersonic_Reservation);

    private
        ...
    end Supersonic_Reservation_System;
```

With the Ada 83 approach extensive recompilation would have been necessary since the variant records would have required redefinition. Thus we see that Ada 9X truly provides Programming by Extension.

EXERCISE 17.2.1

1   Declare the type Object and the functions Distance and Area in a package Objects. Then declare a package Shapes containing the types Point, Circle, Square and Rectangle and appropriate functions returning the area. See Exercise 11.1(**3**).

17.2.2   Class wide programming

The facilities we have seen so far have allowed us to define a new type as an extension of an existing one. We have introduced the different categories of Reservation as distinct but related types. What we also need is a means to manipulate any kind of Reservation and to process it accordingly. We do this through the introduction of the notion of class wide types.

Each tagged type T has an associated type denoted by T'Class. This type comprises the union of all the types in the tree of derived types rooted at T. The values of T'Class are thus the values of T and all its derived types. Moreover a value of any type derived from T can be implicitly converted to the type T'Class.

So, for example, in the case of the type Reservation the tree of types can be pictured as in Figure 17.1.

A value of any of the reservation types can be implicitly converted to Reservation'Class. Note carefully that Nice_Reservation'Class is not the same

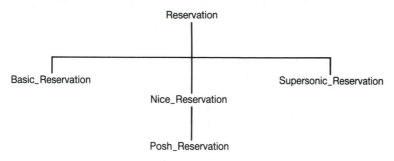

Figure 17.1   A tree of types.

as Reservation'Class; the former consists just of Nice_Reservation and Posh_Reservation.

Each value of a class wide type has a tag which identifies its particular type from other types in the tree of types at run time. Thus the tag acts as a hidden discriminant as mentioned earlier.

The type T'Class is treated as an unconstrained type; this is because we cannot possibly know how much space could be required by any value of a class wide type because the type might be extended. As a consequence, although we can declare an object of a class wide type we must initialize it and it is then constrained by the tag. This is very similar to the behaviour of a discriminated type without defaults and illustrates the notion of the tag being a hidden discriminant.

Furthermore, we can declare an access type referring to a class wide type in which case the access could designate any value of the class wide type from time to time. This is much as an access type could designate values of a discriminated type with different discriminants from time to time as we saw in Section 11.6. The use of access types is obviously a key factor in class wide programming. Moreover, a parameter of a procedure can also be of a class wide type.

We now continue our example by considering how we might buffer up a series of reservation requests and process them in sequence by some central routine. The whole essence of the problem is that such a routine cannot know of the individual types because we need it to work (without recompilation) even if we extend the system by adding a new reservation type to it.

The central routine could thus take a class wide value as its parameter so we might have

```
procedure Process_Reservation(RC: in out Reservation'Class) is
   ...
begin
   ...
   Make(RC);   -- dispatch according to tag
   ...
end Process_Reservation;
```

In this case we do not know which procedure Make to call until run time because we do not know which specific type the reservation belongs to.

However, RC is of a class wide type and so its value includes a tag indicating the specific type of the value. The choice of Make is then determined by the value of this tag; the parameter is then implicitly converted to the appropriate specific reservation type before being passed to the appropriate procedure Make.

This run-time choice of procedure is called dispatching and is key to the flexibility of class wide programming.

Before processing, the reservation requests might be held as a heterogeneous list using an access type such as

```
type Reservation_Ptr is access Reservation'Class;
```

and the central routine could then manipulate the reservations directly from such a list

```
procedure Process_Reservation is
   Next: Reservation_Ptr;
begin
   ...
   Next :=                 – – get next reservation
   ...
   Make(Next.all);    – – dispatch to appropriate Make
   ...
end Process_Reservation;
```

In this case, the value of the object referred to by Next is of a class wide type and so includes a tag indicating the specific type. The parameter Next.**all** is thus dereferenced, the value of the tag gives the choice of Make and the parameter is then implicitly converted before being passed to the chosen procedure Make.

EXERCISE 17.2.2

1 Declare a procedure that will print the area of a geometrical object of any type derived from the type Object of Section 17.2.1.

2 Reformulate the type Person from Section 11.3 as a tagged type just containing the common components. Then declare types Man and Woman.

3 Declare procedures Print_Details for Person, Man and Woman which output information regarding the current values of their components. Then declare a procedure Analyze_Person which takes a parameter of the class wide type Person'Class and calls the appropriate procedure Print_Details.

17.2.3   Abstract types and subprograms

We now introduce the concepts of abstract types and subprograms. An abstract subprogram is a sort of place holder for an operation to be provided.

A tagged type which has one or more abstract operations is said to be an abstract type. An abstract type on its own is of little use because we cannot declare an object of the type. But the purpose of an abstract type is to provide a common foundation upon which useful types can be built by derivation.

Upon derivation from an abstract type we can provide actual subprograms for all the abstract subprograms of the parent type (and it is in this sense that we said they were place holders). Once all the abstract subprograms are provided the type is then no longer abstract and we can then declare objects of the type in the usual way. (This ensures that dispatching always works.)

We can now reformulate our example of processing reservations so that the root type Reservation is just an abstract type and then build the specific types upon it. This will enable us to program and compile all the general infrastructure routines for processing all reservation requests such as Process_Reservation in the previous section without any concern at all for the individual reservation types and indeed before deciding what they should contain.

The baseline package can then simply become

```
package Base_Reservation_System is

    type Reservation is tagged null record;

    procedure Make(R: in out Reservation) is <>;

end Base_Reservation_System;
```

in which we have declared the type Reservation as a tagged null record with just the procedure Make as an abstract subprogram. The notation <> indicates that the subprogram is abstract; it does not have a body. (Note the abbreviated form for a null record declaration which saves us having to write **record**; **null**; **end record**;)

We can now develop our reservation infrastructure and then later add the normal reservation system containing the three types of reservations as follows

```
with Base_Reservation_System;
package Subsonic_Reservation_System is

    type Position is (Aisle, Window);
    type Meal_Type is (Green, White, Red);

    type Basic_Reservation is
        new Base_Reservation_System.Reservation with
    record
        Flight_Number: Integer;
        Date_Of_Travel: Date;
        Seat_Number: String(1 .. 4) := "    ";
    end record;
```

```
                    - - now provide actual subprogram for abstract one
                    procedure Make(BR: in out Basic_Reservation);

                    procedure Select_Seat(BR: in out Basic_Reservation);

                    type Nice_Reservation is new Basic_Reservation with
                       record
                          Seat_Sort: Position;
                          Food: Meal_Type;
                       end record;

                    procedure Order_Meal(NR: in Nice_Reservation);

                    procedure Make(NR: in out Nice_Reservation);

                    type Posh_Reservation is new Nice_Reservation with
                       record
                          Destination: Address;
                       end record;

                    procedure Arrange_Limo(PR: in Posh_Reservation);

                    procedure Make(PR: in out Posh_Reservation);

                 end Subsonic_Reservation_System;
```

In this revised formulation we must provide a procedure Make for Basic_Reservation to meet the promise of the abstract type. The procedure Select_Seat now takes a parameter of type Basic_Reservation and the type Nice_Reservation is more naturally derived from Basic_Reservation.

Note carefully that we did not make Select_Seat an abstract subprogram in the package Base_Reservation_System. There was no need; it is only Make that is required by the general infrastructure such as the procedure Process_Reservation and to add anything else would weaken the abstraction and clutter the base level.

We also have to make corresponding changes to the package body. This is left as an exercise for the reader.

When we now add our Supersonic_Reservation we can choose to derive this from the baseline Reservation as before or perhaps from some other point in the tree picking up the existing facilities of one of the other levels.

For completeness, we mention a few further minor points about abstract types. When we derive from an abstract type we do not have to provide a proper subprogram for every abstract one. However, if we do not, then the newly derived type will also be abstract. On the other hand when we derive from a non-abstract type we can provide abstract operations (either additional ones or to replace inherited ones) and as a consequence the derived type will then be abstract. We will see an example of this when we consider controlled types in Section 17.2.6.

A special situation occurs in the case of a function which returns a type when the type is extended. Clearly the function cannot return a value of the extended type (since it does not know how to provide values for the new components) and so in order for the extended type to use that function it must be overridden with a new definition providing an appropriate result. If we do not provide such a function then it becomes abstract for the derived type and so the type itself is abstract. Moreover, in order to warn us of the situation (it might have been an oversight) we must explicitly provide at least one abstract subprogram for the derived type (so that a < > is visible) and it would indeed be natural for this to be for the function itself.

This is an example of a general rule that we must always provide at least one visible abstract subprogram for any abstract type so that it is clear that it is abstract.

EXERCISE 17.2.3

1   Reformulate the type Object as an abstract type containing no components and where the function Area is abstract. Then declare types Point and Circle etc from the type Object.

2   Write the body of the package Subsonic_Reservation_System.

17.2.4   Discriminants

We have seen how discriminants and variants in Ada 83 can often be replaced by type extension. In Exercise 17.2.2(**2**) we reconsidered the formulation of the type Person as

```
type Person is tagged
   record
      Birth: Date;
   end record;

type Man is new Person with
   record
      Bearded: Boolean;
   end record;

type Woman is new Person with
   record
      Children: Integer;
   end record;
```

We have, perhaps surprisingly, avoided the use of a discriminant and indeed there is no explicit component indicating the sex; this is implicit in the tag. Note that the information is not lost since we could write

```
if P in Woman then
   - - special processing for Women
end if;
```

where P is of the class wide type Person'Class. We could also write

    if P **in** Woman'Class **then** ...

and this would then cover any types derived from Woman as well.

Indeed, it is also possible to test the tag explicitly using the attribute Tag which can be applied to a value of a class wide type and to a tagged type itself. So we could alternatively have written

    if P'Tag = Woman'Tag **then**

The value of the attribute Tag is of the type Tag declared in the package System. We can declare variables of the type Tag in the usual way. It is important to note that the attribute Tag cannot be applied to a value of a specific type. The reason will be explained later.

Returning to our discussion on discriminants, it is still possible to have a discriminant in the root type and we could then choose to make an extension for just a certain value of that discriminant. So an alternative implementation might be based upon

```
type Gender is (Male, Female);

type Person(Sex: Gender) is tagged
   record
      Birth: Date;
   end record;
```

and we can then extend with, for example

```
type Man is new Person(Male) with
   record
      Bearded: Boolean;
   end record;
```

The type Man naturally inherits the discriminant from Person in the sense that a man still has a component called Sex although of course it is constrained to be Male.

The full possibilities are quite complex. We could extend from the unconstrained type and then the new type would inherit the old discriminant just as any other component.

```
type Old_Person is new Person with
   record
      Pension: Money;
   end record;
```

and the Old_Person also has a component Sex (although it is not visible in the declaration but then neither is the Birth component).

Finally it is also possible to provide a completely new set of discriminants when inheriting and in this case the parent must be constrained and the new

discriminants then replace rather than add to the old ones. We might declare a
type Boxer who must be male (ladies don't box in this model of the world) and
then add a discriminant giving his weight

>   **type** Weight **is** (Light, Middle, Heavy);
>
>   **type** Boxer(W: Weight) **is new** Person(Male) **with**
>   **record**
>   – – information according to weight
>   **end record**;

An interesting point to note in this last situation is that the constraint on
the parent could actually be supplied by a new discriminant. So our
Old_Person could have been written as

>   **type** Old_Person(Sex: Gender) **is new** Person(Sex => Sex) **with**
>   **record**
>   Pension: Money;
>   **end record**;

where we have chosen to give the new discriminant the same name as the old
one.

We conclude this section by saying a few words about discriminants in
general (and not specifically relating to tagged types).

An irritating aspect of Ada 83 is that the full type corresponding to a
private type without discriminants cannot be a discriminated type with
defaults. This contrasts with generics where the actual type corresponding to a
formal type without discriminants can be such a type (see Section 13.2 and AI-
37). This anomaly is removed in Ada 9X where we can write

>   **package** P **is**
>   **type** T **is private**;
>   **private**
>   **type** T(N: Natural := 0) **is**
>   ...
>   **end** P;

This enables us to reconsider the problem of ragged arrays and varying
strings which we have met from time to time (see Sections 11.2 and 11.6). We
can now declare a private type without a discriminant and make the full type
discriminated so that we can choose access type storage for very long strings
and direct storage for short strings.

Another interesting facility is the ability to declare a private type with
unknown discriminants such as

>   **type** T (<>) **is limited private**;

One consequence is that no objects can be declared outside the defining
package thereby giving the package complete control over the creation of

objects. The user could of course be given access values referring to such objects as the result of calling subprograms in the package. This provides an alternative approach to the creation of safe keys discussed in Section 9.3.

17.2.5　Operations of tagged types

In this section we consider in a little more detail some of the fundamental properties of tagged types and their operations.

It is important to understand exactly when dispatching is used as opposed to the static resolution of binding familiar from Ada 83. The basic principle is that dispatching is only used when a controlling operand is of a class wide type. Thus the call

Make(RC); – – RC of type Reservation'Class

in the procedure Process_Reservation in Section 17.2.2 is a dispatching call. The value of the tag of RC is used to determine which procedure Make to call and this is determined at run time.

On the other hand a call such as

Make(Reservation(NR));

in the package body of New_Reservation_System in Section 17.2.1 is not a dispatching call because the type of the operand is the specific type Reservation as a result of the explicit type conversion.

It is also possible to dispatch on the result of a function when the context of the call determines the specific type. In order to illustrate this we need to remember that an operation may have several controlling operands. Consider for example

```
package Example is

    type T is tagged ... ;
    procedure P(X: T; Y: T);
    function F return T;
    function G(Z: T) return T;
    procedure Q(U: T; V: T := F);
    type TT is new T with ... ;  – – inherits the operations
    ...
end Example;
```

so that P, Q, F and G are dispatching operations of T. Actual parameters corresponding to U, V, X, Y and Z are controlling operands and the results of calls of F and G are controlling results. Note that the parameter V of Q has a default initial expression consisting of a call of F.

It is an important principle that all controlling operands and results of a call must be of the same type. If they are statically determined then, of course, this is checked at compile time. If they are dynamically determined (for example, variables of a class wide type) then again the actual values must all be of the same specific type and of course this check has to be made at run time (the tags are compared) and Constraint_Error is raised if the check fails. In order to avoid confusion a mixed situation whereby some operands are static and some are dynamic is not allowed.

Now let us suppose that we have variables whose types are as follows

```
A, B: T;
AA, BB: TT;
C: T'Class := ... ;   – – must be initialized
D: T'Class := ... ;   – – because a class wide type
```

then we can write calls such as

```
P(A, B);      – – non-dispatching, type T
P(AA, BB);    – – non-dispatching, type TT
P(C, D);      – – dispatching
```

and in the last case a check is made before the call that C'Tag equals D'Tag. On the other hand the following are illegal for the reasons stated

```
P(A, BB);   – – illegal – mixed specific types
P(A, C);    – – illegal – mixed static and dynamic
```

and both these situations are detected at compile time.

We can now look at the use of the functions F and G which have controlling results. Consider

```
P(A, F);   – – non–dispatching, type T
P(C, F);   – – dispatching
```

In the first case, the controlling operand A is static and determines that the call of F is also static; the call of F is thus chosen at compile time to be the F with result of type T. In the second case the controlling operand C is dynamic and determines the type at run time; in this case the call of F dispatches to the particular F with the same type as C; there is no run-time check because only one controlling operand is used to determine the type. The call of F is thus like a chameleon and adapts to the circumstances; we say that it is tag indeterminate.

The situation can be nested, for example

```
P(C, G(D));   – – dispatching
```

in which case the tags of C and D are checked to ensure that they are the same; Constraint_Error is raised if they are not. A more elaborate expression such as G(F) is also indeterminate so we can have

```
P(A, G(F));   – – non–dispatching
P(C, G(F));   – – dispatching
```

In the second case the call of G is then determined by the specific type of C and this in turn determines the call of F.

We can also use a call of a function such as F to determine a default value. Thus we can have

```
Q(A);   – – non–dispatching
Q(C);   – – dispatching
```

and in the first case the default call of F is statically determined to be that of type T whereas in the second case the call of F is dynamically determined by the specific type of the value of C.

It is interesting to note that a default expression for a controlling operand has to be tag indeterminate and so has to be a call of a function such as F or an expression such as G(F). The reason is that we need to be able to use the default expression in both dispatching and non-dispatching contexts.

Another use for an indeterminate expression is as the initial value for a class wide object or as a class wide actual parameter. For example

```
C: T'Class := F;   – – non–dispatching
```

In this case the type of F is *statically* determined to be T.

Finally note that

```
P(F, F);   – – illegal
```

is ambiguous and thus illegal. Because of inheritance we do not know whether we are dealing with the P and F of the type T or TT. In other words the overload resolution fails. Dispatching is not involved because there are no class wide operands.

The above discussion may have seemed a bit tedious but it is important to grasp the essential ideas which are really quite simple and are aimed to make things as explicit as possible so that surprises are minimized or at least show up at compile time.

Another rule designed to avoid confusion is that it is not possible for a subprogram to have controlling operands or results of different tagged types. Although we can of course declare two tagged types in the same package we cannot in that package declare a subprogram that has operands or result of both types. We can naturally do this outside the package but then in that case the subprogram is not inherited and does not dispatch anyway.

The rules for type conversion are also designed for clarity. The first point is that type conversion is always allowed towards the root of a tree of tagged types and so, as we have seen, we can convert a Nice_Reservation into a Reservation as in the call

```
Make(Reservation(NR));
```

On the other hand we cannot convert a specific type away from the root (there might be missing components); we have to use an extension aggregate even if there are no extra components. So for example we can 'extend' a Reservation into a Basic_Reservation by

    BR := (R **with null record**);

where we have to write **null record** because there are no extra components.

    We can however convert a value of a class wide type to a specific type as in

    NR := Nice_Reservation(RC);

where RC is of the type Reservation'Class as in Section 17.2.2. In such a case there is a run-time check that the current value of the class wide parameter RC is of a specific type for which the conversion is possible. Hence it must be of the type Nice_Reservation or derived from it so that the conversion is not away from the root of the tree. In other words we check that the value of RC is actually in Nice_Reservation'Class. Constraint_Error is raised if the check fails.

    Some conversions are what is known as view conversions. This means that the underlying object is not changed but we merely get a different view of it. (Much as the private view and full view of a type are just different views; the type is still the same.) View conversions of variables exist in Ada 83 although the terminology was not used. For example in Section 7.3 we called the procedure Increment with the view conversion Integer(R) as parameter.

    Most conversions of tagged types are view conversions. For example the conversion in

    Make(Reservation(NR));

is a view conversion. The value passed on to the call of Make (the one with parameter of type Reservation) is in fact the same value as held in NR but we can no longer see the components relating to the type Nice_Reservation. And in fact if we looked at the tag (if we could) we would find it related to the underlying value and this might even be the tag for Posh_Reservation because it could have been view converted all the way down the tree.

    However if we did an assignment as in

    NR := Nice_Reservation(PR);

then the tag of NR is of course not changed. All that happens is that the components appropriate to the type of NR are copied from the object PR. This is not a view conversion but a full blooded value conversion. A conversion (for tagged types) is a view conversion if used as an actual parameter or in a context where a name is required; in other contexts such as on the right hand side of an assignment (where a general expression is allowed) it is a value conversion.

    The reader might well wonder why the view conversion does not change the tag. The reason lies in what is called redispatching.

    If often happens that after one dispatching operation we apply a further common (and inherited) operation and so need to dispatch once more to an operation of the original type. If the original tag is lost then this is not possible. An example of the seeds of this difficulty already lies in our reservation system for Ada Airlines.

Consider again

```
procedure Make(NR: in out Nice_Reservation) is
begin
   Make(Reservation(NR));  – – make as plain reservation
   Order_Meal(NR);
end Make;
```

in which there is a call of the procedure Order_Meal. This call is not a dispatching call because the parameter is of a specific type and indeed there is only one procedure Order_Meal. Inside the body of Order_Meal we would expect to deal just with an order from a nice reservation and would not anticipate having to take account of the fact that the order might have originated from a posh passenger. (Although one would hope that posh meals are indeed better than nice meals.)

Actually we *could* write

```
procedure Order_Meal(NR: Nice_Reservation) is
   NRC: Nice_Reservation'Class := NR;
begin
   if NRC in Posh_Reservation then
      – – order a posh meal
   else
      – – order a nice meal
   end if;
end Order_Meal;
```

where we have regained the original type by converting to the class wide type Nice_Reservation'Class. We could actually avoid the burden of the assignment by writing

```
NRC: Nice_Reservation'Class renames Nice_Reservation'Class(NR);
```

although this is rather a mouthful.

Note also that we could alternatively have written the test as

```
if NRC'Tag = Posh_Reservation'Tag then
```

but remember that we cannot apply the attribute Tag to an object of a specific type. So we could not have avoided the introduction of the class wide variable by writing

```
if NR'Tag = Posh_Reservation'Tag then
```

This is disallowed because it would be very confusing to allow NR'Tag because we would naturally expect this always to be Nice_Reservation'Tag and to find that it had some other value would be strange.

It is of course against the spirit of the game to mess about inside Order_Meal to see if it was ordered by a posh passenger. The whole idea of programming by extension is that one should be able to write the body for Order_Meal without considering how the type system might be extended later. Indeed the type Posh_Reservation (like Supersonic_Reservation) might be in a later package in which case we could not here refer to the type Posh_Reservation at all.

The proper approach is to use redispatching. We write a distinct procedure

procedure Order_Meal(PR: **in** Posh_Reservation);

for posh passengers and redispatch in the body of Make as follows

```
procedure Make(NR: in out Nice_Reservation) is
begin
   Make(Reservation(NR));  – – make as plain reservation
   Order_Meal(Nice_Reservation'Class(NR));  – – redispatch
end Make;
```

This will work properly and our posh passenger will now get a posh meal instead of just a nice one.

It is hoped that the discussion in this section has not seemed overly complex and detailed. Object oriented programming may be very flexible but it has its pitfalls and it is important that the reader be aware of these. Ada 9X strives for clarity. The basic rule is that dispatching is only used if the operand is of a class wide type and this is clear at the point of the call. This simple rule should cause less surprises than the more obscure rules of C++.

We will now leave our reservation system noting that there is an analogous possible difficulty with Select_Seat; it seems likely that the requests of nice and posh passengers for an aisle or window seat might be overlooked. We leave the consideration of this as an exercise.

We conclude this section with a very brief summary of the main points regarding tagged types.

- Record (and private) types can be tagged. Values of tagged types carry a tag with them. The tag indicates the specific type. A tagged type can be extended on derivation with additional components. Discriminants can be replaced or inherited.

- Primitive operations of a type are inherited on derivation. The primitive operations are those implicitly declared, plus, in the case of a type declared in a package specification, all subprograms with a parameter or result of that type also declared in the package specification. Primitive operations can be overridden on derivation and further ones added.

- A subprogram can be declared as abstract (designated by <>). An abstract subprogram does not have a body but one can be provided on derivation. A tagged type with abstract subprograms is an abstract type.

- T'Class denotes the class wide type rooted at T. Implicit conversion is allowed to values of T'Class. Objects and parameters of T'Class are treated as unconstrained. An appropriate access type can designate any value of T'Class.

• Calling a primitive operation with an actual parameter of a class wide type results in dispatching: that is the run-time selection of the operation according to the tag.

One of the main advantages of type extension is that it can be done without recompiling and retesting an existing stable system. This is perhaps the most important overall characteristic of object oriented languages.

EXERCISE 17.2.5

1   Add a procedure Select_Seat appropriate for nice passengers (and better) and rewrite the procedure Make for the type Reservation to dispatch on Select_Seat.

17.2.6   Controlled types

A very interesting example of the use of type extension is provided by considering the Ada 9X facilities for controlled types. These allow a user complete control over the initialization and finalization of objects and also provide the capability for user defined assignment.

This subject is clearly one for the specialist and so we just give a brief sketch. Before proceeding we need to remember that Ada 9X treats objects and values much as the same thing. We recall how we were able to rename the result of a function in Section 15.2 when we were preserving the value of Current_Output.

The general principle is that there are three distinct primitive activities concerning the control of objects

• initialization after creation,
• finalization before destruction,
• duplication upon assignment.

and the user is given the ability to provide appropriate procedures which are called to perform whatever is necessary at various points in the life of an object. These procedures are Initialize, Finalize and Duplicate and they take the object as a parameter.

To see how this works, consider

```
declare
    A: T;           -- create A, Initialize(A)
begin
    A := E;         -- Finalize(A), copy value, Duplicate(A)
    ...
end;                -- Finalize(A)
```

After A is declared and any normal default initialization carried out, the Initialize procedure is called. On the assignment, Finalize is first called to tidy up the old object about to be overwritten and thus destroyed, the physical copy is then made and finally Duplicate is called to do whatever might be required for the new copy. At the end of the block Finalize is called once more before the object is destroyed. Note, of course, that the user does not have to physically write the calls of the three control procedures, they are called automatically by the compiled code.

In the case of a nested structure where inner components might themselves be controlled, the rules are that components are initialized and duplicated before the object as a whole and on finalization everything is done in the reverse order.

There are many other situations where the control procedures are invoked such as when calling allocators, evaluating aggregates and so on; the details are omitted but the principles will be clear.

In order for a type to be controlled it has to be extended from one of two tagged types declared in the library package Finalization whose specification is as follows

```
with System.Finalization_Implementation;
use System;
package Finalization is

   type Controlled is
      new Finalization_Implementation.Root_Controlled with null record;

   procedure Initialize(Object: in out Controlled);
   procedure Duplicate(Object: in out Controlled) is <>;
   procedure Finalize(Object: in out Controlled) is <>;

   Root_Part: Finalization_Implementation.Root_Controlled
                        renames Finalization_Implementation.Root_Part;

   type Limited_Controlled is
      new Finalization_Implementation.Root_Limited_Controlled
                                                    with null record;

   procedure Initialize(Object: in out Limited_Controlled);
   procedure Finalize(Object: in out Limited_Controlled) is <>;
end Finalization;
```

We see that there are distinct types for non-limited and limited types and that these are themselves derived from corresponding types in the package System.Finalization_Implementation. Naturally enough the Duplicate procedure does not exist in the case of limited types because they cannot be copied.

As a simple example suppose we wish to declare a type and keep track of how many objects (values) of the type are in existence and also record the identity number of each object in the object itself. We could declare

```
with Finalization; use Finalization;
package Tracked_Things is
```

```
    type Thing is new Controlled with
      record
        Identity_Number: Integer;
        ... − − other data;
      end record;

  private

    procedure Initialize(Object: in out Thing);
    procedure Duplicate(Object: in out Thing);
    procedure Finalize(Object: in out Thing);

  end Tracked_Things;

  package body Tracked_Things is

    The_Count: Integer := 0;
    Next_One: Integer := 1;

    procedure Initialize(Object: in out Thing) is
    begin
      The_Count := The_Count + 1;
      Object.Identity_Number := Next_One;
      Next_One := Next_One + 1;
    end Initialize;

    procedure Duplicate(Object: in out Thing) renames Initialize;

    procedure Finalize(Object: in out Thing) is
    begin
      The_Count := The_Count − 1;
    end Finalize;

  end Tracked_Things;
```

In this example we have considered each value of a thing to be a new one and so Duplicate is the same as Initialize and we can conveniently use a renaming declaration to provide the body as was mentioned in Section 8.5. An alternative approach might be to consider new things to be created only when an object is first declared (or allocated). This variation is left as an exercise.

The observant reader will note that the identity number is visible to users of the package and thus liable to abuse. We will reconsider this when we discuss child packages in Section 17.4.1.

We finish this section with a few observations on the package Finalization. The procedures Duplicate and Finalize are made abstract so that the user will not forget to provide them. The default implementation of Initialize does nothing and will often be appropriate. The types Controlled and Limited_Controlled are of course abstract.

The package System.Finalization_Implementation defines the ultimate ancestor types from which the controlled types are derived; these ultimate types are not abstract and so it is possible to declare the constant Root_Part. This constant is then renamed in the package Finalization so that it can conveniently be used without reference to the other package. Such a constant is necessary for declaring an extension aggregate of a controlled type such as

```
T: Thing := (Root_Part with ... );
```

Incidentally this aggregate shows that the type of the expression before **with** need not be the immediate ancestor of the type of the aggregate but can be any ancestor type. It would not work in this case if it had to be the immediate ancestor because we cannot have an expression of the type Controlled because it is abstract.

Finally we note that this package illustrates how an abstract type can be obtained by derivation from a non-abstract type.

EXERCISE 17.2.6

1   Rewrite Initialize, Duplicate and Finalize as necessary for the situation where we only consider new things to be created when an object is declared or allocated.

17.3   Access types

One of the advantages of Ada 9X is its much more flexible approach to the manipulation of references. This overcomes the static and closed feel of Ada 83 and makes it much easier to interface Ada 9X programs to systems written in other languages.

This extra flexibility is provided by two new forms of access types. One allows the manipulation of subprograms as values and the other allows the manipulation of references to objects not created through the allocation mechanism.

17.3.1   Subprograms as values

In a previous section we mentioned late binding. All procedure calls are bound early in Ada 83 and this is one reason why the language feels so static; even the generic mechanism only defers binding to instantiation which is still essentially a compile-time process.

There were a number of reasons for taking such a static approach in Ada 83. There was concern for the implementation cost of dynamic binding, it was also clear that the presence of dynamic binding would reduce the provability of programs and moreover it was felt that the introduction of generics where subprograms could be passed as parameters would cater for practical situations where formal procedure parameters were used in other languages.

However, the absence of dynamic binding in Ada 83 has been unfortunate. It is now realized that implementation costs are trivial and not pervasive;

provability is not a relevant argument because we now know that in any safety-critical software where mathematical provability is a real issue, we only use a small subset of the language. And furthermore, the generic mechanism has proved not to be a sufficiently flexible alternative anyway.

We have seen how dispatching in Ada 9X is one mechanism for late binding. Another is provided by the manipulation of subprogram values through an extension of access types.

In Ada 9X an access type can refer to a subprogram; such an access to subprogram value can be created by the Access attribute and a subprogram can be called indirectly by dereferencing such an access value. Thus we can write

> **type** Trig_Function **is access function** (R: Real) **return** Real;
> T: Trig_Function;
> X, Theta: Real;

and T can then 'point to' functions such as Sin, Cos and Tan. We can then assign an appropriate access to subprogram value to T by for example

> T := Sin'Access;

and later indirectly call the subprogram currently referred to by T as expected

> X := T(Theta);

which is really an abbreviation for

> X := T.**all**(Theta);

Just as with many other uses of access types the .**all** is not usually required but it would be necessary if there were no parameters.

The access to subprogram mechanism can be used to program general dynamic selection and to pass subprograms as parameters. It allows program call-back to be implemented in a natural and efficient manner.

There are a number of rules which ensure that access to subprogram values cannot be misused. Subtype conformance matching ensures that the subprogram always has the correct number and type of parameters and there are rules about accessibility that ensure that a subprogram is not called out of context. Flexibility is thus gained without loss of integrity.

Classic numerical codes can now be implemented in Ada 9X in the same way as in languages such as Fortran but with complete security. Thus following the example in Section 13.3 an integration routine might have the following specification

> **type** Integrand **is access function** (X: Real) **return** Real;
>
> **function** Integrate(F: Integrand; A, B: Real) **return** Real;

and we might then write

> Area := Integrate(Log'Access, 1.0, 2.0);

which will compute the area under the curve for log(*x*) from 1.0 to 2.0. Within the body of the function Integrate there will be calls of the actual subprogram passed as parameter; this is a simple form of call-back.

A common paradigm within the process industry is to implement sequencing control through successive calls of a number of interpreter actions. A sequence compiler might interactively build an array of such actions which are then obeyed. Thus we might have

```
type Action is access procedure;
Action_Sequence: array (1 .. N) of Action;

...    - - build the array

       - - and then obey it
for I in Action_Sequence'Range loop
   Action_Sequence(I).all;
end loop;
```

where we note the need for **.all** because there are no parameters.

It is of course possible for a record (possibly private) to contain components whose types are access to subprogram types. We will now consider a package which might be within the system which drives the controls in the cockpit of Ada Airlines. There are a number of physical buttons on the console and we wish to associate different actions corresponding to pushing the various buttons.

```
package Buttons is

   type Button is private;

   type Button_Response is access procedure (B: in out Button);

   procedure Establish(B : in out Button; ... );

   procedure Push(B: in out Button);

   procedure Set_Response(B: in out Button;
                          R: in Button_Response);

   procedure Default_Response(B: in out Button);

   ...

private
   type Button is
      record
         Response: Button_Response := Default_Response'Access;
         ...   - - other aspects of the button
      end record;
end Buttons;
```

A button is represented as a private record containing a number of components describing properties of the button (position of message on the display for example). The component Response is an access to a procedure which is the action to be executed when the button is pushed. Note carefully that the button value is passed to this procedure as a parameter so that the procedure can obtain access to the other components of the record describing the button. The procedure Associate makes the connection between the physical button and the software button and fills in these other components. Other functions (not shown) provide access to them. The procedure Push is called when any physical button is pushed, the parameter indicating its identity. An appropriate default procedure is provided which warns the pilot if the button has not been set. The body might be as follows

```
package body Buttons is

    procedure Push(B: in out Button) is
    begin
        B.Response(B);  – – indirect call
    end Push;

    procedure Set_Response(B: in out Button;
                                       R: in Button_Response) is
    begin
        B.Response := R;  – – set procedure value in record
    end Set_Response;

    procedure Default_Response(B: in out Button) is
    begin
        Display("Button not set");
        Alarm.Sound;
    end Default_Response;

    ...

end Buttons;
```

We can now set the specific actions we want when a button is pushed. Thus we might want some emergency action to take place when a big red button is pushed.

```
Big_Red_Button: Button;

Associate(Big_Red_Button, ... );

procedure Emergency(B: in out Button) is
begin
    Broadcast("mayday");
    ...
    Eject(Pilot);
end Emergency;

...

Set_Response(Big_Red_Button, Emergency'Access);
...

Push(Big_Red_Button);
```

The reader will realize that the access to subprogram mechanism coupled with the inheritance and dispatching facilities described earlier enable very flexible yet secure dynamic structures to be programmed.

EXERCISE 17.3.1

1   Show how Exercise 13.3(**9**) might be reformulated avoiding the use of generics.

17.3.2   General access types

We have just seen how access types in Ada 9X have been extended to provide a means of manipulating subprogram values. Access types have also been extended to provide more flexible access to objects.

In Ada 83 access values could only refer to objects dynamically created through the allocator mechanism. It was not possible to access objects declared in the normal way. This approach was inherited from Pascal which had similar restrictions and was a reaction against the very flexible approach adopted by Algol 68 and C which can give rise to dangerous dangling references.

However, the ability to manipulate pointers is very valuable provided the risks can be overcome. The view taken by Ada 83 has proved unnecessarily inflexible, especially when interfacing to external systems possibly written in other languages.

In Ada 9X we can declare a general access type such as

```
type Int_Ptr is access all Integer;
```

and we can then assign the 'address' of any variable of type Integer to a variable of type Int_Ptr provided that the designated variable is marked as aliased. So we can write

```
IP: Int_Ptr;
I: aliased Integer;
...
IP := I'Access;
```

and we can then read and update the variable I through the access variable IP. Note once more the use of the Access attribute.

As with access to subprogram values there are rules that (at compile time) ensure that dangling references cannot arise.

A variation is that we can restrict the access to be read-only by replacing **all** in the type definition by **constant**. This allows read-only access to any variable and also to a constant thus

```
type Const_Int_Ptr is access constant Integer;
CIP: Const_Int_Ptr;
I: aliased Integer;
C: aliased constant Integer := 1815;
```

followed by

```
CIP := I'Access;  – – or CIP := C'Access;
```

The type accessed by a general access type can of course be any type such as an array or record. We can thus build chains from records statically declared. Note that we can also use an allocator to generate general access values. Our chain could thus include a mixture of records from both storage mechanisms although this would be unusual.

The components of an array can also be aliased as in

```
AI: array (1 .. 100) of aliased Integer;
...
IP := AI(I)'Access;
```

Finally note that the accessed value could be a component of any composite type. Thus we could point into the middle of a record (provided the component is marked as aliased). In a fast implementation of Conway's Game of Life a cell might contain access values directly referencing the component of its eight neighbours containing the counter saying whether the cell is alive or dead.

```
type Ref_Count is access constant Integer range 0 .. 1;
type Ref_Count_Array is array (Integer range <>) of Ref_Count;

type Cell is
  record
    Life_Count: aliased Integer range 0 .. 1;
    Total_Neighbour_Count: Integer range 0 .. 8;
    Neighbour_Count: Ref_Count_Array(1 .. 8);
    ...
  end record;
```

We can now link the cells together according to our model by statements such as

```
This_Cell.Neighbour_Count(1) :=
                        Cell_To_The_North.Life_Count'Access;
```

and then the heart of the computation which computes the sum of the life counts in the neighbours might be

```
C.Total_Neighbour_Count := 0;
for I in Neighbour_Count'Range loop
  C.Total_Neighbour_Count :=
```

C.Total_Neighbour_Count + C.Neighbour_Count(I).**all**;
    end loop;

Note that we have given the type Ref_Count and the component
Life_Count the same static subtypes so that they can be checked against each
other at compile time. This is not necessary but avoids a run-time check that
would otherwise be required if the subtypes did not statically match.

There is a restriction on accessing components of records which is
identical to that for renaming mentioned in Section 11.3. We cannot apply the
Access attribute to a component of an unconstrained variable if the component
depends upon a discriminant.

General access types can also be used to program static ragged arrays as
for example a table of messages of different lengths. The key to this is that the
accessed type can be unconstrained (such as String) and thus we can have an
array of pointers to strings of different lengths. In Ada 83 we would have to
allocate all the strings dynamically using an allocator.

In conclusion we have seen how the access types of Ada 83 have been
considerably enhanced in Ada 9X to allow much more flexible programming
which is especially important in open systems while nevertheless retaining the
inherent security missing in languages such as C and C++.

17.3.3   Access discriminants and parameters

All access types have to be named in Ada 83. However, there are two contexts
in Ada 9X where we can use an access type anonymously. We can have an
access value as a discriminant and also as a parameter of a subprogram.

Object oriented programming is much concerned with manipulating
records and it is a natural style to use access values to refer to records
indirectly. In particular it is often convenient to be able to dispatch on an
access value which is a parameter of a subprogram.

Thus in the case of the Ada Airlines reservation system we might prefer to
declare the procedure Select_Seat as

procedure Select_Seat(AR: **access** Reservation);

Following the answer to Exercise 17.2.5(**1**) we can now dispatch on
Select_Seat from within the body of Make by writing

procedure Make(R: **in out** Reservation) **is**
begin
    Select_Seat(Reservation'Class(R)'Access);
end Make;

where we naturally have to use the Access attribute to create the access value
to the class wide type.

Note that a function can also have access parameters and so this is a sly
way of getting the effect of functions with **out** or **in out** parameters.

An important property of access parameters is that they can never have a null value. We are not allowed to pass null as an actual parameter (this is checked on the call) and of course being of an anonymous type we cannot declare another such object inside the subprogram. As a consequence within the subprogram we never need to check for a null value of the type (neither in the program text nor in the compiled code). Note also that since we cannot declare any other objects of the type, assignment and equality do not apply to access parameters.

The uses of an access parameter are as expected; the accessed object can be manipulated using .**all** in the usual way and the parameter might be passed on as a further access value.

The actual parameter corresponding to an access parameter can be any access referring to the accessed type (or a corresponding class wide type as in the above example).

A particular property of access parameters is their accessibility rules which are dynamic in contrast to the static rules otherwise used to ensure that dangling references do not arise. Violation of an accessibility check raises Program_Error. For details the reader is referred to the Ada 9X Reference Manual.

The final use of access types we have to consider is as discriminants. We are familiar with the use of discriminants from Ada 83 in which all discriminants have to be of a discrete type. In Ada 9X a discriminant can also be of an access type and this access type can be a named type but it can also be an anonymous access type.

A discriminant of an access type is useful for effectively parameterizing one record with another. In the case of an (anonymous) access discriminant this can be used to enable a component of a record to obtain the identity of the record in which it is embedded. This enables complex chained structures to be created and can provide multiple views of a structure. Consider

```
type Outer is limited private;

private

type Inner(Ptr: access Outer) is ...

type Outer is limited
  record
     ...
     Component: Inner(Outer'Access);
     ...
  end record;
```

The Component of type Inner has an access discriminant Ptr which refers back to the instance of the record Outer. This is because the attribute Access applied to the name of a record type inside its declaration refers to the current instance. This is rather similar to the way in which the name of a task type refers to the current task inside its own body rather than to the type itself (see Section 14.9). If we now declare an object of the type Outer

```
Obj: Outer;
```

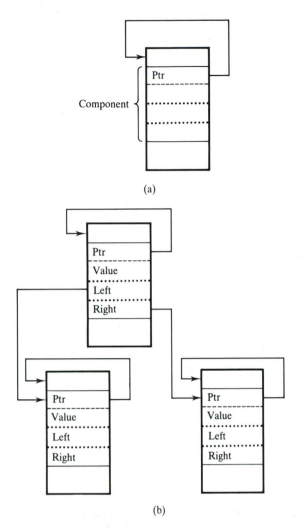

Component {

(a)

(b)

Figure 17.2   Self-referential structures.

then the structure created is as shown in Figure 17.2(a). We call it a self-referential structure for obvious reasons. Note that it becomes self-referential automatically which is not the same as the effect that would be obtained with a record of a type such as Cell in which an instance might happen to have a component referring to itself. All instances of the type Outer will refer to themselves.

This simple example on its own is of little interest. However, the types Inner and Outer can both be extensions of other types and these other types might themselves be chained structures. For example the type Inner might be an extension of some type Node (such as in Section 11.4) containing components which access other objects of the type Node in order to create a tree. Note in particular that Inner could also be

type Inner(Ptr: **access** Outer'Class) **is new** Node **with** ...

so that heterogeneous chains can be constructed. The important point is that we can navigate over the tree which consists of the components of type Inner linked together but at any point in the tree we can reach to the enclosing Outer record as a whole by the access discriminant Ptr as illustrated in Figure 17.2(b).

It should be noted that an access discriminant is only allowed for a limited type. This avoids copying problems with the self-referring components. Moreover a task can have an access discriminant and this enables a task in a record to have automatic access to the record in which it is embedded.

This brings us to the end of our discussion on access types. We have explained the various building blocks available but space precludes us from illustrating the great variety of structures that can be created. We leave the reader to explore the possibilities at leisure.

17.4   Hierarchical libraries

One of the great strengths of Ada is the library package where the distinct specification and body decouple the user interface to a package (the specification) from its implementation (the body). This enables the details of the implementation and the clients to be recompiled separately without interference provided the specification remains stable.

However, although this works well for smallish programs it has proved cumbersome when programs become large or complex. There are two aspects of the problem: the coarse control of visibility of private types and the inability to extend without recompilation.

There are occasions when we wish to write two logically distinct packages which nevertheless share a private type. We cannot do this in Ada 83. We either have to make the type not private so that both packages can see it with the unfortunate consequence that all the client packages can also see the type; this breaks the abstraction. Or, on the other hand, if we wish to keep the abstraction, then we have to merge the two packages together and this results in a large monolithic package with increased recompilation costs. (We discount as evil the use of tricks such as Unchecked_Conversion to get at the details of private types.)

The other aspect of the difficulty arises when we wish to extend an existing system by adding more facilities to it. If we add to a package specification then naturally we have to recompile it but moreover we also have to recompile all existing clients even if the additions have no impact upon them.

In Ada 9X these and other similar problems are solved by the introduction of a hierarchical library structure containing child packages and child subprograms. There are two kinds of children: visible children and private children. We will first consider visible children in the next section; private children will be discussed later.

17.4.1   Child units

Consider first the familiar example of a package for the manipulation of complex numbers described in Section 9.1. It contains the private type itself plus the arithmetic operations and also subprograms to construct and decompose a complex number taking a cartesian view.

```
package Complex_Numbers is
  type Complex is private;
  ...
  function "+" (X, Y: Complex) return Complex;
  ...
  function Cons(R, I: Real) return Complex;
  function Rl_Part(X: Complex) return Real;
  function Im_Part(X: Complex) return Real;

private
  ...
end Complex_Numbers;
```

We have deliberately not shown the completion of the private type since it is immaterial how it is implemented. Although this package gives the user a cartesian view of the type, nevertheless it certainly does not have to be implemented that way as we saw in Chapter 9.

Some time later we might need to additionally provide a polar view by the provision of subprograms which construct and decompose a complex number from and to its polar coordinates as we did in Section 13.4. In Ada 83 we can only do this by adding to the existing package and this forces us to recompile all the existing clients.

In Ada 9X, however, we can add a child package as follows

```
package Complex_Numbers.Polar is

  procedure Cons_Polar(R, Theta: Real) return Complex;
  function "abs" (X: Complex) return Real;
  function Arg(X: Complex) return Real;

end Complex_Numbers.Polar;
```

and within the body of this package we can access the full details of the private type **Complex**.

Note the notation, a package having the name P.Q is a child package of its parent package P. We can think of the child package as being declared inside the declarative region of its parent but after the end of the specification of its parent; most of the visibility rules stem from this model. In other words the declarative region defined by the parent (which is primarily both the specification and body of the parent) also includes the space occupied by the text of the children; but it is important to realize that the children are inside that region and do not just extend it.

In just the same way, library packages in Ada 9X can be thought of as being declared in the declarative region of the package **Standard** and after the end of its specification. It should be noted that this is a slightly different model to Ada 83 necessary to fit in with other rules such as which operations are primitive. (A child subprogram is not a primitive operation of a type declared in its parent's specification because the child is not declared in the specification but after it.)

The important special visibility rule is that the private part (if any) and the body of the child have visibility of the private part of their parent. (They naturally also have visibility of the visible part.) However, the visible part of a (visible) child package does not have visibility of the private part of its parent; if it did it would allow renaming and hence the export of the hidden private details to any client; this would break the abstraction of the private type (this rule does not apply to private children).

The body of the child package for our complex number example could simply be

```
package body Complex_Numbers.Polar is

    - - bodies of Cons_Polar etc

end Complex_Numbers.Polar;
```

In order to access the procedures of the child package the client must have a with clause for the child package. However this also implicitly provides a with clause for the parent as well thereby saving us the burden of having to write one separately. Thus we might have

```
with Complex_Numbers.Polar;
package Client is
    ...
```

and then within Client we can access the various subprograms in the usual way by writing Complex_Numbers.Rl_Part or Complex_Numbers.Polar.Arg and so on.

Direct visibility can be obtained by use clauses as expected. However, a use clause for the child does not imply one for the parent; but, because of the model that the child is in the declarative region of the parent, a use clause for the parent makes the child name itself directly visible. So writing

```
with Complex_Numbers.Polar; use Complex_Numbers;
```

now allows us to refer to the subprograms as Rl_Part and Polar.Arg respectively.

We could of course have added

```
use Complex_Numbers.Polar;
```

and we would then be able to refer to the subprogram in Polar just as Arg.

The reader may recall that a use clause in a context clause can only mention the packages in the with clause (see Section 8.4). So we could not abbreviate this last use clause to just **use** Polar; on the grounds that we already have direct visibility of the parent but we could do so if the use clause were in a declarative part.

Child packages thus neatly solve both the problem of sharing a private type over several compilation units and the problem of extending a package without recompiling the clients. They thus provide another form of programming by extension.

A package may of course have several children. In fact with hindsight it might have been more logical to have developed our complex number package as three packages: a parent containing the private type and the four arithmetic operations and then two child packages, one giving the cartesian view and the other giving the polar view of the type. At a later date we could add yet another package providing perhaps the trigonometric functions on complex numbers and again this can be done without recompiling what has already been written and thus without the risk of introducing errors.

The extension mechanism provided by child packages fits neatly together with that provided by tagged types. Thus a child package might itself have a private part and then within that part we might derive and extend a private type from the parent package. This enables us to provide different views of a type and effectively allows us to create a type with some components visible to the user and some components hidden.

An example is provided by the controlled type Thing we introduced in Section 17.2.6. A problem was that the identity number was visible to the user and thus could be abused. With child packages we can arrange that the identity number is not visible to the user at all. Consider

```
package Tracked_Things is

   type Identity_Controlled is new Controlled with private;
   procedure Finalize(IC: Identity_Controlled) is <>;

private
   type Identity_Controlled is new Controlled with
      record
         Identity_Number: Integer;
      end record;
end Tracked Things;

package Tracked_Things.User_View is

   type Thing is new Identity_Controlled with
      record
         ... - - visible data
      end record;

private
   procedure Initialize...
   - - etc
end Tracked_Things.User_View;
```

In this arrangement we first declare a controlled type just containing the component Identity_Number (this component being hidden from the user) and then in the child package we further extend the type with the visible data which we wish the user to see. Note that the type Identity_Controlled is still abstract so objects of this type cannot be declared (we have explicitly indicated that it is abstract by the declaration of Finalize for it; we recall from Section 17.2.3 that every view of an abstract type must have a visible abstract subprogram). We then declare Initialize, Duplicate and Finalize for the type Thing in the private part of the child package so that the user cannot call them directly.

Note that although the private part of the child package does not need to access the private part of the parent, nevertheless the body of the child package will and that is why the child package is necessary.

Of course many other arrangements are possible. We could provide the control procedures for Identity_Controlled by declaring them in the private part of the main package and then we might derive a variety of other types from Identity_Controlled all sharing the same control mechanism.

Yet another arrangement would be to declare the visible data first and then extend with the hidden identity number.

Finally, it is very important to realize that the child mechanism is hierarchical. Children may have children to any level so we can build a complete tree providing decomposition of facilities in a natural manner. A child may have a private part and this is then visible from its children but not its parent.

With regard to siblings a child can obviously only have visibility of a previously compiled sibling anyway. And then the normal rules apply: a child can only see the visible part of its siblings.

A parent body may access (via with clauses) and thus depend upon its children and grandchildren. A child body automatically depends upon its parent (and grandparent) and needs no with clause for them. A child body can depend upon its siblings (again via with clauses).

EXERCISE 17.4.1

1   Rewrite the package Complex_Numbers as a parent and two children as suggested above.

2   Rearrange the declarations of the types in the package Tracked_Things so that the intermediate type has the visible components and the identity number is then declared in the type extension in the child package.

17.4.2   Private children

In the previous section we introduced the concept of hierarchical child packages and showed how these allowed extension and continued privacy of private types without recompilation. However, the whole idea was based around the provision of additional facilities for the client. The specifications of the additional packages were all visible to the client.

In the development of large subsystems it often happens that we would like to decompose the system for implementation reasons but without giving any additional visibility to clients.

Ada 83 has a problem in this area which we have not yet addressed. In Ada 83 the only means at our disposal for the decomposition of a body is the subunit. However, although a subunit can be recompiled without affecting other subunits at the same level, any change to the top level body (which of course includes the stubs of the subunits) requires all subunits to be recompiled.

Ada 9X also solves this problem by the provision of a form of child unit that is totally private to its parent. In order to illustrate this idea consider the following outline of an operating system.

```
package OS is
   - - parent package defines types used throughout the system
   type File_Descriptor is private;
   ...
private
   type File_Descriptor is new Integer;
end OS;

package OS.Exceptions is
   - - exceptions used throughout the system
   File_Descriptor_Error,
   File_Name_Error,
   Permission_Error: exception;
end OS.Exceptions;

with OS.Exceptions;
package OS.File_Manager is
   type File_Mode is (Read_Only, Write_Only, Read_Write);
   function Open(File_Name: String; Mode: File_Mode)
                                    return OS.File_Descriptor;

   procedure Close(File: in OS.File_Descriptor);
   ...
end OS.File_Manager;

procedure OS.Interpret(Command: String);

private package OS.Internals is
   ...
end OS.Internals;

private package OS.Internals_Debug is
   ...
end OS.Internals_Debug;
```

In this example the parent package contains the types used throughout the system. There are then three child units, the package OS.Exceptions containing various exceptions, the package OS.File_Manager which provides file open/close routines (note the explicit with clause for its sibling

OS.Exceptions) and a procedure OS.Interpret which interprets a command line passed as a parameter. (Incidentally this illustrates that a child unit can be a subprogram as well as a package. It can actually be any library unit and that includes a generic declaration and a generic instantiation.) Finally we have two private child packages called OS.Internals and OS.Internals_Debug.

A private child (distinguished by starting with the word **private**) can be declared at any point in the child hierarchy. The visibility rules for private children are similar to those for normal children but there are two extra rules.

The first extra rule is that a private child is only visible within the subtree of the hierarchy whose root is its parent. And moreover within that tree it is not visible to the specifications of any non-private siblings (although it is visible to their bodies).

In our example, since the private child is a direct child of the package OS, the package OS.Internals is visible to the bodies of OS itself, of OS.File_Manager and of OS.Interpret (OS.Exceptions only has a null body anyway) and it is also visible to both body and specification of OS.Internals_Debug. But it is not visible outside OS and a client package certainly cannot access OS.Internals at all.

The other extra rule is that the visible part of the private child can access the private part of its parent. This is quite safe because it cannot export information about a private type to a client because it is not itself visible. Nor can it export information indirectly via its non-private siblings because, as we have seen, it is not visible to their specifications but only to their bodies.

We can now safely implement our system in the package OS.Internals and we can create a subtree for the convenience of development and extensibility. We would then have a third level in the hierarchy containing packages such as OS.Internals.Devices, OS.Internals.Access_Rights and so on.

We conclude this section by summarizing the various visibility rules which are actually quite simple and mostly follow from the model of the child being located after the end of the specification of its parent but inside the parent's declarative region.

- A specification never needs to with its parent; it may with a sibling (if compiled first) except that a visible child specification may not with a private sibling; it may not with its own child (it has not been compiled yet!).

- A body never needs to with its parent; it may with a sibling (private or not); it may with its own child.

- A private child is never visible outside the tree rooted at its parent.

- The private part and body of any child can access the private part of its parent (and grandparent...).

- In addition the visible part of a private child can also access the private part of its parent (and grandparent...).

- A with clause for a child automatically implies with clauses for all its ancestors.

- A use clause for a unit makes the child units accessible by simple name (this only applies to child units for which there is also a with clause).

These rules may seem a bit complex but actually stem from just a few considerations of consistency. Questions regarding access to children of sibling units and other remote relatives follow by analogy with an external client viewing the appropriate subtree.

EXERCISE 17.4.2

1   Rewrite the body of the package Rational_Numbers of Exercise 9.1(**3**) so that the functions Normal and GCD are in a private child package Rational_Numbers.Slave.

17.4.3   Generic children

We conclude our discussion of hierarchical libraries by considering their interaction with generics. Genericity is also an important tool in the construction of subsystems and it is essential that it be usable with the child concept.

Any parent unit may have generic children. If the parent unit is not generic then a generic child may be instantiated in the usual way at any point where it is visible.

On the other hand, if the parent unit is itself generic, then it can only have generic children and moreover the rules regarding their instantiation are somewhat different. A generic child of a generic parent can be instantiated inside the parent and its hierarchy (as normal) or externally but then only as a child of an instantiation of its parent.

As a simple example, we might wish to make the package Complex_Numbers of the previous section generic with respect to the underlying floating point type. Following Section 13.2 we would write

```
generic
   type Real is digits <>;
package Generic_Complex_Numbers is
   ...
end Generic_Complex_Numbers;

generic
package Generic_Complex_Numbers.Polar is
   ...
end Generic_Complex_Numbers.Polar;
```

and then the instantiations might be

```
with Generic_Complex_Numbers;
package My_Complex_Numbers is
     new Generic_Complex_Numbers(My_Real);
```

```
with Generic_Complex_Numbers.Polar;
package My_Complex_Numbers.Polar is
    new Generic_Complex_Numbers.Polar;
```

We thus have to instantiate the generic hierarchy (or as much of it as we want) unit by unit. This avoids a number of problems that would arise with a more liberal approach but enables complete subsystems to be built in a generic manner.

The reader will now appreciate that the hierarchical library system of Ada 9X coupled with genericity provides a very powerful and convenient tool for the development of large systems from component subsystems.

17.5 Exceptions

We have already observed that Numeric_Error is just a renaming of Constraint_Error in Ada 9X. Furthermore we are allowed to mention the same exception more than once in the same handler. This enables us to continue to write

```
when Constraint_Error | Numeric_Error =>
```

so that programs remain compatible.

Ada 9X also provides additional facilities which enable a program to identify further information about the cause of an exception. This is particularly useful in an others clause where we may require to log the details of all exceptions raised. Thus in our general clean-up clause in Section 10.2 we wrote

```
when others =>
    Put("Something else went wrong");
    Clean_Up;
raise;
end;
```

This is not very helpful since we would really like to record what actually happened. We cannot do this in Ada 83 without writing a handler for every exception in the program and, of course, some of these may not be in scope anyway. Ada 9X introduces the idea of an exception occurrence which identifies both the exception and the instance of its being raised (that is, the circumstances associated with the particular error condition).

In Ada 9X the type Exception_Occurrence is declared in the package System.Exceptions (a child package of System) together with functions Exception_Name, Exception_Message and Exception_Information. These functions take an exception occurrence as their single parameter and return a string. As their names suggest Exception_Name returns the name of the exception and Exception_Message and Exception_Information return two levels of more detailed information which in addition identify the cause and location.

To get hold of the occurrence we write a 'choice parameter' in the handler and this behaves as a constant of the type Exception_Occurrence. We can now more usefully write

```
when Event: others =>
    Put("Unexpected exception:");
    New_Line;
    Put(Exception_Message(Event));
    Clean_Up;
    raise;
end;
```

The object Event of the type Exception_Occurrence acts as a sort of marker which enables us to identify the current occurrence; its scope is the handler. Such a choice parameter can be placed in any handler.

17.6   Numeric types

We mentioned in Chapter 12 that the model of numeric types is somewhat different in Ada 9X. Most of the change is fine detail that need not concern the normal user and is addressed in the Numerics annex. However, one area that is important in the core language is the somewhat different treatment of universal types and the introduction of the anonymous types root integer and root real.

The essence of the root types is that they can be considered as the types from which all other integer and real types are derived. The base range of root integer is thus System.Min_Int .. System.Max_Int.

The universal types are types which can be matched by any specific numeric type of their class. We see therefore that the universal types are rather like class wide types of the respective classes. So universal integer is thus effectively root_integer'Class.

The integer literals are, of course, of the type universal integer and so, as in Ada 83, can be implicitly converted to any integer type including the anonymous root integer. However, an important change is that, in the case of an ambiguity, an expression is by preference converted to the corresponding root type.

A corollary of this preference rule is that the rule for converting universal expressions (which meant that only certain simple expressions could be automatically converted in Ada 83, see Section 12.1) can be liberalized so that all universal expressions can be implicitly converted in Ada 9X. One outcome of all this is that we can now write

```
for I in −1 .. 10 loop
```

as we have already mentioned.

Another small change concerns static expressions. As already mentioned in Section 16.1, static expressions may be more elaborate in Ada 9X. Moreover, an expression which looks static but occurs in a context not demanding a static expression will be evaluated statically; perhaps surprisingly this was not the case in Ada 83 – an expression such as 2 + 3 was only required to be evaluated statically if the context demanded it.

The above changes are fairly marginal and only affect relatively obscure situations. Of more interest is the fact that Ada 9X also includes two new classes of numeric types. These are the modular types (a variation on integer types) and decimal types (a special form of fixed point types) which are described in the next two sections.

17.6.1   Modular types

In Ada 9X the integer types are subdivided into signed integer types and modular types. The signed integer types are those with which we are already familiar from Ada 83 such as Integer and so on. The modular types are new to Ada 9X.

The modular types are unsigned integer types which exhibit cyclic arithmetic. Suppose for example that we wish to perform unsigned 8-bit arithmetic (that is byte arithmetic). We can declare

```
type Unsigned_Byte is mod 256;
```

and then the range of values supported by Unsigned_Byte is 0 .. 255. The normal arithmetic operations apply but all arithmetic is performed modulo 256 and overflow cannot occur.

The modulus of a modular type need not be a power of two although it often will be. It might, however, be convenient to use some obscure prime number as the modulus perhaps in the implementation of hash tables.

The logical operations **and or xor** and **not** are also available on modular types; they naturally treat the value as a bit pattern. No problems arise with mixing these logical operations with arithmetic operations because negative values are not involved and hence the difference in representation on one's and two's complement machines does not matter.

Shift operations are also available through a standard package for certain implementation defined modular types.

The rules for modular type are phrased in terms of principal values in such a way that conversion from modular to signed integer types works in a useful manner. (Modular types really work in terms of equivalence classes.)

Thus suppose we had

```
type Index is range −128 .. +127;
X: Unsigned_Byte := 150;
Y: Index := Index(X);
```

then the type conversion will not cause overflow and the value in Y will be −106. Observe that −106 is congruent to 150, modulo 256.

The modular types form a distinct class of types to the signed integer types. There is thus a distinct form for a generic formal parameter of a modular type namely

    type T **is mod** <>;

and this cannot be matched by a type such as Integer. Nor indeed can the signed integer form with **range** <> be matched by a modular type such as Unsigned_Byte.

EXERCISE 17.6.1

1   Given

    X: Unsigned_Byte := 16#AB#;
    Y: Unsigned_Byte := 16#CD#;

    what are the values of

    (a) X **or** Y
    (b) X + Y
    (c) X − Y
    (d) X * Y

2   Reconsider Exercise 6.2(**2**) using an appropriate modular type.

17.6.2 Decimal types

Decimal types are used in specialized commercial applications and are dealt with in depth in the Information Systems annex which is outside the scope of this book. However, the basic syntax of decimal types is in the core language and it is therefore appropriate to give a brief overview.

A decimal type is a form of fixed point type. The declaration provides a value of delta as for an ordinary fixed point type (except that in this case it must be a power of 10) and also prescribes the number of significant decimal digits. So we can write

    type Money **is delta** 0.01 **digits** 20;

which will cope with values of some currency such as Eurodollars up to one trillion (US, one quintillion) in units of one Eurocent. This allows 2 digits for the cents and 18 for the dollars so that the maximum allowed value is

    $999,999,999,999,999,999.99

The usual operations apply to decimal types as to other fixed point types. Furthermore the Information Systems annex describes a number of special packages for decimal types including conversion to external format using picture strings.

The only other point which we need to make here is that there is also a special form for a generic parameter of a decimal type. Not unexpectedly, it is

type T **is delta** <> **digits** <>;

Again this cannot be matched by an ordinary fixed point type and nor is the form with just **delta** <> matched by a decimal type such as Money.

17.7 Generics

The generic facility in Ada 83 has proved very useful for developing reusable software particularly with regard to its type parameterization capability. However, there were a few anomalies which have been rectified in Ada 9X. In addition a number of further parameter models have been added to match the object oriented facilities and the additional numeric types as described in previous sections.

As mentioned in Section 13.2 the Ada 83 contract model was broken because of the lack of distinction between constrained and unconstrained formal parameters. This is overcome by the introduction of a new form of formal parameter notation for unconstrained types

type T(<>) **is private**;

In this case we are not allowed to declare an (uninitialized) object of type T in the generic body; we can only use T in ways which do not require a constrained type. The actual parameter can then be any unconstrained type such as String; it could, of course, also be a constrained type.

The existing notation

type T **is private**;

can only be matched in Ada 9X by a type such as Integer or a constrained type or a record type with default discriminants (these types are known as definite types in Ada 9X).

17.7.1 Generics and type extension

Other new parameter models are useful for combining genericity with type extension and for writing class-wide generic packages. The formal declaration

type T **is tagged private**;

requires that the actual type be tagged (but it cannot be abstract, see Section 17.2.3).

We can also write

> **type** T **is new** S;

or

> **type** T **is new** S **with private**;

In both cases the actual type must be S or derived directly or indirectly from S. In the second case, **with private** indicates that the actual type must also be tagged. (Remember the rule that all tagged types have **tagged** or **with** in their declaration.)

In all these cases we can also follow the formal type name with (<>) to indicate that the actual may be indefinite (using the terminology introduced above) or we can follow the type name with a list of formal discriminants.

For implementation reasons there are some restrictions on the use of generic parameters in the body. For example, we cannot derive from a formal tagged type in a generic body although we can in the specification.

A common template for a generic package might be

```
generic
   type S is tagged private;
package P is
   type T is new S with private;
   – – operations on T
private
   type T is new S with
      record
         – – additional components
      end record;
end P;
```

where the body provides the operations and the specification exports the extended type.

We can then use an instantiation of P to add the operations of T to any existing tagged type and the resulting type will of course still be in the class of the type passed as actual parameter.

This approach allows us to extend a type privately with generic operations that the client cannot see. For example we recall from Section 17.2.1 that the full type corresponding to

> **type** Shape **is new** Object **with private**;

need not be directly derived from **Object**. We can therefore write

```
private
   package Q is new P(Object);
   type Shape is new Q.T with null record;
```

and then the type Shape will also have all the components and properties of the type T in the generic package. As written, these are, of course, not visible to the client but subprograms in the visible part of the package in which Shape is declared could provide access to them.

This and related techniques provide forms of multiple inheritance which will be found to be very useful for type composition and generally building subsystems from reusable components.

EXERCISE 17.7.1

1 Write a generic package whose visible part is

```
generic
   type Raw_Type is tagged private;
package Tracking is
   type Tracked_Type is new Raw_Type with private;
   function Identity(TT: Tracked_Type) return Integer;
private ...
```

The purpose is to extend the Raw_Type so that objects of the resulting type Tracked_Type contain an identity number as in the controlled type Thing of Section 17.2.6. Although Tracked_Type will not be controlled in the sense that it is directly descended from the type Controlled, it will have a component of a controlled type and this will give the effect of controlling objects of Tracked_Type. The function Identity returns the identity number of the object TT.

2 Using the package Tracking of the previous example, write a package whose visible part is

```
package Hush_Hush is
   type Secret_Shape is new Object with private;
   function Shape_Identity(SS: Secret_Shape) return Integer;
   – – other operations on a secret shape
private ...
```

The intent is that objects of the type Secret_Shape should be controlled and have an identity number which is returned by a call of Shape_Identity plus other hidden components which can be manipulated by the other operations in the visible part of the package.

17.7.2 Package parameters

The last new kind of formal generic parameter is the formal generic package. This greatly simplifies the composition of generic packages. It allows one package to be used as a parameter to another so that a hierarchy of facilities can be created.

As an example we reconsider the package Generic_Complex_Functions described in Section 13.4. This provides the ability to compute functions of complex numbers by building upon two existing packages, one providing the corresponding elementary functions on real numbers and the other providing the complex numbers themselves; both are generic with respect to the underlying floating type.

In the Ada 83 formulation we have to pass the type Complex and many of its operations exported from the instantiation of Generic_Complex_Numbers and the functions exported from the instantiation of Generic_Elementary_Functions back into the complex functions package as distinct formal parameters so that we can use them in that package. The burden is somewhat reduced by using the default mechanism for the operations but it is nevertheless very tedious.

This burden is completely alleviated in Ada 9X by the ability to declare generic formal packages. In the generic formal part we can write

with package P **is new** Q(<>);

and then the actual parameter corresponding to P must be any package which has been obtained by instantiating Q which must itself be a generic package. We can also explicitly indicate the actual parameters required by the instantiation of Q thus

with package R **is new** Q(P1, P2, ...);

and then the actual package corresponding to R must have been instantiated with the given parameters.

Returning to our example, in Ada 9X, having written Generic_Complex_Numbers and Generic_Elementary_Functions as before, we can now write

```
with Generic_Elementary_Functions;
with Generic_Complex_Numbers;
generic
   with package Elementary_Functions is
      new Generic_Elementary_Functions(<>);
   with package Complex_Numbers is
      new Generic_Complex_Numbers
                              (Elementary_Functions.Float_Type);
package Generic_Complex_Functions is
   use Complex_Numbers;

   - - as before

end Generic_Complex_Functions;
```

where the actual packages must be instantiations of Generic_Elementary_Functions and Generic_Complex_Numbers. Note that both forms of formal package are used. Any instantiation of Generic_Elementary_Functions is allowed but the instantiation of Generic_Complex_Numbers must have

Elementary_Functions.Float_Type as its actual parameter. This ensures that both packages are instantiated with the same floating type.

Note carefully that we are using the formal exported from the first instantiation as the required parameter for the second instantiation. The formal parameters are only accessible in this way when the default form (<>) is used. In order to reduce verbosity it is permitted to have a use clause for a formal package in the generic formal list, so we could have written

```
with package Elementary_Functions is
    new Generic_Elementary_Functions(<>);
use Elementary_Functions;
with package Complex_Numbers is
    new Generic_Complex_Numbers(Float_Type);
```

although this is perhaps not so clear.

Finally our instantiations are

```
type My_Real is digits 9;

package My_Elementary_Functions is
    new Generic_Elementary_Functions(My_Real);

package My_Complex_Numbers is
    new Generic_Complex_Numbers(My_Real);

package My_Complex_Functions is
    new Generic_Complex_Functions
        (My_Elementary_Functions, My_Complex_Numbers);
```

which should be compared with those in Section 13.4.

The key point is that we no longer have to import (explicitly or implicitly) the types and operators exported by the instantiations of Generic_ Elementary_Functions and Generic_Complex_Numbers. Hence the parameter list of Generic_Complex_Functions is reduced to merely two parameters which are the packages obtained by the previous instantiations. We no longer even have to pass the underlying type My_Real.

Although this example has been couched in terms of a numerical application, the general approach is applicable to many examples of building a hierarchy of generic packages.

17.8   Tasking

As we mentioned in Chapter 14, there are essentially two sorts of problems in tasking. One concerns the passing of messages from one task to another and the other concerns the protection of shared resources.

Ada 83 uses the rendezvous mechanism to solve both kinds of problems. This works well with message problems since the rendezvous in essence provides a message passing protocol. We have also seen how it can be used to solve shared resource problems such as the protected variable and bounded buffer in Section 14.4.

The rendezvous approach certainly avoids the methodological difficulties encountered by the use of low level primitives such as semaphores. Such primitives suffer from similar problems to gotos; it is obvious what they do and they are trivial to implement but in practice they are easy to misuse and can lead to programs which are difficult to maintain.

However, the rendezvous has not proved entirely satisfactory for the shared data problems. It requires additional tasks to manage the shared data and this often leads to poor performance. Moreover, in some situations, awkward race conditions arise essentially because of abstraction inversion. We remember, for example, the problems with the Count attribute and timed calls in Section 14.5.

Ada 9X overcomes these problems by the introduction of a completely new construction for shared data problems; this is the protected type. A protected type encapsulates and provides synchronized access to the private data of objects of the type without the introduction of additional tasks.

17.8.1   Protected types

A protected type has a distinct specification and body in a similar style to a package or task. The specification provides the access protocol and the body provides the implementation details. We can also have a single protected object by analogy with a single task.

The specification of a protected type is also split into a visible part and a private part. The visible part contains the specifications of subprograms and entries providing the protocol. The private part contains the hidden shared data and also the specifications of any other subprograms and entries which are private to the type.

As a simple example consider the following

```
protected Variable is
   function Read return Item;
   procedure Write(New_Value: in Item);
private
   Data: Item;
end Variable;

protected body Variable is

   function Read return Item is
   begin
      return Data;
   end Read;

   procedure Write(New_Value: in Item) is
   begin
      Data := New_Value;
```

```
    end Write;

end Variable;
```

The protected object Variable provides controlled access to the private variable Data of some type Item. The function Read enables us to read the current value whereas the procedure Write enables us to update the value. Calls are written in the usual way

```
X := Variable.Read;
...
Variable.Write(New_Value => Y);
```

where the familiar dotted notation is used.

Within a protected body we can have a number of subprograms and the implementation is such that (like a monitor) calls of the subprograms are mutually exclusive and thus cannot interfere with each other. A procedure in the protected body can access the private data in an arbitrary manner whereas a function is only allowed read access to the private data. The implementation is consequently permitted to perform the useful optimization of allowing multiple calls of functions at the same time thus automatically solving the basic classic readers and writers problem which caused us so much trouble in Section 14.4.

It is interesting to compare the above protected object with the task Protected_Variable in Section 14.4. An important difference is that we wrote the task in such a way that Write was always accepted first thereby setting the initial value. We leave the modification of the protected object to ensure similar behaviour as an exercise.

By analogy with entries in tasks, a protected type may also have entries. The action of an entry call is provided by an entry body which has a barrier condition which must be true before the entry body can be executed. There is a strong parallel between an accept statement with a guard in a task body and an entry body with a barrier in a protected body, although, as we shall see in a moment, the timing of the evaluation of barriers is quite different to that of guards.

A good illustration of the use of barriers is given by a protected type implementing the classic bounded buffer of Section 14.4. Consider

```
protected type Buffering is
    entry Put(X: in Item);
    entry Get(X: out Item);
private
    A: Item_Array(1 .. N);
    I, J: Integer range 1 .. N := 1;
    Count: Integer range 0 .. N := 0;
end Buffering;

protected body Buffering is

    entry Put(X: in Item) when Count < N is
```

```
begin
   A(I) := X;
   I := I mod N + 1; Count := Count + 1;
end Put;

entry Get(X: out Item) when Count > 0 is
begin
   X := A(J);
   J := J mod N + 1; Count := Count − 1;
end Get;

end Buffering;
```

Like the task Buffering this provides a cyclic bounded buffer holding up to N values of the type Item with access through the entries Put and Get.

As an aside, note that we have had to declare both an array type Item_Array and the constant N external to the protected type; this is because we are only allowed components inside the protected type. There is a general rule that we cannot declare a type inside a type; a similar problem occurred with the type Stack in Section 9.2. These restrictions do not really matter since in practice the protected type is likely to be declared inside a (possibly generic) package.

We can now declare an object of the protected type and access it as expected

```
My_Buffer: Buffering;
...
My_Buffer.Put(X);
```

The behaviour of the protected object is controlled by the barriers. When an entry is called its barrier is evaluated; if the barrier is false then the call is queued in much the same way that calls on entries in tasks are queued. When My_Buffer is declared, the buffer is empty and so the barrier for Put is true whereas the barrier for Get is false. So initially only a call of Put can be executed and a task issuing a call of Get will be queued.

At the end of the execution of an entry body (or a procedure body) of the protected object all barriers which have queued tasks are re-evaluated thus possibly permitting the processing of an entry call which had been queued on a false barrier. So at the end of the first call of Put, if a call of Get had been queued, then the barrier is re-evaluated thus permitting a waiting call of Get to be serviced at once.

It is important to realize that there is no task associated with the buffer itself; the evaluation of barriers is effectively performed by the run time system. Barriers are evaluated when an entry is first called and when something happens which could sensibly change the state of a barrier with a waiting task.

Thus barriers are only re-evaluated at the end of an entry or procedure body and not at the end of a protected function call because a function call cannot change the state of the protected object and so is not expected to change the values of barriers. These rules ensure that a protected object can be implemented efficiently.

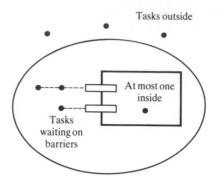

Figure 17.3   The eggshell model.

Note that a barrier *could* refer to a global variable; such a variable might get changed other than through a call of a protected procedure or entry – it could be changed by another task or even by a call of a protected function; such changes will thus not be acted upon promptly. The programmer needs to be aware of this and should not use global variables in barriers without due consideration.

It must be understood that the barrier protection mechanism is superimposed upon the natural mutual exclusion of the protected construct thus giving two distinct levels of protection. At the end of a protected call, already queued entries (whose barriers have now become true) take precedence over other calls contending for the protected object. On the other hand, a new entry call cannot even evaluate its barrier if the protected object is busy with another call until that call (and any processible queued calls) have finished.

This has the following important consequence: if the state of a protected resource changes and there is a task waiting for the new state, then this task will gain access to the resource and be guaranteed that the state of the resource when it gets it is the same as when the decision to release the task was made. Unsatisfactory polling and race conditions are completely avoided.

The two level model has been termed the eggshell model for historic reasons. We can envisage the protected object with its entry queues as surrounded by a shell as illustrated in Figure 17.3. The shell can only be penetrated by a new task trying to call a subprogram or entry when the protected object is quiescent. Tasks can thus be waiting at two levels, outside the shell where they are just milling around in an unstructured way contending for access to the implementation lock which guards the protected object as a whole, and inside the shell in an orderly manner on entry queues. The internal waiting tasks always take priority over the external tasks.

Protected objects are somewhat similar to monitors; they are both passive constructions with synchronization provided by the language run time system. However, protected objects have the great advantage over monitors in that the protocols are described by barrier conditions (which are fairly easy to prove correct) rather than the low level and unstructured signals internal to monitors as found in Modula.

In other words, protected objects have the essential advantages of the high level guards of the rendezvous model but without the overhead and race conditions of an active task.

Protected types enable very efficient implementations of various semaphore and similar paradigms. For example a general semaphore might be implemented as follows

```
protected type Semaphore(Start_Count: Integer := 1) is
   entry Secure;
   procedure Release;
private
   Count: Integer := Start_Count;
end Semaphore;

protected body Semaphore is

   entry Secure when Count > 0 is
   begin
      Count := Count – 1;
   end Secure;

   procedure Release is
   begin
      Count := Count + 1;
   end Release;

end Semaphore;
```

The entry Secure and the procedure Release correspond to Dijkstra's classic P and V operations (from the Dutch *Passeren* and *Vrijmaken*). This example also illustrates that a protected type can have a discriminant which is here used to provide the initial value of the semaphore or in other words the number of items of the resource being guarded by the semaphore. The discriminant has a default value of one which corresponds to the usual binary semaphore. So we can write

```
S: Semaphore;
...
S.P;
...   – – protected statements
S.V;
```

Observe that we have used the default value for the discriminant. However, this does not mean that S is mutable in the sense that we can change its discriminant as we did with the Mutant in Section 11.3. Protected objects and task objects are inherently limited and cannot be changed in any way.

It is important to note that a task type may also have a discriminant in Ada 9X and this can similarly be used to initialize a task. This can for example be used to tell a task who it is without introducing a special entry just for that purpose.

1   Modify the protected object Variable so that a call of Write will be obeyed first.

2   Encapsulate the protected type Buffering inside a generic package with the type Item as a parameter and make the size of the buffer a discriminant of the type.

3   Modify the solution to the Sieve of Eratosthenes in Section 14.9 so that the task type Filter has its prime divisor as a discriminant.

17.8.2   The requeue statement

Our next example introduces the ability to requeue a call on another entry. It sometimes happens that a service needs to be provided in two parts and that the calling task has to be suspended after the first part until conditions are such that the second part can be done. Two entry calls are then necessary but attempts to program this in Ada 83 usually run into difficulties; race conditions can arise in the interval between the calls and there is often unnecessary visibility of the internal protocol.

The example is of a broadcast signal. Tasks wait for some event and then when it occurs all the waiting tasks are released and the event reset. The difficulty is to prevent tasks that call the wait operation after the event has occurred, but before the signal can be reset, from getting through. In other words, we must reset the signal in preference to letting new tasks through. The requeue statement allows us to program such preference control. An implementation is

```
protected Event is
   entry Wait;
   entry Signal;
private
   entry Reset;
   Occurred: Boolean := False;
end Event;

protected body Event is

   entry Wait when Occurred is
   begin
      null;                          -- note null body
   end Wait;

   entry Signal when True is         -- barrier is always true
   begin
      if Wait'Count > 0 then
         Occurred := True;
         requeue Reset;
      end if;
   end Signal;
```

```
    entry Reset when Wait'Count = 0 is
    begin
       Occurred := False;
    end Reset;

  end Event;
```

Tasks indicate that they wish to wait for the event by the call

    Event.Wait;

and the happening of the event is notified by some task calling

    Event.Signal;

whereupon all the waiting tasks are allowed to proceed and the event is reset so that future calls of Wait work properly.

The Boolean variable Occurred is normally false and is only true while tasks are being released. The entry Wait has a null body and just exists so that calling tasks can suspend themselves on its queue while waiting for Occurred to become true.

The entry Signal is interesting. It has a permanently true barrier and so is always processed. If there are no tasks on the queue of Wait (that is no tasks are waiting), then there is nothing to do and so it exits. On the other hand, if there are tasks waiting then it must release them in such a way that no further tasks can get on the queue and, moreover, it must then regain control so that it can reset the flag. It does this by requeuing itself on the entry Reset after setting Occurred to true to indicate that the event has occurred.

The semantics of requeue are such that this completes the action of Signal. However, remember that at the end of the body of a protected entry or procedure the barriers are re-evaluated for those entries which have tasks queued. In this case there are indeed tasks on the queue for Wait and there is also a task on the queue for Reset (the task that called Signal in the first place); the barrier for Wait is now true but of course the barrier for Reset is false since there are still tasks on the queue for Wait. A waiting task is thus allowed to execute the body of Wait (being null this does nothing) and the task thus proceeds and then the barrier evaluation repeats. The same process continues until all the waiting tasks have gone when finally the barrier of Reset also becomes true. The original task which called signal now executes the body of Reset thus resetting Occurred to false so that the system is once more in its initial state. The protected object as a whole is now finally left since there are no waiting tasks on any of the barriers.

Note carefully that if any tasks had tried to call Wait or Signal while the whole process was in progress then they would not have been able to do so because the protected object as a whole was busy. This illustrates the two levels of protection and is the underlying reason why a race condition does not arise.

Another consequence of the two levels is that it still all works properly even in the face of such difficulties as timed and conditional calls and aborts.

The reader may recall, for example, that by contrast, the Count attribute for entries in tasks cannot be relied upon in the face of timed entry calls.

In the case of a protected object a queued entry call can still disappear from the queue as a consequence of abort or a timed call but such removal is treated as a protected operation of the protected object and can only be performed when the object is quiescent. After such removal any barrier using the Count attribute for that queue will be immediately re-evaluated so that consistency is maintained. Removing a task from a queue might thus allow a task queued on a different queue to proceed. In our example aborting the last task on the queue for Wait would allow the task waiting on Reset to proceed.

A minor point to note is that the entry Reset is declared in the private part of the protected type and thus cannot be called from outside. Ada 9X also allows a task to have a private part containing private entries.

The above example has been used for illustration only. The astute reader will have observed that the condition is not strictly needed inside Signal; without it the caller will simply always requeue and then immediately be processed if there are no waiting tasks. But the condition clarifies the description. Indeed, the very astute reader might care to note that we can actually program this example in Ada 9X without using requeue at all.

We conclude this section by reconsidering the package Resource_Allocator of Section 14.8. This can be recast as a protected object as follows

```ada
protected Resource_Allocator is
   entry Request(S: Set);
   procedure Release(S: Set);
private
   entry Again(S: Set);
   procedure Try(S: Set; OK: out Boolean);
   Free: Set := Full;
   Waiters: Integer := 0;
end Resource_Allocator;

protected body Resource_Allocator is

   procedure Try ... - - as Section 14.8

   procedure Release(S: Set) is
   begin
      Free := Free + S;
      Waiters := Again'Count;
   end Release;

   entry Request(S: Set) when True is
      Allocated: Boolean;
   begin
      Try(S, Allocated);
      if not Allocated then
         requeue Again;
      end if;
   end Request;
```

```
     entry Again(S: Set) when Waiters > 0 is
        Allocated: Boolean;
     begin
        Waiters := Waiters − 1;
        Try(S, Allocated);
        if not Allocated then
           requeue Again;
        end if;
     end Again;

  end Resource_Allocator;
```

The general principles are much as before. A first attempt at acquiring the resources is made by calling the entry Request. If it fails then it is requeued on the entry Again. We have to make Request an entry because only an entry can do a requeue; the guard of Request is permanently true since a new call is always allowed an immediate attempt. A call of Release allows all those tasks waiting on Again to have another try. The variable Waiters is set to the number of tasks waiting on the entry Again and is decremented by Again thus allowing each waiting task just one further attempt. The entry Again is similar to Request and requeues on itself if the request still fails.

We have kept the procedure Try as before in order to simplify the comparison although clearly the coding could be shortened by making it a function returning the Boolean result.

In contrast to the tasking model, this solution works exactly; the Count attribute is always correct and no race conditions arise (a task is requeued at once and cannot get out of order and new tasks cannot even enter the system).

Our examples of requeue have shown an entry in a protected object requeuing on another or the same entry of the same protected object. In fact requeue can be from any entry to any other entry including to and from and between entries of tasks.

A requeue can either pass on all the parameters of the original call (implicitly) or none. For implementation reasons no other possibilities are allowed. Thus the destination entry must either have a parameter profile with the same types as the original call in which case all the parameters are passed on or no parameters at all. In either case the requeue statement has no explicit parameters.

Finally a few words about abort. Because a requeue is normally seen as continuing the same service as was asked for by the original call, a requeued call is normally treated specially and is not allowed to be aborted because this might mess up the internal structures of the protected object. If this special treatment is not required then we can requeue with abort thus

     requeue Again **with abort**;

and in this example no problem will arise.

This concludes our discussion of protected types. The key important point is that they provide a data oriented approach to synchronization which combines the high level conditions expressed by the barriers with the efficiency of monitors. Moreover, the two levels of protection and the requeue statement provide a means of programming preference control and thereby enable race conditions to be avoided.

EXERCISE 17.8.2

1   In the protected Event would it be sensible for the requeue on Reset to be **with abort**?

2   Write the protected object Event without the use of requeue. Hint: the last task out switches off the light.

17.8.3 Task scheduling and timing

A criticism of Ada 83 has been that its scheduling rules are unsatisfactory especially with regard to the rendezvous. First-in-first-out queuing on entries and the arbitrary selection from several open alternatives in a select statement lead to conflict with the normal preemptive priority rules. For example, priority inversion occurs when a high priority task is on an entry queue behind a lower priority task.

Furthermore, mode changes may require the ability to dynamically change priorities and this conflicts with the simple static model of Ada 83. In addition, advances in the design of scheduling techniques based on Rate Monotonic Scheduling prescribe a variety of techniques to be used in different circumstances according to the regularity (or otherwise) of events.

Ada 9X allows much more freedom in the choice of priority and scheduling rules. However, because this is a specialized area (and may not be appropriate on some host architectures), the details are contained in the Real Time annex and thus outside the scope of this book.

Timing is another important aspect of scheduling and the delay statement of Ada 83 is supplemented by the delay until statement as already explained in Section 14.3. This overcomes another source of race conditions.

The final new tasking facility to be introduced is the ability to perform an asynchronous transfer of control. This enables an activity to be abandoned if some condition arises (such as running out of time) and an alternative sequence of statements to be executed instead. This gives the capability of performing mode changes.

This can of course be programmed in Ada 83 by the introduction of an agent task and the use of the abort statement but this is a heavy solution not at all appropriate for most applications needing a mode change.

Asynchronous transfer of control is achieved by a new form of select statement which comprises two parts: an abortable part and a triggering alternative. As a simple example consider

```
   select
      delay 5.0;                    - - triggering alternative
      Put_Line("Calculation did not complete");
   then abort
      Invert_Giant_Matrix(M);   - - abortable part
   end select;
```

The general idea is that if the statements between **then abort** and **end select** do not complete before the expiry of the delay then they are abandoned and the statements following the delay executed instead. Thus if we cannot invert our giant matrix in five seconds we give up and print a message.

The statement that triggers the abandonment can alternatively be an entry call instead of a delay statement. If the call returns before the computation is complete then again the computation is abandoned and any statements following the entry call are executed instead. On the other hand if the computation completes before the entry call, then the entry call is itself abandoned. The entry call can, of course, be to a task or to a protected object. Indeed, Ada 9X allows an entry call to be to a protected object or to a task in all contexts.

17.9   Summary of core language

This chapter has described the major new features of Ada 9X. We have covered type extension and class wide programming, the various new forms of access types, the hierarchical library, the ability to manipulate exception occurrences, modular and decimal types, new forms of generic parameters, the protected object, requeue statement and asynchronous transfer of control.

Earlier chapters covered a number of minor improvements which remove various irritations and which together make Ada 9X a major improvement within existing paradigms. They were marked with one, two or three icons according to their potential impact on moving from Ada 83 to Ada 9X.

For convenience we now summarize these in the three categories with section references in brackets.

First there is the category with three icons. These changes can potentially cause an inconsistency; that is a program might execute in both Ada 83 and Ada 9X but with different behaviour. They are

The type Character is now the 8-bit set, Latin–1 (3.3, 6.4).

Rounding of exact halves is now defined as away from zero (4.5).

Applicable subprograms in private part are inheritable (11.7).

Subprograms become inheritable immediately after they are declared (11.7).

Small can be any power of 2 less than or equal to delta (12.4).

Mode Append_File added for sequential and text input–output (15.1).

Although these changes can cause inconsistent behaviour, in most cases it is very unlikely. For example the additional mode Append_File will only cause an inconsistency if the programmer has done something bizarre which essentially uses the fact that the position number of Text_IO.File_Mode'Last is 2 in Ada 9X yet 1 in Ada 83.

Perhaps the most tricky of the above is the fact that the rounding of exact halves is now defined. A program which erroneously relied upon a different behaviour to that now prescribed could go wrong. However, such a program was very dodgy anyway and it is a relief that such an unfortunate omission in the definition of Ada 83 is now corrected in Ada 9X.

The second category with two icons embraces those changes which can cause an Ada 83 program not to compile in Ada 9X. They are

There are five additional reserved words (3.3).
Wide_Character and Wide_String introduced (6.4, 6.6).
Library packages can only have a body if required (8.1).
Numeric_Error renames Constraint_Error (10.1).
The attribute Base no longer allowed for composite types (12.1).
Real model numbers and real attributes changed (12.3, 12.4).
Contract model repaired for indefinite types (13.2).
Sequential_IO has indefinite formal parameter (15.1).
Configuration pragmas such as System_Name removed (15.5).
Static subtype matching required in various contexts (16.2).

Of these, the change to Numeric_Error merits some discussion. It could be argued that this is a three icon change because a program that had different handlers for Constraint_Error and Numeric_Error could execute differently. But this will never happen if the programmer has taken heed of the advice of AI-387 (approved in 1987) to always handle them together. Note that different handlers in the same unit will cause a compile-time error anyway.

The final category with one icon covers those changes which cannot cause any problems and are simply extensions. The main ones are

Incorrect order dependencies removed and bounded errors introduced (2.3).
Alternative characters for |, # and " deprecated (3.2).
Program text is in Latin–1 (3.2).
Trailing underlines permitted in identifiers (3.3).
New functional attributes Min and Max for scalar types (4.8).
Pred and Succ also apply to real types (4.8).
Preference rules for root numeric types allow −1 in loops (5.3, 12.1).
Bounds of an array variable can be deduced from initial value (6.2).
Anonymous array types in declarations may be unconstrained (6.2).
Named aggregates with **others** allowed after := (6.3).
Abbreviated form of null record provided (6.7).
Concatenation more helpful with constrained array types (6.6 answers).
Sliding used widely for array operations (7.1, 16.1).
Rules for "=" and "/=" are relaxed (7.1, 9.2).

An **out** parameter can be read (7.3).

Restriction on the order of declarations removed (7.6, 8.1).

Use type clause provided for operators (8.5).

A library unit can be renamed as another library unit (8.5).

A subprogram body can be provided by renaming (8.5).

A deferred constant can be of any type (9.1).

A deferred constant can have an explicit constraint (9.1).

An **out** parameter can be of a limited type (9.2, 9.3 answers).

A record type can be explicitly marked as limited (9.2).

Discriminant of a variable can be deduced from initial value (11.1).

The attribute Base can now be used as a type mark (12.1, 13.4).

Static expressions are more general (12.1, 12.3 answers, 16.1).

Fixed point multiplication and division now more flexible (12.4).

Generic formal allowed in case or variant with **others** (13.1).

Generic units can be renamed (13.1).

Exception handlers allowed for accept statements (14.2).

Delay until statement added (14.3).

Tasks may have a private part (14.9).

Further pragmas provided for shared data (14.9).

The result of a function call can be renamed (15.2).

Alternative notation for setting representations provided (15.4).

Indefinite parameters in Unchecked_Conversion and _Deallocation (15.6).

Pragma Elaborate replaced by Elaborate_All and Elaborate_Body (16.3).

The above list does not include every entry in the earlier chapters but just those that have not been described in more detail in this chapter.

Finally, the core language is also enhanced by a number of additional predefined packages in the standard library which we have not covered. These include packages for heterogeneous stream input–output, string and character handling, generic elementary functions (see Section 13.4), and generic complex types and functions. The reader is referred to the Ada 9X Reference Manual for details.

For convenience we conclude by presenting the Ada 9X versions of Figure 4.4 and Table 16.1 showing the types and operations of Ada 9X.

As will be seen from Figure 17.4, the type hierarchy in Ada 9X is presented differently to that of Ada 83. Task and protected types are now classed as forms of composite types (they have discriminants) and the term elementary type is introduced (elementary types are always passed by copy).

Private types do not appear in the figure because being private is a property of a view of a type and not that of the type itself. For similar reasons limited and tagged types are not shown. A private view of a type need not be tagged even if the full type is tagged (the reverse is not true) so that tagged is also a view property.

The operations of Ada 9X are shown in Table 17.1. The differences are the addition of operations on modular types, the replacement of the operations on

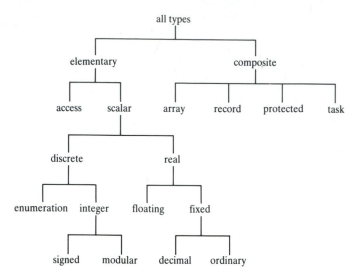

Figure 17.4   Ada 9X type hierarchy.

universal integer and real by corresponding operations on root integer and real, and the use of universal fixed as the operands of fixed point multi-plication and division.

17.10   The annexes

The Ada 9X Reference Manual has seven annexes addressing the needs of various application areas. Although outside the scope of this book, the following is a brief summary of their contents.

Systems Programming. This covers a number of low level features such as in-line machine instructions, interrupt handling, pre-elaboration, shared variable access, task identification and per-task attributes. This annex is a prior requirement for the Real Time annex.

Real Time. This annex addresses various scheduling and priority issues including setting priorities dynamically, scheduling algorithms and entry queue protocols. It also includes detailed requirements on the abort statement for single and multiple processor systems and a monotonic time package (as distinct from Calendar which might go backwards because of time-zone or daylight-saving changes). There are also suggested tasking restrictions which might be appropriate for the development of very efficient run time systems for specialized applications.

Distributed Systems. The core language introduces the idea of a partition whereby one coherent 'program' is distributed over a number of partitions

Table 17.1   Predefined operations of Ada 9X.

Operator	Operand(s)		Result
and or xor	Boolean		same
	one-dim Boolean array		same
	modular		same
and then or else	Boolean		same
= /=	any, not limited		Boolean
< <= > >=	scalar		Boolean
	one-dim discrete array		Boolean
in not in	scalar	range	Boolean
	any	type mark	Boolean
+ − (binary)	numeric		same
&	one-dim array ǀ component		same array
+ −(unary)	numeric		same
*	integer	integer	same
	fixed	Integer	same fixed
	Integer	fixed	same fixed
	univ fixed	univ fixed	univ fixed
	floating	floating	same
	root real	root integer	root real
	root integer	root real	root real
/	integer	integer	same
	fixed	Integer	same fixed
	univ fixed	univ fixed	univ fixed
	floating	floating	same
	root real	root integer	root real
mod rem	integer	integer	same
**	integer	Natural	same integer
	floating	Integer	same floating
not	Boolean		same
	one-dim Boolean array		same
	modular		same

each with its own environment task. This annex defines active and passive partitions and inter-partition communication using statically and dynamically bound remote subprogram calls.

Information Systems. The core language extends fixed point types to include basic support for decimal types. This annex defines additional attributes and a number of packages providing detailed facilities for manipulating decimal values. The child package Text_IO.Picture_IO provides conversion to and from external format using picture strings.

Numerics. This annex addresses the special needs of the numeric community. One significant change is the basis for model numbers. These are no longer described in the core language but in this annex. Moreover, as mentioned in Section 12.2, floating point model numbers in 9X are essentially what were called safe numbers in Ada 83 and the old model numbers and the term safe numbers have been abandoned.

Safety and Security. This annex addresses restrictions on the use of the language and requirements of compilation systems for programs to be used in safety-critical and related applications where program security is vital.

Language Interfaces. This annex defines additional facilities for communication with programs in other languages especially C, COBOL and Fortran.

17.11 Conclusion

We have now come to the end of our discussion on Ada 9X which although not complete in every detail has covered most topics of the core language in reasonable depth. We have not, however, been able to show how all the features fit together particularly in areas such as the use of generics with type extension and child libraries. Space has also precluded any serious discussion of the facilities in the various annexes.

As we have seen, Ada 9X extends Ada 83 in a manner designed to allow the investment in Ada to continue forward into the more demanding applications of the future. The author hopes that the coverage in this book has been sufficient to impart the general principles of Ada 9X plus enough detail to enable the reader to get started on using this powerful and comprehensive language.

APPENDIX 1

Reserved Words, Attributes and Pragmas

This appendix lists the reserved words and predefined attributes and pragmas. An implementation may define additional attributes and pragmas but not additional reserved words.

The lists of attributes and pragmas are taken from Annexes A and B of the *LRM*. The references have been altered to correspond to appropriate sections of this book.

A1.1   Reserved words

The following words are reserved, their use is described in the sections indicated.

abort	14.7
abs	4.5
accept	14.2
access	11.4
all	11.4
and	4.7, 4.9
array	6.1
at	15.4
begin	4.2, 7.1, 8.1, 14.1
body	8.1, 14.1
case	5.2, 11.3
constant	4.1
declare	4.2
delay	14.3
delta	12.4, 13.2

digits	12.3, 13.2
do	14.2
else	4.9, 5.1, 14.5
elsif	5.1
end	4.2, 7.1, 8.1, 14.1, 14.2
entry	14.2
exception	10.1
exit	5.3
for	5.3, 15.4
function	7.1
generic	13.1
goto	5.4
if	5.1
in	4.9, 5.3, 7.3
is	4.3, 5.2, 7.1, 8.1, 11.3, 14.1
limited	9.2, 13.2
loop	5.3
mod	4.5, 15.4
new	11.4, 11.7, 13.1
not	4.7, 4.9
null	5.2, 6.7, 11.3, 11.4
of	6.1
or	4.7, 4.9, 14.5
others	5.2, 6.3, 10.1
out	7.3
package	8.1
pragma	2.8
private	9.1, 13.1
procedure	7.3
raise	10.2
range	4.4, 6.1, 6.2, 13.2, 15.4
record	6.7
rem	4.5
renames	8.5
return	7.1, 7.3, 14.2
reverse	5.3
select	14.4, 14.5
separate	8.3
subtype	4.4

task	14.1
terminate	14.7
then	4.9, 5.1
type	4.3
use	8.1, 15.4
when	5.2, 5.3, 10.1, 11.3, 14.4
while	5.3
with	8.2, 13.3
xor	4.7

The reserved words **delta**, **digits** and **range** are also used as attributes; there is no conflict.

The following words are also reserved in Ada 9X

aliased	17.3.2
protected	17.6.1
requeue	17.6.2
tagged	17.2.1
until	14.3

A1.2 Predefined attributes

This section lists all the predefined attributes. Note that the phrase 'is appropriate for a type' applied to a prefix means that the prefix is of that type or is of an access type which designates that type.

P'Address   For a prefix P that denotes an object, a program unit, a label, or an entry:
Yields the address of the first of the storage units allocated to P. For a subprogram, package, task unit or label, this value refers to the machine code associated with the corresponding body or statement. For an entry for which an address clause has been given, the value refers to the corresponding hardware interrupt. The value of this attribute is of the type Address defined in the package System. (See Section 15.4)

P'Aft   For a prefix P that denotes a fixed point subtype:
Yields the number of decimal digits needed after the point to accommodate the precision of the subtype P, unless the delta of the subtype P is greater than 0.1, in which case the attribute yields the value one. (P'Aft is the smallest positive integer N for which (10**N)*P'Delta is greater than or equal to one.) The value of this attribute is of the type universal integer. (See Section 15.2)

P'Base   For a prefix P that denotes a type or subtype:
This attribute denotes the base type of P. It is only allowed as the prefix of the name of another attribute, for example P'Base'First. (See Section 12.1)

P'Callable   For a prefix P that is appropriate for a task type:
Yields the value False when the execution of the task P is either completed or terminated, or when the task is abnormal; yields the value True otherwise. The value of this attribute is of the predefined type Boolean. (See Section 14.7)

P'Constrained   For a prefix P that denotes an object of a type with discriminants:
Yields the value True if a discriminant constraint applies to the object P, or if the object is a constant (including a formal parameter or generic formal parameter of mode **in**); yields the value False otherwise. If P is a generic formal parameter of mode **in out**, or if P is a formal parameter of mode **in out** or **out** and the type mark given in the corresponding parameter specification denotes an unconstrained type with discriminants, then the value of this attribute is obtained from that of the corresponding actual parameter. The value of this attribute is of the predefined type Boolean. (See Section 11.2)

P'Constrained   For a prefix P that denotes a private type or subtype:
Yields the value False if P denotes an unconstrained nonformal private type with discriminants; also yields the value False if P denotes a generic formal private type and the associated actual subtype is either an unconstrained type with discriminants or an unconstrained array type; yields the value True otherwise. The value of this attribute is of the predefined type Boolean. (See Section 13.2)

P'Count   For a prefix P that denotes an entry of a task unit:
Yields the number of entry calls presently queued on the entry (if the attribute is evaluated within an accept statement for the entry P, the count does not include the calling task). The value of this attribute is of the type universal integer. (See Section 14.4)

P'Delta   For a prefix P that denotes a fixed point subtype:
Yields the value of the delta specified in the fixed accuracy definition for the subtype P. The value of this attribute is of the type universal real. (See Section 12.4)

P'Digits   For a prefix P that denotes a floating point subtype:
Yields the number of decimal digits in the decimal mantissa of model numbers of the subtype P. (This attribute yields the number D of Section 12.3). The value of this attribute is of the type universal integer.

P'Emax   For a prefix P that denotes a floating point subtype:
Yields the largest exponent value in the binary canonical form of model

numbers of the subtype P. (This attribute yields the product 4*B of Section 12.3). The value of this attribute is of the type universal integer.

P'Epsilon   For a prefix P that denotes a floating point subtype:
Yields the absolute value of the difference between the model number 1.0 and the next model number above, for the subtype P. The value of this attribute is of the type universal real. (See Section 12.3)

P'First   For a prefix P that denotes a scalar type, or a subtype of a scalar type:
Yields the lower bound of P. The value of this attribute has the same type as P. (See Section 4.8)

P'First   For a prefix P that is appropriate for an array type, or that denotes a constrained array subtype:
Yields the lower bound of the first index range. The value of this attribute has the same type as this lower bound. (See Sections 6.1 and 6.2)

P'First(N)   For a prefix P that is appropriate for an array type, or that denotes a constrained array subtype:
Yields the lower bound of the nth index range. The value of this attribute has the same type as this lower bound. The argument N must be a static expression of type universal integer. The value of N must be positive (nonzero) and no greater than the dimensionality of the array. (See Sections 6.1 and 6.2)

P'First_Bit   For a prefix P that denotes a component of a record object:
Yields the offset, from the start of the first of the storage units occupied by the component, of the first bit occupied by the component. This offset is measured in bits. The value of this attribute is of the type universal integer. (See Section 15.4)

P'Fore   For a prefix P that denotes a fixed point subtype.
Yields the minimum number of characters needed for the integer part of the decimal representation of any value of the subtype P, assuming that the representation does not include an exponent, but includes a one character prefix that is either a minus sign or a space. (This minimum number does not include superfluous zeros or underlines; and is at least two.) The value of this attribute is of the type universal integer. (See Section 15.2)

P'Image   For a prefix P that denotes a discrete type or subtype:
This attribute is a function with a single parameter. The actual parameter X must be a value of the base type of P. The result type is the predefined type String. The result is the image of the value of X, that is, a sequence of characters representing the value in display form. The image of an integer value is the corresponding decimal literal; without underlines, leading zeros, exponent or trailing spaces; but with a one character prefix that is either a minus sign or a space.
The image of an enumeration value is either the corresponding identifier in upper case or the corresponding character literal (including the two

apostrophes); neither leading nor trailing spaces are included. The image of a character other than a graphic character is implementation-defined.

P'Large   For a prefix P that denotes a real subtype:
   The attribute yields the largest positive model number of the subtype P. The value of this attribute is of the type universal real. (See Sections 12.3 and 12.4)

P'Last   For a prefix P that denotes a scalar type or a subtype of a scalar type:
   Yields the upper bound of P. The value of this attribute has the same type as P. (See Section 4.8)

P'Last   For a prefix P that is appropriate for an array type, or that denotes a constrained array subtype:
   Yields the upper bound of the first index range. The value of this attribute has the same type as this upper bound. (See Sections 6.1 and 6.2)

P'Last(N)   For a prefix P that is appropriate for an array type, or that denotes a constrained array subtype:
   Yields the upper bound of the nth index range. The value of this attribute has the same type as this upper bound. The argument N must be a static expression of type universal integer. The value of N must be positive (nonzero) and no greater than the dimensionality of the array. (See Sections 6.1 and 6.2)

P'Last_Bit   For a prefix P that denotes a component of a record object:
   Yields the offset, from the start of the first of the storage units occupied by the component, of the last bit occupied by the component. This offset is measured in bits. The value of this attribute is of the type universal integer. (See Section 15.4)

P'Length   For a prefix P that is appropriate for an array type, or that denotes a constrained array subtype:
   Yields the number of values of the first index range (zero for a null range). The value of this attribute is of the type universal integer. (See Sections 6.1 and 6.2)

P'Length(N)   For a prefix P that is appropriate for an array type, or that denotes a constrained array subtype:
   Yields the number of values of the nth index range (zero for a null range). The value of this attribute is of the type universal integer. The argument N must be a static expression of type universal integer. The value of N must be positive (nonzero) and no greater than the dimensionality of the array. (See Sections 6.1 and 6.2)

P'Machine_Emax   For a prefix P that denotes a floating point type or subtype:
   Yields the largest value of *exponent* for the machine representation of the base type of P. The value of this attribute is of the type universal integer. (See Section 15.5)

P'Machine_Emin   For a prefix P that denotes a floating point type or subtype:
   Yields the smallest (most negative) value of *exponent* for the machine representation of the base type of P. The value of this attribute is of the type universal integer. (See Section 15.5)

P'Machine_Mantissa   For a prefix P that denotes a floating point type or subtype:
   Yields the number of digits in the *mantissa* for the machine representation of the base type of P (the digits are extended digits in the range 0 to P'Machine_Radix−1). The value of this attribute is of the type universal integer. (See Section 15.5)

P'Machine_Overflows   For a prefix P that denotes a real type or subtype:
   Yields the value True if every predefined operation on values of the base type of P either provides a correct result or raises the exception Numeric_Error in overflow situations; yields the value False otherwise. The value of this attribute is of the predefined type Boolean. (See Section 15.5)

P'Machine_Radix   For a prefix P that denotes a floating point type or subtype:
   Yields the value of the *radix* used by the machine representation of the base type of P. The value of this attribute is of the type universal integer. (See Section 15.5)

P'Machine_Rounds   For a prefix P that denotes a real type or subtype:
   Yields the value True if every predefined arithmetic operation on values of the base type of P either returns an exact result or performs rounding; yields the value False otherwise. The value of this attribute is of the predefined type Boolean. (See Section 15.5)

P'Mantissa   For a prefix P that denotes a real subtype:
   Yields the number of binary digits in the binary mantissa of model numbers of the subtype P. (This attribute yields the number B of Section 12.3 for a floating point type, or of Section 12.4 for a fixed point type). The value of this attribute is of the type universal integer.

P'Pos   For a prefix P that denotes a discrete type or subtype:
   This attribute is a function with a single parameter. The actual parameter X must be a value of the base type of P. The result type is the type universal integer. The result is the position number of the value of the actual parameter. (See Section 4.8)

P'Position   For a prefix P that denotes a component of a record object:
   Yields the offset, from the start of the first storage unit occupied by the record, of the first of the storage units occupied by the component. This offset is measured in storage units. The value of this attribute is of the type universal integer. (See Section 15.5)

P'Pred   For a prefix P that denotes a discrete type or subtype:
   This attribute is a function with a single parameter. The actual

parameter X must be a value of the base type of P. The result is of the base type of P. The result is the value whose position number is one less than that of X. The exception Constraint_Error is raised if X equals P'Base'First. (See Section 4.8)

P'Range   For a prefix P that is appropriate for an array type, or that denotes a constrained array subtype:
Yields the first index range of P, that is, the range P'First .. P'Last. (See Sections 6.1 and 6.2)

P'Range(N)   For a prefix P that is appropriate for an array type, or that denotes a constrained array subtype:
Yields the nth index range of P, that is, the range P'First(N) .. P'Last(N). (See Sections 6.1 and 6.2)

P'Safe_Emax   For a prefix P that denotes a floating point type or subtype:
Yields the largest exponent value in the binary canonical form of safe numbers of the base type of P. (This attribute yields the number E of Section 12.3.) The value of this attribute is of the type universal integer.

P'Safe_Large   For a prefix P that denotes a real type or subtype:
Yields the largest positive safe number of the base type of P. The value of this attribute is of the type universal real. (See Sections 12.3 and 12.4)

P'Safe_Small   For a prefix P that denotes a real type or subtype:
Yields the smallest positive (nonzero) safe number of the base type of P. The value of this attribute is of the type universal real. (See Sections 12.3 and 12.4)

P'Size   For a prefix P that denotes an object:
Yields the number of bits allocated to hold the object. The value of this attribute is of the type universal integer. (See Section 15.4)

P'Size   For a prefix P that denotes any type or subtype:
Yields the minimum number of bits that is needed by the implementation to hold any possible object of the type or subtype P. The value of this attribute is of the type universal integer. (See Section 15.4)

P'Small   For a prefix P that denotes a real subtype:
Yields the smallest positive (nonzero) model number of the subtype P. The value of this attribute is of the type universal real. (See Sections 12.3 and 12.4)

P'Storage_Size   For a prefix P that denotes an access type or subtype:
Yields the total number of storage units reserved for the collection associated with the base type P. The value of this attribute is of the type universal integer. (See Section 15.4)

P'Storage_Size   For a prefix P that denotes a task type or task object:
  Yields the number of storage units reserved for each activation of a task of the type P or for the activation of the task object P. The value of this attribute is of the type universal integer. (See Section 15.4)

P'Succ   For a prefix P that denotes a discrete type or subtype:
  This attribute is a function with a single parameter. The actual parameter X must be a value of the base type of P. The result type is the base type of P. The result is the value whose position number is one greater than that of X. The exception Constraint_Error is raised if X equals P'Base'Last. (See Section 4.8)

P'Terminated   For a prefix P that is appropriate for a task type:
  Yields the value True if the task P is terminated; yields the value False otherwise. The value of this attribute is of the predefined type Boolean. (See Section 14.7)

P'Val   For a prefix P that denotes a discrete type or subtype:
  This attribute is a special function with a single parameter which can be of any integer type. The result type is the base type of P. The result is the value whose position number is the universal integer value corresponding to X. The exception Constraint_Error is raised if the universal integer value corresponding to X is not in the range P'Pos(P'Base'First) .. P'Pos(P'Base'Last). (See Section 4.8)

P'Value   For a prefix P that denotes a discrete type or subtype:
  This attribute is a function with a single parameter. The actual parameter X must be a value of the predefined type String. The result type is the base type of P. Any leading and any trailing spaces of the sequence of characters that corresponds to X are ignored.
  For an enumeration type, if the sequence of characters has the syntax of an enumeration literal and if this literal exists for the base type of P, the result is the corresponding enumeration value. For an integer type, if the sequence of characters has the syntax of an integer literal, with an optional single leading character that is a plus or minus sign, and if there is a corresponding value in the base type of P, the result is this value. In any other case, the exception Constraint_Error is raised.

P'Width   For a prefix P that denotes a discrete subtype:
  Yields the maximum image length over all values of the subtype P (the image is the sequence of characters returned by the attribute Image). The value of this attribute is of the type universal integer. (See Section 15.2)

In Ada 9X, a number of the above numeric attributes are not available, namely: Emax, Epsilon, Large, Safe_Emax, Safe_Large and Safe_Small. Furthermore, the attribute Base is slightly different as explained in Section 12.1. Also the form of the Constrained attribute applying to private types is obsolete.

::: Some attributes have wider applicability. In particular, Succ and Pred also apply to real types and give the adjacent implemented numbers (see Section 4.8).

::: There are a number of additional attributes in Ada 9X which are briefly as follows.

::: The attributes Access (see Sections 17.3.1 and 17.3.2) and Unchecked_Access concern the new forms of access types. The attribute Unchecked_Access is like Access except that accessibility checks are omitted.

::: The attribute Storage_Pool denotes the pool of an access type (storage pool is the Ada 9X term for the space used by an access collection) and the attribute Max_Size_In_Storage_Elements concerns user-defined pools; the use of these attributes is outside the scope of this book.

::: The attribute Valid applies to an object of a scalar type and returns true if its value is valid. This is useful for testing the results of unchecked conversion (see Section 15.6).

::: The size of a component of an array subtype is given by Component_Size. The alignment of a record or object is given by Alignment; the bit number order is given by Bit_Order (see Section 15.4).

::: The attribute Class denotes the class wide type of a tagged type (see Section 17.2.2). The attribute Tag denotes the tag of a class wide or specific type or the tag of the value of an object of a class wide type (see Section 17.2.4).

::: The attributes Max and Min are functions which take two parameters of any scalar subtype and return the maximum or minimum value respectively (see Section 4.8).

::: The attributes Wide_Image and Wide_Value are similar to Image and Value but use Wide_String rather than String in their definition.

::: The attributes Round and Scale apply to decimal types. The function Round takes any real type and returns the nearest value of the decimal type rounded away from zero. The attribute Scale gives the number of digits after the decimal point; this is negative if Delta is greater than one.

::: Finally, the attributes Safe_First and Safe_Last give the range of values of a floating point type over which it behaves according to the requested precision. For further details of these and other specialized attributes the reader is referred to the Ada 9X annexes.

A1.3   Predefined pragmas

The following pragmas are predefined in the language

Controlled   Takes the simple name of an access type as the single argument. This pragma is only allowed immediately within the declarative part or package specification that contains the declaration of the access type; the declaration must occur before the pragma. This pragma is not allowed for a derived type. This pragma specifies that automatic storage reclamation must not be performed for objects designated by values of the access type, except upon leaving the innermost block statement, subprogram body, or task body that encloses the access type declaration, or after leaving the main program. (See Section 11.4)

Elaborate Takes one or more simple names denoting library units as arguments. This pragma is only allowed immediately after the context clause of a compilation unit (before the subsequent library unit or secondary unit). Each argument must be the simple name of a library unit mentioned by the context clause. This pragma specifies that the corresponding library unit body must be elaborated before the given compilation unit. If the given compilation unit is a subunit, the library unit body must be elaborated before the body of the ancestor library unit of the subunit. (See Section 16.3)

Inline Takes one or more names as arguments; each name is either the name of a subprogram or the name of a generic subprogram. This pragma is only allowed at the place of a declarative item in a declarative part or package specification, or after a library unit in a compilation, but before any subsequent compilation unit. This pragma specifies that the subprogram bodies should be expanded inline at each call whenever possible; in the case of a generic subprogram, the pragma applies to calls of its instantiations. (See Section 15.5)

Interface Takes a language name and a subprogram name as arguments. This pragma is allowed at the place of a declarative item, and must apply in this case to a subprogram declared by an earlier declarative item of the same declarative part or package specification. This pragma is also allowed for a library unit; in this case the pragma must appear after the subprogram declaration, and before any subsequent compilation unit. This pragma specifies the other language (and thereby the calling conventions) and informs the compiler that an object module will be supplied for the corresponding subprogram. (See Section 15.7)

List Takes one of the identifiers On or Off as the single argument. This pragma is allowed anywhere a pragma is allowed. It specifies that listing of the compilation is to be continued or suspended until a List pragma with the opposite argument is given within the same compilation. The pragma itself is always listed if the compiler is producing a listing. (See Section 2.8)

Memory_Size Takes a numeric literal as the single argument. This pragma is only allowed at the start of a compilation, before the first compilation unit (if any) of the compilation. The effect of this pragma is to use the value of the specified numeric literal for the definition of the named number Memory_Size. (See Section 15.5)

Optimize Takes one of the identifiers Time or Space as the single argument. This pragma is only allowed within a declarative part and it applies to the block or body enclosing the declarative part. It specifies whether time or space is the primary optimization criterion. (See Section 15.5)

Pack   Takes the simple name of a record or array type as the single argument. The allowed positions for this pragma, and the restrictions on the named type, are governed by the same rules as for a representation clause. The pragma specifies that storage minimization should be the main criterion when selecting the representation of the given type. (See Section 15.5)

Page   This pragma has no argument, and is allowed anywhere a pragma is allowed. It specifies that the program text which follows the pragma should start on a new page (if the compiler is currently producing a listing). (See Section 2.8)

Priority   Takes a static expression of the predefined integer subtype Priority as the single argument. This pragma is only allowed within the specification of a task unit or immediately within the outermost declarative part of a main program. It specifies the priority of the task (or tasks of the task type) or the priority of the main program. (See Section 14.3)

Shared   Takes the simple name of a variable as the single argument. This pragma is allowed only for a variable declared by an object declaration and whose type is a scalar or access type; the variable declaration and the pragma must both occur (in this order) immediately within the same declarative part or package specification. This pragma specifies that every read or update of the variable is a synchronization point for that variable. An implementation must restrict the objects for which this pragma is allowed to objects for which each of direct reading and direct updating is implemented as an indivisible operation. (See Section 14.9)

Storage_Unit   Takes a numeric literal as the single argument. This pragma is only allowed at the start of a compilation, before the first compilation unit (if any) of the compilation. The effect of this pragma is to use the value of the specified numeric literal for the definition of the named number Storage_Unit. (See Section 15.5)

Suppress   Takes as arguments the identifier of a check and optionally also the name of either an object, a type or subtype, a subprogram, a task unit, or a generic unit. This pragma is only allowed either immediately within a declarative part or immediately within a package specification. In the latter case, the only allowed form is with a name that denotes an entity (or several overloaded subprograms) declared immediately within the package specification. The permission to omit the given check extends from the place of the pragma to the end of the declarative region associated with the innermost enclosing block statement or program unit. For a pragma given in a package specification, the permission extends to the end of the scope of the named entity.

  If the pragma includes a name, the permission to omit the given check is further restricted: it is given only for operations on the named object or on all objects of the base type of a named type or subtype; for calls of a named subprogram; for activations of tasks of the named task type; or for instantiations of the given generic unit. (See Section 15.5)

System_Name   Takes an enumeration literal as the single argument. This
pragma is only allowed at the start of a compilation, before the first
compilation unit (if any) of the compilation. The effect of this pragma is to
use the enumeration literal with the specified identifier for the definition of
the constant System_Name. This pragma is only allowed if the specified
identifier corresponds to one of the literals of the type Name declared in
the package System. (See Section 15.5)

The pragmas System_Name, Storage_Unit and Memory_Size are not
predefined in Ada 9X but an implementation may continue to provide them.

There are a number of additional pragmas in Ada 9X which are briefly as
follows.

Interface control to other languages is provided by pragmas Convention,
Export and Import with Import replacing the pragma Interface of Ada 83.

Elaboration order is now specified by Elaborate_All and Elaborate_Body
(see Section 16.4). Elaborate_All is like Elaborate but is transitive and
essentially replaces Elaborate which is retained for compatibility.

Pragmas Pure and Preelaborate concern link time execution and the
sharing of units between partitions. A library unit is pure if it has no state and
is thus free of side effects.

The pragma Restrictions enables the programmer to assert that a program
does not use certain features of the language; this may enable small or certified
versions of the run time system to be employed and is relevant to safety-
critical and similar systems. For full details of this and other specialized
pragmas the reader is referred to the Ada 9X annexes.

APPENDIX 2
Predefined Language Environment

As mentioned earlier, certain entities are predefined through their declaration in a special package Standard. It should not be thought that this package necessarily actually exists; it is just that the compiler behaves as if it does. Indeed, as we shall see, some entities notionally declared in Standard cannot be truly declared in Ada at all. The general effect of Standard is indicated by the outline specification below which is taken from Annex C of the *LRM*.

The operators that are predefined for the types declared in the package Standard are given in comments since they are implicitly declared. Italics are used for identifiers that are not available to users (such as the identifier *universal_real*) and for undefined information (such as *implementation_defined* and *any_fixed_point_type*).

package Standard **is**

type Boolean **is** (False, True);

– – The predefined relational operators for this type are as
– – follows:

– – **function** "=" (Left, Right: Boolean) **return** Boolean;
– – **function** "/=" (Left, Right: Boolean) **return** Boolean;
– – **function** "<" (Left, Right: Boolean) **return** Boolean;
– – **function** "<=" (Left, Right: Boolean) **return** Boolean;
– – **function** ">" (Left, Right: Boolean) **return** Boolean:
– – **function** ">=" (Left, Right: Boolean) **return** Boolean;

– – The logical operators and the logical negation operator are
– – as follows:

function "and" (Left, Right: Boolean) **return** Boolean;
function "or"   (Left, Right: Boolean) **return** Boolean;
function "xor" (Left, Right: Boolean) **return** Boolean;
function "not" (Right: Boolean) **return** Boolean;

– – The universal type *universal_integer* is predefined

type Integer **is** *implementation_defined* ;

-- The predefined operators for this type are as follows:

-- **function** "="   (Left, Right: Integer) **return** Boolean;
-- **function** "/="   (Left, Right: Integer) **return** Boolean;
-- **function** "<"   (Left, Right: Integer) **return** Boolean;
-- **function** "<="   (Left, Right: Integer) **return** Boolean;
-- **function** ">"   (Left, Right: Integer) **return** Boolean;
-- **function** ">="   (Left, Right: Integer) **return** Boolean;

-- **function** "+"   (Right: Integer) **return** Integer;
-- **function** "−"   (Right: Integer) **return** Integer;
-- **function** "abs"   (Right: Integer) **return** Integer;

-- **function** "+"   (Left, Right: Integer) **return** Integer;
-- **function** "−"   (Left, Right: Integer) **return** Integer;
-- **function** "*"   (Left, Right: Integer) **return** Integer;
-- **function** "/"   (Left, Right: Integer) **return** Integer;
-- **function** "rem"   (Left, Right: Integer) **return** Integer;
-- **function** "mod"   (Left, Right: Integer) **return** Integer;
-- **function** "**"   (Left: Integer; Right: Integer) **return** Integer;

-- An implementation may provide additional predefined integer
-- types. It is recommended that the names of such additional
-- types end with Integer as in Short_Integer or Long_Integer.
-- The specification of each operator for the type
-- *universal_integer*, or for any additional predefined integer
-- type, is obtained by replacing Integer by the name of the
-- type in the specification of the corresponding operator of
-- the type Integer, except for the right operand of the
-- exponentiating operator.

-- The universal type *universal_real* is predefined.

type Float **is** *implementation_defined*;

-- The predefined operators for this type are as follows:

-- **function** "="   (Left, Right: Float) **return** Boolean;
-- **function** "/="   (Left, Right: Float) **return** Boolean;
-- **function** "<"   (Left, Right: Float) **return** Boolean;
-- **function** "<="   (Left, Right: Float) **return** Boolean;
-- **function** ">"   (Left, Right: Float) **return** Boolean;
-- **function** ">="   (Left, Right: Float) **return** Boolean;

-- **function** "+"   (Right: Float) **return** Float;
-- **function** "−"   (Right: Float) **return** Float;
-- **function** "abs"   (Right: Float) **return** Float;

-- **function** "+"   (Left, Right: Float) **return** Float;
-- **function** "−"   (Left, Right: Float) **return** Float;
-- **function** "*"   (Left, Right: Float) **return** Float;
-- **function** "/"   (Left, Right: Float) **return** Float;
-- **function** "**"   (Left: Float; Right: Integer) **return** Float;

– – An implementation may provide additional predefined floating
– – point types. It is recommended that the names of such
– – additional types end with Float as in Short_Float or
– – Long_Float. The specification of each operator for the type
– – *universal_real*, or for any additional predefined floating
– – point type, is obtained by replacing Float by the name of
– – the type in the specification of the corresponding operator
– – of the type Float.

– – In addition the following operators are predefined for
– – universal types:

– – **function** "∗" (Left: *universal_integer*,
  Right: *universal_real*) **return** *universal_real*;

– – **function** "∗" (Left: *universal_real*;
  Right: *universal_integer*) **return** *universal_real*;

– – **function** "/" (Left: *universal_real*;
  Right: *universal_integer*) **return** *universal_real*;

– – The type *universal_fixed* is predefined. The only operators
– – declared for this type are

– – **function** "∗" (Left: *any_fixed_point_type*;
  Right: *any_fixed_point_type*)
  return *universal_fixed*;

– – **function** "/" (Left: *any_fixed_point_type*;
  Right: *any_fixed_point_type*)
  return *universal_fixed*;

– – The following characters form the standard ASCII character
– – set. Character literals corresponding to control characters
– – are not identifiers; they are indicated in italics in this
– – definition.

type Character **is**

(nul,	soh,	stx,	etx,	eot,	enq,	ack,	bel,
bs,	ht,	lf,	vt,	ff,	cr,	so,	si,
dle,	dc1,	dc2,	dc3,	dc4,	nak,	syn,	etb,
can,	em,	sub,	esc,	fs,	gs,	rs,	us,
' ',	'!',	'"',	'#',	'$',	'%',	'&',	''',
'(',	')',	'∗',	'+',	',',	'−',	'.',	'/',
'0',	'1',	'2',	'3',	'4',	'5',	'6',	'7',
'8',	'9',	':',	';',	'<',	'=',	'>',	'?',
'@',	'A',	'B',	'C',	'D',	'E',	'F',	'G',
'H',	'I',	'J',	'K',	'L',	'M',	'N',	'O',
'P',	'Q',	'R',	'S',	'T',	'U',	'V',	'W',
'X',	'Y',	'Z',	'[',	'\',	']',	'^',	'_',
'`',	'a',	'b',	'c',	'd',	'e',	'f',	'g',
'h',	'i',	'j',	'k',	'l',	'm',	'n',	'o',
'p',	'q',	'r',	's',	't',	'u',	'v',	'w',
'x',	'y',	'z',	'{',	'|',	'}',	'~',	del);

for Character **use** $--$ 128 ASCII character set without holes
(0, 1, 2, 3, 4, 5, ..., 125, 126, 127);

$--$ The predefined operators for the type Character are the same
$--$ as for any enumeration type.

package ASCII **is**

$--$ Control characters:

NUL:	**constant** Character := *nul*;
SOH:	**constant** Character := *soh*;
STX:	**constant** Character := *stx*;
ETX:	**constant** Character := *etx*;
EOT:	**constant** Character := *eot*;
ENQ:	**constant** Character := *enq*;
ACK:	**constant** Character := *ack*;
BEL:	**constant** Character := *bel*;
BS:	**constant** Character := *bs*;
HT:	**constant** Character := *ht*;
LF:	**constant** Character := *lf*;
VT:	**constant** Character := *vt*;
FF:	**constant** Character := *ff*;
CR:	**constant** Character := *cr*;
SO:	**constant** Character := *so*;
SI:	**constant** Character := *si*;
DLE:	**constant** Character := *dle*;
DC1:	**constant** Character := *dc1*;
DC2:	**constant** Character := *dc2*;
DC3:	**constant** Character := *dc3*;
DC4:	**constant** Character := *dc4*;
NAK:	**constant** Character := *nak*;
SYN:	**constant** Character := *syn*;
ETB:	**constant** Character := *etb*;
CAN:	**constant** Character := *can*;
EM:	**constant** Character := *em*;
SUB:	**constant** Character := *sub*;
ESC:	**constant** Character := *esc*;
FS:	**constant** Character := *fs*;
GS:	**constant** Character := *gs*;
RS:	**constant** Character := *rs*;
US:	**constant** Character := *us*;
DEL:	**constant** Character := *del*;

$--$ Other characters

Exclam: **constant** Character := '!';
Quotation: **constant** Character := '"';
Sharp: **constant** Character := '#';
Dollar: **constant** Character := '$';
Percent: **constant** Character := '%';
Ampersand: **constant** Character := '&';

```
  Colon: constant Character := ':';
  Semicolon: constant Character := ';';
  Query: constant Character := '?';
  At_Sign: constant Character := '@';
  L_Bracketconstant Character := '[';
  Back_Slash: constant Character := '\';
  R_Bracket: constant Character := ']';
  Circumflex: constant Character := '^';
  Underline: constant Character := '_';
  Grave: constant Character := '`';
  L_Brace: constant Character := '{';
  Bar: constant Character := '|';
  R_Brace: constant Character := '}';
  Tilde: constant Character := '~';

  -- Lower case letters
  LC_A: constant Character := 'a';
      ...
  LC_Z: constant Character := 'z';
end ASCII;
```

-- Predefined subtypes:

```
subtype Natural is Integer range 0 .. Integer'Last;
subtype Positive is Integer range 1 .. Integer'Last;
```

-- Predefined string type:

```
type String is array (Positive range <>) of Character;
pragma Pack(String);
```

-- The predefined operators for this type are as follows:

```
-- function "="  (Left, Right: String) return Boolean;
   function "/=" (Left, Right: String) return Boolean;
-- function "<"  (Left, Right: String) return Boolean;
-- function "<=" (Left, Right: String) return Boolean;
-- function ">"  (Left, Right: String) return Boolean;
-- function ">=" (Left, Right: String) return Boolean;
-- function "&"  (Left: String; Right: String) return String;
-- function "&"  (Left: Character; Right: String) return String;
-- function "&"  (Left: String; Right: Character) return String;
-- function "&"  (Left: Character; Right: Character) return String;
```

```
type Duration is delta implementation_defined range
                                    implementation_defined;
```

-- The predefined operators for the type Duration are the same
-- as for any fixed point type.

-- The predefined exceptions

```
Constraint_Error: exception;
Numeric_Error: exception;
```

```
        Program_Error: exception;
        Storage_Error: exception;
        Tasking_Error: exception;

    end Standard;
```

The above specification is not complete. For example, although the type Boolean can be written showing the literals False and True, the short circuit control forms cannot be expressed explicitly. Moreover, each further type definition introduces new overloadings of some operators. All types, except limited types, introduce new overloadings of = and /=. All scalar types and discrete one-dimensional array types introduce new overloadings of & and those with Boolean components also introduce new overloadings of **and**, **or**, **xor** and **not**. Finally, all fixed point types introduce new overloadings of +, −, *, / and **abs**.

In addition there are also certain other predefined library units such as Calendar (see Section 14.3), Sequential_IO and Direct_IO (see Section 15.1), Text_IO (see Section 15.2), System (see Section 15.5) and Unchecked_Conversion and Unchecked_Deallocation (see Section 15.6).

The package Standard for Ada 9X is very similar to the above with the expected additions and variations. It seems unnecessary to give the full details.

APPENDIX 3
Glossary

The following glossary is reproduced from Appendix D of the *LRM*. Italicized terms in the abbreviated descriptions below either have glossary entries themselves or are described in entries for related terms.

Access statement   See *entry*.

Access type   A value of an access type (an *access value*) is either a null value, or a value that *designates* an *object* created by an *allocator*. The designated object can be read and updated via the access value. The definition of an access type specifies the type of the objects designated by values of the access type. See also *collection*.

Actual parameter   See *parameter*.

Aggregate   The evaluation of an aggregate yields a value of a *composite type*. The value is specified by giving the value of each of the *components*. Either *positional association* or *named association* may be used to indicate which value is associated with which component.

Allocator   The evaluation of an allocator creates an *object* and returns a new *access value* which *designates* the object.

Array type   A value of an array type consists of *components* which are all of the same *subtype* (and hence, of the same type). Each component is uniquely distinguished by an *index* (for a one-dimensional array) or by a sequence of indices (for a multidimensional array). Each index must be a value of a *discrete type* and must lie in the correct index *range*.

Assignment   Assignment is the *operation* that replaces the current value of a *variable* by a new value. An *assignment statement* specifies a variable on the left, and on the right, an *expression* whose value is to be the new value of the variable.

Attribute   The evaluation of an attribute yields a predefined characteristic of a named entity; some attributes are *functions*.

485

Block statement   A block statement is a single statement that may contain a sequence of statements. It may also include a *declarative part*, and *exception handlers*; their effects are local to the block statement.

Body   A body defines the execution of a *subprogram*, *package*, or *task*. A *body stub* is a form of body that indicates that this execution is defined in a separately compiled *subunit*.

Collection   A collection is the entire set of *objects* created by evaluation of *allocators* for an *access type*.

Compilation unit   A compilation unit is the *declaration* or the *body* of a *program unit*, presented for compilation as an independent test. It is optionally preceded by a *context clause*, naming other compilation units upon which it depends by means of one or more *with clauses*.

Component   A component is a value that is a part of a larger value, or an *object* that is part of a larger object.

Composite type   A composite type is one whose values have *components*. There are two kinds of composite type: *array types* and *record types*.

Constant   See *object*.

Constraint   A constraint determines a subset of the values of a *type*. A value in that subset *satisfies* the constraint.

Context clause   See *compilation unit*.

Declaration   A declaration associates an identifier (or some other notation) with an entity. This association is in effect within a region of text called the *scope* of the declaration. Within the scope of a declaration, there are places where it is possible to use the identifier to refer to the associated declared entity. At such places the identifier is said to be a *simple name* of the entity; the *name* is said to *denote* the associated entity.

Declarative part   A declarative part is a sequence of *declarations*. It may also contain related information such as *subprogram bodies* and *representation clauses*.

Denote   See *declaration*.

Derived type   A derived type is a *type* whose operations and values are replicas of those of an existing type. The existing type is called the *parent type* of the derived type.

Designate   See *access type*, *task*.

Direct visibility   See *visibility*.

Discrete type   A discrete type is a *type* which has an ordered set of distinct values. The discrete types are the *enumeration* and *integer types*. Discrete types are used for indexing and iteration, and for choices in case statements and record *variants*.

Discriminant   A discriminant is a distinguished *component* of an *object* or value of a *record type*. The *subtypes* of other components, or even their presence or absence, may depend on the value of the discriminant.

Discriminant constraint   A discriminant constraint on a *record type* or *private type* specifies a value for each *discriminant* of the *type*.

Elaboration   The elaboration of a *declaration* is the process by which the declaration achieves its effect (such as creating an *object*); this process occurs during program execution.

Entry   An entry is used for communication between *tasks*. Externally, an entry is called just as a *subprogram* is called; its internal behavior is specified by one or more *accept statements* specifying the actions to be performed when the entry is called.

Enumeration type   An enumeration type is a *discrete type* whose values are represented by enumeration literals which are given explicitly in the *type declaration*. These enumeration literals are either *identifiers* or *character literals*.

Evaluation   The evaluation of an *expression* is the process by which the value of the expression is computed. This process occurs during program execution.

Exception   An exception is an error situation which may arise during program execution. To *raise* an exception is to abandon normal program execution so as to signal that the error has taken place. An *exception handler* is a portion of program text specifying a response to the exception. Execution of such a program text is called *handling* the exception.

Expanded name   An expanded name *denotes* an entity which is *declared* immediately within some construct. An expanded name has the form of a *selected component*: the *prefix* denotes the construct (a *program unit*; or a *block*, loop, or *accept statement*); the *selector* is the *simple name* of the entity.

Expression   An expression defines the computation of a value.

Fixed point type   See *real type*.

Floating point type   See *real type*.

Formal parameter   See *parameter*.

Function   See *subprogram*.

Generic unit   A generic unit is a template either for a set of *subprograms* or for a set of *packages*. A subprogram or package created using the template is called an *instance* of the generic unit. A *generic instantiation* is the kind of *declaration* that creates an instance. A generic unit is written as a subprogram or package but with the specification prefixed by a *generic formal part* which may declare *generic formal parameters*. A generic formal parameter is either a *type*, a *subprogram*, or an *object*. A generic unit is one of the kinds of *program unit*.

Handler   See *exception*.

Index   See *array type*.

Index constraint   An index constraint for an *array type* specifies the lower and upper bounds for each index *range* of the array type.

Indexed component   An indexed component *denotes* a *component* in an *array*. It is a form of *name* containing *expressions* which specify the values of the *indices* of the array component. An indexed component may also denote an *entry* in a family of entries.

Instance   See *generic unit*.

Integer type   An integer type is a *discrete type* whose values represent all integer numbers within a specific *range*.

Lexical element   A lexical element is an identifier, a *literal*, a delimiter, or a comment.

Limited type   A limited type is a *type* for which neither assignment nor the predefined comparison for equality is implicitly declared. All *task* types are limited. A *private type* can be defined to be limited. An equality operator can be explicitly declared for a limited type.

Literal   A literal represents a value literally, that is, by means of letters and other characters. A literal is either a numeric literal, an enumeration literal, a character literal, or a string literal.

Mode   See *parameter*.

Model number   A model number is an exactly representable value of a *real type*. *Operations* of a real type are defined in terms of operations on the model numbers of the type. The properties of the model numbers and of their operations are the minimal properties preserved by all implementations of the real type.

Name   A name is a construct that stands for an entity: it is said that the name *denotes* the entity, and that the entity is the meaning of the name. See also *declaration, prefix.*

Named association   A named association specifies the association of an item with one or more positions in a list, by naming the positions.

Object   An object contains a value. A program creates an object either by *elaborating* an *object declaration* or by *evaluating* an *allocator.* The declaration or allocator specifies a *type* for the object: the object can only contain values of that type.

Operation   An operation is an elementary action associated with one or more *types.* It is either implicitly declared by the *declaration* of the type, or it is a *subprogram* that has a *parameter* or *result* of the type.

Operator   An operator is an operation which has one or two operands. A unary operator is written before an operand; a binary operator is written between two operands. This notation is a special kind of *function call.* An operator can be declared as a function. Many operators are implicitly declared by the *declaration* of a *type* (for example, most type declarations imply the declaration of the equality operator for values of the type).

Overloading   An identifier can have several alternative meanings at a given point in the program text; this property is called *overloading.* For example, an overloaded enumeration literal can be an identifier that appears in the definitions of two or more *enumeration types.* The effective meaning of an overloaded identifier is determined by the context. *Subprograms, aggregates, allocators,* and string *literals* can also be overloaded.

Package   A package specifies a group of logically related entities, such as *types, objects* of those types, and *subprograms* with *parameters* of those types. It is written as a *package declaration* and a *package body.* The package declaration has a *visible part,* containing the *declarations* of all entities that can be explicitly used outside the package. It may also have a *private part* containing structural details that complete the specification of the visible entities, but which are irrelevant to the user of the package. The *package body* contains implementations of *subprograms* (and possibly *tasks* and other *packages*) that have been specified in the package declaration. A package is one of the kinds of *program unit.*

Parameter   A parameter is one of the named entities associated with a *subprogram, entry,* or *generic unit,* and used to communicate with the corresponding subprogram body, *accept statement* or generic body. A *formal parameter* is a designator used to denote the named entity within the body. An *actual parameter* is the particular entity associated with the corresponding formal parameter by a *subprogram call, entry call,* or *generic instantiation.* The *mode* of a formal parameter specifies whether the associated actual parameter supplies a value for the formal parameter, or the formal supplies a value for the actual parameter, or both. The association of actual parameters with formal parameters can be specified by *named associations*, by *positional associations*, or by a combination of these.

Parent type   See *derived type*.

Positional association   A positional association specifies the association of an item with a position in a list, by using the same position in the text to specify the item.

Pragma   A pragma conveys information to the compiler.

Prefix   A prefix is used as the first part of certain kinds of name. A prefix is either a *function call* or a *name*.

Private part   See *package*.

Private type   A private type is a *type* whose structure and set of values are clearly defined, but not directly available to the user of the type. A private type is known only by its *discriminants* (if any) and by the set of *operations* defined for it. A private type and its applicable operations are defined in the *visible part* of a *package*, or in a *generic formal part*. *Assignment*, equality and inequality are also defined for private types, unless the private type is *limited*.

Procedure   See *subprogram*.

Program   A program is composed of a number of *compilation units*, one of which is a *subprogram* called the *main program*. Execution of the program consists of execution of the main program, which may invoke subprograms declared in the other compilation units of the program.

Program unit   A program unit is any one of a *generic unit*, *package*, *subprogram* or *task unit*.

Qualified expression   A qualified expression is an *expression* preceded by an indication of its *type* or *subtype*. Such qualification is used when, in its absence, the expression might be ambiguous (for example as a consequence of *overloading*).

Raising an exception   See *exception*.

Range   A range is a contiguous set of values of a *scalar type*. A range is specified by giving the lower and upper bounds for the values. A value in the range is said to *belong* to the range.

Range constraint   A range constraint of a *type* specifies a *range*, and thereby determines the subset of the values of the type that *belong* to the range.

Real type   A real type is a *type* whose values represent approximations to the real numbers. There are two kinds of real type: *fixed point types* are specified by an absolute error bound; *floating point types* are specified by a relative error bound expressed as a number of significant decimal digits.

Record type   A value of a record type consists of *components* which are usually of different *types* or *subtypes*. For each component of a record value or record *object*, the definition of the record type specifies an identifier that uniquely determines the component within the record.

Renaming declaration   A renaming declaration declares another *name* for an entity.

Rendezvous   A rendezvous is the interaction that occurs between two parallel *tasks* when one task has called an *entry* of the other task, and a corresponding *accept statement* is being executed by the other task on behalf of the calling task.

Representation clause   A representation clause directs the compiler in the selection of the mapping of a *type*, an *object* or a *task* onto features of the underlying machine that executes a program. In some cases, representation clauses completely specify the mapping; in other cases, they provide criteria for choosing a mapping.

Satisfy   See *constraint, subtype*.

Scalar type   An *object* or value of a scalar *type* does not have *components*. A scalar type is either a *discrete type* or a *real type*. The values of a scalar type are ordered.

Scope   See *declaration*.

Selected component   A selected component is a *name* consisting of a *prefix* and of an identifier called the *selector*. Selected components are used to denote record components, *entries*, and *objects* designated by access values; they are also used as *expanded names*.

Selector   See *selected component*.

Simple name   See *declaration, name*.

Statement   A statement specifies one or more actions to be performed during the execution of a *program*.

Subcomponent   A subcomponent is either a *component*, or a component of another subcomponent.

Subprogram   A subprogram is either a *procedure* or a *function*. A procedure specifies a sequence of actions and is invoked by a *procedure call* statement. A function specifies a sequence of actions and also returns a value called the *result*, and so a *function call* is an *expression*. A subprogram is written as a *subprogram declaration*, which specifies its *name*, *formal parameters*, and (for a function) its result; and a *subprogram body* which specifies the sequence of actions. The subprogram call specifies the *actual parameters* that are to be associated with the formal parameters. A subprogram is one of the kinds of *program unit*.

Subtype   A subtype of a *type* characterizes a subset of the values of the type. The subset is determined by a *constraint* on the type. Each value in the set of values of a subtype *belongs* to the subtype and *satisfies* the constraint determining the subtype.

Subunit   See *body*.

Task   A task operates in parallel with other parts of the program. It is written as a *task specification* (which specifies the *name* of the task and the names and *formal parameters* of its entries), and a *task body* which defines its execution. A *task unit* is one of the kinds of *program unit*. A *task type* is a *type* that permits the subsequent *declaration* of any number of similar tasks of the type. A value of a task type is said to *designate* a task.

Type   A type characterises both a set of values, and a set of *operations* applicable to those values. A *type definition* is a language construct that defines a type. A particular type is either an *access type*, an *array type*, a *private type*, a *record type*, a *scalar type* or a *task type*.

Use clause   A use clause achieves *direct visibility* of *declarations* that appear in the *visible parts* of named *packages*.

Variable   See *object*.

Variant part   A variant part of a *record* specifies alternative record *components*, depending on a *discriminant* of the record. Each value of the discriminant establishes a particular alternative of the variant part.

Visibility   At a given point in a program text, the *declaration* of an entity with a certain identifier is said to be *visible* if the entity is an acceptable meaning for an occurrence at that point of the identifier. The declaration is *visible* by *selection* at the place of the *selector* in a *selected component* or at the place of the name in a *named association*. Otherwise, the declaration is *directly visible*, that is, if the identifier alone has that meaning.

Visible part   See *package*.

With clause   See *compilation unit*.

APPENDIX 4
Syntax

The following syntax rules for Ada 83 are taken from Appendix E of the *LRM*. The rules have been reordered to correspond to the order of introduction of the topics in this book but individual rules have not been changed.

The rules for Ada 9X are considerably restructured and are given separately in Section A4.3.

It should be noted that the rules for the construction of lexical elements, which are under the subheading of Chapter 3, have a slightly different status to the other rules since spaces and newlines may be freely inserted between lexical elements but not within lexical elements.

The rules have been sequentially numbered for ease of reference; an index to them will be found in Section A4.2. Note that in rules 65, 81, 124, 131 and 133 the vertical bar stands for itself and is not a metasymbol.

A4.1 Syntax rules

Chapter 2

1 pragma ::= **pragma** identifier [(argument_association
        {, argument_association})];

2 argument_association ::= [*argument*_identifier =>] name
                         | [*argument*_identifier =>] expression

Chapter 3

3 graphic_character ::= basic_graphic_character
        | lower_case_letter | other_special_character

4 basic_graphic_character ::= upper_case_letter | digit
        | special_character | space_character

5 basic_character ::= basic_graphic_character | format_effector

6 identifier ::= letter {[underline] letter_or_digit}

7 letter_or_digit ::= letter | digit

8 letter ::= upper_case_letter | lower_case_letter

9 numeric_literal ::= decimal_literal | based_literal

10 decimal_literal ::= integer [. integer] [exponent]

11 integer ::= digit {[underline] digit}

12 exponent ::= E [+] integer | E − integer

13 based_literal ::= base # based_integer [. based_integer] # [exponent]

14 base ::= integer

15 based_integer ::= extended_digit {[underline] extended_digit}

16 extended_digit ::= digit | letter

17 character_literal ::= 'graphic_character'

18 string_literal ::= "{graphic_character}"

Chapter 4

19 basic_declaration ::=

object_declaration	| number_declaration
| type_declaration	| subtype_declaration
| subprogram_declaration	| package_declaration
| task_declaration	| generic_declaration
| exception_declaration	| generic_instantiation
| renaming_declaration	| deferred_constant_declaration

20 object_declaration ::=
      identifier_list : [**constant**] subtype_indication [:= expression];
      | identifier_list : [**constant**] constrained_array_definition
                                              [:= expression];

21 number_declaration ::=
      identifier_list : **constant** := *universal_static*_expression;

22 identifier_list ::= identifier {, identifier}

23 assignment_statement ::= *variable*_name := expression;

24 block_statement ::= [*block*_simple_name :]
                              [**declare**
                                 declarative_part]
                              begin
                                 sequence_of_statements
                              [**exception**
                                 exception_handler
                                 {exception_handler}
                              end [*block*_simple_name];

25 type_declaration ::=
                           full_type_declaration
                           | incomplete_type_declaration
                           | private_type_declaration

26 full_type_declaration ::=
        type identifier [discriminant_part] **is** type_definition;

27 type_definition ::=
                 enumeration_type_definition | integer_type_definition
                 | real_type_definition | array_type_definition
                 | record_type_definition | access_type_definition
                 | derived_type_definition

28 subtype_declaration ::= **subtype** identifier **is** subtype_indication;

29 subtype_indication ::= type_mark [constraint]

30 type_mark ::= *type*_name | *subtype*_name

31 constraint ::= range_constraint | floating_point_constraint
                 | fixed_point_constraint | index_constraint
                 | discriminant_constraint

32 range_constraint ::= **range** range

33 range ::= *range*_attribute | simple_expression .. simple_expression

34 enumeration_type_definition ::=
        (enumeration_literal_specification
                                  {, enumeration_literal_specification})

35 enumeration_literal_specification ::= enumeration_literal

36 enumeration_literal ::= identifier | character_literal

37 name ::= simple_name | character_literal | operator_symbol
             | indexed_component | slice | selected_component | attribute

38 simple_name ::= identifier

39 prefix ::= name | function_call

40 attribute ::= prefix ' attribute_designator

41 attribute_designator ::= simple_name [(*universal_static*_expression)]

42 expression ::=
  relation {**and** relation}
  | relation {**and then** relation}
  | relation {**or** relation}
  | relation {**or else** relation}
  | relation {**xor** relation}

43 relation ::=
  simple_expression [relational_operator simple_expression]
  | simple_expression [**not**] **in** range
  | simple_expression [**not**] **in** type_mark

44 simple_expression ::=
  [unary_adding_operator] term {binary_adding_operator term}

45 term ::= factor {multiplying_operator factor}

46 factor ::= primary [** primary] | **abs** primary | **not** primary

47 primary ::= numeric_literal | **null** | aggregate | string_literal | name
  | allocator | function_call | type_conversion
  | qualified_expression | (expression)

48 logical_operator ::= **and** | **or** | **xor**

49 relational_operator ::= = | /= | < | <= | > | >=

50 binary_adding_operator ::= + | − | &

51 unary_adding_operator ::= + | −

52 multiplying_operator ::= * | / | **mod** | **rem**

53 highest_precedence_operator ::= ** | **abs** | **not**

54 type_conversion ::= type_mark (expression)

55 qualified_expression ::=
  type_mark ' (expression) | type_mark ' aggregate

Chapter 5

56 sequence_of_statements ::= statement {statement}

57 statement ::= {label} simple_statement | {label} compound_statement

58 simple_statement ::=
                   null_statement | assignment_statement
                   | procedure_call_statement | exit_statement
                   | return_statement | goto_statement
                   | entry_call_statement | delay_statement
                   | abort_statement | raise_statement
                   | code_statement

59 compound_statement ::=
                   if_statement | case_statement
                   | loop_statement | block_statement
                   | accept_statement | select_statement

60 label ::= <<*label*_simple_name>>

61 null_statement ::= **null**;

62 if_statement ::= **if** condition **then**
                        sequence_of_statements
                     {**elsif** condition **then**
                        sequence_of_statements}
                     [**else**
                        sequence_of_statements]
                     end if;

63 condition ::= *boolean*_expression

64 case_statement ::= **case** expression **is**
                          case_statement_alternative
                          {case_statement_alternative}
                       end case;

65 case_statement_alternative ::=
        when choice { | choice} => sequence_of_statements

66 choice ::= simple_expression | discrete_range | **others**
            | *component*_simple_name

67 discrete_range ::= *discrete*_subtype_indication | range

68 loop_statement ::= [*loop*_simple_name :]
                          [iteration_scheme] **loop**
                             sequence_of_statements
                          end loop [*loop*_simple_name];

69 iteration_scheme ::=
   while condition
   I **for** loop_parameter_specification

70 loop_parameter_specification ::= identifier **in** [**reverse**] discrete_range

71 exit_statement ::= **exit** [*loop*_name] [**when** condition];

72 goto_statement ::= **goto** *label*_name;

Chapter 6

73 array_type_definition ::=
   unconstrained_array_definition I constrained_array_definition

74 unconstrained_array_definition ::=
   array (index_subtype_definition {, index_subtype_definition}) **of**
                                    *component*_subtype_indication

75 constrained_array_definition ::=
   array index_constraint **of** *component*_subtype_indication

76 index_subtype_definition ::= type_mark **range** <>

77 index_constraint ::= (discrete_range {, discrete_range})

78 indexed_component ::= prefix (expression {, expression})

79 slice ::= prefix (discrete_range)

80 aggregate ::= (component_association {, component_association})

81 component_association ::= [choice { I choice} =>] expression

82 record_type_definition ::= **record**
                                 component_list
                              end record

83 component_list ::=
            component_declaration {component_declaration}
            I {component_declaration} variant_part
            I **null**;

84 component_declaration ::=
   identifier_list : component_subtype_definition [:= expression];

85 component_subtype_definition ::= subtype_indication

86 selected_component ::= prefix . selector

87 selector ::= simple_name I character_literal I operator_symbol I **all**

Chapter 7

88 subprogram_declaration ::= subprogram_specification;

89 subprogram_specification ::=
    procedure identifier [formal_part]
    I **function** designator [formal_part] **return** type_mark

90 designator ::= identifier I operator_symbol

91 operator_symbol ::= string_literal

92 formal_part ::= (parameter_specification {; parameter_specification})

93 parameter_specification ::=
    identifier_list : mode type_mark [:= expression]

94 mode ::= [**in**] I **in out** I **out**

95 subprogram_body ::= subprogram_specification **is**
        [declarative_part]
    begin
      sequence_of_statements
    [**exception**
      exception_handler
      {exception_handler}]
    end [designator];

96 procedure_call_statement ::=
        *procedure*_name [actual_parameter_part];

97 function_call ::= *function*_name [actual_parameter_part]

98 actual_parameter_part ::=
    (parameter_association {, parameter_association})

99 parameter_association ::= [formal_parameter =>] actual_parameter

100 formal_parameter ::= *parameter*_simple_name

101 actual_parameter ::=
    expression I *variable*_name I type_mark (*variable*_name)

102 return_statement ::= **return** [expression];

Chapter 8

103 package_declaration ::= package_specification;

104 package_specification ::= **package** identifier **is**
                                {basic_declarative_item}
                                [**private**
                                {basic_declarative_item}]
                                end [*package*_simple_name]

105 package_body ::= **package body** *package*_simple_name **is**
                            [declarative_part]
                            [**begin**
                                sequence_of_statements
                            [**exception**
                                exception_handler
                                {exception_handler}]]
                            end [*package*_simple_name];

106 declarative_part ::=
            {basic_declarative_item} {later_declarative_item}

107 basic_declarative_item ::=
            basic_declaration | representation_clause | use_clause

108 later_declarative_item ::= body
                                | subprogram_declaration
                                | package_declaration
                                | task_declaration
                                | generic_declaration
                                | use_clause
                                | generic_instantiation

109 body ::= proper_body | body_stub

110 proper_body ::= subprogram_body | package_body | task_body

111 use_clause ::= **use** *package*_name {, *package*_name};

112 compilation ::= {compilation_unit}

113 compilation_unit ::=
                context_clause library_unit
                | context_clause secondary_unit

114 Library_unit ::=
            subprogram_declaration | package_declaration
            | generic_declaration | generic_instantiation
            | subprogram_body

115 secondary_unit ::= library_unit_body I subunit

116 library_unit_body ::= subprogram_body I package_body

117 context_clause ::= {with_clause {use_clause}}

118 with_clause ::= **with** *unit*_simple_name {, *unit*_simple_name};

119 body_stub ::= subprogram_specification **is separate**;
　　　　　　　　I **package body** *package*_simple_name **is separate**;
　　　　　　　　I **task body** *task*_simple_name **is separate**;

120 subunit ::= **separate** (*parent_unit*_name) proper_body

121 renaming_declaration ::=
　　　identifier : type_mark **renames** *object*_name;
　　I identifier : **exception renames** *exception*_name;
　　I **package** identifier **renames** *package*_name;
　　I subprogram_specification **renames** *subprogram_or_entry*_name;

Chapter 9

122 private_type_declaration ::=
　　　type identifier [discriminant_part] **is** [**limited**] **private**;

123 deferred_constant_declaration ::=
　　　identifier_list: **constant** type_mark;

Chapter 10

124 exception_handler ::=
　　　when exception_choice { I exception_choice} =>
　　　　　sequence_of_statements

125 exception_choice ::= *exception*_name I **others**

126 exception_declaration ::= identifier_list : **exception**;

127 raise_statement ::= **raise** [*exception*_name];

Chapter 11

128 discriminant_part ::=
　　　(discriminant_specification {; discriminant_specification})

129 discriminant_specification ::=
　　　identifier_list : type_mark [:= expression]

130 discriminant_constraint ::=
    (discriminant_association {, discriminant_association})

131 discriminant_association ::=
    [*discriminant*_simple_name { | *discriminant*_simple_name} =>]
                                        expression

132 variant_part ::= **case** *discriminant*_simple_name **is**
                        variant
                        {variant}
                    end case;

133 variant ::= **when** choice { | choice} => component_list

134 access_type_definition ::= **access** subtype_indication

135 incomplete_type_declaration ::= **type** identifier [discriminant_part];

136 allocator ::= **new** subtype_indication | **new** qualified_expression

137 derived_type_definition ::= **new** subtype_indication

Chapter 12

138 integer_type_definition ::= range_constraint

139 real_type_definition ::=
        floating_point_constraint | fixed_point_constraint

140 floating_point_constraint ::=
        floating_accuracy_definition [range_constraint]

141 floating_accuracy_definition ::= **digits** *static*_simple_expression

142 fixed_point_constraint ::=
        fixed_accuracy_definition [range_constraint]

143 fixed_accuracy_definition ::= **delta** *static*_simple_expression

Chapter 13

144 generic_declaration ::= generic_specification;

145 generic_specification ::=
        generic_formal_part subprogram_specification
        | generic_formal_part package_specification

146 generic_formal_part ::= **generic** {generic_parameter_declaration}

147 generic_parameter_declaration ::=
        identifier_list : [**in** [**out**]] type_mark [:= expression];
        | **type** identifier **is** generic_type_definition;
        | private_type_declaration
        | **with** subprogram_specification [**is** name];
        | **with** subprogram_specification [**is** <>];

148 generic_type_definition ::=
    (<>) | **range** <> | **digits** <> | **delta** <>
    | array_type_definition | access_type_definition

149 generic_instantiation ::=
        package identifier **is**
          new *generic_package*_name [generic_actual_part];
        | **procedure** identifier **is**
          new *generic_procedure*_name [generic_actual_part];
        | **function** designator **is**
          new *generic_function*_name [generic_actual_part];

150 generic_actual_part ::= (generic_association {, generic_association})

151 generic_association ::=
        [generic_formal_parameter =>] generic_actual_parameter

152 generic_formal_parameter ::=
                *parameter*_simple_name | operator_symbol

153 generic_actual_parameter ::= expression | *variable*_name
    | *subprogram*_name | *entry*_name | type_mark

Chapter 14

154 task_declaration ::= task_specification;

155 task_specification ::= **task** [**type**] identifier [**is**
           {entry_declaration}
           {representation_clause}
        end [*task*_simple_name]]

156 task_body ::= **task body** *task*_simple_name **is**
        [declarative_part]
      begin
        sequence_of_statements
      [**exception**
        exception_handler
        {exception_handler}]
      end [*task*_simple_name];

157 entry_declaration ::=
    entry identifier [(discrete_range)] [formal_part];

158 entry_call_statement ::= *entry*_name [actual_parameter_part];

159 accept_statement ::=
    accept *entry*_simple_name [(entry_index)] [formal_part] [**do**
      sequence_of_statements
    end [*entry*_simple_name]];

160 entry_index ::= expression

161 delay_statement ::= **delay** simple_expression;

162 select_statement ::= selective_wait | conditional_entry_call
    | timed_entry_call

163 selective_wait ::= **select**
              select_alternative
        {**or**
           select_alternative}
        [**else**
           sequence_of_statements]
        end select;

164 select_alternative ::=
    [**when** condition =>] selective_wait_alternative

165 selective_wait_alternative ::= accept_alternative
    | delay_alternative | terminate_alternative

166 accept_alternative ::= accept_statement [sequence_of_statements]

167 delay_alternative ::= delay_statement [sequence_of_statements]

168 terminate_alternative ::= **terminate**;

169 conditional_entry_call ::= **select**
                entry_call_statement
                [sequence_of_statements]
          else
              sequence_of_statements
          end_select;

170 timed_entry_call ::= **select**
                entry_call_statement
                [sequence_of_statements]
          or
              delay_alternative
          end select;

171 abort_statement ::= **abort** *task*_name { , *task*_name};

Chapter 15

172 representation_clause ::=
    type_representation_clause I address_clause

173 type_representation_clause ::= length_clause
    I enumeration_representation_clause
    I record_representation_clause

174 length_clause ::= **for** attribute **use** simple_expression;

175 enumeration_representation_clause ::=
  for *type*_simple_name **use** aggregate;

176 record_representation_clause ::= **for** *type*_simple_name **use**
     record [alignment_clause]
      {component_clause}
     end record;

177 alignment_clause ::= **at mod** *static*_simple_expression;

178 component_clause ::=
   *component*_name **at** *static*_simple_expression **range** *static*_range;

179 address_clause ::= **for** simple_name **use at** simple_expression;

180 code_statement ::= type_mark ' *record*_aggregate;

A4.2 Syntax index

This index lists the syntactic categories in alphabetical order and gives the number of their definition in the previous section and also the numbers of the categories in which each is used.

Category	Definition number	Used in number		
abort_statement	171	58		
accept_alternative	166	165		
accept_statement	159	59	166	
access_type_definition	134	27	148	
actual_parameter	101	99		
actual_parameter_part	98	96	97	158
address_clause	179	172		

Category	Definition number	Used in number			
aggregate	80	47	55	175	180
alignment_clause	177	176			
allocator	136	47			
argument_association	2	1			
array_type_definition	73	27	148		
assignment_statement	23	58			
attribute	40	33	37	174	
attribute_designator	41	40			
base	14	13			
based_integer	15	13			
based_literal	13	9			
basic_character	5				
basic_declaration	19	107			
basic_declarative_item	107	104	106		
basic_graphic_character	4	3	5		
binary_adding_operator	50	44			
block_statement	24	59			
body	109	108			
body_stub	119	109			
case_statement	64	59			
case_statement_alternative	65	64			
character_literal	17	36	37	87	
choice	66	65	81	133	
code_statement	180	58			
compilation	112				
compilation_unit	113	112			
component_association	81	80			
component_clause	178	176			
component_declaration	84	83			
component_list	83	82	133		
component_subtype_definition	85	84			
compound_statement	59	57			
condition	63	62	69	71	164
conditional_entry_call	169	162			
constrained_array_definition	75	20	73		
constraint	31	29			
context_clause	117	113			
decimal_literal	10	9			
declarative_part	106	24	95	105	156
deferred_constant_declaration	123	19			
delay_alternative	167	165	170		
delay_statement	161	58	167		
derived_type_definition	137	27			
designator	90	89	95	149	
discrete_range	67	66	70	77	79	157

Category	Definition number	Used in number			
discriminant_association	131	130			
discriminant_constraint	130	31			
discriminant_part	128	26	122	135	
discriminant_specification	129	128			
entry_call_statement	158	58	169	170	
entry_declaration	157	155			
entry_index	160	159			
enumeration_literal	36	35			
enumeration_literal_specification	35	34			
enumeration_type_definition	34	27			
enumeration_representation_clause	175	173			
exception_choice	125	124			
exception_declaration	126	19			
exception_handler	124	24	95	105	156
exit_statement	71	58			
exponent	12	10	13		
expression	42	2	20	21	23	41
		47	54	55	63	64
		78	81	84	93	101
		102	129	131	147	153
		160			
extended_digit	16	15			
factor	46	45			
fixed_accuracy_definition	143	142			
fixed_point_constraint	142	31	139		
floating_accuracy_definition	141	140			
floating_point_constraint	140	31	139		
formal_parameter	100	99			
formal_part	92	89	137	139	
full_type_declaration	26	25			
function_call	97	39	47		
generic_actual_parameter	153	151			
generic_actual_part	150	149			
generic_association	151	150			
generic_declaration	144	19	108	114	
generic_formal_parameter	152	151			
generic_formal_part	146	145			
generic_instantiation	149	19	108	114	
generic_parameter_declaration	147	146			
generic_specification	145	144			
generic_type_definition	148	147			
goto_statement	72	58			
graphic_character	3	17	18		
highest_precedence_operator	53				

Category	Definition number	Used in number			
proper_body	110	109	120		
qualified_expression	55	47	136		
raise_statement	127	58			
range	33	32	43	67	178
range_constraint	32	31	138	140	142
real_type_definition	139	27			
record_representation_clause	176	173			
record_type_definition	82	27			
relation	43	42			
relational_operator	49	43			
renaming_declaration	121	19			
representation_clause	172	107	155		
return_statement	102	58			
secondary_unit	115	113			
select_alternative	164	163			
select_statement	162	59			
selected_component	86	37			
selective_wait	163	162			
selective_wait_alternative	165	164			
selector	87	86			
sequence_of_statements	56	24	62	65	68	95
		105	124	156	159	163
		166	167	169	170	
simple_expression	44	33	43	66	141	143
		161	174	177	178	179
simple_name	38	24	37	41	60	66
		68	87	100	104	105
		118	119	131	132	152
		155	156	159	175	176
		179				
simple_statement	58	57			
slice	79	37			
statement	57	56			
string_literal	18	47	91		
subprogram_body	95	110	114	116	
subprogram_declaration	88	19	108	114	
subprogram_specification	89	88	95	119	121	145
		147				
subtype_declaration	28	19			
subtype_indication	29	20	28	67	74	75
		85	134	136	137	
subunit	120	115			
task_body	156	110			
task_declaration	154	19	108		
task_specification	155	154			

Category	Definition number	Used in number			
term	45	44			
terminate_alternative	168	165			
timed_entry_call	170	162			
type_conversion	54	47			
type_declaration	25	19			
type_definition	27	26			
type_mark	30	29	43	54	55	76
		89	93	101	121	123
		129	147	153	180	
type_representation_clause	173	172			
unary_adding_operator	51	44			
unconstrained_array_definition	74	73			
use_clause	111	107	108	117	
variant	133	132			
variant_part	132	83			
with_clause	118	117			

A4.3 Syntax rules for Ada 9X

The syntax rules for Ada 9X are considerably restructured although the change is more apparent than real. A prime goal has been to increase clarity and this has resulted in rather more rules than the number of additional features would lead one to expect.

In order to enable the reader and particularly those familiar with Ada 83 to obtain a reasonably clear view of the new arrangement, the rules are presented as nearly as possible in the same way as in Section A4.1.

Rules have the same number if they are completely unchanged or changed but are clearly the replacement for the previous rule. This does not necessarily mean that all rules with existing numbers have the same category name; for example, the category integer is now called numeral but clearly it is the replacement rule.

The numbers of changed rules are followed by an *. New rules in existing areas are inserted in an appropriate place and are numbered by adding a suffix letter to some closely related rule. Some numbers are now not used. Most of the completely new rules relating to additional areas are grouped under the heading of Chapter 17 and are numbered from 1 with a suffix X.

Chapter 2

1*   pragma ::= **pragma** identifier [(pragma_argument_association
          {, pragma_argument_association})];

2*   pragma_argument_association ::=
          [*pragma_argument_*identifier =>] name
        | [*pragma_argument_*identifier =>] expression

Chapter 3

4*   graphic_character ::= letter | digit
         | space_character | special_character

5*   character ::= graphic_character | format_effector
         | other_control_function

6*   identifier ::= letter {letter | digit | underline}

9   numeric_literal ::= decimal_literal | based_literal

10*   decimal_literal ::= numeral [. numeral] [exponent]

11*   numeral ::= digit {digit | underline}

12*   exponent ::= E [+] numeral | E – numeral

13*   based_literal ::= base # based_numeral [. based_numeral] # [exponent]

14*   base ::= numeral

15*   based_numeral ::= extended_digit {extended_digit | underline}

16*   extended_digit ::= digit | A | B | C | D | E | F

17   character_literal ::= 'graphic_character'

18   string_literal ::= "{string_element}"

Chapter 4

19*   basic_declaration ::=
            object_declaration | number_declaration
            | type_declaration | subtype_declaration
            | subprogram_declaration | package_declaration
            | generic_declaration | exception_declaration
            | generic_instantiation | renaming_declaration
            | abstract_subprogram_declaration

20*   object_declaration ::=
            defining_identifier_list :
                [aliased] **[constant]** subtype_indication [:= expression];
            | defining_identifier_list :
                [aliased] **[constant]** array_type_definition [:= expression];
            | single_task_declaration
            | single_protected_declaration

21*   number_declaration ::=
     defining_identifier_list : **constant** := *static*_expression;

22*   defining_identifier_list ::= defining_identifier {, defining_identifier}

22a   defining_identifier ::= identifier

23   assignment_statement ::= *variable*_name := expression;

24*   block_statement ::= [*block*_statement_identifier:]
                       [**declare**
                         declarative_part]
                       begin
                         handled_sequence_of_statements
                       end [*block*_identifier];

24a   statement_identifier ::= direct_name

25*   type_declaration ::=
                         full_type_declaration
                      | incomplete_type_declaration
                      | private_type_declaration
                      | private_extension_declaration

26*   full_type_declaration ::=
                         type defining_identifier [known_discriminant_part]
                         is type_definition;
                      | task_type_declaration
                      | protected_type_declaration

27   type_definition ::=
                         enumeration_type_definition | integer_type_definition
                      | real_type_definition | array_type_definition
                      | record_type_definition | access_type_definition
                      | derived_type_definition

28*   subtype_declaration ::=
     subtype defining_identifier **is** subtype_indication;

29*   subtype_indication ::= subtype_mark [constraint]

30*   subtype_mark ::= *subtype*_name

31*   constraint ::= scalar_constraint | composite_constraint

31a   scalar_constraint ::=
     range_constraint | digits_constraint | delta_constraint

31b   composite_constraint ::= index_constraint | discriminant_constraint

32   range_constraint ::= **range** range

33*   range ::= range_attribute_reference
     | simple_expression .. simple_expression

34   enumeration_type_definition ::=
     (enumeration_literal_specification
                          {, enumeration_literal_specification })

35*   enumeration_literal_specification ::=
     defining_identifier | defining character_literal

35a   defining_character_literal ::= character_literal

37*   name ::= direct_name | explicit_dereference | indexed_component
     | slice | selected_component | attribute_reference
     | type_conversion | function_call | character_literal

38*   direct_name ::= identifier | operator_symbol

39*   prefix ::= name | implicit_dereference

39a   explicit_dereference ::= name . **all**

39b   implicit_dereference ::= name

40*   attribute_reference ::= prefix ' attribute_designator

40a   range_attribute_reference ::= prefix ' range_attribute_designator

41*   attribute_designator ::= identifier [(*static*_expression)]
     | Access | Delta | Digits

41a   range_attribute_designator ::= Range [(*static*_expression)]

42 expression ::=
                  relation {**and** relation}
               | relation {**and then** relation}
               | relation {**or** relation}
               | relation {**or else** relation}
               | relation {**xor** relation}

43 relation ::=
         simple_expression [relational_operator simple_expression]
        | simple_expression [**not**] **in** range
        | simple_expression [**not**] **in** subtype_mark

44   simple_expression ::=
     [unary_adding_operator] term {binary_adding_operator term}

45   term ::= factor {multiplying_operator factor}

46   factor ::= primary [** primary] | **abs** primary | **not** primary

47*   primary ::= numeric_literal | **null** | aggregate | string_literal | name
                | allocator | qualified_expression | (expression)

48   logical_operator ::= **and** | **or** | **xor**

49   relational_operator ::= = | /= | < | <= | > | >=

50   binary_adding_operator ::= + | – | &

51   unary_adding_operator ::= + | –

52   multiplying_operator ::= * | / | **mod** | **rem**

53   highest_precedence_operator ::= ** | **abs** | **not**

54*   type_conversion ::=
       subtype_mark (expression) | subtype_mark (name)

55*   qualified_expression ::=
       subtype_mark ' (expression) | subtype_mark ' aggregate

Chapter 5

56   sequence_of_statements ::= statement {statement}

57   statement ::= {label} simple_statement | {label} compound_statement

58*   simple_statement ::=
          null_statement | assignment_statement
        | procedure_call_statement | exit_statement
        | return_statement | goto_statement
        | entry_call_statement | delay_statement
        | abort_statement | raise_statement
        | code_statement | requeue_statement

59   compound_statement ::=
          if_statement | case_statement
        | loop_statement | block_statement
        | accept_statement | select_statement

60*   label ::= <<*label*_statement_identifier>>

61   null_statement ::= **null**;

62   if_statement ::= **if** condition **then**
                              sequence_of_statements
                       {**elsif** condition **then**
                              sequence_of_statements}
                       [**else**
                              sequence_of_statements]
                       end if;

63   condition ::= *boolean*_expression

64   case_statement ::= **case** expression **is**
                                case_statement_alternative
                              {case_statement_alternative}
                       end case;

65*   case_statement_alternative ::=
          when discrete_choice_list => sequence_of_statements

65a   discrete_choice_list ::= discrete_choice { | discrete_choice}

66*   discrete_choice ::= expression I discrete_range I **others**

67   discrete_range ::= *discrete*_subtype_indication I range

68*   loop_statement ::= [*loop*_statement_identifier :]
                        [iteration_scheme] **loop**
                           sequence_of_statements
                       end loop [*loop*_identifier];

69   iteration_scheme ::=
          while condition I **for** loop_parameter_specification

70*   loop_parameter_specification ::=
          defining_identifier **in** [**reverse**] discrete_subtype_definition

71   exit_statement ::= **exit** [*loop*_name] [**when** condition];

72   goto_statement ::= **goto** *label*_name;

Chapter 6

73   array_type_definition ::=
          unconstrained_array_definition I constrained_array_definition

74*   unconstrained_array_definition ::=
          array (index_subtype_definition {, index_subtype_definition})
                                       of component_definition

75*   constrained_array_definition ::=
        array (discrete_subtype_definition {, discrete_subtype_definition})
                                         of component_definition

76*   index_subtype_definition ::= subtype_mark **range** <>

76a   discrete_subtype_definition ::= *discrete*_subtype_indication I range

76b   component_definition ::= [**aliased**] subtype_indication

77   index_constraint ::= (discrete_range {, discrete_range})

78   indexed_component ::= prefix (expression {, expression})

79   slice ::= prefix (discrete_range)

80*   aggregate ::= record_aggregate I extension_aggregate I array_aggregate

80a   record_aggregate ::= (record_component_association_list)

80b   record_component_association_list ::=
        record_component_association {, record_component_association}
    I **null record**

80c   record_component_association ::=
        [component_choice_list =>] expression

80d   component_choice_list ::=
        *component*_selector_name{ I *component*_selector_name} I **others**

80e   array_aggregate ::=
        positional_array_aggregate I named_array_aggregate

80f   positional_array_aggregate ::=
        (expression , expression {, expression})
        I (expression {, expression} , **others** => expression)

80g   named_array_aggregate ::=
        (array_component_association {, array_component_association})

80h   array_component_association ::=
        discrete_choice_list => expression

82*   record_type_definition ::= [**tagged**] [**limited**] record_definition

82a   record_definition ::= **record**
                               component_list
                  end record
                  I **null record**

83   component_list ::=
                        component_declaration {component_declaration}
                        | {component_declaration} variant_part
                        | **null**;

84*   component_declaration ::=
               defining_identifier_list : component_definition
                                      [:= default_expression];

84a   default_expression ::= expression

86*   selected_component ::= prefix . selector_name

87*   selector_name ::= identifier | character_literal | operator_symbol

Chapter 7

88   subprogram_declaration ::= subprogram_specification;

89*   subprogram_specification ::=
               procedure defining_program_unit_name parameter_profile
            | **function** defining_designator parameter_and_result_profile

89a   parameter_profile ::= [formal_part]

89b   parameter_and_result_profile ::= [formal_part] **return** subtype_mark

90*   designator ::= [parent_unit_name .] identifier | operator_symbol

90a   defining_designator ::=
           defining_program_unit_name | defining_operator_symbol

90b   defining_program_unit_name ::=
           [parent_unit_name .] defining_identifier

90c   parent_unit_name ::= name

91   operator_symbol ::= string_literal

91a   defining_operator_symbol ::= operator_symbol

92   formal_part ::= (parameter_specification {; parameter_specification})

93*   parameter_specification ::=
         defining_identifier_list : mode subtype_mark
          [:= default_expression]
       | defining_identifier_list : access_definition
          [:= default_expression]

94   mode ::= [**in**] | **in out** | **out**

95*   subprogram_body ::= subprogram_specification **is**
                       declarative_part
                  begin
                       handled_sequence_of_statements
                  end [designator];

96*   procedure_call_statement ::=
        *procedure*_name; | *procedure*_prefix actual_parameter_part;

97*   function_call ::=
        *function*_name | *function*_prefix actual_parameter_part

98   actual_parameter_part ::=
        (parameter_association {, parameter_association})

99*   parameter_association ::=
        [*formal_parameter*_selector_name =>] explicit_actual_parameter

101* explicit_actual_parameter ::=
        expression | *variable*_name

102   return_statement ::= **return** [expression];

Chapter 8

103   package_declaration ::= package_specification;

104* package_specification ::= **package** defining_program_unit_name **is**
                      {basic_declarative_item}
                  [**private**
                      {basic_declarative_item}]
                  end [[parent_unit_name .] identifier]

105* package_body ::= **package body** defining_program_unit_name **is**
                    declarative_part
                  [**begin**
                    handled_sequence_of_statements]
                  end [[parent_unit_name .] identifier];

106* declarative_part ::= {declarative_item}

107   basic_declarative_item ::=
        basic_declaration | representation_clause | use_clause

108* declarative_item ::= basic_declarative_item | body

109   body ::= proper_body | body_stub

110*   proper_body ::= subprogram_body | package_body | task_body
          | protected_body

111*   use_clause ::= use_package_clause | use_type_clause

111a   use_package_clause ::= **use** *package*_name {, *package*_name};

111b   use_type_clause ::= **use type** subtype_mark {, subtype_mark};

112   compilation ::= {compilation_unit}

113*   compilation_unit ::=
             context_clause library_item
             | context_clause subunit

113a   library_item ::=
          [**private**] library_unit_declaration | library_unit_body

114*   library_unit_declaration ::=
             subprogram_declaration | package_declaration
             | generic_declaration | generic_instantiation
             | library_unit_renaming_declaration

114a   library_unit_renaming_declaration ::=
             package_renaming_declaration
             | generic_renaming_declaration
             | subprogram_renaming_declaration

116   library_unit_body ::= subprogram_body | package_body

117*   context_clause ::= {context_item}

117a   context_item ::= with_clause | use_clause

118*   with_clause ::= **with** *library_unit*_name {, *library_unit*_name};

119*   body_stub ::= subprogram_body_stub | package_body_stub
          | task_body_stub | protected_body_stub

119a   subprogram_body_stub ::= subprogram_specification **is separate**;

119b   package_body_stub ::=
          package body defining_identifier **is separate**;

119c   task_body_stub ::=
          task body defining_identifier **is separate**;

119d protected_body_stub ::=
    protected body defining_identifier **is separate**;

120* subunit ::= **separate** (parent_unit_name) proper_body

121* renaming_declaration ::= object_renaming_declaration
                     | exception_renaming_declaration
                     | package_renaming_declaration
                     | subprogram_renaming_declaration
                     | generic_renaming_declaration

121a object_renaming_declaration ::=
    defining_identifier : subtype_mark **renames** *object*_name;

121b exception_renaming_declaration ::=
    defining_identifier : **exception renames** *exception*_name;

121c package_renaming_declaration ::=
    package defining_program_unit_name **renames** *package*_name;

121d subprogram_renaming_declaration ::=
    subprogram_specification **renames** *callable_entity*_name;

121e generic_renaming_declaration ::=
        generic package defining_program_unit _name
        renames_*generic_package*_name;
      | **generic procedure** defining_program_unit _name
        renames_*generic_procedure*_name;
      | **generic function** defining_program_unit _name
        renames_*generic_function*_name;

Chapter 9

122* private_type_declaration ::= **type** defining_identifier
      [discriminant_part] **is** [**tagged**] [**limited**] **private**;

Chapter 10

124* exception_handler ::=
    when [choice_parameter_specification :]
      exception_choice { | exception_choice} =>
      sequence_of_statements

124a handled_sequence_of_statements ::= sequence_of_statements
                          [**exception**
                             exception_handler
                             {exception_handler}]

124b   choice_parameter_specification ::= defining_identifier

125   exception_choice ::= *exception*_name | **others**

126*   exception_declaration ::= defining_identifier_list : **exception**;

127   raise_statement ::= **raise** [*exception*_name];

Chapter 11

128*   discriminant_part ::=
         unknown_discriminant_part | known_discriminant_part

128a   unknown_discriminant_part ::= (<>)

128b   known_discriminant_part ::=
         (discriminant_specification {; discriminant_specification})

129*   discriminant_specification ::=
         defining_identifier_list : subtype_mark [:= default_expression]
         | defining_identifier_list : access_definition [:= default_expression]

130   discriminant_constraint ::=
         (discriminant_association {, discriminant_association})

131*   discriminant_association ::=
         [*discriminant*_selector_name { | *discriminant*_selector_name} =>]
                                                                        expression

132*   variant_part ::=
       case *discriminant*_direct_name **is**
                   variant
                   {variant}
               end case;

133*   variant ::= **when** discrete_choice_list => component_list

134*   access_type_definition ::= access_to_object_definition
                                | access_to_subprogram_definition

134a   access_to_object_definition ::=
         access [general_access_modifier] subtype_indication

134b   general_access_modifier ::= **all** | **constant**

134c   access_to_subprogram_definition ::=
         access [**protected**] **procedure** parameter_profile
         | **access** [**protected**] **function** parameter_and_result_profile

134d   access_definition ::= **access** subtype_mark

135*   incomplete_type_declaration ::=
                            type defining_identifier [discriminant_part];

136   allocator ::= **new** subtype_indication | **new** qualified_expression

137*   derived_type_definition ::=
           new subtype_indication [record_extension_part]

Chapter 12

138*   integer_type_definition ::=
           signed_integer_type_definition | modular_type_definition

138a   signed_integer_type_definition ::=
           range *static*_simple_expression .. *static*_simple_expression

138b   modular_type_definition ::= **mod** *static*_expression

139*   real_type_definition ::=
           floating_point_definition | fixed_point_definition

140*   floating_point_definition ::=
           digits *static*_expression [real_range_specification]

140a   real_range_specification ::=
           range *static*_simple_expression .. *static*_simple_expression

142*   fixed_point_definition ::=
           ordinary_fixed_point_definition | decimal_fixed_point_definition

142a   ordinary_fixed_point_definition ::=
           delta *static*_expression real_range_specification

142b   decimal_fixed_point_definition ::=
           delta *static*_expression **digits** *static*_expression
                                                [real_range_specification]

142c   digits_constraint ::= **digits** *static*_expression [range_constraint]

142d   delta_constraint ::= **delta** *static*_expression [range_constraint]

Chapter 13

144*   generic_declaration ::=
           generic_subprogram_declaration | generic_package_declaration

144a generic_subprogram_declaration ::=
        generic_formal_part subprogram_specification;

144b generic_package_declaration ::=
        generic_formal_part package_specification;

146* generic_formal_part ::=
        generic {generic_formal_parameter_declaration I use_clause}

147* generic_formal_parameter_declaration ::=
              formal_object_declaration
            I formal_type_declaration
            I formal_subprogram_declaration
            I formal_package_declaration

147a formal_object_declaration ::=
        defining_identifier_list : mode subtype_mark
                                        [:= default_expression];

147b formal_type_declaration ::=
        type defining_identifier [discriminant_part] **is**
                                        formal_type_definition;

147c formal_type_definition ::=
                        formal_private_type_definition
                      I formal_derived_type_definition
                      I formal_discrete_type_definition
                      I formal_signed_integer_type_definition
                      I formal_modular_type_definition
                      I formal_floating_point_definition
                      I formal_ordinary_fixed_point_definition
                      I formal_decimal_fixed_point_definition
                      I formal_array_type_definition
                      I formal_access_type_definition

147d formal_private_type_definition ::= [**tagged**] [**limited**] **private**

147e formal_derived_type_definition ::=
        new subtype_mark [**with private**]

147f formal_discrete_type_definition ::= (<>)

147g formal_signed_integer_type_definition ::= **range** <>

147h formal_modular_type_definition ::= **mod** <>

147i formal_floating_point_definition ::= **digits** <>

147j formal_ordinary_fixed_point_definition ::= **delta** <>

147k formal_decimal_fixed_point_definition ::= **delta** <> **digits** <>

147l formal_array_type_definition ::= array_type_definition

147m formal_access_type_definition ::= access_type_definition

147n formal_subprogram_declaration ::=
   with subprogram_specification [**is** subprogram_default];

147o subprogram_default ::= default name | <>

147p default_name ::= name

147q formal_package_declaration ::= **with package** defining_identifier **is**
  new *generic_package*_name formal_package_actual_part;

147r formal_package_actual_part ::= (<>) | [generic_actual_part]

149* generic_instantiation ::=
  package defining_program_unit_name **is**
   new *generic_package*_name [generic_actual_part];
  | **procedure** defining_program_unit_name **is**
   new *generic_procedure*_name [generic_actual_part];
  | **function** defining_designator **is**
   new *generic_function*_name [generic_actual_part];

150 generic_actual_part ::= (generic_association {, generic_association})

151* generic_association ::=
  [*generic_formal_parameter*_selector_name =>]
        explicit_generic_actual_parameter

153* explicit_generic_actual_parameter ::= expression | *variable*_name
  | *subprogram*_name | *entry*_name | subtype_mark
  | *package_instance*_name

Chapter 14

154* task_type_declaration ::=
  task type defining_identifier [known_discriminant_part]
           [**is** task_definition];

154a single_task_declaration ::=
  task defining_identifier [**is** task_definition];

155* task_definition ::= {task_item}
                          [**private**
                            {task_item}]
                          end [*task*_identifier]

155a task_item ::= entry_declaration | representation_clause

156* task_body ::= **task body** defining_identifier **is**
                          declarative_part
                        begin
                          handled_sequence_of_statements
                        end [*task*_identifier];

157* entry_declaration ::=
        entry defining_identifier [(discrete_subtype_definition)]
                                                    parameter_profile;

158   entry_call_statement ::= *entry*_name [actual_parameter_part];

159* accept_statement ::=
            accept *entry*_direct_name [(entry_index)] parameter_profile [**do**
              handled_sequence_of_statements
            end [*entry*_identifier]];

160   entry_index ::= expression

161* delay_statement ::= delay_until_statement | delay_relative_statement

161a delay_until_statement ::= **delay until** *delay*_expression;

161b delay_relative_statement ::= **delay** *delay*_expression;

162* select_statement ::= selective_accept | conditional_entry_call
          | timed_entry_call | asynchronous_select

163* selective_accept ::= **select**
                          [guard]
                            selective_accept_alternative
                        {**or**
                          [guard]
                            selective_accept_alternative}
                        [**else**
                            sequence_of_statements]
                        end select;

163a guard ::= **when** condition =>

165* selective_accept_alternative ::= accept_alternative
          | delay_alternative | terminate_alternative

166 accept_alternative ::= accept_statement [sequence_of_statements]

167 delay_alternative ::= delay_statement [sequence_of_statements]

168 terminate_alternative ::= **terminate**;

169* conditional_entry_call ::= **select**
                              entry_call_alternative
                         else
                              sequence_of_statements
                         end_select;

169a entry_call_alternative ::=
         entry_call_statement [sequence_of_statements]

170* timed_entry_call ::= **select**
                              entry_call_alternative
                         or
                              delay_alternative
                         end select;

171 abort_statement ::= **abort** *task*_name {, *task*_name};

Chapter 15

172* representation_clause ::=
         attribute_definition_clause
         | enumeration_representation_clause
         | record_representation_clause
         | at_clause

174* attribute_definition_clause ::=
         for direct_name ' attribute_designator **use** expression;
         | **for** direct_name ' attribute_designator **use** name;

175* enumeration_representation_clause ::=
         for *first_subtype*_direct_name **use** enumeration _aggregate;

176* record_representation_clause ::= **for** *first_subtype*_direct_name **use**
                                     record [mod_clause]
                                     {component_clause}
                                     end record;

177* mod_clause ::= **at mod** *static*_expression;

178 component_clause ::= component_clause_component_name **at**
                         position **range** first_bit .. last_bit;

178a component_clause_component_name ::=
        *component*_direct_name
        | *component*_direct_name ' attribute_designator
        | *first_subtype*_direct_name ' attribute_designator

178b position ::= *static*_expression

178c first_bit ::= *static*_simple_expression

178d last_bit ::= *static*_simple_expression

179* at_clause ::= **for** direct_name **use at** expression;

180* code_statement ::= qualified_expression;

Chapter 17

1X   record_extension_part ::= **with** record_definition

2X   extension_aggregate ::=
       (expression **with** record_component_association_list)

3X   abstract_subprogram_declaration ::=
       subprogram_specification **is** <>;

4X   private_extension_declaration ::=
       type defining_identifier [discriminant_part] **is**
               new *ancestor*_subtype_indication **with private**;

5X   protected_type_declaration ::=
       protected type defining_identifier [known_discriminant_part] **is**
                    protected_definition;

6X   single_protected_definition ::=
     protected defining_identifier **is** protected_definition;

7X   protected_definition ::= {protected_operation_declaration}
             [**private**
              {protected_element_declaration}]
             end [*protected*_identifier]

8X   protected_operation_declaration ::=
     subprogram_declaration | entry_declaration

9X   protected_element_declaration ::=
     protected_operation_declaration | component_declaration

10X   protected_body ::= **protected body** defining_identifier **is**
              {protected_operation_item}
          end [*protected*_identifier];

11X   protected_operation_item ::=
      subprogram_declaration I subprogram_body I entry_body

12X   entry_body ::=
      entry defining_identifier entry_body_formal_part entry_barrier **is**
        declarative_part
      begin
        handled_sequence_of_statements
      end [*entry*_identifier];

13X   entry_body_formal_part ::=
      [(entry_index_specification)] parameter_profile

14X   entry_barrier ::= **when** condition

15X   entry_index_specification ::=
      for defining_identifier **in** discrete_subtype_definition

16X   requeue_statement ::= **requeue** *entry*_name [**with abort**];

17X   asynchronous_select ::= **select**
                triggering_alternative
      then abort
        abortable_part
      end select;

18X   triggering_alternative ::=
      triggering_statement [sequence_of_statements]

19X   triggering_statement ::= entry_call_statement I delay_statement

20X   abortable_part ::= sequence_of_statements

Answers to Exercises

Specimen answers are given to all the exercises. In some cases they do not necessarily represent the best technique for solving a problem but merely one which uses the material introduced at that point in the discussion.

Answers 2

Exercise 2.2

1   **package** Simple_Maths **is**
      function Sqrt(F: Float) **return** Float;
      function Log(F: Float) **return** Float;
      function Ln(F: Float) **return** Float;
      function Exp(F: Float) **return** Float;
      function Sin(F: Float) **return** Float;
      function Cos(F: Float) **return** Float;
  end Simple_Maths;

The first few lines of our program Print_Roots could now become

  with Simple_Maths, Simple_IO;
  procedure Print_Roots **is**
      use Simple_Maths, Simple_IO;

Exercise 2.6

1   The default field is 11 for a 32-bit type Integer so

  Put(123);   – – "sssssss123"
  Put(–123);   – – "sssssss–123"

Exercise 2.7

1
```ada
with Text_IO, Etc;
use Text_IO, Etc;
procedure Ten_Times_Table is
  use Int_IO;
  Row, Column: Integer;
begin
  Row := 1;
  loop
    Column := 1;
    loop
      Put(Row * Column, 5);
      exit when Column = 10;
      Column := Column+1;
    end loop;
    New_Line;
    exit when Row = 10;
    Row := Row+1;
  end loop;
end Ten_Times_Table;
```

2
```ada
with Text_IO, Etc;
use Text_IO, Etc;
procedure Table_Of_Square_Roots is
  use Int_IO, Real_IO, Real_Maths;
  N: Integer;
  Last_N: Integer;
  Tab: Count;
begin
  Tab := 10;
  Put("What is the largest value please? "); Get(Last_N);
  New_Line(2);
  Put("Number"); Set_Col(Tab); Put("Square root");
  New_Line(2);
  N := 1;
  loop
    Put(N, 4); Set_Col(Tab); Put(Sqrt(Real(N)), 3, 5, 0);
    New_Line;
    exit when N = Last_N;
    N := N+1;
  end loop;
end Table_Of_Square_Roots;
```

Answers 3

Exercise 3.3

1   The following are not legal identifiers

   (b) contains &
   (c) contains hyphens not underlines
   (e) adjacent underlines
   (f) does not start with a letter
   (g) trailing underline (but allowed in Ada 9X)
   (h) this is two legal identifiers
   (i) this is legal – but it is a reserved word

Exercise 3.4

1   (a) legal – real
   (b) illegal – no digit before point
   (c) legal – integer
   (d) illegal – integer with negative exponent
   (e) illegal – closing # missing
   (f) legal – real
   (g) illegal – C not a digit of base 12
   (h) illegal – no number before exponent
   (i) legal – integer – case of letter immaterial
   (j) legal – integer
   (k) illegal – underline at start of exponent
   (l) illegal – integer with negative exponent

2   (a) $224 = 14 \times 16$
   (b) $6144 = 3 \times 2^{11}$
   (c) 4095.0
   (d) 4095.0

3   (a) 32 ways

```
41, 2#101001#, 3#1112#, ...
   10#41#, ... 16#29#
41E0, 2#101001#E0, ... 16#29#E0
```

   (b) 40 ways. As for example (a) plus, since 150 is not prime but $2 \times 3 \times 5^2 = 150$ also

```
2#1001011#E1
3#1212#E1
5#110#E1
5#11#E2
6#41#E1
10#15#E1
15#A#E1
```

and of course

   15E1

Exercise 3.5

1   (a) 7
     (b) 1
     (c) 1
     (d) 12

2   (a) This has 3 units
          the identifier   delay
          the literal   2.0
          the single symbol   ;

     (b) This has 4 units
          the identifier   delay2
          the single symbol   .
          the literal   0
          the single symbol   ;

Case (a) is a legal delay statement, (b) is just a mess.

Answers 4

Exercise 4.1

1   R: Real := 1.0;

2   Zero: **constant** Real := 0.0;
     One: **constant** Real := 1.0;

but better to write number declarations

     Zero: **constant** := 0.0;
     One: **constant** := 1.0;

3   (a) **var** is illegal – this is Ada not Pascal
     (b) terminating semicolon is missing
     (c) a constant declaration must have an initial value
     (d) no multiple assignment – this is Ada not Algol
     (e) nothing – assuming M and N are of integer type
     (f) 2Pi is not a legal identifier

Exercise 4.2

1 There are four errors

(1) semicolon missing after declaration of J, K
(2) K used before a value has been assigned to it
(3) = instead of := in declaration of P
(4) Q not declared and initialized

Exercise 4.4

1 This analysis assumes that the values of all variables originally satisfy their constraints; this will be the case if the program is not erroneous.

(a) the ranges of I and J are identical so no checks are required and consequently Constraint_Error cannot be raised,

(b) the range of J is a subset of that of K and again Constraint_Error cannot be raised,

(c) n this case a check is required since if K > 10 it cannot be assigned to J in which case
Constraint_Error will be raised.

Exercise 4.5

1 (a) −105   (d) −3   (g) −1
    (b) −3   (e) −3   (h) 2
    (c) 0   (f) illegal

2 All variables are real

(a) M*R**2
(b) B**2 − 4.0*A*C
(c) (4.0/3.0)*Pi*R**3   − − brackets not necessary
(d) (P*Pi*A**4)/(8.0*L*Eta)   − − brackets are necessary

Exercise 4.6

1 (a) Sat
    (b) Sat   note that Succ applies to the base type
    (c) 2

2 (a) **type** Rainbow **is** (Red, Orange, Yellow, Green, Blue, Indigo, Violet);
    (b) **type** Fruit **is** (Apple, Banana, Orange, Pear);

3 Groom'Val ((N−1) **mod** 8)

or perhaps better

Groom'Val ((N-1) **mod** (Groom'Pos(Groom'Last) + 1))

4 D := Day'Val((Day'Pos(D) + N – 1) **mod** 7);

5 If X and Y are both overloaded literals then X < Y will be ambiguous. We would have to use qualification such as T'(X) < T'(Y).

Exercise 4.7

1 T: **constant** Boolean := True;
   F: **constant** Boolean := False;

2 The values are True and False, not T or F which are the names of constants.

    (a) False   (c) True   (e) False
    (b) True   (d) True

3 The expression is always True. The predefined operators **xor** and /= operating on Boolean values are the same. But see the note at the end of Section 11.7.

Exercise 4.9

1 All variables are real except for N in example (c) which is integer.

    (a) 2.0*Pi*Sqrt(L/G)
    (b) M_0/Sqrt(1.0 – (V/C)**2)
    (c) Sqrt(2.0*Pi*Real(N))*(Real(N)/E)**N

2 Sqrt(2.0*Pi*X)*Exp(X*Ln(X)–X)

Answers 5

Exercise 5.1

1   **declare**
     End_Of_Month: Integer;
  begin
     if Month = Sep **or** Month = Apr **or** Month = Jun **or** Month = Nov **then**
       End_Of_Month := 30;
     elsif Month = Feb **then**
       if Year **mod** 4 = 0 **then**
         End_Of_Month := 29;
       else
         End_Of_Month := 28;
       end if;
     else
       End_Of_Month := 31;
     end if;

```
    if Day /= End_Of_Month then
       Day := Day+1;
    else
       Day := 1;
       if Month /= Dec then
          Month := Month_Name'Succ(Month);
       else
          Month := Jan;
          Year := Year+1;
       end if;
    end if;
 end;
```

If today is 31 Dec 2099 then Constraint_Error will be raised on attempting to assign 2100 to Year. Note that the range 1901 .. 2099 simplifies the leap year calculation.

2   ```
     if X < Y then
        declare
           T: Real := X;
        begin
           X := Y; Y := T;
        end;
     end if;
     ```

*Exercise 5.2*

1    ```
     declare
        End_Of_Month: Integer;
     begin
        case Month is
           when Sep | Apr | Jun | Nov =>
              End Of Month := 30;
           when Feb =>
              if Year mod 4 = 0 then
                 End_Of_Month := 29;
              else
                 End_Of_Month := 28;
              end if;
           when others =>
              End_Of_Month := 31;
        end case;
        - - then as before
        ...
     end;
     ```

2   ```
     subtype Winter is Month_Name range Jan .. Mar;
     subtype Spring is Month_Name range Apr .. Jun;
     subtype Summer is Month_Name range Jul .. Sep;
     subtype Autumn is Month_Name range Oct .. Dec;
     ...
     ```
     ```

```
case M is
   when Winter => Dig;
   when Spring => Sow;
   when Summer => Tend;
   when Autumn => Harvest;
end case;
```

Note that if we wished to consider winter as December to February then we could not declare a suitable subtype.

3
```
case D is
   when 1 .. 10 => Gorge;
   when 11 .. 20 => Subsist;
   when others => Starve;
end case;
```

We cannot write 21 .. End_Of_Month because it is not a static range. In fact **others** covers all values of type Integer because although D is constrained, nevertheless the constraints are not static.

Exercise 5.3

1
```
declare
   Sum: Integer := 0;
   I: Integer;
begin
   loop
      Get(I);
      exit when I < 0;
      Sum := Sum+I;
   end loop;
end;
```

2
```
declare
   Copy: Integer := N;
   Count: Integer := 0;
begin
   while Copy mod 2 = 0 loop
      Copy := Copy/2;
      Count := Count+1;
   end loop;
   ...
end;
```

3
```
declare
   G: Real := –Ln(Real(N));
begin
   for P in 1 .. N loop
      G := G+1.0/Real(P);
   end loop;
   ...
end;
```

Exercise 5.4

1   **for** I **in** 1 .. N **loop**
        for J **in** 1 .. M **loop**
            if condition_OK **then**
                I_Value := I;
                J_Value := J;
                goto Search;
            end if;
        end loop;
    end loop;

<<Search>>

This is not such a good solution because we have no guarantee that there may not be other places in the program from where a goto statement leads to the label. It is also a silly name for the label anyway – it ought to be Found!

Answers 6

Exercise 6.1

1   **declare**
        F: **array** (0 .. N) **of** Integer;
    begin
        F(0) := 0; F(1) := 1;
        for I **in** 2 .. F'Last **loop**
            F(I) := F(I−1) ₁ F(I−2);
        end loop;
        ...
    end;

2   **declare**
        Max_I: Integer := A'First(1);
        Max_J: Integer := A'First(2);
        Max: Real := A(Max_I, Max_J);
    begin
        for I **in** A'Range(1) **loop**
            for J **in** A'Range(2) **loop**
                if A(I, J) > Max **then**
                    Max := A(I, J);
                    Max_I := I;
                    Max_J := J;
                end if;

```
      end loop;
    end loop;
    – – Max_I, Max_J now contain the result
  end;
```

3 **declare**
```
      Days_In_Month: array (Month_Name) of Integer
          := (31, 28, 31, 30, 31, 30, 31, 31, 30, 31, 30, 31);
      End_Of_Month: Integer;
    begin
      if Year mod 4 = 0 then
        Days_In_Month(Feb) := 29;
      end if;
      End_Of_Month := Days_In_Month(Month);

      – – then as Exercise 5.1(1)

    end;
```

4 Yesterday: **constant array** (Day) of Day
```
        := (Sun, Mon, Tue, Wed, Thu, Fri, Sat);
```

5 Bor: **constant array** (Boolean, Boolean) of Boolean
```
        := ((False, True), (True, True));
```

6 Unit: **constant array** (1 .. 3, 1 .. 3) **of** Real
```
        := ((1.0, 0.0, 0.0),
            (0.0, 1.0, 0.0),
            (0.0, 0.0, 1.0));
```

Exercise 6.2

1 **type** Bbb **is array** (Boolean, Boolean) **of** Boolean;

2 **type** Ring5_Table **is array** (Ring5, Ring5) **of** Ring5;

Add: **constant** Ring5_Table
```
    := ((0, 1, 2, 3, 4),
        (1, 2, 3, 4, 0),
        (2, 3, 4, 0, 1),
        (3, 4, 0, 1, 2),
        (4, 0, 1, 2, 3));
```

Mult: **constant** Ring5_Table
```
    := ((0, 0, 0, 0, 0),
        (0, 1, 2, 3, 4),
        (0, 2, 4, 1, 3),
        (0, 3, 1, 4, 2),
        (0, 4, 3, 2, 1));
```

A, B, C, D: Ring5;

...

D := Mult(Add(A, B), C));

Exercise 6.3

1   Days_In_Month: **array** (Month_Name) **of** Integer
            := Month_Name'(Sep | Apr | Jun | Nov => 30, Feb => 28, **others** => 31);

2   Zero: **constant** Matrix := (1 .. N => (1 .. N => 0.0));

3   This cannot be done with the material at our disposal at the moment. See Exercise
        7.1(**6**).

4   **type** Molecule **is** (Methanol, Ethanol, Propanol, Butanol);
        type Atom **is** (H, C, O);

        Alcohol: **constant array** (Molecule, Atom) **of** Integer
          := (Methanol => (H => 4, C => 1, O => 1),
                Ethanol =>   (6,   2,   1),
                Propanol => (8,   3,   1),
                Butanol =>   (10,   4,   1));

    Note the danger in the above. We have used named notation in the first inner
    aggregate to act as a sort of heading but omitted it in the others to avoid clutter.
    However, if we had written H, C and O in other than positional order then it would
    have been very confusing because the positional aggregates would not have had the
    meaning suggested by the heading.

Exercise 6.4

1   Roman_To_Integer: **constant array** (Roman_Digit) **of** Integer
            := (1, 5, 10, 50, 100, 500, 1000);

2   **declare**
            V: Integer := 0;
        begin
          for I **in** R'Range **loop**
            if I /= R'Last **and then**
                Roman_To_Integer(R(I)) < Roman_To_Integer(R(I+1))
        then
                V := V – Roman_To_Integer(R(I));
            else
                V := V + Roman_To_Integer(R(I));
            end if;
          end loop;
            ...
        end;

    Note the use of **and then** to avoid attempting to access R(I+1) when I = R'Last.

Exercise 6.5

1   AOA(1 .. 2) := (AOA(2), AOA(1));

2   Farmyard: String_3_Array(1 .. 6)
      := ("pig", "cat", "dog", "cow", "rat", "ass");
    ...
    Farmyard(4)(1) := 's';

3   **if** R'Last >= 2 **and then** R(R'Last–1 .. R'Last) = "IV" **then**
    R(R'Last–1 .. R'Last) := "VI";
  end if;

Exercise 6.6

1   White, Blue, Yellow, Green, Red, Purple, Orange, Black

2   (a) Black   (b) Green   (c) Red

3   **not** (True **xor** True) = True
    not (True **xor** False) = False

the result follows.

4   An aggregate of length one must be named.

5   "123", "ABC", "Abc", "aBc", "abC", "abc"

6   (a) 1   (b) 5   (c) 5

We note therefore that & like **and**, **or** and **xor** is not strictly commutative.

7   (a) raises Constraint_Error
    (b) the bounds are 1 .. 10.

This is almost a trick question. In the first case the lower bound of the result of & is the lower bound of the left operand which is 6. The upper bound thus tries to be 15 but this exceeds the upper bound of T thereby raising Constraint_Error. In the second case the left operand of the first call of & is a single component and so the lower bound is the lower bound of the array index subtype which is 1; the rest then follows.

This bizarre behaviour does not occur in Ada 9X where & with a constrained type always produces a result with the lower bound equal to the lower bound of the index subtype. We might say that the result slides before being delivered.

Exercise 6.7

1   **declare**
   Days_In_Month: **array** (Month_Name) **of** Integer
     := Month_Name'(Sep | Apr | Jun | Nov => 30, Feb => 28, **others** => 31);
   End_Of_Month: Integer;
  begin
   if D.Year **mod** 4 = 0 **then**
    Days_In_Month(Feb) := 29;
   end if;
   End_Of_Month := Days_In_Month(D.Month);
   if D.Day /= End_Of_Month **then**
    D.Day := D.Day+1;
   else
    D.Day := 1;
    if D.Month /= Dec **then**
     D.Month := Month_Name'Succ(D.Month);
    else
     D.Month := Jan;
     D.Year := D.Year+1;
    end if;
   end if;
  end;

2   C1, C2, C3: Complex;

  (a) C3 := (C1.Rl+C2.Rl, C1.Im+C2.Im);
  (b) C3 := (C1.Rl*C2.Rl – C1.Im*C2.Im, C1.Rl*C2.Im + C1.Im*C2.Rl);

3   **declare**
   Index: Integer;
  begin
   for I **in** People'Range **loop**
    if People(I).Birth.Year >= 1950 **then**
     Index := I;
     exit;
    end if;
   end loop;
   – – we assume that there is such a person
  end;

Answers 7

Exercise 7.1

1   **function** Even(X: Integer) **return** Boolean **is**
  begin
   return X **mod** 2 = 0;
  end Even;

```
2   function Factorial(N: Natural) return Positive is
    begin
      if N = 0 then
        return 1;
      else
        return N*Factorial(N−1);
      end if;
    end Factorial;
```

```
3   function Outer(A, B: Vector) return Matrix is
      C: Matrix(A'Range, B'Range);
    begin
      for I in A'Range loop
        for J in B'Range loop
          C(I, J) := A(I)*B(J);
        end loop;
      end loop;
      return C;
    end Outer;
```

```
4   type Primary_Array is array (Integer range <>) of Primary;

    function Make_Colour(P: Primary_Array) return Colour is
      C: Colour := (F, F, F);
    begin
      for I in P'Range loop
        C(P(I)) := T;
      end loop;
      return C;
    end Make_Colour;
```

Note that multiple values are allowed so that

```
    Make_Colour((R, R, R)) = Red
```

```
5   function Value(R: Roman_Number) return Integer is
      V: Integer := 0;
    begin
      for I in R'Range loop
        if I /= R'Last and then
           Roman_To_Integer(R(I)) < Roman_To_Integer(R(I+1))
    then
          V := V − Roman_To_Integer(R(I));
        else
          V := V + Roman_To_Integer(R(I));
        end if;
      end loop;
      return V;
    end Value;
```

6   **function** Make_Unit(N: Natural) **return** Matrix **is**
        M: Matrix(1 .. N, 1 .. N);
     begin
        for I **in** 1 .. N **loop**
           for J **in** 1 .. N **loop**
              if I = J **then**
                 M(I, J) := 1.0;
              else
                 M(I, J) := 0.0;
              end if;
           end loop;
        end loop;
        return M;
     end Make_Unit;

We can then declare

Unit: **constant** Matrix := Make_Unit(N);

7   **function** GCD(X, Y: Natural) **return** Natural **is**
     begin
        if Y = 0 **then**
           return X;
        else
           return GCD(Y, X **mod** Y);
        end if;
     end GCD;

or

     function GCD(X, Y: Natural) **return** Natural **is**
        XX: Integer := X;
        YY: Integer := Y;
        ZZ: Integer;
     begin
        while YY /= 0 **loop**
           ZZ := XX **mod** YY;
           XX := YY;
           YY := ZZ;
        end loop;
        return XX;
     end GCD;

Note that X and Y have to be copied because formal parameters behave as constants.

8   **function** Inner(A, B: Vector) **return** Real **is**
        Result: Real := 0.0;
     begin
        if A'Length /= B'Length **then**
           raise Constraint_Error;
        end if;

```
        for I in A'Range loop
           Result := Result + A(I)*B(I+B'First–A'First);
        end loop;
        return Result;
     end Inner;
```

Exercise 7.2

1 ```
   function "<" (X, Y: Roman_Number) return Boolean is
   begin
      return Value(X) < Value(Y);
   end "<";
   ```

2  ```
   function "+" (X, Y: Complex) return Complex is
   begin
      return (X.RI + Y.RI, X.Im + Y.Im);
   end "+";
   ```

   ```
   function "*" (X, Y: Complex) return Complex is
   begin
      return (X.RI*Y.RI – X.Im*Y.Im, X.RI*Y.Im + X.Im*Y.RI);
   end "*";
   ```

3 ```
   function "<" (P: Primary; C: Colour) return Boolean is
   begin
      return C(P);
   end "<";
   ```

4  ```
   function "<=" (X, Y: Colour) return Boolean is
   begin
      return (X and Y) = X;
   end "<=";
   ```

5 ```
   function "<" (X, Y: Date) return Boolean is
   begin
      if X.Year /= Y.Year then
         return X.Year < Y.Year;
      elsif X.Month /= Y.Month then
         return X.Month < Y.Month;
      else
         return X.Day < Y.Day;
      end if;
   end "<";
   ```

*Exercise 7.3*

1  ```
   procedure Swap(X, Y: in out Real) is
      T: Real;
   begin
      T := X; X := Y; Y := T;
   end Swap;
   ```

2   **procedure** Rev(X: **in out** Vector) **is**
         R: Vector(X'Range);
      begin
         for I **in** X'Range **loop**
            R(I) := X(X'First + X'Last − I);
         end loop;
         X := R;
      end Rev;

or maybe

      procedure Rev(X: **in out** Vector) **is**
      begin
         for I **in** X'First .. X'First + X'Length/2 − 1 **loop**
            Swap(X(I), X(X'First + X'Last − I));
         end loop;
      end Rev;

This procedure can be applied to an array R of type Row by

Rev(Vector(R));

3   The fragment is erroneous because the outcome depends upon whether the parameter
      is passed by copy or by reference. If it is copied then A(1) ends up as 2.0; if it is
      passed by reference then A(1) ends up as 4.0. This is an example of a bounded error in
      Ada 9X.

4

		calling mode (actual)		
		in	**in out**	**out**
called mode (formal)	**in**	✓	✓	✕
	in out	✕	✓	✕
	out	✕	✓	✓

Remember that an **out** parameter can be read in Ada 9X and therefore this table
needs suitable modification.

Exercise 7.4

1   **function** Add(X: Integer; Y: Integer := 1) **return** Integer **is**
      begin
         return X + Y;
      end Add;

The following 6 calls are equivalent

```
Add(N)
Add(N, 1)
Add(X => N, Y => 1)
Add(X => N)
Add(N, Y => 1)
Add(Y => 1, X => N)
```

2   **function** Favourite_Spirit **return** Spirit **is**
    begin
        case Today **is**
            when Mon .. Fri => **return** Gin;
            when Sat | Sun => **return** Vodka;
        end case;
    end Favourite_Spirit;

```
procedure Dry_Martini(Base: Spirit := Favourite_Spirit;
                      How: Style := On_The_Rocks;
                      Plus: Trimming := Olive);
```

This example illustrates that defaults are evaluated each time they are required and can therefore be changed from time to time.

Exercise 7.5

1   The named form of call

Sell(C => Jersey);

is unambiguous since the formal parameter names are different.

Answers 8

Exercise 8.1

1   **package** Random **is**
        Modulus: **constant** := 2**13;
        subtype Small **is** Integer **range** 0 .. Modulus;
        procedure Init(Seed: Small);
        function Next **return** Small;
    end;

```
package body Random is
   Multiplier: constant := 5**5;
   X: Small;

   procedure Init(Seed: Small) is
   begin
    X := Seed;
   end Init;

   function Next return Small is
   begin
      X := X*Multiplier mod Modulus;
      return X;
   end Next;

end Random;
```

2
```
package Complex_Numbers is
   type Complex is
      record
         Rl, Im: Real := 0.0;
      end record;

   I: constant Complex := (0.0, 1.0);

   function "+" (X: Complex) return Complex; – – unary +
   function "-" (X: Complex) return Complex; – – unary –

   function "+" (X, Y: Complex) return Complex;
   function "–" (X, Y: Complex) return Complex;
   function "*" (X, Y: Complex) return Complex;
   function "/" (X, Y: Complex) return Complex;
end;

package body Complex_Numbers is

   function "+" (X: Complex) return Complex is
   begin
      return X;
   end "+";

   function "–" (X: Complex) return Complex is
   begin
      return (–X.Rl, –X.Im);
   end "+";

   function "+" (X, Y: Complex) return Complex is
   begin
```

```
   return (X.RI + Y.RI, X.Im + Y.Im);
end "+";

function "–" (X, Y: Complex) return Complex is
begin
   return (X.RI – Y.RI, X.Im – Y.Im);
end "–";

function "*" (X, Y: Complex) return Complex is
begin
   return (X.RI*Y.RI – X.Im*Y.Im, X.RI*Y.Im + X.Im*Y.RI);
end "*";

function "/" (X, Y: Complex) return Complex is
   D: Real := Y.RI**2+Y.Im**2;
begin
   return ((X.RI*Y.RI + X.Im*Y.Im)/D,
           (X.Im*Y.RI – X.RI*Y.Im)/D);
end "/";

end Complex_Numbers
```

Exercise 8.2

1

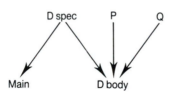

There are 18 different possible orders of compilation.

Exercise 8.3

1

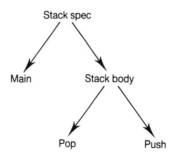

There are 18 different possible orders of compilation.

Exercise 8.5

1   **function** Monday **return** Diurnal.Day **renames** Diurnal.Mon;

2   This cannot be done because Next_Work_Day is of an anonymous type.

3   Pets: String_3_Array **renames** Farmyard(2 .. 3);

Note that the bounds of Pets are 2 and 3.

Answers 9

Exercise 9.1

1   Inside the package body we could write

```
function "*" (X: Real; Y: Complex) return Complex is
begin
   return (X*Y.RI, X*Y.Im);
end "*";
```

but outside we could only write

```
function "*" (X: Real; Y: Complex) return Complex is
   use Complex_Numbers;
begin
   return Cons(X, 0.0)*Y;
end "*";
```

and similarly with the operands interchanged.

2   **declare**
```
   C, D: Complex_Numbers.Complex;
   R, S: Real;
begin
   C := Complex_Numbers.Cons(1.5, –6.0);
   D := Complex_Numbers."+" (C, Complex_Numbers.I);
   R := Complex_Numbers.RI_Part(D) + 6.0;
   ...
end;
```

3   **package** Rational_Numbers **is**
```
   type Rational is private;

   function "+" (X: Rational) return Rational;  – – unary +
   function "–" (X: Rational) return Rational;  – – unary –

   function "+" (X, Y: Rational) return Rational;
   function "–" (X, Y: Rational) return Rational;
   function "*" (X, Y: Rational) return Rational;
   function "/" (X, Y: Rational) return Rational;
```

```
      function "/" (X: Integer; Y: Positive) return Rational;
      function Numerator(R: Rational) return Integer;
      function Denominator(R: Rational) return Positive;

   private
      type Rational is
         record
            Num: Integer := 0;   - - numerator
            Den: Positive := 1;  - - denominator
         end record;
   end;

   package body Rational_Numbers is

      function Normal(R: Rational) return Rational is
         - - cancel common factors
         G: Positive := GCD(abs R.Num, R.Den);
      begin
         return (R.Num/G, R.Den/G);
      end Normal;

      function "+" (X: Rational) return Rational is
      begin
         return X;
      end "+";

      function "-" (X: Rational) return Rational is
      begin
         return (-X.Num, X.Den);
      end "-";

      function "+" (X, Y: Rational) return Rational is
      begin
         return Normal((X.Num*Y.Den + Y.Num*X.Den, X.Den*Y.Den));
      end "+";

      function "-" (X, Y: Rational) return Rational is
      begin
         return Normal((X.Num*Y.Den - Y.Num*X.Den, X.Den*Y.Den));
      end "-";

      function "*" (X, Y: Rational) return Rational is
      begin
         return Normal((X.Num*Y.Num, X.Den*Y.Den));
      end "*";

      function "/" (X, Y: Rational) return Rational is
      begin
         return Normal((X.Num*Y.Den, X.Den*Y.Num));
      end "/";
```

```
function "/" (X: Integer; Y: Positive) return Rational is
begin
   return Normal((X, Y));
end "/";

function Numerator(R: Rational) return Integer is
begin
   return R.Num;
end Numerator;

function Denominator(R: Rational) return Positive is
begin
   return R.Den;
end Denominator;

end Rational_Numbers;
```

4 Although the parameter base types are both Integer and therefore the same as for predefined integer division, nevertheless the result types are different. The result types are considered in the hiding rules for functions. See Section 7.5.

Exercise 9.2

1 ```
   package Stacks is
      type Stack is limited private;
      Empty: constant Stack;

      ...
   private

      ...
      Empty: constant Stack := ((1 .. Max => 0), 0);
   end;
   ```

Note that Empty has to be initialized because it is a **constant** despite the fact that Top which is the only component whose value is of interest is automatically initialized anyway.

2  ```
   function Empty(S: Stack) return Boolean is
   begin
      return S.Top = 0;
   end Empty;

   function Full(S: Stack) return Boolean is
   begin
      return S.Top = Max;
   end Full;
   ```

3 ```
   function "=" (S, T: Stack) return Boolean is
   begin
      return S.S(1 .. S.Top) = T.S(1 .. T.Top);
   end "=";
   ```
   ```

4
```
function "=" (A, B: Stack_Array) return Boolean is
begin
   if A'Length /= B'Length then
      return False;
   end if;
   for I in A'Range loop
      if A(I) /= B(I + B'First – A'First) then
         return False;
      end if;
   end loop;
   return True;
end "=";
```

Note that this uses the redefined = (via /=) applying to the type Stack. This pattern of definition of array equality clearly applies to any type. Beware that we cannot use slice comparison (as in the previous answer) because that always uses predefined equality – surprise, surprise!

5
```
procedure Assign(S: in Stack; T: out Stack) is
begin
   T.Top := S.Top;
   for I in 1 .. S.Top loop
      T.S(I) := S.S(I);
   end loop;
end Assign;
```

The loop could be replaced by the slice assignment

```
T.S(1 .. S.Top) := S.S(1 .. S.Top);
```

6
```
package Stacks is
   type Stack is private;
   procedure Push(S: in out Stack; X: in Integer);
   procedure Pop(S: in out Stack; X: out Integer);
private
   Max: constant := 100;
   Dummy: constant := 0;
   type Integer_Vector is array (Integer range < >) of Integer;
   type Stack is
      record
         S: Integer_Vector(1 .. Max) := (1 .. Max => Dummy);
         Top: Integer range 0 .. Max := 0;
      end record;
end;

package body Stacks is
   procedure Push(S: in out Stack; X: in Integer) is
   begin
      S.Top := S.Top+1;
      S.S(S.Top) := X;
   end;
```

```
   procedure Pop(S: in out Stack; X: out Integer) is
   begin
      X := S.S(S.Top);
      S.S(S.Top) := Dummy;
      S.Top := S.Top-1;
   end;
end Stacks;
```

Note the use of Dummy as default value for unused components of the stack.

Exercise 9.3

1
```
   private
      Max: constant := 1000;  -- no of accounts
      subtype Key_Code is Integer range 0 .. Max;
      type Key is
         record
            Code: Key_Code := 0;
         end record;
   end;

   package body Bank is
      Balance: array (Key_Code range 1 .. Key_Code'Last) of Money := (others => 0);
      Free: array (Key_Code range 1 .. Key_Code'Last) of Boolean := (others => True);

      function Valid(K: Key) return Boolean is
      begin
         return K.Code /= 0;
      end Valid;

      procedure Open_Account(K: in out Key; M: in Money) is
      begin
         if K.Code = 0 then
            for I in Free'Range loop
               if Free(I) then
                  Free(I) := False;
                  Balance(I) := M;
                  K.Code := I;
                  return;
               end if;
            end loop;
         end if;
      end Open_Account;

      procedure Close_Account(K: in out Key; M: out Money) is
      begin
         if Valid(K) then
            M := Balance(K.Code);
            Free(K.Code) := True;
```

```
        K.Code := 0;
    end if;
end Close_Account;

procedure Deposit(K: in Key; M: in Money) is
begin
    if Valid(K) then
        Balance(K.Code) := Balance(K.Code)+M;
    end if;
end Deposit;

procedure Withdraw(K: in out Key; M: in out Money) is
begin
    if Valid(K) then
        if M > Balance(K.Code) then
            Close_Account(K, M);
        else
            Balance(K.Code) := Balance(K.Code)-M;
        end if;
    end if;
end Withdraw;

function Statement(K: Key) return Money is
begin
    if Valid(K) then
        return Balance(K.Code);
    end if;
end Statement;
```

```
end Bank;
```

Various alternative formulations are possible. It might be neater to declare a record type representing an account containing the two components Free and Balance.

Note that the function Statement will raise Program_Error if the key is not valid. Alternatively we could return a dummy value of zero but it might be better to raise our own exception as described in the next chapter.

2   An alternative formulation which represents the home savings box could be that where the limited private type is given by

```
type Box is
    record
        Code: Box_Code := 0;
        Balance: Money;
    end record;
```

In this case the money is kept in the variable declared by the user. The bank only knows which boxes have been issued but does not know how much is in a particular box. The details are left to the reader.

3   Since the parameter is of a private type, it is not defined whether the parameter is passed by copy or by reference. If it is passed by copy then the call of Action will succeed whereas if it is passed by reference it will not. The program is therefore erroneous. However this does not seem a very satisfactory answer and might be considered a loophole in the design of Ada.

A slight improvement would be for Action to check (via Valid say) whether the passed key is free or not by reference to the array Free but this would not be any protection once the key were reissued. However, a foolproof solution can be devised using access types which will be described in Chapter 11.

4   He is thwarted because of the rule mentioned in the previous section that, outside the defining package, a procedure cannot be declared having an **out** parameter of a limited type. The purpose of this rule is precisely to prevent just this kind of violation of privacy. (As a minor aside note that in any case the parameter may be passed by reference.)

In Ada 9X we can have an **out** parameter but if any components have defaults it is copied in (like access values) just to be safe.

Answers 10

Exercise 10.1

1   ```
procedure Quadratic(A, B, C: in Real;
            Root_1, Root_2: out Real; OK: out Boolean) is
   D: constant Real := B**2 – 4.0*A*C;
begin
   Root_1 := (–B+Sqrt(D)) / (2.0*A);
   Root_2 := (–B-Sqrt(D)) / (2.0*A);
   OK := True;
exception
   when Constraint_Error =>
      OK := False;
end Quadratic;
```

2   ```
function Factorial(N: Integer) return Integer is

   function Slave(N: Natural) return Positive is
   begin
      if N = 0 then
         return 1;
      else
         return N*Slave(N–1);
      end if;
   end Slave;

begin
   return Slave(N);
exception
   when Constraint_Error | Storage_Error | Numeric_Error =>
      return –1;
end Factorial;
```

Exercise 10.2

```
1   package Random is
       Bad: exception;
       Modulus: constant := 2**13;
       subtype Small is Integer range 0 .. Modulus;
       procedure Init(Seed: Small);
       function Next return Small;
    end;

    package body Random is
       Multiplier: constant := 5**5;
       X: Small;

       procedure Init(Seed: Small) is
       begin
         if Seed mod 2 = 0 then
           raise Bad;
         end if;
         X := Seed;
       end Init;

       function Next return Small is
       begin
         X := X*Multiplier mod Modulus;
         return X;
       end Next;

    end Random;

2   function Factorial(N: Integer) return Integer is

       function Slave(N: Natural) return Positive is
       begin
        if N = 0 then
          return 1;
        else
          return N*Slave(N–1);
         end if;
       end Slave;

    begin
       return Slave(N);
    exception
       when Numeric_Error | Storage_Error =>
         raise Constraint_Error;
    end Factorial;
```

3 **function** "+" (X, Y: Vector) **return** Vector **is**
　　　R: Vector(X'Range);
　　begin
　　　if X'Length /= Y'Length **then**
　　　　raise Constraint_Error;
　　　end if;
　　　for I **in** X'Range **loop**
　　　　R(I) := X(I) + Y(I + Y'First − X'First);
　　　end loop;
　　　return R;
　　end "+";

4 No. A malevolent user could write **raise** Stack.Error; outside the package. It would be nice if the language provided some sort of 'private' exception that could be handled but not raised explicitly outside its defining package.

Exercise 10.3

1 Three checks are required. The one inserted by the user plus the two for the assignment to S(Top) which cannot be avoided since we can say little about the value of Top (except that it is not equal to Max). So this is the worst of all worlds thus emphasizing the need to give appropriate constraints.

Exercise 10.4

1 **package** Bank **is**
　　　Alarm: **exception**;
　　　subtype Money **is** Natural;
　　　type Key **is limited private**;
　　　− − as before
　　private
　　　− − as before
　　end;

　　package body Bank **is**
　　　Balance: **array** (Key_Code **range** 1 .. Key_Code'Last) **of** Money := (**others** => 0);
　　　Free: **array** (Key_Code **range** 1 .. Key_Code'Last) **of** Boolean := (**others** => True);

　　　function Valid(K: Key) **return** Boolean **is**
　　　begin
　　　 return K.Code /= 0;
　　　end Valid;

　　　procedure Validate(K: Key) **is**
　　　begin
　　　　if not Valid(K) **then**

　　　　　raise Alarm;
　　　　end if;
　　　end Validate;

```ada
procedure Open_Account(K: in out Key; M: in Money) is
begin
   if K.Code = 0 then
      for I in Free'Range loop
         if Free(I) then
            Free(I) := False;
            Balance(I) := M;
            K.Code := I;
            return;
         end if;
      end loop;
   else
      raise Alarm;
   end if;
end Open_Account;

procedure Close_Account(K: in out Key; M: out Money) is
begin
   Validate(K);
   M := Balance(K.Code);
   Free(K.Code) := True;
   K.Code := 0;
end Close_Account;

procedure Deposit(K: in Key; M: in Money) is
begin
   Validate(K);
   Balance(K.Code) := Balance(K.Code)+M;
end Deposit;

procedure Withdraw(K: in out Key; M: in out Money) is
begin
   Validate(K);
   if M > Balance(K.Code) then
      raise Alarm;
   else
      Balance(K.Code) := Balance(K.Code)−M;
   end if;
end Withdraw;

function Statement(K: Key) return Money is
begin
   Validate(K);
   return Balance(K.Code);
end Statement;

end Bank;
```

For convenience we have declared a procedure Validate which raises the alarm in most cases. The Alarm is also explicitly raised if we attempt to overdraw but as remarked in the text we cannot also close the account. An attempt to open an account with a key which is in use also causes Alarm to be raised. We do not however raise the Alarm if the bank runs out of accounts but have left it to the user to check with a call of Valid that he was issued a genuine key; the rationale is that it is not the user's fault if the bank runs out of keys.

2   Suppose N is 2. Then on the third call, P is not entered but the exception is raised and handled at the second level. The handler again calls P without success but this time, since an exception raised in a handler is not handled there but propagated up a level, the exception is handled at the first level. The pattern then repeats but the exception is finally propagated out of the first level to the originating call. In all there are three successful calls and four unsuccessful ones. The following diagram may help.

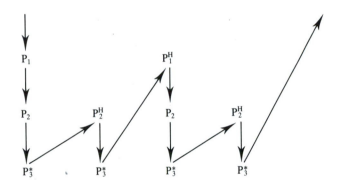

An * indicates an unsuccessful call, H indicates a call from a handler.
    More generally suppose C_n is the total number of calls for the case $N = n$. Then by induction

$$C_{n+1} = 2C_n + 1$$

with the initial condition $C_0 = 1$ since in the case $N = 0$ it is obvious that there is only one call which fails. It follows that the total number of calls C_N is $2^{N+1} - 1$. Of these 2^N are unsuccessful and $2^N - 1$ are successful.
    I am grateful to Bob Bishop for this example.

Answers 11

Exercise 11.1

1   Trace((M'Length, M))

If the two dimensions of M were not equal then Constraint_Error would be raised. Note that the lower bounds of M do not have to be 1; all that matters is that the number of components in each dimension is the same.

```
2   package Stacks is
        type Stack(Max: Natural) is limited private;
        Empty: constant Stack;
        ...
    private
        type Integer_Vector is array (Integer range <>) of Integer;
        type Stack(Max: Natural) is
            record
                S: Integer_Vector(1 .. Max);
                Top: Integer := 0;
            end record;
        Empty: constant Stack(0) := (0, (others => 0), 0);
    end;
```

We have naturally chosen to make Empty a stack whose value of Max is zero. Note that the function "=" only compares the parts of the stacks which are in use. Thus we can write S = Empty to test whether a stack S is empty irrespective of its value of Max.

```
3   function Full(S: Stack) return Boolean is
    begin
        return S.Top = S.Max;
    end Full;
```

```
4   S: constant Square := (N, Make_Unit(N));
```

Exercise 11.2

```
1   Z: Polynomial := (0, (0 => 0));
```

The named notation has to be used because the array has only one component.

```
2   function "*" (P, Q: Polynomial) return Polynomial is
        R: Polynomial(P.N+Q.N) := (P.N+Q.N, (others => 0));
    begin
        for I in P.A'Range loop
            for J in Q.A'Range loop
                R.A(I+J) := R.A(I+J) + P.A(I)*Q.A(J);
            end loop;
        end loop;
        return R;
    end "*";
```

It is largely a matter of taste whether we write P.A'Range rather than 0 .. P.N.

```
3   function "−" (P, Q: Polynomial) return Polynomial is
        Size: Integer;
    begin
        if P.N > Q.N then
```

```
        Size := P.N;
      else
        Size := Q.N;
      end if;

      declare
        R: Polynomial(Size);
      begin
        for I in 0 .. P.N loop
          R.A(I) := P.A(I);
        end loop;
        for I in P.N+1 .. R.N loop
          R.A(I) := 0;
        end loop;
        for I in 0 .. Q.N loop
          R.A(I) := R.A(I)–Q.A(I);
        end loop;
        return Normal(R);
      end;
  end "–";
```

There are various alternative ways of writing this function. We could initialize R.A by using slice assignments

```
    R.A(0 .. P.N) := P.A;
    R.A(P.N+1 .. R.N) := (P.N+1 .. R.N => 0);
```

or even more succinctly by

```
    R.A := P.A & (P.N+1 .. R.N => 0);
```

4   ```
     procedure Truncate(P: in out Polynomial) is
     begin
       if P'Constrained then
         raise Truncate_Error;
       else
         P := (P.N–1, P.A(0 .. P.N–1));
       end if;
     end Truncate;
     ```

5    Any unconstrained Polynomial could then include an array whose range is 0 .. Integer'Last. This will take a lot of space. Since most implementations are likely to adopt the strategy of setting aside the maximum possible space for an unconstrained record it is thus wise to keep the maximum to a practical limit by the use of a suitable subtype such as Index.

6    ```
     function "&" (X, Y: V_String) return V_String is
     begin
       return (X.N + Y.N, X.S & Y.S);
     end "&";
     ```

7   **function** "+" (V: V_String) **return** String **is**
     begin
        return V.S;
     end "+";

and then Put(+Zoo(3)); will output the string "camel".

Exercise 11.3

1   **procedure** Shave(P: **in out** Person) **is**
     begin
        if P.Sex = Female **then**
           raise Shaving_Error;
        else
           P.Bearded := False;
        end if;
     end Shave;

2   **procedure** Sterilize(M: **in out** Mutant) **is**
     begin
        if M'Constrained **and** M.Sex /= Neuter **then**
           raise Sterilize_Error;
        else
           M := (Neuter, M.Birth);
        end if;
     end Sterilize;

3   **type** Figure **is** (Circle, Square, Rectangle);

     type Object(Shape: Figure) **is**
        record
           case Shape **is**
              when Circle =>
                 Radius: Real;
              when Square =>
                 Side: Real;
              when Rectangle =>
                 Length, Breadth: Real;
           end case;
        end record;

4   **function** Area(X: Object) **return** Real **is**
     begin
        case X.Shape **is**
           when Circle =>
              return Pi*X.Radius**2;
           when Square =>
              return X.Side**2;
           when Rectangle =>

```
      return X.Length*X.Breadth;
   end case;
end Area;
```

Note the similarity between the case statement in the function Area and the variant part of the type Object.

5 **function** F(N: Integer) **return** Integer_Vector;

```
type Polynomial(N: Index := 0) is
   record
      A: Integer_Vector(0 .. N) := F(N);
   end record;

function F(N: Integer) return Integer_Vector is
      R: Integer_Vector(0 .. N);
begin
   for I in 0 .. N–1 loop
      R(I) := 0;
   end loop;
   R(N) := 1;
   return R;
end;
```

In order to declare both the function and the type in the same declarative part we have to give the function specification on its own first. This is because a type declaration may not follow a body as explained in Section 7.6. It does not matter that F is referred to before its body is elaborated provided that it is not actually called. Thus if we declared a polynomial (without an initial value) before the body of F then Program_Error would be raised.

Remember that the restriction on the order of declarations does not apply in Ada 9X.

6 If the user declared a constrained key with a nonzero discriminant thus

```
   K: Key(7);
```

then he will have bypassed Get_Key and be able to call the procedure Action without authority. Note also that if he calls Return_Key then Constraint_Error will be raised on the attempt to set the code to zero because the key is constrained.

Hence forged keys can be recognized since they are constrained and so we could rewrite Valid to check for this

```
   function Valid(K: Key) return Boolean is
   begin
      return not K'Constrained and then K.Code /= 0;
   end Valid;
```

We use the short circuit form so that we only test K.Code when we are sure it exists. We must also insert calls of Valid into Get_Key and Return_Key.

7 **package** Rational_Polynomials **is**
    Max: **constant** := 10;
    subtype Index **is** Integer **range** 0 .. Max;
    type Rational_Polynomial(N, D: Index := 0) **is private**;

    function "+" (X: Rational_Polynomial) **return** Rational_Polynomial;
    function "−" (X: Rational_Polynomial) **return** Rational_Polynomial;

    function "+" (X, Y: Rational_Polynomial) **return** Rational_Polynomial;
    function "−" (X, Y: Rational_Polynomial) **return** Rational_Polynomial;
    function "*" (X, Y: Rational_Polynomial) **return** Rational_Polynomial;
    function "/" (X, Y: Rational_Polynomial) **return** Rational_Polynomial;

    function "/" (X, Y: Polynomial) **return** Rational_Polynomial;
    function Numerator(R: Rational_Polynomial) **return** Polynomial;
    function Denominator(R: Rational_Polynomial) **return** Polynomial;

private

    function Zero(N: Index) **return** Polynomial;
    function One(N: Index) **return** Polynomial;

    type Rational_Polynomial(N, D: Index := 0) **is**
        record
            Num: Polynomial(N) := Zero(N);
            Den: Polynomial(D) := One(D);
        end record;
end;

The functions Zero and One are required in order to supply appropriate safe initial values. It is not possible to write a suitable aggregate for One although it is for Zero. Nevertheless the function Zero is written for symmetry

    function Zero(N: Index) **return** Polynomial **is**
    begin
        return (N, (0 .. N => 0));   − − all coefficients zero
    end;

    function One(N: Index) **return** Polynomial **is**
        R: Polynomial(N) := Zero(N);
    begin
        R.A(0) := 1;   − − coefficient of x^0 is one
        return R;
    end;

We make no attempt to impose any special language constraint on the denominator as we did in the type Rational where the denominator has subtype Positive.

Exercise 11.4

1   ```
     procedure Append(First: in out Link; Second: in Link) is
        L: Link := First;
     begin
        if First = null then
           First := Second;
        else
           while L.Next /= null loop
              L := L.Next;
           end loop;
           L.Next := Second;
        end if;
     end Append;
     ```

2    ```
     function Size(T: Tree) return Integer is
     begin
        if T = null then
           return 0;
        else
           return Size(T.Left)+Size(T.Right)+1;
        end if;
     end Size;
     ```

3   ```
     function Copy(T: Tree) return Tree is
     begin
        if T = null then
           return null;
        else
           return new Node'(T.Value, Copy(T.Left), Copy(T.Right));
        end if;
     end Copy;
     ```

*Exercise 11.5*

1    ```
     procedure Push(S: in out Stack; X: in Integer) is
     begin
        S := new Cell'(X, S);
     exception
        when Storage_Error =>
           raise Error;
     end;
     ```

     ```
     procedure Pop(S: in out Stack; X: out Integer) is
     begin
        if S = null then
           raise Error;
        else
           X := S.Value;
           S := S.Next;
        end if;
     end;
     ```

2   **procedure** Push(S: **in out** Stack; X: **in** Integer) **is**
```
   procedure Push(S: in out Stack; X: in Integer) is
   begin
      S.List := new Cell'(X, S.List);
   end;

   procedure Pop(S: in out Stack; X: out Integer) is
   begin
      X := S.List.Value;
      S.List := S.List.Next;
   end;

   function "=" (S, T: Stack) return Boolean is
      SI: Link := S.List;
      TI: Link := T.List;
   begin
      while SI /= null and TI /= null loop
         SI := SI.Next;
         TI := TI.Next;
         if SI.Value /= TI.Value then
            return False;
         end if;
      end loop;
      return SI = TI;
   end "=";
```

3   **package** Queues **is**
```
   package Queues is
      Empty: exception;
      type Queue is limited private;
      procedure Join(Q: in out Queue; X: in Item);
      procedure Remove(Q: in out Queue; X: out Item);
      function Length(Q: Queue) return Integer;
   private
      type Cell;
      type Link is access Cell;
      type Cell is
         record
            Data: Item;
            Next: Link;
         end record;
      type Queue is
         record
            Count: Integer := 0;
            First, Last: Link;
         end record;
   end;

   package body Queues is

      procedure Join(Q: in out Queue; X: in Item) is
         L: Link;
```

```
  begin
     L := new Cell'(Data => X, Next => null);
     Q.Last.Next := L;
     Q.Last := L;
     Q.Count := Q.Count+1;
  end Join;

  procedure Remove(Q: in out Queue; X: out Item) is
  begin
     if Q.Count = 0 then
        raise Empty;
     end if;
     X := Q.First.Data;
     Q.First := Q.First.Next;
     Q.Count := Q.Count-1;
  end Remove;

  function Length(Q: Queue) return Integer is
  begin
     return Q.Count;
  end Length;

end Queues;
```

Exercise 11.6

```
1   function Heir(P: Person_Name) return Person_Name is
       Mother: Womans_Name;
    begin
       if P.Sex = Male then
          Mother := P.Wife;
       else
          Mother := P;
       end if;
       if Mother = null or else Mother.First_Child = null then
          return null;
       end if;
       declare
          Child: Person_Name := Mother.First_Child;
       begin
          while Child.Sex = Female loop
             if Child.Next_Sibling = null then
                return Mother.First_Child;
             end if;
             Child := Child.Next_Sibling;
          end loop;
          return Child;
       end;
    end Heir;
```

2 **procedure** Divorce(W: Womans_Name) **is**
   begin
      if W.Husband = **null or** W.First_Child /= **null then**
         return;   − − divorce not possible
      end if;
      W.Husband.Wife := **null**;
      W.Husband := **null**;
   end Divorce;

3 **procedure** Marry(Bride: Womans_Name; Groom: Mans_Name) **is**
   begin
      if Bride.Father = Groom.Father **then**
         raise Incest;
      end if;
      − − then as before
   end Marry;

Note that there is no need to check for marriage to a parent because the check for bigamy will detect this anyway. Our model does not allow remarriage.

4 **function** No_Of_Children(P: Person_Name) **return** Integer **is**
      Mother: Womans_Name;
   begin
      if P.Sex = Male **then**
         Mother := P.Wife;
      else
         Mother := P;
      end if;
      if Mother = **null then**
         return 0;
      end if;
      declare
         Child: Person_Name := Mother.First_Child;
         Count: Integer := 0;
      begin
         while Child /= **null loop**
            Count := Count+1;
            Child := Child.Next_Sibling;
         end loop;
         return Count;
      end;
   end No_Of_Children;

   function No_Of_Siblings(P: Person_Name) **return** Integer **is**
   begin
      return No_Of_Children(P.Father)−1;
   end No_Of_Siblings;

```
.function No_Of_Grandchildren(P: Person_Name) return  Integer is
   Mother: Womans_Name;

begin
   if P.Sex = Male then
      Mother := P.Wife;
   else
      Mother := P;
   end if;
   if Mother = null then
      return 0;
   end if;
   declare
      Child: Person_Name := Mother.First_Child;
      Count: Integer := 0;
   begin
      while Child /= null loop
         Count := Count + No_Of_Children(Child);
         Child := Child.Next_Sibling;
      end loop;
      return Count;
   end;
end No_Of_Grandchildren;

function No_Of_Cousins(P: Person_Name) return Integer is
begin
   return No_Of_Grandchildren(P.Father.Father)
        + No_Of_Grandchildren(P.Father.Wife.Father)
        – 2 * No_Of_Children(P.Father);
end No_Of_Cousins;
```

We and our siblings get counted twice among the grandchildren and have to be
deducted. We have assumed no intermarriage between our maternal and paternal
aunts and uncles. If there is then some of our cousins may have been counted twice as
well. We leave further contemplation of this complication to the reader.

Exercise 11.7

1
```
package P is
   type Length is new Real;
   type Area is new Real;
   function "*" (X, Y: Length) return Length;
   function "*" (X, Y: Length) return Area;
   function "*" (X, Y: Area) return Area;
end;

package body P is

   function "*" (X, Y: Length) return Length is
   begin
      raise Constraint_Error;
   end "*";
```

```
function "*" (X, Y: Length) return Area is
begin
 return Area(Real(X)*Real(Y));
end "*";

function "*" (X, Y: Area) return Area is
begin
 raise Constraint_Error;
end "*";

end P;
```

Answers 12

Exercise 12.1

1 P: on A: Integer, on B: Short_Integer
   Q: on A: Long_Integer, on B: Integer
   R: on A: cannot be implemented, on B: Long_Integer

2 No, the only critical case is type Q on machine A. Changing to one's complement changes the range of Integer to

   −32767 .. +32767

   and so only Integer'First is altered.

3 (a) Integer
   (b) illegal – type conversion must be explicit
   (c) My_Integer'Base
   (d) Integer
   (e) universal integer
   (f) My_Integer'Base

4 **type** Longest_Integer **is range** System.Min_Int ..
   System.Max_Int;

Exercise 12.2

1 (a) illegal
   (b) Integer
   (c) universal real
   (d) Integer
   (e) universal real
   (f) universal integer

2 R: **constant** := N*1.0;

Exercise 12.3

1 $^1/_{16}$

2   Real has B=18.
      The values of the variables P and Q are model numbers. However, the result P/Q = $^2/_3$ is not. The nearest model numbers can be determined by considering $^2/_3$ as a binary recurring fraction

   0.10101010...

The model number below (L say) is obtained by truncating after 18 digits. The difference between $^2/_3$ and L is clearly $^2/_3$ shifted down by 18 places. So L is $^2/_3(1 - 2^{-18})$. The model number above is obtained by adding 2^{-18} to L. Hence P/Q lies in the model interval

   $^2/_3(1 - 2^{-18}), \ ^2/_3(1 + 2^{-19})$

The mathematical bounds for (P/Q)*Q are obtained by multiplying the bounds of this interval by 3. The lower bound is then $2(1 - 2^{-18})$ and this is a model number. The upper bound is
$2(1 + 2^{-19})$ but this is not a model number; the next model number above is $2(1 + 2^{-17})$. So the final model interval in which R must lie is

   $2(1 - 2^{-18}), \ 2(1 + 2^{-17})$

3   In this example P and Q are numbers of type universal real and since the operators * and / apply to the type universal real we might think that the expression (P/Q)*Q is always of type universal real and thus evaluated exactly at compilation. However, remember that implicit conversion of the universal types is only performed in the case of single literals, numbers and attributes and that general expressions must be converted explicitly. In the case of the assignment to R the only interpretation is that the individual numbers are implicitly converted to type Real before the operations * and / are performed. The result is that R is assigned a value in the same model interval as in the previous exercise. In the case of S, however, an explicit conversion is given and the complete expression is thus of type universal real. The result is that S is assigned the model number 2.0.
      The conversion rules are more liberal in Ada 9X and a general universal expression can be implicitly converted. As a consequence both cases give the exact result.

4   1313 = 16 (= possible mantissae)
      ×   41 (= possible exponents)
      ×   2 (= possible signs)
      +   1 (= zero)

5
```
function Hypotenuse(X, Y: Real) return Real is
   Tiny: constant Real := 2.0**(–Real'Emax/2);
begin
   if abs X < Tiny and abs Y < Tiny then
      return Sqrt((X/Tiny)**2+(Y/Tiny)**2)*Tiny;
   else
```

```
      return Sqrt(X**2+Y**2);
   end if;
end Hypotenuse;
```

Note that Real'Emax is always even.

6   In the case of type Rough we have requested one decimal digit which implies a
maximum relative precision of 1 in 10. If we took $B = 4$ then the relative precision
would vary from 1 in 8 to 1 in 16. There would therefore be occasional places where
the binary numbers are slightly further apart than the decimal ones. In fact, around 10
000 the decimal model numbers for
$D = 1$ are

8000,   9000,   10 000,   20 000

whereas the binary model numbers for $B = 4$ are

7680,   8192,   9216,   10 240

and we see that 8192 and 9216 are more than 1000 apart. Hence we have to take $B = 5$
so that the minimum relative precision is 1 in 16. The general result follows.

7   The ratio is 2^{B-1} or 1/Epsilon. Thus the hole around zero is relatively more dangerous
for higher values of B.

8
```
function Inner(A, B: Vector) return Real is
   type Long_Real is digits 14;
   Result: Long_Real := 0.0;
begin
   for I in A'Range loop
      Result := Result + Long_Real(A(I))*Long_Real(B(I));
   end loop;
   return Real(Result);
end Inner;
```

9   R*R*R*R lies in the model interval $[1^1/_2, 1^{11}/_{16}]$ whereas (R*R)*(R*R) lies in the model
interval $[1^9/_{16}, 1^3/_4]$. The upper bound of the latter interval is outside the former one.
Thus the optimization of using repeated squaring for R**4 can give a formally
incorrect answer. Nevertheless AI-868 allows this optimization although the earlier
AI-137 confirmed that repeated multiplication was indeed required.

Exercise 12.4

1 $^1/_{10}(1 - 2^{-12})$, $^1/_{10}(1 + 2^{-14})$

2   The operation * cannot be universal real because the general expression 2.0*Pi cannot be
implicitly converted to type Angle before the subtraction. Nor can it be the * applying to
two operands of type Angle because that delivers a result of the type universal fixed
which always has to be explicitly converted and moreover a universal real operand of
fixed point multiplication cannot be implicitly converted because of lack of uniqueness.
It is fortunate that this is so; otherwise we would have got the wrong answer because 2.0
is not a model number of type Angle.

3

```
function "**" (X: Complex; N: Integer) return Complex is
   Result_Theta: Angle := 0.0;
begin
   for I in 1 .. abs N loop
      Result_Theta := Normal(Result_Theta+X.Theta);
   end loop;
   if N < 0 then Result_Theta := –Result_Theta; end if;
   return (X.R**N, Result_Theta);
end "**";
```

We cannot simply write

```
return (X.R**N, Normal(X.Theta*N));
```

because if **abs** N is larger than 3 the multiplication is likely to overflow; so we have to repeatedly normalize. A clever solution which is faster for all but the smallest values of **abs** N is

```
function "**" (X: Complex; N: Integer) return Complex is
   Result_Theta: Angle := 0.0;
   Term: Angle := X.Theta;
   M: Integer := abs N;
begin
   while M > 0 loop
      if M rem 2 /= 0 then
         Result_Theta := Normal(Result_Theta + Term);
      end if;
      M := M/2;
      Term := Normal(Term*2);
   end loop;
   if N < 0 then Result_Theta := –Result_Theta; end if;
   return (X.R**N, Result_Theta);
end "**";
```

This is a variation of the standard algorithm for computing exponentials by decomposing the exponent into its binary form and doing a minimal number of multiplications. In our case it is the multiplier N which we decompose and then do a minimal number of additions. Note that we cannot write Term*2.0 because a universal real operand cannot be implicitly converted in the case of fixed point multiplication. In any event such a product would be of type universal fixed and as mentioned in a previous answer 2.0 is not a model number and so errors would be introduced.

One of the major points about fixed point is the ability to do exact addition; multiplication by integers is treated conceptually as repeated addition which is why it produces a result of the same fixed point type. Multiplication by real values (universal or otherwise) is to be treated with suspicion and hence the concept of universal fixed and compulsory conversion which draws the matter to the programmer's attention. It is hence very appropriate that we are using repeated addition in order to multiply by our integer N.

Recognizing that our repeated addition algorithm is essentially the same as for exponentiation, we can in parallel compute X.R**N by the same method. A little manipulation soon makes us realize that we might as well write

```
function "**" (X: Complex; N: Integer) return Complex is
    One: constant Complex := Cons(1.0, 0.0);
    Result: Complex := One;
    Term: Complex := X;
    M: Integer := abs N;
begin
    while M > 0 loop
        if M rem 2 /= 0 then
            Result := Result * Term;    - - Complex *
        end if;
        M := M/2;
        Term := Term * Term;            - - Complex *
    end loop;
    if N < 0 then Result := One / Result; end if;
    return Result;
end "**";
```

This brings us back full circle. This is indeed the standard algorithm for computing exponentials and we are now applying it in the abstract to our type Complex. Note the calls of the functions "*" and "/" applying to the type Complex. This version of "**" can be declared outside the package Complex_Numbers and is quite independent of the internal representation (but it will be very inefficient unless the internal representation is polar).

4   private
```
    type Angle is delta 0.05 range −720.0 .. 720.0;
    type Complex is
      record
          R: Real;
          Theta: Angle range 0.0 .. 360.0;
       end record;
    I: constant Complex := (1.0, 90.0);
end;
...
function Normal(A: Angle) return Angle is
begin
    if A >= 360.0 then
       return A − 360.0;
    elsif A < 0.0 then
       return A + 360.0;
    else
       return A;
    end if;
end Normal;
```

The choice of delta is derived as follows. We need 10 bits to cover the range 0 .. 720 plus one bit for the sign thus leaving 5 bits after the binary point. So *small* will be 2^{-5} and thus any value of delta greater than that but less than 2^{-4} will do. We have chosen 0.05.

Answers 13

Exercise 13.1

1   **generic**
        type Item **is private**;
    package Stacks **is**
        type Stack(Max: Natural) **is limited private**;
        procedure Push(S: **in out** Stack; X: **in** Item);
        procedure Pop(S: **in out** Stack; X: **out** Item);
        function "=" (S, T: Stack) **return** Boolean;
    private
        type Item_Array **is array** (Integer **range** <>) **of** Item;
        type Stack(Max: Natural) **is**
            record
                S: Item_Array(1 .. Max);
                Top: Integer := 0;
            end record;
    end;

The body is much as before. To declare a stack we must first instantiate the package.

    package Boolean_Stacks **is new** Stacks(Item => Boolean);
    use Boolean_Stacks;
    S: Stack(Max => 30);

2   **generic**
        type Thing **is private**;
    package P **is**
        procedure Swap(A, B: **in out** Thing);
        procedure Cab(A, B, C: **in out** Thing);
    end P;

    package body P **is**
        procedure Swap(A, B: **in out** Thing) **is**
            T: Thing;
        begin
            T := A; A := B; B := T;
        end;

        procedure Cab(A, B, C: **in out** Thing) **is**
        begin
            Swap(A, B);
            Swap(A, C);
        end;
    end P;

Exercise 13.2

1   **function** "not" **is new** Next(Boolean);

2   **generic**
       type Base **is range** <>;
   package Rational_Numbers **is**
       type Rational **is private**;
       function "+" (X: Rational) **return** Rational;
       function "−" (X: Rational) **return** Rational;
       function "+" (X, Y: Rational) **return** Rational;
       function "−" (X, Y: Rational) **return** Rational;
       function "*" (X, Y: Rational) **return** Rational;
       function "/" (X, Y: Rational) **return** Rational;

       subtype Pos_Base **is** Base **range** 1 .. Base'Last;
       function "/" (X: Base; Y: Pos_Base) **return** Rational;
       function Numerator(R: Rational) **return** Base;
       function Denominator(R: Rational) **return** Pos_Base;
   private
       type Rational **is**
         record
            Num: Base := 0;
            Den: Pos_Base := 1;
         end record;
   end;

3   **generic**
       type Index **is** (<>);
       type Floating **is digits** <>;
       type Vec **is array** (Index **range** <>) **of** Floating;
       type Mat **is array** (Index **range** <>, Index **range** <>) **of** Floating;
   function Outer(A, B: Vec) **return** Mat;

   function Outer(A, B: Vec) **return** Mat **is**
       C: Mat(A'Range, B'Range);
   begin
      for I **in** A'Range **loop**
        for J **in** B'Range **loop**
           C(I, J) := A(I)*B(J);
        end loop;
      end loop;
      return C;
   end Outer;

   function Outer_Vector **is new** Outer(Integer, Real, Vector, Matrix);

4   **package body** Set_Of **is**

       function Make_Set(X: List) **return** Set **is**
         S: Set := Empty;
       begin
         for I **in** X'Range **loop**

```ada
      S(X(I)) := True;
   end loop;
   return S;
end Make_Set;

function Make_Set(X: Base) return Set is
   S: Set := Empty;
begin
   S(X) := True;
   return S;
end Make_Set;

function Decompose(X: Set) return List is
   L: List(1 .. Size(X));
   I: Positive := 1;
begin
   for E in Set'Range loop
      if X(E) then
         L(I) := E;
         I := I+1;
      end if;
   end loop;
   return L;
end Decompose;

function "+" (X, Y: Set) return Set is
begin
   return X or Y;
end "+";

function "*" (X, Y: Set) return Set is
begin
   return X and Y;
end "*";

function "−" (X, Y: Set) return Set is
begin
   return X xor Y;
end "−";

function "<" (X: Base; Y: Set) return Boolean is
begin
   return Y(X);
end "<";

function "<=" (X, Y: Set) return Boolean is
begin
   return (X and Y) = X;
end "<=";
```

```
function Size(X: Set) return Natural is
   N: Natural := 0;
begin
   for E in Set'Range loop
      if X(E) then
         N := N+1;
      end if;
   end loop;
   return N;
end Size;

end Set_Of;
```

5   ```
    private
       type Base_Array is array (Base) of Boolean;
       type Set is
          record
             Value: Base_Array := (Base_Array'Range => False);
          end record;

       Empty: constant Set := (Value => (Base_Array'Range => False));
       Full: constant Set := (Value => (Base_Array'Range => True));
    end;
    ```

We have to make the full type into a record containing the array as a single
component so that we can give it a default initial expression. Unfortunately, this
means that the body needs rewriting and moreover the functions become rather
untidy. Sadly we cannot write the default expression as Empty.Value. This is because
we cannot use the component name Value in its own declaration. In general, however,
we can use a deferred constant as a default value before its full declaration. Note also
that we have to use the named notation for the single component record aggregates.

*Exercise 13.3*

1   First we have to declare our function "<" which we define as follows: if the
    polynomials have different degrees, the one with the lower degree is smaller; if the
    same degree, then we compare coefficients starting at the highest power. So

    ```
    function "<" (X, Y: Polynomial) return Boolean is
    begin
       if X.N /= Y.N then
          return X.N < Y.N;
       end if;
       for I in reverse 0 .. X.N loop   -- or X.A'Range
          if X.A(I) /= Y.A(I) then
             return X.A(I) < Y.A(I);
          end if;
       end loop;
    ```
    ```

      return False;   − − they are identical
  end "<";

  procedure Sort_Poly **is new** Sort(Integer, Polynomial, Poly_Array);

2   **type** Mutant_Array **is array** (Integer **range** <>) **of** Mutant;

  function "<" (X, Y: Mutant) **return** Boolean **is**
  begin
    if X.Sex /= Y.Sex **then**
      return X.Sex > Y.Sex;
    else
      return Y.Birth < X.Birth;
    end if;
  end "<";

  procedure Sort_Mutant **is new** Sort(Integer, Mutant, Mutant_Array);

Note that the order of sexes asked for is precisely the reverse order to that in the type Gender and so we can directly use ">" applied to that type. Similarly younger first means later birth date first and so we use the function "<" we have already defined for the type Date but with the arguments reversed.

    We could not sort an array of type Person because we cannot declare such an array anyway. See the end of Section 11.3.

3   We cannot do this because the array is of an anonymous type.

4   We might get Constraint_Error. If C'First = Index'First then the attempt to evaluate Index'Pred(C'Last) will raise Constraint_Error. Considerable care can be required to make such extreme cases foolproof. The easy way out in this case is simply to insert

  if C'Length < 2 **then return**; **end if**;

5   The generic body corresponds closely to the procedure Sort in Section 11.4. The type Vector is replaced by Collection. I is of type Index. The types Node and Tree are declared inside Sort because they depend on the generic type Item. The incrementing of I cannot be done with "+" since the index type may not be an integer and so we have to use Index'Succ. Care is needed not to cause Constraint_Error if the array embraces the full range of values of Index. However, the important thing is that the generic specification is completely unchanged and so we see how an alternative body can be sensibly supplied.

6   Assuming

  type Bool_Array **is array** (Integer **range** <>) **of** Boolean;

  we have

  function And_All **is new** Apply(Integer, Boolean, Bool_Array, **"and"**);

7   A further generic parameter is required to supply a value for zero.

```
generic
   type Index is (<>);
   type Item is private;
   Zero: in Item;
   type Vec is array (Index range <>) of Item;
   with function "+" (X, Y: Item) return Item;
function Apply(A: Vec) return Item;

function Apply(A: Vec) return Item is
   Result: Item := Zero;
begin
   for I in A'Range loop
    Result := Result+A(I);
   end loop;
   return Result;
end Apply;
```

and then

```
function And_All is new Apply(Integer, Boolean, True, Bool_Array, "and");
```

8
```
generic
   type Item is limited private;
   type Vector is array (Integer range <>) of Item;
   with function "=" (X, Y: Item) return Boolean is <>;
function Equals(A, B: Vector) return Boolean;

function Equals(A, B: Vector) return Boolean is
begin
   – – body exactly as for Exercise 9.2(3)
end Equals;
```

We can instantiate by

```
function "=" is new Equals(Stack, Stack_Array, "=");
```

or simply by

```
function "=" is new Equals(Stack, Stack_Array);
```

in which case the default parameter is used.

9
```
function G(X: Real) return Real is
begin
   return Exp(X)+X–7.0;
end;
...
function Solve_G is new Solve(G);
...
Answer: Real := Solve_G;
```

Exercise 13.4

1   **with** Generic_Elementary_Functions;
package body Simple_Maths **is**

    package Float_Functions **is**
      new Generic_Elementary_Functions(Float);

    function Sqrt(F: Float) **return** Float **is**
    begin
      return Float_Functions.Sqrt(F);
    exception
      when Float_Functions.Argument_Error =>
        raise Constraint_Error;
    end Sqrt;

    function Log(F: Float) **return** Float **is**
    begin
      return Float_Functions.Log(F, 10.0);
    exception
      when Float_Functions.Argument_Error =>
        raise Constraint_Error;
    end Log;

    function Ln(F: Float) **return** Float **is**
    begin
      return Float_Functions.Log(F);
    exception
      when Float_Functions.Argument_Error =>
        raise Constraint_Error;
    end Ln;

    function Exp(F: Float) **return** Float **is**
    begin
      return Float_Functions.Exp(F);
    end Exp;

    function Sin(F: Float) **return** Float **is**
    begin
      return Float_Functions.Sin(F);
    end Sin;

    function Cos(F: Float) **return** Float **is**
    begin
      return Float_Functions.Cos(F);
    end Cos;

end Simple_Maths;

We did not write a use clause for Float_Functions largely because it would not have enabled us to write simply

return Sqrt(F);

since this would have resulted in an infinite recursion.

2   **package body** Generic_Complex_Functions **is**

```
function Sqrt(X: Complex_Type) return Complex_Type is
begin
  return Cons_Polar(Sqrt(abs X), 0.5*Arg(X)));
end Sqrt;

function Log(X: Complex_Type) return Complex_Type is
begin
  return Cons(Log(abs X), Arg(X));
end Log;

function Exp(X: Complex_Type) return Complex_Type is
begin
  return Cons_Polar(Exp(Rl_Part(X)), Im_Part(X));
end Exp;

function Sin(X: Complex_Type) return Complex_Type is
  Rl: Real_Type := Rl_Part(X);
  Im: Real_Type := Im_Part(X);
begin
  return Cons(Sin(Rl)*Cosh(Im)), Cos(Rl)*Sinh(Im));
end Sin;

function Cos(X: Complex_Type) return Complex_Type is
  Rl: Real_Type := Rl_Part(X);
  Im: Real_Type := Im_Part(X);
begin
  return Cons(Cos(Rl)*Cosh(Im)), -Sin(Rl)*Sinh(Im));
end Cos;

end Generic_Complex_Functions;
```

3   **function** Cons_Cartesian(R, I: My_Real) **return** Complex **renames** Cons;

4   **generic**
```
  type Real is digits <>;
  with function Sqrt(X: Real) return Real is <>;
  with function Sin(X: Real) return Real is <>;
  with function Cos(X: Real) return Real is <>;
  with function Arctan(Y, X: Real) return Real is <>;
package Generic_Complex_Numbers is
  type Complex is private;
```

-- as in Section 9.1 plus

```
function Cons_Polar(R, Theta: Real) return Complex;
function "abs" (X: Complex) return Real;
function Arg(X: Complex) return Real;
private

   -- as before

end;


package body Generic_Complex_Numbers is

   -- as before plus

   function Cons_Polar(R, Theta: Real) return Complex is
   begin
      return (R*Cos(Theta), R*Sin(Theta));
   end Cons_Polar;

   function "abs" (X: Complex) return Real is
   begin
      return Sqrt(X.Rl**2 + X.Im**2);
   end "abs";

   function Arg(X: Complex) return Real is
      return Arctan(X.Im, X.Rl);
   end Arg;

end Generic_Complex_Numbers;
```

Numerical analysts will writhe at the poor implementation of **abs** which can
unnecessarily overflow in computing the parameter of Sqrt. This can be avoided by
suitable rescaling.

Note also that if the private type Complex is implemented in polar form then the
same set of auxiliary functions will suffice. Thus the formal functions provided do not
dictate the internal representation and so the abstraction is not compromised.

Answers 14

Exercise 14.1

```
1   procedure Shopping is

       task Get_Salad;

       task body Get_Salad is
       begin
          Buy_Salad;
       end Get_Salad;
```

```
      task Get_Wine;

      task body Get_Wine is
      begin
         Buy_Wine;
      end Get_Wine;

      task Get_Meat;

      task body Get_Meat is
      begin
         Buy_Meat;
      end Get_Meat;

   begin
      null;
   end Shopping;
```

Exercise 14.2

```
1   task body Build_Complex is
       C: Complex;
    begin
      loop
        accept Put_RI(X: Real) do
          C.RI := X;
        end;
        accept Put_Im(X: Real) do
          C.Im := X;
        end;
        accept Get_Comp(X: out Complex) do
          X := C;
        end;
      end loop;
    end Build_Complex;

2   task body Char_To_Line is
       Buffer: Line;
    begin
      loop
        for I in Buffer'Range loop
          accept Put(C: in Character) do
            Buffer(I) := C;
          end;
        end loop;
        accept Get(L: out Line) do
          L := Buffer;
        end;
      end loop;
    end Char_To_Line;
```

Exercise 14.3

1   **generic**
    First_Time: Calendar.Time;
    Interval: Duration;
    Number: Integer;
    with procedure P;
  procedure Call;

```
   procedure Call is
      use Calendar;
      Next_Time: Time := First_Time;
   begin
      if Next_Time < Clock then
         Next_Time := Clock;
      end if;
      for I in 1 .. Number loop
         delay Next_Time–Clock;
         P;
         Next_Time := Next_Time+Interval;
      end loop;
   end Call;
```

2   The type Duration requires at least 24 bits.

Exercise 14.4

1   **task body** Build_Complex **is**
    C: Complex;
    Got_Rl, Got_Im: Boolean := False;
  begin
    loop
      select
        when not Got_Rl =>
        accept Put_Rl(X: Real) **do**
          C.Rl := X;
        end;
        Got_Rl := True;
      or
        when not Got_Im =>
        accept Put_Im(X: Real) **do**
          C.Im := X;
        end;
        Got_Im := True;
      or
        when Got_Rl **and** Got_Im =>
        accept Get_Comp(X: **out** Complex) **do**
          X := C;
        end;
        Got_Rl := False;

```
        Got_Im := False;
      end select;
    end loop;
 end Build_Complex;
```

An alternative solution is

```
task body Build_Complex is
  C: Complex;
begin
  loop
    select
      accept Put_RI(X: Real) do
        C.RI := X;
      end;
      accept Put_Im(X: Real) do
        C.Im := X;
      end;
    or
      accept Put_Im(X: Real) do
        C.Im := X;
      end;
      accept Put_RI(X: Real) do
        C.RI := X;
      end;
    end select;
    accept Get_Comp(X: out Complex) do
      X := C;
    end;
  end loop;
end Build_Complex;
```

At first reading this might seem simpler but the technique does not extrapolate easily when a moderate number of components are involved because of the combinatorial explosion.

Exercise 14.5

```
1   procedure Read(X: out Item; T: Duration; OK: out Boolean) is
    begin
      select
        Control.Start(Read);
      or
        delay T;
        OK := False;
        return;
      end select;
      X := V;
      Control.Stop_Read;
      OK := True;
    end Read;
```

```
procedure Write(X: in Item; T: Duration; OK: out Boolean) is
   use Calendar;
   Start_Time: Time := Clock;
begin
   select
      Control.Start(Write);
   or
      delay T;
      OK := False;
      return;
   end select;
   select
      Control.Write;
   or
      delay T-(Clock-Start_Time);
      Control.Stop_Write;
      OK := False;
      return;
   end select;
   V := X;
   Control.Stop_Write;
   OK := True;
end Write;
```

Note how a shorter time out is imposed on the call of Write.

Exercise 14.7

1   ```
     task Buffering is
        entry Put(X: in Itom);
        entry Finish;
        entry Get(X: out Item);
     end;

     task body Buffering is
        N: constant := 8;
        A: array (1 .. N) of Item;
        I, J: Integer range 1 .. N := 1;
        Count: Integer range 0 .. N := 0;
        Finished: Boolean := False;
     begin
        loop
           select
              when Count < N =>
              accept Put(X: in Item) do
                 A(I) := X;
     ```
     ```

```
        end;
        I := I mod N+1; Count := Count+1;
    or
        accept Finish;
        Finished := True;
    or
        when Count > 0 =>
        accept Get(X: out Item) do
            X := A(J);
        end;
        J := J mod N+1; Count := Count-1;
    or
        when Count = 0 and Finished =>
        accept Get(X: out Item) do
            raise Done;
        end;
    end select;
  end loop;
exception
  when Done =>
    null;
end Buffering;
```

This example illustrates that there may be several accept statements for the same
entry in the one select statement. The exception Done is propagated to the caller and
also terminates the loop in Buffering before being quietly handled. Of course the
exception need not be handled by Buffering because exceptions propagated out of
tasks are lost, but it is cleaner to do so.

2 The server aborts the caller during the rendezvous thereby placing the caller into an
   abnormal state. Although the caller cannot be properly completed until after the
   rendezvous is finished (the server might have access to the caller's data space via a
   parameter), nevertheless the caller is no longer active and does not receive the
   exception Havoc. See AI-446.

Exercise 14.8

1 The select statement becomes

```
select
  when Waiters = 0 =>
  accept First(S: Set; OK: out Boolean) do
      Try(S, OK);
    if not OK then
      Waiters := Waiters+1;
    end if;
  end;
or
  accept Release(S: Set) do
    Free := Free+S;
  end;
```

```
      accept Again(S: Set; OK: out Boolean) do
         Try(S, OK);
         if OK then
            Waiters := Waiters-1;
         end if;
      end;
   end select;
```

2 ```
   package Controller is
      procedure Request(P: Priority; D: Data);
   end;

   package body Controller is

      task Control is
         entry Sign_In(P: Priority);
         entry Request(Priority)(D: Data);
      end;

      task body Control is
         Total: Integer := 0;
         Pending: array (Priority) of Integer := (Priority => 0);
      begin
         loop
            if Total = 0 then
               accept Sign_In(P: Priority) do
                  Pending(P) := Pending(P)+1;
                  Total := 1;
               end;
            end if;
            loop
               select
                  accept Sign_In(P: Priority) do
                     Pending(P) := Pending(P)+1;
                     Total := Total+1;
                  end;
               else
                  exit;
               end select;
            end loop;

            for P in Priority loop
               if Pending(P) > 0 then
                  accept Request(P)(D: Data) do
                     Action(D);
                  end;
                  Pending(P) := Pending(P)-1;
                  Total := Total-1;
                  exit;
               end if;
```
```

```
        end loop;
      end loop;
   end Control;

   procedure Request(P: Priority; D: Data) is
   begin
      Control.Sign_In(P);
      Control.Request(P)(D);
   end Request;

end Controller;
```

The variable Total records the total number of requests outstanding and the array
Pending records the number at each priority. Each time round the outer loop, the task
waits for a call of Sign_In if no requests are in the system, it then services any
outstanding calls of Sign_In and finally deals with a request of the highest priority.
We could dispense with the array Pending and scan the queues as before but there is a
slight risk of polling if a user has called Sign_In but not yet called Request.

Finally, note that the solution will not work if a calling task is aborted; this could
be overcome by the use of agents.

Exercise 14.9

```
1   package Cobblers is
      procedure Mend(A: Address; B: Boots);
    end;

    package body Cobblers is
      type Job is
        record
          Reply: Address;
          Item: Boots;
        end record;

      package P is new Buffers(100, Job);
      use P;
      Boot_Store: Buffer;

      task Server is
        entry Request(A: Address; B: Boots);
      end;

      task type Repairman;
      Tom, Dick, Harry: Repairman;

      task body Server is
        Next_Job: Job;
      begin
```

```
   loop
      accept Request(A: Address; B: Boots) do
         Next_Job := (A, B);
      end;
      Put(Boot_Store, Next_Job);
   end loop;
end Server;

task body Repairman is
   My_Job: Job;
begin
   loop
      Get(Boot_Store, My_Job);
      Repair(My_Job.Item);
      My_Job.Reply.Deposit(My_Job.Item);
   end loop;
end Repairman;

   procedure Mend(A: Address; B: Boots) is
   begin
      Server.Request(A, B);
   end;

end Cobblers;
```

We have assumed that the type **Address** is an access to a mailbox for handling boots.
Note one anomaly; the stupid server accepts boots from the customer before checking
the store – if it turns out to be full, he is left holding them. In all, the shop can hold
104 pairs of boots – 100 in store, 1 with the server and 1 with each repairman.

2 ```
procedure Gauss_Seidel is
   N: constant := 5;
   subtype Full_Grid is Integer range 0 .. N;
   subtype Grid is Full_Grid range 1 .. N–1;
   type Real is digits 7;
   Delta_P: Real;
   Tolerance: constant Real := 0.0001;
   Error_Limit: constant Real := Tolerance * (N–1)**2;
   Converged: Boolean := False;
   Error_Sum: Real;

   function F(I, J: Grid) return Real is separate;

   task type Iterator is
      pragma Priority(1);
      entry Start(I, J: in Grid);
   end;
```
```

```
task type Point is
  pragma Priority(2);
  entry Set_P(X: in Real);
  entry Get_P(X: out Real);
  entry Get_Delta_P(X: out Real);
  entry Set_Converged(B: in Boolean);
  entry Get_Converged(B: out Boolean);
end;

Process: array (Grid, Grid) of Iterator;
Data: array (Grid, Grid) of Point;

task body Iterator is
  I, J: Grid;
  P, P1, P2, P3, P4: Real;
  Converged: Boolean;
begin

  accept Start(I, J: in Grid) do
    Iterator.I := Start.I;
    Iterator.J := Start.J;
  end Start;

  loop    -- needs modification if adjacent to boundary
    Data(I-1, J).Get_P(P1);
    Data(I+1, J).Get_P(P2);
    Data(I, J-1).Get_P(P3);
    Data(I, J+1).Get_P(P4);
    P := 0.25 * (P1 + P2 + P3 + P4 - F(I, J));
    Data(I, J).Set_P(P);
    Data(I, J).Get_Converged(Converged);
    exit when Converged;
  end loop;

end Iterator;

task body Point is
  Converged: Boolean := False;
  P: Real;
  Delta_P: Real;
begin
  loop
    select
      accept Set_P(X: in Real) do
        Delta_P := X - P;
        P := X;
      end;
    or
```

```
      accept Get_P(X: out Real) do
        X := P;

      end;
    or
      accept Get_Delta_P(X: out Real) do
        X := Delta_P;
      end;
    or
      accept Set_Converged(B: in Boolean) do
        Converged := B;
      end;
    or
      accept Get_Converged(B: out Boolean) do
        B := Converged;
      end;
    or
      terminate;
    end select;
  end loop;
end Point;

begin   -- of main program; the tasks are now active

  for I in Grid loop
    for J in Grid loop
      Process(I, J).Start(I, J);   -- tell them who they are
    end loop;
  end loop;

  loop
    Error_Sum := 0.0;
    for I in Grid loop
      for J in Grid loop
        Data(I, J).Get_Delta_P(Delta_P);
        Error_Sum := Error_Sum + Delta_P**2;
      end loop;
    end loop;

    Converged := Error_Sum < Error_Limit;
    exit when Converged;
  end loop;

  -- tell the data tasks that it has converged

  for I in Grid loop
    for J in Grid loop
      Data(I, J).Set_Converged(True);
    end loop;
  end loop;
```

```
-- output results

end Gauss_Seidel;
```

The main problem with this solution is that we have not taken account of the boundary. Nor have we considered how to initialize the system. However, it must now be clear that using the rendezvous rather than shared variables means that the communication must completely overwhelm the computation unless the function F is extremely complex. Practical applications of distributed tasks of this kind will have much larger computational tasks to perform.

The main loop of the Iterator task is a bit painful. It is a pity that we cannot have entry functions. However, it could be made neater by using renaming in order to avoid repeated evaluation of Data(I, J) and so on; this would also speed things up. Thus we could write

```
procedure Get_P1(X: out Real) renames Data(I-1, J).Get_P;
procedure Get_P2(X: out Real) renames Data(I+1, J).Get_P;
...
procedure Set_P(X: in Real) renames Data(I, J).Set_P;
procedure Get_Converged(B: out Boolean) renames Data(I, J).Get_Converged;
```

and then

```
Get_P1(P1); Get_P2(P2); Get_P3(P3); Get_P4(P4);
Set_P(0.25 * (P1 + P2 + P3 + P4 - F(I, J)));
Get_Converged(Converged);
exit when Converged;
```

Answers 15

Exercise 15.1

```
1   with Direct_IO;
    generic
       type Element is private;
    procedure Rev(From, To: String);

    procedure Rev(From, To: String) is
       package IO is new Direct_IO(Element);
       use IO;
       Input: File_Type;
       Output: File_Type;
       X: Element;
    begin
       Open(Input, In_File, From);
       Open(Output, Out_File, To);
       Set_Index(Output, Size(Input));
       loop
          Read(Input, X);
```

```
    Write(Output, X);
    exit when End_Of_File(Input);
    Set_Index(Output, Index(Output)-2);
  end loop;
  Close(Input);
  Close(Output);
end Rev;
```

Remember that **reverse** is a reserved word. Note also that this does not work if the
file is empty (the first call of Set_Index will raise Constraint_Error). However, this is
an improvement on the solution in earlier editions of this book which always raised
Constraint_Error. I am very grateful to Vittorio Frigo of CERN for pointing out this
blunder.

Exercise 15.2

1   The output is shown in string quotes in order to reveal the layout. Spaces are
    indicated by s. In reality of course, there are no quotes and spaces are spaces.

    (a) "Fred"
    (b) "sss120"
    (c) "sssss120"
    (d) "120"
    (e) "−120"
    (f) "ss8#170#"
    (g) "−3.80000E+01"
    (h) "sssss7.00E−2"
    (i) "3.1416E+01"
    (j) "1.0E+10"

2   **with** Text_IO;
    package body Simple_IO **is**

        package Float_IO **is new** Text_IO.Float_IO(Float);

        procedure Get(F: **out** Float) **is**
        begin
          Float_IO.Get(F);
        end Get;

        procedure Put(F: **in** Float) **is**
        begin
          Float_IO.Put(F);
        end Put;

        procedure Put(S: **in** String) **is**
        begin
          Text_IO.Put(S);
        end Put;
```
```

```
procedure New_Line(N: in Integer := 1) is
begin
   Text_IO.New_Line(Text_IO.Count(N));
end New_Line;

end Simple_IO;
```

Note that we have chosen to call the instantiated package Float_IO; this causes no confusion (except perhaps for the reader) since the new package merely prevents direct access (via a use clause) to the generic one of the same name. This does not matter since we are using the full dotted notation to access the generic one. In any event we have to use the full notation in the procedures in order to avoid recursion so there is little point in a use clause for Text_IO.

The other point of note is the type conversion in New_Line.

Answers 16

Exercise 16.1

1 (a) dynamic – Integer
   (b) static – Integer
   (c) static – universal integer

Exercise 16.4

1

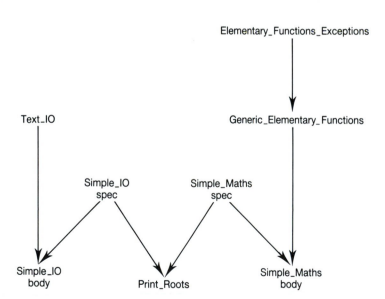

We have assumed that Text_IO and Generic_Elementary_Functions are self-contained. Note moreover that insisting that generic specifications and bodies are compiled together requires that the specification and body of Text_IO are also compiled together; this is because the specifications and bodies of the generic units Integer_IO, Float_IO and so on are themselves in the specification and body of Text_IO respectively.

Exercise 16.5

1 (a) The order of evaluation of the operands I and F of "+" is not defined. As a result the effect
could be

	I := 1+2;	– – I first
or	I := 2+2;	– – F first

(b) The order of evaluation of the destination A(I) and the value F is not defined. The effect
could be

	A(1) := 2;	– – I first
or	A(2) := 2;	– – F first

(c) The order of evaluation of the two indexes is not defined. The effect could be

	AA(1, 2) := 0;	– – I first
or	AA(2, 2) := 0;	– – F first

Answers 17

Exercise 17.2.1

1
```
package Objects is

    type Object is tagged
        record
            X_Coord: Real;
            Y_Coord: Real;
        end record;

    function Distance(O: Object) return Real;
    function Area(O: Object) return Real;

end Objects;

package body Objects is

    function Distance(O: Object) return Real is
    begin
        return Sqrt(O.X_Coord**2 + O.Y_Coord**2);
    end Distance;
```

```
    function Area(O: Object) return Real is
    begin
        return 0.0;
    end Area;

end Objects;

package Shapes is

    type Point is new Object with null record;

    type Circle is new Object with
        record
            Radius: Real;
        end record;

    function Area(C: Circle) return Real;

    type Square is new Object with
        record
            Side: Real;
        end record;

    function Area(S: Square) return Real;

    type Rectangle is new Object with
        record
            Length, Breadth: Real;
        end record;

    function Area(R: Rectangle) return Real;

end Shapes;

package body Shapes is

    function Area(C: Circle) return Real is
    begin
        return Pi*C.Radius*2;
    end Area;

    function Area(S: Square) return Real is
    begin
        return S.Side*2;
    end Area;

    function Area(R: Rectangle) return Real is
    begin
        return R.Length * R.Breadth;
    end Area;

end Shapes;
```

Exercise 17.2.2

1   **procedure** Print_Area(Obj: Object'Class) **is**
    begin
        Put(Area(Obj)); – – dispatch to appropriate Area
    end;

2   **type** Person **is tagged**
        record
            Birth: Date;
        end record;

    type Man **is new** Person **with**
        record
            Bearded: Boolean;
        end record;

    type Woman **is new** Person **with**
        record
            Children: Integer;
        end record;

3   **procedure** Print_Details(P: **in** Person) **is**
    begin
        Print_Date(P.Birth);
    end;

    procedure Print_Details(M: **in** Man) **is**
    begin
        Print_Details(Person(M));
        Print_Boolean(M.Beard);
    end;

    procedure Print_Details(W: **in** Woman) **is**
    begin
        Print_Details(Person(W));
        Print_Integer(W.Children);
    end;

    procedure Analyze_Person(P: Person'Class) **is**
    begin
        Print_Details(P); – – dispatch
    end;

Exercise 17.2.3

1   **package** Objects **is**

    type Object **is tagged null record**;

    function Area(O: Object) **return** Real **is <>**;

  end Objects;

  package Shapes **is**

    type Point **is new** Object **with**
     record
      X_Coord: Real;
      Y_Coord: Real;
     end record;

    function Area(P: Point) **return** Real;
    function Distance(P: Point) **return** Real;

    type Circle **is new** Point **with**
     record
      Radius: Real;
     end record;

    function Area(C: Circle) **return** Real;

    − − etc

  end Shapes;

2   **package body** Subsonic_Reservation_System **is**

    procedure Make(BR: **in out** Basic_Reservation) **is**
     Select_Seat(BR);
    end Make;

    procedure Make(NR: **in out** Nice_Reservation) **is**
     Make(Basic_Reservation(NR));
     Order_Meal(NR);
    end Make;

    procedure Make(PR: **in out** Posh_Reservation) **is**
     Make(Nice_Reservation(PR));
     Arrange_Limo(PR);
    end Make;
    ...
  end Subsonic_Reservation_System;

Exercise 17.2.5

1 **procedure** Select_Seat(NR: **in out** Nice_Reservation) **is**
   begin
       if NR.Seat_Sort = Aisle **then**
           – – choose aisle seat
       else
           – – choose window seat
       end if;
   end Select_Seat;

   ...
   procedure Make(R: **in out** Reservation) **is**
   begin
       Select_Seat(Reservation'Class(R)); – – redispatch
   end Make;

Observe that we know that the component NR.Seat_Sort must exist because this is a nice reservation or derived from it. Naturally enough all seats are window or aisle seats in nice and posh categories.

Exercise 17.2.6

1 **procedure** Duplicate(Object: **in out** Thing) **is**
   begin
       The_Count := The_Count + 1;
   end Duplicate;

The procedures Initialize and Finalize are as before.

Exercise 17.3.1

1 **type** Operand **is access function** (X: Real) **return** Real;

   function Solve(F: Operand) **return** Real;
       ...

   function G(X: Real) **return** Real **is**
   begin
       return Exp(X)+X–7.0;
   end G;
       ...

   Answer := Solve(G'Access);

Exercise 17.4.1

1 **package** Complex_Numbers **is**
       type Complex **is private**;

       ...
       function "+" (X, Y: Complex) **return** Complex;
       ...

```
    private
        ...
    end Complex_Numbers;

    package Complex_Numbers.Cartesian is
        function Cons(R, I: Real) return Complex;
        function RI_Part(X: Complex) return Real;
        function Im_Part(X: Complex) return Real;
    end Complex_Numbers.Cartesian;

    package Complex_Numbers.Polar is
        -- as before
    end Complex_Numbers.Polar;
```

The bodies are as expected.

2   ```
    package Tracked_Things is

        type Intermediate is new Controlled with
            record
                -- visible data
            end record;
        procedure Finalize (I: Intermediate) is <>;

    end Tracked Things;

    package Tracked_Things.User_View is

        type Thing is new Intermediate with private;

    private
        type Thing is new Intermediate with
            record
                Identity_Number: Integer
            end record;

        procedure Initialize...
        -- etc
    end Tracked_Things.User_View;
    ```

Again the intermediate type is abstract so that the user cannot declare objects of the type. But somehow this solution does not feel so good. Moreover the child package mechanism is not really required since the parent package does not have a private part. Nevertheless the commonality of naming is helpful.

*Exercise 17.4.2*

1   ```
    private package Rational_Numbers.Slave is
        function Normal(R: Rational) return Rational;
    end;
    ```

```
package body Rational_Numbers.Slave is

   function GCD ... etc

   function Normal(R: Rational) return Rational is
      G: Positive := GCD(abs R.Num, R.Den);
   begin
      return (R.Num/G, R.Den/G);
   end Normal;

end Rational_Numbers.Slave;

with Rational_Numbers.Slave;
package body Rational_Numbers is
 use Slave;
   – – as before without the function Normal
end Rational_Numbers;
```

Exercise 17.6.1

1   (a) 16#EF#
       (b) 120
       (c) 222
       (d) 239

2   **type** Ring5 **is mod** 5;
       A, B, C, D: Ring5;
       ...
       D := (A + B) * C;

Exercise 17.7.1

1   **with** Finalization;
       generic
          type Raw_Type **is tagged private**;
       package Tracking **is**
          type Tracked_Type **is new** Raw_Type **with private**;
          function Identity(TT: Tracked_Type) **return** Integer;
       private
          type Control **is new** Finalization.Controlled **with**
             record
                Identity_Number: Integer;
             end record;

          procedure Initialize(C: **in out** Control);
          procedure Duplicate(C: **in out** Control);
          procedure Finalize(C: **in out** Control);

          – – Control now not abstract

```
    type Tracked_Type is new Raw_Type with
      record
        Component: Control;
      end record;
  end Tracking;


  package body Tracking is

    The_Count: Integer := 0;
    Next_One: Integer := 1;


    function Identity(TT: Tracked_Type) return Integer is
    begin
      return TT.Component.Identity_Number;
    end Identity;


    procedure Initialize(C: in out Control) is
    begin
      The_Count := The_Count + 1;
      C.Identity_Number := Next_One;
      Next_One := Next_One + 1;
    end Initialize;


    procedure Duplicate ...
    procedure Finalize ...


  end Tracking;
```

```
2   with Tracking;
    package Hush_Hush is
      type Secret_Shape is new Object with private;
      function Shape_Identity(SS: Secret_Shape) return Integer;
      ...
    private
      package Q is new Tracking(Raw_Type => Object);
      type Secret_Shape is new Q.Tracked_Type with
        record
          ... - - other hidden components
        end record;
    end Hush_Hush;


    package body Hush_Hush is

      function Shape_Identity(SS: Secret_Shape) return Integer is
      begin
        return Q.Identity(SS);
      end Shape_Identity;
      ...
    end Hush_Hush;
```

Exercise 17.8.1

1   **protected** Variable **is**
       entry Read(Value: **out** Item);
       procedure Write(New_Value: **in** Item);
     private
       Data: Item;
       Value_Set: Boolean := False;
     end Variable;

     protected body Variable **is**

       entry Read(Value: **out** Item) **when** Value_Set **is**
       begin
         Value := Data;
       end Read;

       procedure Write(New_Value: **in** Item) **is**
       begin
         Data := New_Value;
         Value_Set := True; – – clear the barrier
       end Write;

     end Variable;

The problem with this solution is that it no longer allows multiple readers because the function has been replaced by an entry. We leave further consideration of this to the reader.

2   **generic**
       type Item **is private**;
     package Buffers **is**
       type Item_Array **is array** (Integer range <>) **of** Item;
       protected type Buffering(N: Integer) **is**
       – – as before
       end Buffering;
     end Buffers;

3   **task type** Filter(P: Integer) **is**
       entry Input(Number: Integer);
     end Filter;

     type A_Filter **is access** Filter;

     function Make_Filter(N: Integer) **return** A_Filter **is**
     begin
       return new Filter(N);
     end Make_Filter;

```
task body Filter(P: Integer) is
   N: Integer;
   Here: Position := Make_Frame(P);
   Next: A_Filter;
begin
   loop
      accept Input(Number: Integer) do
         N := Number;
      end;
      Write_To_Frame(N, Here);
      if N mod P /= 0 then
         if Next = null then
            Next := Make_Filter(N);
         else
            Next.Input(N);
         end if;
      end if;
      Clear_Frame(Here);
   end loop;
end Filter;

procedure Sieve is
   First: A_Filter := new Filter(2);
   N := Integer := 3;
begin
   loop
      First.Input(N);
      N := N + 1;
   end loop;
end Sieve;
```

This may not seem much of an improvement but the solution in Chapter 14 was 'optimized' in that the same entry was used for telling the task its prime divisor and then also supplying the numbers to try. This might be considered rather confusing.

Exercise 17.8.2

1   If we wrote

requeue Reset **with abort**;

then there would be a risk that the task that called Signal was aborted before it could clear the occurred flag. This might result in some waiting tasks missing the signal and having to wait for a further signal.

2
```
protected Event is
   entry Wait;
   procedure Signal;
private
   Occurred: Boolean := False;
end Event;
```

protected body Event **is**

   entry Wait **when** Occurred **is**
   begin
     if Wait'Count = 0 **then**
       Occurred := False;
     end if;
   end Wait;

   procedure Signal **is**
   begin
     if Wait'Count > 0 **then**
       Occurred := True;
     end if;
   end Signal;

end Event;

The last of the waiting tasks to be let go clears the occurred flag back to false (the last one out switches off the light). It is important that the procedure Signal does not set the occurred flag if there are no tasks waiting since in such a case there is no waiting task to clear it and the signal would persist (remember this is a model of a transient signal).

Bibliography

The following selection for further reading comprises a number of books which the author believes will be found helpful. It is by no means exhaustive and omits many other books which make a valuable contribution to the Ada literature. However, if you are new to Ada and wish to build a library then this list is a good starting point.

Booch, G. (1986). *Software Engineering with Ada*, 2nd edn. Benjamin Cummings

This well-known classic was one of the first books to discuss how to design programs in Ada; it is especially famed for Object Oriented Programming.

Burns, A. (1986). *Concurrent Programming in Ada*. Cambridge University Press

This is a very complete account of Ada tasking and contains further examples which complement those in Chapter 14.

Cohen, N. H. (1986). *Ada as a Second Language*. McGraw-Hill

This is a rather comprehensive account of the Ada language. It is a large book and contains many examples explored in detail. Its coverage of Ada is not quite complete; it omits a number of minor issues which we have addressed in this book but on the other hand it discusses some topics that we have skimped (especially the pragmas and machine dependent bits). It also has myriads of exercises but no solutions (just as well because otherwise it would be 2000 pages!).

Dawes, J. (1988). *Ada*. Pitman

This useful little book is a handy reference guide to Ada. It covers the whole language in 200 pages.

Ford, B., Kok, J. and Rogers, M. W., eds. (1986). *Scientific Ada*. Cambridge University Press

Do not be put off by the apparently specialized topic. This book does indeed deal in depth with the use of Ada for numerical calculations. But it also includes much useful discussion about separate compilation and generics which is relevant to all applications.

Gautier, R. J. and Wallis, P. J. L., eds. (1990). *Software Reuse with Ada*. Peter Peregrinus

This contains a very good discussion on how to design reusable software components in Ada.

Hibbard, P., Hisgen, A., Rosenberg, J., Shaw, M. and Sherman, M. (1983). *Studies in Ada Style*, 2nd edn. Springer-Verlag

This excellent book contains a detailed analysis of a small number of intricate programs which explore important issues of structure. A lot can be learnt from really understanding them.

Jones, Do-While (1989). *Ada in Action*. Wiley

This down-to-earth and amusing book contains some valuable practical advice on using Ada. It also contains a number of listings of useful programs.

Le Verrand, D. (1985). *Evaluating Ada* (English translation). North Oxford Academic

This is a critical review of Ada and gives the reader further insight into the design of Ada and how to get the most out of it.

Pyle, I. P. (1991). *Developing Safety Systems: A Guide using Ada*. Prentice-Hall

It has now been realized that software is a key issue in the development of many life critical systems. This book illustrates the advantages of Ada in this area.

Shumate, K. (1988). Understanding Concurrency in Ada. Intertext Publications

This is another very detailed account of Ada tasking. It contains a fascinating discussion of many variations on the cobblers example at the end of Chapter 14.

Software Productivity Consortium, The (1989). *Ada Quality and Style*. Van Nostrand Reinhold

This is an excellent guide to writing good Ada programs. Topics covered include portability and reuse as well as stylistic issues. A must for every programmer.

Sommerville, I. and Morrison, R. (1987). *Software Development with Ada*. Addison-Wesley

This book covers a broad number of topics concerning how to develop well structured reliable Ada programs. A good book to dip into. It contains a large bibliography.

The following books are of a more general nature.

Gibson, W. and Sterling, B. (1991). *The Difference Engine*. Bantam Books

This colourful novel contemplates a Victorian world in which Babbage's engines are in widespread use, Lord Byron becomes Prime Minister of Britain and Ada is known as the Queen of Engines. A good read for a flight to an Ada conference!

Langley Moore, D. (1977). *Ada, Countess of Lovelace*. John Murray

This is a classical biography of Lord Byron's daughter after whom the language is named.

Nabakov, V. (1969). *Ada*. Weidenfeld and Nicolson

The title of this book is an illustration of overloading. It has nothing to do with either Ada the language or the Countess of Lovelace. However, if you are fed up with programming languages, this novel brings light relief and will provoke interesting comment if placed in your library.

Stein, D. (1985). *Ada, A Life and a Legacy*. MIT Press

This biography contains more about Ada's relationship and technical work with Charles Babbage.

Toole, Betty A. (1992). *Ada, the Enchantress of Numbers*. Strawberry Press

This recent biography of Ada is written by someone familiar with the Ada language community and captures more of the spirit of Ada as the first programmer.

Index

This index applies to both Ada 83 and Ada 9X. Those entries relating especially to Ada 9X are distinguished by being followed by the letter x.

Index to Examples

This index lists the more significant examples. The entries give the section numbers where they are declared or referenced. Predefined entities such as the type String will be found in the main index.